CH00687581

English Historical Linguistics
Approaches and Perspectives

Written by an international team of leading scholars, this engaging textbook on the study of English historical linguistics is uniquely organized in terms of theoretical approaches and perspectives. Each chapter features textboxes, case studies, suggestions for further reading, and exercises, enabling students to understand the strengths and weaknesses of each approach and guiding them on undertaking further research. The case studies and exercises guide students in approaching and manipulating empirical data, providing them with hands-on experience of conducting linguistic research. An extensive variety of approaches, from traditional to contemporary, is treated, including generative approaches, historical sociolinguistic and pragmatic approaches, psycholinguistic perspectives, grammaticalization theory, and discourse-based approaches, as well as perspectives on standardization and language variation. Each chapter applies the concepts discussed to data from the history of English, and a glossary of key terms enables easy navigation and quick cross-referencing. An essential resource for advanced undergraduate and graduate students of the history of English linguistics.

LAUREL J. BRINTON is the (co-)author of four scholarly books (and one forthcoming) and the (co-)author of two textbooks (in the history of English and structure of modern English). She has (co-)edited three collections of papers as well as a two-volume handbook of historical linguistics (2,312 pages, 70+ authors). She was co-editor of the *Journal of Historical Pragmatics* and is currently co-editor of *English Language and Linguistics*. She is a recipient of a Killam Research Prize and a Killam Research Fellowship.

English Historical Linguistics

Approaches and perspectives

Edited by

LAUREL J. BRINTON

University of British Columbia,
Vancouver

CAMBRIDGE
UNIVERSITY PRESS

University Printing House, Cambridge CB2 8BS, United Kingdom

One Liberty Plaza, 20th Floor, New York, NY 10006, USA

477 Williamstown Road, Port Melbourne, VIC 3207, Australia

4843/24, 2nd Floor, Ansari Road, Daryaganj, Delhi – 110002, India

79 Anson Road, #06–04/06, Singapore 079906

Cambridge University Press is part of the University of Cambridge.

It furthers the University's mission by disseminating knowledge in the pursuit of education, learning, and research at the highest international levels of excellence.

www.cambridge.org
Information on this title: www.cambridge.org/9781107113640
DOI: 10.1017/9781316286562

© Laurel J. Brinton 2017

This publication is in copyright. Subject to statutory exception and to the provisions of relevant collective licensing agreements, no reproduction of any part may take place without the written permission of Cambridge University Press.

First published 2017

Printed in the United Kingdom by Clays, St Ives plc

A catalogue record for this publication is available from the British Library.

ISBN 978-1-107-11364-0 Hardback
ISBN 978-1-107-53421-6 Paperback

Cambridge University Press has no responsibility for the persistence or accuracy of URLs for external or third-party internet websites referred to in this publication and does not guarantee that any content on such websites is, or will remain, accurate or appropriate.

Contents

Figures

Tables

Case Studies

Contributors

Cynthia L. Allen is a Fellow Emerita at the Australian National University, where she taught courses in Linguistics and History of English until her retirement in 2015. She is a Fellow of the Australian Academy of the Humanities in recognition of her work in the history of English morphosyntax. She has authored two monographs examining the loss of case marking in English and its relationship with syntactic changes. She has recently contributed chapters to *English Historical Linguistics: An International Handbook* (2012) and *The Cambridge Handbook of English Historical Linguistics* (2016) and contributed the entry on Middle English to the *Online Research Encyclopedia of Linguistics*. She is a co-founder and current editorial board member of the series Studies in Language Change and serves on the editorial board of the series Studies in Diachronic and Historical Linguistics. For more information, see https://researchers.anu.edu.au/researchers/allen-cl

Lieselotte Brems is Associate Professor of English language and linguistics at the University of Liège and Research Fellow at the KU Leuven. Her research interests include grammaticalization and (inter)subjectification, specifically within the English noun phrase. She has published a monograph on size and type noun constructions, e.g., *a bunch of lies* and *a quirky type of love song*, which discusses the synchronic functional variation of these constructions and argues for this being the result of grammaticalization processes (*Layering of Size and Type Noun Constructions in English*, 2011). Recent research looks at nominal complementation constructions in which negation markers interact with a set of nouns that synchronically layer lexical and (epistemic, deontic, and mirative) modal meanings, e.g., *no doubt/question/fear/wonder that/of*. For further information, see www.arts.kuleuven .be/ling/func/members/lieselotte-brems

Laurel J. Brinton is a Professor of English Language in the Department of English at the University of British Columbia, Vancouver. Her research interests include grammaticalization and lexicalization, historical pragmatics, phrasal verbs and composite predicates, and verbal aspect. In addition to two textbooks (on the structure of Modern English [co-authored with Donna M. Brinton] and on the History of English [co-authored with Leslie K. Arnovick]), she has authored four monographs: on comment clauses, on pragmatic markers, on verbal aspect, and on lexicalization (co-authored with Elizabeth Closs Traugott). Most recently she co-edited *Studies in the History of the English Language* IV with Michael Adams and R. D. Fulk (2014) and the two-volume *English Historical Linguistics: An International Handbook* with

Alexander Bergs (2012). She is co-editor of the journal *English Language and Linguistics* (Cambridge University Press). For further information, see faculty.arts.ubc.ca/lbrinton/

Claudia Claridge is Professor of English Linguistics at the University of Augsburg, Germany. Her research interests include Early Modern English, (historical) pragmatics, figurative language, text linguistics, subordinate clauses, intensifiers, and verb and adjective usage. She is one of the compilers of the *Lampeter Corpus of Early Modern English (1640–1740)*. She has authored two monographs (*Multi-word Verbs in Early Modern English*, 2000, and *Hyperbole in English*, Cambridge University Press, 2011) and co-edited two volumes (*Developments in English: Expanding Electronic Evidence*, 2014, with Irma Taavitsainen, Merja Kytö, and Jeremy Smith, and *Fiasko: Scheitern in der frühen Neuzeit*, 2015, with S. Brakensiek). She has contributed articles on historical corpora, historical registers and genres, pragmaticalization, news discourse, and lying vs. hyperbole/metaphor to various recent handbooks. For further information, see philhist.uni-augsburg.de/lehrstuehle/anglistik/sprachwissenschaft/1-staff/claridge

Anne-Christine Gardner is currently a research and teaching assistant in the English Department at the University of Zurich. After studying at the Ruprecht-Karls-Universität Heidelberg and Newcastle University, she received her PhD in 2013 from the University of Zurich with a corpus-based investigation of regional and text type variation in Middle English word formation. Her postdoctoral research project aims at conducting a linguistic analysis of selected diaries written by Lady Mary Hamilton (1756–1816) between 1776 and 1797, contextualizing her linguistic profile through social network analysis and corpus-linguistic case studies. The project also involves preparing transliterations of selected diary entries for a digital edition working with TEI-conformant XML mark-up. Her wider research interests also include the development of the English lexicon, and language contact and pragmatics.

Peter J. Grund is Associate Professor of English Language Studies at the University of Kansas. He is the author of *Misticall Wordes and Names Infinite: An Edition and Study of Humfrey Lock's Treatise on Alchemy* (2011). Together with Merja Kytö and Terry Walker, he is the co-author of *Testifying to Language and Life in Early Modern England*, including a CD containing *An Electronic Text Edition of Depositions 1560–1760 (ETED)* (2011), and, as part of a twelve-member team, he co-edited *Records of the Salem Witch-hunt* (Cambridge University Press, 2009, 2014). He also serves as the co-editor of the *Journal of English Linguistics*. His interests include English historical sociolinguistics and sociopragmatics, stance, evidentiality, and speech representation in historical periods, and he has published extensively on these topics. For further information, see english.ku.edu/peter-j-grund

Raymond Hickey is Professor of English Linguistics at the University of Duisburg and Essen, Germany. His main research interests are varieties of English (especially Irish English and Dublin English), sociolinguistics, and general questions of language contact, variation, and change. Among his recent book publications are *Motives for Language Change* (Cambridge University Press, 2003), *Legacies of Colonial English* (Cambridge University Press, 2004), *Dublin English: Evolution and Change* (2005), *Irish English: History and Present-day Forms* (Cambridge University Press, 2007), *The Handbook of Language Contact* (2010), *Eighteenth-century English* (Cambridge University Press, 2010), *Areal Features of the Anglophone World* (2012), *The Sound Structure of Modern Irish* (2014), *Researching Northern English* (2015), *Sociolinguistics in Ireland* (2016), and *Listening to the Past: Audio Records of Accents of English* (Cambridge University Press, 2016) For further information, see www.uni-due.de/~lan300/HICKEY.htm

Martin Hilpert is Professor of English Linguistics at the University of Neuchâtel. He holds a PhD in Linguistics from Rice University (2007). He conducted post-doctoral research at the International Computer Science Institute in Berkeley and the FRIAS (Freiburg Institute for Advanced Studies). In 2012, he completed his Habilitation Thesis in English Philology at the University of Freiburg. His research interests include Construction Grammar, cognitive linguistics, language change, and corpus linguistics. He is the author of *Germanic Future Constructions* (2008), *Constructional Change in English* (Cambridge University Press, 2013), and *Construction Grammar and its Application to English* (2014). He is one of the editors of the journal *Functions of Language*. For further information, see members.unine.ch/martin.hilpert/

Sebastian Hoffmann is Professor of English Linguistics at Trier University. He received his doctoral degree from the University of Zurich, where he also worked for several years as a postdoctoral researcher. Before moving to Trier, he spent three years at Lancaster University (UK) as Lecturer in English Linguistics (2006–2009). His research predominantly focuses on the application of usage-based approaches to the study of language; recent research topics include: syntactic change (e.g., *Grammaticalization and English Complex Prepositions: A Corpus-based Study*, 2005), tag questions, the lexico-grammar of New Englishes, and corpus linguistic methodology involving internet-derived data. He is a co-author of BNCweb, a user-friendly web interface to the *British National Corpus*, which also forms the basis for his textbook publication *Corpus Linguistics with BNCweb: A Practical Guide* (2008; with S. Evert, N. Smith, D. Lee, and Y. Berglund-Prytz) For further information, see www.uni-trier.de/index.php?id=29525

Marianne Hundt is Professor of English Linguistics at Zurich University. Her research interests range from grammatical change in contemporary and late Modern English to varieties of English as a first and second language (New Zealand, British and American English; English in Fiji and South Asia) and language in the Indian diaspora. She has been involved in the compilation of various electronic corpora: the extension of the Brown family corpora and ARCHER, *A Representative Corpus of Historical English Registers* (completed), and the Fiji component of the *International Corpus of English* (ongoing). She has also explored the use of the

World Wide Web as a corpus and for corpus building. She is the author of *English Mediopassive Constructions* (2007) and *New Zealand English Grammar – Fact or Fiction?* (1998) and co-author of *Change in Contemporary English: A Grammatical Study* (Cambridge University Press, 2009). She has edited various monographs, and since 2013 has been co-editor of *English World-Wide*. For further information, see www.es.uzh.ch/en/subsite/personal/mhundt.html

María José López-Couso is an Associate Professor at the University of Santiago de Compostela and a member of the Research Unit for Variation, Linguistic Change and Grammaticalization. Her research interests include morphosyntactic change and grammaticalization and (inter)subjectification processes in the history of English. She has published extensively on these topics and co-edited the following volumes: *English Historical Syntax and Morphology* (2002; with Teresa Fanego and Javier Pérez-Guerra), *Rethinking Grammaticalization: New Perspectives* (2008; with Elena Seoane), *Theoretical and Empirical Issues in Grammaticalization* (2008; with Elena Seoane), *Information Structure and Syntactic Change in the History of English* (2012; with Anneli Meurman-Solin and Bettelou Los), and *Corpus Linguistics on the Move: Exploring and Understanding English through Corpora* (2016; with Belén Méndez-Naya, Paloma Núñez-Pertejo, and Ignacio M. Palacios-Martínez). She is also a member of the Executive Board of ICAME (International Computer Archive of Modern and Medieval English). For further information, see www.usc-vlcg.es/MXLC.htm

Edgar W. Schneider holds the Chair of English Linguistics at the University of Regensburg, Germany. He is an internationally renowned sociolinguist and World Englishes scholar, known widely for his "Dynamic Model" of the evolution of Postcolonial Englishes. He has lectured on all continents, given many keynote lectures at international conferences, and published many articles and books on the dialectology, sociolinguistics, history, semantics, and varieties of English, including *American Earlier Black English* (1989), *Introduction to Quantitative Analysis of Linguistic Survey Data* (1996), *Focus on the USA* (1996), *Englishes around the World* (2 vols., 1997), *Degrees of Restructuring in Creole Languages* (2000), *Handbook of Varieties of English* (2 vols., 2004), and the Cambridge University Press books *Postcolonial English* (2007) and *English around the World* (2011). For many years he edited the journal *English World-Wide* and its associated book series, Varieties of English Around the World. For further information, see www.uni-regensburg.de/language-literature-culture/english-linguistics/staff/schneider/index.html

Merja Stenroos is Professor of English Linguistics in the Department of Cultural Studies and Languages at the University of Stavanger, Norway. She leads the Middle English Scribal Texts Programme at Stavanger and is the main compiler of two corpora of Middle English: the *Middle English Grammar Corpus* (MEG-C) and the *Middle English Local Documents Corpus* (MELD). Her research interests include historical sociolinguistics and pragmatics, historical dialect geography, medieval literacy and text production as well as writing systems. Together with Inge

Særheim and Martti Mäkinen, she edited the volume *Language Contact and Variation Around the North Sea* (2012).

Ingrid Tieken-Boon van Ostade has a chair in English Sociohistorical Linguistics at the Leiden University Centre for Linguistics (Leiden, the Netherlands). She specializes in the English standardization process (particularly in codification and prescription), and is interested in the relationship between grammar rules and actual usage. Her most recent books are *An Introduction to Late Modern English* (2009), *The Bishop's Grammar: Robert Lowth and the Rise of Prescriptivism* (2011) and *In Search of Jane Austen: The Language of the Letters* (2014). She is the director of the research project "Bridging the Unbridgeable: Linguists, Prescriptivists and the General Public," which studies English usage guides and usage problems, and is writing a monograph on the English usage guide. A recent book is *Prescription and Tradition in Language: Establishing Standards across Time and Space*, which she co-edited with Carol Percy (2017).

Abbreviations

General terms

AdvP	adverb phrase
AmE	American English
Aux	auxiliary, auxiliary node
BrE	British English
DAT	dative
Det	determiner
E-Language	external language
EModE	Early Modern English
FLB	faculty of language in a broad sense
FLN	faculty of language in a narrow sense
HUGE	*Hyper Usage Guide of English* database
I	inflection
IITSC	Invited Inferencing Theory of Semantic Change
I-Language	internal language
IP	inflection phrase
LModE	Late Modern English
M	modal auxiliary
ME	Middle English
MED	*Middle English Dictionary*
N	noun
Neg	negative
NegP	negative phrase
NOM	nominative
NP	noun phrase
OBJ	object
ODNB	*The Oxford Dictionary of National Biography*
OE	Old English
OED	*Oxford English Dictionary*
OV	object-verb word order
PDE	Present-day English
PP	prepositional phrase
SBJ	subject
SV	subject-verb word order

SVO	subject-verb-object word order
V	(main) verb
V2	verb-second word order
VO	verb-object word order
VP	verb phrase

Corpora (for full information, see the References at the end of the book)

AE06	*American English 2006*
ANC	*American National Corpus*
ARCHER	*A Representative Corpus of Historical English Registers 3.2*
B-Brown	*The 1930s Brown Corpus*
BE06	*British English 2006*
B-LOB	*The BLOB-1931 Corpus*
BNC	*British National Corpus*
Brown	*A Standard Corpus of Present-day Edited American English*
CED	*A Corpus of English Dialogues 1560–1760*
CEEC	*Corpus of Early English Correspondence*
CEECS	*Corpus of Early English Correspondence Sampler (1418–1680)*
CEEM	*Corpus of Early English Medical Writing (1375–1800)*
CLMET	*Corpus of Late Modern English Texts*
COCA	*The Corpus of Contemporary American English: 520 million words, 1990–present*
COERP	*Corpus of English Religious Prose*
COHA	*The Corpus of Historical American English: 400 million words, 1810–2009*
COOEE	*Corpus of Oz Early English*
DCPSE	*Diachronic Corpus of Present-day Spoken English*
DOEWC	*Dictionary of Old English Web Corpus*
EAF	*Early American Fiction Collection (1789–1875)*
ECCO	*Eighteenth Century Collections Online*
ED	*English Drama*
EEBO	*Early English Books Online*
EMEMT	*Early Modern English Medical Text*
ETED	*An Electronic Text Edition of Depositions 1560–1760*
FLOB	*Freiburg–LOB Corpus*
Frown	*Freiburg–Brown Corpus*

HC	*The Helsinki Corpus of English Texts: Diachronic and Dialectal*
LAEME	*A Linguistic Atlas of Early Middle English, 1150–1325*
LALME	*A Linguistic Atlas of Late Mediaeval English*
LC	*The Lampeter Corpus of Early Modern English Tracts*
LOB	*Lancaster–Oslo–Bergen Corpus*
MEG-C	*The Middle English Grammar Corpus*
MELD	*Middle English Local Documents Corpus*
NCF	*Nineteenth-century Fiction, 1782–1903*
OBC	*The Old Bailey Corpus 2.0*
PCEEC	*Parsed Corpus of Early English Correspondence*
PPCEME2	*The Penn–Helsinki Parsed Corpus of Early Modern English*
PPCME2	*The Penn–Helsinki Parsed Corpus of Middle English*
YCOE	*The York–Toronto–Helsinki Parsed Corpus of Old English Prose*
York Poetry corpus	*The York–Helsinki Parsed Corpus of Old English Poetry*

1

The Study of *English* Historical Linguistics

LAUREL J. BRINTON

Introduction

Students of English will find a wealth of textbooks on the history of the language, as well as a substantial number of textbooks introducing them to the principles of historical linguistics in general.[1] In the last ten years we have also seen a spate of "handbooks" on the history of English or English historical linguistics published.[2] How do all of these approaches to the history of English differ, and how is the following textbook distinguished?

In broad outline, textbooks on historical linguistics tend to be organized around linguistic levels of change – phonological change, morphological change, syntactic change, and semantic change. Of course, they also cover a variety of other topics, such as internal and external reconstruction, causes of change, language birth and death, language contact, language classification, and so on. In contrast, histories of the English language – with very rare exceptions – are organized chronologically, following the different "periods" of English (see below on "periodization"). Principles of linguistic change, if discussed explicitly at all in these textbooks, are subsumed to the overall presentation of a "narrative" of change from Old English to the present day. The more recent handbooks of English – all impressive works in their own right, collecting work by many of the best scholars in the field today – are typically organized by period (like histories of English) or by linguistic level (like introductions to historical linguistics), though again they may treat a myriad of other topics.

The linguistic study of the English language has a long history, as will be described briefly in the next section, and over time scholars have made different assumptions about the nature of language and language change, have adopted different theoretical perspectives, and have utilized different methodologies in studying the history of English. There is not one monolithic, coherent approach to the history of English. Some of the recent handbooks of English present discussions of these different approaches and perspectives,[3] but these handbooks are generally addressed to the scholarly researcher, not the student of English, and often focus on the "state of the art" in research rather than providing descriptive information on methodology and approach. The range of advanced research articles published in academic journals, while utilizing many different approaches, typically do not supply the contextual information necessary for the student to understand where they fit within the broader framework of approaches.

This focus of this textbook, then, is the different **approaches** and **perspectives** taken in the study of English over time, ranging from more "traditional" approaches such as language contact and dialectology to the most contemporary approaches, including psycholinguistic, sociolinguistic, and pragmatic ones. A basic knowledge of the history of the English language is assumed, and the textbook does not strive for comprehensive coverage of either the details of specific changes in the history of English or all principles of linguistic change, both of which are handled more ably by histories of English and historical linguistics textbooks. Rather, what is undertaken here is a description of eleven varied approaches to English historical linguistics: each chapter first describes the theoretical approach and its methodologies, challenges, and successes and then illustrates it with case studies that highlight the strengths and scope of the approach (see overview of chapters below). The overall goal of this textbook is to give you a sense of how English historical linguistic study is (and has been) undertaken over the years

A Short History of English Historical Linguistics[4]

English historical linguistics grew out of the philological tradition (with its focus on older stages of English and manuscript studies), but the discipline itself (as a scientific endeavor) can be traced most directly to the Neogrammarians (*Junggrammatiker*), a group of scholars originally working in Leipzig at the end of the nineteenth century. Their approach spread to other countries in Europe and to England as chairs in English linguistics were established at various universities. Great strides in understanding developments in English and the Germanic languages generally were made by assuming the "Neogrammarian hypothesis" (with its assertion of the exceptionlessness of sound change – see Chapter 2), despite the fact that it has ultimately been proven wrong. It is also during this period that large-scale dialect studies began to be undertaken, which although focused on contemporary dialects, were also inherently concerned with dialect change; such studies ultimately led to the development of historical dialectology in the twentieth century (Chapter 12).

The Neogrammarian approach was replaced by structuralism (of both European and American varieties) in the early part of the twentieth century. The focus of structuralism – as the name suggests – was on the overall structure of language systems and the systemic effects of language change, such as mergers or splits affecting the phonological system or analogy affecting the morphosyntactic system. The extent to which structural changes are functionally motivated was also investigated. It was proposed, for example, that certain changes were consciously made to achieve some goal (for example, avoiding the development of "homonyms") or, on a larger scale, that languages could be seen as moving, unconsciously, in a particular direction, e.g., from synthetic (highly inflected) to analytic (less highly inflected). Although the notion of teleology in language change has been discredited to a large extent, this focus on both structure and function provided important insights into development of English.

The generative approach, which took hold in the mid-twentieth century, shifted attention from the history of individual languages to the study of more abstract principles of language; initially its focus was rigidly synchronic. But by 1970, generativists began to turn their attention to language change, seeing it as the result of sudden changes or reanalyses (later understood as changes in parameter settings) and to incomplete or imperfect transmission of grammatical structure during language acquisition. Generative approaches to change are described in detail in Chapter 3.

In reaction to the focus on the abstract system of language ("competence") in the generative approach, an alternative "usage-based" approach has gained strength. In it, usage (the forms speakers use) is understood as crucial for our understanding of language, and variation (an intrinsic part of "performance") is seen as the locus of change. Linguistic structures emerge as a result of frequently used forms, which, in appropriate contexts, invite reinterpretation, thus eventually leading to a change in the grammar. A strongly usage-based focus underlies grammaticalization studies (see Chapter 6), an approach which began to assume a significant part in English historical linguistics in the 1980s.[5] The study of standardization (Chapter 11) also views variation and usage as central to change.

What perhaps most obviously characterizes approaches to English historical linguistics in the latter part of the twentieth century and the beginning of the twenty-first century is the merger of historical linguistics with other fields whose focus was initially synchronic. These include corpus linguistics (Chapter 5), discourse studies (Chapter 8), sociolinguistics (Chapter 9), pragmatics (Chapter 10), and language contact as well as pidgin and creole studies (Chapter 13).

Overview of Chapters

Chapter 2 "The Scope of English Historical Linguistics" by Raymond Hickey provides a sweeping overview of what is covered by English historical linguistics. It begins with a comparison of the major approaches, exemplifying some of the fundamental principles of each: the exceptionless nature of sound change (Neogrammarian), sound shifts, mergers and distinctions, internal and external motivation, the force of analogy (structuralist), simplification and repair, avoidance of merger, functional load, gradual and discrete change, the notion of drift (functionalist), reanalysis by children, and sudden change (generative).

Grammaticalization and lexicalization (treated in detail in Chapter 5) represent newer approaches. The chapter then describes the techniques by which linguistic forms and processes are established: use of the comparative method, of internal reconstruction, of general knowledge of linguistic processes, and of the evidence of relative chronology. The transmission of change is shown to follow an S-curve, with remnants of older forms and processes continuing to exist. The chapter then provides five extended examples of changes in the sound system which exemplify many of the principles discussed: the Great Vowel Shift, the loss of /h/ (also discussed in Chapter 9), the replacement of interdental fricatives, the vocalization of /l/ and /r/, and the adoption of dialect forms. (Note that because most of the later chapters treat syntax, the focus of this chapter is phonology.)

Chapter 3 "Generative Approaches" by Cynthia L. Allen begins with a brief discussion of the development of generative grammar before turning to generative approaches to linguistic change. Lightfoot's study of the rise of the modal auxiliaries (1979) is presented as an example of the importance of child language acquisition as the locus of change, in which younger speakers construct new grammars based on contraints imposed by Universal Grammar. The chapter moves on to more recent generative views of change (within the "Minimalism Program") in which syntactic change happens when language learners reset one or more "parameters" in language. Changes in the expression of negation in the history of English are used as a case study of this approach. The treatment of variation as an instance of "competing grammars" in the generative approach is exemplified with the regulation of *do* in English (Kroch 1989); here, the declining frequency of one grammar (that allows verb-raising) is seen as regulating the increasing frequency of *do* at the same rate in different environments, but the ultimate loss of that grammar allows *do* to develop independently in different contexts. The chapter ends with a discussion of generative approaches to phonological change within Optimality Theory, in which historical change involves differences in the ranking of the constraints that generate linguistic forms. Originally introduced as an approach to phonology, it has been extended to other linguistic levels.

Chapter 4 "Psycholinguistic Perspectives" by Martin Hilpert presents a survey of some of the most important psychological processes that are thought to underlie linguistic change. "Categorization," or the ability to view things as belonging to the same group, may – on the linguistic level – be behind the modal auxiliaries as a distinct category and the rise of "emerging modals." "Analogy" (also discussed in Chapter 2) is the capacity to perceive identity in relations; it is the type of rule generalization that leads irregular verbs to become regular in the history of English. "Automatization" occurs when an action (or a linguistic string) is repeated often enough that it is processed as a single unit; it may be partially responsible for the development of complex prepositions (discussed in Chapter 5). "Reanalysis" happens when a hearer analyzes a speaker's utterance as a structure that deviates from what the speaker intended; it accounts for the development of the perfect periphrasis from an originally possessive construction. "Metaphor" establishes a conceptual relation between two distinct ideas from different domains, while "metonymy" involves mapping within a single domain between things that tend to be experienced together. Both processes are prominent in semantic change, accounting for meaning changes in the modal auxiliaries. "Inferencing," the ability to read intended meanings into utterances, has been seen as a primary motivation in grammaticalization, Finally, "priming," or the cognitive activation of one element facilitating the subsequent processing of a similar element, may create an opportunity for speakers to extend the ways in which certain constructions are used. The chapter ends with a discussion of ways in which such a psycholinguistic approach relates (or does not relate) to the generative approach and to other usage-based approaches, such as Construction Grammar.

After defining what constitutes a corpus, describing different types of corpora, and cataloguing available historical corpora of English, Chapter 5 "Corpus-based Approaches" by Marianne Hundt and Anne-Christine Gardner provides an introduction to corpus linguistic methodology (how to conduct, and analyze the results of, a corpus search). The chapter includes two detailed studies of corpus studies, one grammatical and one lexical, which provide comprehensive illustrations of how to conduct corpus-based studies of language variation and change. The first study involves changes in the use of the inflected subjunctive in three contexts: in *if*-clauses, following suasive verbs (the "mandative subjunctive"), and in conditional clauses. Using a variety of corpora (including the Brown family of corpora, ARCHER, and COHA), the searches show that American and British English are developing differently, with American English reviving the mandative subjunctive and preserving the subjunctive in *if*-clauses and conditionals at a higher rate than British English. The second study involves the competition between a number of deadjectival suffixes in Middle English, *-ity, -ness*, and *-hood*. Using data from LAEME and other Middle English corpora, the study shows the introduction of the borrowed suffix *-ity* and the competition between *-ness* and *-hood*, ultimately leading to the decline of the latter.

Chapter 6 "Approaches to Grammaticalization and Lexicalization" by Lieselotte Brems and Sebastian Hoffmann begins by surveying the (often divergent) conceptualizations of grammaticalization and lexicalization in the field. The chapter argues that definitions of grammaticalization have moved from more formal (morpho-syntactic) to more pragmatic-semantic, with increasing emphasis placed on context. However, questions of what to subsume under the lexicon have led to a lack of consensus on how to define lexicalization. After discussing the corpus methodology utilized in grammaticalization studies – and some of the difficulties of obtaining adequate historical data – the chapter presents three case studies. The development of connective *while* is seen as a paradigm case of grammaticalization which exemplifies Hopper's (1991) principles of decategorialization, divergence, layering, and persistence as well as many of the other principles proposed by Lehmann (1985). The case of *methinks* emphasizes the blurred distinction between grammaticalization and lexicalization since the fusion of two words into one and demotivation of the original impersonal construction suggest the latter, while the rise of a (fairly) closed-class adverb marking evidentiality with discourse functions suggests the former. The third case study reviews work on complex prepositions such as *instead of* or *in terms of* as cases of grammaticalization but notes that problems in this analysis (e.g., the lack of crucial data for transitional periods, the low frequency of these items, and for many, such as *with respect to* or *in relation to*, no known change from concrete to abstract) may point to a different explanation altogether. The chapter ends with a discussion of degrammaticalization, admitting that its existence does not invalidate grammaticalization research.

Chapter 7 "Inferential-based Approaches" by María José López-Couso discusses how pragmatic inferences arising in the context of speaker–hearer negotiations play a fundamental role in language change, specifically through the processes of subjectification and intersubjectification. After presenting Traugott's "Invited Inferencing Theory of Semantic Change," the chapter defines subjectification and intersubjectification, seeing the rise of (inter)subjective meanings as the result of the conventionalization of pragmatic inferences. These processes provide predictable paths for some (but not all) types of semantic change and may be found in some (but not all) types of grammaticalization. Four case studies exemplifying (inter)subjectification are given. The rise of epistemic meanings from deontic meanings in the modal auxiliaries shows an increase in meanings expressing speaker assessment, attitude, or viewpoint. For example, *must* originates in a modal expressing 'ability' or 'permission' and over time acquires a meaning of 'obligation,' out of which arises the meaning of 'deontic necessity' and finally the fully epistemic meaning of 'logical deduction.' In their development from matrix clauses, the parentheticals *(it) seems like, (it) looks like*, and *(it) sounds like* undergo (inter)subjectification as they come to serve as mitigators or hedges on the speaker's commitment to the veracity of the clause to which they are adjoined as well as a means of attending to the interlocutor's negative face. The rise of condition, contrast, and causal meanings from original temporal meanings in the connective *while* is the result of invited inferences in the context of use, some of which have been conventionalized, and shows clear signs of (inter)subjectification. Finally, the interjection *gee!* – as well as undergoing euphemistic phonological change from the religious invocation *Jesus!* – involves conventionalization of the invited inference of subjective surprise or annoyance arising in its use outside its original contexts.

Chapter 8 "Discourse-based Approaches" by Claudia Claridge provides a means of entering language history through the door of discourse. The importance of vernacularization and standardization in shaping the language, as well as that of multilingualism and the effects of genre, are described. The chapter identifies three ways in which the role of discourse in language change can be investigated and presents a case study of each. First, in *discourse-oriented diachronic linguistics*, the focus is on what role discourse plays in the distribution of features, as well as in the origin and diffusion of changes. As an example, the increase in three syntactic structures – *there* sentences, *it*-clefts, and certain passive constructions – can be seen as filling discourse needs for expressing topics and linking brought about by the loss of verb-second word order in early Middle English. Second, *diachronic(ally oriented) discourse analysis* focuses on changes in discourse types as changing entities over time. The differentiation of texts into more informational, elaborate, and abstract as opposed to more involved and situation-dependent based on the presence or absence of certain linguistic features underlies studies of stylistic shifts toward a more literate style during standardization and an opposing shift toward more oral or colloquial style in the modern period. Third, *historical discourse analysis* is concerned with the linguistic form of texts or genres, their communicative aims, and their embedding in a sociocultural context at a certain point in time. Here, a detailed study of the changing form of letters is provided.

Chapter 9 "Sociohistorical Approaches" by Peter J. Grund defines a field which applies the tools and concepts of sociolinguistics to historical study. Within this field a diachronic approach, which focuses on the connection between various social factors and change over time, may be distinguished from a synchronic approach, which focuses on the social dynamics of language use at one point in time. The chapter discusses the problems of acquiring appropriate source material for sociohistorical study (the problem of "bad data," a problem also taken up in Chapters 7 and 10). Sufficient social information – on the gender, age, social rank of the interlocutors or on their social networks, communities, or practices – may also be difficult to access, though it becomes more readily available in the modern period. Two detailed case studies show sociohistorical research at work. The first involves the distinction of *you* and *thou* in Early Modern English. As a variety of works on this topic have shown, the choice between these pronouns is dynamic and fluid and is determined by a range of social, situational, and textual factors. The second case study involves *h*-dropping; here, the evidence of spelling and contemporary commentary shows that, whatever its origin, this phenomenon became strongly stigmatized by the early nineteenth century.

After defining the field of historical pragmatics, its three subfields, and the range of pragmatic units studied, Chapter 10 "Historical Pragmatic Approaches" by Laurel J. Brinton turns to questions of methodology. Historical corpus pragmatics – facilitated now with the existence genre-specific corpora containing more "speech-based" data – is seen as the primary means of addressing the "bad data" problem. The chapter then moves on to two case studies. The study of speech acts may be undertaken via a form-to-function approach through the study of performative verbs, but this approach is seen as minimally fruitful. Speech acts – as communicative acts expressed linguistically by a wide variety of linguistic means – require a function-to-form approach which, however, causes difficulties for corpus approaches (which typically require explicit search terms). A number of studies that have attempted to overcome these limitations are summarized. The study of comment clauses (parentheticals usually formed with first- or second-person pronouns and simple present-tense verbs) is much more amenable to a corpus-linguistic approach. The chapter provides a detailed examination of the development of *you see* comment clauses. Whether this development is best understood as grammaticalization, or lexicalization (as discussed in Chapter 6), or pragmaticalization is examined.

Chapter 11 "Perspectives on Standardization" by Ingrid Tieken-Boon van Ostade traces the path from codification to prescriptivism, the last two stages of the standardization process (Milroy and Milroy 2012). Interest in codifying English arose in the mid-seventeenth century when John Dryden revised Shakespeare's plays. Calls for the establishment of a language academy for English to produce grammars and dictionaries were ultimately unsuccessful. Rather, in the early eighteenth century, grammars codifying the language came to be written by individuals, including clergymen, schoolmasters (and mistresses), scientists and mathematicians, wealthy merchants and even publishers themselves. Competition among publishers was often fierce. The chapter provides guidance on how to study these developments using primary sources. The publication of grammars led to a next step in the process, the birth of the English usage guide, both in Britain and America, in response to a need among the people for linguistic guidance in an era characterized by social and geographical mobility. The legacy of the Fowler brothers on usage guides is described in detail. The HUGE (*Hyper Usage Guide of English*) database is presented as a tool for studying the history of usage guides. Finally, a number of studies comparing actual usage (gleaned from corpus data) with the dictates of usage guides are summarized.

Chapter 12 "Perspectives on Geographical Variation" by Merja Stenroos begins with a "thought experiment" imagining how future generations might be able to reconstruct Present-day English were all sound recordings lost and only written evidence remained. The chapter then briefly discusses variation in Old, Middle, and (Early) Modern English, focusing on the difficulties faced by scholars, who must rely solely on the evidence of the written form (spelling) and manuscripts whose history may be unknown or complex. The methodology of historical dialectology developed out of the large-scale dialect surveys of Britain and America in the late nineteenth and twentieth centuries (using informants), and was adapted to historical periods (using textual materials). Here, two approaches are possible, one which localizes texts on the basis of their language, the other which focuses on texts for which the provenance is known (so-called "local documents"). Changes in historical dialectology reflect a merger with sociolinguistics – the recognition that geographical variation cannot be studied in isolation but must be considered along with a host of (non-linguistic) variables. The chapter than presents three case studies. The first involves the distribution of forms of the third-person plural pronoun, "they," in the ME Kentish dialect. Here, what looks like a geographical spread of the innovative form outwards from London must be seen instead as a diachronic spread over the course of the fifteenth century. The second case study uses local documents to trace the decline of four characteristic Northern ME forms over the course of the fifteenth and early sixteenth centuries (pointing to the effects of standardization). The third case study examines the merger of the [ʍ] and [w] (as in the homophonous pronunciation of *whales* and *Wales* for many speakers). The textual evidence (based on variant spellings including <w>, <wh>, and forms like <qu>) is shown to be complex but suggests that the sounds had indeed already merged in some varieties of Middle English.

Chapter 13 "Perspectives on Language Contact" by Edgar W. Schneider sets out to explain how our conception of English as a single coherent language has given rise to recognition of a variety of "World Englishes," each with its own distinctive properties. Moreover, even Standard English itself is a language that has emerged from contact processes to a large extent. After a discussion of language contact effects in general, where it is argued that extralinguistic history predominates over internal processes of change and that a correlation exists between degree of contact and the range of contact effects, the chapter examines five case studies which illustrate important and typical contact scenarios. The first looks at vernacular contact during the Old English period, placing emphasis on Celtic and Scandinavian influence, both of which had significant effects. The second examines French contact in the Middle Ages, suggesting that its impact may not actually have been as far-reaching as traditionally assumed, and Latin influence during the Renaissance. New Zealand English, the third case study, represents a case of settler English, which often results in mutual dialect accommodation but involves minimal (exclusively lexical) effect from the indigenous language(s). The fourth case study discusses issues surrounding the rise of Singapore Colloquial English, or "Singlish," a product of language contact, with transfer phenomena from some varieties of Chinese and from the other local Asian languages. The last case study examines language attitudes in diglossic Nigeria, where Nigerian Pidgin (a contact language illustrating the fuzziness between "creole" and "pidgin") and Standard English evoke competing ideologies.

Excursus on Periodization[6]

The periods of English used in this textbook are those most commonly used today (with some minor differences in dating):

Old English (OE)	*c.* 450–1100
Middle English (ME)	1100–1500
Early Modern English (EModE)	1500–1700
Late Modern English (LModE)	1700–1920
Present-day English (PDE)	1920–today

Like all such schemas, this one includes a high degree of idealization, suggesting absolute boundaries between periods (perhaps based on the presence or absence of a particular linguistic feature), a single linguistic system with long periods of stability and then sudden (cataclysmic) changes from one stage to another, and a straight linear progression form one stage to another. However, we know that the transition from one period to another is continuous and gradient and that languages always contain variation and are in flux, with different components changing at different rates and subject to contact effects yielding mixed languages.

Despite the current acceptance of this periodization (or something like it), you should be aware that such a classification has not always been the accepted one. Early scholars proposed quite different periods, with categories such as "Anglo-Saxon" and "Semi-Saxon" for the earliest periods, with "Old English" beginning only in 1250. The present differentiation into "Old," "Middle," and "Modern" can be traced back to various works by Henry Sweet (1874) and James Murray (1879) (see Curzan 2012: 1237–1244). Sweet initially distinguishes "Old English" as the period of full inflections, "Middle English" as the period of leveled inflections, and "Modern English" as the period of lost inflections, but both Sweet and Murray later add external events to the mix (the Norman Conquest, the Proclamation of 1250, the Tudor dynasty, Caxton and the printing press, the King James Bible, the English Revolution, and literary productions).

The most important question raised by periodization concerns the criteria to be used in making period divisions. It is not intuitively obvious whether periods should be differentiated by internal linguistic criteria (by the retention of archaic features or the development of innovative ones, or both), by extralinguistic (political/historical/cultural) criteria, or by some combination of these criteria. Relying exclusively on linguistic features risks the possibility of arriving at different divisions, depending on the features selected. Reliance on external features alone emphasizes the (linguistically) artificial nature of the proposed periods. Therefore, more recent views favor considering a mix of internal and external criteria.

Curzan concludes that "the now canonical historical periods have been, since their inception, scholarly fictions [but t]hey are important and useful scholarly fictions" (2012: 1243).

Notes

1. To name just a few histories of English referred to in this textbook, we can cite Fennell (2001), Crystal (2004), Algeo (2010), Baugh and Cable (2013), and Brinton and Arnovick (2016). Some of these have gone through numerous revisions and iterations – Baugh's history, for example, was originally published in 1935 and is still in print today! We must, of course, not neglect to mention the monumental *Cambridge History of the English Language* (Hogg [general ed.] 1992–2001).

   A few general historical linguistics textbooks cited in the following text include McMahon (1994), Crowley and Bowern (2010), Campbell (2013), and Miller (2015).

   But textbooks showing the intersection of these two disciplines are very limited (however, see Smith 1996 and Jucker 2000).

2. These include Hogg and Denison (2006), van Kemenade and Los (2006), Bergs and Brinton (2012a, 2 volumes), Mugglestone (2012), Nevalainen and Traugott (2012), and Kytö and Pahta (2016).
3. See, especially, the second volume of Bergs and Brinton (2012a).
4. For a longer discussion, see Bergs and Brinton (2012b) and the contributions to section XI "History of English historical linguistics" in Bergs and Brinton (2012a).
5. On the history of grammaticalization studies, see Hopper and Traugott (2003: 19–38).
6. This section is based on Curzan (2012); see her discussion for a much fuller treatment of problems of periodization.

2

The Scope of English Historical Linguistics

RAYMOND HICKEY

Introduction

When studying linguistics as an English student one is confronted with configurations of language and processes of change which are attested both in the
homeland of the English language, Britain, and in many other locations across
the world where English is spoken, both as a first and as a second language.
In this sense the scope of English linguistics is bounded by the structural range of
today's language. However, when viewed from a historical perspective many
other aspects come to light which present students with insights into language
states and language change. This applies on all levels of language, but also to
possible sociolinguistic scenarios which are known to have existed in the history
of English. In addition, there are many more features and configurations of
language, not attested in English, either today or in its history. This fact is
often highlighted by non-Anglicist scholars attempting to demonstrate just how
much languages can vary and how restrictive it can be to confine the primary data
one considers solely to the English language. So the student of English should be
aware that the history of the language tells us about certain types of change but by
no means covers all.[1]

There are many features of pronunciation and grammar which are found in
languages other than English and which are part of the possible set of features in
human language. For instance, word order is a parameter of syntax which varies
greatly across languages. English now only has SVO (Subject–Verb–Object) for
simple declarative sentences but it used to have SOV (Subject–Object–Verb)
word order as well. Other languages, like Irish, Welsh or Classical Arabic, show
VSO (Verb–Subject–Object) with the verb at the beginning in normal declarative
sentences. There are languages which have series of related sounds distinguished
by some secondary feature, e.g., Russian has sets of palatal (those produced by
raising the tongue towards the palate) and non-palatal sounds. There are languages with double consonants, like /kp/ and /gb/ (spoken together), e.g.,

indigenous languages of West Africa, or click sounds found in Khoisan and Nguni languages of South Africa (the latter are Bantu languages which borrowed them from the former group). Some languages have a small number of distinct sounds (phonemes), e.g., Hawaiian (a Polynesian language) with only eight consonants; others, like many Caucasian languages, have very large inventories of over 70–80 distinctive sounds, almost twice as many as English.

Despite the absence of so many structural features of human language in English it is a fruitful undertaking to outline what types of language change are attested in the history of English and to discuss these as a subset of possible changes in language. In considering such changes one can see how English, especially in its early history, moved away from its inherited early Germanic type. This can be seen, for instance, in morphology where English lost most of the verb endings characteristic of its Germanic input, in syntax where the old SOV word order was replaced by SVO and where the inherited V2 (verb-second) rule was later abandoned. It can also be seen in phonology where English lost long consonants and the rules governing syllable structure which are connected to this (still present in Norwegian and Swedish). English also lost front rounded vowels which form an integral part of the sound systems of the remaining Germanic languages in Europe.

In this chapter different models and processes of language change will be presented. Then the techniques of historical linguistics are described. The final section looks at various items of language change in the history of English which illustrate the principles discussed in previous sections. The examples given in this chapter are largely from phonology. Examples of language change from grammar, lexis, and pragmatics are presented in other chapters of the book.

Language Change: Models and Processes

The study of the historical development of language within the Indo-European language family was known in the nineteenth century as "comparative philology." This had its beginning at the end of the previous century with the discovery that classical languages like Greek, Latin, and Sanskrit are related to each other. Soon after this a number of scholars independently established interconnections between the languages of the Germanic, Romance, Celtic, Slavic, and Baltic groups of languages. Notable among these authors is Jacob Grimm, who established a series of sound laws which applied to Germanic in its earlier stages. A sound law refers to a change or a series of related changes in the phonology of a language. The term "sound law" (German *Lautgesetz*) is used to stress the regularity of the change. The classic example is the Germanic Sound Shift or Grimm's Law (Minkova 2014: 61–68). This states

Table 2.1 *The Germanic Sound Shift / Grimm's Law*

Latin	English	Old English
pes	*foot* (p ~ f)	*fot*
tres	*three* (t ~ θ)	*þrēo*
collis	*hill* (k ~ x)	*hyl*
quod	*what* (kw ~ xw)	*hwæt*

that very early on, when Germanic was differentiating itself from the remaining dialects of Indo-European, all voiceless stops were shifted to voiceless fricatives, i.e., /p/ became /f/, /t/ became /θ/ and /k/ became /x/ (among other shifts[2]).

With *hill* and *what* one must consider the development of the /x/-sound. Within the Old English period /x/ was weakened to /h/ in word-initial position and represented as *h* in writing. From this fact one can conclude that those words which had been inherited from Germanic and which were written with initial *h* originally had /x-/. The sequence /xw/ in Germanic later developed analogically to /hw/. Through assimilation of /w/ to the preceding voiceless glottal fricative the voiceless [ʍ] developed; this was voiced in the early modern period in southern England to [w].

The Neogrammarians

The examination of language change in the heyday of historical linguistics – in the nineteenth century – was done within a framework which saw language change as proceeding continuously for all elements which could in principle be affected by a change in progress (see the discussion of the Germanic Sound Shift just given). This approach is known as the "Neogrammarian hypothesis" (derived from the German word *Junggrammatiker*) and was formulated most clearly by the German linguist Hermann Paul in his book *Prinzipien der Sprachgeschichte* 'Principles of Language History,' first published in 1880 (Paul 1891 [1880]).

Working within this hypothesis, linguists stressed the exceptionless character of sound laws (German *Ausnahmslosigkeit*). According to this view, the only exceptions to a valid sound law can occur due to the force of analogy. This is where an expected change is not found because another element in a grammatical paradigm blocked or masked a change at some later point. Thus, the attested change of /s/ to /r/ (from an earlier /z/ due to "rhotacism" [see below]) in the past tense of the verb *sein* 'be' in German was later masked by the analogical spread of /r/ to all elements of the verbal paradigm, e.g., *ich war, du warst*, etc. In English we can still see the original alternation between /s/ and /r/: *I was, you were*, etc. (the /-z/ at the end of *was* is a later development from an earlier /-s/; the /r/ is from the original /z/).

The Structuralist Point of View

An aspect of language backgrounded by the Neogrammarians is its overall structure – they seem to have been overly concerned with detail. This shortcoming was later remedied by a number of linguists who were active at the beginning of the twentieth century. Because they emphasized the necessity of categorizing changes and taking the whole structure of a language into account when offering explanations of language change, they are termed "structuralists." The father of this approach is the Swiss-French scholar Ferdinand de Saussure (1857–1913).

To begin with one can give an example of how structure can explain language change or the lack of it. In English there are two interdental fricatives, a voiced and a voiceless one: /θ, ð/. Their functional load (the degree to which a distinction is utilized in a language – see section on avoidance of mergers below) is slight, i.e., there are only a few minimal pairs in which the sounds contrast, e.g., *thigh* /θaɪ/ – *thy* /ðaɪ/; *teeth* /tiːθ/ – *teethe* /tiːð/. However, the contrast voiced–voiceless is central to the phonology of English and so a peripheral set of distinctions is retained for reasons of conformity to the overall pattern. The appeal to the overall organization of the sounds in a language can also be made when considering sounds entering a language with lexical borrowings: French loans like *vision* and *pleasure* introduced the sequence /zj/ which later became /ʒ/ thus providing a voiced equivalent to the /ʃ/ sound (as in *shoe*) which already existed in English.

A structuralist view of language change can be used to explain series of changes in a language. Take the example of Grimm's Law again. The Neogrammarians simply described the law. The structuralists considered its origin and its course. Assuming that one sound began to shift, it is obvious that this upset the structure of the entire sound system. If /p/ shifted to /f/, what happened to the original /f/? If /f/ first shifted to /v/ what happened to the "vacuum" which it left behind? Because one has no way of determining in retrospect (and without any written records) what part of the entire sound law occurred first, one speaks of a "push–pull" chain which led to a reshuffling of the sound system of Proto-Germanic. In such an overall view of sound structure, no one element can change without affecting the remaining elements in the system.

Another example of a push–pull chain is the Great Vowel Shift in English (see section below). This is a change in the values for long vowels beginning in the Middle English period and more or less completed by the eighteenth century. Basically it consisted of a raising of long vowels by one level, e.g., /oː/ became /uː/ (as in *fool*), /eː/ became /iː/ (as in *feet*). At the same time the two high vowels of Middle English, /iː/ and /uː/, diphthongized, as in *time* and *house* respectively. While we cannot say what occurred first, one can maintain that either a raising of monophthongs or a diphthongization of high vowels upset the system (altered the relations in phonological space) and this led to a restructuring of the entire long vowel pattern. These vowel shifts led to spelling and sound no longer being in sync and are in large part responsible for the divergence of the two in Present-day English.

Incidentally, both instances just discussed do not either expand the entire phonological system or cause it to contract. However, there are many changes which lead to a loss of phonological contrast ("system contraction," as in the loss of /x/ through vocalization, written <-gh>, in later Middle English in words like *plough, although, through*) and many which led to an increase ("system expansion," as in the process of umlaut,[3] the anticipation of a high front vowel in a preceding syllable, e.g., /o/ expands to /o/ and /ø/ as well as /u/ to /u/ and /y/ in Germanic).

Mergers and Distinctions

A particular type of sound change is where two sounds are reduced to one, technically termed a "merger." A good example of this is the coalescence of Middle English /a:/ and /aɪ/ under /eɪ/ in Modern English, e.g., *tale* and *tail*, now both /teɪl/. The orthography shows that the original pronunciation was /ta:l/ and /taɪl/ in the late Middle English period before the Great Vowel Shift set in.

A merger is generally taken to be irreversible because for a later generation it is not possible to recognize that one form may have originally consisted of two. There are cases which seem to contradict this, however. For instance, the realization of *boil* and *bile* as /baɪl/ is a merger which was reversed because it did not occur in all varieties of eighteenth-century English. The pronunciation /bɔil/ was re-established for *boil* because speakers had access to varieties of English with this pronunciation.

In Old English there were two words *cwēn* 'queen' and *cwene* 'slut, prostitute.' They continued up to about the time of Shakespeare as two separate words, then with the pronunciations [kwi:n] and [kwe:n] respectively. But sometime afterwards both pronunciations became the same as the /e:/ was raised to /i:/. The derogatory meaning was then lost and 'queen' became the sole meaning of the merged form.

Internal versus External Motivation

All the above examples of language change can be considered as internally motivated. There are many changes which are externally motivated (Hickey 2012c), particularly at times when a language is under the influence of a further language, i.e., in a situation of language contact (Hickey 2012a; see Chapter 13). At the outset of Old English there was contact with Celtic (Hickey 2012b) and in later centuries there were two main periods in which Scandinavian and French influence was felt. The nature of the change is dependent on the type of contact: with the close everyday contact during the Scandinavian period one has many daily lexical items but also a series of morphological borrowings, whereas with French one has mainly lexical borrowings but with sounds hitherto unsystemic in English, such as /ʒ/ mentioned above. Both influences on English can be interpreted from a structural point of view.

With the loss of inflections in Middle English (see section on "drift" below), new systemic distinctions arose. Consider that in Old English voiceless fricatives were found in voiceless contexts (initially and finally and next to voiceless consonants) while voiced fricatives were found in voiced contexts (between voiced sounds, e.g., intervocalically). But frequently the intervocalic position was due to an ending, as in *teðan* 'to teethe,' so that when these endings were lost the voiced fricatives now occurred word-finally and contrasted with the voiceless fricatives which already existed in this position. This accounts for the contrast in voice found in modern word pairs like *teeth* [ti:θ]: *teethe* [ti:ð], *knife* [naɪf]: *knives* [naɪvz], etc. This fact seems to have furthered the adoption of the voiced fricatives /v, z/ in French words into English (e.g., *virtue*, *zeal*), leading to a later phonemic distinction /f/ : /v/, e.g., *file* : *vile*, and /s/ : /z/, e.g., *seal* : *zeal*. Contrast this situation with other languages: in Swedish, the voiced fricative in *journal* from French is always voiceless as Swedish has no voiced [z] or [ʒ] and thus no motivation to introduce this extraneous sound with borrowings.

For a discussion of Scandinavian influence on English, see the section on "Simplification and repair" below.

The Force of Analogy

The term "analogy" is used in a number of different senses, but basically it refers to a change on the basis of an already existing pattern in the language.

- ***Proportional analogy***. This can be summarized as a change on the basis of the following formula.

  A : B :: C : D (A is to B as C is to D, where D is an innovation)

  This can be seen working in the occasional change of weak to strong verbs, a change attested in varieties of southern American English (1) and found as a shift of conjugational type in the history of English (2).

(1) A: *sing*: B : *sang*	C: *bring* : D: *brang* (for *brought*)
(2) A: *teach*: B : *taught*	C: *catch* : D: *catched* → *caught*

- ***Analogical remodeling.*** This refers to a change under the influence of another form. It can be seen in the phonetic alteration of words because of semantic similarity, as with the following French loans after they entered English.

  denizen and *citizen* (changed from the original French *citeain*)
  male and *female* (changed from the original French *femelle*)

The spread of a pattern frequently involves a leveling of phonological contrast in order to attain regularity in a grammatical paradigm. Consider types of plural: in Old English there were various patterns, some of which survived into the

Middle English period. Of these the *-en* plural lasted a considerable time but was finally replaced by the *-s* plural, e.g., *eye* has the plural *eyen* in Chaucer but later shows a final *-s*. Here *-s*, the dominant plural suffix in English, came to replace the nasal which is nowadays only present in *ox : oxen* as well as in *children* and *brethren* (actually "double" plurals as they contain the former /r/ suffix as well). Such irregular plurals are only found in the core vocabulary of English, e.g., *man : men, foot : feet* which contain reflexes of former umlaut.

Because analogical remodeling makes a minority form conform to majority usage, it may render a former distribution invisible. For instance, the word *roof* frequently has a plural with a voiceless fricative – *roofs* – despite the original voiced fricative (still recognizable in *rooves* and found in *wife ~ wives* and *leaf ~ leaves*, etc.).

The common ground for both meanings of analogy discussed here is the creation of symmetry. This would seem to suggest that speakers value symmetry in an abstract way and that their knowledge of language and its possible forms includes the concept of system regularity.

- *Analogical maintenance.* In general /w/ after /s/ and before /o/ was lost in English. However, in those cases where the /w/ is present elsewhere in a paradigm this exerted pressure to maintain it. Hence *sword* lost the /w/ but the past tense form *swore* has retained the /w/ because this also occurs in the present tense *swear* /swe:r/.

- *Analogical creation.* Here again one form acts as a model for another. In this instance, however, a new word is created on the basis of another. *Moonscape* modeled on *landscape* is an example. *Regardless* leading to *irregardless* on the basis of *irrespective* would be another.

The Functionalist Approach

Considering a language's structure leads one to the question of its function and whether there is an implicit goal in language change, i.e., whether change is teleological (from Greek *telos* 'goal'). If language change is motivated, then this presupposes that speakers have an unconscious knowledge of what constitutes an optimizing change. On this assumption, speakers will on the whole avoid changes which involve great homophony and further changes which lead to system regularity.

The functionalist view is, however, fraught with anomalies. To begin with, if all languages change in such a way that they are optimized, then this implies that to begin with, all languages were inefficient and that the end stage will be one of perfection after which no more change occurs. However, there could be changes which do not lead to optimization and hence prevent the system from reaching complete equilibrium. Another difficulty is defining what is optimal in a language. Furthermore, optimization can refer variously to communication and to the internalized system of language.

Consider firstly that there is a natural tension between the tendency among humans to inertia (inactivity) and the need for communication. According to this, language systems should move towards a reduction in complexity, but this would be constrained by the necessity to guarantee communication. At first sight this appears to be true. Throughout the history of English there has been a tendency to simplify English grammar with the loss of nominal and verbal inflections. From Edward Sapir we have the term "drift" (see the discussion below), intended to describe the gradual and largely imperceptible direction of language change. But for drift to work, each generation must have an (unconscious) awareness of the direction of the drift – otherwise how would speakers know how their language is changing?

Simplification and Repair

Language change in the sense of simplification is limited by the needs of communication. Changes which would seriously impair individuals understanding each other are avoided, or if they occur, are very often "repaired."

In late Old English some third-person pronouns had become homophones or near homophones; i.e., /hi:/ could have caused confusion between 'he' and 'they,' at least in some varieties of Old English. This situation was "remedied" by borrowing Scandinavian forms in *th*- [θ] from the north of England (Modern English: *they, them, their*), replacing those beginning with *h* /h-/.

Reparational changes are of interest in their own right. Their basic motivation is the maintenance of system clarity and consistency. Consider the following case: in Germanic a phonological change occurred called "rhotacism" where /z/ (from an original /s/ due to Verner's Law[4]) changed to /r/. This led to original morphological alternations of /s/ and /z/ becoming alternations of /s/ and /r/. Furthermore, if the /s/ was later voiced (after rhotacism had declined as a phonological process) then the alternation may have become /z/ ~ /r/, which is what one has in *was* : *were* in Present-day English. What one can see here is that a regular phonological change (/z/ > /r/) resulted in irregularity in the morphology of English.

In Modern English the /z/ ~ /r/ alternation is preserved in the past of the verb *be*, but in other forms later regularization may conceal the original alternation. Compare the /s/ in English *lose* (now voiced due to a later development) / *lost* (from Old English *forleas* ~ *forloren*) but /r/ in the German verb *verlieren* 'to lose'/ *verloren*. That is, all the /r/-forms were changed in English to conform to those in /s/, whereas in German all the /s/ forms changed to /r/. See Table 2.2. This is known as "analogical levelling." However, remnants may provide evidence of the older pattern: in German the noun *Verlust* 'loss' shows that an /s/ was originally found in the paradigm, while in English the adjective *forlorn* 'abandoned, scarcely likely' as in *a forlorn place, a forlorn hope* (derived from a past participle) shows that there was originally an /r/ in the paradigm.

Another instance where the /s/ ~ /r/ alternation was reversed to maintain paradigmatic regularity is the Old English verb *cēosan* 'choose,' which had the

Table 2.2 *Effects of regularization (analogical leveling) of s ~ r variation in English and German*

	English	German
infinitive	*lose*	*verlieren*
preterite	*lost*	*verlor*
past participle	*lost*	*verloren*

past participle *gecoren*. This is now *chosen* and there is no *r*-form in the paradigm of the verb *choose* today.

Avoidance of Mergers and Functional Load

While the avoidance of mergers may play a role in inhibiting language change, one should not overemphasize its importance. Above all one should remember that it is not possible to predict language change on the basis of merger avoidance. In English many instances of language change have given rise to very considerable homophony, just consider the outcome of the merging of Middle English /ai/ and /a:/ to /eɪ/ as in *tail, tale; sail, sale* or the vocalization of /r/ which led to homophones like *caught, court; horse, hoarse* in Received Pronunciation (Upton 2008).[5]

With examples of this kind comprehension is not impaired. The context is in all cases enough to clarify the intention of the speaker. Recall that the degree to which a distinction is utilized in a language is known as its "functional load." The smaller this load, the easier it is for elements to be subject to merger or loss.

Gradual and Discrete Change

If language change is something which takes places slowly, over at least a few generations, then it is obvious that it is gradual by nature. This poses a problem for the interpretation of certain attested types of language change. In some cases it is clear that the change is discrete by nature. For example, the change from Old English *niman* to *take* cannot have had intermediary stages (in form) as can, for example, the shift of /u:/ to /au/ in *house*. The answer to the question posed by discrete change is that there must have been a period (of at least one generation) in which both the older and the newer form were valid alternatives and that, in the course of time, the newer variant became dominant, finally suppressing the older one entirely.

The Notion of "Drift"

The early twentieth-century American linguist Edward Sapir spoke of "drift" in the history of languages, meaning a gradual movement over time in a consistent direction. Whether drift exists for individual speakers is disputed, but nonetheless one can observe a movement in the history of English away from a synthetic language type, with many case endings and complex verb forms, to a more analytic type in which the morphology has been greatly simplified. This is widely assumed to have triggered further changes, notably less freedom in word order, SVO for declarative sentences, and the loss of the stringent V2 rule (which demanded, for instance, that after a sentence-initial adverb the order of verb and subject be reversed, as in Modern German *Hoffentlich kommt er morgen*, lit. 'hopefully comes he tomorrow').[6] The demise of inflectional morphology has furthermore meant that subject agreement in Present-day English is based more on content than on form, e.g., *The police have come at last*, *The majority are in favor of the measure*, where the singular subjects take plural verb forms.

The Generative Approach

Since the advent of generative grammar in the late 1950s the seminal ideas of its inventor, Noam Chomsky, have been applied to developments in the history of English. The essential premise of this approach is that speakers have an internalized grammar of their native language and it is this which underlies their ability to speak. This grammar is constructed during early childhood when language learners combine their inherited knowledge of language structure with the external input of the language in their surroundings (or more than one in a multilingual environment). Children reach conclusions about the structure of the language they are exposed to by analyzing the linguistic input. When a language is changing, however, children may interpret this input differently from preceding generations, leading to reanalysis which is a sudden type of change, assuming that the majority of language learners in a community perform the same reanalysis at approximately the same time. Furthermore, they may construct different interpretations of the primary linguistic data they are exposed to, leading to competing internalized grammars. Examples of these phenomena are discussed in detail in Chapter 3 of this volume.

Grammaticalization

The process labeled "grammaticalization" involves a shift in status of words from full lexical items to grammatical endings or words (Hopper and Traugott 2003). There is usually a sequence of steps which the words pass through during grammaticalization.

Table 2.3 *Process of grammaticalization*

Status	Steps in process
lexical word, semi-lexical word	loss of meaning through semantic bleaching
clitic	frequent attachment to another lexical word
affix (inflection)	permanent loss of independence and retention of grammatical meaning only

A few examples from the history of English can illustrate this principle clearly. Old English *līc* meant 'form, body' and existed as an independent word but later was lost in this capacity and was retained only as an ending *-lice* which led to the modern suffix *-ly*. A northern pronunciation of the word without palatalization of the final segment gave *like* which is both an independent grammatical word and an element of a compound as in *childlike*.

Another instance is provided by Germanic /au/, which became /æɑ/ in Old English but remained /au/ in Old Norse. *Leas* /læɑs/ was therefore an Old English form while *lauss* was the shape in Old Norse. This was borrowed into English and resulted in Modern English *loose*, whereas the Old English form is still to be seen in the suffix *-less* which has been grammaticalized to a privative ending, as in *homeless, hapless*.[7]

The Old English word *hwīl* 'time' occurred in the dative plural *hwīlom* meaning 'during.' This was reduced to *while* by inflectional loss and the original noun came to be used primarily as an adverb/conjunction of time, e.g., *She rang while he was having his lunch*, and is now only found as a noun in more or less fixed phrases such as *worth my while* or *once in a while*. Later still a concessive meaning developed, seen in a sentence like *While she likes linguistics, she took the literature course*.

Again in Old English there was a word *dōm* meaning 'judgment; condition' (Modern English *doom*), which as an ending lost its original meaning but survived as a suffix indicating a quality noun. Hence forms like *kingdom* and *wisdom* are taken to consist of stem + derivational suffix.

The situation just described is very common and is attested in Present-day English with such endings as *-burger* (from the original *hamburger*), which came to be used in other cases like *cheeseburger, veggieburger, fishburger* where meat is not necessarily found. Yet another example would be modern English *lemonade*, which has been expanded to include drinks from other fruits, e.g., *orangeade*. This ending is also found in another sense, namely, 'location with a specific function': from an original *arcade* one now has formations like *parkade* 'building with parking facilities.'

Any word class can be subject to grammaticalization. Consider the use of *go* for the future. This was originally locative in meaning (and still is in cases like *She goes to work at eight*), but the lexical meaning of movement forward in space came to be interpreted as a movement in time and sentences like *She's going to buy some new clothes* show that both a locative and a temporal interpretation are possible, while instances like *She's going to say something about her new clothes* show a purely temporal meaning.

The context in which a word or phrase is used can lead to grammaticalization, frequently if it is reduced phonologically. An example in Present-day English is *lets* which went through a development as follows: *Let us* (< 'allow us to do something') > *let's* > *lets* 'why don't we,' as in *We could go for a walk. Yeah, lets.* (Further discussion of grammaticalization is found in Chapter 6.)

Lexicalization

At any one time in a language certain words are transparent in their composition or in the derivational process used to construct them. A simple example can be offered with the word *asleep* which derives from Old English *on slæpe* but which in Modern English is not understood as 'on sleep.' In Old English what one had was a transparent phrase, in Modern English one has an opaque compound. Thus the phrase became lexicalized; i.e., speakers can no longer derive it from *on* + *sleep* but learn it as a single indivisible word.

Lexicalization (Brinton and Traugott 2005) is most often connected with phonetic developments. Consider the following example. The word *pan* has full stress as it is a monosyllable, /pæn/. However, *saucepan* has a reduced vowel due to lack of stress on the second syllable so that the word is no longer necessarily interpreted as being 'a pan for cooking sauce in.'

Phonological developments may lead to lexicalization as forms are no longer associated with each other by speakers. For instance, *sloth* 'laziness' comes from *slow* + the ending *-th* as in *warm* ~ *warmth*, but the difference in vowel length probably led to *slow* and *sloth* moving apart semantically.

Names frequently show lexicalized elements, e.g., *Clapham, Greenham*, which contain as second element the Old English word *hām* 'home,' which, because unstressed, did not undergo later vowel raising. This situation is also to be seen with the word *hamlet* 'small village,' which now has a short /æ/ from Old English /ɑ:/, which was raised to /o:/ and diphthongized in Early Modern English and is variously realized in *home* as /hɔʊm/, /hoʊm/ in different varieties of modern English. The result is that speakers no longer see a connection between *home* and *hamlet* and the latter word is lexicalized. Another instance of such lexicalization is *Lambeth*, the name of a London suburb, which contains the words for *lamb* + *heath* but where the latter is reduced to an unstressed vowel, whereas the independent word *heath* retained the long vowel and went through all later vowel changes.

Lexicalization can also occur when one or more elements of a compound disappear from the language. For example, *garlic* comes from Old English *gar* 'sharp' + *lēc* 'leek,' i.e. the word meant 'sharp leek.' But with the loss of *gar* 'sharp,' the compound *garlec* (> modern *garlic*) became opaque.

Examining common words from the core vocabulary of a language shows that lexicalization is a frequent process. For instance, the words *husband* (a Norse loan) and *woman* are now indivisible forms but they each derive from two words, i.e., *hūs* + *bond* 'house' + 'servant' and *wīf* + *mann* 'female' + 'man' respectively. Further instances which involve the shortening and reduction of vowels and which have led to a dissociation between the compound and its elements are *holiday* < *holy* + *day*; *breakfast* < *break* + *fast*; *gospel* < OE *gōd* + *spel* 'the good news'; *sheriff* < *shire* + *reeve* 'county warden.' (Further discussion of lexicalization can also be found in Chapter 6.)

The Techniques of Historical Linguistics

So far in this chapter examples of different kinds of language change have been presented and discussed. You could justifiably ask how linguists know what forms from the history of English were like and what changes took place. The answer is by using established techniques for tracking historical data and change in languages. In the course of the nineteenth century, when linguistics evolved as a science in its own right, various techniques and methods were developed to help linguists gain reliable information about previous stages of languages.

The Comparative Method

This refers to the practice of comparing forms in two or more languages with a view to discovering regularities of correspondence. A simple instance from English and German concerns /t/ and /s/. With a series of native words – not loans – one can see that where English has /t/ German has /s/: *water* : *Wasser*, *better* : *besser*, *foot* : *Fuss*. So English /t/ corresponds to German /s/ in non-initial position. The question is whether /t/ or /s/ is original. Here one can quote other Germanic languages – e.g., Swedish has *vatten*, *betra*, *fot* for *water*, *better*, *foot* – and this would imply that it is German which has changed the original /t/ to its present /s/. One could also use the argument that a fricative is more likely to develop from a stop, through a general process of weakening, rather than vice versa (unless through assimilation to another stop).

As a further instance consider the reconstruction of morphological endings, in this case, the nominative singular masculine ending of Germanic. This is postulated to have been /-z/. Icelandic, which is particularly archaic, has /–r/, as in Icelandic *ulfr* 'wolf'; neither Swedish *ulf* or English *wolf* retain this ending. We can deduce from a number of well-preserved old Germanic loans in Finnish such as *rengas* 'ring' which shows a final /-s/ that Icelandic /-r/ is the result of rhotacism. Since Finnish does not have /z/ and since we know from rhotacism in other languages (such as Latin, compare *flōs* : *flōris* 'flower') that /r/ arises from a voiced sibilant, we are justified in assuming the nominative masculine singular in Germanic ended in /-z/.

Another major concern of the comparative method is justifying a postulated original form which is not attested. An example would be the vowel originally present in English *home* and German *Heim*. The assumption is that it was a low back vowel with the following development:

Scottish [hem], southern German [heim]; English *home* ← OE *hām*

/e/, /eɪ/   /ou/, /əʊ/

ɑː

The reason for assuming /ɑ:/ as the original vowel is that this requires the shortest movement through articulatory space to both a mid-front and a mid-back vowel, that is to /e, ei/ and /ou, əʊ/ respectively.

Dialect information can also be used in reconstruction. As noted above, the sequence <wh-> was formerly pronounced /ʍ/, although it is currently /w/ in most dialects of Standard English. However, if one looks at conservative dialects, like rural Irish or Scottish English, one sees the older pronunciation still. Across languages one can find supportive evidence of assumptions about pronunciation as well. Take the word *kyning* 'king' in Old English. Linguists assume that the *y* refers to a front rounded vowel. Now Modern English has /ɪ/ in this word, but the German word *König* shows a front rounded vowel (albeit mid rather than high). Again a look at Finnish can be revealing: *kuningas* 'king' is a very old Germanic loan and hence the first syllable must have had /u/ initially in Germanic. This helps us also because linguists assume that there was a later phenomenon of umlaut whereby back vowels were fronted when a high vowel was present in a following syllable (as is the case here).

Internal Reconstruction

This is the second major technique in reconstructing previous stages of languages. The basic principle is that one uses evidence from within a single language to gain knowledge of an earlier stage, e.g., by examining the reflexes of older pronunciations. Such evidence is usually available in forms which embody unproductive processes, themselves remnants of formerly active processes.

An example from the English verbal system is offered by word pairs like *sleep* : *slept*; *keep* : *kept*; *creep* : *crept*. These are not strong verbs like *sing* : *sang* : *sung* although they do show a vowel alternation, i.e., /i:/ : /e/ between the present and past. This vowel change can be traced to a tendency in the history of English to shorten vowels before clusters of consonants in syllable-final position. Thus the original vowel in all the verb forms was /e:/. This was shortened to /e/ when followed by two or more consonants, this condition being met by the past forms of certain verbs (such as *slept, kept, crept*) where /t/ was added to the final /p/. Later the Great Vowel Shift led to the raising of Middle English /e:/ to /i:/ (in *sleep, keep, creep*) resulting in the present-day alternation of /i:/ and /e/ in these verbs.

Examining the Orthography

The orthographic conventions of older languages can give us evidence of earlier pronunciations and sound systems. For instance, Latin orthography is known in its entirety and much is known of other systems as well. For instance, we know that *þ*, *ð* in Old English (not part of the Latin alphabet) were realized phonetically as [θ, ð], because the first letter is a known Runic symbol and the second, a "crossed d," a fricative voiced alveolar stop, was used elsewhere as well. *Æ* (lowercase: *æ*) is a ligature and is understood to symbolize a sound between [a] and [e].

The orthography is not always reliable, however. Take the practice in Early Modern English of writing *ye* as a shorthand for *the*. The *y* never had any phonetic basis although it has led to a curious spelling pronunciation /ji:/, which is found in names of supposedly traditional pubs and restaurants such as *Ye Olde Shippe* /ji: əuld ʃɪp/.

At any one stage of a language the orthography can show "reverse" spellings which can be useful in dating a sound change. Consider the following example: in southern Middle English the voiceless fricative /x/, indicated in writing by <gh> and then present in words like *night, light, right*, was gradually lost. Now there are spellings from the fourteenth century, like *wright* for *write*, which was always pronounced with a long /i:/ and never had /x/. This suggests that the scribe using this spelling assumed that <*igh*> represented /i:/ because, for example, the pronunciation /ni:t/ for <*night*>, from earlier /nɪxt/, had already been established.

Rhyme Material

If a word is made to rhyme with another whose pronunciation is known, then the same sound value can be assumed for the first word. Consider the following opening of a well-known piece from Act IV, Scene 2 of Shakespeare's *Cymbeline*.

> Fear no more the frown o'th' great;
> Thou art past the tyrant's stroke.
> Care no more to clothe and eat;
> To thee the reed is as the oak:

(internetshakespeare.uvic.ca)

This shows that, for Shakespeare, the word *eat* was pronounced with the same vowel as is the word *great* today, i.e., as a mid-front vowel /e:/, because it is known from other sources that *great* did not change its pronunciation as did *eat, beat, seat*, etc.

Prescriptive Comments on Language

In the Early Modern English and especially Late Modern English periods, there are many prescriptive comments on contemporary language use (for the eighteenth century see the contributions in Hickey 2010a). Such comments are a valuable source of information on pronunciation. For instance, we know from contemporary remarks that the high back vowel in *but* /but/ was lowered to an unrounded low vowel during the seventeenth century in the south of England ultimately yielding present-day /bʌt/ (Dobson 1968).

Many prescriptive authors of the eighteenth century, foremost among them Thomas Sheridan (1719–1788) and John Walker (1732–1807), condemned or favored older or newer pronunciations of their day. For instance, Sheridan preferred a long /a:/ in the first syllable of *merchant*, a pronunciation which is established in words like *barn, dark, marsh* and in the first syllable of county names like *Berkshire, Derbyshire* in England, thus showing that this pronunciation was much more widespread in previous centuries than it is today.

For standard British English, Walker also preferred the retention of a non-prevocalic /r/, the sound /r/ when it does not occur before a vowel, e.g., *car* /kɑːr/ and *card* /kɑːrd/ (Ihalainen 1994), something which was on the way out during his lifetime. Such comments can help us to date the loss of /r/ at the end of syllables, a development which is responsible for the modern Received Pronunciation seen in words like *car* /kɑː/ and *card* /kɑːd/. (See further Chapter 11 on the influences of prescriptivism.)

General Knowledge of Linguistic Processes

Finally, one can appeal to what linguists know about general processes in language change. Applying general knowledge in particular cases assumes that linguists have an accurate conception of what constitutes a typical and what an unusual change. There is not always agreement among scholars on this point and it is difficult to define "typical" and "unusual" objectively. Despite these difficulties, the notions are nonetheless useful. For instance, palatalization, the shift forward in the mouth for place of articulation, often with a change in manner of articulation as well, is a very common phenomenon. This is seen in Slavic and Romance languages, e.g., Latin *camera* (with /k/) became *chambre* in French (first with /tʃ/ then with /ʃ/ by simplification). Old English also shows this change with /tʃ/ in southern forms and /k/ in northern forms, as well as in Scandinavian and German, e.g., *chin* versus German *Kinn*. Thus, if two related languages have the sounds [k] and [tʃ] respectively, one can safely assume that the language with [tʃ] has this from an earlier [k], as the shift [tʃ] to [k] is a non-attested sound change (palatalization as a process normally involves a forward movement from the velum to the palate). Another example of a general process would be rhotacism, the development of /r/ from /z/. This is attested in a wide variety of languages and language groups such as Latin and Germanic (see above). The direction is generally from the fricative to the sonorant, though examples in the opposite direction are not unknown.

Yet another example of general reasoning would concern front vowels. If a language has /y/ and /ø/ then one can assume that umlaut has occurred, as this is generally the source of front rounded vowels. There is a second possible origin in language contact, though this type of source is not accepted by all linguists.

Again an instance of general knowledge helping in an individual case would be with morphology. If a language has fewer inflections than another related one, then it is probably right to assume that the latter is older – at least more conservative – as inherited inflections tend to be lost by phonetic attrition; the acquisition of inflections by the grammaticalization of semantically bleached lexical elements is much less frequent.

A common principle may be seen to apply to a specific process in language change. For instance, there is a general principle that words normally maintain

Table 2.4 *Palatalization and* i-*umlaut in Old English*

palatalization	*cinn*	→	*chin*	[tʃin] (shift of *c* [k] to [tʃ] before front vowels like /i/ or /y/)
umlaut	*cuning*	→	*cyning*	[kynɪŋ] (fronting of back [u] to [y])

their quantity, despite segmental changes within them. Thus on consonant loss, there is frequently compensatory lengthening by a short vowel becoming long. In Middle English the /x/ sound was lost in southern English and the vowels before this segment were lengthened, thus maintaining the entire quantity of the word, e.g., *light* was originally /lixt/ and later became /li:t/ (and /laɪt/ with the Great Vowel Shift). If one considers single consonants and short vowels as consisting of one unit of quantity then one can interpret the long vowel (a segment with two units of quantity) as arising due to the adoption of the quantity released by the loss of /x/.

Relative Chronology

It is rare that one can date a certain change precisely. But a relative rather than absolute chronology can often be established. By this is meant that two or more changes can be put in chronological order relative to each other. This is usually possible because the result of one change would have been different if it had preceded or followed the other. Here are some examples to illustrate what is meant.

In Table 2.4, we see that there are two processes involved in a definite chronological order: first palatalization then umlaut. We know this because if the order was the other way around then the present-day pronunciation of the word for 'king' would be [tʃiŋ], i.e. *cyning* would have been palatalized to [tʃynɪŋ] (> [tʃiŋ] through vowel unrounding and loss of second syllable). We conclude that palatalization became inactive before umlaut set in, so that those words which experienced umlaut did not go through palatalization.

As shown in Table 2.5, a tendency in the history of English is for long /u:/ to be shortened. This starts in the early modern period and continues to the present-day. The forms affected by this change differ in their realizations today depending on when the shortening took effect. With these changes one can also specify the environment in which they took place. The earliest shortening affects many instances of /u:/ before /d/, as in *blood* (but not all, cf. *food*). This vowel was then affected by the general lowering of /ʊ/ to /ʌ/ in southern English. After this shortening came that of /u:/ before /k/, as in *took*. This occurred after the lowering of /ʊ/ to /ʌ/ had become inactive, hence the pronunciation /bʊk/ for *book* and not /bʌk/. Finally, the shortening before /m/ occurs. This shortening has not been completed yet as can be seen from words which have variable realizations in Received Pronunciation: *broom* /brʊm/ or /bru:m/.

Table 2.5 *Vowel shortenings in the history of English*

	Great Vowel Shift	Shortening	17th century	19th century	
fool	/oː/ → /uː/				(no shortening)
blood	/oː/ → /uː/	→ /ʊ/	/ʌ/		(early shortening)
took	/oː/ → /uː/			→ /ʊ/	(later shortening)
roof	/oː/ → /uː/			→ /ʊ/	(present-day shortening, partial)

Table 2.6 *Great Vowel Shift and French loans*

ME	vowel shift	EModE	
divine	/iː/ → /aɪ/	*machine* /iː/	(no shift)
gout	/uː/ → /au/	*rouge* /uː/	(no shift)

Table 2.7 *Latin /w/ and /v/*

Latin *vinum* /winum/	→	Germanic *wīn* (later English *wine*) with /w-/
Old French *vine* /viːn/	→	(Middle + Modern) English *vine* with /v-/ (< Latin *vinea* 'vine(yard)')

The earlier shortenings may or may not be present in different varieties of English, for instance northern English and Scottish English do not have the lowering of /ʊ/ to /ʌ/; Irish English does not have the shortening before velars in all cases, e.g., *cook* /kuːk/ and not /kʊk/.

The Great Vowel Shift in English (see below for details) is a process which began in late Middle English. By this time most of the French loans (Anglo-Norman and Central French) had already entered the language and thus underwent the Great Vowel Shift, e.g., *doubt* /daut/ from an earlier /duːt/. However, a significant number of loans did not undergo the expected shift – see the examples in Table 2.6 – and so one must assume that they were borrowed after the Great Vowel Shift had been completed.

One must also consider the operation of later analogy. There are a few instances where orthographic *ou* is realized as /au/, for example, with *route* /raut/ in American English whereas British English still has /ruːt/.

Finally, in Table 2.7, we see that Old English *wine* from Latin *vinum* /winum/ has an initial /w/, as did Latin at the time of the borrowing (in common with West Germanic, on the continent). Later, the word was reborrowed with the pronunciation /viːn/ to give *vine* which in Modern English means the bush on which the wine grapes grow. The latter pronunciation arose because in Latin an original /w/ had developed to /v/ between the periods when the two forms of the word were borrowed.

Transmission and Propagation of Change

If one assumes that language does not exist separately from the speakers who use it, then a major question arises for language change: how will a following generation know what changes are in progress in a current generation? The answer to this is that at any one time there co-exist two or more competing variants (Bermúdez-Otero 2007: 2–4). Of these one is dominant and the other recessive.

In the period of first language acquisition children note not only what forms a language possesses but also what the variation among these forms is. For instance, a child would note that both *dived* and *dove* are possible preterit forms of the verb *dive* and would furthermore register other relevant aspects of the distribution, e.g., if one form is more common among older speakers, only used in more formal styles or conversely predominant in colloquial usage, etc. By these means children can observe the direction in which language change is moving and later contribute to this by unconsciously favoring forms which are in keeping with their own linguistic preferences (see Figure 2.1).

This conception of how language change is transmitted enables one to understand the notion of "drift" better. If speakers at any point in time are aware of which variants are preferred and which are being increasingly neglected, then the language can move in a definite direction, as was the case with the drift from synthetic to analytic in the history of English.

The propagation of change, in this case through the linguistic forms used by a speech community, would seem to follow a pattern which is found in other spheres apart from language. The pattern is termed an "S-curve" because of its approximate shape (see Figure 2.2). In essence an S-curve describes a change which starts slowly, picks up speed, and proceeds rapidly but which stops – or at least slows down considerably – before it reaches completion. The change itself may be actuated by small numbers of innovative individuals within a speech community. The acceptance of a change by the majority probably has to do with the form coming to function in group identity.

The shift of /u/ to /ʌ/, in words like *cut, luck, fun*, in Early Modern English illustrates an S-curve. This change would appear to have started in the

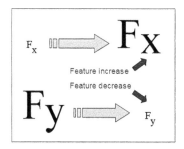

Figure 2.1 *Linked development of features over time*

No. of forms

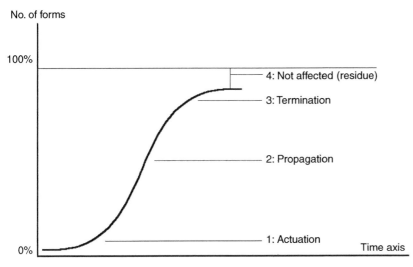

Figure 2.2 *S-curve as model of language change*

mid-seventeenth century and was probably active into the following century in the south of England. However, not all instances of /u/ were unrounded and lowered to /ʌ/. The small set of forms which did not undergo the shift are those which were phonetically resistant to the change, i.e., which were both preceded and followed by sounds with inherent rounding. The elements which have such rounding are labial plosives /p, b/, palato-alveolar fricatives /ʃ, ʒ/, and a velarized syllable-final [ɫ]; hence *pull, bull, push, bush, should* still have /ʊ/ in standard English. These words occupy the gap between the top of the S-curve and the 100 percent mark on the vertical axis.

Remnants of Former Processes

At any stage a language will contain remnants of processes which were once productive, i.e., part of the synchronic grammar. Such remnants are important in reconstructing previous stages of the language concerned. For instance, umlaut is a process which was once productive in English. The principle was that a high vowel or /j/ in a syllable (usually a grammatical ending) caused the vowel of the preceding syllable, if a back vowel, to be moved to a front position. Now the umlaut process became inactive in the Old English period and no new instances of it arose in Middle English. But because the words affected by umlaut belonged to the core of the vocabulary, for instance, names for humans, animals, or parts of the body, and because such words change slowly if at all, traces of umlaut are still to be found in English:

Nouns   *tooth : teeth, man : men, goose : geese, mouse : mice*
Verbs   *blood : bleed, doom : deem*

Various changes have obscured the original process. For example, *tooth* now has /u:/ but formerly had /o:/, as the orthography suggests. The original change between singular and plural in this form was /o:/ > /ø:/ (the front rounded vowel), but /ø:/ unrounded to /e:/, which was then raised by the Great Vowel Shift to give us the /i:/ we find today in *teeth*. Umlaut was not confined to the alternation of number in nouns. It could also occur with verbs; for instance those which were originally derived from nouns and adjectives by adding the ending *-jan* underwent umlaut in the stem vowel, hence *deem* and *doom* from a very much earlier *dømjan* from an even earlier *dōmjan*.

Reflexes of Older Words

Older words may still be found in fixed expressions and so may be helpful in linguistic reconstruction. In English there is an alliterative expression *to wend one's weary way* which contains the old verb *wend* 'to go.' This verb has now virtually died out but the past form of the verb *go* – *went* – derives from this source. This process is known as suppletion, the appearance of a form from one paradigm in another paradigm in which it did not originally occur.

Reflexes of older words may be available in different word classes. For instance, the only reflex of Old English *wyrd* 'destiny' is the present-day adjective *weird* (with a semantic shift). A reflex may also be contained in a compound as with Old English *wer* 'man' (a common Indo-European word; cf. Latin *vir*) which does not exist anymore but is found in the compound *werewolf* 'man-wolf.' Another Old English word for 'man' *guma* is contained in *bridegroom* (originally *brydguma*) where the second element was mistakenly reinterpreted as *groom*.

Fixed expressions are also worth considering in this respect. These very often contain older words no longer found elsewhere. For instance, Old English has a word *sweltan* 'to die, perish' with no continuation in Modern English; however, the expression *sweltering heat* contains a reflex of this verb. Another case is the adjective *hale* 'healthy, free from disease' which can occur in northern England and Scotland but which in standard English is only found in the fixed expression *hale and hearty* 'robust and healthy.'

Remnants of processes involving vowels are also to be found in Modern English (Minkova 2014: 212). For instance, long consonants (called "geminates" and written with two letters) used to exist in Old English and were preceded by short vowels. This applied, for instance, to cases of gemination (consonant doubling) as with *blēdan* 'bleed' : *bledde* 'bled.' However, geminates were later lost (and often only one letter was then used in writing), but the short vowel which preceded them was maintained, leading to contrastive vowel patterns in Modern English such as *bleed* : *bled*.

The techniques illustrated above all involve the undoing of changes in order to arrive at an original form of some earlier stage of a language. This process of

Table 2.8 *Unraveling sound changes to arrive at original forms*

		Change "undone"		
Singular	/maus/	– Great Vowel Shift	=	/muːs/
Plural	/maɪs/	– Great Vowel Shift	=	/miːs/
	/miːs/	– unrounding	=	/myːs/
	/myːs/	– inflectional loss	=	/myːsi/
	/myːsi/	– umlaut	=	/muːsi/
Original alternation:	/muːs/-SG : /muːsi/-PL			

working backwards is a common method for gaining knowledge of former periods of languages. It consists basically of reversing known changes in order to add time depth to an investigation. A complete example of this technique is offered in Table 2.8. The goal of this exercise is to show what the original singular ~ plural alternation was for a word pair which shows an irregular alternation in Modern English: *mouse* ~ *mice*. We begin with the present-day forms /maus/ and /maɪs/ and "undo" the relevant sound changes to arrive at the original form. The symbol "–" in the table means that the sound change is reversed. Note that the original plural inflection for this noun class was *-i*.

Change and the Sound System of English

This section discusses some major changes in the historical phonology of English. The purpose of the section is to illustrate the principles of language change and the methods of historical linguistics outlined in the preceding sections. The examples are selective, of course; many more examples, treated in greater detail, can be found in the histories of English cited in the Suggestions for Further Study section below.

The Great Vowel Shift

By the end of the thirteenth century alternative spellings for *e* and *o* as *i* and *u* begin to appear. These shifts are most likely the beginning of a development which changed the long vowel system of English radically. This development is known by the general label "Great Vowel Shift." It affected only the long vowels, both monophthongs and diphthongs. In order to understand the basic mechanism of the Great Vowel Shift one should imagine a vowel rectangle and see the shifts in relation to this.

Many linguists assume that the closed mid vowels were first raised somewhat. After this raising had reached a certain level it was represented orthographically, *i* was written for *e* and *u* for *o*. This could be understood as a "push" chain, as the raised *e* and *o* would eventually have put pressure on the vowels above to shift.

Table 2.9 *Overview of the Great Vowel Shift*

	(1300)	1400	1500	1600	1700	1800	1900
drive	/iː/	/ɪi/	/ei/	/əi/	/ʌi/	/aɪ/	
house	/uː/	/ʊu/	/ou/	/əu/	/ʌu/	/au/	
feet	/eː/			/iː/			
fool	/oː/			/uː/			
beat	/ɛː/			/eː/	/iː/		
foal	/ɔː/			/oː/	/ou/		/əʊ/
take	/aː/			/æː/	/ɛː/	/eː/	/eɪ/
sail	/ai/	/æi/	/ei/	/eː/			/eɪ/
law	/au/	/ɒu/	/ɒːu/	/ɒː/		/ɔː/	

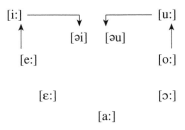

Figure 2.3 *Movement of long vowels in the early Great Vowel Shift*

However, it could also have been that the two high vowels /iː/ and /uː/ were shifted first. Middle English /iː/ and /uː/ correspond to Modern English /aɪ/ and /au/ (as in *time* and *house*). From this one can conclude that the Great Vowel Shift also caused the diphthongization of both high vowels. The initial diphthongization of the high vowels would have created a "gap" at the top, which would be filled by the vowels below moving up. This would be a "pull" chain.[8]

If one observes the Great Vowel Shift over its entire period, then one can recognize clearly the starting and end points for the long vowels. These can be represented in the form of a diagram (see Figure 2.3). The basic principle of the Great Vowel Shift is that each long vowel was raised by a single level and that the two highest vowels were diphthongized. This rule of thumb does not hold for all vowels but offers a fairly accurate orientation in the system of vowel shifts. The low vowel /aː/ went through two intermediary stages until it arrived at the position it occupies today. The open mid vowel /ɛː/ went through one intermediary stage.

Although not all researchers would agree with the details of the Great Vowel Shift set out in Table 2.9, certain aspects of it are undisputed. For example, the raising of monophthongized Middle English /ai/ (as in *sail*) can never have "caught up" with the open front vowel /ɛː/ (as in *beat*) as otherwise a collapse of the difference between the two vowels would have resulted, with common further development as the consequence, i.e., *sail* would be /siːl/ in Modern English. The development of Middle English /aː/ and /ai/ must have been similar as the result of the shift in both these cases is the same (as in the homophones *tale* and *tail*).

H in the History of English

The story of this sound reaches back beyond Old English. The sound in Germanic is represented by χ, a cover symbol for a velar–uvular voiceless fricative which in turn derives from Indo-European /k/ by the Germanic Sound Shift (Grimm's Law). There was also a labialized version of the sound: /xw/ < /kw/.

By the Old English period an allophony had developed whereby in initial position the sound was weakened to a glottal fricative /h-/, the velar form /x/ being retained in medial and final position. The original situation in Old English involved /h/ before sonorants as well – /hw-, hl-, hn-, hr-/ – but these clusters were simplified quite early on by the loss of pre-consonantal /h/.

During the Middle English period and afterwards all instances of /x/ were lost except in Scottish and Ulster English where it is still found as a relic pronunciation, e.g., *enough* /ɪˈnʌx/. In Modern English the distribution of /h/ is quite restricted. It can only occur in the onset of a stressed syllable, normally in word-initial position, but occasionally word-internally, e.g., *behave* /bɪˈheɪv/.

Initial /h-/ was often lost in unstressed grammatical forms, e.g., Old English *hit* > *it*. A more general loss of /h-/ is found in colloquial varieties of southern British English, but the standard and other varieties, such as American English and Canadian English, retain /h-/. Instances of hypercorrection may occur in *h*-less varieties, as in *hobviously, hearring* 'earring' with an initial /h-/; i.e., speakers who normally do not pronounce initial /h-/ insert it in words in which it was not present historically in the attempt to use more standard speech. Generalized *h*-insertion is known from some lesser-known varieties of English (Schreier et al. 2010; Williams et al. 2015), such as Newfoundland English and that of Tristan da Cunha in the South Atlantic. *H*-dropping, and its opposite *h*-insertion, are of some vintage in English: the phrase *to eat humble pie* shows insertion of /h-/ in the word *umble* 'animal entrails' (itself from French *numble* by false segmentation). This insertion implies that *h*-dropping must have been common at the time. Varieties which do not have *h*-dropping do not have *h*-insertion either as speakers always know where *h* occurs in words. (The sociolinguistics of *h*-dropping is dealt with in detail in Chapter 9.)

Interdental Fricatives

English is somewhat unusual, when compared to other languages, in having the interdental fricatives /θ/ and /ð/. These sounds have existed in English for as long as there are records and they are attested in the earliest stages of Germanic. The source of /θ, ð/ in English is (i) pre-Germanic /tʰ/, through fricativization, as in *three* from */tʰreː/ or (ii) Greek borrowings / creations, e.g., *theology*, based on θeos 'God.'

Table 2.10 *Realization of interdental fricatives in varieties of English*

(a)	TH-fronting	*breath* > [bref], *brother* > [brʌvə]
(b)	TH-stopping	*breath* > [breṯ], *brother* > [brʌḏər]
(c)	TH-alveolarization	*breath* > [bret], *brother* > [brʌdə(r)]
(d)	TH-debuccalization	*breath* > [breh], *brother* > [bʌhər]
(e)	TH-assibilation	*breath* > [bres], *brother* > [brʌzə(r)]
(f)	TH-lateralization	*other* > [ʌlər] (in intervocalic position)

In the history of English /θ, ð/ have undergone different developments, as shown in Table 2.10. The sounds were frequently fronted to equivalent labio-dental fricatives (a); this shift is found in varieties as far apart as Cockney English and African American English. In other varieties the sounds were realized as stops (b), e.g., in colloquial New York or Liverpool English, especially in grammatical words such as *the, they, them, with*. This shift can also be to alveolar stops (c), as in rural Irish English. In varieties of Scottish and Ulster English the oral gesture may be removed (debuccalization) and only a glottal fricative /h/ remains, if any sound at all (d). The use of /s, z/ for the interdental fricative is generally a second-language phenomenon (e), e.g., with German speakers of English, but it has been reported for the first-language variety of Tristan da Cunha. Lastly, the shift of the voiced /ð/ to /l/ (f) is a feature of English in the city of Derry.

In the history of English many words have vacillated in the occurrence of /d/ or /ð/. For instance, at Shakespeare's time words like *burden* and *murder* were written *burthen, murther*, implying that the voiced interdental fricative was used in this position.

L- and R-sounds

These two types of sounds are often classed as liquids. The sounds are highly sonorous, i.e., vowel-like, and this fact might explain the tendency both show to be vocalized (shift from a consonant to a vowel).

The laterals, *l*-sounds, generally show a secondary articulation, or coloring, which is clear or dark, i.e., alveolar or velar. The dark coloring, realized by lowering the body of the tongue and raising the back toward the velum, often triggers the vocalization of the /l/ with time. This is attested in the history of English since at least the Middle Ages (and is widely found in the histories of other languages, e.g., Dutch and Polish). It can be recognized in those words where the <l> is still written, e.g., *talk, walk, palm, Stockholm*. Dialect literature from the early modern period, e.g., Ray (1674), testifies to just how widespread *l*-vocalization was previously, e.g., in words like *soul, bold, old*. Today, many varieties show a dark *l* in syllable coda position and a tendency to vocalize this, e.g., Cockney English *milk* [mɪʊk], *help* [eʊp] (with *h*-dropping).

Rhotics, or *r*-sounds, refer to a class of consonants which can have a variety of realizations: (i) alveolar frictionless continuant [ɹ], (ii) alveolar trill [r], (iii) flap [ɾ], (iv) retroflex [ɻ], (v) uvular [ʁ]. All these occur in present-day varieties of English. In addition, there are many varieties – most forms of British English, those in the north-eastern USA (recessive), African American English and all varieties in the Southern Hemisphere – where /r/ is not found in syllable-final position (also called non-prevocalic /r/ to cover cases like *very* [veri]). In such varieties word pairs like *caught* : *court, paw* : *pour* are generally homophones.

Dialectal Forms in Standard English

The scope of English historical linguistics is not just the story of how south-eastern English became the standard, that is, its history is not a direct line from the main dialect of the late Old English period (450–1100) in the south of England – West Saxon – down to the present-day.[9] Rather the emerging lead variety, educated English of London and the Home Counties, which was later to become the standard, interacted with the dialects from different regions during its history and was itself derived from more southern varieties: toward the end of the Middle English period (1100–1500) there was a swing around from a broadly southern form to a largely east midland form, which was centered around London, the city which, as the capital, was to represent, in its more prestigious varieties, the input to the later standard.

But already in Old English we find marked dialect differences which, if not clearly localizable regionally, are at least recognizable in different texts from the period. Nonetheless, three broad dialect areas are recognized: (1) West Saxon in the south along with Kentish in the extreme south-east, (2) Mercian in the center of England, and (3) Northumbrian in the north (the term "Anglian" is a cover term for Mercian and Northumbrian together). For the ensuing Middle English period a similar dialect picture is posited traditionally: (1) Southern (with Kent a special case), (2) Midland, East and West, and (3) Northern. With the rise of large urban centers in England, sociolects arose which did not necessarily show the same features as the dialects of the regions where they were located.

(i) ***Northern forms in standard English****. Like* goes back to *līc* /liːk/ in the North of England whereas *līc* /liːtʃ/ in the south was further reduced in its affixed form to /liː/ which gives us the modern ending *-ly* as in *friendly*. This can lead to cases of contrast such as the adjectives *lively* and *lifelike*, which contain the same elements but with a northern and a southern derived second element respectively. *Uncouth* /ʌnkuːθ/ is evidently from the north as it has not gone through the Great Vowel Shift; otherwise it would be pronounced /ʌnkauθ/. Northern forms in morphology include the *th-* variants from Old Norse for 'they,' 'their,' 'them' in Old English (the southern forms began in *h-*), which were adopted into Southern English.

(ii) ***Anglian forms as input to the later standard.*** Anglian in Old English refers to the dialects in the middle and northern parts of England, i.e., Mercia and Northumbria respectively. Here certain vowels were different from the West Saxon dialect in the south and some modern forms are continuations of the Anglian rather than the West Saxon pronunciations, e.g., present-day *cold*, *old* come from *cald* and *ald*. The continuation of the Old English forms *cēald* and *ēald* would have been /tʃiːld/ and /iːld/ respectively.

(iii) ***Southern/Kentish forms in standard English.*** One of the typical features of the south is the initial voicing of consonants. This can be seen in the words *vat*, *vixen* (the Kentish for female fox), *vane* which had an initial /f-/ in Old English but now show the voiced fricative found in the southern dialects. Kentish pronunciations are also recognizable in *merry*, *bury*, *evil* because in Old English, the /e(:)/ was typical of this area while West Saxon (the mid-south) had /iː/ or /yː/. With the word *evil* the present-day pronunciation would have been /aivl/ if the West Saxon form *ȳfel* had continued into the later standard.

(See further Chapter 12 on historical dialectology.)

Concluding Remarks

The nature and range of language change has provided the background for the current chapter, which is concerned with how this is manifest in the history of English. In particular the changes in the sound system of English have been highlighted to show both types and instances of phonological change. The examples discussed are selective, given the restrictions of space, but hopefully they will help to improve your awareness of what has happened in the history of English. Discussing the approaches to interpreting language change is intended to focus your attention on the analysis of such change and to aid you in understanding the pathways such change has taken and the contexts in which it occurred in the history of English.

Suggestions for Further Study

The most comprehensive treatment of the history of English is Hogg (general ed.) (1992–2001). Introductions to the history of English include Lass (1987), Bailey (1991), Crystal (2003), Smith (2005), Hogg and Denison (2006), van Kemenade and Los (2006), Barber, Beal, and Shaw (2009), Algeo (2010), Mugglestone (2012), Nevalainen and Traugott (2012), Baugh and Cable (2013), and Brinton and Arnovick (2016). On the phonological history of

English, see Smith (2007) and Minkova (2014). More specialized treatments of Late Modern English include Hickey (2010a) and Hundt (2014). On the backgrounds of English, see Robinson (1992), König and van der Auwera (1994), and Clackson (2007).

General treatments of historical linguistics – at different levels of detail and complexity – include McMahon (1994), Lass (1997), Joseph and Janda (2003), Hock and Joseph (2009), Crowley and Bowern (2010), Aitchison (2013), Campbell (2013), and Miller (2015). Brinton and Traugott (2005) and Hopper and Traugott (2003) treat lexicalization and grammaticalization, as does Fischer, Rosenbach, and Stein (2000). Lefebvre, Comrie, and Cohen (2013) is a recent discussion of the origins of language. Milroy (1992a) is a classic discussion of historical sociolinguistics, and Hernández-Campoy and Conde-Silvestre (2012) is a recent handbook on the topic. Pintzuk, Tsoulas, and Warner (2001) treat models and mechanisms of syntactic change.

Discussions of varieties of English include Wells (1982), Crystal (2004), Hickey (2004, 2012d), Kortmann (2008), Schreier, Trudgill, Schneider, and Williams (2010), Cruttenden (2014), and Williams, Schneider, Trudgill, and Schreier (2015). (See further Chapter 13.)

Exercises

1. A comparison of approaches
   Explain how the Neogrammarians thought languages changed (mention exceptionlessness and analogy). Contrast this with possible structural and functional interpretations.

2. Internal and external motivation
   Which of the following changes appears to be internally and which externally motivated, i.e., determined by linguistic factors (internal) or by sociolinguistic considerations (external)? (1) /u/ > /ʌ/ as in *cup, sun, pub*; (2) *-th* as third-person singular ending > *-s* as in *hath* > *has*. Do you think that combinations of these factors can exist?

3. Analogy
   Explain how at least two types of analogy work and give appropriate examples to illustrate this. For instance, explain how the form *strove* as the past for *strive* (a verb ultimately from French) might have arisen or state why some people say *roofs* for *rooves*.

4. Grammaticalization and lexicalization
   Which of the following changes represents grammaticalization and which lexicalization? Explain. (1) *wedlock* < Old English *wed* 'wedding vow' + *lāc*,

an action suffix; (2) *fatherhood, motherhood, priesthood* all with *-hood* < Old English *hād* meaning 'person, quality'; (3) *She has to learn Russian.*

5. Reconstruction
   What is understood by (i) the comparative method and (ii) internal reconstruction? Which of the following cases illustrate (i) and which (ii): English *foot* is related to Latin *pes* as are English *heart* and Greek *kardia*; the words *five* and *wise* have a long vowel/diphthong but *fifth* and *wisdom* have a short vowel (hint: vowel shortening occurred before consonant clusters).

6. Relative chronology of change
   Give an example for relative chronology showing how one change must have taken place before another. For instance, account for why *routine* and *police* have the same vowel as *deep* in the second syllable but *resign* and *polite* have that of *time.*

7. Avoidance of homophony
   Discuss an example from the sound system of English where the avoidance of homophony seems to have been the motivating factor and one where this appears not to have been the case. Here are some examples of change which you can discuss: Kentish *vat* replaced previous *fat* 'barrel for wine, spirits'; *horse* and *hoarse*; *which* and *witch*; *meat* and *meet* are now pronounced the same by most English speakers (hint: think of word class).

8. Vowel changes
   What major change in English vowels helps to explain the present-day pronunciation of *tale, tail, fool, foal, down*? Which of the following words did it apply to: *mouth, come, time, police, young, serene, doubt, polite, mail, home*?

9. The history of /h/
   Outline the development of /h/ in the history of English in (i) clusters and (ii) initial position. Explain in this connection what hypercorrection is.

10. Regional origins
    Can the pronunciation of a word betray its regional origins? Give appropriate examples illustrating northern and southern dialect words in present-day standard English.

Notes

I would like to thank Cynthia Allen and Laurel Brinton for their detailed and useful comments. All shortcomings are clearly my own.
1. Textbooks on language structure and language change do in general present data from a whole range of languages, often representing the scholarly interests of the authors. The introduction to historical linguistics by Crowley and Bowern (2010) contains discussions of languages from Australia and the Pacific region, the book by Campbell (2013) has much material from the native languages of America, whereas that by Hock and Joseph (2009) deals extensively with data from Indo-European languages, to which English as a (West) Germanic language belongs.

2. The Germanic Sound Shift also included the shift of voiced stops to voiceless stops and of voiced aspirated stops to voiced fricatives (and later to voiced stops).
3. For a fuller discussion of umlaut, see the sections on "Relative chronology" and "Remnants of former processes."
4. In essence Verner's Law specifies that if the accent does not fall on an immediately preceding syllable then the onset of the following syllable is voiced. Thus, one had 'V/s/V but V'/z/V in verbal paradigms, for example.
5. If you are a speaker of a dialect that preserves /r/ before consonants, *court* and *caught* will, of course, not be homophones.
6. The V2 rule can be applied in cases of restrictive or negative adverbs/adverbial phrases in Modern English, such as *Only recently has he concerned himself with the matter, Never had he seen such a sight*. For more on V2, see Chapter 8.
7. The first element of the second word form is also a bound lexical morpheme; i.e., there is no *hap* in Modern English.
8. One piece of evidence supporting the notion that it was a push chain is that in northern English dialects of Middle English /u:/ is traditionally unshifted but /i:/ is shifted, as in *town* /tu:n/ and *time* /taɪm/ respectively. This has led scholars like Roger Lass to postulate that the trigger was the raising of /o:/ to /u:/ in the south of England because in the north Middle English /o:/ was frequently fronted and so the diphthongization of Middle English /u:/ to /au/ did not happen (Lass 1987: 226–227; see Minkova 2014: 248–270 for a detailed discussion of various views on how the vowel shift proceeded).
9. On the plurality of standards, see Hickey (2012d).

3 Generative Approaches

CYNTHIA L. ALLEN

Introduction

William Shakespeare and his contemporaries of the late sixteenth and early seventeenth century wrote sentences like these:

(1)   a. for the eye sees not itself / But by reflection
        (*Julius Caesar* I.ii.52)
    b. What means this shouting? I do fear, the people
       Choose Caesar for their king.
       (*Julius Caesar* I.ii.79–80)

We can still understand such sentences, but these two examples illustrate three instances of syntax that is no longer normal in Present-day English. To start with, sentence negation is no longer expressed by placing the negator *not* after a main verb. Today, we can only place a negator after an auxiliary verb, as in *the eye cannot see itself*, a sentence which Shakespeare could also have written. Similarly, we need an auxiliary to form the question of (1b), turning it into *What does this shouting mean?* And rather surprisingly, given that he could leave out auxiliaries where modern-day speakers need one, Shakespeare could use an auxiliary where we could not – *I do fear* could indeed be uttered today, but only in emphatic speech, as in *I do not fear that Brutus will betray Caesar, but I DO fear that the people will choose Caesar for their king.*

Although we cannot assume that people in Tudor England produced speeches exactly like Shakespeare's in their everyday language, we can assume that these particular constructions reflected syntactic possibilities in more pedestrian spoken language. The essence of the generative approach to analyzing linguistic change between period A and period B is to make a formal and explicit description of the differences between the internalized grammar of a speaker of stage A and that of a speaker of stage B.

Generative theory is primarily focused on synchronic analysis, and shifts in the treatment of changes such as those illustrated by the sentences of (1) reflect developments in the synchronic theory. However, diachronic generative linguists assume that the results of their studies can help shape synchronic theory as well as elucidate the history of a given language and add more generally to our understanding of how languages change. As we'll see below, it has been argued that a single change in a hypothesized **parameter setting** between Shakespeare's period and later led to a cluster of apparently unrelated changes, including the loss of a speaker's ability to produce questions and negatives without an auxiliary. If this analysis holds up to scrutiny, it is a powerful argument that the proposed parameter is on the right track.

Before we can look in detail at diachronic generative linguistics, we need to make a brief sketch of generative theory and how it has evolved.

The Development of the Generative Approach

Generative grammar burst upon the scene in 1957 with the publication of Noam Chomsky's *Syntactic Structures*. It is not an exaggeration to say that this little book caused a revolution among linguists who took a structuralist approach to language. Generative grammar can be regarded as the inheritor of the American structuralist tradition, an approach to language which focuses on the structure of sentences in a language and does not concern itself with explanations of why one structure might be chosen by a speaker as more appropriate than an alternative structure. A generative grammar seeks to give a formal characterization of an idealized native speaker's knowledge about what constitutes a grammatical sentence in his or her language.

Early generative work made a distinction between a speaker's competence – what the speaker knew about the possible structures of their language – as opposed to a speaker's performance, which might result in ungrammatical output due to tiredness, stress, or anything else that might cause speech errors. Currently, the internalized grammar is referred to as the **I-Language**. The I-Language generates the **E-Language** (E for "external"), which is the output or speech. It is the I-Language of an idealized speaker–hearer that the generative linguist seeks to model.

The big difference between American structuralism and generative grammar is that the previous approach used static models of language, describing a language in terms of the categories and patterns found in it. For example, an American structuralist treatment of English syntax would analyze a sentence like *the linguist analyzed the data* to break the sentence up into its immediate constituents, the noun phrase (NP) *the linguist* and the verb phrase (VP) *analyzed the data*, further breaking the NP up into its constituents, the determiner *the* and the noun *linguist*, and the VP into the verb *analyzed* and an NP, which could be broken down into its components, etc. The **transformational grammar** introduced in *Syntactic Structures* treated language as a dynamic system which involved more abstract underlying forms and processes which derived surface forms. In syntax, it retained the approach to structures as hierarchical, but treated sentences as being **generated** by a dynamic interaction between underlying or "deep" structures by the phrase structure rules and syntactic processes or transformations. The phrase structure rules generated an underlying structure for a sentence, which would be operated on by transformations to create the "surface" structure, the final form of the sentence. Even a simple sentence like *the linguist analyzed the data* would involve at least one transformation, because it was assumed that the form *analyzed* was not generated by "the base." That is, tense was assumed to be an abstract category generated in the syntax, and its initial position was before the first verb (whether main verb or auxiliary). A transformation (Affix Hopping) moved the tense affix from its "base-generated" position before the verb to its final position after the verb.[1] So the underlying structure of our example sentence would be very similar to its surface structure, but it would differ in containing the string $_T$[Past] $_V$[analyze]. With a negative sentence such as *the linguist did not analyze the data*, things got more abstract. This sentence provides an illustration of how a speaker's grammar was assumed to contain ordered transformations which produced intermediate structures before reaching the surface structure. The negative (realized as *not* or *n't*) was assumed to be moved into its position by a transformation which placed it directly before the verb, resulting in an intermediate structure $_T$[Past] $_{NEG}$[n't] $_V$ [analyze]. This transformation (Negative Transportation) prevented Affix Hopping from applying, since it prevented the past tense affix from being adjacent to the verb. The only way to rescue the structure from ungrammaticality was to apply another transformation, Do Support, which would insert *do* before the negative, allowing the affix to hop onto it. Another important transformation was the Passive transformation, which converted a base-generated active sentence into a passive sentence such as *the data was analyzed by the linguist* by moving the post-verbal NP to the front of the sentence, adding a participle, etc.

The Passive transformation has played an important role in more than one respect. First, it gave an attractive way of capturing the relationship between active and passive sentences, in a way that static descriptions of possible sentence patterns could not. Second, it played a crucial role in the development of generative grammar, for example in arguments resulting in the addition of a semantic component to the grammar (see below for further discussion of this component in more recent treatments). It is obvious that the phonological shape of a sentence is a function of the surface structure, but in early transformational grammar, it was assumed that the meaning of a sentence was encoded by the deep structure. It became apparent, however, that at least some aspects of meaning, such as the scope of quantifiers, which is affected by the surface position of the quantifier, required a separate semantic component which received input from the surface structure. This is because a sentence like *Three languages are spoken by everyone in this room* has different possible readings from *Everyone in this room speaks three languages*.

In generative approaches to phonology, synchronic phonological rules are assumed to operate on underlying inputs to create the surface forms of words.

The underlying forms of early generative phonology were sometimes very abstract. As with transformations, the rules were assumed to be ordered, with the result that the output of one rule might create or remove contexts for the next rule to apply. So for example Chomsky and Halle's seminal *The Sound Pattern of English* posits an underlying structure [mænVgeriæl] (V=vowel) for the word *managerial* (1968: 53). The journey to the surface form involves the application of six phonological rules (one assigning stress, one inserting a glide, and four affecting vowels).

Morphology was not treated separately from phonology and syntax in the earliest generative work, as it was at first assumed that the interaction between syntax and phonology would remove any necessity of a separate morphological component. It became clear by the 1970s that there were issues that rendered this assumption problematic. Morphology continues to play a very important role in many generative syntactic analyses today which assume that a morpheme or morphological features in a particular position may "drive" a particular movement, such as the movement of a verb to give an inflectional morpheme a host to attach itself to.

The generative approach was immediately appealing to formally inclined linguists because it offered not simply a way of formally describing the patterns of a language and the relationship between semantically similar sentences, but a principled way of predicting the intuitions of native speakers about what a possible utterance in their language was, and it quickly eclipsed earlier structuralist approaches. One of the reasons for formalizing descriptions is that formalism makes the predictions of an analysis explicit, and so problems with that analysis become glaringly evident. Formal descriptions also make it evident when generalizations are not being adequately captured by a theory. It soon became clear that early analyses raised a number of problems, and this led to numerous developments. Some of these developments will be introduced in the following discussion of generative approaches to linguistic change.

Generative Approaches to Linguistic Change

Generative approaches to linguistic change have evolved as a result of developments in the assumptions about the synchronic nature of a possible grammar. However, some fundamental assumptions have remained constant. Children learning their first language are assumed to be the primary locus of language change as they each **abduce** a grammar from the primary linguistic data they encounter. This grammar is constrained by an innate knowledge of what constitutes a possible grammar of a language. It is also assumed that there must be some sort of innate knowledge guiding the child in selecting the best possible grammar to account for his or her data. Otherwise, it is impossible to explain the apparently miraculous ability of children to learn a language so quickly, and particularly so because they are dealing with impoverished data – no child is presented with negative data, such as the fact that a sentence like *Which hat did you resent the fact that I wore?* is ungrammatical. It is rather mysterious that we would construct a grammar which allowed all sorts of questions not heard in the acquisition process, such as *Which polka-dotted elephant did you swear that you saw?* but would rule the ungrammatical question out. This problem of how to account for a person's knowledge based on apparently inadequate information is known as "Plato's problem" among generativists.

Assuming that child language acquisition is the locus of linguistic change, normal linguistic change from one generation to another (that is, changes excluding drastic changes found in creolization; see Chapter 13) must result from some change to the data that children encounter. Changes to this data might result from language contact. In the case of English, for example, contact with Scandinavian speakers who settled in England after the massive invasions which started in the Old English period has been seen as a "trigger" for a number of changes. It has long been suggested that the similarity between the stems of words used by the Scandinavian and English speakers led speakers to simplify the inflection of English by stripping off endings to facilitate communication, with a concomitant fixing of SVO (subject–verb–object) word order. Previously, SVO had only been an order which was common for pragmatic reasons, rather than a grammatically mandated order. Diachronic generative linguists have largely been in agreement that the loss of case marking rendered one or more features of the earlier grammar of English unlearnable, although the details of what was not learned vary according to the specific version of the framework assumed by the linguist proposing an analysis.

Language contact is undoubtedly one reason why children might get exposed to different data from that heard by the older members of their community. Another possible cause of a syntactic change might be a phonological change. So, for example, the loss of final nasals in the Early Middle English period, along with the reduction and eventual loss of the unstressed vowels of inflections, caused substantial syncretism (that is, conflation) of inflections. For example, the Old English case suffixes *-um* and *-an* fell together into a form written *-e*, but presumably pronounced [ə]. Morphological change of this sort has been widely regarded as causing language learners to be unable to abduce the grammars of the preceding generation. For example, a speaker of generation A might have a category of dative case in her grammar. However, in her output, the same speaker might use a distinctive marker of that category only occasionally. This speaker's child might not hear enough examples of the distinctive marker to conclude that his language had a category of dative case. So, for example, the child might hear *cild* 'child' used as an indirect object instead of the old dative form *cilde*. The child fails to learn that his language has (overt) dative case, leading to a loss of the category distinction in his grammar, essentially because of phonological reduction which took place in the earlier generation. The syntactic effect might be that the child would be more likely to rely on the preposition *to* for expressing what was previously expressed by the case marker *-e*, and to rely more on a fixed position for indirect objects when he didn't use *to*, as in *he gave the child a gift.*

The generative view does not completely discount the possibility of change to speakers' grammars over their lifetime. There is no doubt, for example, that people's accents can change a good deal as they grow older. Furthermore, Weinreich, Labov, and Herzog (1968) pointed out that the speech of older peers can be more important in the final shape of a person's language than the speech of his or her parents, and recent studies have confirmed this view beyond doubt, at least in some aspects of language. However, generativists usually assume that adjustments made to the grammar that is acquired in early childhood are limited to fairly superficial ones. It is usually assumed that although older speakers may tinker at the edges of their grammars by adding some rules of adjustment as they encounter speakers of other dialects (regional or social) in later life, such adjustments will be superficial add-ons and will not affect what is currently referred to as their "core grammar," which is fixed early on in life.

Another important type of change by adult speakers is a change of frequency in the use of a given construction. If OV (object–verb) and VO (verb–object) word orders are both possible, for example, the speaker might use OV order a lot in early life, but later on, perhaps because of contact with Scandinavian speakers' English, might switch to using VO order more frequently. This could affect the linguistic data that this speaker's child is exposed to. However, it does not represent a change to the mother's grammar, because VO is not a new option, just one that she has started to use more frequently.

Constraints Replace Rules

As discussed above, early generative theory posited underlying structures and rules which acted on those structures (and other, intermediate structures) to arrive at the surface form of a sentence. Language change was seen primarily in terms of changes to those rules and underlying structures. The earliest generative studies noted that while the grammarian may have some interest in what causes these changes, this was not really part of the job of the diachronic linguist, whose central concern was to describe how the grammar of one stage differed from that of a preceding period. Descriptions were made in terms of rules being added, lost, reordered, or becoming either more or less general in their application. Restructuring of the lexicon resulted in rule inversion. An example comes from the history of the indefinite article. In Modern English, we say *an apple* but *a tree.* Originally, the /n/ was always present, since the article developed from Old English *an* 'one.' In Middle English, the /n/ began to be dropped if the following word started with a consonant. So for a period, speakers had a synchronic rule dropping the /n/ in this situation. Since other words did not drop /n/ when a consonant followed, this was not a general phonological rule, but a phonological rule that was restricted to a particular morpheme (a morphophonemic rule). While there was still variation between an /n/ pronounced before consonants and the omission of the /n/, language learners had evidence for an underlying form /æn/. However, as omission of the /n/ became more common, language learners reanalyzed the base form as having no final /n/. This means that modern speakers have a synchronic rule which is the inverse of the rule that Middle English speakers followed. In formal notation, generative phonologists would write the rules this way:

(2)   Middle English n → ø]art / __ #C
             Modern English ø → n]art / __ #V

The rule for Middle English says that the article loses -n at the end of a word when a consonant follows (beginning the next word). In contrast, in Modern English the -n appearing in *an* is assumed not to be part of the basic form, so the new rules adds -n when the next word begins with a vowel. Thus a reanalysis of the base form has led to a new rule.[2]

One of the problems that drew attention early on in the development of generative grammar was the excessive power of the theory in some respects. For example, the syntactic side of the theory allowed in principle the positing of transformations of the sort that seemed never to occur in any language. Problems also arose when it became apparent that some types of historical change that were predicted as theoretically possible never seemed to be attested. This did not satisfy the goal, as stated by Chomsky in *Syntactic Structures*, "of determining the fundamental underlying properties of successful grammars." Similarly, pho-nological processes of some sort are quite common cross-linguistically – the deletion of unstressed final vowels that happened in Middle English is comple-tely unremarkable – but the rule-based approach did not by itself distinguish between expected and unexpected rules. From the rule-based perspective, a rule adding a vowel to the end of a final unstressed syllable would be just as well-formed as one reducing an unstressed vowel, but a language having such a rule would certainly make a linguist sit up and take notice. The rule-based approach made it look like a coincidence that similar rules had to be written for many languages, but clearly this was not satisfactory.

Because of such problems, the focus of the generative approach shifted to **constraints** on processes. Specific transformations were replaced with more general processes which were made available in Universal Grammar, which also contained universal constraints on those processes. Universal Grammar not only constrains possible linguistic systems, it also makes first language learning possible as it drastically reduces the possible grammars that children might build from the linguistic data they hear.

This new emphasis on constraining the possible grammars a language learner can construct led naturally to a change in the treatment of linguistic change. Lightfoot (1979) can be regarded as a foundational work in the current generative approach to syntactic change. Lightfoot noted that earlier generative treatments had been unconstrained in the changes they proposed and had paid little attention to the question of what constituted a possible change. Lightfoot applied the new assumptions about possible grammars to some case histories of syntactic change. One of these case histories was the development of modal verbs in English.

Case Study: Modal Verbs

Lightfoot (1979) presented the history of English modals as a "paradigm case" of reanalysis which was triggered by other changes. Lightfoot argues that the modal verbs of Modern English (e.g., *can*) had the characteristic properties of ordinary verbs in Old English and therefore did not represent a separate class of Modal (or Auxiliary). For example, they could typically take direct objects:

(3)   se deofol ... **cann** fela searacræfta (ÆHom 30 97)[3]
         'the devil ... knows many artifices.'

Here, *cann* has the meaning of 'know.' These "premodals" were frequently followed by (bare) infinitives:

(4)   and ic **cunne** tocnawan betwux god and yfel (ÆCHom II, 45 336.28)
         'and I know-subjunctive (how to) discriminate between good and evil.'

Here, the premodal is in the same position in the string as it would be in Modern English, i.e., before the main verb. This is typical of main clauses. However, in subordinate clauses, the premodal could be in final position:

(5)   þæt hy þæt ece lif mid him habban **mihton** (ÆHom_7:135.1121)
         'that they might have eternal life with him' (lit. 'that they the eternal life with him have might').

This final position was also characteristic of main verbs in subordinate clauses.

Lightfoot therefore proposes a biclausal analysis in Old English for sentences containing such premodals:

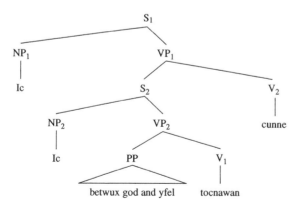

This analysis assumes that the Old English speaker had a transformation which moved verbs to a position between the subject and object. This transformation was obligatory in main clauses but optional in subordinate clauses.

By applying this transformation both in the subordinate clause and in the main clause (and another transformation that deletes the coreferential subject in the subordinate clause), we derive the string *ic **cunne** tocnawan betwux god and yfel.*

Lightfoot argues that in the sixteenth century such strings were reanalyzed as being base-generated, rather than derived by transformation. This happened because a number of independent changes had taken place which caused the modals to become increasingly distinct from ordinary verbs, such as the loss of the ability to take objects. Most crucially, the old analysis became opaque when the underlying order of English changed from SOV to SVO and language learners had less evidence for a transformation moving verbs into their final (medial) position. The surface strings with medial verbs were analyzed as being generated by phrase structure rules rather than as derived by transformation, and because the premodals had become so different from other verbs, they were analyzed as members of a distinct modal word class.

The most important aspect of this analysis is that it is supposed to account for a cluster of apparently unrelated and essentially simultaneous changes as the result of this single reanalysis, including a new inability of the modals to occur in non-finite forms such as **to can do that is impressive* or **canning do that is impressive*; cf. *to be able/being able to do that is impressive.*

The fundamental principles that Lightfoot espoused have continued to be mainstays of diachronic generative syntax. First, we have the fundamental role of Universal Grammar in making the grammar of older speakers unlearnable when those speakers – for whatever reason – produce E-Language which makes the language learner unable to produce the same analysis for a string like (the Middle English variant of) *ic **cunne** tocnawan betwux god and yfel.* The older generation generates this string using a verb-final base structure and a movement transformation, but younger speakers are unable to learn this analysis because the evidence for it has become too weak, and so they come up with a new analysis to account for the same word order. Lightfoot emphasized that we should not think in terms of mechanisms of language change, but rather in terms of how a grammar could be constructed from the available data. So while we would use the traditional term *reanalysis* to describe the change from a grammar which achieves verb-medial position by a transformation to a grammar which generates the verb in this position in the base structure, we must keep in mind that from the language learner's point of view, there is no change of analysis. Second, we see the idea of one change immediately causing other, superficially unrelated, changes. If a number of changes can be linked to a single "triggering" change, this is taken as a powerful argument for the correctness of the analysis.

While these fundamental ideas have continued to underpin much current work in diachronic generative syntax, the details of Lightfoot's analysis have been demonstrated to be open to criticism on a number of fronts. Warner (1993) showed that the sharpening of the category of auxiliaries (not just modals) was not as cataclysmic as Lightfoot suggested; there was a "cluster of changes," but this was more in the nature of a tidying up after more gradual changes took place than a radical restructuring. Furthermore, the modals did not simply behave like main verbs in Old English but already showed some auxiliary-like properties. More recent treatments of the development of modals in English generally accept that modals with specific meanings were always generated in a position that distinguished them from ordinary verbs. For example, van Kemenade (1992) follows Lightfoot in seeing the change of basic word order from OV to VO as playing a role in making the special status of some modals evident, but unlike Lightfoot she does not treat the loss of main verb behavior as a sudden change resulting from a single reanalysis. Rather, it was a gradual, verb-by-verb change.

In the earliest generative treatments, phrase structure rules were assumed to produce the sequence of an Aux (auxiliary) node followed by a VP (verb phrase). The Aux node consisted of T (M) (*have* + *-en*) (*be* + *-ing*) V. The Affix Hopping transformation moved the affixes onto the verb (whether auxiliary or main verb) to its right, with the effect that a sentence beginning with a modal (M) had tense on the modal, while in a sequence like *has eaten*, the tense hopped onto *have* to attach to it, while the participial *-en* hopped onto the main verb *eat*. Important changes in the conception of phrase structure have taken place since these early treatments. Originally, a clause was denoted by S (sentence). S has been replaced by IP 'inflection phrase.' The Aux node has disappeared and tensed verbs, including auxiliary verbs, are assumed to reside (whether by base generation or after movement) in I, the head of IP. In most contemporary analyses, the tense affix is assumed to get its position either by raising the verb to I, where the tense affix is found, or lowering the affix to V. In Modern English, raising to I is only available for the auxiliary verbs; with main verbs, only lowering of the affixes (the more recent equivalent of Affix Hopping) is possible. In frameworks that do not incorporate movement, however, verb forms are assumed to be inserted fully inflected from the lexicon.

Meanwhile, developments in generative syntax made new analyses possible which sought to link changes in the behavior of modals and other changes in the auxiliary system. In the earliest treatments, the Aux(iliary) node generated a "flat" structure with a string of auxiliary verbs all on the same level. In more recent analyses, the Aux node has disappeared, and a string of auxiliary verbs is assumed to involve a series of recursive (nested) VPs. Roberts (1985) proposed the following development of auxiliary verbs in English. Before the sixteenth century, the modals were (at least sometimes) generated as main verbs (V), and raised to INFL (essentially Aux) to pick up their inflection, as shown below:

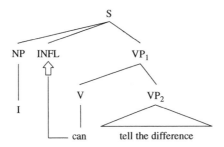

The major difference with Lightfoot's earlier analysis of pre-sixteenth-century English is that the modal (which by Middle English was no longer sentence-final) is assumed to have been raised up to its final position in INFL, rather than generated in the main clause as a verb. Roberts argues that by the sixteenth century, certain morphological changes which we will not discuss here made it impossible for verbs to raise to INFL. From a language learners' point of view, the modals and the other auxiliary verbs, including *do*, clearly were in INFL, but they could no longer construct grammars that raised the verb to that position. They accordingly reanalyzed these verbs as being generated in INFL, rather than raised there. Thus the modern situation, with auxiliary verbs being generated in INFL rather than within a VP, was the result of a reanalysis.

Many generativists treat the development of modals in English as an instance of grammaticalization.

"Grammaticalization," the evolution of grammatical forms from lexical items and constructions, will be treated in depth in Chapter 6. As the previous discussion of modals and upcoming discussion of negation in this chapter illustrate, current generative syntax treats grammaticalization as the reanalysis of a form as a functional head or "moving up the tree."

The reason is that grammaticalization is the change in status of a form from lexical to grammatical. In this instance, the premodals were members of V, so lexical. As V, they had the ability to take complements and engage in the other behavior of verbs. Now they are members of I, a functional category, so they have become "more grammatical" and are unable to take complements, etc. The grammatical nature of the modals is most obvious with *will*, which usually merely serves as a marker of future tense.

Functional Heads, Parameters, and Features

The mention of grammaticalization leads naturally to a discussion of the most recent developments in generative syntax. The **Principles and Parameters** framework postulated a limited number of universal syntactic principles and attributed cross-linguistic variation to different settings of universal parameters of variation. Within this framework, syntactic change happens when language learners reset one or more parameters in language, as proposed by Roberts (1985). That is, they do not encounter enough evidence in the speech they hear for parameter settings that had previously existed in the language. Naturally, there has been a good deal of debate about what might count as "sufficient evidence" for a particular parameter setting. In the case of the loss in English of the parameter setting allowing the raising of verbs to collect inflection, the explanation which is usually given is that the verbal morphology of English became too impoverished for this process to be possible anymore. This reflects the observation that cross-linguistically, languages with rich inflection typically behave quite differently from languages with little inflection. The basic idea is that language learners can only learn that the language they are acquiring has Verb-Raising if they get clear morphological cues in the right places.

Let us assume that young Margaret, born in the sixteenth century, had parents who had Verb-Raising as a part of their I-Language. They had sufficiently clear evidence in their own acquisition data to incorporate Verb-Raising into their grammars. However, they learned English at a time when certain verbal inflections had become optional, such as the old infinitival suffix -en (the reflex of the -an found on the infinitives we have seen in the Old English examples). For whatever reason, Margaret's parents and others in the speech community started using these inflections only infrequently. The result was that little Margaret had insufficient evidence to force her to the conclusion that she was learning a Verb-Raising language, and so she came up with a different way to account for the patterns that were in fact a result of Verb-Raising in the language of older people. Margaret may be the only child making this "mistake" because of some peculiar aspect of the speech to which she is exposed, in which case her grammar dies with her and is only likely to become the object of study by future linguists if she has left written records for some reason – in which case Margaret's writings will be the source of heated debate, since examples from her writings will not fit well with the picture of the grammar of the "English" of her period that can be constructed from other sources. If Margaret was simply doing what many other children were doing at the same time, however, then the change would eventually have propagated through the community and be destined to be one of the facts that the diachronic syntactician seeks to explain about the history of English.

In addition to the theoretical developments already mentioned, generative syntacticians working in this framework also started to posit an increasing number of **functional heads**. Functional heads are heads that carry grammatical information like tense rather than lexical information, for instance I, the head of IP (inflection phrase). Verb-Raising is the raising of a verb to be in the position of a functional head. Pollock (1989) influenced the study of English syntax profoundly by demonstrating that a number of differences between Modern English and French, for example, the inability of main verbs to front in questions, could be tied together by the assumption that verbs in general raise to a higher functional head in French than in English. In other words, English and French have different settings for the parameter of Verb-Raising. Pollock's analysis also assumed a more articulated IP than previously. The analysis depends on there being two functional heads that could serve as landing sites for verbs, T (Tense) and Agr (Agreement). Pollock also added a new phrase NegP (negative phrase). Many new phrases with functional heads quickly followed in later work.

   In the most recent version of mainstream generative syntax, the Minimalist Program, introduced in Chomsky (1993) and further developed in Chomsky (1995), phrase structure rules have disappeared, replaced by an operation Merge, which combines syntactic elements to build up a sentence step-by-step. There is only one other syntactic operation, Move.[4] Both Merge and Move are highly constrained by principles of Universal Grammar, facilitating the child's task of building a grammar. In this version of the theory, the lexicon plays a starring role. A separate lexical component was not even present in *Syntactic Structures*; in the model introduced there, lexical items were introduced by phrase structure rules such as N → *dog*, etc. The lexicon played an increasingly important role after the introduction of the lexical component in Chomsky's (1965) *Aspects of the Theory of Syntax*. Possible phrase structure configurations were constrained by the **X-bar** theory (Jackendoff 1977), in which phrases of different types have to conform to the same overall structure, consisting of an optional specifier modifying another phrase containing the head and optionally, a phrasal complement.[5] The phrase is projected from the lexicon: e.g., a noun projects an NP; that is, where N can occur, N' can occur above it, and NP can occur above that. In this way, phrases and sentences could be seen as built up from the lexicon in a bottom-up way rather than generated in a top-down way by phrase structure rules, although phrase structure rules continued to provide a convenient notation for expressing possible phrase structure configurations.

X-bar theory postulates that phrases follow this schema:

   XP → Spec X'
   X' → X YP

XP stands for any phrase, such as NP, IP, or VP. A phrase of type X has a specifier (Spec), which is itself some type of phrase, and a second level, X'. This second level consists of the head X, which may itself be followed by a complement, YP, which is a phrase of some type. For example, in the tree below IP instantiates XP, NP is the Spec(ifier), I' is the X', and the VP is the YP:

Although this is the basic schema, there are other possibilities involving adjuncts, etc.

In Minimalism, lexical items are assumed to be generated with **interpretable** or **uninterpretable** features. The interpretable features are meaningful ones, which the semantic component can interpret, such as number on nouns. The uninterpretable features are purely grammatical features which the semantic component cannot interpret, and they must not be present at the end of the derivation of a sentence, or the derivation will "crash"; that is, the attempt to create a grammatical sentence will fail. For example, we might assume that a verb has an uninterpretable feature for number, which must be matched up with an interpretable number feature on a noun phrase. This matching can only be done under the right conditions. Extensive verbal morphology of the sort found in Old English can provide the matching, but in a language like Modern English, in which the verbal morphology is impoverished, this matching of features can only be done when the noun phrase with the interpretable feature for number is in the "right" configuration (that is, the subject position). Thus uninterpretable features in essence drive the syntax of a language, and important typological differences in syntax are attributable to differences in the feature composition of elements in different languages.

In recent versions of Minimalism, it is assumed that an uninterpretable feature must be given a value somehow before it can be eliminated. One way to value an uninterpretable feature is through the relationship Agree. An uninterpretable feature can send out a Probe to find a Goal within the phrase structure with a non-distinct (i.e., agreeing) interpretable feature. If the interpretable and uninterpretable features are in the right structural configuration, the uninterpretable feature is valued by agreement with the interpretable feature. It may be necessary for an element to move in order to get into the right position for the uninterpretable feature to be valued.

The impoverishment of morphology is a traditional account for why word order is more fixed in Modern English than in Old English. The approach sketched above attempts to give a formal account of the mechanisms that link morphology and syntax. In addition, recent developments in generative syntax have resulted in analyses of syntactic change as involving changes of bar-level status – (phrasal) specifier to head – as well as changes of feature type (interpretable to uninterpretable). We can look at the history of sentence negation in English to illustrate both the workings of interpretable and uninterpretable features in a synchronic grammar and how these can be used to account for syntactic change.

Case Study: Clausal Negation

In Present-day English, we use the negator *not* to negate a clause. The position of this negator must be between an auxiliary verb such as *can* or *do* and the main or lexical verb. So, for example, we can say *Hubert must not play his tuba again at the meeting* or *Hubert does not play his tuba at meetings* but not **Hubert plays not his tuba at meetings* or **Hubert not plays his tuba at meetings*. This pattern has only emerged relatively recently in the history of English, however.

Table 3.1 *Negation in the history of English*

Stage	Pattern	Example
a. Old English	Neg (*ne*) + V	Ic ne singe 'I do not sing'
b. Middle English	Neg (*ne*) + V + Neg (*nawt*)	Ich ne singe nawt 'I do not sing'
c. Early Modern English	V + Neg (*not*)	I sing not
d. Present-day English	Aux + Neg (*not*) + V	I do/may not sing

In Shakespeare's language, which belongs to the Early Modern English period, it would have been perfectly acceptable to say *plays not*, as indicated by the grammaticality of example (1a). When we go back further, we find a different dominant pattern in every major period of English.

The Danish grammarian Otto Jespersen is responsible for bringing it to the attention of linguists (in 1917) that negation in English has gone through stages which are similar to stages which have occurred in other languages. In the case of English, we have four stages, illustrated by the (hypothetical) examples[6] in Table 3.1. The stages present an oversimplified picture, since the patterns overlapped, as already noted for Shakespeare's language, and of course the patterns are not so neatly packaged into periods. Nevertheless, the patterns are those that the generative linguist seeks to analyze formally, and they are characteristic of the periods specified.

This sequence can be regarded as a process of renewal as one form of negation is replaced by another. This process has been dubbed the "Jespersen Cycle." This process of renewal has caused great interest among generative linguists, and the Jespersen Cycle has been the subject of several generative studies. The introduction of new features and NegP makes it possible to describe the stages in a way which relates the history of negation in English to cross-linguistic parameters of variation.

Negation in the world's languages has been the subject of fairly intense synchronic study by generative linguists for some time, and before proceeding, it will be useful to set out some widely held cross-linguistic assumptions. The main negator of a language is commonly analyzed as the head of NegP (at least initially, although it may move further up in the structure). A language may have a "secondary negation" exemplified by stage b (in Table 3.1) for English. It is widely assumed that this negative "reinforcer" is phrasal, and occupies the Specifier position of NegP. Languages exhibiting a secondary negator of this sort are usually said to have "negative concord." It should be noted that the term "negative concord" is also used for languages that use a negative form of a quantifier such as *nobody* in the scope of sentence negation. This sort of "double negative" is actually found at the Old English stage. For the moment, let's ignore sentences with negative quantifiers and focus on the explanations of negative concord of the sort exhibited in English stage b.

The interaction between the negative head *ne* and the secondary negator *nawt* (and variants, which developed into *not*) in Middle English is generally treated as an instance of the Agree relationship. This is a relationship holding between a specifier and a head.

The graphic descriptions of stages a and b are presented below to give an idea of the basic ingredients of the sort of analyses that have been proposed for the development of negation from Old to Middle English. The structures that are represented here are for *ne singe (nawt)* in Old English and *(ne) singe nawt* 'don't sing' in Middle English.[7]

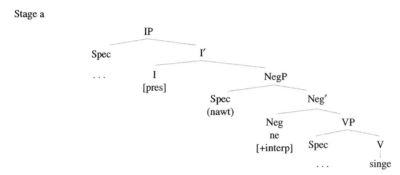

Stage a

This is not the final structure, because the verb will move up to Neg to collect *ne*, and then raise to I. It will be cancelled out in its original position. *Nawt* has a meaning beyond pure negation at this stage, and does not need to appear, since *ne* has an interpretable feature and so can stand on its own.

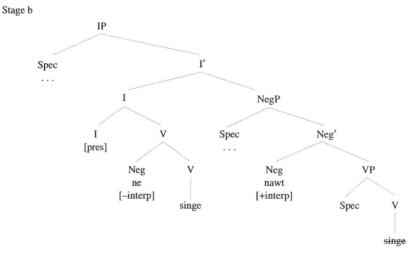

Stage b

At this stage, *nawt* has been reanalyzed as the head of the negative phrase. It now has an interpretable feature, and so can stand on its own. The word *ne* can still be used, but it has become uninterpretable, meaning that it cannot be used except in combination with the interpretable *nawt*. The (optional) *ne* could start out in a number of positions, but we can assume that somewhere in the derivation it has been collected by the verb as it moves up to I, getting valued by *nawt* along the way. This tree shows the derivation after the verb has moved to I, creating a new I node as it is adjoined to the original I and taking *ne* along with it. The result is the string *ne singe nawt* 'don't sing.' These trees are not meant to represent the details of any specific analysis which has been proposed but simply to give a (simplified) visual representation of some current proposals.

The current minimalist conception of Agree is that it is the satisfaction of the need to dispense with an uninterpretable feature borne by one element by pairing it with an interpretable feature carried by another element which is in a suitable structural relationship with the first element. Thus we can assume that the first negator (*ne*) in stage b, being a purely grammatical element, has an uninterpretable negative feature and needs reinforcement by *nawt* (or some other negative), which is meaningful and has an interpretable negative feature. So the change from Old to Middle English was that the negative feature of the head *ne* was interpretable in Old English, but became uninterpretable in Middle English. This could have happened because the *nawt*, originally an intensifier, was used so frequently that it had been reanalyzed as obligatory. The secondary negators started out as emphatic elements but became semantically bleached as they were frequently used in contexts where their emphatic nature was ambiguous. This caused them to become seen as the essential part of the negative, and so they were reanalyzed as carrying the main negative feature (the interpretable one), while the *ne* feature became uninterpretable. The *ne* therefore became optional, as elements which carry only uninterpretable features are not crucial to the grammar, and eventually disappeared.

Generative Approaches to Variation

Early work in generative grammar did not pay much attention to variation in synchronic grammar, but variation could be accounted for by such devices as optionality of transformations or phonological rules. With the increasing focus on constraining the power of generative grammars, however, optional rules became impossible – a parameter setting either forced movement, for example, or prevented it. This was problematic for linguists working on diachronic analyses, however. If syntactic change was a matter of the resetting of a parameter, it should become impossible for a language learner to generate constructions which depended on the earlier parameter setting, at least in any productive way. This predicts the rather sudden death of a construction. However, sufficiently detailed studies of syntactic change have consistently found that it is implemented gradually. Change typically begins with variation.

The use of corpora, especially syntactically parsed corpora, has greatly advanced the study of the syntax of earlier periods. Older generative studies typically based their analyses of earlier English syntax on examples culled from sources such as handbooks, but today diachronic generative syntacticians standardly use the more systematic data made available through electronic corpora. The use of these corpora has increased our awareness of variation in all periods of English. See Chapter 5 for a detailed discussion of English historical corpora currently available. The corpora most frequently used in generative studies of diachronic English morphosyntax are *The York–Toronto–Helsinki Parsed Corpus of Old English Prose* (YCOE), *The York–Helsinki Parsed Corpus of Old English Poetry* (York Poetry corpus), *The Penn–Helsinki Parsed Corpus of Middle English* (PPCME2), and *The Penn–Helsinki Parsed Corpus of Early Modern English* (PPCEME).

The existence of variation within a speech community is not problematic, because we can assume that Margaret may have one parameter setting and William may have another. This parameter setting causes some difference in their E-Language, but not enough to create output that makes the differences in their I-Language apparent except with careful and systematic observation. So if we find one Middle English scribe writing E-Language that is diagnostic for setting A of a given parameter and a second scribe showing evidence of the opposite setting for the same parameter, there is no problem. However, textual evidence points to variation at the level of the individual, not just at the community level. That is, we find the same scribe writing some sentences which suggest the older parameter and some which could only be generated by the new one, all in the same work. If we maintain that a speaker can only have a single parameter setting, there are a number of explanations we might put forward. Our scribe (let's assume it is William)[8] might be copying an exemplar from an earlier period, sometimes faithfully reproducing the original sentences but occasionally updating the language to match his own speech, for example. However, explanations of this sort are incapable of being tested and allow us to make up any story that suits us. An analysis that accounts for the variation in William's E-Language by somehow allowing variation to be generated by his I-Language explains the variation in the text without further assumptions and is surely superior.

Within the Principles and Parameters framework, the notion of **competing grammars** within the individual was introduced in an important paper by Kroch (1989). Kroch proposed that when speakers learning a language realize that there is variation in the community between two forms, they acquire grammars that generate both forms. In effect, they acquire two grammars, one with one setting for a particular parameter, and another with the opposite setting. They use the different grammars with approximately the frequency that they hear around them. This frequency may be modified as a result of their life experience (for example, in not being understood by some speakers if they use the "wrong" form), and if they increase the frequency of the innovative form, the younger generation learns a higher base frequency of this form, and so on. Eventually, the old parameter setting gets lost. Thus we get the gradual spread of a syntactic change, although it is important to note that the change is abrupt in its initiation, in keeping with the generative view of the language learner as the locus of syntactic change: the new parameter setting is discretely distinct from the old one. This model of competing grammars has been adopted by many syntacticians interested in explaining syntactic change as originating in variation, for example by Pintzuk (1999), who argues that the shift from OV to VO base word order in English was not the result of a cataclysmic reanalysis in the twelfth century, as some generativists had previously proposed. Pintzuk provides evidence that VO order was generated by the base rules already in Old English as an alternative to the older OV order, albeit at a low rate.

Case Study: The Story of *Do*

Kroch (1989) uses the detailed data gathered by Ellegård (1953) concerning the frequency of the auxiliary *do* in English in different environments (negation, questions, positive assertions) to illustrate how the assumption of competing grammatical forms can account for the gradual propagation of a syntactic change in English. When *do* started being used as a "dummy" verb in English, it was used in positive affirmative declarative sentences, as in (1b). As we have noted, it is no longer found in declarative sentences except in emphatic statements. For a period of more than 300 years, the use of *do* was optional in the environments where it is now required.

The requirement to use *do* or some other auxiliary in questions and with the negator *not* in Present-day English is widely ascribed to the inability of verbs generally to rise to I, as they can in languages like French and earlier English. In Shakespeare's time, a sentence like *The people choose Caesar* could have been generated by Verb-Raising, as illustrated above in the discussion of Roberts' analysis. This sentence is still possible today, but because of the loss of Verb-Raising it is generated differently: when I and the main verb are in the right structural configuration, the verb is able to get its inflection by lowering the tense affix to V. *The people choose Caesar* is possible because nothing blocks the lowering of the tense affix onto *choose*. But when NegP intervenes between I and the main verb or I is moved to form a question, an auxiliary is needed to carry the tense of the sentence because the lowering of the affix is blocked when a phrase intervenes between I and the verb. In the absence of any other auxiliary, *do* is pressed into service.

It is generally assumed in generative grammar that questions are formed by fronting I.[9] Since all verbs fronted in Old English, that means even main verbs were in I, and so raising to I must have applied to verbs generally. As we noted in the discussions of modals and negation, it is generally assumed that this raising became impossible in the sixteenth century. But since there was such a long period of variation when either the main verb or a dummy *do* fronted in questions and preceded *not*, it cannot be a simple matter of a parameter being reset (or some sudden change in features). At the same time when *do* was becoming more and more the norm in questions and negative sentences, it was declining in positive affirmative sentences. Kroch (1989) treats variation in the use of *do* in different syntactic environments, leading up to the establishment of obligatory *do* in most of those environments, as an instance of grammars in competition.

Kroch assumes that the establishment of obligatory *do* is a result of the same loss of Verb-Raising in the mid-sixteenth century that accounts for the restrictions on modal verbs in Present-day English. Since Verb-Raising was clearly not lost as an option overnight, Kroch assumes that during the long period when *do* was optional, different grammars were in competition both in the speech community and within individual speakers. So a single speaker had at his or her disposal one grammar which generated structures using Verb-Raising and another grammar which lacked Verb-Raising. There was no true optionality within either grammar. After Verb-Raising was lost, some of the string types that had been generated by Verb-Raising previously remained because they could be generated by other means, such as the lowering of affixes.

As evidence for his notion of competing grammars, Kroch pointed to the fact that the rate of change was the same in different environments. It is the rate of change, not overall frequency of *do* in a given context, that is important here. That is, *do* was not found at the same rate in positive declarative sentences, negative declarative sentences, positive questions, and negative questions. However, Kroch argued that a proper statistical treatment of the rate of increase of *do* showed that the rate of increase remained common to all these environments up to the point where the grammar with Verb-Raising was completely lost. Furthermore, the rate of change was the same in the placement of adverbs like *never.* The grammar with Verb-Raising had generated sequences like *saw never*, which are not possible in Present-day English. The reason is that the verb could raise from its initial position, placing it to the left of the adverb. The innovative grammar generated the modern *never saw* because the verb stayed in its initial position and the affix lowered to inflect it. Kroch gives evidence that the new order with *never* increased at the same rate as *do*.

Kroch took this identical rate of change as strong evidence that a single difference in two grammars underlay the behavior of apparently unrelated constructions. Kroch suggested that the Constant Rate Effect could in fact be used as a diagnostic of competing grammars that differed in a single feature. Importantly, the frequency of increase in *do* in the different environments became independent after the assumed loss of Verb-Raising in the sixteenth century. Up to Kroch's Period 7 (1550–1575), *do* increases in all environments. After that, the frequency of *do* changes at different rates in negative declaratives, positive questions, and negative questions, and disappears from affirmative declaratives. Kroch's contention is that the declining frequency of use of the grammar with Verb-Raising was what had regulated the increasing frequency of *do* in the different environments, but now there was no grammar with Verb-Raising, and the use of *do* developed independently in the different contexts where it was used.

Within the Minimalist framework, new ways have emerged to account for optionality. One way to deal with optionality is to allow a lexical item to be generated with either an interpretable or an uninterpretable feature. This could happen when an item is becoming "semantically bleached," with one variant that is purely grammatical and another variant that is fully meaningful. If the variant with an uninterpretable feature is generated, this will have consequences for the syntactic processes which must take place. We can assume, for example, that the change of status of the Old English preverbal negator *ne* from having an interpretable feature to one with an uninterpretable feature did not happen in one step. Rather, there must have been periods when *ne* could be generated with either type of feature, namely, the periods when we find both patterns a and b in Table 3.1 co-existing. A child hearing pattern a would conclude that *ne* could be interpretable, since it could stand on its own. But the frequent presence of b made the child conclude that *nawt* was an alternative interpretable negative to *ne*, and so *ne* was uninterpretable in that pattern.

Optimality Theory in Generative Historical Linguistics

In line with the new emphasis on constraints rather than rules, Optimality Theory, introduced in Prince and Smolensky (1993), replaced rules in phonology with constraints. Optimality Theory assumes that speakers have a mental lexicon that they have postulated on the basis of primary linguistic data. This lexicon provides the inputs to a mechanism GEN which generates all possible outputs from each input. So for example we have the input /kæt/, and possible outputs for this input include [æt] (with loss of the initial consonant), [tæt] (with /k/ replaced by [t]), among many others. The possible outputs which are generated are then evaluated as candidates for the final form according to constraints. One constraint might require that the output should be faithful to the input, which would rule out both candidates just mentioned and favor [kæt] as the output, identical to the input. Another constraint might conflict with this FAITHFULNESS constraint, however. For example this input form is not compatible with a MARKEDNESS constraint which values a CVCV (consonant–vowel–consonant–vowel) word structure and would favor an output such as [kætə].

Since the constraints sometimes contradict each other, they are assumed to be given a ranking in each language. The candidates are then evaluated against the ranked constraints. The candidate which violates the fewest constraints will win as the surface form. Language-specific parameter settings are replaced with differential rankings in different languages.

McMahon (2006) offers the following hypothetical example to illustrate this point. Suppose two closely related languages differ in whether they require every

Table 3.2 *Optimality in Language B*

Input: /atel/	ONSET	DEP-IO
☞ [ʔatel]		*
[atel]	*!	

Table 3.3 *Optimality in Language A*

Input: /atel/	DEP-IO	ONSET
[ʔatel]	*!	
☞ [atel]		*

syllable to have an onset (an initial consonant). Language A has words of the form VCVC (vowel–consonant–vowel–consonant) but language B does not tolerate word-initial vowels, using a glottal stop as the universal word-initial consonant when the input does not have a consonant in this position. The evaluation of competing forms is often presented visually in the form of a tableau. The tableaux for languages B and A are presented in Tables 3.2 and 3.3.[10]

In language B, the form [ʔatel] violates the constraint DEP-IO, which requires the output form to be dependent on the input form; that is, the output should faithfully reflect the input. A violation of a constraint is marked with *. However, in this language this is the lesser of two evils because in language B, Onset is ranked higher than DEP-IO. That is, in this language it is more important to have an onset than to have an output that matches the input. This fatal violation is marked with !.

In language A, the situation is reversed: DEP-IO is ranked higher than Onset. Although the form [atel] violates the constraint that a syllable should have an onset, it is faithful to the input, and so it is the optimal output candidate.

The intuitive appeal of Optimality Theory is that all linguists are aware that languages are subject to different pressures leading them in different directions. So, for example, speakers of a language want to be able to articulate words easily, which pushes the language towards a small phonemic system, but they also want to communicate efficiently, and this provides a pressure towards more phonemic distinctions or long words, if massive homophony is to be avoided. It seems clear enough that languages (or rather their speakers) differ in the comparative value they put on the conflicting desiderata, a fact which is satisfyingly captured by the idea that languages rank constraints differently.

If language differences are due to different rankings, then historical change must involve changes in these rankings. In our example just presented, we can assume that the original ranking allowed syllables without onsets, a situation preserved in language A, but language B reranked the constraints. This assumption follows from the use of a universal word-initial consonant to satisfy this constraint.

As with parameters, there is a challenge here in modeling variability. Do we assume that speakers internalize competing grammars? We must also face the question of what would cause language learners to come up with a different ranking that generated the primary linguistic data that they hear. The fairly recent development of Stochastic Optimality Theory offers a possible way to deal with these matters. The crucial difference between Stochastic Optimality Theory and earlier Optimality Theory is that instead of having discrete rankings, it assumes that constraints are ranked along a gradient. This means that some constraints will be ranked very close to each other, while others are ranked far apart. It is furthermore assumed that in speech production, there is a random "noise" element that can perturb the rankings. The result will be that constraints which are ranked very close to each other may occasionally have their rankings reversed. In this way Stochastic Optimality Theory can model the fact that what are "hard constraints," i.e., absolutely inviolable constraints, in one language may be "soft" constraints in another, that is, strong tendencies rather than absolutes.

To apply this to a concrete example, let's consider the simplification of initial /kn/ in the sixteenth century, as in *knight* or *knee*. We can assume that at one point, the DEP-IO constraint might be ranked just a short way above whatever constraint discouraged initial consonant clusters, meaning that speakers would sometimes come out with [ni:] instead of [kni:] for *knee*. In the language learning process, children will learn a ranking which closely approximates the ranking that generated the data they hear, but they will be exposed to different frequencies of the two variants from different speakers, since each individual will have a slightly different ranking, and they will make small mistakes. Eventually, the majority of speakers may rank the markedness constraint a bit higher than the DEP-IO constraint. The rankings become progressively so far apart that eventually language learners restructure the lexicon – they no longer hear enough evidence for underlying forms with initial /kn/, and do not include any such forms in their lexicons.

Optimality Theory was introduced as a theory of phonology, but it has been adapted to morphology and syntax. Different rankings of features for person and number, etc. have been argued to underlie the different paradigms for the verb BE in varieties of British English, for example. In syntax, Stochastic Optimality analyses have been proposed to model the gradual transition from verb-final to verb-medial clauses. For example, Clark (2004) uses the changing interaction of a constraint that favors the projections of verbs aligning to the right of clauses and a conflicting constraint that favors heads to the left and gives pressure for a medial position of the verb.[11]

The application of (Stochastic) Optimality Theory to syntax is especially attractive to linguists who work in frameworks which do not incorporate movement as a syntactic process. This introduction to generative approaches has focused on "mainstream" generative grammar, but frameworks such as Head-Driven Phrase Structure Grammar (HPSG) and Lexical-Functional Grammar (LFG) are also generative approaches because they formally model speakers' internalized grammars. They differ from the majority position in assuming analyses which are closely based on surface structures, making only very limited use of empty nodes and not assuming any movement processes. Such analyses contrast sharply with the very abstract analyses which are sometimes proposed within the Minimalist Program, which might incorporate phonologically null nodes which carry a semantically interpretable feature. Students wishing to learn about how such approaches work can consult the readings listed below. Optimality Theory is well suited to such approaches because the possible structures can be expressed in terms of ranked constraints. Syntactic change can be expressed as changes to the lexicon, to the feature inventory, and to a change in what sort of structures are favored.

Concluding Remarks

This chapter has shown how generative approaches to language change have evolved as synchronic generative theory developed from its original form in the late 1950s. The various generative frameworks share the common goal of formally modeling the internalized grammar of a native speaker. The rule-based grammars assumed in early generative treatments have been replaced by constraint-based grammars, and the lexicon has gained an ever-increasing importance as the repository of features which determine syntax. Diachronic analyses have accordingly shifted from viewing change as predominately involving changes to rule systems to changes in the strength of competing constraints. A basic idea that has remained constant is that language learners are the primary locus of linguistic change as they construct a grammar from the linguistic data they hear around them. In this process, they sometimes come up with a novel grammar because something has happened to make the correct analysis (from the point of view of older speakers) opaque. Linguistic variation at the level of the speaker is difficult to model in generative frameworks that assume on–off parameter settings, and the increased attention which has been given to this problem as generative approaches have developed is especially important to diachronic linguistics, since it is widely acknowledged that change to a language as a whole begins with variation.

Suggestions for Further Study

For an overview of some of the major problems in collecting data facing diachronic generative syntacticians studying the earliest English periods, see Allen (2016). Fischer et al. (2000) is a good introduction to the study of Early

English syntax with the Principles and Parameters framework, while van Gelderen (1993) is an important early study of the introduction of functional categories. The rapidly changing nature of the Minimalist Program means that some details of the analyses presented by Roberts (2007) will have been superseded, but this textbook remains an excellent introduction to the treatment of syntactic change within the generative approach, setting out fundamental assumptions of the most widely practiced current variant of generative grammar and offering some English changes among the case studies presented. Some of the papers of Jonas et al. (2012) illustrate the application of recent developments in diachronic generative syntax to problems in the history of English. Advanced readers (graduate students and researchers) will also benefit from Picallo's more recent (2014) volume on treatments of variation within generative grammar. Allen (1995) offers a detailed account of changes to the case marking system of English in the Middle English period and remains a standard reference for generative discussions of the interaction of these changes and syntactic changes. While Adger and Smith (2010) is a synchronic study rather than a diachronic one, its focus on the treatment of morphological variation has obvious applications to students interested in accounting for the development of the famous "Northern Subject Rule" in English within a generative framework (for an account of this rule, see Chapter 13). In addition to general theoretical discussions of the use of Optimality Theory to model historical changes, Holt (2003) contains some important case studies of phonological change in English. The Rutgers Optimality Archive (http://roa.rutgers.edu/) is a distribution point for work in Optimality Theory generally. Stochastic Optimality Theory was introduced for phonology in Boersma (1997) and soon extended to morphology and syntax. An accessible study of how morphological variation within Stochastic Optimality Theory can be modeled is given in Bresnan et al. (2007); this investigation into variant forms of BE in British English suggests approaches to accounting for changes in morphological paradigms. An example of a generative treatment of diachronic syntax in a framework which does not assume movement is Allen (2007), which suggests a Lexical–Functional account of the loss of combinations like *my the beloved son* in Early Middle English. Finally, the journal *English Language and Linguistics* publishes a large number of historical papers written within a generative framework.

Exercises

1. Linking /r/ and intrusive /r/
   a. Most North American varieties of English are "rhotic," meaning, for example, the phoneme /r/ (phonetically [ɹ]) is pronounced postvocalically, as in the words *car* [kɑɹ] or *cart* [kɑɹt]. Many other varieties of English, however, have lost the original /r/ phoneme in postvocalic position, with compensatory vowel lengthening. In many of these "non-rhotic" varieties,

we find the phenomenon of "linking /r/" as a "hiatus consonant" before vowels, so we have [ðə kɑː mɛi] 'the car may' but [ðə kɑɹ ɪz] 'the car is.' First, say how this change from having an /r/ in both positions to only having it as a hiatus consonant would be dealt with in early generative phonology. Then outline how you might describe the development using Optimality Theory. Hint: for the early generative phonology approach, you should be able to write a new phonological rule that non-rhotic speakers have added to their grammars. For the Optimality approach, you need not present tableaux or formulate a specific constraint; just give an outline of how a change in the ranking of constraints could describe the change from one stage to another. The markedness constraint discussed in the chapter is not the only markedness constraint that is likely to be necessary to describe the world's languages.

b. Next, consider the fact that in some non-rhotic dialects, /r/ is added even where historically there would be no /r/, so we have [ðə aidiːə keim] 'the idea came' but [ðə aidiːəɹ ɪz] 'the idea-r is.' Such dialects are said to have "intrusive /r/." Assume that this "intrusive /r/" is a development from a "linking /r/" variety. How could this development be described in early generative phonology? How might you describe it using an Optimality Theory approach? Hint: for the early generative phonology approach, pay close attention to the discussion of "rule inversion" in this chapter. Remember also that both these approaches must allow restructuring of the lexicon; in the Optimality approach, this is treated as a reanalysis of the input.

2. Modals

> Lordis, ye **muste** do othirwyse than ye do
> Lords, you must do otherwise than you do'
> (CMMALORY, 27.853 [PPCME2])

This sentence, from Sir Thomas Malory's *Morte Arthure*, was probably written in the 1460s. It is highly comprehensible to modern readers, who only have to make adjustments in the spelling and substitute *you* for the archaic nominative *ye*. In terms of word order, it is identical with the Present-day English translation. However, according to both Lightfoot's and Roberts' accounts (discussed in this chapter), Malory's grammar would have generated this sentence quite differently from the way a Present-day English speaker's grammar generates its modern equivalent, since these linguists both assume that crucial reanalyses of modals such as *muste* 'must' took place in the sixteenth century, later than Malory's period. Say how a fifteenth-century English speaker's grammar would generate the modal *muste* in this sentence according to Lightfoot's approach, then how Roberts' more recent analysis would differ. Hint: what different assumptions do the two make about clause structure in the earlier period, and what crucial reanalysis do they assume?

3. *Do* in negatives and questions

As discussed in the chapter, the grammars of the speakers of Present-day English must differ from the grammars of English speakers of Shakespeare's time. Specifically, Present-day English grammars no longer generate either the V + *not* sequence of (la) or the question with fronting of the main verb in (lb). In generative treatments, it is assumed that both these differences stem from a single difference in the grammars of Shakespeare's time and later periods. Explain what this difference is, drawing on the discussions of Roberts' treatment of modals and Kroch's treatment of *do*. Hint: what syntactic process do both Roberts and Kroch assume was responsible for the sequence V + *not* and for the fronting of a main verb?

4. Loss of negative concord

In many non-standard variants of Present-day English, sentences like *I didn't do nothing*, with a meaning 'I didn't do anything,' are grammatical. In other words, these varieties exhibit negative concord. Since negative concord was a feature of earlier English, it seems reasonable to treat the standard variety as the innovative one here.

Using the concept of interpretable and uninterpretable features discussed in this chapter, how could we describe the change? Do not concern yourself with accounting for the obligatoriness of words like *anything* in negative contexts in Standard English, and assume that it is possible for a language to have a negative feature that is optionally interpretable or uninterpretable. Hint: sentences with a single negator, e.g., *I don't see it*, are also possible in the non-standard dialect, and so your account of this dialect must allow for both a single and a "double" negator. Start with working out how the non-standard dialect can be analyzed, then think about how the standard dialect differs.

Notes

I would like to acknowledge Manuel Delicado, who kindly read and commented on a draft of my chapter.

1. For further discussion of Affix Hopping and later developments, see the box in the "Constraints Replace Rules" section of this chapter.
2. Rule inversion was first discussed in Vennemann (1972). Vennemann used the example of the "intrusive /r/" found in many non-rhotic varieties of English. Intrusive /r/ is the subject of exercise 1.
3. The Old English examples are taken from the YCOE; see the box on the use of corpora by generative syntacticians in the "Generative Approaches to Variation" section of this chapter and Corpora and Electronic Databases in the References.
4. In more recent Minimalist treatments, Move has been treated as a type of Merge, Internal Merge, in which elements already in the structure are added to a higher part of the structure.
5. The name "X-bar" derives from the fact that the levels of the phrase were presented with bars over them in the earliest work, for example N̄ became N' (both pronounced "N bar"). In early work on X-bar theory, there was debate over the number of possible "bars" (two or three levels above the head), but the schema presented in the box above is now widely accepted.

6. I have used hypothetical examples because actual examples introduce irrelevant complications. However, all these types are attested in texts.
7. Non-branching nodes are left out for simplicity.
8. But Margaret could have been a scribe too! There were some female scribes in medieval England.
9. In a generative framework that does not assume movement operations, such as Head-Driven Phrase Structure Grammar and Lexical Functional Grammar, it is assumed that the constraints on phrase structure allow INFL to be generated in this position.
10. Adapted from April McMahon, "Change for the better? Optimality Theory versus history," in Ans van Kemenade and Bettelou Los (eds.), *The Handbook of the History of English* (Oxford: Blackwell, 2006), p. 5, reprinted by kind permission of Blackwell Publishing Ltd.
11. Unlike the majority of generative linguists, for whom the positioning of verbs in early English is accomplished by assuming a basic position for verbs and subsequent movement of either the verb or some other element, Clark works within a framework that assumes no movement processes. Clark (2012) offers a non-movement account of another favorite puzzle for generative linguists, the positioning of pronominal versus nominal subjects.

4

Psycholinguistic Perspectives

MARTIN HILPERT

Introduction

To most of you, it will not be immediately obvious why a textbook on English historical linguistics should contain a chapter on psycholinguistics. What do the two have to do with one another? Historical linguistics is the study of how languages change in the long term, over many generations of speakers, while psycholinguistics is concerned with the cognitive processes that take place when an individual speaker produces or processes language. It could thus be argued that historical linguists look at language at the level of entire linguistic communities, while psycholinguists try to understand how language works in the mind of a single human being. Against this dichotomy, this chapter will make the case that historical linguistics and psycholinguistics are much more deeply connected than it might initially appear. The centerpiece of that argument is the observation that language gradually changes in the long term simply because individual speakers in the here-and-now process it when they communicate. This idea was formulated in the nineteenth century by the historical linguist Hermann Paul:

> The changes in language fulfil themselves in the individual, partly through his spontaneous activity, by means of speaking and thinking in the forms of language, and partly through the influence which each individual receives from others. A change in linguistic usage can hardly be brought about without the co-operation of both.   (1891: 15)

Comments like these make Hermann Paul an intellectual grandfather of what is nowadays called usage-based linguistics (Bybee and Hopper 2001; Bybee 2010). As the name suggests, this framework assigns a fundamental role to language use, which is seen as the basis of speakers' knowledge of language. As you experience language in use, you retain detailed memories of that experience and build up linguistic knowledge. This knowledge is flexible, and it is continually reshaped as you encounter new uses of language. This means that over time, your knowledge of language changes. With it changes your language production, which in turn influences the linguistic knowledge of the speakers around you.

Through repeated cycles of small changes in usage, languages can change rather dramatically in the long term.

When language change is viewed in this way, it becomes apparent that it is closely intertwined with the psychological processes that shape language use in the here-and-now. The main purpose of this chapter is to present and discuss those psychological processes, and to offer examples from the history of English in which their effects become apparent. Hence, the two leading questions of this chapter are the following. First, what are the psychological processes that underlie language change as it unfolds in language use? Second, what structures in the English language exemplify how these processes shape language change? With regard to the first question, the list below offers a first sketch of an answer. Some of the terms in the list have been discussed already in this textbook; others are new and will be explained in the sections below.

- categorization
- analogy
- automatization
- reanalysis
- metaphor and metonymy
- invited inferencing
- priming

More processes could be added to this list, but in its present state the list includes those that are most frequently discussed in analyses of language change. Many if not all of these processes are not only found in language, but are in fact general traits of human cognition: they are so-called "domain-general cognitive processes." What is meant by this is that human beings use a process such as categorization not only when they engage in language use, but also in other, non-linguistic activities. To illustrate this, a simple activity such as unloading a dishwasher and putting the clean dishes, forks, and knives into their right places would constitute an act of non-linguistic categorization. In this chapter, each process from the list will be explained in a separate section, on the basis of actual linguistic phenomena from the history of English.

A second aim of the chapter is to explain what roles these psychological processes play in three current linguistic theories. The framework of usage-based linguistics has already been mentioned as a theory in which domain-general cognitive processes have a designated place. However, this is not to say that other linguistic theories disregard them. For instance, the processes of analogy and invited inferencing are central to grammaticalization theory, as is discussed in Chapters 6 and 7 of this book. The process of reanalysis has been first treated comprehensively in work on generative grammar (Langacker 1977), which was the topic of Chapter 3. The final section of this chapter will revisit some of the ideas that are covered in these other chapters and complement them with a few comments on usage-based linguistics, specifically Construction Grammar (Goldberg 1995, 2006; Hilpert 2014). It will become clear that in all three theories cognitive processes are viewed as relevant, but that the theories differ with regard to the relative importance that is assigned to each of the processes, and also with regard to the question of whether these processes take effect only during language acquisition or over the entire lifetime of speakers. The discussion will not attempt a thorough review of the three theories, but it will highlight several differences so as to provide a point of entry.

Psychological Processes in Language Change

Categorization

Categorization is the ability to view things and ideas as belonging to a certain group, that is, as members of a category. Categorization happens involuntarily, for instance when a person sits down next to you on the bus, and you realize without conscious reflection that that person is a woman. The word *woman*, like any other noun of the English language (*book, guitar, cloud, departure, beauty*), is a label for a category, not an individual entity. Hence, whenever you use a noun, categorization is taking place in your mind and also in the mind of your interlocutor. As will be explained in more detail below, not only nouns, but also other linguistic structures relate to the process of categorization.

In order for categorization to occur, two prerequisites need to be in place. First, in your mind, there has to be a schema that allows you to classify a certain entity as an instance of a category. As a proficient speaker of English, your vast linguistic knowledge reflects the many categories that enable you to make sense of the world. Through the words you know, language allows you to categorize objects (*book, guitar*), events (*departure, party*), emotions (*happiness, love*), qualities (*hot, green*), and relations (*in, after*), but also more schematic concepts such as 'an event that happened in the past,' as expressed by the verbal suffix *-ed* (*walk-ed*), or the idea of 'more than one,' as expressed by the plural morpheme *-s* (*cucumber-s*). To be clear, categorization is not dependent on language, but language tellingly reveals just how human beings divide up the world into categories. If a language provides a structure such as a noun, a grammatical morpheme, or a syntactic pattern for a certain idea, that means that its speakers habitually access this idea.

The second prerequisite for categorization is that you must be able to perceive similarities and differences between things in the world so that you can match an entity with its category. If, for example, a metal object is flat and elongated, with a handle on one end and parallel pointed ends on the other, you would realize that it looks similar to objects that you have previously categorized as a fork. Viewing an entity as belonging to a certain category means that you see similarities between that entity and the other members of the category. A rather important point is that new categories can come into being via the ability to perceive similarities between different entities. This process shows itself very vividly in young children's acquisition of new words. It is particularly obvious when a newly formed category does not quite match the adult use of a word, such as when a child excitedly utters 'bow-wow' while pointing at a giraffe.

Much has been written about the internal organization of categories. In his book on *Linguistic Categorization*, Taylor (1989) offers an overview for a linguistic audience. In the simplest of terms, we can distinguish a "classical view," which defines categories in terms of necessary and sufficient features (e.g., a *bird* is an animal with a beak, feathers, two wings, and two feet), from a "prototype view," according to which categories are organized around a central, particularly typical member (e.g., a typical *game* is an activity that is pursued for fun, that involves an element of luck, and that has a winner). On the classical view, all members need to share the features that define the category; on the prototype view, it is possible that more peripheral members only share a certain subset of similarities with the prototype (so that there are, for example, games without a winner). Since the 1970s, substantial empirical evidence has been gathered in support of the prototype view (Labov 1973; Rosch 1977, amongst others). Hence, this view of categories is adopted in the discussion that follows.

Importantly, not only entities in the world are categorized, but also the structures of language themselves behave like categories with a prototype and more peripheral members. You are actually very familiar with some linguistic categories, namely word classes such as nouns, verbs, adjectives, and prepositions. Prototypical nouns like *cat* share certain morphosyntactic behaviors: they can be preceded by determiners and adjectives (*the black cat*), they can be pluralized (*cats*), and they can be used to coin new words with a derivational suffix such as *-less* (*catless*). A more peripheral member of the category of nouns would be the word *kith*, which in Present-day English is practically restricted to the idiom *kith and kin*. As a proficient speaker of English, you will probably recognize *kith* as a noun, even though it fails the three structural tests for nounhood that *cat* passes. Word classes are not the only examples of linguistic categories. There are linguistic categories that represent syntactic constructions, such as the ditransitive construction (*John gave Mary the book*), and there are categories that correspond to morphological word formation processes, such as the suffix *-ment* (*payment, punishment*, etc.). To say that these are linguistic categories essentially makes the point that speakers, in language processing, subconsciously recognize forms such as *cat, payment*, or *John gave Mary the book* as instances of their respective categories.

With all this in mind, how does the process of categorization relate to language change? Language change crucially involves the emergence of new linguistic categories, and the processes of adding new members to that category. Whenever a new word class, grammatical construction, or word formation process appears in a language, this means that its speakers have formed a new category. A particularly prominent example of this from the history of English is the emergence of the modal auxiliaries (*could, should, might*, etc.), which was discussed in Chapter 3, so that only a few basic points will be taken up again here. In Present-day English, the core modal auxiliaries collectively differ from

Table 4.1 *Characteristics of the modal auxiliaries*

	Modal auxiliaries	Lexical verbs
Negation	*I could not sleep.*	* *I slept not.*
Inversion	*Should he help you?*	* *Helped he you?*
Pro-form	*I haven't tried it, but I might.*	* *I haven't tried it, but I like.*
Infinitive	* *I want to can.*	*I want to go.*
Past tense	* *He musted leave.*	*He left.*
3rd person sg.	* *He wills sing.*	*He sings.*

lexical verbs in their structural behavior, for instance with regard to negation, inversion, the use as pro-forms, as well as the lack of an infinitive, a past tense,[1] and inflection for the third person singular, as shown in Table 4.1.

Examples such as those in the table show that modal auxiliaries nowadays form a category that is markedly different from the category of lexical verbs. Importantly, however, this was not always the case. The examples below show historical uses of lexical verbs that pattern like modern auxiliaries (1a–b), and conversely, ancestors of the modal auxiliaries that behave like modern lexical verbs (1c–d).

(1)   a. negation: *I heard not of it before.* (*c.* 1604 Shakespeare)
      b. inversion: *How understand we that?* (*c.* 1604 Shakespeare)
      c. infinitive: *Cryseyde shal not conne knowen me.* (*c.* 1385 Chaucer)
      d. with object: *Yet can I Musick too.* (1649 Lovelace)

Note that in example (1c), the form *conne* co-occurs with *shal*. This co-occurrence pattern is an important characteristic of the English pre-modals (i.e., the elements that gradually turned into the modal auxiliaries of Present-day English). Pre-modals were also found with nominal objects, as illustrated in (1d). Over time, the broad grammatical category of English verbs diversified, so that today, lexical verbs and modal auxiliaries represent two different categories, rather than one heterogeneous category. A recent review of diachronic work on how the modal auxiliaries emerged is offered by Fischer (2007b: 159–202). Whereas it is largely uncontroversial what morphosyntactic and semantic changes led up to the current state of affairs, there are different claims with regard to the relative timing of those changes and the discreteness of the respective categories. As was discussed in Chapter 3, Lightfoot (1979: 80) proposes that various small changes have accumulated to trigger what he calls a catastrophic change, i.e., the sudden emergence of a new linguistic category that is sharply different from other categories. This view has been challenged, among others, by Plank (1984) for two reasons. First, the changes in question can be shown to span several centuries for the entire set of modal auxiliaries. Second, there is considerable diachronic variability in the morphosyntactic behavior of the elements that constitute today's modal auxiliaries. The changes that the premodals underwent happened at different times. These observations are more in line with the view of modal auxiliaries as a prototypical category, rather than a classical category. They are furthermore in line with the idea that the cognitive process of categorization is a force that continually shapes language change. As speakers process language, they subconsciously match the utterances they hear with the linguistic categories they know, thereby updating their memory records of those categories. You can thus imagine that speakers of English around the year 1600 had an intuitive understanding of how the ancestors of Present-day English *would*, *should*, and *can* were typically used. To the extent that these elements showed similarities in their usage, speakers would have been encouraged to view them as instances of the same category, perhaps as a subcategory of verbs in general. With enough evidence of dissimilarities between them and typical lexical verbs, speakers would have been prompted to view them not as a subcategory of lexical verbs, but in fact as a category of their own. Repeated acts of categorization can thus yield the result that we see in Present-day English.

Further evidence for such an understanding of the English modal auxiliaries comes from research on more recent developments, in which a range of constructions, notably *be going to*, *have to*, *have got to*, and *want to*, exhibit gradual behavioral changes that reflect the formation of a new modal-like category. Krug (2000: 214) calls these forms "emerging modals" and views them as "a subcategory within the higher-level class of modal verbs." This new category shares certain semantic traits with the core modal auxiliaries, most notably the deontic meaning of obligation that is present in *have to* and *got to*. At the same time, there are a number of formal differences. The emerging modals do not invert with the subject in questions (**Wanna you go?*) and they do not occur with negative clitics (**I wannan't*). In the light of these observations, we can conclude that the emergence of new linguistic categories is thus not something that is restricted to the past, but something that is constantly happening in living languages. And indeed, if the emergence of new linguistic categories is held to be the outcome of language processing in the minds of ordinary speakers, this would be expected.

Analogy

The human ability to form analogies can be seen as a special case of the ability to see similarities between entities in the world. As was argued above, being able to make judgments of similarity and dissimilarity is a crucial ingredient in the process of categorization. Analogy is a special case of seeing similarity because it is just concerned with similarity between relations. To draw an analogy is to perceive identity in relations. Let us consider a non-linguistic example of this. Suppose that you show a friend of yours two pictures. On the first picture, there is a woman giving a glass of juice to a child. On the second picture, there is the same child, using a watering-can to water a sunflower. Figure 4.1 shows what these pictures could look like.

Figure 4.1a *Child receiving drink*

Figure 4.1b *Child watering flower*

Now imagine asking your friend whether these two pictures are similar. What would she say? Probably she would say that yes, the pictures are similar. But why are they similar? One very simple answer could be that both pictures show the same child. You could probe this possibility by asking your friend what element from the second picture is similar to the child in the first picture. Again, what do you think she would respond? One answer that your friend might give is that the child receiving a drink in the first picture corresponds to the watered sunflower from the second picture. If you think about it for a minute, this response is a bit surprising, since the child and the sunflower have relatively few objective traits in common that would justify seeing them as similar. Yet participants in experiments with pictures of this kind tend to give exactly that response (Markman and Gentner 1993). What makes the child and the sunflower similar are their respective roles in the relations that the pictures show. Both are receiving something, that is, they are in a momentary relation with a "giver" and "something that is given." As a human observer, your attention to such relational similarities even trumps objective similarities. In both pictures there is a child, in both pictures the child is involved in the handling of a container filled with a liquid. Yet Markman and Gentner's respondents judged that non-relational similarity as relatively unimportant. Why would this be? It could be argued that it is in fact language that prompts human beings to think in terms of relations, as many elements in language, notably verbs, encode relations. Note that both pictures in Figure 4.1 show an action that in English could be expressed with the verb *to give*:

(2)   The woman gave the child a glass of juice.
             The child gave the flower some water.

The pivotal role that analogy plays in language is, however, not limited to lexical elements such as *give*. Rather, it is in the domain of grammar that analogical thinking is most visible. Analogy manifests itself, for example, in children's overgeneralization errors, such as *His doggie bited him* or *Don't giggle me!* (examples from Bowerman 1988). These utterances are ungrammatical from the perspective of an adult speaker of English, but at the same time, they betray some rather sophisticated analogical reasoning on the part of the child. In both cases, the child's utterance reflects a relation between two linguistic elements that is identical to a relation that does occur in conventionalized grammatical English. More specifically, in order to produce a form such as *bited*, the child would have to know that there are systematic correspondences between pairs of words such as *wait* and *waited*, *start* and *started*, or *shout* and *shouted*. In each case, there is a correspondence between the base form and the past tense form. The tremendous benefit of being able to see the similarities across those pairs is that the child, faced with a new verb, can simply "fill in the blank," as suggested in the list below.

(3)   wait   >> waited
             start >> started
             shout >> shouted
             bite   >> ?

Similarly, the utterance *Don't giggle me!* can be explained as the result of an analogy that the child formed across different sentence types, namely intransitive and transitive sentences. The first type encodes a spontaneous action whereas the second type is used to express that something is done to an entity. Verbs such as *roll*, *drop*, and *walk* are routinely used across both types, so that the child would have some reason to suppose that *giggle* works in just the same way.

(4)   The ball is rolling down.   >> She kept rolling the ball.
             The plate dropped to the floor. >> He dropped the plate.
             We were walking to the park.   >> We were walking the dog.
             I giggled.   >> ?

These examples could be taken to suggest that linguistic analogies always result in ungrammaticality, but that is not the case. It is just that analogies are plainly visible as such when they go against established patterns. When they are successful, they pass as ordinary language use. Neither is it the case that only children take recourse to analogy. Adult speakers as well use analogy as the basis for creative linguistic utterances. Take for instance the following example.

(5)   The organization criticizes that too many wild animals are privately owned.

The verb *criticize* is very rarely followed by a *that*-clause in Present-day English. If you are a native speaker of English, you might have the strong intuition that you yourself would never produce such an utterance. However, the speaker who did produce it selected this combination of *criticize* and a *that*-clause for a reason. Verbs such as *complain*, *object*, or *protest* share some of their meaning with *criticize*, and are at the same time regularly used with *that*-clauses.

Analogy has been recognized as a major force in language change. Hopper and Traugott (2003: 63), who view it as a counterpart to reanalysis (see below), associate analogy with the concept of "rule generalization," which is very much in line with the examples that were given above. In those examples, the respective speakers applied a rule somewhat more generally than the rest of the speech community. As it turns out, phenomena of rule generalization are regularly encountered in the history of English. As an example of this, consider the irregular verb forms that are shown in bold in (6).

(6)   a. Swiche teres scedde M. Magdalene þa heo **wosch** ure drihtenes fet
            (OE, Homilies in Lambeth)
            'Such tears shed M. Magdalena as she washed the feet of our Lord'
         b. that hem hath **holpen** (ME, Chaucer's *Canterbury Tales*)
            'who has helped them'
         c. It shall not be **baken** with leauen (EModE, Holy Bible, Authorized Version)
            'It shall not be baked with leaven'

In Present-day English, the forms *washed*, *helped*, and *baked* are used in both the past tense and the past participle. As the examples above illustrate, that was not always the case. Over time, the irregular forms have disappeared, as speakers started to use regularized formations. The diachronic regularization of irregular verbs, rather than vice versa, is no coincidence. Speakers are more likely to draw an analogy if the basis for that analogy is strongly present in their minds. With regard to verb regularization, the sheer number of regularly inflected verbs in the English lexicon explains why speakers use those verbs as a model. Conversely, the irregular verbs that are most likely to be regularized are those that occur very rarely. With a rare verb such as *wade*, it is not hard to imagine that speakers simply had not encountered the irregular past tense form (ME *wod*) too often, so that they mistook that verb for a regular one. Bybee and Slobin (1982) demonstrated this frequency effect in experiments in which the participants had to produce past tense forms as quickly as possible. Regularization errors were made more often with less frequent irregular verbs. More recently, this finding has been substantiated on the basis of diachronic corpus analysis. Lieberman et al. (2007) have argued that irregular verbs behave a little bit like radioactive materials: they have a half-life. The half-life of an irregular verb is a mathematical function of its frequency, so that a verb that is 100 times less frequent regularizes 10 times as fast.

Automatization

The cognitive process of automatization goes by several different names, among them "routinization," "entrenchment," and "chunking" (Bybee 2010). What is meant by these terms is the change by which a sequence of deliberately executed actions, through extensive repetition, comes to be cognitively represented as a single action, a unified whole. As a process becomes automatized, it can be accomplished more quickly and efficiently, while at the same time, it becomes more and more difficult to break up the process into its component parts and carry out each component on its own. Non-linguistic examples for automatized processes abound. Think for example of tying your shoelaces. You accomplish this task in the blink of an eye. Now, as a thought experiment, do you think you could write down a list of steps, so that someone who has never done this before would be able to follow your instructions and end up with properly tied laces? Chances are that in order to write this list, you would actually have to observe yourself tying your shoes, extracting the sequence of steps in the process. The process has become automatized to such a degree that you are left with very little explicit knowledge of how you actually accomplish it.

Also in language, automatization comes about as the result of repetition. If you repeat a string of words in the same form often enough, two things will happen. The string will become a processing unit, that is, a unified cognitive routine, and by the same token, its pronunciation will become more and more reduced. Examples for this are common expressions such as *How are you doing?* or *I don't know*. Phonetic reduction in automatized linguistic units is an effect of frequency, either sheer text frequency, as in the case of *I don't know* (Bybee and Scheibman 1999), or relative frequency, that is, high frequency in a given context (Jurafsky et al. 2001). To illustrate the latter, let us suppose that you are at a bar and a friend of yours utters a sequence of three words that begins with the word *gin* and ends with the word *tonic*. Even if you did not manage to properly hear the second word, you know that there is a very high likelihood that the word in the middle is *and*. Now of course the word *and* is highly frequent to begin with, but in places such as these, it has such high relative frequency that it can be heavily reduced and still be understood. In summary, the more frequent a linguistic expression is, or the more predictable it is in a given context, the more it will be phonetically reduced.

Phonetic reduction via automatization is a highly common phenomenon in language change. This is illustrated for instance by the *be going to* construction, which is often realized as *gonna*, or the cliticization (contraction) of the auxiliaries *have* and *be* in *I've seen it* or *It's under the sofa*. However, besides reduction there is a second effect by which automatization leaves its mark on language change, and that is change in syntactic constituency. Bybee (2010: 136) proposes that syntactic constituency, i.e., the hierarchical syntactic structure of phrases and sentences, is an emergent outcome of automatization. An example for automatization-derived constituency can be found in the seemingly simple question *What are you sitting and waiting for?*, which contains the highly frequent string *sitting and waiting*. What is unusual about the question is that the initial *wh*-word questions the prepositional object of the verb *waiting*. As has been shown by Ross (1967: 89), questioning parts of a coordinated structure in English typically renders a sentence ungrammatical. A question such as **What are you sleeping and waiting for?* is simply unacceptable to many speakers. This is evidence that *sitting and waiting*, to all intents and purposes, is no longer a coordination of phrases. Automatization has taken place, so that speakers process the string *sitting and waiting* as a unified verbal constituent. A similar example discussed by Beckner and Bybee (2009: 35) is the complex preposition *in spite of* (cf. the discussion of complex prepositions in Chapter 6). To a speaker of Present-day English, a string such as *in spite of the weather* consists of a preposition (*in spite of*) and a noun phrase (*the weather*). To a speaker of earlier English, the phrase would have a different constituent structure, namely one in which a prepositional phrase headed by *in* contains the bare noun *spite* and the prepositional phrase *of the weather*. These phrase boundaries have been erased and re-drawn with the automatization of *in spite of*. Consider the two different bracketings in example (7):

(7) a. earlier English: [in$_{PREP}$ spite$_N$ [of the weather]$_{PP}$]$_{PP}$
     b. Present-day English: [[in spite of]$_{PREP}$ the weather]$_{PP}$

To stay on the topic of complex prepositions, the expression *by dint of* nicely illustrates the phenomenon that once automatization has occurred, it becomes harder to analyze the components of the automatized unit. In the same way that you have trouble spelling out the steps that are involved in tying your shoelaces, you would be hard-pressed to define the meaning of the word *dint*, even if you know the complex preposition.

In summary, the psychological process of automatization has the effect that frequently repeated linguistic units undergo phonetic reduction and come to be cognitively processed as units. The drift towards holistic processing means that complex syntactic strings can become more tightly integrated syntactic constituents and that the individual processing of their component parts can become more difficult.

Reanalysis

The process of reanalysis holds a prominent position in discussions of language change, specifically syntactic change. Hopper and Traugott (2003: 39) see it as a central mechanism of change that is only rivaled in importance by analogy. Nonetheless, its inclusion in this chapter could be viewed critically. The reason for that is that reanalysis is rarely discussed as a domain-general cognitive process – it is usually seen as a process that exclusively operates on linguistic structures. Whether or not reanalysis runs deeper and in fact extends to other domains of human cognition is a question that will be briefly touched upon at the end of this section. With regard to language, reanalysis can be characterized as a kind of misunderstanding. Reanalysis happens when a hearer analyzes a speaker's utterance morphosyntactically, and assigns to it a structure that deviates from what the speaker intended. Importantly, the results of reanalysis can only persist in language if this process is a "happy misunderstanding" that does not lead to communicative failure. To illustrate this with a well-known example, consider the English word *adder*, which refers to a snake. If you consult the *OED*, you will learn that the word used to begin in an alveolar nasal, which is still visible in other Germanic cognates of the word, for instance German *Natter* or Icelandic *naðra*. Where did the nasal go in English? It fell prey to the process of reanalysis, which would have been possible in utterances such as *Watch out! A nadder!* The hearer could have analyzed the speaker's warning as *Watch out! An adder!* without either of them ever knowing that a misunderstanding had occurred. Through such a misunderstanding, however, a new linguistic structure was created that was then passed on to other members of the speech community. Reanalysis is thus implicated in the emergence of new linguistic structures, and that is what makes it so fundamental for the study of language change.

An example for reanalysis in the domain of grammar is the emergence of the English perfect. In Present-day English, this construction involves the auxiliary verb *have*, a past participle, and optionally also an object of that verb, as in *I have locked the door*. The presence of the verb *have* is no coincidence, as the perfect is thought to have emerged out of a possessive construction (Visser 1984: 2189; Mitchell 1985: 292). That source construction crucially involved a participial form that described the possessed object, as in the Old English examples in (8), which are taken from Denison (1993: 347–349):

(8) a. hwæðer he ... þa stafas mid him awritene hæfde (Bede 4 23.328.6)
       'whether he the letters with him written-out had'
     b. hæfde se cyning his fierd on tu tonumen (Chron A 84.31)
       'had the king his army in two divided'
     c. oþ þæt hie hine ofslægenne hæfdon (Chron A 48.4)
       'until they him killed had'

The first of these could be rendered into Present-day English as *whether he had the letters with him, in writing*. The misunderstanding that examples of this kind make possible is an analysis of the verb *have* as belonging to the past participle to indicate the completion of an action, so that the example would be understood as *whether he had written the letters, and had them with him*. As in the case of *a nadder / an adder*, this misunderstanding does not lead to a communicative failure. With regard to the second example, nobody would notice that a hearer understands *the king has divided his army in two* when what the speaker actually wanted to say was *the king has his army in a state of division*. Despite the new analysis, the utterance itself is a grammatical structure for both speaker and hearer. With this in mind, consider a classic definition of reanalysis: Langacker (1977: 55) describes it as a "change in the structure of an expression or class of expressions that does not involve any immediate or intrinsic modification of its surface manifestation." What is captured by this definition is that the outer appearance of a construction remains the same while the underlying structure that speakers assign to the construction has changed. However, although the act of reanalysis itself is covert, that is, invisible to speaker and hearer, the consequences of reanalysis tend to leave visible traces (Hopper and Traugott 2003: 50). This phenomenon is called "actualization." For instance, the hearer who has reanalyzed *a nadder* as *an adder* might actualize that reanalysis by forming the utterance *Look! Another adder!*, which would render the new form visible as such. Similarly, a hearer who has reanalyzed the sequence of *have* and a past participle as a perfect construction might actualize it in sentences such as *I have spent all my money* or *I have danced*. The first of these is incongruent with the idea of possession (you no longer have money that you already spent), the second even lacks an object that could denote a possessed entity.

With these examples and a definition in place, we can return to the question of whether reanalysis is a purely linguistic phenomenon or whether it can be thought of as a domain-general cognitive process. The position that will be taken here can be summarized as "neither nor." First, reanalysis, seen as a covert misunderstanding through which new ideas emerge, can in fact be shown to exist outside the realm of language.

> The physicist Richard Feynman has, in a different context, discussed the example of "cargo cults," that is, the religious practice of South Pacific islanders of building replicas of landing strips and airports, complete with light signals, in order to attract airplanes full of cargo (Feynman 1985). Tragic as this misunderstanding may seem, it reveals that the islanders had a precise theory of how cargo shipping worked. Once this theory was actualized in the construction of a replica airstrip, the misunderstanding became apparent.

If we accept the idea that reanalysis can be non-linguistic, why is it not a domain-general cognitive process? The answer is that it is not one single process, but in fact a higher-order phenomenon that involves categorization, analogy, and automatization. Harris and Campbell (1995: 61) point out that reanalysis can mean that structures are categorized differently (e.g., the modal auxiliaries), segmented differently (e.g., *an adder*), and assigned different hierarchical constituent structures (e.g., *in spite of*), amongst other things. Hence, including reanalysis in this chapter is perhaps a category mistake, but since it is so deeply interconnected with the processes discussed above, and since it is so central to many discussions of language change, leaving it out would not be appropriate either.

Metaphor and Metonymy

The terms metaphor and metonymy are frequently used as labels for linguistic expressions with non-literal meaning. To illustrate, the poem "The road not taken" by Robert Frost describes the choice between two roads that diverge in a forest. Arguably, the poem is in fact describing a turning point in life, that is, a decision far more consequential than the choice between taking a left or taking a right during a hike through the forest. The title of the poem thus conveys non-literal meaning, more specifically, metaphorical meaning. If metaphor and metonymy are defined as expressions in which words mean something other than what they ordinarily mean, that definition portrays them as purely linguistic phenomena. The perspective taken in this section is a different one, namely one in which metaphor and metonymy are more than a matter of words. Rather, they are seen as domain-general cognitive processes, on a par with categorization and analogy. This view is held for instance by Lakoff and Johnson (1980: 5), who define metaphor as "understanding and experiencing one kind of thing in terms of another." Human beings have the cognitive ability to understand complex and abstract things, such as for example a turning point in life, in terms of something that is more concrete and graspable, such as a fork in a road. Language reveals such patterns of thought, but the patterns themselves are conceptual, not linguistic. Accordingly, this view of metaphor goes by the name of "conceptual metaphor theory."

   While both metaphor and metonymy are conceptual in nature, they differ in terms of the processes that underlie them. Metaphor, as exemplified above, establishes a conceptual relation between two distinct ideas. Taking decisions in life is something very different from hiking through the forest. In the parlance of conceptual metaphor theory, these two ideas are called "domains." Conceptual metaphors consist of multiple links, so-called "mappings," between those domains. Some mappings of the conceptual metaphor that underlies expressions such as "The road not taken" are shown in Table 4.2. More mappings could be added to that list, but the general principle should be clear. The ideas on the right-hand side, i.e., living life, can be conveyed with linguistic expressions that belong to the left-hand side, i.e., going on a hike. For that reason, the latter is called the "source domain" (it is the source of linguistic material) while the former is called the "target domain" (it is the target of what the speaker wants to express).

   Whereas a conceptual metaphor consists of several cross-domain mappings, a conceptual metonymy involves just a single domain and a single mapping

Table 4.2 *Mapping in a conceptual metaphor*

Domain 1: going on a hike	Domain 2: living life
a hiker ———————————————	the living person
a destination —————————————	goals in life
choosing a destination ——————————	choosing a life goal
roads towards the destination —————————	ways to reach those goals
little-traveled roads ———————————	uncommon ways of living
choosing a road —————————————	adopting a certain way of life
obstacles in the terrain —————————————	difficulties to reach the goals

Table 4.3 *Examples of metonymic mappings*

Brazil won the World Cup.	COUNTRY FOR TEAM
Three Picassos were reported stolen.	ARTIST FOR ARTIST'S WORK
The violin has the flu today.	INSTRUMENT FOR PLAYER
I slept during linguistics this morning.	SUBJECT FOR COURSE
Table 14 didn't leave a tip.	TABLE FOR CUSTOMER

within that domain. Metonymy is thus a conceptual pattern of associating things that tend to be experienced together. Several different metonymic mappings are exemplified in Table 4.3.

What unites metaphor and metonymy, and thus justifies their joint treatment in this section, is that both are based on patterns of thought that involve domains (which are sometimes also called scripts or frames). Like categories, domains are cognitive structures that reflect how human beings make sense of the world. As was explained above, categories are organized in terms of similarity; they group together entities that are similar. For domains, on the other hand, the organizing principle is that of contiguity. Domains thus group together entities and actions that occur together in the same situation. You understand what it means to go on a hike or to leave a tip at a restaurant because you know what elements are typically involved in situations of that kind. It is this kind of "world knowledge" that underlies metaphorical and metonymical reasoning.

In the history of English, metaphor and metonymy show themselves prominently in lexical semantic change. Over time, the meanings of words can change, and many of the semantic developments that are known today can be explained as sequences of metaphorical and metonymical meaning extensions. Nerlich and Clarke (2001) offer the example of the word *toilet*, which has undergone a whole series of metonymic shifts.

(9)   *toilet* (Nerlich and Clarke 2001: 262)
        piece of cloth covering clothes >> cloth worn over shoulders while
        hairdressing >> cloth covering a dressing table >> articles on the
        dressing table >> act of dressing which involves using those articles

>> dressing table >> room where this activity took place >> room with various facilities involved in dressing and other things >> room to do certain bodily functions in

It is also possible to point to semantic shifts of this kind in grammatical construc-tions. As will be discussed in Chapter 7, a metaphorical change can be seen in the emergence of epistemic meanings in the English modal (see Table 4.1 above and the examples following the table). The examples below contrast deontic and epistemic uses of the modal auxiliaries *must, should,* and *may.* Historically, the latter develop out of the former. The deontic uses convey meanings of obligation and permission whereas the epistemic uses encode degrees of certainty. Sweetser (1990) suggests that these uses represent two domains, namely the domain of interpersonal forces on the one hand, and the domain of logical forces on the other.

(10)   deontic (interpersonal force)   epistemic (logical force)
            You must be home by ten!   He must be married.
            You should do your homework. He should arrive very soon.
            You may now kiss the bride.   He may be a little surprised.

The first deontic sentence, which includes the modal *must,* could be paraphrased as *You are obliged to be home by ten.* The first epistemic sentence, with the same modal, means that *I deduce (from his behavior, his wedding ring, etc.) that he is married.* As will be noted in Chapter 7, what unites these examples is the idea of a compelling force: In the first sentence, the speaker exerts an interpersonal, social force that obliges the hearer to take a certain action. In the second sentence, *must* does not convey the meaning of a social force, but rather that of a logical force: There are compelling reasons that force the speaker to arrive at a certain conclusion.

In both lexical semantic change and the semantic development of grammatical constructions, the respective roles of metaphor and metonymy are central. The meanings of linguistic forms change as speakers use them in ways that stretch the limits of their conventionalized meanings. Importantly, new meanings conventionalize and old meanings fall out of usage, so that to a speaker of Present-day English, the noun *toilet* no longer refers to a dressing table, but rather just to a water closet. Very often metaphorical and metonymical extensions result in synchronic polysemy. The English modals that were discussed above provide an example of this. An example from the lexical domain is the noun *date,* which can refer to a point in time, the event of meeting someone, and even the person you meet. Over time, older meanings may also become obsolete, as was observed in the case of *toilet.* The loss of intermediary meanings will sometimes cover the tracks of metaphor and metonymy.

Invited Inferencing

Not every meaning in linguistic interaction needs to be overtly expressed; much is only hinted at, and yet understood by the hearer. Especially with people you know very well, you share so much common ground that there is little need to spell everything out. Consider a seemingly innocent question, uttered by your partner or roommate, namely *When are you going to be home?* Depending on the tone of their voice, you will figure out immediately whether this is just a request for information or whether there is in fact a hidden agenda. The question might be a friendly reminder to please be home in time so you can fix that broken drawer, or it could be the recommendation that you not stay out as late as last night, or else. Understanding the unsaid goes by the name of inferencing, which will also be discussed in more detail in Chapter 7. You infer that the speaker wants to communicate something that goes beyond the meaning of the words that are pronounced. Inferencing is a fundamental principle of how linguistic communication works, and as will be explained below, it is a major driving force of language change. The term "invited inferencing" stresses the fact that often speakers design their utterances in such a way as to encourage certain inferences. The hearer is "invited" to flesh out the meaning of what is said and to enrich the communicated message.

Psychologically, what lies at the heart of drawing inferences is the ability to see other people as intentional agents. You work on the assumption that your fellow human beings have ideas, feelings, and intentions, just like yourself. When you interact with other people, part of that interaction is the coordination of your ideas with theirs. In order to navigate your social surroundings successfully, you need to understand what your fellow human beings want. The first steps towards reading the thoughts of other people develop in infants around 9–12 months of age, just before the onset of their first words (Tomasello 2003: 21). At this age, infants begin to engage in what is called triadic joint attention, which is the ability to focus on an object such as a toy together with a fellow human being, typically the mother or father. The baby is aware of both the toy and the mother, and crucially, is able to form the idea that handling the toy is a mutually shared experience. In other words, for the duration of triadic joint attention, the baby understands what goes on in the mother's mind. This kind of behavior can be seen as the beginning of examining other people's ideas and intentions. At around 16 months of age, toddlers routinely understand whether something that an adult did was a fully intended action. In experimental settings, children of that age tend to imitate adults' actions selectively, re-enacting intentional actions but not accidents (Carpenter et al. 1998). Since these experiments do not involve language, it is clear that intention-reading is not limited to linguistic communication. That said, our habit of monitoring other people's knowledge states clearly shows itself in the language we use. Whether we say *There's a mouse*, *There's the mouse*, or *There it is* depends on our assessment of how present the said mouse is in the mind of the addressee.

To return to invited inferencing, when hearers draw an inference they are venturing a guess as to what the speaker really wants to communicate. Reading intended meanings into the utterances of other people can give rise to meaning change. If a linguistic form triggers the same inference often enough, the intended meaning will slowly but surely become conventionally associated with that form. A linguistic form that has undergone this development is the sub-ordinating conjunction *since*. Consider the following sentence.[2]

(11)   Since I've started my gym classes, I've been feeling a lot fitter.

Hearing this sentence, you are likely to understand that the speaker has recently started working out, and as a result has been feeling a lot fitter. The sentence conveys the idea of two events that are located in time, with the first one taking place earlier and causing the second. This causal interpretation of *since* has come about diachronically as a conventionalization of an inference. Originally, *since* just encoded a temporal sequence of events, and technically, the above example is still ambiguous between a causal reading and a purely temporal reading. Meanwhile, the purely temporal reading has not completely disappeared. It is still present in examples such as the following.

(12)   Since Apple first introduced the iPad, four new models have been launched.

Also this sentence presents a temporal sequence of events, but in contrast to the gym class example, introducing iPad number one is not understood as causing the introduction of iPad number two, and so on. What it takes for invited inferencing to shape language is many examples like the gym example, where the hearer is likely to infer causality from mere temporal sequence. The ultimate proof that causality has entered the semantics of *since* is provided by examples in which a temporal reading is simply not possible. One example of this kind is shown below.

(13)   Since Martin is German, he knows a lot about beer.

Let us assume that Martin has been German for all his life, so that no temporal sequence of events can be at issue here. All that is communicated by the sentence is a causal relation between two states of affairs, namely being German on the one hand, and being knowledgeable about beer on the other. Examples such as this one show that the conventionalization of invited inferences shapes the historical development of language. A speaker may use a word such as *since* to describe a sequence of events that is temporal, but also causal. The hearer then follows the invitation to understand an enriched meaning that includes causality. As exchanges of this kind repeat themselves, this enriched meaning convention-alizes, that is, it becomes part of the "normal" way of using and understanding the word *since*. Eventually, the conjunction *since* becomes intrinsically charged with the meaning of causality. It is then that speakers start to produce utterances in which the original temporal meaning is no longer an option. This is not only a theoretical hypothesis; there are actual attested examples from the history of English that are open to both interpretations, thereby illustrating how the tem-poral and causal meanings of *since* overlap. Hopper and Traugott (2003: 83) discuss the following example from Mitchell (1985):

(14)   þa   siþþan   he   irre   wæs &   gewundod,
        then   after/because   he   angry   was and wounded
        he ofslog micel þæs   folces
        he killed much of that   troop

Examples like (14) illustrate what is known as the bridging context (Heine 2002) that allows the gradual meaning shift of *since* to conventionalize: Meanings that start out as an invited inference become, as time goes on, more intimately attached to a linguistic form. At this point, the question could be raised whether invited inferencing is related to, or even instantiates metaphor or metonymy. Traugott and Dasher (2002: 282) explicitly link invited inferencing to metonymy, as the crucial cognitive step in both cases is an association of two ideas within one domain. As with the case of reanalysis, it could be argued here that invited inferencing is in fact a higher-order phenomenon that combines several cognitive processes that are in themselves more basic. The process of intention-reading, coupled with metonymic reasoning, goes a long way towards explaining how invited inferencing works.

Priming

One widely used experimental technique in psycholinguistics is the so-called "lexical decision task." The basic set-up of such a task is that participants are instructed to read a string of letters that is presented on a computer screen, and to decide as fast as they can whether or not that string of letters is a real word of English. In response to a string such as *nsrop* the appropriate decision would be negative, whereas a string such as *sport* should trigger a positive response. What the participants of a lexical decision task have to do in order to succeed is to access their mental lexicon and see whether there is an entry that matches the stimulus on the screen. Interestingly, the verification of a stimulus such as *sport* is accomplished faster when it relates semantically to previously shown stimuli. In a classic study, Meyer and Schvaneveldt (1971) showed their participants pairs of strings, asking them to determine whether or not both strings were words. The participants had to respond with a "no" whenever one or both strings were non-words (*bread – marb*, *lurse – marb*), and they had to respond with a "yes" when both strings were actual words. The crucial variable in the experiment was that certain word–word pairs were semantically related (*bread – butter*) whereas others were not (*bread – nurse*). What Meyer and Schvaneveldt observed was that semantically related pairs were verified faster and with lower error rates (1971: 229). The conclusion that is to be drawn from this result, which has been confirmed in many subsequent studies (McNamara 2005), is that the cognitive activation of one element facilitates the subsequent processing of a similar element, suggesting that human knowledge is organized in a network-like system. This phenomenon has come to be known as priming. A word such as *bread* primes *butter*, that is, processing *bread* facilitates the subsequent processing of *butter*.

Priming is a domain-general cognitive process that is not restricted to language. This has been shown for instance by Palmer (1975), who presented experimental participants with visual scenes such as a drawing of a kitchen counter. After inspecting that visual scene for a while, the participants saw a second picture, but only for a few milliseconds, leaving them very little time to process that picture in detail. Then, the participants were asked to identify the object shown in the second picture. The responses were more accurate, and given with more confidence, when the object in the second picture was related to the visual scene that the participants saw earlier. For example, after seeing a kitchen counter, the participants identified a loaf of bread more accurately than a mailbox or a tin drum (1975: 521). The kitchen counter had primed the idea of bread and so had facilitated the visual processing of the second picture.

The examples of priming given above instantiate a particular type of priming that is driven by meaning. In the literature, phenomena of that kind are referred to as "semantic priming." With regard to language, a second, very important type of priming is known as "structural priming" or "syntactic priming." What these terms refer to is the phenomenon that the processing of a syntactic structure facilitates the subsequent processing of that same structure. Speakers even show a marked preference for primed structures in their language production. A central reference for this is Bock (1986: 364), who showed that exposure to a structure such as the ditransitive construction (*The undercover agent sold the rock star some cocaine*) influenced how participants described a picture that showed a grandfather reading a book to his grandchild. As the two examples below illustrate, both the ditransitive construction and the prepositional dative construction would be appropriate for such a description.

(15)   The grandfather read his grandchild a book.
         The grandfather read a book to his grandchild.

When primed with the ditransitive construction, the participants were relatively more likely to use the first option and to repeat the ditransitive structure, even though semantically, reading stories and selling drugs do not have much in common.

Both syntactic priming and semantic priming have been argued to be implicated in processes of language change. With regard to syntactic priming, Bock and Griffin (2000) show that effects of the kind described above are surprisingly long-lasting. Even when more than ten stimuli intervene between a prime and a picture description task, speakers still favor the primed structure. This is consonant with the hypothesis that syntactic priming is not a transient phenomenon, but actually a process of learning. In current usage-based linguistics, this idea is embodied in the claim that speakers keep a highly detailed memory record of the language they encounter (Bybee 2010: 14). Every instance of a construction that is heard leaves a little trace and so updates the memory record of that construction. Syntactic priming further creates an opportunity for speakers to extend the ways in which certain constructions are used, which is relevant for language change. Consider the following two sentences.

(16)   The canoe floated down the river sank.
         The man thrown down the stairs died.

In all likelihood, the first of these struck you as ungrammatical or weird. It is only when the verb *float* is understood as a transitive verb with the meaning 'push a floating object over water' that the sentence makes sense. You have to process the word *floated* as a transitive verb in the passive in order to arrive at a grammatically correct parse. Matthews (1979: 212) reports that speakers who had been primed with the second sentence, which includes a transitive verb in the passive, were more accepting of the first one than speakers who saw them in the reverse order. This means that syntactic priming may cognitively activate a construction to such a degree that speakers are encouraged to pair it with verbs that the construction does not usually accommodate. In other words, syntactic priming may drive linguistic creativity, or at least make hearers more sympathetic towards creative utterances. This creative extension of syntactic constructions is a process that has been documented for instance by Israel (1996) in a study of the so-called *way*-construction, which is exemplified by sentences such as *Fred dug his way out of prison*. Diachronically, this construction has come to be used with an ever increasing range of verbs. Whereas early examples of the *way*-construction are found only with verbs that explicitly encode movement along a path (*go, walk*, etc.), uses soon extend to verbs that encode laborious or difficult movement (*plod, limp*), and from there on to verbs that can encode laborious motion through space, but that are not strictly speaking movement verbs (*fight, cut*). In Present-day English, the *way*-construction is even used with verbs such as *sing* (as in the headline *Ed Sheeran singing his way to his first UK no. 1*).

Turning to semantic priming, it has been suggested that this phenomenon explains regularities in semantic change, particularly the unidirectionality of semantic change in grammaticalizing forms. Jäger and Rosenbach (2008) propose a hypothesis that draws on a special case of semantic priming, namely "asymmetric priming." In asymmetric priming, one idea strongly evokes another, while that second idea does not evoke the first one with the same force. For instance, given the word *paddle*, the first association for many speakers is the word *water*. The reverse is not true. Given the word *water*, many speakers think of *sea, drink*, or *wet* before offering *paddle*. Asymmetric priming would elegantly explain the observation that many semantic changes in grammar are unidirectional. Expressions of spatial relations evolve into markers of temporal relations (*be going to*), expressions of temporal relations evolve into markers of causal relations (the conjunction *since*), and expressions of possession evolve into markers of completion (the perfect with *have*). Crucially, the inverse processes are unattested.

To sum up this section, priming is the cognitive activation of one element that facilitates the subsequent processing of a similar or the same element. It is a pervasive and well-researched psychological phenomenon that goes beyond language but that is clearly visible in language processing, through which it also influences processes of language change.

How Do Linguistic Theories Incorporate These Processes?

The discussion above has outlined several psychological processes that shape language use, and in the long term, language change. To round off that discussion, it is important to consider how different linguistic theories deal with those processes. Do theories of language change take into account psychological processes, and if so, how? The following paragraphs will outline a number of views that are held in generative linguistics, in grammaticalization theory, and in Construction Grammar. As these frameworks are neither homogenous nor static, it is clear that no single view can be thought of as being fully representative, or true for all future versions of a theory. Nonetheless, the contrasts should give you a general sense of how different linguistic theories incorporate psychological processes.

Chapter 3 already discussed how historical linguistics is approached from the perspective of generative grammar; some of the points in that discussion will be complemented here. A core idea of the generative research program is the assumption of an innate, specifically human language faculty that allows infants to learn language. In current generative work, a distinction is made between the faculty of language in a broad sense and in a narrow sense, FLB and FLN for short (Hauser et al. 2002). While FLB is thought to include a broad portfolio of perceptual and conceptual processes that presumably show substantial overlap with the processes discussed above, FLN is more restricted, and is thought to include merely the capacity of recursion. In language, recursion describes the phenomenon of nested structures: a structure such as a clause may itself be part of a larger clause, as shown in the example below.

(17)   I think [that you know [that Hauser et al. said [that FLN includes recursion]]]

This view of human language puts the ability to discern the hierarchy of syntactic structures above everything else, so that one psychological process takes center stage, namely reanalysis. Processes such as categorization or automatization do not figure in generative theories of language for two reasons. First, these processes are well attested in primates, and second, human beings use them for things other than language. For generativists, if only one of these points is met, that shows that a process cannot be part of FLN. Reanalysis, contrary to what has been suggested above, is thought to be a purely linguistic phenomenon, and it thus lies at the heart of generative approaches to language change. More specifically, it is syntactic reanalysis by children during language acquisition that is seen as the driving force of language change. New syntactic structures come into being as children "misunderstand" an utterance in their input and analyze it in terms of a structure that the speaker had not intended. Lightfoot (1979: 137) points out that such reanalyses tend to bring about structural simplifications:

> [T]he child learning the language will pick the simplest grammar consistent with the data. If the grammar of the models is more complex (opaque) than

the data require, then the child will pick a simpler grammar and thereby effect a re-structuring.

Also in grammaticalization theory (see Chapter 6), reanalysis is assigned a central role, but the idea that it only takes effect through intergenerational transmission is rejected. The position that also adolescents and adults contribute to language change is voiced for example by Hopper and Traugott (2003: 44):

> [I]t is becoming increasingly widely accepted among sociolinguists and researchers on language acquisition that people continue to develop language skills throughout their lives, and also to innovate.

Next to reanalysis, the process that has figured most prominently in grammaticalization research is analogy. Hopper and Traugott (2003: 65–66) point out that many instances of grammaticalization can only be properly understood as sequences of changes that draw on both reanalysis and analogy. Reanalysis brings about the creation of a new structure, analogy brings about the spread of this new structure to new environments, which may in turn trigger further processes of reanalysis, and so on. A well-worn example for this interplay of reanalysis and analogy is the English *be going to* future. Once *be going to* was reanalyzed as a complex future auxiliary, it was no longer limited to the co-occurrence with verbs expressing purposeful activities, and through analogy, it could be paired with a new set of verbs. The sentences in (18) adapt a scenario presented by Hopper and Traugott (2003: 93).

(18)   Reanalysis   Analogy
        I am going [to get water] >> I am going to [get water] >> I am going to [get wet]

Another process that is intimately related to grammaticalization theory is categorization, although perhaps in a somewhat unusual way. Hopper (1991: 30) coined the term "decategorialization," which describes how nouns and verbs during grammaticalization gradually shed the morphosyntactic behaviors that mark them as members of those categories. The results of decategorialization can be seen in the uses of *while*, originally a noun (as in *a short while*), and *considering*, originally a verbal form, that are shown in (19) below. Here, the element *while* is no longer a noun, but a clause connector, and *considering* is no longer a verb, but rather a preposition.

(19)   While the design is nice, the usability is not great.
         Considering the hefty price, I would have expected higher quality.

The term decategorialization highlights the loss of categorial features, but of course grammaticalizing elements also gain features of the categories that they join. Both the loss and the gain of categorial features betray the fact that speakers continually analyze the utterances they hear, linking the elements of those utterances to linguistic categories and assessing degrees of similarity between different category members.

The last theory to be covered here is usage-based Construction Grammar (see Hilpert 2014 for a basic introduction). This theory in many ways compatible with the assumptions that are made in grammaticalization theory. The closeness of the two frameworks is evidenced by recent works that draw in equal measures on both of them (Hilpert 2013a; Traugott and Trousdale 2013). What distinguishes the two is thus not so much a difference in theoretical views, but rather a difference in the goals that the respective research traditions set themselves and the role that psychological processes have to play with respect to those goals. For usage-based Construction Grammar, the overarching goal of linguistic research is the development of a theory of language that is reduced as far as possible to domain-general cognitive processes (Diessel 2015). The challenge for usage-based Construction Grammar is to show that language-specific, innate mental structures are not in fact needed to explain the characteristics of human language. An explanation of why language is the way it is should only make reference to the human ability to categorize, to draw analogies, to think meta-phorically, and so on and so forth. In order to investigate whether the construction of such a theory is feasible, it is crucial to analyze in detail how these psycho-logical processes are implicated in language change, and whether they are enough to explain what is going on. To contrast this project with the approach of grammaticalization theory, many researchers interested in grammaticalization do take a very sympathetic attitude towards explanations of language change that involve psychological processes, but this is not fundamentally necessary. In fact, there are branches of grammaticalization theory that are fully endorsing the generative idea of an innate language faculty (Roberts and Roussou 2003; van Gelderen 2004; Eckardt 2006). The difference, then, between grammaticaliza-tion theory and usage-based Construction Grammar is a commitment of the latter to the hypothesis that language is a phenomenon emerging from the interplay of domain-general cognitive processes.

Concluding Remarks

Regardless of the differences between the theoretical positions that have been presented in the previous section, the points made in this chapter should have clarified why historical linguistics and psycholinguistics are not quite as distinct as they might appear at first sight. While it certainly is possible to study language change without taking psychological processes into account, it will be very hard to explain the observed facts without reference to what goes on in speakers' minds, and so virtually all current linguistic theories reserve a special role for those processes. By the same token, any meaningful explanation of language change will also have to take into account the social factors that shape human interaction. These factors, which inform Chapters 7 to 10, are unjustly neglected here. It is only through the conjoint study of cognitive and social factors that a full understanding of language and language change can be achieved. It is one of the major challenges for future work in English historical linguistics to establish a dialogue between these research traditions and to develop a unified research agenda.

Suggestions for Further Study

An excellent short introduction to usage-based linguistics, the theoretical framework that lies behind much of what has been discussed in this chapter, is Holger Diessel's review article on Joan Bybee's book *Language, Usage, and Cognition* (Diessel 2011). The review does much more than summarize Bybee's findings, but naturally, it is also a very good primer for the book itself, which is also very highly recommended. For the most important concepts that were covered in this chapter, the following references offer more comprehensive information. John Taylor (1989) remains a central reference for linguistic categorization and prototype theory. Fischer (2008) is a good point of entry for the notion of analogy in grammaticalization. For automatization, Bybee's (2010) book that was just mentioned is highly relevant, especially chapter 3 (pp. 33–56). The concept of reanalysis is discussed in chapter 3 of Hopper and Traugott (2003). The role of metaphor and metonymy in language change is described in Sweetser (1990). Invited inferencing is presented in chapter 1 of Traugott and Dasher (2002). With regard to structural priming, Bock (1986) is a classic reference.

Exercises

1. Domain-general cognitive processes
   What are domain-general cognitive processes and why should linguists care about them?

2. The categorization of *much*
   Many words of English can easily be classified into a category such as noun, verb, or preposition, using their respective morphosyntactic behavior as a clue. However, some words are not easily classified. Consider the following uses of the word *much*:

   - Much has happened since last year.
   - Much money has been spent.
   - He must be rich if he spends that much money.
   - We arrived at much the same conclusion.
   - That is too much of a hassle.
   - I don't travel much these days.

   How would you categorize *much*? Is it perhaps necessary to assume several different words that have the same phonological form?

3. Analogy and overgeneralization
   What does analogy have to do with children's overgeneralization errors?

4. Automatization and orthographical change
   A regular question to grammar advice pages on the internet is whether sentences such as *I would of liked to see that movie* are grammatical or not. Given what you have learned about automatization in this chapter, how would you respond?

5. The special status of reanalysis
   Why is syntactic reanalysis not a domain-general cognitive process?

6. From motion to future time
   In many languages, grammatical markers of future time derive historically from verbs that mean 'go' or 'come.' Examples include English *be going to* or French *aller faire quelque chose*. Can you explain how metaphor or metonymy are implicated in this phenomenon?

7. Deriving concessivity and causality from the same source
   The English clause connector *while*, which can sometimes mean 'although,' is actually etymologically related to the German clause connector *weil*, which means 'because.' Consider the two examples below:

   - While I see your point, I firmly stand by my opinion.
   - Er kann heute nicht kommen, weil er krank ist.
     'He cannot come here today because he is sick.'

   Can you explain how invited inferencing gave rise to both of these interpretations?

8. Priming and the lexical decision task
   What is a lexical decision task and what does it have to do with priming?

Notes

1. Note that the modals *would, should, might*, and *could* are historically the past tense forms of *will, shall, may*, and *can* (Bybee 1995: 503). In Present-day English, however, only *could* is still used with past time reference, as in *When John was four years old, he could already read and write*.
2. For further discussion, see Chapter 2.

5

Corpus-based Approaches: Watching English Change

MARIANNE HUNDT AND ANNE-CHRISTINE
GARDNER

Introduction

Strictly speaking, all historical English linguistic studies are corpus-based in the sense that historical linguists, who cannot use native-speaker informants or their own intuition as a source of information, have always had to rely on historical texts as their source of information. The main difference between modern-day, computer-based historical linguistics and traditional historical linguistics is that, before the advent of computer-readable text collections, researchers had to read through (large) amounts of texts for their data and record individual relevant examples on slips of paper.[1] Digitized texts offer a much more efficient way of retrieving data. But the question is whether every kind of digital text collection constitutes a corpus or not. We might also want to ask whether all historical linguistic research that draws on computerized text collections as a source of information is automatically corpus-based or whether we want to define "corpus-based historical linguistics" more narrowly.

According to Biber et al. (1998: 4), the defining characteristics of a corpus-based approach are that

- it is empirical, analysing the actual patterns of use in natural texts;
- it utilizes a large and principled collection of natural texts, known as a "**corpus**," as the basis for analysis;
- it makes extensive use of computers for analysis, using both automatic and interactive techniques; and
- it depends on both quantitative and qualitative analytical techniques.

As regards the first characteristic, we need to be aware of the relation between method and theory: unlike research done within the generative tradition (see Chapter 3), corpus-based approaches typically make use of functional and cognitive models of grammar (see Chapter 4).

The idea of a principled text collection means that corpus compilation typically relies on a **sampling frame**, i.e., a clear idea as to which text extracts from which (sub)period and which range of text types will be included in the corpus. In order for this sampling frame to make the text collection representative of a language or a specific subsection of it, it needs to include "the full range of variability in a population" (Biber 1993: 243) and be based on a clear understanding of what that target population is. For Present-day (written) American English, for instance, the target population would be all texts written by native speakers in the US (whether published or not). Biber (1993: 243) further says:

> Whether or not a sample is "representative" ... depends first of all on the extent to which it is selected from the range of text types in the target population; an assessment of this representativeness thus depends on a prior full definition of the "population" that the sample is intended to represent, and the techniques used to select the sample from that population.

Representativeness in historical corpus linguistics is typically restricted by availability of material (examples are given in the next section).

Databases of historical writing (e.g., *Early English Books Online* [EEBO], *Early American Fiction* [EAF], *Nineteenth-century Fiction* [NCF]) or electronic editions of parallel versions of the Bible in English are not typically compiled with a view to using them as a corpus.[2] They are representative of fictional writing of a particular period or biblical writing, but certainly not of the language of a particular period in more general terms. Additionally, such databases typically consist of complete texts whereas corpora tend to sample (representative) text segments of similar length. Notable exceptions are some corpora covering early periods of English from which only a limited amount of writing survives and where the objective is to include as much material as possible (e.g., the *Dictionary of Old English Web Corpus* [DOEWC], *A Linguistic Atlas of Early Middle English, 1150–1325* [LAEME]).

A special case of a database is the quotations included as illustrations in historical dictionaries, such as the *Oxford English Dictionary Online* (OED). However, these are somewhat problematic methodologically, as they were not sampled from a representative corpus themselves (i.e., there is a certain bias towards individual authors and text types), and since their primary purpose is to illustrate a particular sense of a word in the dictionary, they are taken out of context.[3] A similar case in point is the electronic *Middle English Dictionary* (*MED*), which is founded on more than three million citation slips.

A further resource which can be useful when studying medieval English is digitized manuscripts. Some of these come replete with transcriptions, for instance the *Digital Vercelli Book* (Roselli Del Turco 2013), featuring an OE homily and the poem *Dream of the Rood*. Others also offer advanced search functions, e.g., *The Auchinleck Manuscript* (Burnley and Wiggins 2003), a compilation of ME texts including saints' lives and romances. A number of scholarly editions of medieval texts can be accessed online, ranging from digitized printed editions, such as the collection of Middle English texts hosted by the University of Rochester, to more sophisticated online editions.[4] One such example is Honkapohja's (2013) edition of a Middle English treatise on the Seven Planets, which makes use of hyperlinks for glosses, textual and editorial notes, as well as links to the manuscript images. The *Electronic Beowulf* (Kiernan 2011) transcends the concept of a traditional edition: it presents not only a transcription of the poem alongside the manuscript images, but also a critical apparatus, translation, glossary with grammatical information, and detailed analysis of the meter of each verse.

This chapter gives an overview of the most important historical corpora for English. We provide detailed information on the basic steps in corpus-based historical analysis as background for two case studies. While the corpus-based approach is a *methodology* that can be used for virtually all branches of historical linguistic analysis and is, in principle, compatible with different theoretical models (functional, cognitive), the focus in the case studies will be on morpholexical and morphosyntactic change. (Corpus-based research in other areas, for example, historical discourse analysis, historical sociolinguistics, and historical pragmatics, is discussed in Chapters 8–10; for an overview of corpus-based approaches to constructional change, i.e., within a cognitive framework, see Hilpert 2013b).

Overview of Historical Corpora of English

Corpora in the narrow sense typically rely on some kind of sampling frame. If the aim is to compile a corpus that can be used as a general reference corpus for a variety of studies, this sampling frame will cover the most important text types that survive from a particular period of the language, preferably in a way that enables comparison across subsequent periods in the history of a language. Examples of such general reference corpora are *The Helsinki Corpus of English Texts* (HC) and *A Representative Corpus of Historical English Registers* (ARCHER). Other corpora are more specialized in that they sample a more narrow selection of texts (such as private letters, newspapers, or court proceedings), typically with a very specific research agenda in mind (e.g., historical sociolinguistics, the diachronic development of a text type, or the analysis of historical "spoken" data). We give examples of such specialized corpora below. Both kinds of corpora are typically available as raw text in various formats, ideally following the international standards of the Text Encoding Initiative (TEI) and with XML (Extensible Markup Language). They are increasingly provided with rich layers of **annotation**, including spelling normalization, but also lemmatization, Part-of-Speech (PoS) tagging, and parsing. In a lemmatized corpus, the head word in a dictionary entry (lemma) is given for each word; for instance, inflected words like *goes, going,* or *went* would be labeled with the lemma GO. In a tagged corpus, every **token** (or linguistic unit, usually a word) in the corpus is (automatically) assigned a word class label such as "NNS" (for plural noun) or "VVN" (for verb, past participle).[5] A parsed corpus additionally provides information on phrase structure and syntactic functions such as "subject" and "object" relation.

An obvious problem for corpus compilation that aims for **representative** sampling of language use in a previous period of the language is availability of surviving evidence. Any scholar of OE dialectology, for instance, faces a serious problem from a corpus-linguistic point of view, namely that of extremely patchy data: "about a dozen fairly extensive texts spread over nearly three centuries, leaving most of the country unattested most of the time" (Toon 1992: 428). For most periods of English, achieving representativeness in the strict sense (e.g., Biber 1993; Woods et al. 1986: 52–54) is impossible. This does not mean that statistical modeling, which assumes that the underlying data are sampled in an unbiased way, is impossible. Rather, the more pragmatic approach suggested by Woods et al. (1986: 55) can be adopted:

> a sensible way to proceed is to accept the results of each study, in the first place, as though any sampling had been carried out in a theoretically "correct" fashion. If these results are interesting – suggesting some new hypothesis or contradicting a previously accepted one, for example – then is time enough to question how the sample was obtained and *whether this is likely to have a bearing on the validity of the conclusions reached.*

Another limitation concerns the fact that available historical evidence is typically restricted to written texts. This means that historical corpora (especially for early periods) tend to come with a built-in bias towards relatively formal (often literary) language use. Predominance of writing as a source also means that data in historical corpora are usually skewed with respect to the social background of the informants: even as late as the beginning of the seventeenth century, literacy was often limited to the better educated (and typically male) part of the population (see also Chapters 9 and 11).

While genuine spoken data are not available for most of the history of almost any language, linguists have studied texts that may serve as a proxy for speech. The most systematic to date is Culpeper and Kytö's (2010) study of EModE dialogues. They distinguish between

(a) "speech-like" genres – such as personal letters – that are not designed to be like speech but still contain "oral" features such as second-person pronouns, contractions, and discourse markers;

(b) "speech-based" text types – such as trial proceedings – that are based on real speech events, and

(c) "speech-purposed" writing – such as sermons or plays – that is supposed to be read out or performed (Culpeper and Kytö 2010: 16f.).

Their corpus-based investigation shows that play texts (i.e., a speech-purposed genre) score highest on the gradient of "most speech-like" (Culpeper and Kytö 2010: 402). The relevance of this approach to historical sociolinguistics and to historical pragmatics is discussed in Chapters 9 and 10.

Some historical corpora are diachronic in that they cover more than one period in the history of the language. The prime example of such a corpus is

The Helsinki Corpus of English Texts. Other corpora provide samples of an individual period of the language, e.g., *The Lampeter Corpus* for Early Modern English and ARCHER for the LModE period. A broad definition of what "historical linguistics" means also includes the study of recent change, i.e., developments that have taken place in the twentieth century and right up to the present. These can also be studied with the help of corpora, such as the Brown family of corpora or *The Corpus of Contemporary American English* (COCA). In the following, we give a chronological overview first of the most important general reference corpora and then some more specialized corpora of English.[6]

The Helsinki Corpus of English Texts (HC) spans almost a millennium of English writing from Old English to Early Modern English (730–1710). As not all genres are equally well represented throughout this period, the texts have been grouped into "prototypical text categories":

- religious instruction (e.g., homilies and sermons, religious treatises),
- secular instruction (e.g., astronomy, medicine, philosophy),
- expository (e.g., certain scientific texts and educational treatises),
- non-imaginative narration (e.g., history, biography),
- imaginative narration (e.g., fiction, romance), and
- statutory (e.g., laws, legal documents).

Divided into eleven subperiods of 70 to 100 years, the HC has been successfully used as a "diagnostic" corpus for observing linguistic change over a long period of time ("long diachrony"), despite its comparatively small size (*c.* 1 million words). In a subsequent step, the more general findings from the HC can be usefully complemented by more in-depth studies based on larger corpora dedicated to particular subperiods or specialized corpora (see below).

ARCHER – short for *A Representative Corpus of Historical English Registers* – samples texts from the seventeenth to the end of the twentieth century (in subperiods of 50 years), covering both British (BrE) and American English (AmE). Originally aimed to run to 1.7 million words (see Biber et al. 1994), the corpus has been growing thanks to the collaborative effort of an international consortium of universities and comprises approximately 3.3 million words at the time of writing. It includes advertisements, drama, fictional writing, sermons, journals and diaries, legal documents, medical writing, news reportage, scientific texts, and personal letters. However, coverage for all periods and genres is currently not distributed evenly across the two varieties. For the first subperiod, early prose texts rather than fiction was sampled. This illustrates a problem with (non-)continuity of certain kinds of text that diachronic corpora may run into.

For the diachronic study of twentieth-century BrE and AmE, the Brown family of corpora (named after the nucleus Brown corpus from 1961) provides a valuable source. These are relatively small (one-million-word) standard reference corpora of written English sampled from texts printed in the early 1930s, 1960s, and 1990s, respectively, i.e., roughly one generation apart (see Figure 5.1). They comprise

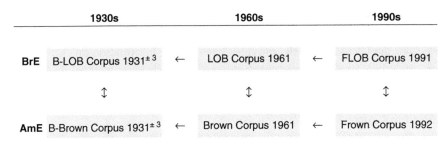

	1930s		1960s		1990s
BrE	B-LOB Corpus 1931±3	←	LOB Corpus 1961	←	FLOB Corpus 1991
	↕		↕		↕
AmE	B-Brown Corpus 1931±3	←	Brown Corpus 1961	←	Frown Corpus 1992

Figure 5.1 *The Brown family of corpora (including the nucleus* Brown Corpus *of AmE, the* Lancaster–Oslo–Bergen Corpus *of BrE from the 1960s, as well as their sequels and prequels from the 1990s and 1930s; see Hundt and Leech 2012)*

four macro-text categories, namely, news texts, general prose, academic writing and fiction. The sampling frame of the Brown family has also been used to sample web-based corpora from material at the beginning of the twenty-first century (AE06, BE06), thus providing data that allow us to track changes into the more recent past.

In addition to these general reference corpora, there are more specialized corpora that sample a particular type of texts, often with the aim of showing its development across time. We give examples of five such electronic text collections.

The *Corpus of Early English Medical Writing* (CEEM) contains *c.* 2.5 million words of scientific texts from the ME and EModE periods (1375–1700) and covers genres such as remedies, recipes, surgical and anatomical treatises, as well as scientific journals. The wide coverage of CEEM allows a diachronic linguistic analysis of a specific register, while also offering a perspective on the shift in scientific thought styles from medieval scholasticism to early-modern empiricism. A LModE component is currently in preparation.

The *Corpus of Early English Correspondence* (CEEC) was designed to enable socio-historical research. The original corpus samples letters from the late ME into the EModE period (1410–1681). The novelty of this corpus is that, in addition to the text files, it provides background information on a number of social parameters, such as regional background, gender, and social rank, thus enabling historical linguists to apply sociolinguistic insights from studies of ongoing language change to previous stages of the language. The corpus is currently being extended into the Late Modern period.[7]

The Lampeter Corpus of Early Modern English Tracts (LC) is a corpus comprising a little over 1 million words of prose writing from the Early Modern period sampled in decades from material printed between the 1640s and the 1730s. The texts stem from the following subject domains: science, economy, law, religious writing, politics, and "miscellaneous," the latter comprising biographical writings, texts that were of current interest as well as those that offered advice.

The Old Bailey Corpus (OBC) is a large, 24.4 million-word corpus of speech-based language from between 1720 and 1913, i.e., spanning a large part of the LModE period. Like the CEEC, the OBC provides background information on social variables, including gender, age, occupation, and social class, as well as social role (defendant, judge, victim, witness, etc.); a somewhat larger, off-line version includes data from 1674 onwards.[8]

A very similar time range (1710–1920) is covered by the *Corpus of Late Modern English Texts* (CLMET), which comprises 34 million words of texts written by (predominantly male) British English authors. The corpus is divided into three subperiods of 70 years each and covers the genres narrative (non-) fiction, drama, letters, and treatises. Its current version (CLMET3.0) also offers Part-of-Speech tagging.

Finally, there is a growing body of historical corpora that aim to represent the historical evolution and development of the English language outside the British Isles, such as the *Corpus of Historical American English* (COHA), which runs up to 400 million words of text sampled from 1810 to the present. This resource is particularly useful for the study of less frequent phenomena. The *Corpus of Oz Early English* (COOEE), another variety-specific corpus, consists of a broad selection of texts written in Australia between the years 1788 and 1900. For a rare source of spoken data – ONZE – documenting the development of the New Zealand accent from the generation of the first New Zealand-born speakers, see Chapter 13.

Corpus Methodology

A corpus is always only a means to an end. In other words, any kind of corpus-based study starts with a research question (typically obtained or emerging from the close study of previous research). From this vantage point, the study proceeds in essentially three steps:

(a)   the definition of the linguistic variable (this is an essential prerequisite for data retrieval);

(b)   data retrieval and post-editing (if necessary);

(c)   analysis and description (including statistical modeling).

This sounds quite abstract, and while the three steps will be illustrated in more detail in the case studies below, let us start with a simple example to show how corpus-based research designs work in principle. Let us assume that you have recently read a study on variation in the complementation patterns of the near-synonymous verbs *start* and *begin* in Present-day English (e.g., Biber et al. 1998: 95–100). You have also come across a comment in the literature on LModE syntax (e.g., Denison 1998) that complementation patterns of certain verbs have undergone substantial changes in the course of the eighteenth and nineteenth centuries. Combining the two, you would hypothesize

Table 5.1 *Variant complement patterns of* start *and* begin

	Complementation type	Example
Intransitive	no complement	*Before we begin/start, we need to define the variable.*
Transitive type I	NP	*He started/began a new page in his paper.*
Transitive type II	*-ing* clause	*The students started/began collecting their data.*
Transitive type III	*to*-infinitival clause	*It started/began to rain heavily.*

that the relative proportion of transitive and intransitive patterns with *start* and *begin* have changed over time and that, within the transitive patterns, there has been change in the relative proportion of non-finite *-ing* clauses and *to*-infinitival clauses (i.e., this would be your research question). You would then proceed to define the variable context as all forms of the verbs *start* and *begin* and retrieve relevant instances from a suitably large corpus of LModE texts (e.g., COHA or CLMET3.0). The search would retrieve the variants shown in Table 5.1.

In the analysis, you would record the frequency of the different variants across time, maybe also with respect to certain other variables (text type, author background, syntactic context), and verify whether these changes are significant. In the discussion of your data, you would situate the findings of your own research vis-à-vis earlier research (e.g., Rudanko 2012), evaluating your case study on lexico-grammatical change of two verbs against changes in the complementation patterns in Late Modern English more generally.

Some corpora, such as ARCHER or COHA, come with online search facilities so that you can conduct your linguistic inquiries through an interface on the web. In the case of most corpora, however, you will have to use concordance software like AntConc or WordSmith Tools in order to be able to retrieve data from the corpora.[9]

In formulating your actual corpus query or search algorithm, you will have to find the right balance between what corpus linguists call **precision** and **recall**: precision refers to the number of relevant examples retrieved with a search (measured as a proportion against false positives), while recall measures the success rate of retrieving relevant data (against instances that are missed). The two tend to be in inverse relation: increase in precision usually goes hand in hand with a decrease in recall, and vice versa. If you wish to increase recall, for instance, you are likely to have to do more manual post-editing of concordance entries in order to remove false positives (see examples below) from your dataset.

Very often you need to compare data from (sub)corpora which differ in size. Here it is important to remember that you cannot compare raw frequencies directly because, say, 40 attestations of a feature in a corpus of 100,000 words carry more weight than 40 attestations in a corpus of 1 million words. One way of dealing with this problem is to **normalize** raw frequencies, for instance per

10,000 or 1,000,000 words. You can find examples of this method in the second case study below (see Figures 5.9, 5.11, and 5.13). Another approach is to work with percentages which show the proportions of two or more features in a (sub) corpus, which is illustrated in the first case study (see Figures 5.2 or 5.6). Whichever approach you choose, you also need to determine whether the difference between two figures is **statistically significant**, i.e., whether the results are likely to be due to chance or not. This likelihood is expressed by a p-value such as $p < 0.05$, which means that there is only a 5 percent chance that the difference between the two values is a random occurrence. In such cases it is particularly worthwhile to try and figure out possible reasons behind this difference. There are a number of significance tests for a variety of purposes, and the ones used in the following case studies are log-likelihood and chi square. You can calculate log-likelihood online at http://ucrel.lancs.ac.uk/llwizard, a website run by Paul Rayson. Calculation of chi square significance levels is possible with standard applications such as EXCEL.[10]

Finally, in reporting the results of your analyses, note that the underlying raw frequencies always need to be given since proportions and statistical tests can only be reliably interpreted if this information is supplied, as Woods et al. (1986: 9) point out:

> A table of relative frequencies is not really informative (and can be down-right misleading) unless we are given the total number of observations on which it is based.

Case Studies

The following two case studies demonstrate how corpora can be used as powerful tools to track language change and variation in the recent and more distant past – the first study focuses on the development of the subjunctive from Early Modern to Present-day English, while the second study concentrates on changes in the word formation system in Middle English. The case studies illustrate the value of combining quantitative and qualitative analyses: the interpretation of statistical results and close contextual readings of corpus texts fruitfully complement each other, leading to a more comprehensive understanding of the data. For each case study, we will outline hypotheses to test on the basis of corpus data, define the variable context and detail methods of data retrieval before moving on to the results.

Morphosyntactic Change: The Subjunctive from Early Modern to Present-day English

In previous periods of the English language, verbs inflected not only for tense, person, and number, but also for mood; that is, there were distinct verbal paradigms for the indicative and the subjunctive. The subjunctive only distinguished between singular and plural, however (and not between first, second, and third person). Over time, there has been considerable reduction in the paradigm so that in PDE, the only remnants are the third-person singular present tense forms (1a), the verb *be* in its bare form (1b) and (2), and the past subjunctive *were* with the first and third person singular (3). The trigger expression in the following examples is underlined, the subjunctive verbs are in bold.

(1)   a. ... he turned upon her with his mock fury and <u>demanded</u> that she **give** him another pickled peach before the jar was disposed of. (1913 COHA: FIC)

        b. She felt that her position as a future poet <u>demanded</u> that she **be** finely dressed. (1911 COHA: FIC)

        c. Beware, <u>lest</u> she **create** as much dissension in our congregation as did the beautiful Susannah in the days of old among the elders. (1836 COHA: FIC)

(2)   ... and yet <u>if</u> the truth **be** told, ... (1908 COHA: FIC)

(3)   you were shifting the gears <u>as if</u> this **were** an ordinary car ... (1973 COHA: MAG)

Moreover, in PDE, the use of the subjunctive is limited to a very small number of contexts:

- formulaic expressions such as *Long live the Queen, If need be ...*;
- after certain subordinators (such as *on condition that* or *lest*; see (1c) and (16));
- so-called mandative subjunctives following "suasive" verbs, nouns, and adjectives (such as *demand, requirement* or *important*; see (1a) and (1b));
- in the *if*-clause or "protasis" of conditional sentences (see (2) and (3)).

In Old English and Middle English, the subjunctive was used in many more contexts than it is in PDE, e.g., after verbs of saying, as in the following example:

(4)   and norðeweard hē <u>cwæð</u>, þær hit smalost **wǣre** ...
        'and in the north, he said, where it was (literally 'were') the most narrow, ... '
        (*The Voyages of Ohthere and Wulfstan*, Ohthere's first voyage; Lauderdale and Cottonian MSS)

Subjunctives in hypothetical sentences, the mandative subjunctive, and the conditional subjunctive after *on condition that* provide interesting topics for case studies on variation and change in the (recent) past: they illustrate instances of (imminent) loss and revival, as well as regional divergence between AmE and BrE.

In Early and Late Modern English, both present and past subjunctives were used in conditional *if*-clauses; the following are examples of present subjunctives in this context:

(5)   If he **come**, I meane to give him that answere you advise (1626, R. Mountague 89; quoted from Gonzáles-Álvarez 2003: 303)

(6)   If ye Lord **have** pleasure in us, he will defeat their councells (1659 J. Jones 285; quoted from Gonzáles-Álvarez 2003: 306)

In Early Modern English, present subjunctives of a large range of verbs are found in this context, whereas in Late Modern English, only *be* is common. Evidence from private letters shows that the present subjunctive with *be* also gave way to the past subjunctive in the course of the modern period (see Gonzáles-Álvarez 2003: 308) and now is extremely rare. The discussion in this section therefore focuses on **past subjunctive** *were* in hypothetical *if*-clauses. The subjunctive dominates over the indicative in previous stages of the history (e.g., Rissanen 1999: 308), but then decreases in Late Modern English.

    Variation in hypothetical *if*-clauses is between subjunctive *were* (see (7)) and indicative *was* (see (8)) with first- and third-person singular subjects (in all other contexts, *were* is used for both indicative and subjunctive).

(7)   ... it was a pity the Miss Gunns did not show that judgment which she herself would show if she **were** in their place ... (1861 ARCHER, elio_f6b)

(8)   They never would leave her, if wreck there **was**. (1872 ARCHER, blac_f6b)

Subordinating conjunctions triggering the subjunctive – in addition to simple *if* – are *as if, (as) though/tho*, and *even if*. A suitable search algorithm to retrieve data from corpora thus combines these subordinating conjunctions with *were(n't)* and *was(n't)*, allowing for several words to occur between conjunction and verb. The resulting concordances have to be post-edited, eliminating all plural subjects and singular *you* (where there is no distinction between the subjunctive and the indicative). Among the false positives, instances where *if* is used to mean 'whether' also need to be excluded (see (9)).

(9)   I wonder if it **was** sweet? (1851 ARCHER, low_j6a)

Auer (2009: 76–79), using data from ARCHER, further limits her analysis to third person subjects. Figure 5.2 shows the development of the two variants in Late Modern English.

    We can see a sharp decline in the use of subjunctive *were* at the beginning of the Late Modern period followed by a slight revival towards the second half of the nineteenth century, which Auer (2009: 86) attributes to the influence of prescriptive grammars. In the twentieth century, the ARCHER evidence indicates a further decline followed by another revival of the subjunctive. Data in this

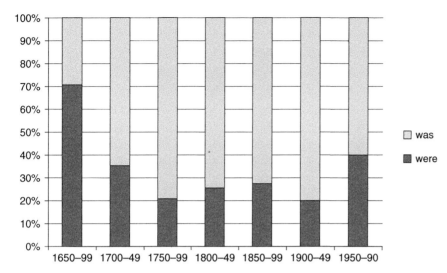

Figure 5.2 *Proportion of indicative* was *and subjunctive* were *in the protasis of conditional clauses with third-person singular subjects in Late Modern English (ARCHER 3.1 data from Auer 2009: 77)*
Note: The author has been unable to supply the raw numbers to accompany this chart. Best practice in corpus linguistics, however, dictates that raw numbers always be provided.

diachronic corpus are too sparse to clearly distinguish trends in the recent past, however. Evidence from the Brown family of corpora shows that we are actually dealing with a divergent development in BrE and AmE (see Figure 5.3). While the subjunctive decreases in BrE in the course of the twentieth century, it remains relatively stable in AmE (the differences between FLOB and Frown prove significant in a log-likelihood test at $p < 0.001$). In other words, we see a divergent trend in the two varieties. This may well have to do with an overall greater propensity of Americans to use subjunctives, as we will see in the next part of this case study.

Now, let's look at the second context in which the subjunctive is found in PDE, the mandative subjunctive (see (1a) and (1b) above). After having decreased in previous periods of the language, the **mandative subjunctive** has been shown to increase again in the twentieth century, with AmE leading this revival (see, e.g., Övergaard 1995; Hundt 1998; Leech et al. 2009). According to Övergaard, the most significant increase in the rate of subjunctives in AmE occurred between 1900 and 1920 (from 36 to 77 percent), with the increase in the 1940s, 1960s, and 1990s being more gradual. One problem with her study is that she used only two computerized corpora (LOB and Brown) and collected the remainder of her material by reading through comparable amounts of text for earlier and later periods. Moreover, she added an additional text category in all periods that is not sampled in the Brown family of corpora, namely drama. It is therefore interesting to see whether data from the Brown-family corpora confirm that the decisive

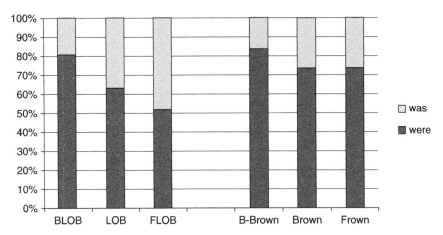

Figure 5.3 *Proportion of indicative* was *and subjunctive* were *(following first- and third-person singular subjects) in the protasis of conditional clauses in the Brown family of corpora (1960s and 1990s data from Johansson and Norheim (1988) and Leech et al. (2009), respectively; for raw figures, see Table 5.1-a in the Appendix)*

change in AmE occurred before the 1940s. For a more long-term perspective, we will be looking at data from ARCHER and COHA.

Since a full set of mandative subjunctives cannot be retrieved automatically, the data in this case study are based on the same set of trigger expressions that were used in Johansson and Norheim's (1988) study, which provides the evidence from LOB and Brown.[11] These verbs were *advise, ask, beg, demand, desire, direct, insist, move, order, propose, recommend, request, require, stipulate, suggest, urge,* and *wish.* The related nouns were *demand, desire, proposal, recommendation, request, requirement, suggestion,* and *wish.* The set of adjectives consisted of *anxious, essential, important, necessary,* and *sufficient.*

For verbs other than *be,* the subjunctive and indicative are formally distinct in affirmative contexts only after third-person singular subjects. In other words, a sentence such as *I propose we/they/you all use fewer subjunctives in future* is underspecified with respect to mood (i.e., indeterminate between a subjunctive and an indicative interpretation). With a past tense in the main clause, however, the unmarked verb (e.g., *He insisted that they go*) counts as a subjunctive since the indicative would require back-shifting to the past tense in the main clause (e.g., *He insisted that they* **went**). Thus, a sentence like *He insisted that they go* needs to be included in the relevant dataset. As a variant, we will limit our analysis to the periphrastic construction with modal *should.* While the mandative semantics is also expressed in constructions with *must* or *have to,* these are a lot less frequent than *should* in the twentieth century (see Crawford 2009). Another variant, the indicative (as in *I recommend that she uses fewer passives*), is really only a (relatively rare) alternative in BrE. Indicatives are not attested in the American corpora of the Brown family.[12]

The data are retrieved from the corpora by searching for all forms of the trigger expressions. Because the subordinate clauses may or may not be introduced by *that*, better recall is achieved by not limiting the search to instances with the subordinating conjunction. Again, the concordances have to be manually post-edited to exclude "false positives" (among them instances where the trigger does not have suasive meaning). Thus, example (10) from COHA is a false positive for two reasons: *advised* is used with the meaning 'inform,' and a different modal than *should* is used.

(10)   As regards the former, we are advised that "reciprocity must be treated as the handmaiden of protection." (1901 COHA: MAG)

The results of the analysis of corpus data from the Brown family of corpora in Figure 5.4 confirm that AmE in the 1930s was already fairly advanced in the revival of the mandative subjunctive and that BrE has been very slow in following suit in the twentieth century. The differences between the BrE and AmE corpora prove statistically significant in a chi square test.

Beyond this quantitative analysis it is interesting to take a closer look at the contexts favoring the subjunctive. As the subjunctive is increasingly used after suasive verbs, nouns, and adjectives, it starts to lose its previous connotations of being a formal syntactic variant. But even in BrE from the 1930s, the subjunctive is not predominantly used in administrative writing. In fact, there is only one example from category H in B-LOB (i.e. the section of the corpus that samples government documents, foundation reports and similarly formal texts); moreover, it combines with a phrasal verb *be set up* instead of a more formal Latinate

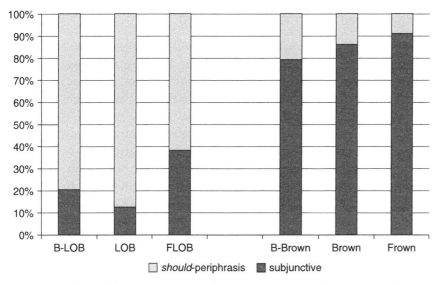

Figure 5.4 *Proportion of periphrastic constructions and mandative subjunctives in the Brown family of corpora (for raw figures, see Table 5.2-a in the Appendix)*

loan word such as *establish* (see example (11)). At the same time, we also find instances in the less formal registers such as newspaper writing (9 of the 19 subjunctives) and fiction (see examples (12) and (13) respectively).

(11)   We make one central <u>recommendation</u> that a National Film Institute **be set up** in Great Britain, financed in part by public funds and incorporated under Royal Charter. (B-LOB: H08)

(12)   The letter <u>demanded</u> that a special national conference of the Labour Party, analogous in representation to the Annual Conference, **be called** prior to January 28 to discuss the question of unemployment. (B-LOB: A04)

(13)   Collins did not see how he was going to get along without them and he almost had made up his mind to follow Lucy's <u>suggestion</u> that he **install** himself in one of the Biarritz hotels. (B-LOB: K22)

Passives were another "formal" context that originally favored the subjunctive. And in the earlier B-LOB, the majority (14 of 19) of the subjunctives are, indeed, attested from passive constructions, while in the later FLOB, they are distributed more evenly (25:24) across actives and passives. The change in the American corpora is even more marked: passive subjunctives in Brown are still more frequent than actives (63:54), while in Frown, active subjunctives clearly out-number passives (66:39). Finally, Leech et al. (2009: 60) report on the wide-spread use of the subjunctive in spoken American data, where it reaches proportions comparable to its use in written texts. The following example from the spoken component of COCA illustrates such a use:

(14)   She also <u>recommended</u> that he **go** to an ear, nose, and throat doctor which he declined. (2012 COCA: SPOK, CNN)

All this evidence indicates that the mandative subjunctive is losing its previous connotations of formality, more so in AmE than in BrE. Evidence from the *Diachronic Corpus of Present-day Spoken English* (DCPSE), in fact, indicates that the mandative subjunctive does not increase in spoken BrE (see Waller 2005).

We also retrieved data from ARCHER, using the same algorithm as above. The results (Table 5.2) confirm that the mandative subjunctive after suasive expressions was used extremely rarely in both varieties during most of the Late Modern period. Note that proportions have to be interpreted with caution as the overall frequencies are rather low. Testing for statistical significance is also problematic as soon as there are cells with expected frequencies < 5.

For AmE, the drastic increase occurs in the twentieth century, but since ARCHER samples texts in subperiods of fifty years, it is impossible to pinpoint the changeover from the periphrastic to the subjunctive in AmE. COHA is much larger and allows us to look at more data points, for instance by retrieving evidence at thirty-year intervals from the 1840s onwards. A comprehensive

Table 5.2 *Proportion of periphrastic constructions with* should *versus mandative subjunctives in ARCHER*

	1700–1799		1800–1899		1900–1999	
	raw freq.	% subj.	raw freq.	% subj.	raw freq.	% subj.
BrE	2:14	12.5	5:23	17.9	6:26	18.9
AmE	1:5	17	5:10	33.3	29:4	87.9

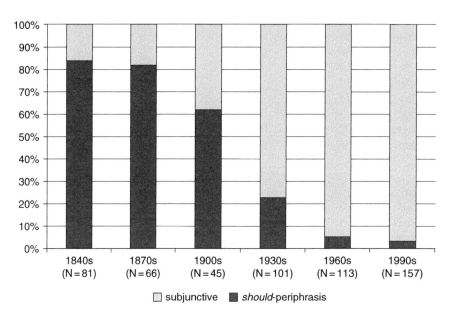

Figure 5.5 *Proportion of periphrastic constructions and mandative subjunctives following forms of* REQUIRE *in COHA (N = total number of relevant contexts)*

study using this approach would merit book-length treatment, but we can limit our search for the purposes of illustration to a single trigger, such as the verb *require* in all its variant forms immediately followed by the subordinating conjunction *that* and repeat this search in the relevant synchronic subsections of the corpus. The results show that subjunctives after *require* start increasing around 1900 but that the most drastic increase appears to have occurred between the 1900s and 1930s (see Figure 5.5).

We can also retrieve additional data from around 1900 in COHA using the same set of trigger expressions as for the investigation of the Brown family of corpora. The results of such a search yield an even higher proportion of subjunctives (i.e., 46.4 percent) than the 37.8 percent obtained for the single trigger used for Figure 5.5 (see Table 5.3). We also see that nouns and verbs trigger the

Table 5.3 *Mandative subjunctives and* should-*periphrasis in COHA (1901$^{\pm3}$)*

	Subjunctive	*should*
ADVISE	6	4
ASK	12	4
BEG	0	1
DEMAND	9	8
DESIRE	8	17
DIRECT	11	5
INSIST	2	5
MOVE	23	3
ORDER	20	27
PROPOSE	14	19
RECOMMEND	17	5
REQUEST	15	4
REQUIRE	3	5
STIPULATE	2	6
SUGGEST	6	11
URGE	15	4
WISH	1	13
anxious	0	10
essential	2	12
important	1	14
necessary	2	19
sufficient	1	0
Total	170	196
	(46.4%)	(37.8%)

subjunctive in COHA more often than suasive adjectives: the proportion of subjunctives rises to 53.8 percent if adjectives are taken out of the equation.

On the whole, the COHA data further substantiate the results reported in Övergaard (1995): the marked revival of the mandative subjunctive in AmE dates back to the first thirty years of the twentieth century.

Now let's turn to the third context of use for the subjunctive, following certain subordinating conjunctions. Schlüter (2009) uses corpus data from fictional databases of BrE and AmE to study the development of the **conditional subjunctive** after *(up)on (the) condition (that)*. Her case study is the first to investigate subjunctives after this complex conjunction. Hypotheses on the development of subjunctives therefore have to draw on previous research on the use of the subjunctive in (hypothetical) conditional contexts more generally. On the basis of the rather sparse data from HC and ARCHER, Auer (2008: 153) provides evidence of a sharp decline of subjunctives following *lest* during the EModE period. Since subjunctives in other conditional contexts increase again towards the end of the LModE period (see above), a larger corpus might provide evidence of a revival of the subjunctive after the complex conjunction *(up)on (the) condition (that)*, particularly in AmE.

Auer (2008: 153) found only a total of 33 instances of *lest* in the HC and ARCHER, which indicates that for any study that focuses on a single subordinating conjunction, a much larger dataset than the standard reference corpora is needed. Schlüter (2009: 284) uses fictional databases of AmE and BrE amounting to between approximately 5 million and 30 million words per period. Her case study further differs slightly from the previous ones in that she does not take the date of publication as the reference point for the diachronic analysis but the birth dates of the authors (2009: 287). Such an approach is based on the assumption that an individual's grammar, once acquired, remains stable throughout that person's lifetime. This assumption has recently been challenged (see, e.g., Raumolin-Brunberg 2009).

In order to retrieve her data, Schlüter searched for all variant forms of the subordinator, i.e., including both *on* and *upon* as well as variants with and without the definite article and *that*. Her definition of the relevant verb forms distinguishes between constructions with a modal auxiliary (15), present subjunctives (16), indicatives (17), and ambiguous verb phrases (18).

(15)   I consented, <u>on condition that</u> he **should be** very temperate. (1823 COHA: FIC)

(16)   a. ... it must be <u>upon the condition that</u> he **depend** on the fortunes of war for his reward. (1858 COHA: FIC)

       b. ... Collector Gulbenkian ... later offered the gallery all the paintings as an outright gift <u>on condition that</u> they **be housed** separately ... (1957 COHA: MAG)

       c. A man may even be willing to burden himself with a few parasites ... <u>on condition that</u> they **not cast** stones into the well they drink from. (1993 COHA: FIC)

(17)   ... he will only do so <u>upon condition that</u> she drops all intercourse with her mother ... (1845 COHA: FIC)

(18)   This truism is the end of the whole matter – <u>upon the condition that</u> we **frame** our theory of knowledge in accord with the pattern set by experimental methods. (1929 COHA: NF)

As past subjunctives were extremely rare, Schlüter (2009: 286) decided to restrict her analysis to present subjunctives. Evidence for this kind of case study can be obtained by searching for all variants of the complex subordinating conjunction. In a second step, the resulting concordances have to be manually analysed for the choice of verb phrase. Figure 5.6 shows the results for both BrE and AmE fictional writing.

Figure 5.6 reveals that the indicative has a much stronger foothold in BrE, where the subjunctive really is a marginal variant (at around 1–2 percent).

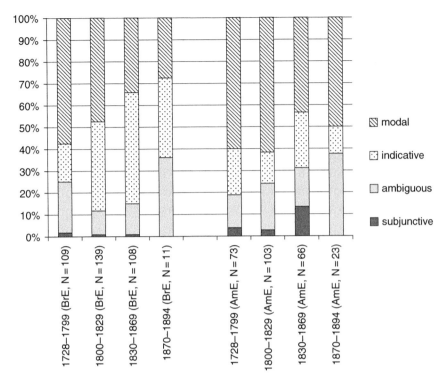

Figure 5.6 *Relative frequency of subjunctives and alternative verb patterns following* (up)on (the) condition (that) *in Late Modern BrE and AmE; data from Schlüter (2009: 288 and 289) (N = overall number of relevant contexts)*

In AmE, on the other hand, subjunctives take a more substantial share at up to 15 percent in the second half of the nineteenth century. Note that for the last subperiod, the overall number of hits from the fiction databases is very low so that the percentages only indicate a general trend. Data from COHA for the 1870s, 1880s, and 1890s (see Figure 5.7) show that the subjunctive was, in fact, on the increase towards the end of the LModE period.

The following are typical examples of subjunctives from COHA:

(19)   It is bound to print all that is offered it, but prints it only <u>on condition that</u> the author **defray** the first cost out of his credit (1887 COHA: FIC)

(20)   The gift came <u>on condition that</u> the laboratory **be** suitably endowed, ... (1897 COHA: MAG)

For the twentieth century, Schlüter (2009) used evidence from two other corpora, the *British National Corpus* (BNC) and the *American National Corpus* (ANC). The results based on these two corpora (see Figure 5.8) indicate a remarkable revival of the subjunctive in AmE, which merits further study, for instance on the basis of data from COHA or COCA (see Exercise 3).

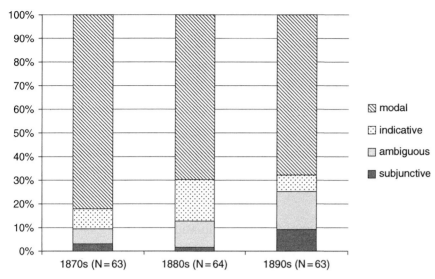

Figure 5.7 *Relative frequency of subjunctives and alternative verb patterns following* (up)on (the) condition that *in the last three decades of COHA (N = overall number of relevant contexts)*

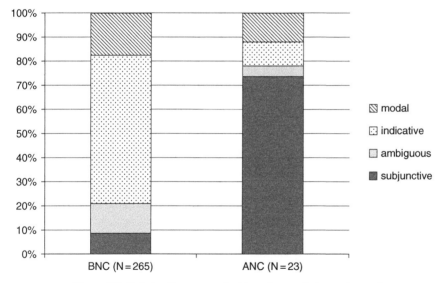

Figure 5.8 *Relative frequency of subjunctives and alternative verb patterns following* (up)on (the) condition (that) *in twentieth-century BrE and AmE; data from Schlüter (2009: 288 and 289)*

Even though the case studies provided in this section have looked at quite different syntactic environments where the subjunctive is used, they all show that it was a moribund option in Late Modern English, but that the subjunctive is far from extinct today. The most marked revival has occurred with the subjunctive following suasive expressions, a change led by AmE in the twentieth century. Övergaard (1995: 44–49) attributes a major role in this revival to substrate influence in speakers from the Mid-West with first languages such as Dutch, German, or Swedish. But the past subjunctive is also going strong in this variety, with the decline in BrE having led to a divergence over the last thirty years. Finally, AmE also shows a greater propensity for using subjunctives after the complex subordinator *(up)on (the) condition (that)* than does BrE. It might be that the recent revival of the subjunctive in mandatives, where it is the majority variant in AmE today, has served to support its survival in counterfactual conditionals and fostered what looks like a revival (in speech) after the complex subordinator.

Lexical Change: The Development of Suffixation in Middle English

The following section discusses developments in the ME word formation system, some of which are the result of language-external events.[13] The Norman Conquest in 1066 brought about far-reaching changes in English society, which was consequently dominated by a French-speaking elite for a considerable time (see Chapter 13). With this change in power, French was established as a high-prestige language in England alongside Latin, resulting in the introduction of thousands of borrowings from French and/or Latin between 1150 and 1500 (Durkin 2014: 255f.). Many loanwords ended in suffixes like -ITY (e.g., *chastity*), -ERY (e.g., *robbery*), or -AGE (e.g., *baronage*), which became recognizable for English speakers through transparent loans, i.e., words whose morphological structure (base + suffix) could be perceived by English speakers (see Durkin 2009: 99). The structure was easier to discern when the base was already part of the English lexicon. An example of a transparent or analyzable word is *stability*, which is composed of the base *stable* and the suffix -ITY; according to the *OED*, the base was first attested in the late thirteenth century, and *stability* at the beginning of the fourteenth. Frequently encountered in transparent borrowings, Romance suffixes like -ITY eventually became integrated into the English word formation system and, in analogy to earlier borrowings, began to be used productively for the creation of new words in English.

The ME word formation system was not only affected by the introduction of Romance suffixes, but also underwent changes within the group of Germanic suffixes, in particular those which, like -ITY, are used to derive abstract nouns from adjectives (called "deadjectival" suffixes). The three most productive suffixes in this group are shown in Table 5.4, with the period in which new derivatives reached their peak. The suffix -NESS was the most productive and most frequently used suffix of this set. To a large extent, these suffixes had overlapping semantic properties and, as a result, were interchangeable to some degree. The entries in *MED* and *OED* show that parallel derivatives like *idleness*, *idlehood*, and *idleship*, i.e., formations with the same base but different suffixes, do not diverge significantly in meaning. Also -ITY can be

Table 5.4 *Productive periods of three deadjectival suffixes in Middle English*

Suffix	Example	Peak period of productivity
-SHIP	*hardship*	mid-thirteenth century
-HOOD	*falsehood*	first half of the fourteenth century
-NESS	*goodness*	second half of the fourteenth century

found in sets of parallel derivatives involving Germanic suffixes, for instance *chastity, chasteness,* and *chastehood.*

Our case study focuses on deadjectival formations in -ITY, -HOOD, and -NESS, and aims to shed light on the following issues:

- At which rate were analysable formations in -ITY introduced during the ME period?
- When was a "critical mass" of transparent formations reached, which then favored the use of -ITY as an English word formation element?
- Did particular groups of texts or authors play a significant role in the introduction of analyzable -ITY formations?
- To what extent did deadjectival -HOOD "compete" with the generally more productive -NESS?
- Which contexts promote the selection of a particular suffix (-ITY, -HOOD, or -NESS) in sets of parallel derivatives?

The data come from *A Linguistic Atlas of Early Middle English* (LAEME) for the period 1150–1350, and from selections of the following three corpora for Late Middle English (1350–1500): *The Penn–Helsinki Parsed Corpus of Middle English* (PPCME2), *The Middle English Grammar Corpus* (MEG-C), and *The Helsinki Corpus* (HC), giving us a total of *c.* 1.6 million words.[14] The texts are divided into eight subperiods spanning forty years in Early Middle English (EMidE I–V) and fifty years in Late Middle English (LMidE I–III) as this allows us to study changes in suffixal frequency and productivity in smaller steps (see Table 5.3a in the Appendix).

In order to be able to understand how suffixes developed and competed with each other in Middle English we need to assess their **productivity**, i.e. to what extent they are used to form new words. We will be concerned with both tokens (the number of attestations of a word) as well as types (the number of different words) in our corpus, as well as other measures:

- *Token frequency*: How often are words with a particular suffix attested?
- *Type frequency*: How many different derivations with a particular suffix are attested?

- *Type/token ratio*: Are the tokens based on a wide variety of types or does a small number of types occur repeatedly? A high number of tokens based on a limited number of types indicates low productivity.
- *New types*: How many words are recorded in the corpus for the first time? The more new types are documented, the higher the productivity of a suffix.
- *Hybrid formations*: Are there formations in which a foreign suffix (-ITY) is attached to an English base, or in which an English suffix like -HOOD follows a borrowed (i.e., French- or Norse-derived) base? In the first scenario, hybrids demonstrate that the foreign suffix has been integrated into the English word formation system, in the second that the native suffix is productive because it can be combined with more recent lexical innovations.
- *Hapax legomena*: How many words occur in the corpus only once? A large number of hapaxes is typically interpreted as a sign of productivity.

As Figures 5.9 and 5.10 show, deadjectival -ITY formations such as *poverty* and *privity* are gradually introduced during the Early ME period, both in terms of frequency and number of new types entering the lexicon (for all suffixes raw frequencies for tokens, types and new types are provided in Table 5.4-a in the Appendix). The early fourteenth century (EMidE V) then sees a strong increase in frequency ($p < 0.0001$), yet here only a relatively small number of types is attested often, among them *chastity* and *soberty*. Since these few types account for over 46 percent of all occurrences, the type/token ratio is very low ($p < 0.05$).[15] At this stage -ITY is therefore not very productive yet. In the following subperiod, however, this changes dramatically: in the second half of the

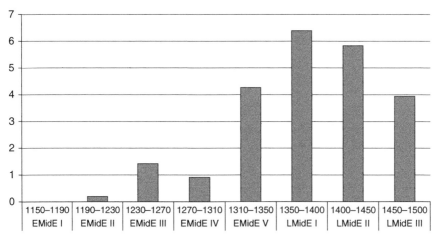

Figure 5.9 *Token frequency of deadjectival formations in -*ITY *in Middle English by subperiod, normalized per 10,000 words*
(Reprinted from Gardner (2014) by permission of Société Néophilologique, Helsinki)

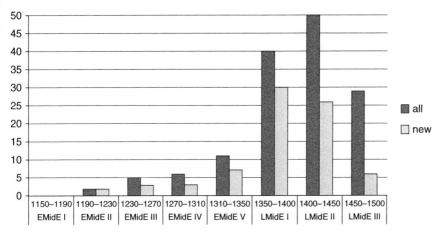

Figure 5.10 *Total type count and new types of deadjectival formations in -ITY in Middle English by subperiod*
(Reprinted from Gardner (2014) by permission of Société Néophilologigue, Helsinki)

fourteenth century (LMidE I), the frequency of -ITY formations reaches its height and we witness an explosion of different -ITY types ($p < 0.05$) – as many as 30 of these 40 different -ITY formations are new types. These include one hybrid, *scantity*, which contains an English base (originally a borrowing from Old Norse) and clearly demonstrates the productive use of -ITY (as well as the nativization of the Old Norse loan). How are we to interpret this evidence? It suggests that by the second half of the fourteenth century a "critical mass" of transparent -ITY formations is reached and that this supports the creation of new words with this suffix on English bases.

Concerning the question of whether particular groups of texts or authors played a role in the introduction of analyzable -ITY formations, a distinct pattern emerges. The majority of new types can be found in texts which have a French/Latin connection: religious writings, romances, translations and works by Chaucer.

1. In religious writings formations in -ITY are attested from the beginning, and this text category continues to be the dominant source for new -ITY types throughout the ME period. One reason for this could be that words like *chastity*, *debonairty* 'mildness,' and *poverty* denote abstract quali- ties typically discussed in religious works on Christian life and values rather than in, say, legal documents or scientific texts. We also need to consider the socio-historical background of the time. After the Norman Conquest many French clerics relocated to England and often obtained leading positions (Berndt 1969, 1976). Consequently French was a language of considerable importance in the religious domain.
2. Romances as a text type originate in French literary traditions, which might explain why new -ITY formations (e.g., *Christianity, falsity*) are present at a comparatively early stage, in the later thirteenth century.

3. A further group of texts in which (new) -ITY types appear more dominantly are translations of French or Latin texts, many of which have a religious subject matter. The originals naturally contain derivatives in -ITY and, as a result, may serve as a model for the translator. For instance, in his translation of Boethius' *De Consolatione Philosophiae* Chaucer renders *aeternitatis* as *eternyte* (Benson 1987: 419, l. 96), staying very close to the original.

4. Finally, one author stands out in his prolific use of -ITY formations: Geoffrey Chaucer. Most new types in LMidE I (20 out of 30) are recorded in his writings (among them translations), and the hybrid *scantity* mentioned before occurs in his *Parson's Tale*. Chaucer was immersed in French language and culture both through his marriage and through his work at court and on the continent (Gray 2004), and we can detect his close contact with French in his lexical choices.

A further interesting question in this context is whether deadjectival -ITY spread more rapidly in spoken than in written language. For that purpose, we can adopt Culpeper and Kytö's taxonomy and compare different text types from the same domain. For religious writing we can look at "written-based and purposed" religious treatises and compare them with "speech-purposed" sermons and homilies. There are some indications that sermons and homilies were in fact more progressive in the adoption of suffixal innovations than religious treatises. For example, sermons and homilies contain a new type with deadjectival -HOŎD (*goodhood*) already around the mid-thirteenth century (EMidE III), whereas in religious treatises this new word formation pattern only occurs towards the end of that century (EMidE IV). Similarly, denominal -ERY, another suffix introduced via French loanwords, is attested in sermons and homilies as early as the twelfth century (*robbery* in EMidE I), but does not appear in new types in religious treatises until the mid-thirteenth century (EMidE III). Unfortunately, these two text types are not equally well represented in each subperiod so that it is very difficult to study differences between them systematically.[16]

Let's now turn to Germanic suffixes and look into the "competition" between -HOOD and the more widely used -NESS. For that we first need to assess the productivity of -HOOD. Throughout the entire ME period deadjectival -HOOD occurs very infrequently (see Figure 5.11), with the exception of the late thirteenth and early fourteenth centuries (EMidE IV–V). In EMidE IV the frequency of deadjectival -HOOD rises and reaches a peak in EMidE V before falling almost out of use again in LMidE I (all changes are significant at $p < 0.0001$). Is this frequency peak correlated with a rise in productivity? It clearly is:

- we encounter 12 and 44 new derivatives in EMidE IV and V, respectively (see Figure 5.12);
- there is a high diversity of types in EMidE V ($p < 0.0001$);

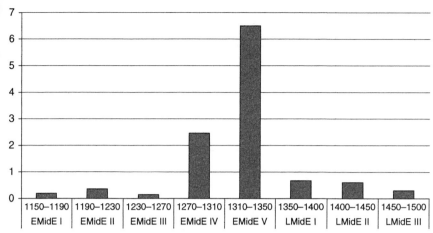

Figure 5.11 *Token frequency of deadjectival* -HOOD *in Middle English by subperiod, normalized per 10,000 words*
(Reprinted from Gardner (2014) by permission of Société Néophilologigue, Helsinki)

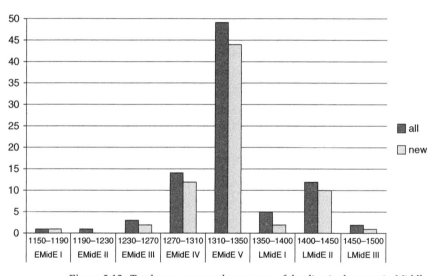

Figure 5.12 *Total type count and new types of deadjectival* -HOOD *in Middle English by subperiod*
(Reprinted from Gardner (2014) by permission of Société Néophilologigue, Helsinki)

- there are three hybrids on French bases in EMidE IV: *felhood* 'cruelty' as well as *chastehood* and *poorhood*, which are synonymous to the parallel derivatives in -ITY;
- 32 of the 44 new derivatives in EMidE V are hapax legomena.

These findings unmistakeably attest to the productivity of -HOOD. At the same time, the hapax legomena also reveal that the new coinages are not common

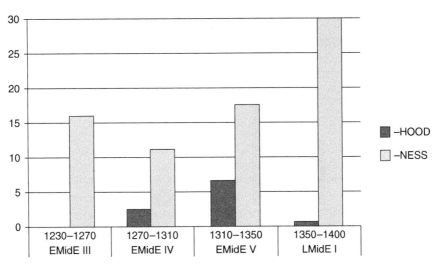

Figure 5.13 *Normalized frequencies of deadjectival* -HOOD *and* -NESS *during the most productive phase of* -HOOD

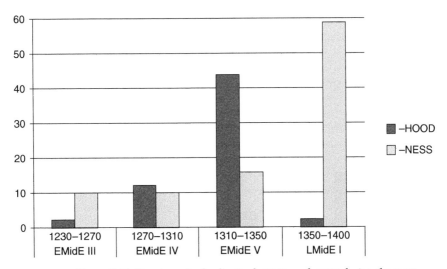

Figure 5.14 *New types in deadjectival* -HOOD *and* -NESS *during the most productive phase of* -HOOD

enough to become integrated into the English lexicon – foreshadowing the subsequent decline of deadjectival -HOOD.

For the discussion of the **competition** between deadjectival -HOOD and -NESS we now focus on the time around the subperiod in which -HOOD is most productive, i.e., the first half of the fourteenth century (EMidE V). Figure 5.13 displays the frequency of -HOOD and -NESS, and Figure 5.14 the number of new derivatives attested for both suffixes between the mid-thirteenth century and the end of the fourteenth century (EMidE III to LMidE I). We can see that -NESS is

Table 5.5 *Regional distribution of new derivatives in*
-HOOD and -NESS in the late thirteenth century and first
half of the fourteenth century (EMidE IV–V)

Region	-HOOD	-NESS
East Midlands	23	3
South-East	18	6
South-West	5	1
West Midlands	7	8
North	4	10

clearly much more frequent than -HOOD, and also that the two suffixes peak in their productivity in two adjacent subperiods: -HOOD in EMidE V, -NESS in LMidE I.

A striking fact is visible in Figure 5.14: despite the high frequency of -NESS overall, -HOOD exceeds the other suffix in productivity in EMidE V; it occurs in over three times as many new derivations as -NESS. If you look at Table 5.5, you will see that -HOOD is not equally productive in all dialect areas, but mainly in two regions: the South-East and the East Midlands. Table 5.5 contrasts the number of new derivatives in -HOOD with those in -NESS during the most productive phase of -HOOD (EMidE IV–V), for each of the five major dialect areas in Middle English. You can also see that only in the East Midlands and the South-East do the new types in -HOOD far outnumber those in -NESS. By contrast, there is no such clear dominance of -HOOD in the remaining regions.[17] These findings suggest that the productivity of -HOOD is indeed regionally restricted, and that the suffix does not succeed in catching on successfully in all dialect areas. In the long term, -HOOD could not compete against the productive power of -NESS, which had already been the most frequent and productive abstract noun forming suffix in Old English and as such was commonly used in all regions in Middle English.

Parallel derivatives like *chastity, chasteness,* and *chastehood,* or *idleness* and *idlehood,* provide valuable additional evidence for the competition between suffixes. Since parallel derivatives such as these are synonymous in Middle English,[18] we can assume that the suffixes are to a certain degree interchangeable. So studying parallel derivatives involving -HOOD, -NESS, and -ITY gives us further insights into why a particular suffix was chosen when other options are available in the same subperiod. If the suffix selection in parallel derivatives mirrors our previous findings, this lends further support to the validity of the analysis.

In the light of the discussion above, we would expect parallel derivatives in -ITY to appear first in text groups which were shown to be instrumental for the introduction of this suffix. And this turns out to be the case: 14 of 15 -ITY formations for which parallel derivatives exist in -HOOD and/or -NESS are first attested in such texts, 12 in religious writings (e.g., *chastity, poverty*), one (*falsity*) in a romance, three in Chaucer's works (*ability, scantity, scarcity*) and five in translations (e.g., *cruelty, preciosity*). Note that the text groups overlap – some religious writings are by Chaucer and/or translations.

When we trace competition between -HOOD and -NESS in pairs of parallel derivatives, the same picture emerges as before, confirming the earlier results: the first attestation of most parallel derivatives in -HOOD are from East Midland and South-Eastern texts (13 instances), while only three new types (*brighthood, darkhood, micklehood* 'greatness') are from other regions.

Is it always the case that the derivation which is most frequent at a given point in time is also the preferred option? Not necessarily, and this becomes apparent when we look more closely at individual texts. *Chastity*, for instance, is attested 82 times and *poverty* 66 times from the thirteenth century onwards, yet there are also parallel derivatives in -HOOD and -NESS, which occur only once each. There are several reasons why a formation in -NESS or -HOOD may have been chosen rather than -ITY:

- Rhyme. *Poorness* <pouernesse> in *The Sayings of St. Bede* (LAEME text #2002, fol. 128rb) may have been coined to complete the rhyme with the preceding *miss* <misse>.
- Regional "preference." *Poorhood* and *chastehood* occur in texts from the South-East and East Midlands, respectively, so in regions where -HOOD was highly productive.
- Semantic differentiation. *The Book of Margery Kempe* contains both *chasteness* and *chastity*. Here it seems that a difference might have been made between purity of the soul (*chasteness*) and sexual purity (*chastity*). It is worth noting that this appears to be a semantic choice made by the author because in other texts from the same era both derivatives are used with the same meanings (see *MED*).
- Audience. *Chastehood* can be found in *Genesis and Exodus*, a text whose author avoids formations in -ITY (as well as -ERY): despite the general currency of -ITY at the time, only unanalyzable *charity* occurs once, in rhyming position (*fre ... charite*; LAEME text #155, fol. 20 r). It appears that the author made a conscious effort to employ predominantly Germanic vocabulary and keep Latinate vocabulary to a minimum – perhaps this biblical paraphrase was intended for a largely lay audience with little knowledge of Latin or French.

The examples show that regional preferences, stylistic considerations as well as semantic choices by individual authors can play an important role in the selection of a parallel derivative. A less frequent word may be chosen or a new parallel derivative coined even if a more common alternative is available.

In sum, combining quantitative and qualitative analyses, this case study focused on three abstract-noun forming suffixes, tracing the dissemination of -ITY in the English lexicon through identifiable text groups and highlighting competition between the native suffixes -HOOD and -NESS. The creation of larger corpora for Middle English which are Part-of-Speech tagged (LAEME, PPCME2) or even lemmatized (LAEME), as well as advances in statistical testing, call for a (re-)examination of developments also in other areas of the word formation system, uncovering greater detail than previously possible.

Concluding Remarks

The corpus-based approach to the study of English allows you to test whether your hypotheses about change in historical stages of the language or ongoing developments are correct or not. Available computer-readable corpora are a convenient means to collect the necessary hard evidence to do this. These data can be subjected to statistical testing, provided the corpus that you extracted them from is representative (of the language or at least the variety of the language that you wish to study) and the number of examples sufficient. Corpus-based studies of lexical and semantic change typically require larger corpora than investigation of most grammatical phenomena. You can use corpora to study innovations or the rise of new patterns, but also the loss of lexical items or demise of grammatical patterns. Whether you make use of raw text corpora or syntactically annotated versions, corpora preserving original spelling or offering normalization, will depend not only on the availability of resources but also the research question you aim to answer. Annotated corpora, for instance, will be a requirement for certain searches (e.g., post-nominal participle clauses, e.g., *the man driving the car* or *the glass located next to you*), whereas other studies (e.g., lexical change) are possible on the basis of raw text or lemmatized data.

The case studies provided in this chapter serve as illustrations on how to conduct corpus-based studies of language variation and change, in principle, starting with the formulation of a research question or hypothesis to the definition of the variable context that you need to investigate in order to answer this question. We gave examples of search algorithms needed to retrieve the data from different kinds of corpora, criteria for excluding individual examples from your datasets, as well as discussions of relevant examples to complement the quantitative findings. The statistical tests employed were fairly simple, and advanced students are strongly encouraged to try their hand at more complex modelling.

Much remains to be discovered, and exploring language variation and change through corpora, combining quantitative and qualitative analyses, will enable you to gain valuable insights into the history of the English language.

Suggestions for Further Study

Rissanen (2009) is a useful handbook article that introduces basic concepts of historical corpus-based research of the variationist kind (see also Chapters 9 and 12, this volume). A good overview of historical corpora (with a focus on English) is provided in Claridge (2009) and Kytö (2012a), but it might be useful to look for updates at the *Corpus Resource Database* (CoRD) maintained at Helsinki University. General introductions to corpus linguistic methodologies (including statistics) are Oakes (1998), McEnery and Wilson (2001), Anderson and Corbett (2009), Lindquist (2009), Mukherjee (2009), and McEnery and Hardie (2012). For background reading on mark-up and PoS-tagging, see Lehmberg and Wörner (2008) and Atwell (2009), respectively.

Auer (2009) discusses changes in the frequency of the subjunctive against comments from eighteenth-century grammars, thus contextualizing language change within the discourse of prescriptivism. Övergaard (1995) discusses additional factors to substrate influence that may have played a role in the revival of the mandative subjunctive in AmE. The greater prevalence of the subjunctive in AmE has frequently been interpreted as an instance of colonial lag, a notion that is discussed critically in Hundt (2009).

The first corpus-linguistic investigation of ME derivational morphology is Dalton-Puffer (1996), which is based on the *Helsinki Corpus* and treats abstract and concrete noun suffixes, as well as adjectival and verbal suffixes. Gardner (2014), on which the second case study is based, relies on larger ME corpora to examine abstract noun suffixes. Students interested in a more detailed discussion of corpus design for this topic are referred to chapter 3 of the book. Säily (2014) specializes on -NESS and -ITY to study sociolinguistic variation on the basis of the CEEC corpora, the OBC, and the BNC.

Exercises

1. The mandative subjunctive
   Conduct studies parallel to the one presented in Figure 5.5 with data from COHA for additional triggers that allow for variation between modal periphrasis and subjunctive. As triggers you can use any or all of the verbs, nouns, and adjectives listed above (i.e. *advise, ask, beg*, etc.; *proposal, recommendation* etc. and/or *anxious, essential, important*, etc.) or select from the triggers listed in Crawford (2009: 274–276). Remember that the case study above focused on the years around 1900 and that the search algorithm included the subordinating conjunction *that* after the trigger word. If you do this as a group exercise rather than individually, you can include more triggers. Can you observe differences in the revival of the mandative subjunctive depending on the trigger? Compare your results with those in Crawford (2009) on the propensity of certain suasive expressions to be followed by a subjunctive.

2. The conditional subjunctive
   Replicate Schlüter's (2009) study of *on/upon (the) condition (that)* + subjunctive/indicative/modal for AmE on the basis of COHA and/or COCA. This will enable you to verify whether the development towards a greater use of

subjunctives in AmE proceeds faster in certain registers (e.g., non-fictional writing or newspapers) and/or give you more data points for the twentieth century. Since the corpora yield too many instances to post-edit exhaustively, create sub-samples (e.g., by analysing data from 1830s, 1860s, 1890s etc. in COHA). Again, working as a group will allow you to cover more data.

3. The history of -NESS in American English

Working with COHA, you can explore -NESS from a diachronic perspective and study how some words come in or go out of fashion. Select the "List" display, enter "*?ness.[nn*]" in the search string, and select two different decades under "Section," for instance "1820" and "2000." Once you have clicked on "Find matching strings," you will get two lists of words ending with -ness, where the ones highlighted in green are words which are not or only rarely used in the other decade. Browse through the list of words more thoroughly – are all of them derivatives of -NESS? You can find out more about the context(s) in which a particular word occurs if you click on it – you are then given a list of all its attestations in the corpus with surrounding co-text.

Now focus only on derivatives in the list for "1820"; are there any words which you would not use yourself? Pick some words from the list for "2000" which do not occur in the 1820s (so words for which it says "0" in the column "Tokens 1"), and look them up in the *OED*. When were they first attested? Are they more recent formations or do they simply happen not to be included in the corpus?

You can also examine the changing frequencies of particular words by searching for a specific word and selecting the "chart" display. This will give you a bar chart covering each decade from 1810 to 2000, allowing you to see at a glance any rise or fall in frequency through time.

Notes

We would like to thank Lot Brems, Laurel Brinton, and Sebastian Hoffmann as well as our students Rose Weinstein and Nina Benisowitsch for comments on earlier versions of this chapter.

1. An exception to this general rule are concordances of important texts such as the Bible (see Meyer 2008). Some collections of citation slips have been digitized (e.g., the *OED* database).
2. See Hundt (2008: 178–181) and Schlüter (2013).
3. For more details, see Rohdenburg (2013).
4. See http://d.lib.rochester.edu/teams/catalog.
5. Note that there are different taggers, which rely on different sets of tags. The Tree Tagger (with a set of 58 different tags) has been used to annotate the "Penn(–Helsinki) Parsed" historical corpora and ARCHER, for instance. The CLAWS tagset (with over 160 tags) was adopted to annotate the ARCHER corpus. It is obvious that these different tagsets allow for different degrees of granularity in the analysis.
6. This survey does not aim at completeness. For a description of other corpora, see the *Corpus Resource Database* (CoRD) at www.helsinki.fi/varieng/CoRD/index.html.
7. Only part of the corpus is publicly available. In order to make full use of all texts and the social background information, users need to access the database at the University of Helsinki.
8. The OBC is based on material from *The Old Bailey Proceedings Online*. The OBC provides additional background information and comes with a search interface more directly suitable to the needs of linguists.

9. AntConc is freely available at www.laurenceanthony.net/software.html. For WordSmith Tools, see www.lexically.net/wordsmith/.

10. For variables with only two variants, regression analysis allows you to model the relative significance of factors that play a role in the choice of one variant over the other. Students interested in this somewhat more advanced statistical approach are referred to Tagliamonte (2007) for a case study based on Present-day English data.

11. In a recent PhD thesis, Waller (2016) shows that Johansson and Norheim's definition of the subjunctive is slightly different from the one used in follow-up research in that they did not include subjunctives after past tense triggers for plural subjects. This results in differences in significance levels rather than in overall results (general development, regional differences).

12. For a more detailed discussion on how the variable can be defined and the effects this has on the statistics, see Hundt (1998: 159–163) and Waller (2016).

13. This case study is based on Gardner (2014), which presents more detail concerning the methodology, as well as the suffixes and their development in Middle English.

14. LAEME is a lemmatized corpus and Germanic suffixes are annotated, so it is possible to search for "hood" and "ness," but for -ITY it is necessary to search for nouns ending in "ty" and "te." In the case of the other three, non-lemmatized, corpora you are required to perform wildcard searches (i.e., searches including characters such as *, which are used as substitute for any other character) with the potential spellings of the individual suffixes (culled from the *OED*, *MED*, and secondary literature) and then post-edit your results manually. With PPCME2, however, you can increase precision by adding the Part-of-Speech tag for nouns ("_N") to your search queries.

15. Gardner (2014) provides details on permutation testing (Suomela 2007, 2014; Säily 2014), the method used to determine the statistical significance of type frequency and type/token ratio.

16. To investigate the "progressiveness" of sermons and homilies more thoroughly, we would need to study more linguistic variables and more material, perhaps also taking the study further into the EModE period with the *Corpus of English Religious Prose* (COERP).

17. The number of new types recorded in the South-West is too low to be conclusive.

18. Only for parallel derivatives based on *false* (*falsehood, falseness, falsity*) is it possible to observe semantic tendencies which develop into differentiation at a later stage; see Gardner (2014: 68–69, 174f.).

Appendix

Table 5.1-a *Subjunctive* were *vs. indicative* was *in hypothetical/unreal conditional constructions*

	B-LOB	LOB	FLOB	B-Brown	Brown	Frown
	were:was	were:was	were:was	were:was	were:was	were:was
as if	15:5	33:15	19:19	34:4	35:8	32:8
as though	17:4	22:9	13:9	8: 3	19:1	9:3
even if	4:0	7:10	2:6	4: 0	3:4	4:4
if	71:17	64:38	46:40	90: 20	56:28	53:20
Total	107:26	126:72	80:74	136:27	113:41	98:35

Table 5.2-a *Subjunctive vs.* should-*periphrasis in the Brown family of corpora (figures for Brown and LOB are from Johansson and Norheim 1988: 29; figures for FLOB and Frown from Leech et al. 2009: 281)*

	B-LOB		LOB		FLOB	
	subj.	*should*	subj.	*should*	subj.	*should*
ADVISE	0	0	0	3	0	3
ASK	0	3	1	2	1	3
BEG	0	0	0	0	0	0
DEMAND	2	4	2	3	8	6
DESIRE	0	2	0	1	0	0
DIRECT	0	0	0	1	0	1
INSIST	0	4	0	8	3	3
MOVE	3	0	1	0	0	0
ORDER	2	0	1	0	4	3
PROPOSE	0	6	0	5	1	7
RECOMMEND	4	9	1	13	6	20
REQUEST	2	2	2	0	6	1
REQUIRE	0	3	1	6	8	5
STIPULATE	0	0	0	1	1	1
SUGGEST	5	15	2	34	4	13
URGE	1	2	0	2	2	1
WISH	0	1	1	2	0	0
anxious	0	4	0	2	0	0
essential	0	3	1	7	0	1
important	0	7	0	0	1	3
necessary	0	8	0	5	1	0
sufficient	0	0	1	2	0	0
Total	19	73	14	97	46	71
% subjunctive	20.7		12.6		38.3	

	B-Brown		Brown		Frown	
	subj.	*should*	subj.	*should*	subj.	*should*
ADVISE	0	0	2	1	0	0
ASK	6	0	5	0	5	0
BEG	0	0	1	0	1	0
DEMAND	8	4	19	0	14	0
DESIRE	1	0	1	1	1	0
DIRECT	3	2	2	0	0	0
INSIST	4	3	9	2	12	2
MOVE	0	0	1	0	0	0
ORDER	0	0	2	1	4	0
PROPOSE	4	0	9	1	4	1
RECOMMEND	6	2	10	1	8	1
REQUEST	5	1	6	0	7	0
REQUIRE	5	2	14	0	15	0
STIPULATE	0	0	2	0	1	0
SUGGEST	21	4	12	7	25	6
URGE	8	0	6	0	3	0

Table 5.2-a (*cont.*)

	B-Brown		Brown		Frown	
	subj.	*should*	subj.	*should*	subj.	*should*
WISH	0	0	3	0	1	0
anxious	0	0	1	0	0	0
essential	1	1	2	0	0	0
important	3	1	4	4	4	0
necessary	1	0	5	0	0	0
sufficient	0	0	0	0	0	0
Total	76	20	116	18	105	10
% subjunctive	79		85.9		91.3	

Table 5.3-a *Subperiodization of Middle English corpus selection*

Subperiod		Years	Words
Early Middle English	EMidE I	1150–1190	53,785
	EMidE II	1190–1230	107,478
	EMidE III	1230–1270	183,620
	EMidE IV	1270–1310	142,425
	EMidE V	1310–1350	161,493
Late Middle English	LMidE I	1350–1400	233,957
	LMidE II	1400–1450	453,650
	LMidE III	1450–1500	267,428
Total			1,603,836

Table 5.4-a *Token and type frequency of deadjectival* -ITY, -HOOD, *and* -NESS *in Middle English by subperiod*

		EMidE I (1150–1190)	EMidE II (1190–1230)	EMidE III (1230–1270)	EMidE IV (1270–1310)	EMidE V (1310–1350)	LMidE I (1350–1400)	LMidE II (1400–1450)	LMidE III (1450–1500)
-ITY									
tokens		0	2	26	13	69	150	264	105
types		0	2	5	6	11	40	50	29
new types		0	2	3	3	7	30	26	6
-HOOD									
tokens		1	4	3	35	105	16	28	8
types		1	1	3	14	49	5	12	2
new types		1	0	2	12	44	2	10	1
-NESS									
tokens	205	495	292	157	285	771	1035	330
types	46	109	64	54	65	125	127	74
new types	10	14	10	10	16	59	36	10

6

Approaches to Grammaticalization and Lexicalization

LIESELOTTE BREMS AND SEBASTIAN HOFFMANN

Introduction

Grammaticalization[1] has without a doubt become one of the most productive frameworks for studying diachronic change as well as synchronic variation in language, especially within functional-cognitive linguistics and a usage-based approach. As a framework it has evolved both in terms of the topics studied and its methodology. Grammaticalization has been defined in many different ways, both narrowly as 'a process that makes lexical or less grammatical units or constructions, more grammatical,' or more broadly as a 'change that creates grammar' or simply 'grammatical change' as such. Consequently, different characteristics have been argued to be essential for this type of change and different concrete developments have been labeled "grammaticalization." Its relation to lexicalization is complex and has been described in various ways, reflecting the wide variety of definitions of the latter. Lexicalization in a fairly general sense refers to the process that leads to new conventionalized lexical items, phrases, or idioms. However, maybe even more so than grammaticalization, the term has been used to encompass conceptually rather disparate phenomena. It need not always involve a diachronic dimension, for instance when it pertains to how more abstract notions, such as MOTION, MANNER, and SPACE, are lexicalized, i.e., expressed, in English for instance by such verbs as *float*, *stumble*, or *swim*.

Grammaticalization and lexicalization have been described as being completely opposite types of changes, but also as being orthogonal, distinct processes that may intersect or occur in sequence. Confusion about the nature of grammaticalization, lexicalization, and their relationship to a large extent arises from the various ways in which the lexicon and grammar and their relationship have been defined.

Because of the prolific output of research within these frameworks any introduction to either grammaticalization or lexicalization is necessarily incomplete. This chapter is hence restricted to discussing the main approaches

131

to grammaticalization and lexicalization studies and the changes in focus that they have gone through.

Approaches to Grammaticalization

In this chapter we will restrict ourselves to the narrow sense of grammaticalization, which refers to a specific type of language change in which lexical material develops a more grammatical function and status, and already grammatical material develops more grammatical functions. Such an approach incorporates "unidirectionality," predicting that grammatical constructions typically have lexical origins, whereas the opposite, lexical items having grammatical origins, is dramatically less common (see below on degrammaticalization). It is in the context of a narrow approach that linguists have put forward various (types of) characteristics, referred to as parameters (Lehmann 1985), principles (Hopper 1991), diagnostics, mechanisms, etc. that seem to cluster together in a significant way and give grammaticalization an independent status with regard to other types of changes. These parameters help to assess whether a change qualifies as an instance of grammaticalization or to measure degrees of grammaticalization, i.e., the extent to which a construction has grammaticalized diachronically. Crucially, this requires studying diachronic and synchronic sets of data, preferably drawn from corpora (see below). The principles put forward in the literature are sometimes explicitly said to apply both diachronically and synchronically. Lehmann (1985), for instance, argues that his parameters can be used to describe what happens when a construction acquires a grammatical status over time, but also to describe synchronic variation in Present-day English grammar, for instance, in terms of more and less grammatical (or less or more recent) ways of expressing a concept, e.g., *will* vs. periphrastic *be going to* to express future reference. With regard to these two, Lehmann's parameters will predict that *will* is more grammatical and an older future marker than *be going to*.

Oversimplifying matters, one can say that within grammaticalization research there has been a move from a focus on the formal, i.e., morphosyntactic, effects of grammaticalization to an interest in reconstructing the pragmatic–semantic changes involved in the process, which ties in with great attention to context and the notion of constructions. These different foci have yielded different principles, which are often combined in actual case studies, as we will see when we discuss the development of the connective *while* below.

Lehmann (1985) is often seen as fitting in with the first, more formal wave. His six correlated parameters – attrition, paradigmaticization, obligatorification, condensation, coalescence, and fixation – characterize grammaticalization as a series of losses on different levels of linguistic analysis, and remain very influential today. The first three parameters pertain to paradigmatic aspects, and the latter three to syntagmatic ones (see Lehmann 1985: 308–310, from which all examples are taken).

- With attrition, Lehmann argues that as units grammaticalize, they lose semantic and/or phonological substance. Types of attrition such as semantic bleaching (or "desemanticization") and phonetic erosion are illustrated by the change from Latin *ad* to Romance *a*, which is shorter and lacks the locative meaning that was present in *ad*.
- Paradigmaticization is the process of increasingly stronger integration of an item within a paradigm; e.g., grammaticalized French primary auxiliaries *avoir* and *être* are completely integrated within the conjugational paradigm, whereas their Latin predecessors *habere* and *esse/stare* were not.
- Obligatorification is the loss of paradigmatic variability. For instance, whereas Latin *de* could often be replaced by *ab* or *ex*, grammaticalized French *de* can no longer be replaced or omitted.
- Condensation pertains to the shrinking of scope of a grammaticalizing sign; a grammaticalizing item combines with structurally increasingly less complex constituents, e.g., Latin *habere* takes a full NP as its complement, even in its auxiliary use, e.g., *habeo epistulam scriptam*, whereas French *avoir* as an auxiliary only has scope over the perfect participle with which it combines, as in *J'ai écrit la lettre* (see also Ramat 1982).
- Coalescence refers to the increase in bondedness, from juxtaposition to cliticization and beyond; e.g., Latin *clara mente*, a combination of an adjective and a noun, has grammaticalized in French to *clairement*.
- Finally, fixation refers to the loss of syntagmatic variability when grammaticalized signs typically occupy a fixed syntactic slot. An example is French *de* and *à* which have to precede the NP, whereas Latin *de* and *ad* could occupy various positions within it.

Lehmann's examples almost always involve changes that have taken a long time to be completed. They are less straightforwardly applicable to changes that are ongoing or to grammaticalization in its initial stages. In addition, examples such as the development of *clairement* have been disputed as illustrations of grammaticalization. Some people have argued that since a new adverb was created it is rather a case of lexicalization (see below).

Linguists like Traugott, Hopper, and Himmelmann (representing the second focus in grammaticalization studies) have questioned the validity of some of Lehmann's parameters, specifically the one describing what happens semantically in grammaticalization; the notion of bleaching has been argued to be too simplistic. Rather than a pure loss of meaning, Traugott and König (1991) argue that in the initial stages, new (grammatical, more abstract) meaning is gained or reinforced, not lost. They argue that there are typical and predictable semantic pathways in grammaticalization. One of these is subjectification – or "the development of a grammatically identifiable expression of speaker belief or speaker attitude to what is said" (Traugott 1995b: 32) – which often accompanies grammaticalization but is not exclusive to it (see Chapter 6).

In a similar vein, Himmelmann (2004) argues that grammaticalization typically involves a number of expansions rather than losses, i.e., host class expansion, syntactic context expansion, and semantic–pragmatic context expansion, which typically result in a dramatic increase of the frequency of the grammaticalizing construction.

Hopper (1991) presents his principles of divergence, layering, decategorialization, persistence, and specialization as diagnostics to detect grammaticalization in its early stages, thus complementing Lehmann's parameters. We will apply and explain these concepts in the case study of *while* below. In the context of the semantic turn in grammaticalization research, Hopper's principle of persistence is interesting since it further nuances the idea of bleaching. Persistence refers to the fact that aspects of the original lexical meaning may continue to shine through in or influence the development of the grammatical meaning of a construction. Hopper (1991: 29) illustrates this by means of the future auxiliary *will*, which started out as a main verb meaning 'desire.' Even in its grammaticalized future auxiliary sense, the original volitional meaning can still be rekindled in appropriate contexts, as in *Give them the name of someone who will sign for it* (Hopper 1991: 29), which is about the willingness to sign. Ultimately, then, semantic changes in grammaticalization are argued to amount not to a general loss, but to a redistribution of meaning: the loss of referential lexical meaning is compensated for by an increase in grammatical meaning, which Traugott and König (1991: 191–192) have referred to as "strengthening of informativeness."

Finally, attention has shifted to a constructional approach in which the importance of analyzing the relevant (linguistic) context in which units grammaticalize is stressed. Unlike morpheme-based definitions, such as those of Meillet (1912) and Lehmann (1985), constructional approaches emphasize that grammaticalization processes work on multiword strings in addition to individual words, and on (strings of) items in very specific environments. For example, the source of the future auxiliary *gonna* is not just the verb *go*, but the entire BE *going to*-construction, involving progressive aspect and an infinitival complement clause with purposive meaning (see Hopper and Traugott 2003: 87–93). This is why Traugott (2003a: 627) states that "[g]rammaticalization then becomes centrally concerned with the development of lexemes in context-specific constructions (not merely lexemes and constructions)."

Himmelmann's (2004) factors, referred to above, explicitly incorporate the notion of changes in context(s) in describing grammaticalization. Whereas host class expansion has to do with the range of collocates expanding as a construction grammaticalizes, the other two factors (i.e., syntactic context expansion and semantic–pragmatic context expansion) refer to the fact that as a construction grammaticalizes it typically extends to new or other syntactic and semantic contexts. The development of *bunch*, within NP *of* NP patterns such as *a bunch of roses*, from a noun (denoting a specific way in which plants grow or are tied together) into a quantifier illustrates host class expansion. In its lexical use it was restricted to concrete nouns such as *a bunch of flowers/parsley/grapes*, etc., but as a quantifier it can combine with other types of nouns, including concrete count nouns (*Ned wanted to give me a bunch of suits*), abstract nouns (*I spent a bunch of time when I was visiting the country talking to his neighbours*), and animate nouns (*Isn't that pretty painful stuff to express in front of a bunch of strangers?*) (Brems 2011: 176–182).

To conclude, different linguists have proposed different principles and have emphasized changes at different levels of analysis. In some cases the findings lead to opposing insights; for instance, whereas Lehmann argues that grammaticalization is accompanied by a reduction in scope, Traugott (1995a) has argued that it can also involve an expansion of scope, as in the development of discourse markers such as *well*. As an adverb, *well* originally had scope over the verb, adjective, or adverb it modified, as in *You did well*. As a discourse marker, it can for instance express hesitation and impacts on the entire sentence and preceding utterances, as in

> A: Are you from Philadelphia?
> B: **Well** I grew up uh out in the suburbs. (Schiffrin 1987: 106)

As indicated before, the importance attributed to the various factors largely depends on the view one has of grammar. Traugott considers discourse markers, which manage turn-taking and speaker/hearer interaction, as part of grammar, and hence a potential outcome of grammaticalization, while Lehmann would not. Traugott (1995a) has argued that different parameters or principles may apply to different parts of grammar. Some scholars disagree and have used the term pragmaticalization to describe the development of discourse-specific phenomena (for more on pragmaticalization, see Chapter 9).

Diverging views on what is in the grammar and in the lexicon similarly explain important differences in approaches to lexicalization, to which we will turn next.

Approaches to Lexicalization

As already indicated above, the term "lexicalization" has been applied to a highly disparate set of phenomena, and space does not permit us to capture the full extent of the discussions relating to the definition of the concept – and particularly its delimitation from the processes of grammaticalization. Readers are instead referred to the much more extensive overview presented in Brinton and Traugott (2005: chapters 2–4). In what follows, we will only concentrate on a cursory outline of some prominent issues at hand.

In its most inclusive sense, lexicalization is taken to mean 'any addition to the lexicon' and it thus incorporates all types of word formation (derivation, compounding, blending, etc.) in addition to a number of less rule-governed processes of fusion that result in fossilization – and often univerbation – of previously autonomous elements. Typical examples of the latter type are shown in (1):

(1)   *either* < OE *ǽ-ge-hwæðer* 'always each of two'
             handicap < *hand in the cap*
             goodbye < *God be with you*
             lammas < OE *hlaf* 'loaf ' + *mæsse* 'mass'
             gospel < OE *god* 'good' + *spell* 'tidings'
             lord < OE *hlaf* 'loaf ' + *weard* 'guardian'

In the first three of these, we observe a reduction/fusion of a syntagmatic structure into a morphologically and semantically opaque lexical item, while in the second set of examples a previously complex lexeme (here: all compounds) loses its internal structure and can no longer be interpreted as the result of a productive word formation process. A further type of fusion can be seen in the processes of idiomatization and demotivation (i.e., "the loss of identifiable compositional forms" (Brinton and Traugott 2005: 69)). Idioms are typically semantically opaque (e.g., *kick the bucket, shoot the breeze*) and allow little if any internal modification (**kick the buckets, *shoot some breeze*). As such, they must be stored in memory as wholes and are therefore also part of the lexicon. Taking such an all-inclusive view of lexicalization is problematic since it conflates a considerable number of different phenomena into a single category. As a result, most approaches to lexicalization tend not to deal with regular word formation.

Even setting aside regular word formation, the question of what to subsume under the lexicon and lexicalization remains. Grammatical (or closed-class) items such as *the* or *will* are of course stored in memory and are thus presumably also part of the lexicon or – in an expression preferred by many scholars – the inventory. Although grammatical elements are thought to be the result of grammaticalization processes, their presence in the lexicon would also point to the need to include them under both lexicalization and grammaticalization. Yet this is not generally considered a satisfactory option. As a result, many scholars have been concerned with the delimitation of the categories of grammaticalization and lexicalization, but no consensus has so far been formed.

A simple solution would be to fall back on the distinction between open and closed-class items, with the addition of a new member of the former category being a case of lexicalization while new closed-class items would be added via grammaticalization. However, while this will certainly help in clear-cut cases, the boundary between open and closed word classes is often blurred, as in the case of adverbs, which form a veritable ragbag category of different types of lexical items. As a result, some forms can be considered to be examples of both concepts. For example, Wischer (2000: 359–360) points out that Meillet's (1925) example of the grammaticalization of the German adverb *heute* 'today' from the nominal expression **hiu tagu* 'this day' (in the instrumental case) involves phonological, morphological, and semantic lexicalization, yet results in a new member of a fairly closed class of adverbials.

In recent research, the differentiation between grammaticalization and lexicalization has become less central to the discussion. Thus, Traugott and Trousdale (2013) stress the common factors of the two processes and subsume both under the label of constructionalization, with grammaticalization being referred to as "procedural constructionalization" and lexicalization as "contentful constructionalization."

In the next section we will highlight the importance of quantitative work for the analysis of grammaticalization and lexicalization before presenting a number of case studies of grammaticalization and/or lexicalization. We will first provide an outline of a straightforward case of grammaticalization by looking at the development of *while*. This will then be followed by two sections on the marker of evidentiality *methinks* and the class of complex prepositions, respectively. Particularly in the case of *methinks*, this will allow us to revisit the blurred boundary between grammaticalization and lexicalization. The chapter concludes by examining the notion of degrammaticalization,

Data and Methodology

As indicated in the introduction, grammaticalization represents a usage-based approach to explaining language change. In other words, it is assumed that language structure emerges as a result of – frequently repeated – uses in appropriate contexts that invite (re)interpretation of existing meanings and structures on the part of the speakers of the language, thus eventually leading to a change in the grammar of the whole language community. This functional–cognitive approach is in stark contrast to theories of language change that consider incomplete transmission of grammatical structure during language acquisition to be the main impetus for language change (see Chapter 3). Given this focus on language use, large collections of authentic language production should be best suited to trace processes of grammaticalization over time – or alternatively to assess levels of grammaticalization of particular structures in synchronic data. Corpus linguistics offers the tools and the methodology to carry out such studies, and the increasing number of historical corpora that have been compiled over the last two decades have greatly improved the opportunities for linguists to trace grammatical change in real time. For example, the 400-million-word *Corpus of Historical American English* (COHA) covers the period from 1810 to 2009 and allows the investigation of recent grammatical change in previously unprecedented detail. For earlier periods, too, larger amounts of data are accessible today than a generation ago, when the pioneering 1.6-million-word *Helsinki Corpus* was the only electronic corpus available that offered access to Old, Middle, and Early Modern English.

Tracing a process of grammaticalization in a corpus will typically first involve retrieving all potential examples of the construction at hand, then manually discarding irrelevant cases and finally categorizing each of the remaining hits into one of several stages of grammaticalization. Retrieving all relevant instances may pose difficulties in the case of older texts since spelling variants need to be considered. Also, constructions often display considerable variability, which may result in relevant instances not being retrieved. Furthermore, uncritical use of electronic corpora – both historical and of present-day language use – carries the risk of misinterpretation and some methodological comments are therefore required.

> The current chapter naturally cannot function as a complete introduction to corpus linguistics; readers are referred to Chapter 4 and to textbooks such as McEnery et al. (2006) and Lindquist (2009) instead. In the present context, we will only be able to focus on a few of the most important issues that are relevant to studies of grammaticalization.

According to Sinclair's (1996) definition, "[a] corpus is a collection of pieces of language that are selected and ordered according to explicit linguistic criteria in order to be used as a sample of the language." A carefully compiled corpus should thus be representative of the language use of the community or the text type from which it was sampled. The degree to which this is in fact achieved depends on a number of factors; for the compilation of historical corpora, the availability of relevant data is often the most prominent stumbling block, particularly for older periods of the language, for which only a limited number of texts from a restricted range of text types have survived. Furthermore, the radically different levels of literacy in medieval societies mean that only the language of a very small proportion of the population is represented, which renders a comparison with more recent time periods difficult.

In the context of a usage-based approach, an additional problem is constituted by the fact that historical data are always written data, while most language change is assumed to originate in spoken contexts. As a result, researchers are less likely to be able to trace incipient change in real time; instead, some changes may only be reflected in writing decades after they have been conventionalized in spoken interaction. The historical evidence available may thus mask the processes that led to these changes in the first place. For example, it is typically quite difficult to find clear-cut examples of so-called "bridging contexts" (Evans and Wilkins 2000), i.e., contexts where a new meaning of a construction is contextually implicated (but not yet available to speakers as an alternative option). A possible example is given by Traugott (2010a: 46) in her discussion of the grammaticalization of *a bit of* (from a literal nominal expression *a bite of* to the quantifier *a bit of*) here reproduced as example (2), where *bete* "could be interpreted not as 'a bite' but as 'a mouthful'":

(2)   this appyl *a bete therof* thou take (*c.* 1475 *Ludus* C. 23/220; *MED*)
        'This apple, a bite of it take'

(3)   He badd tatt gho shollde himm ec / *An bite brædess* brinngenn
             (*c.* 1200 Orm 8640; *MED*)
             'He commanded that she should him also a bite/bit of bread bring'

However, as example (3) shows – also taken from Traugott – the partitive 'morsel, unit bitten out' meaning suggested for (2) was available much earlier: in the case of (3), the literal 'a bite' meaning is highly unlikely. It is thus impossible to say how example (2) would have been interpreted by its readers in the year 1475 – and whether it is a usage-event that actively contributed to the changes affecting *a bit of*.[2]

Given that many examples of grammaticalization involve medium to low-frequency phenomena, they often cannot be reliably traced in the carefully compiled historical corpora available. As a result of this, historical linguists typically turn to electronic collections of language use that are less likely to be representative of a particular language community or text type, but that can nevertheless provide relevant additional information: dictionaries such as the *Oxford English Dictionary* (*OED*) or the *Middle English Dictionary* (*MED*) and large collections of texts such as *Early English Books Online* (EEBO) or *Eighteenth Century Collections Online* (ECCO) that aim at completeness rather than representativeness. In the case of dictionaries, the database of illustrative quotations provides many million words of authentic language use, but the lack of available context for these quotations will often render a plausible interpretation of a particular usage event problematic.[3] EEBO and ECCO dramatically increase the data available for the time period of 1473 to 1800, but their sheer size and the limitations of existing search interfaces currently still pose some difficulties to scholars.[4] In addition, the relative lack of metatextual information available – at least via the currently available search interfaces – makes it more difficult to trace the development and diffusion of a newly developed construction across the language community.

Case Studies

A Prototypical Grammaticalized Construction: *While*

As the preceding sections have shown, there is disagreement on the boundaries between the lexicon and grammar and on the definitions of lexicalization and grammaticalization. As an example of grammaticalization that is fairly unproblematic, we have chosen to illustrate the emergence of *while* as a connective from an originally lexical nominal origin. This example is, for instance, discussed by Traugott and König (1991). It illustrates nicely how grammaticalization typically affects a string of words or a construction in a specific context. The source construction for connective *while* is the Old English adverbial phrase *þa hwile þe*, which had the temporal meaning 'at the time that.' In that phrase *hwile* is quite clearly a noun, preceded by a demonstrative *þa* (in the accusative case). It is followed by the invariable complementizer *þe*. According to Traugott and König (1991: 201), by late Old English the phrasal expression had been reduced to the one-word expression *wile*. This illustrates Lehmann's parameters of phonological attrition and coalescence, i.e., a loss of substance. In addition, the fact that *while* no longer takes a demonstrative can be seen as "decategorialization" (see Hopper 1991) in the sense that *while* functionally behaves less like a noun and also no longer has the morphosyntactic properties associated with nouns, such as taking determiners, having a singular and plural form, etc. Mirroring the formal changes, and specifically the loss of the demonstrative element, *while* no longer expresses strict simultaneity between two events at this stage, which allows inferences of causality in certain contexts. Take a look at the following example (from Traugott and König 1991: 201):

(4)   ðæt lasted þa [xix] winter **wile** Stephne was king (ChronE(Plummer) 1137.36)
         'That lasted those 19 winters while Stephen was king'

The clause introduced by *wile* does not just specify the "temporal frame of reference" (Traugott and König 1991: 201) for the state of affairs in the main clause. The explicit mentioning that the events lasted 19 years and that Stephen was king at the time can be taken to suggest that the events are also causally linked to Stephen's reign. This process of reading as much information as possible into a sentence is referred to as strengthening of informativeness or the conventionalization of invited conversational implicatures. Heine, Claudi, and Hünnemeyer (1991) refer to this as "context-induced reinterpretation." The co-occurrence of events often suggests, or invites, an additional causal link between these two events, even if it is not literally mentioned in the context. The German cognate *weil*, for instance, similarly developed a causal meaning from an earlier temporal meaning of the noun.

Interestingly, the older temporal function of *while* signaling simultaneity continues to exist, as does its nominal use, as in *I waited for a while*. Hopper (1991) referred to this phenomenon as "divergence": as a unit grammaticalizes in some contexts its lexical origins may continue to exist and it may undergo developments of its own. In Hopper and Traugott (2003) and many other studies this is referred to as "layering," in the sense that *while* layers the functions of a temporal connective and a causal one as well as a lexical nominal use.

In a later stage the causal meaning itself invited a further inference, i.e., of adversity or concession. This new implicature or inference could arise in contexts where the causal relation between certain events could be construed as surprising, or the explicit juxtaposition of two events in terms of causality or simultaneity suggested some kind of incompatibility between the events, as in (5) (from Hopper and Traugott 2003: 91):

(5)   **Whill** others aime at greatness boght with blod,
        Not to bee great thou stryves, bot to bee good (1617 Sir W. Mure,
        Misc. Poems xxi.23; *OED*)
        'While others aim at greatness that is bought with blood, you strive to
        be not great but good'

Traugott and König (1991: 200) state that for some speakers examples with concessive *while* in which there is an anteriority relation between the two events are awkward. They explain this with reference to Hopper's (1991) concept of persistence, which, as we have seen, says that even when a construction has grammaticalized it may be restricted in its development by its original lexical semantics. In this case the temporal origins of indicating simultaneity can explain why its use cannot be generalized to all kinds of contexts, at least for a certain number of speakers. Syntactic context expansion, as defined by Himmelmann (2004), hence may have its limits. Other concessive connectives such as *although*, which has a different origin, for instance, do seem more generally acceptable in the following example with *while* (6) according to Traugott and König (1991: 200):

(6)   ?**While** our business was extremely successful last year, this year
        does not look too promising.

We will now apply some of the other parameters and principles discussed in our introduction to grammaticalization to this case study. In terms of changes in scope it seems that there is an increase in scope rather than a decrease, as suggested by Lehmann's parameter of condensation. *While* first functioned within one clause as an adverbial phrase, whereas as a connective it links two clauses and thus is involved in a construction of greater complexity. Other parameters suggested by Lehmann only help to describe the aftermath of grammaticalization, such as paradigmaticization, or the fact that *while* has joined the paradigm of connectives upon its grammaticalization. In terms of semantic changes, bleaching seems insufficient to describe the attested changes. Instead, the former lexical meaning has become enriched with grammatical meaning that is (inter)subjective. By using *while*, the speaker links up two states of affairs in terms of simultaneity, contrast, or concession. Older layers of meaning, such as nominal temporal *while* and older connective meanings persist alongside newer ones. *While* has also decategorialized (see Hopper 1991) in the sense that as a connective it no longer occurs with a preposition or determiner and is no longer followed by a complementizer. As discussed above, *while* displays syntactic context expansion (see Himmelmann 2004) and context-induced reinterpretation (Heine, Claudi, and Hünnemeyer 1991).

Hence, while the development of *while* into a connective with grammatical meaning illustrates a significant number of parameters and principles put forward in the literature, it goes against some others, such as Lehmann's concept of condensation.

Methinks – Lexicalization or Grammaticalization?

In the present subsection, we will briefly concentrate on the development of the Old English free syntactic construction *me ðynceð* 'it seems to me' into the Early Modern English marker of evidentiality *methinks*, as discussed in Wischer (2000).[5] As will become apparent, this development displays features of both grammaticalization and lexicalization.

The Old English precursor of *methinks* was an impersonal construction – i.e., it does not have a nominative subject – with full syntactic flexibility with respect to person, number, tense, and mood. Typical examples are shown in (7) and (8); the verb form is indicative in (7) and subjunctive in (8). It combined with a dative (DAT) RECIPIENT (*me* 'to me' (7), *monnum* 'to men' (8)) and, usually but not always, a nominative (NOM) AFFECTED to form a clause. Various types of verb complements – e.g., adjective phrases or *that*-clauses – were normally present, and word order was flexible.

(7)   *me   þincð eac   þæt þu sadige hwæthwugununges*
         me-DAT seems also that you are satisfied somewhat
         'It seems to me also that you are somewhat satisfied.'
         (O2 XX Philo Boethal 1007)

(8)
         þeah   monnum   ðynce þæt hit long sie
         although men-DAT seem   that it long be
         'Although to men it may appear to be long.'
         (O2 XX Philo Boethal 117)

Old English also had the semantically fairly similar personal verb *ðencan*, which required a subject (semantically, the ACTOR [ACT]) and an object (OBJ), as for example shown in (9):

(9)   *þa   þohte   he   þæt he sceolde worulde wiðsacan,*
         then thought he (ACT) [that he should world forsake] (OBJ)
         'And he thought that he should forsake the world.'
         (O2 NN Hist Bedehe 264)

The situation in Middle English was in many ways the same, but with a crucial difference with respect to the range of available syntactic combinations: Both the AFFECTED participant of the impersonal construction and adjective-phrase com-plementation are now rarely present, and the RECIPIENT and the verb are usually adjacent. Thus, variability is reduced and the impersonal verb construction becomes formulaic in nature. In addition, as Wischer (2000: 361) points out,

> the impersonal construction is frequently complemented by *that*-clauses with the subordinator in many examples deleted. Since in Middle English the word order has already changed to SVO in main and subordinated clauses, the former complementing clause can easily be analysed as the main clause, and the impersonal construction, formerly the dominating clause, is now consequently interpreted as a subordinated disjunct, which allows for its parenthetical use.

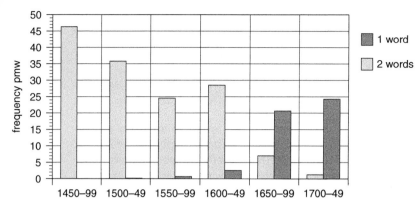

Figure 6.1 *Frequency of* methinks/methought *written as one or two orthographic words in EEBO (per million words) (n=34,406)*

Typical examples are shown in (10) and (11):

(10)   My lord **me thynketh** / my lady here hath saide to you trouthe and gyuen yow good counseyl . . . (M4 Ni Fict Reynard 54)

(11)   I se on the firmament, **Me thynk**, the seven starnes. (M4 XX Myst Town 25)

Due to sound changes taking place during the Middle English period, the two verbs *þyncan* 'seem' and *þencan* 'believe, cogitate' gradually merge in their realization and can therefore no longer be formally distinguished. As a result, the use of impersonal constructions decreases dramatically, even in contexts where Old English *þyncan* would formerly have been employed. By the Early Modern English period, the impersonal construction only survives in the first person singular (*methinks/methought*), and it is also increasingly written as a single orthographic word. Figure 6.1 confirms the development shown in Wischer's (2000: 363) table 1, which was based on a much smaller dataset, namely the 55 instances that are found in the Early Modern English part of the *Helsinki Corpus*. As Wischer (2000: 363) points out, *methinks/methought* "is no longer complemented by other elements and as a rule it functions syntactically as a disjunct. Formally it resembles an adverb, except for its present and past tense forms, which are traits of its verbal origin."

What are we to make of this development? Is it a case of lexicalization, because a former sequence of two orthographic words has become petrified/fossilized and partly demotivated, given that impersonal constructions are no longer productive? However, the resulting lexical item belongs to a fairly closed class of adverbs and is thus (also) grammatical in nature. As Wischer (2000: 363) points out, there are indeed many reasons to regard the development as a case of grammaticalization, too, since it involved syntactic change and, crucially, subjectification, acquiring an exclusively speaker-oriented, interpersonal, meaning.

By the Early Modern English period, it has become an adverbial marker of evidentiality. The parallels to other types of grammaticalizing constructions whose scope can be seen to expand – such as the discourse marker *well* mentioned above – are clearly apparent.

Wischer (2000: 364) concludes that grammaticalization and lexicalization "are not at all contradictory processes," but operate on different levels of the system:

> Both processes ... are accompanied by very similar syntactic and phonetic mechanisms: gradual phonetic reduction, syntactic reanalysis, demotivation, fossilization, conventionalization. The semantic changes, however, differ: When a free collocation or an ordinary word formation is lexicalized, a specific semantic component is added, so that the new lexical meaning differs from the former compositional meaning. Both are related to each other in a metaphorical or metonymical sense. When a linguistic term is grammaticalized, specific semantic components get lost and an implied categorial or operational meaning is foregrounded.   (Wischer 2000: 364–365)

Complex Prepositions

In this third case study, we turn our attention to the somewhat controversial grammatical category of complex prepositions. In contrast to simple prepositions such as *on, under*, or *with*, complex prepositions are formed by sequences of two or three orthographic words (e.g., *contrary to, exclusive of, in terms of, by dint of*). In addition, some complex prepositions feature an optional – usually definite – article (e.g., *in (the) light of, in (the) process of*), thus resulting in sequences of four orthographic words. Examples (12) and (13), taken from the *British National Corpus* (BNC) display typical uses of complex prepositions in Present-day English:

(12)   He sat **in front of** the fire and found his place. (BNC: B1X:1113)

(13)   When you have been so **close to** death and even closer to permanent serious injury then every day becomes a bonus. (BNC: A7 W:1159)

As the very similar uses in (14) and (15) show, both complex prepositions could have been replaced by a simple preposition with little – if any – change in meaning:

(14)   Myles sat **before** the fire, waiting for Father Poole to arrive. (BNC: B1X:1126)

(15)   The 'angel of the Lord' calls from heaven, just as he did when Ishmael was so **near** death. (BNC: ACG:316)

The important question in the present context relates to the syntactic status of sequences like *in front of* and *close to*: Do they have an internal syntactic structure and are thus constructed according to the compositional rules of English syntax or are they indivisible units that are retrieved as a whole from memory? If they have an internal syntactic structure, there would be little sense

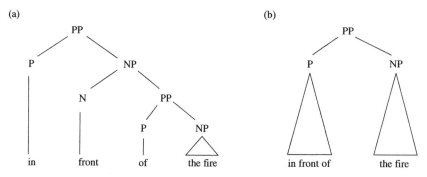

(a)   (b)

Figure 6.2 *Two possible syntactic representations of the complex preposition* in front of

in postulating a class of complex prepositions at all. If they are indivisible units, we have to determine how a multiword sequence involving an open-class item (*front, close*) developed into a single grammatical unit functioning as a preposition. The two options are shown in Figure 6.2, with (a) displaying the compositional interpretation and (b) treating *in front of* as an indivisible unit.

A number of scholars – e.g., Seppänen, Bowen, and Trotta (1994) and Huddleston and Pullum (2002: 620–623) – use a range of syntactic tests to argue for the structure shown in Figure 6.2a. They claim that "the motivation for grouping together two or more words into a complex unit is essentially semantic, and the analysis is unable to provide a satisfactory account of the syntactic data" (Huddleston and Pullum 2002: 621). However, other studies have provided quantitative evidence in favor of a unit-like status, for example by investigating their level of fixedness (or lack of variability) – see for example Smith (2013) and Hoffmann (2005: Chapter 3).[6] Perhaps the strongest argument in this connection stems from an analysis of filled pauses (*uh, uhm*) in the immediate context of complex prepositions. As Hoffmann (2005: 43–46) shows, filled pauses are very rarely found within complex prepositions, but do occur fairly frequently just before and after the sequences in question. Filled pauses have been associated with the effects of planning in the psycholinguistic literature, and they are said to occur prominently at syntactic boundaries (see, e.g., Clark and Clark 1977: 267–268). Given their near absence within complex prepositions, an interpretation corresponding to structure (b) in Figure 6.2 appears justified. Scholars who accept the existence of a class of complex prepositions typically view them as the result of a process of grammaticalization (but see further below for a different view).

In what follows, we will briefly outline the grammaticalization paths of some complex prepositions as discussed in the literature. However, as will soon become clear, a number of difficulties arise when investigating the development of complex prepositions. These most prominently relate to the data used (or available) for such studies, the delimitation of the grammaticalizing elements to be studied, and the interpretation of the observed changes as cases of grammaticalization or lexicalization (or both).

Schwenter and Traugott's (1995) study of the grammaticalization of the substitutive complex prepositions *instead of*, *in place of*, and *in lieu of* covers some of the oldest complex prepositions of the English language. All three are originally noun–preposition–noun sequences; the spelling *instead of* became common in the sixteenth century.[7] The noun *stede* 'place' is a Germanic word; *place* is an Old English borrowing from Latin that is "modelled on a French lexical item" (*OED*, s.v. *place*). Schwenter and Traugott (1995: 252) mention, however, that *in (the) place of* was borrowed from French as a locative construction in Middle English. The noun *lieu* is clearly of French origin.

In their study, Schwenter and Traugott investigate to what extent these three complex prepositions followed the typical path of grammaticalizing elements. Using data from the *Helsinki Corpus*, the *Dictionary of Old English Web Corpus*, and the *OED*, they consider both the changes in meaning in the nominal element itself (e.g., the possibility of *stede* referring to social roles in addition to its original locative meaning) and the nature and syntactic realization of the two slots involved in substitution, i.e., the process whereby an entity X replaces another entity Y. Thus, both *instead of* and *in place of* are shown to occur with animate entities (i.e., a person replacing – or taking over the role of – another person) before they can be used with inanimate referents (as in *a gum called turpentine instead of balsam*). All three constructions undergo the typical semantic shift of grammaticalizing constructions from denoting concrete reference – i.e., a literal place – to the expression of more abstract relations. However, *in lieu of* appears to have been borrowed (or calqued) from French with its substitutive meaning, while early variants of *instead of* and *in place of* can be seen to have a purely locative sense (i.e., referring to a particular place without involving a change in participants). There is also decategorialization in that the definite article or adjectival premodification of the nominal element is no longer possible in the more advanced stages of the development (**in the stead/place/lieu of*, **in the nearest place of*). Furthermore, Schwenter and Traugott (1995: 246) observe the typical features of subjectification; thus, indicating that one lexical referent can replace another referent implies a previous evaluation of the substitutability of the two:

> [T]he classes of lexical referents that can be treated as instances of substitution require pragmatic access to assessments of appropriateness of fit between referents, as well as attitudes based in experience, expectation, and other types of temporal distance.

The complex preposition *instead of* has developed furthest in that it occurs with a wider range of environments than the other two items, including for example gerunds as in (16) and tensed clauses as in (17), and it can be used in metalinguistic contexts, as shown in (18).

Table 6.1 *Stages of development of* instead of *(Schwenter and Traugott 1995: 259)*

Stage	Description
0 (preOE)	locative
I (OE)	role
II (lOE)	slot Y = person/being in an abstract social or spiritual position
III (lME)	slot Y may be inanimate object in a functional slot; loss of constraint that X must be in the same physical location as Y
IV (EModE)	slot Y may be gerund
V (PDE)	slot Y may be tensed clause

Table 6.2 *Stages of development of* in place of *(Schwenter and Traugott 1995: 259–60)*

Stage	Description
0 (French, ME)	locative
I (ME)	slot Y = person/being in an abstract social or spiritual position
II (EModE)	slot Y may be inanimate object in a functional slot; inference that X and Y also occupy the same physical location
III (EModE)	slot Y not necessarily emptied prior to substitution; X not necessarily prototypical
IV (PDE)	X and Y have little or no functional similarity, but share the same physical location

(16)   **Instead of** going into private practice, ... the solicitor may seek an appointment. (BNC: FRA:1816)

(17)   The babe coughed **instead of** cried, and the mother gave him no name for fear the spirit of the old king would be angry and take the life of the small baby. (2015 COCA: FICT)

(18)   ... if they externalized **instead of** internalized the causes of their failure ... (2001 COCA: ACAD)

Tables 6.1 and 6.2, adapted from Schwenter and Traugott (1995), summarize the development of *instead of* and *in place of* as suggested by the data.

But what motivates such changes, and why is it that they almost invariably proceed in the same direction (see above on the concept of unidirectionality)? You will recall the case of *while*, which developed a causal meaning due to inferences drawn by conversational participants. The same can be seen to be at work in the development of complex prepositions:

> [I]t is no more possible for one person to have exactly the same role as another than it is possible for one place to be exactly where another is ... the

> speaker implies a mismatch ... and the hearer is invited to make the
> construction relevant by drawing a subjective inference. Out of repeated
> uses the expectation (i.e. substitution) meaning was semanticized ... by
> context-induced reinterpretation.   (Schwenter and Traugott 1995: 266)

Such an explanation perfectly conforms to the basic principles of usage-based
approaches to language change: repeated events that invite a different interpretation over time lead to changes in the system, even though this may not have been
intended by the individual speakers/writers.

Very similar paths of development can be observed for many other complex
prepositions. For a concise overview, the reader is referred to Hoffmann (2005:
chapter 5); only one further item will be discussed in some detail here. This is *in
terms of*, which starts out in Middle English as a fully compositional sequence with
the noun *terms* referring to literal terms, as shown in example (19). The expression
then develops via the use of *term* in the mathematical sense where one entity is
expressed "in terms of" another entity, as shown in (20), to a meaning that is
compatible with contexts outside the restricted area of mathematics and related
fields of science and which denotes a much looser relationship of equivalence.
A typical example is shown in (21), where the three elements *pitch, intensity,* and
duration together fully describe the nature of a particular sound. In example (22),
finally, the concept of mathematical equivalence is further weakened; *political
manipulability* cannot be considered as a defining feature of ideas in general.
Instead, *in terms of* is employed to highlight one particular aspect of the ideas
relevant within the larger context of the current situation.

(19)   So oure clerkis ... whan þai will speke **in termis of** her religion.
         (*c.* 1380 Wyclif, *Wks.* (1880) 384; *OED*)
         'So our clergymen ... when they want to speak in specific words of
         their religion.'

(20)   If a Series be required to be express'd **in Terms of** that Quantity
         whose 2d, 3d Fluxion, &c. is in the Equation. (1743 Emerson,
         Fluxions 38; *OED*)

(21)   Music ... defines each sound **in terms of** its pitch, intensity, and
         duration ... So should color be supplied with an appropriate system,
         based on the hue, value, and chroma of our sensations. (1905
         A. H. Munsell, *Color Notation* i. 8; *OED*)

(22)   Every idea is judged **in terms of** its political manipulability. (1947
         Partisan Rev. Sept.–Oct. 473; *OED*)

The expansion of possible contexts that are compatible with *in terms of* goes hand
in hand with the typical increase in frequency exhibited by grammaticalizing
constructions. The data shown in Figure 6.3 suggest that an important part in the
grammaticalization of *in terms of* took place in the first half of the twentieth
century, where a dramatic increase in overall frequency can be observed.

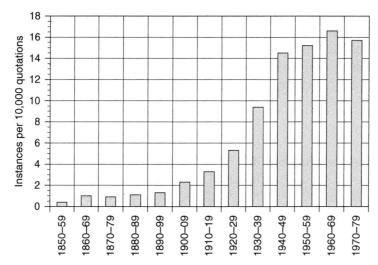

Figure 6.3 *The number of occurrences of in terms of in the* OED *quotations (instances per 10,000 quotations) (from Sebastian Hoffmann,* Grammaticalization and English complex prepositions: A corpus-based study. *London: Routledge, 2005, p. 123; reprinted with kind permission from Routledge, Taylor & Francis Group)*

Interestingly, the development of *in terms of* does not stop at this, however. Rather, the complex preposition is nowadays used as a discourse marker, as examples (23) and (24) demonstrate:

(23)   What I will do is emphasize what we you know where you can go **in terms of** money-wise. (JA4: 167; BNC)

(24)   and we were talking mainly, an elderly, a female elderly client group, let's be honest you know, **in terms of** blind you know, and just wait till you see it, it's lovely (J8B: 187; BNC)

Neither *money-wise* nor *blind* are compatible with a prepositional interpretation of *in terms of*. Instead, typical discourse markers such as *like* or *you know* could replace *in terms of* with very little change in meaning. As mentioned in the introduction, scholars disagree about whether this development should still be considered a case of grammaticalization. Ultimately, this depends on one's view of what is 'in the grammar.' We side with Traugott (1995a), who also considers phenomena that experience scope expansion as relevant cases of grammaticalization.

Having depicted the development of complex prepositions as uncontroversial cases of grammaticalization, it is now time to mention some more problematic aspects of the studies introduced and of the data available that might to some extent qualify the overall picture presented so far. Returning to Schwenter and Traugott (1995), it can be noted that the development as outlined in Tables 6.1

and 6.2 covers periods for which in fact no instances of the sequences *instead of* or *in place of* can be found. Thus, the first three stages of Table 6.1 refer to changes in the meaning and use of *stede* alone rather than the full preposition–noun–preposition sequence. Stage II, for instance, which refers to a substitution of one person and his role by another person, is exemplified by the sequence *on Iudan stede*:

(25)   Mathias bodode   on Iudea   se þe wæs gecoren **on Iudan**
                                       lande,   **stede**.
           Mathias preached in   who   was chosen   in Judas'
                                       Judealand   place
           'Mathias, who was chosen in Judas' place, preached in the land of Judea'
           (Ælfric, *Letter Sigeweard* P60; Schwenter and Traugott 1995: 248)

By the time of the first occurrence of *in stede of* around the year 1400, the substitutive sense of the sequence is already fully in place – see example (26):

(26)   He may right lyghtly ben disceyued For men sellen a gomme tat men
           clepen Turpentyne *in stede of* bawne. (*c.* 1400 Mandeville P 32 [HC];
           Schwenter and Traugott 1995: 249)
           'A person may very easily be deceived, for people sell a gum called
           turpentine instead of balsam.'

In fact, this example displays a fairly advanced point of the grammaticalization path depicted in Table 6.1 in that it is located in the fourth of a total of six stages. As mentioned above, constructional approaches to grammaticalization stress the point that developments typically affect multiword strings in very specific environments. As a consequence, it may be necessary to question the development as outlined by Schwenter and Traugott (1995) and instead suggest that the grammaticalization of *instead of* starts at a much later time.

The second comment we wish to make relates to sparseness of data. As indicated in the section on methodology and data above, grammaticalization studies crucially rely on adequate corpus data to trace the development of the constructions at hand. Particularly in the context of less frequent phenomena, however, such data are often difficult to find. This was also the case for Schwenter and Traugott's (1995) study, which had to rely on a handful of relevant examples to describe developments that span a number of centuries. In the meantime, additional material has become available, for example, in the form of the electronically searchable quotations database of the *MED*. This alone adds several hundred relevant cases of *in stede of* and about twenty instances of *in place of* to the database. These added data reveal earlier relevant uses of the constructions at hand; for example, the earliest instance of *instead of* (in the form of *i stude of*) can be ante-dated to the first half of the thirteenth century:

(27)   Requiescant in pace, **i stude of** Benedicamus, seggeð on ende.
            (*c*. 1230 Ancrene Wisse (Corp-C 402) 16/3; *MED*)
            'Say "Requiescant in pace" instead of "Benedicamus" at the end.'

It is noteworthy that the substitutive meaning of the complex preposition as exemplified by (27) was thus already in place in early Middle English. Also, some Middle English uses of *in place of* can be found that suggest that Stage II ('slot Y may be inanimate object in a functional slot') was reached before early Modern English. While we do not wish to question the general validity of the sequence of stages shown in Table 6.2, these discrepancies highlight the importance of having access to sufficient amounts of data. Otherwise, there is a certain danger in interpreting individual examples from the viewpoint of what is to be expected – i.e., in the form of an idealized sequence of stages – rather than what actually happened.[8]

A third comment about the grammaticalization of complex prepositions relates to the fact that there are many other members of the class for which no centuries-long development from literal to more abstract uses can be found. Typical examples are *in relation to*, *with regard to*, and *with respect to*, but many more of a similar type exist. By the time of their first occurrences, all three nominal elements could be used to denote abstract concepts, and no significant change in the complex prepositional sequences as a whole can be observed since their first occurrences in the seventeenth and eighteenth centuries. This raises a number of interesting questions. Quantitative evidence suggests that these complex prepositions are just as much invariable, fixed units as other sequences that can be shown to be the result of a grammaticalization process. However, how did they achieve this status? Is this really a case of grammaticalization, or are we not instead looking at the result of lexicalization processes?

In this context, it may be helpful to look at complex prepositions as lexical instances of a more abstract schema or construction of the type "preposition–noun–preposition" (and with a meaning that relates clausal or phrasal elements to each other). This construction was presumably established on the basis of common features of grammaticalized complex prepositions such as *in place of* and *in terms of*. Once it is available to speakers, new members of this abstract schema can then be added instantaneously by analogy. Such an interpretation is suggested by recent approaches to grammaticalization from the perspective of Construction Grammar – see Traugott and Trousdale (2013). This view would perhaps also be compatible with the view proposed in Lehmann (2002), who claims that complex prepositions first lexicalize before they can undergo further development in the context of grammaticalization.

To end this section on complex prepositions, we would like to mention one member of the category which displays the exact opposite of the expected development: *by way of*. All of the early examples – starting in 1340, as shown in (28), where *grace* is obviously a metaphorical rather than a literal "way" – carry an abstract meaning, while the first uses of *by way of* that refer to a literal way that is taken are only found by the second half of the eighteenth century, as shown in (29):

(28)   Þan may þe saules in purgatory, **By way of** grace specialy,
          Be delivered of pyn. (1340 Hampole *Pr. Consc.* 3603; *OED*)
          'Then may the souls in purgatory through grace particularly be
          delivered from pain.'

(29)   I . . . left the city **by way of** the Bowery. (1787 M. Cutler in W. P. &
          J. P. Cutler *Life & Corr.* [1888] I. 305; *OED*)

This is highly puzzling, and it goes against the principle of unidirectionality that was mentioned in the introduction.

In sum, the development of complex prepositions has been shown to be both a paradigm case of grammaticalization and at the same time – at least in the case of some members of the category – a fairly tricky linguistic phenomenon that opens up further avenues of research. Furthermore, this section has also highlighted the need for a thorough quantitative basis for this type of research.

Degrammaticalization

Over the years several key issues in grammaticalization theory have become the focus of debate, both within and outside the grammaticalization framework. Particularly contentious is the notion of unidirectionality, incorporated into many so-called narrow definitions of grammaticalization. As mentioned above, many grammaticalization studies are mostly concerned with how a lexical or less grammatical construction changes into a (more) grammatical construction. It is grammaticalization in the narrow sense that can be described in a number of cross-linguistically valid hypotheses to do with predications about typical pathways of change on the various linguistic levels.

The opposite phenomenon, i.e., from grammatical to lexical or from more to less grammatical, is generally considered to be far less common or even impossible, also on functional grounds. Lehmann (1995 [1982]) coined the term "degrammaticalization" to refer to what he thought was a "supposedly non-existent phenomenon" (Norde 2010: 1). Human beings have the need to continually recruit lexical items in grammaticalization processes to express their message more vividly or more creatively with regard to other grammatical means already in place. The opposite movement (from grammatical to lexical) is far less likely from a functional point of view because speakers do not have "a constant desire for understatement," nor "a predilection for litotes" (Lehmann 1985: 11). However, since the early 1990s more people have wanted to challenge the unidirectionality hypothesis and potential counterexamples of various kinds have been referred to as degrammaticalization (see, e.g., Campbell 2001a or Traugott 2001).

Just like grammaticalization and lexicalization, degrammaticalization has been defined in many different ways (for a more comprehensive overview see

Heine 2003a). It has, for instance, also been equated with lexicalization in the context of the creation of lexical items out of function words, as in the nominal use of *isms* from the derivational affix *-ism* or adjectives such as *iffy* from the conditional connective *if* (see, e.g., Ramat 1992). This has turned degrammaticalization into a bit of a wastebasket for all sorts of changes which seemed to have little in common. Brinton and Traugott (2005: 57–60) discuss a third type of lexicalization that involves an increase in autonomy of the elements involved (e.g., in the form of decliticization or when previously bound morphemes acquire lexeme status, as in the case of *ology* or *bus*). This is a minor type which will not be dealt with here.

We will focus on Muriel Norde's approach here since her 2009 monograph on the topic proposes a classification of types of degrammaticalization. She reverses Lehmann's parameters of grammaticalization to do with autonomy to define degrammaticalization as "a change whereby a gram in a specific context gains in autonomy or substance on one or more linguistic levels (semantics, phonology, syntax, and phonology)" (Norde 2010: 5). She acknowledges that degrammaticalization is rarer than changes typically captured by grammaticalization, but still needs to be recognized as a type of change (or rather a set of types of changes) in its own right. She first distinguishes between primary and secondary degrammaticalization, respectively, the change "whereby a function word becomes a full lexical item" and the one "whereby a bound morpheme (inflectional, derivational or clitic) becomes 'less grammatical'" (Norde 2010: 17). Degrammaticalization may involve inverse processes of those seen in grammaticalization, such as resemanticization, phonological strengthening, recategorialization, deparadigmaticization, deobligatorification, scope expansion, and severance, in the sense of a decrease in bondedness, and flexibilization, i.e., an increase in syntactic freedom (Norde 2010: 18–19). Combining this with Andersen's (2006: 232) levels of observation in language change, Norde puts forward three types of degrammaticalization.

- "Degrammation" involves resemanticization from grammatical content to lexical content and is a type of primary degrammaticalization impacting on the content level. The example discussed by Norde is Pennsylvania German *wotte* which has developed into a full main verb with the lexical meaning 'to wish or desire' from an earlier preterite subjunctive use of the modal *welle* 'will.' The resemanticization is accompanied by the loss of syntactic properties associated with auxiliaries and concomitant acquisition of the syntactic properties of lexical verbs, such as the ability to be nominalized, the acquisition of verbal inflections, and the ability to serve as complement of a modal auxiliary like *mussen* (e.g., *Ich muss wotte er brauch net lang Schmaetze hawwe* 'I must wish, he doesn't need to have pain for long'; Norde 2010: 21).

- "Deinflectionalization" is a type of secondary degrammaticalization involving the "shift from 'more grammatical' to 'less grammatical,' or movement out of a paradigm accompanied by a change in grammatical content" (Norde 2010: 19). Norde's (controversial) example is the *s*-genitive as found in English. Genitive *s* is argued to be a clitic in current English and Continental Scandinavian, as in *the Queen of England's hat*, whereas previously it was an affix. A clitic is a morpheme that depends phonetically on another word or phrase, but has syntactic independence. When comparing Old and Modern Swedish it can be seen that previously inflectional genitive *-s* was marked on the article, adjective. and noun, whereas, as an enclitic in Modern Swedish it is only marked onto the noun. Parallel to this the Swedish *s*-genitive has extended its meaning from possession to that of a determiner and as a clitic it displays "a weaker degree of attachment" to its host (Norde 2010: 25).
- "Debonding" is also a type of secondary degrammaticalization, which happens at the morphosyntactic level and makes a bound (affixal or clitic) morpheme shift to a free morpheme in specific contexts. One of Norde's examples is the derivational suffix *-ish*, as in *greenish*, which can now also be used independently as a qualifier, as in *Is everyone excited? I am ish*. Norde (2010: 28) argues that such cases are different from lexicalizations of derivational affixes such as *isms* for instance (pace Ramat 1992), because *ish*, as opposed to *isms*, does not become part of a major word class (i.e., noun or verb for Norde 2010: 29). In addition, *ish* does not become a hypernym for all adjectives in *-ish*, unlike *isms* for instance. The shift from affix to independent word is construction-internal in the case of debonding. *Ish* still has qualifier meaning as an independent word.

In sum, degrammaticalization, as carefully defined by Norde, does seem to exist, but most authors agree that it is far less frequent than grammaticalization changes in the narrow sense. It is not the complete opposite of grammaticalization and different types of degrammaticalization have to be distinguished. Importantly, the existence of degrammaticalization in no way invalidates grammaticalization research. They are simply two different types of changes.

Concluding Remarks

As this chapter will have shown, grammaticalization studies have come a long way since the concept was first formulated by Meillet (1912) over a century ago. Starting with Lehmann's (1995 [1982]) seminal work, which resulted in a revival of interest in the field, grammaticalization has been one of the "hot topics" in linguistics. During this time, it has gone through various phases, changing from an approach with a predominantly morphosyntactic focus to one that highlights semantic–pragmatic motivations for language change. In recent years, further progress has been made by combining insights from Construction Grammar with grammaticalization theory.

One of the vexing questions in the field has been the delimitation of grammaticalization from processes of lexicalization. In our chapter, we have followed the approach of scholars who emphasize the common features of the two concepts. Finally, we have also stressed the need for studies of grammaticalization and lexicalization studies to have a quantitative base. Thanks to a dramatic increase in diachronic data available and the development of suitable linguistic tools that can handle these data, today's researchers are in a much better position to discover the exact workings of mechanisms of language change than ever before.

Suggestions for Further Study

An obvious starting point is Hopper and Traugott (2003), which is the second edition of a classic textbook on grammaticalization. For a shorter, handbook-style overview of the field, Heine (2003b) can be consulted. We also strongly recommend Brinton and Traugott's (2005) book-length treatment of lexicalization and its intersection with grammaticalization. Their study discusses many of the issues mentioned in our chapter in more detail. In recent years, scholars have increasingly combined the approaches of grammaticalization/lexicalization studies and Construction Grammar. Traugott and Trousdale (2013) provide an excellent discussion of the issues at hand. For readers who need further information on the basic principles of Construction Grammar and its application to English, see Hilpert (2014).

For a critical approach towards the concept of grammaticalization, see the papers in the 2001 special issue of *Language Sciences*, edited by Lyle Campbell.

Exercises

1. Principles of grammaticalization and lexicalization
   Throughout this chapter we have discussed various factors offered in the literature to characterize grammaticalization and lexicalization, such as subjectification, phonetic attrition, host class expansion, etc. Try to draw up a table listing the factors that apply to (i) grammaticalization, (ii) lexicalization, and (iii) both. Make use of the factors discussed in the present chapter and in the suggestions for further study. Where do the processes overlap in terms of the mechanisms that underlie them?

2. Intensifiers in the history of English
   Words such as *very, extremely, terribly, awfully,* and *perfectly* can be used to intensify the meaning expressed by an adjective (e.g., *very good, extremely*

powerful). Use COHA to investigate how *terribly* functions as a premodifier of adjectives in American English over the last 200 years (the query for this is "terribly [jj]"). Can you detect any changes? If yes, are these changes suggestive of a process of grammaticalization? Finally, does the relative frequency of *terribly* + adjective develop in a way that is typical of grammaticalizing constructions?

3. Size nouns

The following set of synchronic corpus examples all contain what Brems (2011) calls size nouns, i.e., words like *bunch, heap(s), load(s)*, etc. which are typically complemented by *of* and another noun. These constructions have grammaticalized, but older and younger forms coexist (cf. Hopper's (1991) concept of layering). Can you distinguish the lexical from the grammatical uses? Which formal and semantic parameters/principles discussed in this chapter apply? Are there any bridging examples?

(i) A 55-year-old Muslim survived a massacre near the town of Karakaj by staying motionless under a **pile** of *bodies.*

(ii) Those who must deal with them on a regular basis and wish to get the better of them must employ much patience, deviousness, and duplicity, as well as lorry-**loads of** *flattery.*

(iii) A police spokesman said more than a dozen cars have been stolen with "**heaps of** *cars* broken into."

(iv) All stop a moment when Linda, in clothes of mourning, bearing a little **bunch** of *roses*, comes through the draped doorway into the kitchen.

(v) However, many of the tunnels had been completed and were now filled with untidy **heaps** of military *hardwear-helmets.*

(vi) "We have a ranking of 92nd in the FIFA world lists. That's a depressing record." Jim Boyce Cliftonville was re-elected IFA president for the third successive year. "What a **heap of** *shit.*"

(vii) Your editorial calling for warnings in the brochures of non-ABTA travel agents makes holidaymakers look like a **bunch of** *morons.*

(viii) Thanks so much for the cards and letters and faxes regarding mango mania. We received **heaps of** mango chutney *recipes*, all different, and all sorry to say now that the season is finished, for green mango cooking.

(ix) There's now a whole **bunch of** *studies* from different cities that show the same thing.

(x) I miss the old Valley Pool. The new one is **heaps** *better*, of course, but I pity the children who have to attend school carnivals there.

(xi) Six plane **loads** of *food* are also being flown today to the city of Baidoa.

(xii) I got plenty of chocolates, **loads of** chocolates.

(Examples from *Collins Wordbanks Online* www.collins.co.uk/page/Word banks+Online)

4. Criticism of the grammaticalization framework

   Grammaticalization as a framework or field of study has also come in for criticism – see for example the 2001 special issue of *Language Sciences* (Campbell 2001a). Authors in this issue primarily challenged the independent theoretical status of grammaticalization. Can you summarize their main points? Do you think their views are justified?

5. Complex prepositions in other languages

   If you speak a language other than English: Are there any complex prepositions in this language? If yes, did they develop in a similar fashion as English complex prepositions? If this is the case, how can you explain the fact that very similar processes of grammaticalization are at work in different languages?

6. The development of *indeed*, *in fact*, and *besides*

   Use some diachronic corpus data – for example the *Helsinki Corpus* and ARCHER – to look at the development of *in fact*, *indeed*, and *besides*. In what way does their development display typical features of grammaticalizing constructions? Are there important differences that can be observed?

Notes

We would like to thank Gunnel Tottie for her helpful comments on a draft version of this chapter.

1. *Grammaticization* and *grammatization* are other names used by some authors to refer to more or less the same types of change (see Hopper 1991; Himmelmann 2004, etc.). We will use the term *grammaticalization* except when citing authors who use a different term.
2. An added difficulty is of course the fact that intuitions of modern readers can be radically different from those of contemporary readers, who may not have approached the passage shown in (2) with the knowledge that it was potentially ambiguous.
3. See Hoffmann (2004) and Rohdenburg (2013) for an evaluation of the usability of the *OED* for corpus-linguistic research.
4. At the time of writing, EEBO was available through CQPweb (see Hardie 2012) on the Lancaster Corpus Server while access to ECCO was only possible via an interface that is not optimized for linguistic research. For example, it implements stopwords, thus making it effectively impossible to search for phrases that contain highly frequent words such as *the* or *in*.
5. All of the examples are from the *Helsinki Corpus*. Examples 8–11 and their glosses are from Wischer (2000: 360–362).
6. Quirk et al. (1985: 671–672) also favor the inclusion of the grammatical category of complex preposition and introduce a "scale of 'cohesiveness'" to capture the fact that complex prepositions exhibit different degrees of "syntactic separateness."
7. Compare also *because of*, which displays the same kind of univerbation.
8. A similar comment can be made about the research presented in Hoffmann (2005), where the development of *in view of* is claimed to have moved from literal uses – i.e., actual ocular vision – to an abstract (often causal) meaning only "in texts by authors whose year of birth is later than 1800" (2005: 54). Newly available data from EEBO suggest not only that much earlier abstract examples can be found, but also that interesting different uses, e.g., *in view of* meaning 'on behalf of,' were missed due to the lack of adequate data.

7

Inferential-based Approaches

MARÍA JOSÉ LÓPEZ-COUSO

Introduction

One of the most fascinating and intriguing features of linguistic interaction is the widely recognized fact that we, as speakers, frequently use language to convey much more than what we actually utter. Put differently, not every scrap of meaning we want to convey to our interlocutors must be explicitly expressed. Consider the following made-up conversational exchange:

(1)   A: Are you going to the beach this afternoon?
       B: I have to work.

B's response to A's question does not say that B is not going to the beach, but rather that she has to work. However, just as if she had answered with a simple "No," the implication of her response is clear: she is not going to the beach. The implied meaning is inferred correctly by speaker A, who, by not pursuing the matter further, would appear to be satisfied with B's reply. As this simple example shows, it is not possible to grasp what our interlocutors mean without knowing what they have implied in addition to what they have said.

Starting from the premise of usage-based linguistics that language change originates in language use, it will become apparent from the contents in this chapter that "implicatures" and "inferences" play a decisive role in semantic change and that meaning shifts involved in processes such as metonymization, metaphorization, semanticization, subjectification, and intersubjectification – all of which will be discussed in the following sections – owe much to what speakers "implicate" and to what addressees infer from those implicatures in the context of speaker–hearer negotiation of meaning.

The outline of the chapter is as follows. First, I discuss the role that pragmatic inferencing plays in semantic change, paying special attention to the most relevant inferential-based theories of change, in particular to Traugott's "Invited Inferencing Theory of Semantic Change." In the next section, I examine in detail the processes of subjectification and intersubjectification and their relation to grammaticalization, providing illustrative examples from different stages in the history of English.

The final section of the chapter reviews in greater detail four selected areas where subjectification and/or intersubjectification are found to be at work: epistemic modals, *like*-parentheticals, adverbial clauses introduced by the subordinator *while*, and expletives. This small selection of examples will provide you with further insight into how (inter)subjectification operates in various domains.

The Role of Pragmatic Inferencing in Semantic Change

Grice's Conversational and Conventional Implicatures

For several decades now research on semantic change has suggested the existence of different mechanisms of meaning change, mostly in the form of dichotomies such as metonymy vs. metaphor, widening, broadening or generalization vs. narrowing or specialization, and (a)melioration or elevation vs. pejoration or deterioration (see, among others, Ullmann 1957, 1962).[1] Though useful for the analysis of individual meaning shifts and for the purposes of classification, these taxonomies reveal very little about potential regularities – that is, whether semantic change follows predictable paths which derive from the same or similar cognitive and communicative processes across languages and across domains. The search for such regularities did not arouse much interest among scholars until quite recently, given that semantic change has generally been considered as essentially irregular, unsystematic, or even arbitrary, in contrast to, for instance, phonological change (see Chapter 2).

The search for some kind of regular and predictable paths of development in semantic change was given considerable impetus with the idea that pragmatic contextual conditions play a crucial role in such developments. This was explicitly stated by Paul Grice, who affirmed that "it may not be impossible for what starts life, so to speak, as a conversational implicature to become conventionalized" (1975: 58). To understand how conversational and conventional implicatures work in the Gricean sense, we must start from what Grice called the "Cooperative Principle," the principle which the participants in a communicative act are expected to observe in order to achieve effective communication. The formulation of this principle is as follows: "Make your conversational contribution such as is required, at the stage at which it occurs, by the accepted purpose or direction of the talk exchange in which you are engaged." Conversational cooperation manifests itself in four "maxims" (Grice 1975: 45–47):[2]

Maxim of Quantity	"Make your contribution as informative as is required (for the current purposes of the exchange)."
	"Do not make your contribution more informative than is required."
Maxim of Quality	"Try to make your contribution one that is true."
Maxim of Relation	"Be relevant."
Maxim of Manner	"Be perspicuous."

However, participants in a conversational exchange do not always follow these maxims, but may unconsciously or deliberately violate or flout them. For example, the Maxim of Quality is violated if the speaker tells a lie or it is flouted when uttering an ironic comment such as *Lucy is a great friend*, when both the speaker and his interlocutors know that Lucy has betrayed him by disclosing his most closely guarded secret.

Grice provides the following example to illustrate the crucial distinction between what is said through the conventional meaning of words and what the speaker conversationally implicates by using those words. Here A is standing by the side of an immobilized car, and B approaches him. B's observation is implicitly connected with A's remark, and A infers what B wants to communicate beyond the meaning of the words that are pronounced: that the garage is or may be open and has petrol to sell. As shown by this example, conversational implicatures are not part of the conventional meaning of the sentence uttered, but strongly dependent on features of the conversational context.

(2)   A: I am out of petrol.
       B: There is a garage round the corner.
       A: Great, then I can get my petrol can filled.

> In more technical terms, Grice's conversational implicatures can be defined as follows: by saying p, a speaker conversationally implicates q provided that
>
>   (i)   the speaker is presumed to be observing the Cooperative Principle;
>   (ii) the speaker's supposition q is required to make the utterance consistent with the Cooperative Principle; and
>   (iii) the speaker knows or believes that the hearer will realize that the supposition is true.

Conversational implicatures of this kind are predictable and "cancelable" (i.e., they can be denied): e.g., *There is a garage round the corner, but it is closed at this time of the day*. They must be distinguished from conventional implicatures, which are included among the semantic meanings of a given word. As will be shown later on in this chapter (see, for example, the development of concessive meanings of the conjunction *while* from its original temporal sense), the conventionalization of conversational implicatures plays a crucial role in semantic change.

To illustrate how conventional implicatures differ from conversational ones,[3] let us consider the classic example of the conjunction *since*, illustrated in (3) (see, e.g., Hopper and Traugott 2003: 80–81). (3a) shows the original temporal meaning of *since* in the history of English; the sentence presents a temporal sequence of events, the event in the subordinate clause occurring earlier in time than that in the main clause. By contrast, in (3b) *since* conveys a causal meaning, and the temporal reading is ruled out: the subordinate clause identifies the motivation for what is stated in the main clause. It has been shown that historically, the causal reading of *since* emerged in the Late Middle English period from sequences of the type shown in (3c), which are ambiguous between the two possible interpretations: a temporal reading (two events occurring in a temporal sequence, i.e., "after she left home") and a causal reading (the event in the subordinate clause, which occurs earlier in time, is the cause for the state of affairs described in the main clause, i.e., "because she left home"). It is only when speakers use *since* with enough frequency in sequences such as (3c) and the implicature 'temporal > causal' is understood by hearers with the new meaning of causality that the causal meaning conventionalizes as part of the meanings of *since*. The conjunction then comes to be used in cases such as (3b), where the original temporal reading is no longer possible. Given that the causal meaning of *since* in (3b) is conventional, it cannot be canceled, as shown in (3d).

(3)   a. **Since** I last saw him, he has progressed a lot. [temporal]
        b. **Since** I have to finish this paper today, I won't be able to go to the cinema with you. [causal]
        c. **Since** she left home, I have been feeling very depressed. [temporal or causal]
        d. ***Since** I have to finish this paper today, I won't be able to go to the cinema with you, but not because of the paper.

For further discussion of invited inferencing in the development of *since*, see Chapter 4.

The "Invited Inferencing Theory of Semantic Change"

Building on Grice's distinction between what is said (sentence meaning) and what is conventionally implicated (utterance meaning) – and on the idea that conversational implicatures may become conventionalized over time – Elizabeth Traugott proposed her "Invited Inferencing Theory of Semantic Change" (IITSC), which uncovers the existence of certain cross-linguistic regularities or trends frequently replicated over time and across domains (see Traugott 1999a; Traugott and Dasher 2002). In order to highlight the importance of *both* the speaker and the addressee in the process of change, Traugott prefers the term "invited inferences" over implicatures.[4] As explained by Traugott and Dasher (2002: 5), the label "invited inference" was chosen to encompass "the complexities of communication in which the speaker/writer (SP/W) evokes implicatures and invites the addressee/reader (AD/R) to infer them." It is precisely this emphasis on the relevance of both speaker/writer and addressee/reader that underlies the processes of subjectification and intersubjectification discussed in the next section.

   A key concept in the IITSC is that of "polysemy," i.e., the existence of "families" of conceptually related meanings which arise out of processes of invited inferencing. In this context, in Traugott's model semantic change is seen as deriving from the conventionalization as semantic polysemies of pragmatic inferences that arise in language use in the negotiation of meaning between speaker and addressee. The development of such polysemies is captured in the following cline (Traugott and Dasher 2002: 34–40):

(4)   coded meaning > utterance-token meaning (invited inference) > utterance-type meaning (generalized invited inference) > new coded meaning (new polysemy).

A coded meaning is the conventional meaning that a form has in a language at a particular point in time. The conjunction *since*, for example, has two meanings in Present-day English, namely 'from the time that' and 'because' (see examples (3a–b) above). Utterance-token meanings, in turn, are invited inferences that arise in context "on the fly" (Traugott and Dasher 2002: 17); as such, they are largely idiosyncratic and have not become frequently used implicatures. Utterance-type meanings come about when an invited inference is generalized, is socially accepted, and spreads through the speech community. Generalized invited inferences continue being considered as such as long as the original coded meaning prevails or is at least equally possible as the new meaning, as happens with *since* in our earlier example (3c). Finally, when the original coded meaning is ruled out as a possible interpretation, as in example (3b) above, for which the only likely reading of *since* is that of causality, the generalized invited inference becomes semanticized, and a new coded meaning arises as part of the polysemies of the form.

Two major mechanisms of semantic change play a role in the emergence of new coded meanings in the cline in (4), namely metaphor and metonymy or, put in their dynamic dimension, metaphorization and metonymization (see Traugott and Dasher 2002: 27–34). Lakoff and Johnson (1980: 5) define metaphor as "understanding and experiencing one kind of thing in terms of another." This implies that metaphorization is based on analogical similarities and iconic relations, so that an element belonging to a given conceptual domain is conceptualized in terms of an element from a different (usually more concrete) domain. Since metaphorization works across conceptual boundaries, metaphors are usually explained as projections or mappings from one to another domain (see Sweetser 1990: 19; see further Chapter 4). An example of a metaphorization process from a "source" to a "target" domain is that of the shift of the adverb *behind* from the domain of SPACE (5a) to the domain of TIME (5b).

(5)   a. He was driving down the road with the dog running **behind**.
        b. He is terribly **behind** in his work.

Metonymization also involves a mapping from source to target, but in contrast to metaphor, the relationship between them is based on association rather than on similarity. In metonymy, therefore, source and target are linked by a relation of semantic contiguity, i.e., they belong to closely related conceptual spheres, as shown by the literal and metonymic meanings of the noun *bottle* in (6a–b), which illustrate the metonymic mapping CONTAINER FOR CONTENTS.

(6) a. She said she would buy a **bottle** of Galician white wine.
     b. She said she only drank a **bottle** of Galician white wine.

More interesting are instances of so-called serial metonymy (see Nerlich 2010: 204–207; Nerlich and Clarke 2001), as shown in (7a–c) for the noun *paper*, which results in synchronically polysemous metonymic chains.

(7) a. You can write your name and address on this piece of **paper**.
     b. She has just published a **paper** in *Language Sciences*.
     c. She has been invited to give a **paper** at our next annual conference.

Metaphor and, especially, metonymy can also be considered as potential triggers for semantic change in the realm of grammar. Thus, it would be possible to conceptualize the Late Middle English development of causal *since* out of temporal *since* summarized above in terms of a metaphoric projection across domains (the temporal and the causal domains).

In view of the crucial role that metaphor and metonymy play in semantic change in general, it is no wonder that metaphorization and, especially, metonymization are so closely related with the processes of subjectification and inter-subjectification discussed in the following section.

Subjectification and Intersubjectification

The Notions of Subjectivity and Intersubjectivity

Although it has been traditionally accepted that the main function of language is that of conveying propositional content, it has now become widely recognized that communication entails much more than the mere transfer of information. This becomes clear from a comparison of examples such as (8a–d) below, which though sharing the same referential content, clearly differ as regards the degree of (in)directness of the request which is being conveyed and, therefore, as regards politeness.

(8) a. Pass me the biscuits.
     b. I want you to pass me the biscuits.
     c. Will you pass me the biscuits, please?
     d. I wonder if you could possibly pass me the biscuits.

To account for these and similar examples, it is certainly useful to recognize the existence of different components in the communicative event. As far back as 1934, Bühler distinguished three distinct semantic functions of language:

(i)   the representational function (*Darstellung*), which is related to objects and states of affairs;

(ii) the expressive function (*Ausdruck*), which involves the expression of the speaker's subjective stance toward the proposition; and

(iii) the appealing function (*Appell*), which is centered around the addressee.

In Bühler's classification of the basic components of language, the latter two functions clearly go beyond the referential content of the message by paying attention to the notions of subjectivity and intersubjectivity, respectively (see Bühler 1990 [1934]).

The importance and the pervasiveness of the subjective and intersubjective dimensions of language were also duly acknowledged by Benveniste (1966 [1958]). For him, since the communicative dyad is made up of two complementary terms, the "I" and the "you," every act of communication is tinged with both subjectivity and intersubjectivity. As a consequence, in addition to its representational or referential function, language may also convey the speaker's attitudes, feelings, and points of view toward the proposition, as well as pay attention to the addressee's self-image and his/her needs. The relevance of the notion of subjectivity was also brought to the fore by Lyons (1977, 1982, 1994), who defined it as "the way in which natural languages, in their structure and their normal manner of operation, provide for the ... agent's expression of himself and of his own attitudes and beliefs" (1982: 102).

From Synchrony to Diachrony

All the accounts of (inter)subjectivity mentioned in the preceding paragraphs share the now widespread view that language is certainly much more than "an instrument for the expression of propositional thought" (Lyons 1982: 103). However, they look at the notions of subjectivity and intersubjectivity from a synchronic angle and therefore tell us very little as to how these subjective and intersubjective meanings and functions come into being diachronically. Taking these synchronic analyses of (inter)subjectivity as a point of departure, for more than three decades now Elizabeth Traugott has explored various types of semantic–pragmatic changes which occur in grammaticalization, and has explained those shifts from the perspective of overarching processes of semantic change known as subjectification and intersubjectification.[5] She establishes here an essential distinction between *-ity* (i.e., the synchronic state) an *-ation* (i.e., the diachronic process). In Traugottian terms, subjectivity is described as the relationship to the speaker and his/her beliefs and attitudes toward what is said, while intersubjectivity refers to the relationship to the addressee and his/her self-image. In this context, subjectification is broadly understood as the semantic–pragmatic process whereby meanings develop from the objective description of the external situation to the expression of the speaker's own viewpoint or attitude toward the proposition. Intersubjectification, on the other hand, involves the further development of subjectified meanings to signal the speaker's attention to the addressee. As suggested in these definitions and as will become clear in the sections that follow, both subjectification and intersubjectification occur in the context of speaker–hearer negotiation of meaning through the semanticization of invited inferences (see above).

The Traugottian View of Subjectification

Traugott (1982: 248) distinguishes three functional–semantic components within the linguistic system, namely the propositional, the textual, and the expressive:[6]

- **The propositional component** is concerned with "the resources of the language for making it possible to talk about language." At this level are located relations used for the description of the speech event, including truth-conditional categories as well as deictics to places (e.g., *here*, *there*), times (e.g., *now*, *then*), and persons (e.g., *I*, *you*).
- **The textual component** involves "the resources available for creating a cohesive discourse," thus comprising connectives such as *but* and *therefore*, but also other devices used by speakers to unfold the speech event by, for example, partitioning a discourse into smaller units (e.g., adverbial subordinators, relativizers, and complementizers).
- **The expressive component** has to do with "the resources a language has for expressing personal attitudes to what is being talked about, to the text itself, and to others in the speech situation." Examples of devices situated in the expressive component include turn-taking and turn-giving markers, vocatives, and various types of elements conveying modal meanings, such as epistemic modals (e.g., epistemic uses of *must*), modal adverbs (e.g., *possibly*), and parenthetical expressions of the type *I think*, all of which convey the speaker's evaluation toward the proposition.

By looking into the semantic–pragmatic shifts occurring in grammaticalization processes, Traugott identifies a strong diachronic tendency toward an increase in "expressiveness" and formulates the hypothesis that items originating in the propositional domain develop over time from less to more personal types of meaning along the unidirectional path given in (9) (Traugott 1982: 257):

(9)   propositional > (textual >) expressive

At this stage, Traugott does not use the term "subjectification" to refer to this tendency toward expressive meaning, but the proposed trend comes close to her later definition of subjectification (see below).

Some of the examples of grammaticalization discussed by Traugott (1982: 248ff.) as illustrating this increase in expressiveness concern the development of conjunctives from spatial phrases (e.g., *instead* < preposition *in* + *stead* 'place') and the emergence of intensifiers from content words (e.g., the intensifier *very* from the Middle English adjective *very* 'true').

The shift from the propositional through the textual to the expressive component can easily be grasped by considering the historical development of *where* in English, as reflected in (10)–(13) (from Traugott 1982: 254–255). In Old English *hwær* was an interrogative item conveying spatial meaning in *wh*-questions, as in (10), where it has a propositional value only. It could also be used to introduce complement clauses after predicates of knowing, thinking, asking, and so on, as in (11), where in addition to propositional content, *hwær* also expresses textual meaning. In the course of the Middle English period, *where* came to be used as a locative relative, as in (12), which also illustrates the textual function of the connective. At a later stage, *where* developed a concessive meaning 'although,' shown in (13), within the expressive domain.

(10)   **hwær** syndon ure godas þe swylcra mana gyrnen swilce hiora wæron? (*Orosius* 40. 29)
'Where are our gods who would desire that such crimes were as theirs?'

(11)   He nyste **hwær** he ut sceolde. (*Orosius* 286. 20)
'He didn't know where he could get out.'

(12)   Hi kam over þo huse **war** ure lauerd was (*Kentish Sermons*)
'He came over to the house where our Lord was'

(13)   And **where** hit please you to say I have holdyn my lady, your quene, yerys and wynters, unto that I shall make ever a large answere (Malory, *Morte Arthur* 1188. 10)
'And whereas/although it pleases you to say that I have embraced my lady, your queen, for many years, (yet) I shall always answer freely that'

Although Traugott's hypothesis of the shift from propositional to textual and expressive meanings finds support in examples such as (10)–(13), the ordering suggested in her unidirectional path of change seemed to be too strong. This led her to revise her original proposal in later work (see, e.g., Traugott 1989 on the development of epistemic meanings) and to suggest three general tendencies of semantic change which may overlap:

Tendency I   Meanings based in the external described situation > meanings based in the internal (evaluative/perceptual/cognitive) described situation.

Tendency II   Meanings based in the external or internal described situation > meanings based in the textual and metalinguistic situation.

Tendency III   Meanings tend to become increasingly based in the speaker's subjective belief state/attitude toward the proposition.

In her view, a crucial distinction should be made between the first two tendencies, on the one hand, and Tendency III, on the other. While the shifts corresponding to Tendency I and Tendency II represent cases of metaphorical transfer from one to another domain, the changes characteristic of Tendency III are best described in terms of the conventionalization of pragmatic inferences (or conversational implicatures) used "in the speakers' attempt to communicate with others" (Traugott 1989: 51). Given that the meaning shifts illustrating Tendency III involve pragmatic strengthening of speaker perspective (Traugott 1995b: 36, 49), the process came to be known as "subjectification." The relevance of this tendency is made evident in Traugott and Dasher's statements that Tendency III is "the dominant tendency" and that it can be considered "the major type of semantic change" (2002: 97). These authors provide the following definition of subjectification:

> Subjectification is the … process whereby SP[eaker]/W[riter]s come over time to develop meanings for L[exeme]s that encode or externalize their perspectives and attitudes as constrained by the communicative world of the speech event, rather than by the so-called "real-world" characteristics of the event or situation referred to.   (Traugott and Dasher 2002: 30)

Intersubjectification

The discussion of subjectification provided in the preceding section suggests that semantic change typically proceeds in the direction from non-subjective to subjective meaning, though potential counterexamples to unidirectionality can be adduced. Relying heavily on Benveniste's (1966 [1958]) concept of inter-subjectivity (see above), Traugott has proposed expanding the synchronic continuum of (inter)subjectivity to accommodate not only (subjective) indicators of speaker assessment or evaluation, but also (intersubjective) markers of the speaker's attention to the "self" of the addressee. This yields the following synchronic cline (Traugott 2010a: 34):

(14)   non-/less subjective – subjective – intersubjective

Here "intersubjective" is taken to cover the "explicit expression of the SP[eaker]/W[riter]'s attention to the 'self' of addressee/reader in both an epistemic sense (paying attention to their presumed attitudes to the content of what is said), and in a more social sense (paying attention to their 'face' or 'image needs' associated with social stance and identity)" (Traugott 2003b: 128). Understood in this way intersubjectivity lays the emphasis on the functions of the speaker and addressee as interlocutors in the speech event, rather than on their roles as referents in the situation being described in the proposition. Examples of intersubjective expressions include politeness markers (e.g., *please*),[7] euphemisms (e.g., *the Lord* for *God*), and expletives (e.g., *gosh!*).

Viewed diachronically, the continuum in (14) above suggests that subjectified expressions may be recruited over time to convey intersubjectified meanings, giving as a result the historical unidirectional cline in (15) below (Traugott and Dasher 2002: 40; Traugott 2003b: 134; 2010a: 35), which implies that intersubjectified meanings of an expression always develop later than subjectified ones:

(15)   non-/less subjective > subjective > intersubjective

It must be noted that the shifts along the cline in (15) are only possible (not necessary) changes and that the new (inter)subjectified meanings may coexist with the old ones, in accordance with the concept of "layering" (Hopper 1991), which Hopper and Traugott describe as a "synchronic result of unidirectionality" (2003: 124).[8] The process through which a subjective item or construction becomes intersubjective is known as "intersubjectification," which is defined by Traugott as the "development of meanings that encode speaker/writers' attention to the cognitive stances and social identities of addressees" (2003b: 124). On the close relationship between subjectification and intersubjectification, Traugott writes:

> There cannot be intersubjectification without some degree of subjectification because it is SP[eaker]/W[riter] who designs the utterance and who recruits the meaning for social deictic purposes. Like subjectification, it is part of a mechanism of recruiting meanings to express and regulate beliefs, attitudes, etc. Therefore intersubjectification can be considered to be an extension of subjectification rather than as a separate mechanism.   (Traugott 2003b: 134)

From intersubjectivity to interactiveness? If intersubjectification is taken as an extension of subjectification, as Traugott (2003b: 34) maintains, one may wonder whether Traugott's unidirectional cline of (inter)subjectivity (non-/less subjective > subjective > intersubjective) can be further expanded to cover additional meanings occurring in the communicative event. In line with this, Fitzmaurice (2004) suggests that discourse markers, such as *you know*, *you see*, and *you say*, have shifted over time from intersubjectivity to interactiveness. She shows how from the eighteenth century onward these markers lose their subjective and intersubjective functions, moving away from attention to the addressee, to become interactive markers in an exchange which serve merely to "keep things going on in a conversation" (Fitzmaurice 2004: 438). In Traugott's view (2010a: 36), however, it is at least questionable whether the shift proposed by Fitzmaurice from the intersubjective use to the interactive function of *you know*, *you see*, and *you say* (that is, as expressions associated with the dynamics of the interactive process itself) does in fact represent the development of a new coded meaning, which would justify the addition of "interactiveness" as a further step along the cline of (inter) subjectivity.

On the Relation Between (Inter)subjectification and Grammaticalization

A quick look at the examples of (inter)subjectification offered in the preceding sections suggests the existence of a strong correlation between subjectification and grammaticalization (see Chapter 6), since the latter process normally involves a shift from more concrete items toward more abstract markers and, therefore, toward increased attention to the speaker's perspective. It seems, however, that defining subjectification solely as "a kind of grammaticalization" (Company 2008: 204) or as "the discourse-pragmatic type of grammaticalization" (Fischer 2007b: 260) does not provide a completely accurate picture of the relation between these two mechanisms of linguistic change.

On the one hand, subjectification is typical of semantic change in general and is therefore not restricted to grammaticalization. For example, subjectification operates in processes such as amelioration and pejoration, which involve the conventionalization of more positive or more negative connotations of a word, and are therefore totally unrelated to grammaticalization. Consider in this connection the meaning changes undergone over time by the noun *knight*, originally 'a boy employed as a servant' (amelioration), and the adjective *silly*, from Old English *sellig* 'blessed, innocent' (pejoration). Examples such as these clearly demonstrate that subjectification is not restricted to developments in the grammatical domain, but also occur in the lexical domain. In Traugott and Dasher's words, "[a]melioration and pejoration are the direct outcomes of subjectification at the content level" (2002: 282).

On the other hand, subjectification is only minimally involved or not involved at all in certain grammaticalization processes, such as the development of case markers in some languages from terms for body parts or relational space, such as the Finnish postposition *kohdalla* 'at' (e.g., *talon kohdalla* 'at the house'), which derives from an oblique case form of the noun *kohta* 'place, spot' (see Anttila 1989: 149). Given that the main function of argument structure is to express events or situations and the participants involved in them, the grammaticalization of case markers does not entail a more speaker-based view. Note also that given that the strengthening of pragmatic inferences characteristic of subjectification is more typical of the early stages in the process of grammaticalization, subjectification is more likely to take place in primary grammaticalization (lexical > grammatical) than in secondary grammaticalization (less grammatical > more grammatical).[9]

It seems therefore that, though acknowledging that subjectification and grammaticalization interact at times, it is reasonable to keep the two processes apart. Examples of the intersection between grammaticalization and intersubjectification are even more difficult to find in English,[10] though they do sometimes occur, especially in the historical development of some interjections and discourse markers, for which some scholars prefer the term "pragmaticalization" to grammaticalization (see Chapter 10 for a discussion of pragmaticalization). A case in point is that of the rise of the hedging function of *well*.[11] According to Jucker (1997), the most likely ultimate source of the discourse marker *well* is the Old English manner adverb *wel* with the full propositional meaning 'in a good or proper manner,' as shown in (16).[12] Through subjectification of the manner adverb, *well* is also attested clause-initially in sequences such as (17), where it has the epistemic meaning 'certainly, definitely.' In the course of the Late Middle English period *well* develops a textual function as a "frame-marker and text-sequencing device" (Jucker 1997: 99), used in reported speech at the beginning of a conversational turn, as in (18), with the meaning of acceptance 'if this is so' or 'OK then.' The hedging intersubjective use of *well* arises in Early Modern English instances of the type in (19). Here it serves as a face-threat mitigator, showing a strong orientation to the addressee in a situation where a possible disagreement exists. As shown by examples (16)–(19), the diachronic cline of (inter)subjectification is a layered one, where the earlier and later meanings coexist.

(16)   ... oð ðone first ðe hie **wel** cunnen Englisc gewrit arædan (Alfred, *Preface to Gregory's Pastoral Care*; DOEWC)
           ' ... until the time they are able to read English writing well.'

(17)   Cwæð he: **Wel** þæt swa mæȝ, forþon hi englelice ansyne habbað (Bede, *Eccl. Hist.* ii.i (Schipper) 110; *OED*, from Jucker 1997: 100)
           'He said: "Well may that be so, since they have the faces of angels".'

(18)   "Ye sey well," sayde the kynge, "Aske what ye woll and ye shall have hit and hit lye in my power to gyff hit." "**Well**," seyde thys lady, "than I aske the hede of thys knyght that hath wonne the swerde." (1485 Malory, *Le Morte d'Arthur* 48; HC, from Jucker 1997: 99)
           '"You say well," said the king. "Ask what you will and you shall have it if it lies within my power to give it." "Well," said this lady, "then I ask the head of the knight who has won the sword."'

(19)   Tom: Yes, you must keep a Maid, but it is not fit she should know of her Masters privacies. I say you must do these things your self.
           Ione: **Well** if it must be so, it must.
           (1680 Samuel Pepys' *Penny Merriments*; HC, from Jucker 1997: 102)

As is the case with subjectification, intersubjectification also operates outside grammaticalization. Paradigmatic examples come from the development of taboo meanings, such as the use of the noun *bathroom* to refer to any kind of toilet, either with or without a bath (Traugott and Dasher 2002: 58–59; Traugott 2010b: 108). In taboo-motivated instances of semantic change such as that of *bathroom*, intersubjectification affects a lexical item which acquires a new attitudinal meaning and therefore grammaticalization does not play a role in the development.

Case Studies

As we have seen in the previous section, subjectification can be defined as a

> *gradient* phenomenon, whereby forms and constructions that at first express primarily concrete, lexical, and objective meanings come through repeated use in local syntactic contexts to serve *increasingly* abstract, pragmatic, interpersonal, and speaker-based functions.   (Traugott 1995b: 32; emphasis added)

The notion of gradience is also relevant to the emergence of intersubjectified meanings from earlier subjectified ones along the (inter)subjectification cline. The remainder of the chapter presents more detailed evidence of how these two gradient processes operate. Since epistemicity is a particularly rich domain for (inter)subjectification across languages, our two first illustrative cases concern the emergence of the epistemic meaning of the modal verb *must* and the development of the epistemic/evidential parenthetical *looks like*, respectively. Our third example comes from the domain of clausal connectives and examines the shift from temporal *while* to concessive, contrast, and causal readings of the subordinator. The section closes with a brief discussion of the effects of (inter)subjectification beyond the realm of grammar by looking into the history of the expletives *Jesus* and *gee*.

Modal Verbs: From Deontic to Epistemic

A classic case of subjectification is that of the historical development of deontic uses of modal verbs into epistemic ones. Deontic modality is concerned with the meanings of obligation and permission, as in (20a–b) below; by contrast, epistemic modality conveys degrees of the speaker's certainty toward the truth of the proposition, as shown in (21a–b).

(20)   *Deontic*
         a. You must go home now.
         b. You may now leave.

(21)   *Epistemic*
         a. He must be home by now.
         b. He may have missed his train.

While the meaning of (20a) is 'I demand that you go home now,' (21a) could be paraphrased as 'I infer that he is at home now' (e.g., because he is always at home at this time of the day or because he phoned me half an hour ago on his way home and told me that he was almost there). Similarly, (20b) means 'I allow you to leave,' in contrast to (21b), where the speaker arrives at the conclusion that it is probably the case that he missed the train (e.g., because he left home too late). Sweetser (1990: 59) suggests that in both the (a) and (b) examples above, *must* and *may* involve the idea of a compelling force, but in different domains: while *must* and *may* in (20a) and (20b) express the meaning of an interpersonal, social force on the part of the speaker so that the hearer takes a certain action, the modals in (21a) and (21b) convey the meaning of logical force: there are reasons that compel the speaker to believe that what he/she is saying may be true.

Diachronically, epistemic uses of the modals have been shown to develop out of deontic uses through processes of grammaticalization and subjectification, and illustrate very nicely Traugott's (1989) Tendency III, since the development involves an increase in speaker assessment, attitude, or viewpoint. Let us consider the way in which speakers of English came over time to use the modal verb *must* to express the epistemic meaning 'I conclude that' in addition to the deontic meaning 'be obligated to.'[13]

In Early Old English *motan, the ancestor of *must*, expressed the meanings of ability, as in (22), and permission, as in (23):

(22)   Wilt ðu, gif þu **most**, wesan usser her aldordema, leodum lareow? (eighth century *Genesis* 2482)[14]
         'Are you willing, if you are able, to be the leader of the army, the teacher of the people?'

(23)   he ne **mot** na beon eft gefullod. (*c.* 1000 Ælfric, *Lives of Saints* I, 270.142)
         'It is not permitted for him to be baptized again.'

The ability meaning of *motan was gradually lost over the history of English; the modal *may* 'have the physical ability to' replaced *motan in this sense. In turn, the meaning of permission of *motan became progressively restricted in Late Middle English to occur only in fossilized expressions of the type *so mot I then* 'so may I thrive,' typically found in prayers, oaths, curses, and so on. *Motan acquired a new meaning in Late Old English and Early Middle English, namely that of obligation, a meaning it retains up to the present day. An early example is (24) below, where in the context of a homily the obligation meaning derives from a compelling religious force.

(24)   Hit is halig restendæg; ne **most** ðu styrigan þine beddinge. (*c.* 1000 Ælfric *Catholic Homilies* II, 42)
         'This is holy rest-day: you may/must not move your bed.'

This example can be compared to (25), which shows a more subjective use of the form *moste* with the first-person singular pronoun *I*, but still implying deontic meaning, more specifically deontic necessity ('it is necessary for me to eat some pears'). Subjectification takes place in this context, where no normative force (religious, social, etc.) is at work.

(25)   I **moste** han of the perys that I se, Or I moot dye. (1395 Chaucer, *The Merchant's Tale*, p. 167, line 2331)
         'I must have some of the pears that I see, or I will die.'

Instances of the type shown in (26) below are likely to have played a crucial role in the semanticization of the epistemic meaning in *must* (see Goosens 2000: 161; Traugott and Dasher 2002: 128). This example is indeterminate between a deontic and an epistemic reading, so that two interpretations are possible here: on the one hand, the deontic reading 'it is necessary for a man to submit if he is fettered'; on the other, the epistemic interpretation 'it can be logically concluded that a man necessarily submits if he is fettered.'

(26)   Ah heo **mot** nede beien, þe mon þe ibunden bið. (*c.* 1225 Layamon, *Brut* 1051)
         'But he who is bound must necessarily submit.'

Side by side with indeterminate examples of this kind, unambiguous instances of epistemic *must* are found from the fourteenth century onward, and became more common in the Early Modern English period. (27) provides a late seventeenth-century example of the subjective epistemic use of the modal: *must* here indicates Lord Touchwood's confidence in the inference that he is making from Lady Touchwood's words and behavior (i.e., 'from what she says, I come to the conclusion that something extraordinary is involved here'). In other words, subjectification operates in the history of *must* a second time.

(27)   Lady Touchwood: Don't ask me my reasons, my lord, for they are not fit to be told you.
         Lord Touchwood: (Aside) I'm amazed; here **must** be something more than ordinary in this. (Aloud) Not fit to be told, madam?
         (1693 Congreve, *Double Dealer*, III, p. 154)

In the context of the Invited Inferencing Theory of Semantic Change, the diachronic development of the increasingly subjectified polysemies of *must* involves shifts along a cline of the following kind: coded meaning > invited inferencing > generalized invited inferencing > new coded meaning. A similar path of development seems to have been followed by other modals, such as *ought to*, which started life as a verb expressing possession, then developed the meaning of deontic obligation in Late Old English, and finally became an epistemic modal in Early Modern English times, as in *He ought to be home by now* (see, e.g., Nordlinger and Traugott 1997; Traugott and Dasher 2002: 137–143).

Epistemic/Evidential *Like*-Parentheticals

If the shift from deontic to epistemic in the history of English modals has long been a recurrent topic in the literature on grammaticalization and (inter)subjecti-fication, interest in the origin and development of parentheticals has gained in popularity over the last couple of decades or so, especially after the publication of Thompson and Mulac's (1991) influential article on *I think*.[15]

The *Cambridge Grammar of the English Language* defines parentheticals as "expressions which can be appended parenthetically to an anchor clause but which also have a non-parenthetical use in which they take a declarative content clause as complement" (Huddleston and Pullum 2002: 895). The difference between parenthetical clauses and their non-parenthetical counterparts becomes obvious from the examples shown in (28). In (28a) *I think* is a matrix clause taking a following *that*-clause as complement, while in (28b–c) *I think* bears no such relationship to the rest of the utterance.

(28)   a. **I think** that the riding of bicycles in the front parking area is prohibited.
         b. The riding of bicycles in the front parking area is prohibited, **I think**.
         c. The riding of bicycles in the front parking area is, **I think**, prohibited.

Salient features of clausal parentheticals as in (28b–c) are their syntactic and prosodic independence, their positional mobility, and their non-propositional status. This implies that from the semantic–pragmatic point of view, parentheticals of this kind typically serve what Kaltenböck, Heine, and Kuteva (2011: 865) call "metacommunicative or metatextual" functions, including the organization of discourse, the expression of speaker viewpoint, or the marking of speaker–hearer interaction, that is, pragmatic functions which, as seen above, are characteristic of processes of subjectification and intersubjectification. Since clausal parentheticals frequently express a comment, they are also known as "comment clauses" (see Chapter 10).

While most studies devoted to clausal parentheticals have focused on constructions containing either a first person (e.g., *I think, I mean, I'm afraid*) or a second-person subject (e.g., *you see, you know*), much less attention has been paid to third-person parenthetical clauses (e.g., *it seems, as it were*). A particularly interesting type of these third-person parentheticals is that of the epistemic/evidential markers *(it) looks like, (it) seems like*, and *(it) sounds like*, illustrated in these examples from COCA.

(29)   a. And in China, which may – potentially the biggest story of all, Deng Xiaoping, **it looks like**, is not going to last out another year. (1994 COCA: SPOK)
         b. We now, **it seems like**, get an annual letter. (2005 COCA: SPOK)
         c. they don't stay down, **sounds like**. (2005 COCA: FIC)

Like-parentheticals seem to have gained some currency in contemporary (informal) American English over the last two decades, as shown in Figure 7.1, which provides the distribution of this parenthetical pattern in COCA from the early 1990s to the year 2009.

The most distinctive feature of this parenthetical type is the retention of the "comparative complementizer" *like* of its non-parenthetical (main clause) counterpart shown below:

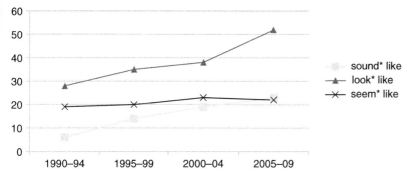

Figure 7.1 Like-*parentheticals in COCA (from María José López-Couso and Belén Méndez-Naya, "From clause to pragmatic marker: A study of the development of* like-*parentheticals in American English,"* Journal of Historical Pragmatics *15 (2014), 36–61, p. 45; reprinted with kind permission of John Benjamins Publishing Company)*

(30) a. In fact, we were the first ones to report earlier today that according to a White House source, **it did look like** those talks broke down. (1998 COCA: SPOK)

b. and so many people to look at that **it seemed almost like** they weren't narrowing it down. (2009 COCA: SPOK)

c. "**It did sound like** he had lost the plot a bit," said Johns, whose eyes twinkle when he grins, although he warns that he can be difficult. (1995 COCA: NEWS)

The comparison of the morphosyntactic and semantic–pragmatic characteristics of the *like*-parentheticals in (29a–c) above with those of the complementation patterns in (30a–c) reveals that the former have undergone over time processes of grammaticalization, subjectification, and intersubjectification. On the structural level, for example, they show decategorialization: an originally complement-taking clause has been downgraded to a parenthetical construction which is syntactically incomplete. Once they acquire parenthetical status, *like*-combinations are free to occupy different positions in the sequence (e.g., medial (29a–b) and final (29c)), a sign of their syntactic and prosodic independence. In addition to decategorialization, *like*-parentheticals show a high degree of morphosyntactic fixation, with a tendency to occur in the simple present form and to disallow adverbial modification. In this respect, *like*-parentheticals contrast starkly with their related complementation patterns, which exhibit a much wider range of variability, as testified by examples (30a–c).

Given that parentheticals typically convey a "second-order reflection, comment, or evaluation upon the anchor" (Brinton 2008: 8), they are very likely candidates for the expression of subjective and intersubjective meanings. As can be gathered from our earlier examples (29a–c), *like*-parentheticals constitute no exception. In all three instances, the use of the parenthetical mitigates the speaker's commitment toward the truth of the proposition, suggesting that he/she possesses only second-hand information about the content in the anchor, casts some doubts on the veracity of the information, or hedges a potentially controversial statement. In their hedging function, *like*-parentheticals also serve an intersubjective function as face-saving devices which make it possible for the interlocutor to disagree. Intersubjectivity is also at work in cases such as (31), where the parenthetical *sounds like* is used by the second speaker as a confirmation (though tentative) in answering his/her interlocutor's question. On other occasions, *like*-parentheticals can function as repair strategies, which allow the speaker to reconsider his/her words. An example is given in (32), where the clausal parenthetical *looks like* co-occurs with the discourse markers *well* and *I mean*.

(31)   He swaggered back and wiped his hands off on his pants. "So. You tell me. Crazy?" # "**Sounds like.**" (2005 COCA: FIC)

(32)   But speaking about the GOP, you have Bobby Jindal, Michael Steele, who's going to – **looks like**, well, I mean, he's put his hat in the ring for Republican National Party Chairman. (2008 COCA: SPOK)

Clause Connectives: From TIME to the CCC Domain

From epistemic modals and parentheticals we now move on to the domain of clause connectives, focusing on the developments affecting the adverbial subordinator *while* from Old English to the present day. As will become apparent from the description that follows, the history of *while* represents a clear illustration of the syntactic and semantic polyfunctionality characteristic of a good number of adverbial subordinators across languages. Moreover, and most importantly for the purposes of this chapter, *while* represents a paradigmatic example of the operation of subjectification from content-based temporal meanings, as in (33), to abstract readings belonging to more complex adverbial domains, such as contrast in (34).

(33)   She got ill **while** she was on holiday in Kenya.

(34)   **While** the first act was excellent, the second seemed rather dull. (from Huddleston and Pullum 2002: 737)

In his detailed typological study of adverbial subordinators in European languages, Kortmann (1997) divides the adverbial semantic space into 32 different interclausal relations, which are conveniently grouped together in four major networks: TIME, CCC (causal, conditional, concessive, and related circumstantial relations), MODAL, and OTHER (e.g., Place). For the subordinator *while*, he identifies up to six different semantic readings through time:

- three belong to the TIME network, namely simultaneity duration, simultaneity co-extensiveness, and *terminus ad quem*,[16] and
- three correspond to the set of CCC relations, namely contrast, cause, and concession.

Table 7.1 *Semantic development of* while *from Old English to Present-day English (adapted from Kortmann 1997: 321)*

		SD	SC	TAQ	Contrast	Cause	Concession
OE	*þa hwile (þe)*	+ +	+ +				
ME	*(the) whyle (that)*	+ +	+ +	+ +	+		
	(the) whyles (that)	+ +	+ +	+ +	+		
	whylst	+ +	+				
EModE	*while (as, that)*	+ +	+	+ +	+ +		
	whiles (that)	+ +	+	+ +	+ +	+ +	
	(the) whilst (that)	+ +	+	+ +	+ +		
PDE	*while*	+ +	+		+ +		+
	whilst	+ +	+		+ +		+

SD = simultaneity duration; SC = simultaneity co-extensiveness; TAQ = *terminus ad quem*

The semantic development of *while* proposed by Kortmann (1997: 321) is summarized in Table 7.1, where the double plus mark indicates a primary reading of the subordinator and a single plus mark signals a secondary reading.

As was discussed in Chapter 6,[17] the origins of the modern conjunction *while* are found in the Old English noun *hwil* 'time, period,' when occurring in the phrasal combination *þa hwile (þe)* 'at/during the time that,' which is made up of the accusative feminine singular form of the distal demonstrative (*þa*), the accusative of the noun *hwil*, and the optional invariable marker of subordination *þe*. An example where the phrase *þa hwile þe* expresses the temporal meaning of simultaneity is the following:

(35)   Him geaf ða se cyngc twa hund gildenra pænega and hæfde hine to geferan **þa hwile þe** he lifede. (950–1050 *Apollonius of Tyre*; HC)
'Then the king gave him two hundred gold pennies and had him as companion while he lived.'

Over time, *while* gradually starts occurring in sequences of the type illustrated in the mid-twelfth-century example in (36). Here the absence of both the determiner and the subordinating marker *þe* points at a new status of *while* which comes close to the modern temporal use of the connective.

(36)   Þe ærcebiscop ... makede ðat sahte ðat te king sculde be lauerd and king **wile** he liuede and æfter his dæi ware Henri king. (1140 *Peterborough Chronicle* 67; MED)
'The archbishop ... made the agreement that the king should be lord and king while he lived, and after his time Henry would be king.'

Although temporal simultaneity has remained the main reading of *while* through the history of English, after the medieval period the connective gradually developed additional meanings beyond the domain of TIME relations. More specifically, the available historical evidence confirms the existence of a diachronic shift of temporal *while*, where meaning is based on the observation of the real world, toward cognitively more complex relations belonging to the CCC network, where meaning arises from the speaker's reasoning (see Table 7.1). The following twentieth-century examples illustrate the derived meanings of concession (37), contrast (38), and cause (39).

(37)   My job is dissolving under me – I have very little to do when I go in. **While** I'm sick of the work, I'm frightened of not making money. (1978 Ryan, *Pregnancy Journal*; ARCHER)

(38)   In young spruce with few wounds the resin canals are in isolated groups associated with the individual wounds, **while** in old trees which have undergone many injuries the delimitation is not complete, because of overlapping among the responses. (1925 Thomson, *Resin Canals in the Canadian Spruce*; ARCHER)

(39)   **While** they are incapable of defence and without a right to call for the protection of the League, they expect the Poles and Czecho-Slovaks will each possess larger armies than they are allowed to retain. (1919 *Daily Herald* 5/7/1919; ARCHER)

In concessive relations, the facts described in one proposition are incompatible or in conflict with those in the other proposition, although both are presented as valid. In (37), for instance, in the *while*-clause the speaker expresses her unhappiness with her job, but offers in the main clause a good reason for keeping it. In turn, in the semantic relation of contrast, two or more propositions belong to the same conceptual domain (the delimitation of resin canals in (38) above) and are simultaneously valid, but differ as regards other properties (the main and subordinate clauses have different subjects with different qualities: young spruces with few wounds vs. old trees with many injuries). Given that in contrast relations there is no general incompatibility between the propositions, a marker of temporal simultaneity such as *while* turns out to be a very likely candidate for the diachronic development of contrastive inferences, which may become conventionalized over time. Finally, causal overtones are present in *while* in examples such as (39) above. Since the temporal interpretation (though backgrounded) still remains here, the reading of causality should probably be taken as an invited inference rather than as a true new coded meaning of the connective. This would explain why contemporary English dictionaries do not normally include the meaning 'cause, reason' as part of the semantic config-uration of *while*, whereas concession and contrast do appear in the dictionary entries for the conjunction.

Whether fully conventionalized meanings (as in the case of the readings of concession and contrast) or generalized invited inferences (as happens with cause), it is the original meaning of simultaneity present in *while* from its earliest occurrences that allows the reinterpretation of the temporal connective as one belonging to the so-called CCC domain. Subjectification is definitely at work in the development: the change from content-based temporal meanings (co-occurrence in time) to increasingly more abstract ones (e.g., concession). Similar diachronic shifts account for the rise of the causal reading of *since* (consider our earlier example (3b), *Since I have to finish this paper today, I won't be able to go to the cinema with you*) and of the conditional meaning 'provided that, if' of *as long as* (e.g., *You can have a cat as long as you promise to take care of it*) (see, e.g., Traugott and Dasher 2002: 36–37), both originating in temporal connectives.

The Development of Expletives: *Jesus!* and *Gee!*

Our last example concerns the development of the historically related expletives *Jesus!* and *gee!* and thus testifies to the existence of (inter)subjectification outside grammaticalization. Biber et al. (1999: 1094–1095) subdivide expletives into two groups:

- taboo expletives – those referring to the taboo domains of religion (e.g., *my God*), sex (e.g., *fuck*), and bodily excretion (e.g., *shit*); and
- moderated or euphemistic expletives – those whose origin is camou-flaged by phonological alterations of various kinds (e.g., *gosh* for *God*) or by substitution for a related word (e.g., *goodness* for *God*).

The origin of the milder, less offensive expletives is often obscured by these modifications, so that the taboo expletives from which they originate are not always recognizable any longer by speakers. Biber et al.'s classification can be complemented with the widely established distinction between primary and secondary interjections (see, e.g., Ameka 1992): primary interjections do not have homonyms in other parts of speech, while secondary interjections do.

In accordance with these classifications, *Jesus!* is a taboo expletive (secondary interjection) deriving from the religious proper name *Jesus*. Gehweiler (2008: 82) shows how the frequent use of the proper name in religious oaths, invocations, and prayers as a vocative, as in (40), led to its pragmatic enrichment in the course of Middle English and its occurrence outside religious contexts, where the form no longer had its earliest referential meaning of invocation, but rather expressed the invited inference of speaker perspective (e.g., surprise, annoyance), as shown in (41). Through repeated use in the latter contexts, the original meaning of the expression is backgrounded, while the invited inference of surprise or annoyance becomes part of its coded meaning. As a result, *Jesus!* becomes established as a new interjection by the end of the Middle English period through subjectification, encoding speaker attitude. In (42), for example, the interjection expresses a negative reaction on the part of the speaker. As examples (40)–(42) suggest, subjectification of the original proper name *Jesus* in vocative function to the taboo expletive *Jesus!* was aided by the sentence-initial position of the vocative expression and its detachment from the rest of the utterance.

(40)   **Jesu** defende us from dethe ['death']! (1470 *The works of Sir Thomas Malory; MED*)

(41)   **Bi ihesus** with here ieweles, ʒowre iustices ['judges'] she shendeth ['corrupts'] (1377 Langland, *Piers Plowman B* Prol. 154; *OED*)

(42)   **Jesu!** madam, what will your mother think is become of you? (1676 Etheredge, *Man of Mode* 283; *OED*)

Interestingly, in the latter part of the nineteenth century the secondary interjection *Jesus!* underwent further change along the cline of subjectification, as a result of which the moderated expletive (primary interjection) *gee!* emerged. Gehweiler (2008) explains that in the Victorian period *Jesus!* was phonologically and ortho-graphically reduced to *gee!* (also *geez, jebus, jeepers, jeeze*) for euphemistic reasons (one should not break the third commandment 'You shall not take the name of the Lord your God in vain'), losing thus its connection to the proper name *Jesus* in the eyes of both speakers and hearers. The lack of transparency of the new interjection had important consequences for its later use: in contrast to the second-ary interjection *Jesus!*, which is heavily loaded with a negative meaning compo-nent from the very beginning (see example (42) above), *gee!* is not restricted to the expression of negative evaluation, but has the general implication of surprise and unexpectedness. In fact, the *OED* (s.v. *gee* int.) defines it as "an exclamation of surprise or enthusiasm; also used simply for emphasis." The following examples from COCA illustrate the use of *gee* encoding a positive (43) and a negative (44) reaction on the part of the speaker, respectively.

(43)   And we shook hands and then he embraced me and made me feel like, "**Gee**, the war is really over, you know, after all of these years." (1991 COCA: SPOK)

(44)   Mr. DONALDSON: Well, let me just say this. The President has already said that we would make up whatever is lost in the way of money in that delay time, but Israel seemed to want a confrontation with George Bush over who controlled the United States Congress, Bill. Mr. SAFIRE: **Gee**, I disagree completely there, Sam. I think the confrontation was a challenge issued by George Bush. (1991 COCA: SPOK)

Concluding Remarks

This chapter has shown how pragmatic inferences in the context of speaker–hearer negotiation of meaning play a fundamental role in the development of language through processes such as subjectification and intersubjectification. The illustrations provided in the preceding sections represent but a small selection of how inferential-based mechanisms of change work in language, but may provide you with some sense of the pervasive nature of such processes. The range of examples and domains where the effects of inferencing can be felt in English could be considerably enlarged. What is more, many of the changes examined here for English find parallels in other languages, which may be suggestive of the existence of significant cross-linguistic regularities, most likely deriving from similar cognitive and communicative processes. Consider, for example, the widespread development of epistemic uses of modals out of originally deontic readings or the emergence of epistemic/evidential parentheticals analogous to English *looks like* in various Romance languages (e.g., Latin-American Spanish *dizque*, Galician *disque*, and Sicilian *parica*). These striking similarities across languages are probably something more than mere coincidence and may indicate that semantic change is far less irregular and unsystematic than was believed until not too long ago.

Suggestions for Further Study

Useful summaries of the development of theories of semantic change can be found in chapter 2 of Traugott and Dasher (2002) and in Geeraerts (2010). The most relevant readings on Gricean and neo-Gricean theories are Grice (1975) and Levinson (1995, 2000). Traugott and Dasher (2002) remains a central reference for the Invited Inferencing Theory of Semantic Change. The book deals with several key issues in this chapter, including invited inferencing (chapter 1), (inter)subjectification and grammaticalization (chapter 2), and the development of modal verbs (chapter 3). Chapter 4 in Hopper and Traugott (2003) is a very good introduction to the role of pragmatic factors in meaning change, with sections on invited inferencing, metaphorical and metonymic processes, etc. The role of metaphor and metonymy in language change is also described in Sweetser (1990). The *Handbook of Historical Pragmatics*, edited by Jucker and Taavitsainen (2010), contains chapters on many of the topics relevant to the present chapter, including metaphor and metonymy (Nerlich 2010), (inter)subjectification (López-Couso 2010), grammaticalization (Traugott 2010b), pragmaticalization (Claridge and Arnovick 2010), and interjections and expletives (Gehweiler 2010), among others. (Inter)subjectification and related processes of change are dealt with in several of the articles included in Davidse, Vandelanotte, and Cuyckens (2010) and Degand and Simon-Vandenbergen (2011). On connectives see the volume edited by Lenker and Meurman-Solin (2007). Brinton (2008) has already become a classic reference for the study of parentheticals/comment clauses. Chapter 8 in Jucker and Taavitsainen's (2013) textbook offers a good introduction to the kind of semantic–pragmatic changes examined here.

Exercises

1. Violating Grice's Cooperative Principle

   The following examples illustrate different ways in which speakers may fail to observe some of the maxims of Grice's Cooperative Principle. Which conversational maxims are not followed by speaker B in each of these examples? Explain why.

   (i) A: Hi, Dad. I'm afraid your car broke down while I was driving home.

      B: That's great! This really makes my day!

   (ii) A: Do you already know the placement test results?

      B: Some more pudding?

2. Semantic change: *shambles*

   The noun *shambles* is a particularly good example of diachronic semantic change. With the help of the *OED* and other etymological dictionaries, trace the various extensions of meaning that the noun has undergone from its original sense in Old English 'stool, bench' to the contemporary (informal) meaning 'confusion, mess' (e.g., *After the party the apartment was a complete shambles*; *The country's economy is in a shambles*).

3. Amelioration and pejoration

   The following words have undergone processes of lexical semantic change over time. Indicate whether their contemporary meanings are the result of amelioration or of pejoration and explain why.

   (i) *mistress*

   (ii) *success*

   (iii) *stink*

4. The development of *ought*

   Taking the following examples as a starting point, comment on the semantic changes undergone by *ought* in the course of history. Which is the meaning of *ought* in each of these instances? Does the semantic development of *ought* suggested by these examples illustrate subjectification? Why/why not?

   (i) ... ealle þa land þe his modor **ahte** ... (1042)

      '... all the lands that his mother possessed ...'

   (ii) Other dispisethe more then they **oughte**, the thyng that they cannot suffer (1556)

   (iii) The next street on the right **ought** to be Glentworth Street.

5. Parenthetical *it looks like*

   Discuss the most salient morphosyntactic and semantic-pragmatic features of the parenthetical clause *it looks like* in the following examples from the *Corpus of Contemporary American English* (COCA), paying special attention to its subjective and intersubjective functions.

(i) They soon entered a clearing of trampled grass. Several tents stood on the far side, and men moved in the trees beyond, soldiers **it looked like**, in leather armor. Most were tending animals. Their mounts resembled horses, but with tufts for tails. (2008 COCA: FIC)

(ii) They have not been kind to her. "The Village Voice" – now this is not "The American Spectator." This is "The Village Voice" doing this to the first lady of the United States. Check out this cover this week, the June 22 issue. This is Hillary coming out of a toilet. And you go to the fold, "The Hillary Clinton Cheat Sheet." It's got the first lady as a prostitute, and the president as, **it looks like**, a disco pimp. This from "The Village Voice." (1999 COCA: SPOK)

(iii) WILLIE-GEIST # She got a little on her thumb, **it looks like**. AL ROKER: Yes. Yeah. (2015 COCA: SPOK)

6. *As long as*

What kind of adverbial relations are expressed by the connective *as long as* in examples (i) and (ii) below? Which of these do you believe is the original meaning of the subordinator in the history of English? Why? What does example (iii) tell you about the possible path of development undergone by *as soon as* over time?

(i) You can go out tonight, **as long as** you are back home by 10.

(ii) He promised he would stay with her **as long as** she was asleep.

(iii) I buy clothes I'm not sure I'll ever wear **as long as** they are on sale.

7. Expletive *jeeze(e)*

Search for uses of the expletive *jeeze(e)* in the *Corpus of Historical American English* (COHA). Analyze the kind of evaluations expressed by the speaker by means of the use of the expletive. What do these corpus data tell you about its semantic development?

Notes

I gratefully acknowledge the financial support of the European Regional Development Fund and the Spanish Ministry of Economy and Competitiveness (grants FFI2014–52188–P and FFI2014–51873–REDT).

1. For example, see Brinton and Arnovick (2016: ch. 3) for a discussion of some of these mechanisms of semantic change.
2. A whiteboard video on Grice's Cooperative Principle and its four maxims is available at: www.youtube.com/watch?v=we6uSVf4qss
3. Another excellent whiteboard video on conversational and conventional implicatures can be found at: www.youtube.com/watch?v=YD821_bUhLc
4. The term "invited inference" is borrowed from Geis and Zwicky (1971); another label used for this kind of implicatures is "context-induced inferences" (Heine, Claudi, and Hünnemeyer 1991).
5. See, for example, Traugott (1982, 1989, 1995b, 1999a, 1999b, 2003b, 2007, 2010a) and Traugott and Dasher (2002).

6. Traugott draws partly on Halliday and Hasan's (1976) tripartite distinction between the ideational, the textual, and the interpersonal functional domains of language at the synchronic level.

7. On politeness, see Brown and Levinson (1987). Nevala (2010) offers a good overview of research on historical politeness.

8. See Chapter 6 on the concept of "layering."

9. See Hopper and Traugott (2003: 82), Fischer (2007b: 259), and Traugott (2010a: 40–41).

10. Intersubjectification is strongly grammaticalized in just a few languages. One of these is Japanese, which has developed addressee honorifics marking politeness or intimacy with respect to the social status of the addressee independently of the content of the proposition (see, for example, Traugott and Dasher 2002: 263–276 on the development of Japanese *saburahu* as a politeness marker).

11. The history of the discourse marker *well* is particularly well documented. See, among others, Finell (1989), Jucker (1997; 2002: 221–224), Traugott and Dasher (2002: 175–176), and Defour (2008, 2010).

12. Jucker does not see the Old English interjection *wel la* or *wella*, which collocates with a vocative and serves as an attention-getting device, as directly contributing to the rise of the Present-day English discourse marker *well*.

13. The semantic development of *must* has attracted considerable attention in the grammaticalization literature. See, among many others, Traugott (1989), Goossens (2000), and Traugott and Dasher (2002: 120–137).

14. The examples in this section (examples (22)–(27)) are from Traugott and Dasher (2002: 122–130).

15. See, among many others, Dehé and Kavalova (2007), Brinton (1996, 2008), and Kaltenböck, Heine, and Kuteva (2011), who use the alternative label "theticals."

16. In simultaneity duration, the proposition in the main clause is only partially simultaneous with that in the subordinate clause, which normally extends for a longer period of time (e.g., *I learnt all about flowers while we lived in the country*). In simultaneity co-extensiveness, by contrast, the propositions in both main and sub-clauses extend for the same time interval (e.g., *As long as we lived in the country our children were happy*). Finally, in *terminus ad quem* the adverbial clause identifies a point or period of time up to which the proposition expressed in the main clause lasts (e.g., *We had a wonderful summer until my mother arrived*).

17. Chapter 6 focuses on the grammaticalization of *while*; here the focus is on its semantic–pragmatic development.

8

Discourse-based Approaches

CLAUDIA CLARIDGE

Introduction

Consider the following two text-initial passages:

(1)   a. **FIRE NUT CAGED** A PSYCHOPATH was jailed for life yesterday for killing a mother and her two kids by torching their home. (2000 *Sun*; *Rostock Newspaper Corpus*)

        b. One of the things we celebrate as we gather for worship week by week is God's ability to bring good out of evil. We often have to do so, don't we, in the teeth of much evidence to the contrary. Evidence that God has lost the plot, as it were. For, as we look around our world we see a never-ending catalogue of headline-grabbing events which, again and again, spell bad news. (*c.* 2000 David Stone; see Claridge and Wilson 2000)

We recognize these texts more or less immediately for what they are, i.e., what genres they represent, and to which larger discoursal and social contexts they belong – namely, newspaper reportage and a sermon, respectively. We can do this because texts consist of features that are not only functional, but also conventional, and because we have acquired textual competence by growing up in a given culture. Even with altered layout, the news report headline (with characteristic ellipsis; cf. *was/has been caged*) and the following lead, referring to the major journalistic questions in a nutshell (who, when, what, why), are probably easily recognizable as typical genre features of (1a). Similarly, the sermon beginning (1b), which we recognize by the reference to the communicative situation (*gather for worship*) and the topic (*God*), contains interactive features (the pronoun *we*, the tag question *don't we*, colloquial expressions such as *lost the plot*) typical of face-to-face communication. Now look at beginnings of the "same" discourse of earlier times for a contrast:

(2)   a. *Newcastle, Dec. 29.* Thursday arrived here, by the London Waggon, the Arms for the Northumberland Militia. (1760 *London Evening Post; Rostock Newspaper Corpus*)

b. The eternall HappineVsse of our immortall souls is to be found only in union and communion with Iesus Christ; Religion is that which gathers and binds up the spirit to close fellowship with Him; . . . " (RelA1642; *Lampeter Corpus*)

(2a) contains neither a proper headline (but a dateline instead) nor a lead. While (1a) is followed by a report that spells out the lead in more detail, the older news text continues with different information on unrelated company movements and officer deaths (not cited here). While (2b) also contains one pronoun (*our*), it does not sound very interactive or colloquial nor does it link to the situation. As these small examples illustrate, texts evolve and conventions as to what is situationally and thus textually necessary and appropriate alter with time. In fact, there was no news report genre before the first newspapers appeared in the seventeenth century. Together with the evolution of genres, linguistic features and/or their distribution (may) develop and transform – like the distinctive conglomeration of features in headlines or the particular narrative features of reports. Sermons and their functional environment have existed since the beginning of the English textual tradition, however; here it is not the genre as such but its stylistic realizations that change with time and fashion(s).

Entering language history through the door of discourse thus means dealing with individual texts (entities "above the sentence"), both as forms with specific requirements for linguistic realizations (e.g., how sentences are linked to build up a coherent argument) and as forms of sociocultural practice (e.g., how ideology is produced and transmitted in texts). It also means dealing with the textual variation which we describe by the terms "register," "genre," and "style." Let's illustrate these terms with the help of the example of newspaper language: This is a register because of its common communicative situation (public print media, professional writers, wide anonymous readership, informational purpose) and shared linguistic features (e.g., frequent use of nouns and past tense verbs; see (1a) and (2a)). Leafing through any newspaper you will find a variety of genres within this register, i.e., texts which share a specific communicative purpose and a conventional text structure, such as news report, editorial, review or interview.

The genre of obituary, for example, follows a small set of text templates (often to be found on "help" websites), e.g.:

{Title or Position} {Name} {Nickname} {Last Name} (née {Maiden Name}) died {unexpectedly/peacefully} in {location} on {date} in {City, State} at the age of {age}. {Name} is survived by {his/her} {relatives, Names}, of {Locations} etc.

Obituaries often contain restricted lexical choices and structures not necessarily found elsewhere (e.g., *be survived by*).

Zooming into the text of one or more newspapers you will then notice differences in style, i.e., linguistic forms used not for functional but for aesthetic, idiosyncratic reasons; the style used by different columnists in newspapers will certainly be distinctive, for example.

The discourse approach allows us to answer questions like the following:

- Which linguistic features are typically associated with a register/genre and how and why do these feature inventories change over time?
- What are the genres within a register and what are their rules for text structure (beginnings, middles, and endings)?
- Are styles important beyond the individual, e.g., across whole groups of people or entire periods?
- And of course how do discourse-based changes connect with and feed into larger linguistic developments?

It is apparent that this approach is not only functionalist in nature, but also one which needs to pay considerable attention to the cultural embedding of language.

The Roles of Discourse in Language History and Change

Imagine living in a country where your native language will be useful for you mostly for everyday conversation, whereas you need foreign languages for most types of writing and specialized communication: this is the situation Görlach (1999: 462) visualizes for England for a long time, as shown in Figure 8.1. It shows that English shared the literary register almost equally with other languages, but was completely outranked by them in the legal and scholarly fields up to about 1350.

We need to be aware of the fact that for a considerable time some registers and genres were not available to exert an influence on the history of English, but also that, once they had to be (re)constructed in English, users found it necessary to innovate or change linguistic features which would be suitable for a particular text variety. Thus, the following aspects are important for the roles of discourse in linguistic history:

(a) What happens with(in) registers and genres during "vernacularization" (the shifting from French and Latin to English) and standardization (the development of a non-regionalized variety with little linguistic variability and maximal discourse functionality)?
(b) Which foreign influences are transmitted by texts in the long-lasting multilingual situation?
(c) What functions precisely do registers and genres fulfill with regard to language change: as sites of innovation, catalysts for spreading change, or the last habitat for obsolescent features?

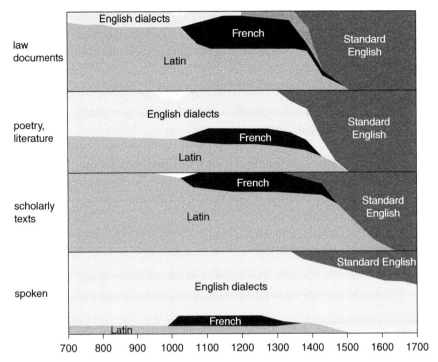

Figure 8.1 *Languages used in discourse (from Manfred Görlach, "Regional and social variation," in Roger Lass (ed.),* The Cambridge History of the English Language, *vol. III*: 1476–1776. *Cambridge: Cambridge University Press, 1999, p. 462; reprinted with kind permission from Cambridge University Press)*

Vernacularization and Standardization

The processes of vernacularization and standardization are closely linked, both functionally and temporally: both were ongoing roughly from the late fourteenth century and both expanded the range of English. Before that we find the prestigious alternatives, French and Latin, covering many registers and carrying the functions that standard English would later take over. Although verse in English existed continuously from Old English, as did religious prose, other types of vernacular prose were late in (re)emerging in English. Medical writing is among the first types of scientific language to appear in the vernacular in late Middle English, and other native scientific prose followed, but the whole of science remained multilingual for a long time (for example, Isaac Newton still wrote in both Latin and English). And English legal writing shows a large gap after the Norman Conquest. On the whole, the process of vernacularization was long and only completed by the nineteenth century, with the mid-seventeenth century providing the turning point in favor of English.

Shaping English to fill the needs of such registers and their genres is part of what Haugen (1972) called "maximal variation or elaboration of function" within the larger process of standardization. In order to be optimally useful for different topics, professions, and user groups, structural linguistic adjustments were necessary that ranged from lexical expansion, including borrowing, to new or adapted morphosyntactic constructions. Words, for example, might be borrowed in a specialized, register-based sense first, and only acquire a more general use later. Published writing also became increasingly less oral in style as its communicative situation (distance between interactants, informational purposes) favored more "literate" features such as participles, subordination, and passives (see below). These developments were driven by the specific textual needs of a register/genre; some of them remained confined to these environments, but others spread out into the language as a whole and were included in the emerging standard. An example of the former are compound adverbs with the first element *here-* (e.g., *hereafter*), a useful cohesive element in legal writing, but not successful in the language as a whole. A productive export from administrative genres, in contrast, is the conjunction *provided that*, which originated in formulaic contexts in legal documents and is found in general contexts by 1700.

In so far as features of the standard emerge out of written registers and genres, they will often involve examples of "change from above"; in other words they are (at least partly) based on conscious decisions of what is functionally necessary and stylistically appropriate for a given genre. The prestigious patterns shared by the community of practice (see Chapter 9) shaping a register undoubtedly played a role in this process.

Foreign Influences and Multilingualism

If we look at Figure 8.1 again, it is clear that foreign influence and multilingualism are especially relevant for the Middle Ages and for the early modern period, as well as for the administrative and the scientific registers. With regard to the administrative registers the so-called "curial style," originating in Anglo-French, exerts its influence through English writers using both Anglo-French and English. Curial style is commonly found in letters and documents, such as those found in *An Anthology of Chancery English* (Fisher et al. 1984), but extends also to other writings in a London context (e.g., the *Chronicles of London*) and to paratexts (dedications, prologues, epilogues, e.g., Caxton's *Eneydos*), in which its ceremonious features are exploited for sounding weighty or respectful. This style is characterized by features which enhance precision and ceremoniousness, namely (i) nominal and verbal groups consisting of near-synonyms (e.g., *we pray and beseech you*), (ii) extremely explicit cohesive devices, e.g., *the (afore) said, the same, the which*, and (iii) Latinate (and often abstract) lexis (e.g., *labour* vs. *work, governance*). Going beyond the curial style, Latinate style in general lends itself as a marker of formality or learning (see Chapter 13 for Latinate borrowing).

As most early English scientific texts were adaptations or translations of Latin (sometimes French) originals, we can expect that English writers will appropriate a number of Latinate discourse conventions, such as methods of text-structuring (e.g., question–answer format), the strong orientation towards authorities and secure knowledge (see the use of attributions, referencing), and the borrowing of classical argumentative patterns. Some of these characteristics eventually fall out of use, especially with the rise of empirical science from the seventeenth century onwards, but others have left an imprint in Present-day English, including the use of complex NP structures (e.g., *correlation coefficients* 'coefficients that report correlations') and the use of Latinate lexis (e.g., *mortality* vs. native *death*), which have always distinguished the more learned from the more popular (handbook-like) texts.

Translations may also introduce further complexities. Translations are often not verbatim translations but rather paraphrases, adaptations, and imitations. If the changes in the "translation" process are extensive, the resulting texts can give an impression of a register/genre that deviates from the foreign-language original. A case in point is the OE translation of Bede's Latin *Ecclesiastical History*, which does not advertise very clearly that it is a translation. Discenza (2002) shows us that one of the most drastic changes the translation introduces is the systematic omission of the vast majority of the documentation (mostly papal letters) that Bede had included in his text as authoritative proof. Bede had been very aware of the great importance of external testimony for the reliability and credibility of his historical narrative, in line with historiographical traditions reaching back to classical and early Christian times. Indeed, it was for this methodological care that Bede was praised as a model of history writing throughout the Middle Ages. An important genre characteristic was thus tacitly removed by the translator, giving readers ignorant of Latin an erroneous impression of the text and indeed of the whole genre.

Multilingual texts were frequent in the Middle Ages and even later, showing different degrees of mixing. The most extreme degree is described as two or more languages being so intricately integrated in a text that they constitute a single grammatical system, as is found, for example, in the late medieval administrative/accountancy register. Lesser degrees of mixing, called code-switching, range from clearly foreign words, phrases, or whole sentences being interspersed in an otherwise English text (in different amounts) to the occurrence of non-, semi-, or even fully integrated borrowings – the borderline of what is foreign and native will not necessarily be clear at all times and in all texts. It is obvious that types of code-switching are a mechanism in language change, most clearly for borrowing (see Chapter 13). Mixed-language texts have been used in various domains, but they are common especially religion, science, business, administration, and law.

Genres and Language Change

Here we need to think of two partly interconnected aspects:

(a) The emergence, change, and loss of genres (or even whole registers), and

(b) The specific functions played by genres in language change, especially with regard to the development of linguistic features.

Thinking of the first aspect we might come up with the following possibilities. New genres emerge, for example, in the wake of technological change: printing in time led to newspapers, a publication format or "higher level genre" (Kohnen and Mair 2012) that accommodated various subgenres, such as news report, review, editorial, advertisement. These new types borrowed and evolved their textual structures partly from other genres; e.g., news reports followed the conventions of letters and chronicles. Once established, genres may go on transforming, e.g., news reports first changed from chronological to non-chronological treatments of events and later, due to competition from other media (television), began using so-called "extracted topics" (focusing on aspects related to the event) and the "package approach" (combining reporting with, e.g., interviews, comments, etc.) (Ungerer 2000). Loss of a genre may be illustrated by the historical annals and the modern telegram; together with their loss, their particular combination of features also falls out of use. Individual linguistic constructions might even be lost completely from the language due to genre change or loss. A case in point is the annalistic use of *here* in a temporal sense, as in this example from the *Anglo-Saxon Chronicles*: *772 Her Milred biscep forþ-ferde* ('772 in this year Bishop Milred died').

If we now move to the function that genres can play in language change, we find that generic developments may lead to linguistic innovation, to the increase of features (diffusion), or to their decline, the latter ending in potential obsolescence. An example of an innovative feature comes from the area of conjunctions: *notwithstanding* originates towards the end of the fourteenth century as a calque on French *non obstant* most likely in legal discourse, i.e., in texts which need to state rules, conditions, and exceptions precisely and where concessive (and other) links are therefore vital. From there it then spread to other domains. It is still most common in these texts, but notably infrequent in speech-related material. An instance of the spread of a feature is the adverbial participial construction (e.g., *these men, **thus gathered**, purposed to fall on the king*). Kohnen (2001) shows us how the construction moved its way into the language with genres as stepping-stones: first religious treatises (around 1340), then both homilies/sermons and petitions/statutes (about 1390), next chronicles (around 1470), and finally narrative prose and private letters (*c.* 1520). The fact that this construction started out in prestigious genres fostered its spread, as did the fact that it could be adapted to genre-specific needs in each case. Kohnen terms this the "catalyst" function of genres. We also find the opposite in language change, with obsolescent features surviving in genre or register "niches." Here *thou* provides an example. While *thou* is not a living form of modern Standard English, it is "protected" by religious (and perhaps poetic) uses, the Bible, prayers, hymns, and liturgy in general. The occurrences in other domains are thus notably secondary uses, i.e., either quotations from religious (literary) texts or clear allusions to those. For example, an example from the *British National Corpus* (AYK 719) is written in jocular commandment style: *Thou shalt not have a lie-in on Sunday morning.*[1]

Researching Historical Discourse: Approaches

We can identify three approaches, or subfields, of research, which overlap with pragmatic concerns (see Chapter 10, in particular Table 10.1). These are:

> *historical discourse analysis proper* – pragmaphilology
> *diachronic(ally oriented) discourse analysis* – diachronic pragmatics
> *discourse-oriented diachronic linguistics* – pragma-historical
>   linguistics

While Chapter 10 puts the emphasis more on the level of (pragmatic) features and therefore prefers the second terms in each line, we will focus here more on text and thus on the italicized expressions.

Historical discourse analysis is concerned with the linguistic/stylistic makeup of texts/genres, their communicative aims, and their embedding in a sociocultural context at a certain point in time (i.e., a historically synchronic approach). Research here may typically deal with the structural characteristics of a genre or a certain grouping of texts (e.g., witchcraft pamphlets), with features highly relevant for textuality such as discourse deixis (as in the use of an expression such as *see below for further discussion*), or with constitutive features of a given text or activity type, e.g., questions and answers in courtroom discourse. A critical discourse analytical approach is successfully applied to historical texts by Prentice and Hardie (2009), when they investigate the portrayal of the anti-English Glencairn Uprising in Scotland in London-based newsbooks published in 1653–4. They find a fairly clear *us* vs. *them* (English vs. Scots) depiction, which is complicated by Scottish lowlanders constituting a third group evaluated differently from the highlanders, and by the fact that the groups can be described in positive and negative terms in close proximity. Nevertheless, the dominantly negative semantics associated with Scottish highlanders serves to disempower and discredit them in the eyes of English readers.

Diachronic(ally oriented) discourse analysis focuses on texts/genres/registers as changing entities over time. Changes can be due to fairly general stylistic shifts such as texts becoming more colloquial and informal. For example, some newspaper writing has increasingly become more "popular" in outlook (Bös 2012). This may be due to external factors leading to the more popular nature of a newspaper, such as a wider range of social classes among its readership, a lower price, and wider circulation. But text-related factors may also play a role, namely the newspaper's structural accessibility (appealing/"easy" layout/structure, sensationalist headlines, pictures), type of content (personal interest stories, more non-news content, "moralistic" tone), and the linguistic realizations (conversational and personalized style, emotionality, humor, emphasis). Many features are traceable, even if in incipient form, to early popular print in the seventeenth and eighteenth centuries, but the most recent stage of popular news is reached only by the full tabloid newspapers in the twentieth century, such as the British newspaper *The Sun*, which we saw an excerpt from in (1a). Here there is colloquial word choice (*nut* 'lunatic,' *kids*) and normative and emotional evaluation (*nut, psychopath*). While not all of the press has been affected by wholesale popularization, a complete transformation is seen in scientific writing from 1675 to 1975, as investigated by Atkinson (1996, 1999). Earlier scientific texts are author-centered with attention to genteel and polite behavioral norms, but later texts become increasingly more distanced and object-centered, the modern norm. The use of the letter genre form, common in early periods of scientific writing, is replaced by experimental reports with an increasingly stricter conventionalized structure which emphasizes precision, namely the format of introduction, methods, results, and discussion. The treatment of theory is also more and more foregrounded. This reflects an overall change in the discourse community, from the "gentleman-scholar" engaging in personalized dialogue to individual researchers retreating behind the content and normative communal practices.

As we see in the label *discourse-oriented diachronic linguistics*, the emphasis here lies not on discourse but on language variation and change, or in other words on what kind of role texts, genres, and registers play in the distribution of features, as well as in the origin and diffusion of changes. The participial construction mentioned in the preceding section is a case in point for the latter. With the now widespread availability of historical corpora paying attention to register/genre coverage,[2] it is fairly common to investigate the textual distribution of historical linguistic features. Researching the quantifiers *a x deal of* and *much* in nineteenth-century English, Smitterberg (2009) finds *deal* virtually only in the genres drama, fiction, letters, and trials, whereas *much* also occurs in debates, history, and science writing. We can learn from this that there is a stylistic distinction between the two forms, that language change proceeds with different speeds in various genres, and that more colloquial forms enter through more interactive genres.

After briefly discussing some of the challenges scholars face, I present case studies undertaken in each of these three approaches.

Researching Historical Discourse: Challenges

The so-called "bad data" problem is treated in Chapters 9 and 10, i.e., the problem that transmitted historical "speech" is not equivalent to modern naturally occurring conversation and does not give access to all uses, speakers, and contexts. As you can see there, the problem is not as acute as was thought earlier; nevertheless, some typical features of conversation such as disfluency phenomena, e.g., repeats and repairs, or the negotiation process underlying turn-taking will not be accessible.

Written discourse, in contrast, is extant throughout the history of English, but is nevertheless not entirely without its own "bad-data" problems. Written sources become more infrequent the further we go back in time, in particular in the era before print. What has survived has done so at least partly by chance – thus we cannot necessarily assume that our resources are representative of the entire discourse world or practices of a community. For Old English, for example, we have mainly religious, legal, and literary texts, but we do not have many "business" documents (sales, leases, etc.). Another problematic aspect concerns our knowledge about the cultural embedding of extant texts. We often know very little about the settings, participants, aims, norms of interaction/interpretation, and stylistic status of the transmitted texts, thus complicating a comprehensive communicative analysis. What may be helpful in this respect are metatexts, a type of source that has perhaps not received sufficient attention in the past. Handbooks, manuals, etiquette books, and guides of all kinds, whether they are for foreigners in an English environment, for servants or tradesmen, or for all potential letter writers, can provide prototypical discourses that tell us something about prevailing conventions. The following excerpt from Jacques Bellot's *Familiar Dialogues*, written for teaching English (conversation) to French Protestant refugee-immigrants in England, shows haggling behavior in an English market, which we might find surprising given our ideas of English interactions:

(3)   THE POULTER. What doe you buye? What doe you lacke?
           RALF.   Showe me a coupell of good, and fatte Rabettes, A fat
                                Capon. . . . [list omitted]
           THE POULTER. Here be them, that be very good and fat.
           RALF.   They be very stale.
           THE POULTER. Truely, they be very new.
           RALF.   How sell you them? How much?
           THE POULTER. Ten pence the couple.
           RALF.   It is to much, you are to, deare, They be not worth so
                                much. They be worth but a grote.
           THE POULTER. They be not mine for that price. They coast me more.
           RALF.   Tell me your lowest word.
           THE POULTER. Are you willing to buye?
           RALF.   Yes, if you will, be reasonable.
           THE POULTER. At one word: you shall pay two grotes for them.
           RALF.   I will pay but six pence for.
           THE POULTER. I may not sell them so.
           RALF.   Fare you well then.

THE POULTER. Here ye Syr: Cast th'other penye.

RALF. I will pay no more for.

THE POULTER. You are a very hard man: Well, you shall haue them: I sell this day. Robin-hoodes peners: Shall I fleae them? (1586 D1HEBELL; CED)

The text may indicate that conventions and norms for the genre service interaction were very different from today's, with more direct and confrontational strategies, and less politeness, as is visible in the blunt imperatives (e.g., *show me*), unmitigated critical statements (e.g., *they be very stale*), categorical refusals (e.g., *I will pay no more*), and expressed or implied negative beliefs about the other (e.g., *if you will, be reasonable*; *you are a very hard man*).

A last aspect we need to think of here concerns material circumstances of another kind, namely the visual aspects of written texts. Much discourse-related historical research is conducted with the help of corpora, digital, and/or edited texts. What is often lost in these cases is the specific layout, idiosyncratic visual structures (e.g., placement of marginalia), particular fonts/writing styles, means of highlighting and the like. All of these aspects can (and often do) have communicative import or a specific effect on the reader(ship). Williams (2013: chapter 6) shows how the particularly sensitive nature of a letter exchange between two mothers whose children had contracted a clandestine marriage contributes to features that are not usual for other letters of the two writers: there is extreme care with the orderly management of space, with an ornate italic script and exquisite flourishes, illustrating audience design and accommodation to a great extent. Without looking at the originals or facsimiles this effect would be lost.

Case Studies

Discourse-oriented Diachronic Approach: Information Packaging and Syntactic Options

When we produce a text, we all unconsciously pay attention not only to *what* we want to say but also to *how* we want to present it. Part of this *how* is "information packaging" (or structure), i.e., the way we order elements in a sentence so as to integrate it effectively into the surrounding text. There is ample evidence that we follow certain "rules," such that (i) given (old, known) information precedes new information in sentences and (ii) different clausal positions fulfill different functions in the so-called topic–comment structure. Topics – what the clause is about – are put in initial position, usually realize the first content-carrying constituent of a clause, and typically provide given information. Thus, the first position also fulfills a linking function with preceding discourse.

With a language whose syntactic rules permit a variety of constituents in first position we can pay attention to discourse-pragmatic considerations fairly easily.

Such freedom was the case in English up to Middle English, when the rule of verb-second (V2) word order, which requires that the finite verb be in second position, allowed a variety of constituents to fill the initial, or topic, position (e.g., *she said loudly to him then, loudly said she ..., then said she ..., to him said she ...*). The situation changed in late Middle English with the loss of V2 and the increasing fixation of the subject–verb (SV) order. From a structural point of view, this meant less freedom for linking and topicalization options and an increasing connection between subject and givenness/topic. With regard to discourse pragmatics, language users needed to pursue strategies beyond SV – which in turn meant the emergence of new constructions and/or higher frequencies for some constructions. We will now have a brief look at how constructions like the existential/presentational *there*-constructions, *it*-clefts, and the passive evolved/increased from late Middle English onwards to fulfill general discourse needs, and how the passive in particular fares in meeting genre-/register-specific requirements.

We use *there*-sentences in Present-day English to provide information that is new to the reader (existential type: *there's no milk*) or new to the discourse (presentational type: *there remain two problems*); both kinds of newness may of course coincide. In his diachronic study of *there* Breivik (1990) considers three types of (semantic) existentials/presentationals, two without (4a, b) and one with dummy *there* (4c):

(4)   a. Type A/B: *ðre þing* ben þat elch man habben mot ... (a1225 OEH 1 147: 25–6)
          'three things are that every man needs to have'
       b. Type C: *On þa ilca tyma* com an Legat of Rome (1123 Peterborough)
          'at the same time came a legate from Rome'
       c. Type D: *þer* wunieð i þan grunde; tweien draken stronge. (1250 Laȝamon 7952)
          'there live in the ground two strong dragons'

While type A/B (4a) is V2 and has an initial or preverbal subject (*ðre þing*), type C (4b) is V2 with variable first position, here an adverbial of time, with the subject following the verb (*an Legat of Rome*). In type D *there*-sentences, the dummy subject allows the sentence to adhere to SV order and places the semantic subject (*tweien draken stronge*) in final position. Investigating the distribution of these types across four periods, Breivik finds that the proportion of type D (*there*) of all existentials rises steadily, beginning at 15.1 percent in Old English and increasing steadily over Middle English from 29.9 percent (–1225) to 81.6 percent (1225–1425), and finally to 88.1 percent (1425–1550). That is, type D *there* is the most common existential by late Middle English/Early Modern English. Both C and D types fulfill the same purpose, namely shifting new material to the end of the clause, but with the weakening and eventual loss of V2 as a regular option, the formerly dominant type C constructions are ousted by type D *there*-sentences.

Turning now to clefts, we find that these also existed already in Old English, but a generally greater range of *it*-clefts emerged from late Middle English.

Table 8.1 *The development of* it-*clefts (frequency per 500,000 words, raw total: 493)*[a]

		it-clefts	Focal category in the it-cleft			
			NP	PP	AdvP	clause
OE	−1150	2.4	2.4			
ME	1150–1250	5.8	3.9	1.9		
	1250–1350	10.2	10.2			
	1350–1420	12.3	11.3	1.0		
	1420–1500	32.0	32.0			
EModE	1500–1569	22.6	20.8	0.9		0.9
	1570–1639	30.6	29.1	1.5		
	1640–1710	91.1	65.5	16.8	8.0	0.9
LModE	1700–1769	137.2	87.0	43.5	3.3	3.3
	1770–1839	142.4	56.9	73.2	9.5	2.7
	1840–1914	168.8	101.3	49.8	10.7	7.1

[a] Compiled from Patten's table 1 (2012: 194) and table 2 (2012: 197).

Clefts split the clause and the information in such a way that one part is foregrounded (bold-faced in (5)) and the other, in the relative clause, is backgrounded and marked as presupposed. In other words, the meeting (5a), the fear (5b), or the losing of God (5c) are not at issue here but taken for granted, while the bold elements specify something more newsworthy. These elements bear the "focus," often contrastively (e.g., the contrasting *rather then paine* in (5b) and the negation in (5c)) and they are often emphatic (e.g., the additional emphasizer *just* in (5a)).

(5)   a. It is **just twenty years** that we had that very very happy meeting at dear Coburg, when you and dear Louise were there! (Victoria-186x:1271.694; Los and Komen 2012: 892)

b. for 'tis **shame of the fault and the disgrace that attends it** that they should stand in feare of, rather then paine, if you would have them a temper truly ingenuous. (1685 Locke-E3-H,57.206; Patten 2012: 201)

c. It is **not wantonly, nor altogether willfully,** that man has so often lost his God. (Talbot-1901,95.93; Patten 2012: 203)

The older method of moving foregrounded material to first position in the sentence – possible in a V2 system – is impossible in Modern English; thus clefts can be seen to fill a gap. As Patten (2012) shows (see Table 8.1), clefts increase over the history of English, with their rise being particularly pronounced from the later EModE period onwards.

Table 8.1 also shows the expansion to a greater variety of focal elements, from originally only NPs (see (5a, b)), to prepositional phrases, adverbials (see (5c)), and clauses. These developments are especially notable from EModE onwards. But the expansion does not only extend to formal possibilities but also to a greater semantic range. Whereas at first proper names and clearly identifiable personal references are put in focal positions, an increasing number of abstract nouns, such as (5b) (from late Middle English), and adverbial relations, such as time (5a), place, means, reason, manner (5c) (from Early Modern English), make clefts very versatile. Over time the construction also becomes more flexible with regard to information structure, admitting not only given information (e.g., (5a)), but also information only presented as given, including finally the expression of opinion as in (5c). If one singles out clearly emphatic cases, like (5a), as Los and Komen (2012: 888) do, one finds that this type within all clefts becomes more important over time as well, expanding in Middle and Early Modern English.

Let's finally have a look at passive(-like) constructions, which have always been present in English. In Middle and Early Modern English there is an increase of new types of passives which are cross-linguistically rare, namely the prepositional passive (e.g., *He was sent for*) and passive exceptional case marking (ECM) constructions (e.g., *John was said to be lying*). What these and more traditional passives have in common is that they are an information-rearranging and argument-reversing strategy which can create subjects (from non-subject complements) and unmarked (i.e., non-contrastive, non-emphatic) topics, and provide discourse links. While (6a) is an OE V2 sentence, which is active and has a topicalized object *us*, the PDE version achieves the same effect by passivization, putting *we* in subject as well as topic position.

(6)   a. *And ðy   us   deriað 7 ðearle dyrfað   fela ungelimpa*
          ADV   OBJ   V   SBJ
          And then   us   harm and severely injure   many misfortunes
       b. *And then   we   will be severely harmed and injured   by many misfortunes*
          ADV   SBJ   V   ADV
       (examples from Seoane 2006: 369)

Both versions have an unmarked topic, whereas a fronted object in Present-day English would be highly marked (emphatic, contrastive, cf. ?*to us many accidents happened*). The translation in (6b) illustrates a "long" passive (with the *by*-phrase), where all complements from the corresponding active are structurally and semantically retained. The preservation of the *by*-phrase in long passives suggests that the reordering was made for information structure reasons whereas in "short" passives (without the *by*-phrase), the omission of (redundant) information alone might provide sufficient cause for the use of a passive. Seoane (2006) charted the steady rise of passives in general in a corpus comprising various registers/genres from 1420 to 1710. The factors influencing the choice of the passive in this corpus are predominantly discourse-pragmatic:

(i) the order given/new is most frequently found (64.3%) whereas the reverse occurs only very rarely (3.6%; the remainder of the data is taken up by given/given, new/new combinations),

(ii) the subject is usually more definite than the agent-phrase (70%).

Items more familiar to writer and reader are thus preferably put in subject/initial position. The only other factor to play a role is end-weight, i.e., the overwhelming tendency to move longer constituents to the end of the clause (applies to 76% of the passives).

Diachronic(ally oriented) Discourse Analysis: Style Shifts and Tendencies

We will use style to denote a conglomeration of textual features which are not inherently necessary for the register or genre but due to certain choices, for example aesthetic ones, by the language user. While the repetition of noun phrases, with their high degree of specificity (e.g., *any question, finding or verdict mentioned in that article*), is a functional characteristic of the legal register, the preference for long or short sentences in an essay, for example, is a matter of style. Styles can be very idiosyncratic and personal, but they can also be group-, genre-/register-, or period-specific. We will be interested in the last three types here. Register and period styles may apply not necessarily to all possible writers in a field or period but only to some. Not all members of the press, for example, participate in the drive towards more popular outputs and styles. Here we will look at stylistic tendencies that apply to larger sections of the language, namely (i) the opposed trends towards more literate and more oral/colloquial linguistic realizations as well as (ii) the link between lexical choice and style.

As we have seen above, the standardization process of English implied making the written language less oral in nature, making the language "fit" for the many functions of a standard language. Thus, it is not surprising that research by Biber and Finegan (Biber 1995; Biber and Finegan 1989, 1992) on the development of several genres (personal essays, medical research articles, science research articles, legal opinions, fiction, personal letters, dialogue from drama and from fiction) from the seventeenth to the twentieth century found that styles start out as fairly literate (standardization had already been in progress for more than a century) and continue to become even more literate for 200 years. However, the eighteenth century stands out as being especially pronounced in this respect, a finding that was confirmed also by Biber's (2001) separate investigation of the eighteenth century and by McIntosh's (1998) research on what he labeled "gentrification." So what does this mean linguistically? It means that features such as those listed in Table 8.2 under positive features of dimensions A and B and all features of dimension C (co-)occur commonly across (many) texts in the eighteenth century and that in contrast the negative features of A and B are not noticeably frequent or widespread.

Table 8.2 *Three dimensions of style (adapted from Biber and Finegan 1992: 690; corresponding to dimensions 1, 3, and 5 in Biber 1988)[a]*

Dimension A "Informational vs. involved production"	Dimension B "Elaborate vs. situation-dependent reference"	Dimension C "Abstract style"
positive features	*positive features*	conjuncts
nouns	*wh*-relative clauses on	agentless passives
word length	object positions	past participial adverbial
prepositions	pied-piping constructions	clauses
type–token ratio	*wh*-relative clauses on	*by*-passives
attributive adjectives	subject positions	past participial WHIZ
	phrasal coordination	deletions
	nominalizations	other adverbial subordinators
negative features	*negative features*	
private verbs	time adverbials	
that deletion	place adverbials	
contractions	other adverbs	
present tense verbs		
2nd person pronouns		
DO as pro-verb		
analytic negation		
demonstrative pronouns		
general emphatics		
1st person pronouns		
pronoun IT		
BE as main verb		
causative subordination		
discourse particles		
indefinite pronouns		
general hedges		
amplifiers		
sentence relatives		
wh-questions		
possibility modals		
non-phrasal coordination		
wh-clauses		
final prepositions		

[a] Such feature bundles are the result of statistical factor analysis aimed at identifying feature groups that commonly co-occur (e.g., the positive features among themselves), but also tend not to co-occur with another bundle (e.g., the negative vs. the positive ones). From these co-occurrences and exclusions one can draw conclusions about the functional characteristics of registers (see the dimension labels, e.g., features in A divide information-focused texts from interactive, interpersonal types). The method was originally outlined and applied in Biber (1988). If you are unsure about the terms used for features in Table 8.2 read up on them in the appendix to Biber (1988) and/or in a grammar (e.g., Quirk et al. 1985).

Thus, eighteenth-century texts – more so than texts either before or after that century – tend, generally speaking, to be more information-heavy, explicit in their references, syntactically elaborate, and abstract as opposed to having features typical of more interpersonal, situational communication. If we look at the following passages from narrative fiction from the seventeenth, eighteenth, and twentieth centuries respectively, keeping in mind the features from Table 8.2, the outstanding nature of the eighteenth-century text becomes clear in comparison (the texts are cited in Biber and Finegan 1989: 503):

(7) a. Seventeenth century: The prince return'd to court with quite another Humour than before; and tho' he did not speak much of the fair *Imoinda*, he had the Pleasure to hear all his Followers speak of nothing but the Charms of that Maid, insomuch, that, even in the Presence of the old King, they were extolling her, and heightning, if possible, the Beauties they had found in her: so that nothing else was talk'd of, no other Sound was heard in every Corner where there were whisperers, but *Imoinda! Imoinda!* (1688 Aphra Behn, *Oroonoko*; www.gutenberg.org/files/29854/29854-h/29854-h.htm)

   b. Eighteenth century: The place which the wisdom or policy of antiquity had destined for the residence of the Abyssinian princes was a spacious valley in the kingdom of Amhara, surrounded on every side by mountains, of which the summits overhang the middle part. The only passage by which it could be entered was a cavern that passed under a rock, of which it has long been disputed whether it was the work of nature or of human industry. The outlet of the cavern was concealed by a thick wood, and the mouth which opened into the valley was closed with gates of iron, forged by the artificers of ancient days, so massive that no man, without the help of engines, could open or shut them. (1759 Samuel Johnson, *Rasselas: Prince of Abyssinia*; www.gutenberg.org/files/652/652-h/652-h.htm)

   c. Twentieth century: He could not sleep. He could not keep still. He rose, quietly dressed himself, and crept out on to the landing once more. The women were silent. He went softly downstairs and out to the kitchen.

      Then he put on his boots and his overcoat and took the gun. He did not think to go away from the farm. No, he only took the gun. As softly as possible he unfastened the door and went out into the frosty December night . . . He went stealthily away down a fence-side, looking for something to shoot. (1922 D. H. Lawrence, *The Fox*; http://gutenberg.net.au/ebooks02/0200801h.html)

We can see that the text by Johnson (7b) is the most informational: almost half of the words in this passage are nouns, prepositions, and attributive adjectives (A: positive features), whereas the percentages are (much) lower in Behn's and especially Lawrence's texts. Johnson also amply uses all of the positive features of the dimension B, elaborated (= explicit, not context-dependent) reference, e.g., *residence* (nominalization), *of which* (*wh*-relative with pied-piping), *wisdom or policy* (phrasal coordination). Passives, with or without *by* (e.g., *be entered, was concealed by a thick wood*), and past participials (e.g., *surrounded*) are also clearly in evidence, making for a fairly abstract style (dimension C). Again, (7a, c) show few or none of these features; (7c) rather exhibits the negative, i.e., situation-dependent, features of dimension B. While Johnson may be a good eighteenth-century representative, he is nevertheless not completely typical; Biber and Finegan remark on the comparatively great variability of styles in the eighteenth century and McIntosh (1998) sees a progress across the century from more oral, loose styles at the beginning to more compact and orderly structures later on. Remarking on *which*-clauses, for example, he points out that they tended to be only loosely added on in early texts, but become more carefully planned and integrated over time (as in Johnson above). Sentence structure on the whole moves towards more compact linking, less structural repetition (such as several *that*-clauses in a row) and a tighter pairing of meaning and structure (e.g., in parallelisms or antithetical structures). McIntosh chose the term "gentrification" for this whole group of changes (cf. also on lexical characteristics below) because he sees it as driven by class-consciousness and a feeling of social propriety. If this was indeed a prevailing feeling it may also explain why none of the eighteenth-century genres investigated by Biber (2001) except for drama appear extremely oral – the oral features would simply have been a thing to avoid in prose writing.

   In contrast to the literate trends in the wake of early standardization, more recent developments in English are often marked by the opposite trend, namely the so-called "oral drift" (Biber and Finegan 1989, 1992; Biber 1995) or colloquialization (Leech et al. 2009). This means, in terms of the dimensions presented above, that texts become more involved, more situated in context and less abstract in style – by exhibiting, relatively speaking, *more* of the negative features of dimensions A and B, and *fewer* features of dimension C. A good example is the following excerpt from a letter by Virginia Woolf, which is conversational in tone and contains many relevant features (e.g., first and second person pronouns, progressives, contractions, *wh*-questions, amplifiers*, discourse particles*, present tense, private verbs* – the starred items are underlined in (8)):

(8)   I'm reading David Copperfield for the sixth time with <u>almost complete</u> satisfaction. I'd <u>for-gotten</u> how magnificent it is. What's wrong, I can't help asking myself? Why wasn't he the greatest writer in the world? For <u>alas</u> – no, I won't try to go into my crabbings and diminishings. <u>So</u> enthusiastic am I that I've got a new life of him: which makes me dislike him as a human being. Did you <u>know</u> – you who <u>know</u> everything – the story of the actress? He was an actor, I <u>think</u>; <u>very</u> hard; meretricious? Something had shriveled? And then

his velvet suit, and his stupendous genius? But you won't want to be discussing Dickens at the moment. (Virginia Woolf, letter, from Biber and Finegan 1992: 501)

Similarly we saw this at the very beginning of this chapter in the difference between the distinctly oral and situated modern sermon excerpt as opposed to the more literate seventeenth-century example. It is important to realize that these characteristics do not apply to individual texts but form a pattern that builds up and holds across the *majority* of texts in a given period; i.e., it is a typical fact. Individual texts in the eighteenth century can be oral in nature, but then they go against the trend, as we have seen above. From the nineteenth century onwards, however, a greater number of oral characteristics become ever more common and "normal," until one finds distinctly oral texts in and across the twentieth century – like (8). Biber and Finegan (1992) adduced three potential reasons for this development:

(a) the increase and growing social diversification of the reading public (together with the rise of literacy),
(b) the functional needs of new informational, expository genres, such as found in (early) press writing, and
(c) changing aesthetic attitudes with more emphasis on "naturalness."

Nevertheless, it need not be *all* registers or genres without exception that partake in such shifts at a given time. In fact, there is a split between modern registers. More popular types such as fiction, drama, essays, and letters show pronounced oral/colloquial styles, while more academic types such as scientific and legal prose continue, sometimes emphasize, literate stylistic characterizations and even develop new, non-oral features, such as very dense modification patterns (e.g., *the value of full doses in treating cancer*). These are due to the pressures of linguistic "economy," i.e., the attempt to present a high amount of information in efficient and concise ways. Oralization or colloquialization of written texts also has its natural limits, because the production circumstances of speech and writing are different in ultimately unbridgeable ways: there is simply no shared extra-linguistic context or true immediate interaction in writing (previous to digital forms such as synchronous chats). The link of colloquialization to language change has also been pointed out. It is not only texts that are changing in nature, but their changes cause the overall rise or decline of individual linguistic features. The increase of the progressive and of some semi-modals, as well as the decrease of *wh*-relatives may be linked to this stylistic trend. The change known as grammaticalization (see Chapter 6) may or may not contribute to colloquialization: increasing fusion may show up as colloquial features (e.g., contracted *let's* versus *let us*) but at the same time writing may resist new grammaticalized forms as informal (e.g., the merged *gotta*).

In what we have seen so far, the features in focus are structural and grammatical, in referring to whole groups of words or constructions with identical characteristics (such as all amplifiers). A complementary approach is to look more closely at the characteristics of individual words with regard to style. Gordon in his history of English prose (1966) highlighted the importance of the balanced use of both native Germanic and borrowed, especially Romance vocabulary as well as the effects an excess of the latter can have. Since the first great influx of French lexis in the Middle Ages, writers have (increasingly) been confronted with the choice between words from different etymological sources and in various stages of integration. Consider two examples from the sixteenth century, which apart from grammatical structure and interactiveness also clearly differ in lexical choice (borrowings of French/Latin origin underlined) (the texts are given in Gordon 1966):

(9)   a. Amonge the <u>romanes</u>, Caius Julius Cesar, whiche first toke upon him the <u>perpetuall rule</u> and <u>gouernaunce</u> of the Julius <u>empire</u>, is a <u>noble</u> <u>example</u> of <u>Industrie</u>, for in his . . . <u>incomparable</u> warres and busy-nesse <u>incredible</u> . . . he dyd nat onely <u>excogitate</u> moste <u>excellent</u> <u>policies</u> and <u>deuises</u> to <u>vainquisshe</u> or <u>subdue</u> his <u>enemies</u>, but also <u>prosecuted</u> them with such <u>celeritie</u> and <u>effecte</u>, that <u>diuers</u> and many tymes he was in the <u>campe</u> of his <u>enemies</u> . . . whan they <u>supposed</u> that he and his <u>hoste</u> had ben two days <u>iournay</u> from thens . . . (1531 Elyot, *The governour*; https://archive.org/stream/bokenamedgouerno01 elyouoft/bokenamedgouerno01elyouoft_djvu.txt)

       b. In some <u>countryes</u> thei go on hunting <u>comonly</u> on good friday in the morninge for a <u>comon custome</u>. Wyll ye breke that evyll <u>custome</u> or, cast away good friday? There be <u>cathedrall</u> churches unto which the <u>countre</u> commeth with <u>procession</u> at whytsuntyde and the women folowing the crosse wyth many an unwomanly songe, and that such <u>honest</u> wyves as out of the <u>procession</u> ye could not heare to speke one such foule <u>rybaudrie</u> worde as thei there synge for gods sake hole <u>ribaudous</u> songes, as lowd as theyr throte can <u>cry</u>. Wil ye mend that lewde <u>manner</u>, or put away whytsontide? (1528 More, *Dialogue against Tyndale*; Gordon 1966: 88)

In terms of word tokens Elyot (9a) uses twice as many Romance items as More (9b) (29% vs. 13%). Elyot's choices are more Latinate, less assimilated (e.g., *excogitate*), more redundant (e.g., *policies and devices*) than More's, and they are chosen also where a native form might have been easier for a contemporary reader (e.g., "overcome his enemies" rather than *vainquisshe or subdue his enemies*). Elyot's striking choices are clearly deliberate, aimed at "improving" the language but more immediately at giving his text a more elevated and refined character – i.e., at sounding less "oral" and down-to-earth in the way that (9b) does. It might be almost possible to write a text wholly based on native Germanic word stock, whereas a text with entirely Romance items is impossible. It is in the middle ground of, say, 95% – 50% Germanic in a given text that the interesting stylistic ground lies. Some words become so assimilated into a language that they lose their

Table 8.3 *Lexicon and style*

Word (to be used in a text)	Usual register / style	Type of meaning	Donor languages	Likely period of origin
ask, hearty, skill	general, "neutral," also informal	wide, general, suitable for many contexts	Germanic: Anglo-Saxon, Old Norse	OE
question (v.), *cordial, ability*	formal	somewhat more specific; contextual restrictions	French (also Latin)	ME
interrogate, cardiac, ingenuity	learned, technical, scientific	narrower, precise; register-restricted	Latin, Greek	EModE / ModE

historical baggage, but many do retain it. As shown in Table 8.3, we find large-scale stylistic and semantic tendencies in the modern English lexicon which are based on the historical development of the lexicon, i.e., on when and from which source a word entered the English language (see Hughes 2000: chapters 1, 8).

We can also link the three-fold stylistic division of the lexicon shown in Table 8.3 to the low, middle, and high (or grand) styles which are appropriate to certain speech situations and speaker roles. Note, for example, Shakespeare's King Lear dividing his kingdom and voicing his royal anger at his daughter's disobedience: befitting his status and the official state occasion, he uses the grand and formal style with many French- and Latin-based words, "Here I *disclaim* all my *paternal* care, *Propinquity* and *property* of blood" (I.i). In contrast, in the same scene, the Earl of Kent strategically switches into a lower (also more emotive) style with a concomitant higher level of Germanic words, e.g., "*What wouldest thou do, old man? Think'st thou that* duty *shall have dread to speak when* power *to* flattery *bows?*" The eighteenth century developed a keen sense of linguistic decorum (appropriateness to situation), increasingly preferring those parts of the lexicon that were more polysyllabic, precise or abstract, learned, and thus more genteel, to the detriment of everyday idioms with their often earthy, blunt character (McIntosh 1998). An exploitation of these differences has also been noted in the modern press, for example, with so-called quality and tabloid papers preferring the more formal vs. more informal lexical choices respectively (e.g., *confrontation, disagreement* vs. *clash, row*).

Historical (and Diachronic) Discourse Analysis: Focus on the Genre of Letters

If we investigate individual letters or letter exchanges, this constitutes a classical case of historical discourse analysis (or pragmaphilology), but if we are additionally interested in how the letter genre changes over time, the undertaking turns into diachronic discourse analysis. The long history of the letter genre, its wider range of authors than many other genres, and its stability, as well as interesting diversity and transformations, raise many questions and allow this genre to be approached in many different ways.

What then characterizes the letter genre? Following initially Görlach's (2001: 54) analysis, we can list the following features as characteristic of the text in question:

(a) written,
(b) prose,
(c) independent/free-standing,
(d) original,
(e) non-fictional, and
(f) non-technical.

Letter texts are heterogeneous, however, with regard to the following:

(g) degrees of conventionality,
(h) formality of language,
(i) fields and topics, and
(j) speech act/intention.

While Görlach characterizes the speech act of letters as 'inform[ative],' letters can in fact fulfil the whole possible functional range; e.g., they may instruct (directive), thank (expressive), or entertain the reader, and in general manage the social relationship between writer and addressee.

Adding to Görlach's features, we can mention the following:

(k) interactive,
(l) non-public or private,
(m) spontaneity, and
(n) (non)standardness of language.

The involvement of (at least) two people means that letters are typically inter-active, even though the individual letter, because of the geographical distance of the correspondents, is a monologue. Typical letters are non-public or private, although it must be born in mind that more than just the correspondents might share in the contents (especially in the past) and that some letters may have been written already with a view to or knowledge of later publication (e.g., the letters written to the editor/secretary of the scientific journal *Philosophical Transactions*). The spontaneity and (non-)standardness of language relate to the fact that letters are often used to approach more involved, oral historical styles (see above). A letter can be drawn up spontaneously and sent off in this form (as is often the case with modern email correspondence), but in the case of many historical letters, we have to factor in careful revision(s). The overall form of the letter, after all, positions its writer socially. There is also a link to feature (d) above: early letters are not always "autograph" (i.e., written by the sender him/herself) but may have been written by a secretary. This may imply not only revision but perhaps even non-original formulation resulting from cursory dictation or even just general instructions given to the secretary. The presence of non-standard features (feature (n)) has potential sociolinguistic relevance. Before the rise of a standard, letters, like any other text, would be written in the dialect of the writer; from Early Modern English onwards, letters – as a mostly non-public genre – could contain either standard or non-standard forms, depending on the sociolinguistic competence of the writer and/or on strategic stylistic choices (in contexts with relaxed social control). In this context, it is also noteworthy that letters can in principle (given literacy) be produced by everyone, in contrast to "public" manuscript and print texts, which exclude the majority of the population from production. Thus, we have letters from writers of both sexes, from all social ranks, including the lower/working classes, and also from people with little schooling – although not in all cases for all periods.

In sum, the letter genre, as most genres, is a prototype category (see Chapter 4): features need not apply always or may allow some relaxation. This gives us, for example, fictional letters, still clearly recognizable as letters, in epistolary novels (e.g., Richardson's *Pamela*, 1740), or letters whose interactiveness is reduced to virtually zero (e.g., the *Newdigate Newsletters*; see below).

Looking more closely at feature (i), field and topic, will show us the great range of possible letters and thus also subgenres. Letters may be strictly private, written between relatives, friends, good acquaintances, or lovers. These are open to all kinds of topics of interest to the respective correspondents, and provide room for a great range of speech acts and intentions. They may be based to a large extent on shared knowledge (also attitudes and emotions), and they are thus most likely to contain involvement, oral and even informal features (refer again to Table 8.2, dimensions A and B). In fact, the aspect of relationship management will often be foregrounded here. Letters also have functional roles in professional fields or domains, however, and thus there are official letters of various kinds, such as administrative, diplomatic, business, and news correspondence. The correspondents in these cases may know each other (well) of course, which may lead to mixed private–official content of the letters. But often the relationship of the correspondents here may be purely professional and distanced. There will then be greater emphasis on informative content, potentially a clear restriction to one function, and on the whole more informational, more elaborate, and abstract styles (again Table 8.2). Such letters may also play a significant role in language change: the government letters of the chancery and especially the signet office in the reign of Henry V have been given a role, though not an undisputed one, in early standardization. An interesting case is presented by letters containing socio-economic requests that are perhaps more common in the past, such as letters seeking patronage or charity (e.g., so-called "pauper letters"). These are typically directed to strangers, usually people of higher rank and/or in authority, and they contain face-threatening acts (see Chapter 10) for either addressee or writer. Such letters are therefore of even greater interest than others for discourse containing face work and politeness.

Before we proceed with a closer look at letters, a brief indication of possible sources for further study is in order. Many corpora contain letters, some of which are mentioned in Chapters 9 and 10. The *Corpus of Early English Correspondence* (CEEC), a whole family of corpora spanning the years 1402 to 1800, is the largest collection of historical letters, of which two (CEECS and PCEEC) are published. PCEEC contains almost 5,000 letters from 666 writers written between 1410 and 1681. The emphasis is on private letters, though not exclusively. The *Corpus of Scottish Correspondence* comprises 719 letters written between 1500 and 1715 by 225 writers, while the *Corpus of Irish English Correspondence* (CORIECOR) contains emigrants' letters from 1740 to 1940. Another particular type of letters is available in the *Newdigate Newsletters* (2,100 letters), namely newsletters sent thrice weekly from the Secretary of State's office to Sir Richard Newdigate from 1673 to 1692. Needless to say, there are also many book editions of historical letters, sometimes by whole families and often by persons of historical significance.

Let us have a look at four letters from different periods of the English language, which illustrate different types of letters and various sender–recipient constellations: religious instruction, abbot to layman (10); business, between brothers (11); official, king to subjects (12); private, father to daughter (13).

(10)   OE

ÆIfric abbod gret Sigefyrð freondlice. *Me* is gesæd, þæt *þu* sædest be *me*, þæt *ic* oðer tæhte on Engliscum gewritum, oðer eower ancor æt ham mid eow tæhð, forþan þe he swutelice sægð, þæt hit sy alyfed, þæt mæssepreostas wel moton wifian, and *mine* gewritu wiðcweðað þysum. Nu secge *ic þe*, leof man, þæt *me* is lað to tælenne agenne godes freond, gyf he godes riht drifð, ac *we* sceolon secgan and forswigian ne durron þa halgan lare, þe se hælend tæhte: Seo lare mæg eaðe *unc* emlice seman. *Ure* Hælend Crist cydde, þæt he lufode þa clænnysse on his þeowum swutelice, þa þa he mædenmann him to meder geceas. . .

    And swa byð æfre oð þissere worulde geendunge, þæt þa clænheortan on Cristes lufe þeonde beoð on halgum

'Abbot Ælfric kindly greets Sigefyrð. *I* am told that *you* said about *me* that *I* taught differently in English writing than your hermit at home, because he clearly says that it is permitted that priests be allowed to have wives, and *my* writing contradicts this. Now *I* am telling *you*, dear man, that *I* am loath to blame God's own friend, if he pursues God's right, but *we* should announce and dare not conceal the holy word that Christ taught: This teaching may easily reconcile *both of us* alike. *Our* Saviour Christ made clear that he loved the pureness of his servants, when he chose a virgin for his mother . . .

    And so be it always until this world's end that the pure of heart shall thrive in Christ's love by holy intercessions, until they

geþingðum, oð þæt hi becumon to come to Christ himself. He be
Criste sylfum. Þam sy a wuldor to always praised to the world.
worulde. Amen. (Ælfric, *Letter to* Amen.'
Sigefyrth; DOEWC)

(11)   ME

A° lxxvj   'Year 1476
   Welbelouyd brother,   Wellbeloved brother,
I recomaund *me* herttely to *yow*, *I* recommend *myself* heartily to
fferthermore informynge *yow* that *you*, furthermore informing *you*
the xiij day of Aprell the ʒeere   that on the 13th day of April
aboue sayd, *I* Robard Cely haue   the year said above, *I* Robert Cely
ressayuyd off Wylliam Eston,   have received from William
mersar of London, xij li. ster. to Eston, merchant of London
pay at Andewarpe in Sencyon   twelve pound sterling to pay at
martte the xxiiij day of June, for Antwerp at Whitsun Market the
euery nobyll of vj s. viij d. ster., 24th day of June for every noble
vij s x d. Fllemeche, and *I* pray [= English gold coin] with the
yow to delyuer to the sayd   value 6 s. [= shillings] 8 d.
Wylliam Eston xij li. starlynge at [= pence] sterling, 7 s. 10
the same ratte, takynge a byll of d. Flemish currency, and *I* ask *you*
ys honde to paye at London the   to deliver to the said William
sayd xij li. at a day as longe hafter Eston twelve pound sterling at the
þe day as *I* toke the mony wp   same rate, taking a bill from his
beffore.   hand to pay at London the said
   In wettnes herof *I* sette my seell twelve pounds at a day as long
at London the xiij day of Aprell. after the day as *I* took the money
    per Robard Cely.   with before. In witness hereof
    A George Cely.   *I* set my seal at London the
    (1476 Cely letters; CEEC) 13th day of April.
                                       Robert Cely.
                                       Addressed to George Cely.'

(12)   EModE

Henry R.

Trusty and welbiloved we grete *you* wele. Signifieng unto *you* it is
shewed unto *us* that albeit *our* welbiloved servant Edward Vaux,
oon of the purveyors of our wynes, hath been with *you* sundry
tymes in *our* name to cause provision to be made for cariage of *our*
wynes from that our Citie of London, for th'expenses of *our*
Household, into these parties: yet nevertheless *ye* have litle
regarded the said provision, as it is sayed, whereby *we* be destitute
of suche wynes as *we* wold have here: of the which *your* demeanur
herin *we* cannot a litle mervaile: wherfor *we* advertise *you* of the

same, willing and commaunding *you* that whansoever any *our* Surveyors either for Wynes or other stuf, from hensforth, shall reasorte unto *you* in *our* name for provision of cariage of the same hither or elliswhere where it shall fortune *us* to be, *ye* will effectually endevoir *yourself* for the qwyk expedicion therof, without any failing as *ye* entende to please *us*.

Yeven under our Signet at our Monasterie of Abendon the xjth. day of Aprill. (King Henry VIII to the citizens of London; HC)

(13)   ModE
4 Marlborough Place, July 19, 1879.
My dear Lucy,
I am just off to Gloucester to fetch M– back, and *I* shall have a long talk with that sage little woman over *your* letter.

In the meanwhile keep quiet and do nothing. *I* feel the force of what *you* say very strongly – so strongly, in fact, that *I* must morally ice *myself* and get *my* judgment clear and cool before *I* advise *you* what is to be done.

I am very sorry to hear *you* have been so ill. For the present dismiss the matter from *your* thoughts and give *your* mind to getting better. Leave it all to be turned over in the mind of that cold-blooded, worldly, cynical old fellow, who signs himself,
     Your affectionate Pater.
(Thomas Henry Huxley, http://gutenberg.net.au/ebooks/fr100108.txt)

What these letters all have in common is certain more or less conventional boundary signals (underlined) that characterize the (sub)genre. All four letters contain a salutation, either by way of a performative verb (*greet* in (10) and (12)) or by an endearment form (*wellbeloved*, *dear*); the salutation also refers to the addressee, either by name (*Sigefyrð, Lucy*), by a relationship term (*brother*), or a pronoun-cum-characterization (*you, trusty*). Titles (e.g., *Sir, Your Highness*) are another option, as are variations of the above such as name or kinship term only (*Lucy . . ., Sister . . .*), first name or surname etc. Letters without salutations are rare and not typical; some OE letters appear not to have them, but this may be due to their secondary transmission in manuscript collections (or the opening and closing may have been in Latin). The choice of salutation reveals much about the (aimed-at) relationship between correspondents, and calibration can take place over a longer exchange. Address forms can of course be repeated and varied throughout the letter, e.g., to emphasize the relationship bond (e.g., *leof man* 'dear man' in (10)). Similar effects can be achieved by calibrating the closing formula. We may find – in isolation or combination – names, first, last, or pet (*Robard Cely*), relationship terms (*Pater, friend*), pronoun (*your(s) . . .*), and various adjectives or adverbs (*affectionate*, also: *loving, obliged, truly, sincerely . . .*). It is noteworthy that of the two family letters here, the one dealing with business matters (11) simply has the signed name while the one dealing with an emotional private matter (13) uses a more elaborate form. In Ælfric's letter (10) we do not find a proper signing off (though again this might be an accident of transmission), but the word *Amen*; the transfer of this classical closer of prayers is perhaps not surprising for an abbot, and it may also be seen as a sign of authority. King Henry VIII's official letter (12) closes with a reference to the stamp of authority, so to speak (*under our signet*), as well as the time and place of writing – information that in other letters may also be given at the top, as in (11) and (13).

Another common aspect we can see in the four letters in spite of their different subject matters is their clear interactiveness, indicated by the high incidence of first- and second-pronoun forms (in italics above). The dialogic nature of much correspondence is especially clear in Ælfric's formulations: 'I was told that you said that I taught … now I tell you …' While this may sound somewhat confrontational, Ælfric also uses inclusive forms of *we* (dual *unc*; *ure*) to bond with the addressee. Interesting pronoun choices are found in the ME and EModE letters. Robert Cely uses *you* to address his brother, i.e., he chooses the more polite, distanced form instead of intimate *thou* (see Chapter 9), which may have been induced by the factual business content of the letter, which concerns a bill of exchange. In order to judge the implications of this usage one would need to look at the larger correspondence contexts of Robert and George Cely. We know from other letters that there is often variation between the two pronouns, even within the same letter. Henry VIII employs the royal *we* as a sign of majesty in this official letter, which he does not use in his private letters (e.g., to Anne Boleyn). The *pluralis majestatis* is essentially a ME development; thus we do not find it in King Alfred's letter to Wærferð (preface to *Pastoral Care*); he uses *ic* 'I' instead.

The salutation and closing formulae, the pronominal uses, as well as some other features (e.g., request realizations: *I pray yow* (11)/*commaunding you* (12), emotive uses: *I feel very strongly/I am very sorry* in (13)) have clear relevance to the assertion and management of social relations, face-work, and politeness (see Chapter 10). The way these aspects are realized may vary not only according to time, but also to subgenre of letter, and to characteristics of the writer (social class, education, gender, age). It may also be influenced by prescriptive works.

The fact that some aspects are very constant across letter(-like) forms may have to do with their "naturalness" (after all we also say *hello* and *good-bye* when we meet face-to-face) but also with some overt teaching and prescription of forms.[3] The medieval *ars dictaminis* ('art of prose composition/letter writing'), for example, which described and taught the conventions for official (i.e., usually Latin) letters, existed in the form of many treatises dealing with the structure, style, and socially appropriate forms used in letters. One standard method was to describe five typical parts and their realizations, namely (i) the Salutation, (ii) the Securing of Good Will, (iii) the narration or statement of facts, (iv) the petition or request, and (v) the conclusion, i.e., summation and complimentary closing (Sloane 2001). Parts (iii) and (iv) clearly make up the bulk of Henry VIII's letter above (12), for example. Similar schemes have been described for the English context by Richardson (1984) and Davis (1965); the influence of such models on

English-language letters can be at least partially attested. The print culture of early modern England produced many letter writing manuals and handbooks, including numerous model letters, that will also have exerted an influence. To mention just three examples, there are Angel Day's *The English Secretorie* (1586), Henry Care's *The Female Secretary* (1671), and the anonymous *The Complete Letter-Writer; Or, Polite English Secretary* (1778, 16th edn.). As in the *ars dictaminis*, the origin of letter writing in rhetoric is still clearly visible in Day's work (e.g., the three levels of style: *sublime, mediocre, humile*), whereas in later works the social aspect, i.e., the encoding of the relationship between correspondents, comes more to the fore.

Concluding Remarks

This chapter has scratched the surface of a wide area which is not (yet) established as an independent, clearly delimited field of research. In contrast to Historical Pragmatics or Historical Sociolinguistics one does not find books with titles like "English Historical Discourse Studies" or "English Diachronic Text Linguistics." Nevertheless, the last twenty years have witnessed unprecedented interest in the characteristics and the evolution of historical texts. This is at least partly due to modern digital possibilities. Corpus linguistic and computational methodology have enabled the study of large bodies of discourse and the unearthing of regularities across many texts (see Biber and Finegan's stylistic studies treated above). The potentials of "cheap" electronic facsimile copies and/or of adequate electronic encoding of visual text characteristics have in recent years again raised awareness of the significance of paralinguistic textual features. Thus, modern technology meets "old" philology to produce new questions and findings.

Suggestions for Further Study

Biber and Conrad's (2009) *Register, Genre, and Style* treats the relevant concepts for discourse studies in theoretical and methodological detail and includes also a historical chapter (chapter 6). The *Handbook of Historical Pragmatics*, edited by Jucker and Taavitsainen (2010), contains chapters on the discourse domains religion, science, news, courtroom, literature, and correspondence, as well as pragmaphilological chapters on Chaucer and Shakespeare. The first four volumes of the *Cambridge History of the English Language* (Hogg 1992–2001) each contain a chapter on literary language with relevant information on stylistic developments. Görlach's *Text Types and the History of English* (2004) is a collection of various individual studies, e.g., on dedications, recipes, the Scottish textual situation. Multilingualism and code-switching are treated in the contributions in Trotter (2000) and Schendl and Wright (2011). With regard to science, there is research on the medical field, treating its development from Middle English onwards (Taavitsainen and Pahta 2010; Taavitsainen et al.

2005), and on the changing discourse in the *Philosophical Transactions* from the late seventeenth to the twentieth century (Atkinson 1996, 1999). Hiltunen (1990) investigates legal writing from Old English onwards, while Archer (2005) focuses on EModE transcriptions of spoken legal interactions. Press language, including newspapers, pamphlets, online publications etc., is dealt with in Facchinetti et al. (2012), Studer (2008), and CHINED conference proceedings (e.g., Brownlees 2006; Jucker 2009). Advertising in newspapers was investigated by Gieszinger (2001). Letters have received extensive attention recently, e.g., Nurmi et al. (2009), Fitzmaurice (2002), Dossena and Del Lungo Camiciotti (2012). Peikola et al. (2009) focuses on the textual function of instruction in the history of English.

Exercises

1. Vernacularization in the sixteenth century
   Use the two reproductions of title pages of early print works below to connect their content to what has been said about multilingualism, foreign influences, and vernacularization in the textual history of English.

Example a:

✠ **The copie of**
a **Sermon pronounced by the**
Byshop of Salisburie at **Paules**
**Crosse the second Sondaye before E-
ster in the yere of our Lord.1560.wher-
upon B. Cole first sought occasion to
encounter, shortly set forthe as
nere as the authour could call it to
remembraunce, without any
alteration or addition.**

TERTVLLIANVS.
Præiudicatum est aduersus omnes
hæreses: id esse verum, quodcunque
primum : id esse adulterum quodcunque posterius.
¶**This is a preiudice against all here-
sies: that that thinge is true, what soe-
uer was first: that is corrupt, whatsoe-
uer came after.**

Concilium Nicinum.
Εθη ἀρχαῖα χρατείτω
Mores antiqui obtineant.

Example b:

A REGISTRE
Of Hystories, conteining
Martiall exploites of worthy war-
riours, Politique practises of Ciuil
Magistrates, wise Sentences of famous
Philosophers, And other matters
manifolde and me-
morable.

*Written in Greeke by Ælianus a Ro-
mane : and deliuered in Englishe
(as well, according to the truth of
the Greeke text, as of the La-
tine) by Abraham
Fleming.*

Seene and allowed.

*Speculum vitæ, memoriæq, The-
saurus, Hystoria.*

¶ Imprinted at London,
for Thomas Woodcocke: dwelling
in Paules Churchyarde, at the signe
of the blacke Beare.

Anno a Messia nato, 1576.

Note: The layout has been reproduced as far as possible, apart from the decorative border surrounding example b. The original pages can be accessed by searching in EEBO for the STC numbers 14612 and 164 respectively.

2. Information structure in parallel Bible passages

In the Bible we find the "same" text (content-wise) throughout the history of English in different "packaging," with regard to linguistic forms and information structure.

Compare the three parallel sentences from Luke 2 (verses 8, 11, and 13) given below, taken from four historical Bibles ranging from Old English to Present-day English:

Parallel verses 8, 11, and 13:

Wessex Gospels (OE) (<u>subject</u> / <u><u>object</u></u>)	Wycliffe Bible (late 14th century, ME)	King James Bible (1611 EModE)	Message Bible (1993–2002, PDE)
8 and <u>hyrdas</u> wæron on þam ylcan rice waciende: and nihtwæccan healdende ofer heora heorda ('and <u>shepherds</u> were on this same country awake and nightwatch holding over their flock')	& shepherdis weren in þe same kuntre wakende & kepende þe wacchis of þe niȝt on her floc	And there were in the same countrey shepheards abiding in the field, keeping watch ouer their flocke by night.	*There were sheepherders camping in the neighborhood. They had set night watches over their sheep.*
11 forþam todæg <u><u>eow</u></u> ys hælend acenned. <u>se</u> is drihten crist on dauides ceastre; ('because today <u><u>to us</u></u> is <u>Savior</u> born. <u>who</u> is Lord Christ in David's city')	for a saueour is born to day to vs, þat is crist a lord in þe cite of dauid	For vnto you is borne this day, in the citie of Dauid, a Sauiour, which is Christ the Lord.	*A Savior has just been born in David's town, a Savior who is Messiah and Master.*
13 And þa wæs færinga geworden mid þam engle mycelnes heofonlices werydes god heriendra. and þus cweþendra; ('And then was suddenly with the angel a multitude of the heavenly host God praising and thus saying')	& sodeinli þer is mad wiþ þe aungil, a multitude of heueneli kniȝþed, heriende god & seyinge-	And suddenly there was with the Angel a multitude of the heauenly hoste praising God, and saying,	*At once the angel was joined by a huge angelic choir singing God's praises:*

In order to supply a fuller context for the parallel sentences, Luke 2 (7–13) is given in Present-day English (*Message Bible*):

(7) She gave birth to a son, her firstborn. She wrapped him in a blanket and laid him in a manger, because there was no room in the hostel.

(8) There were sheepherders camping in the neighborhood. They had set night watches over their sheep.

(9) Suddenly, God's angel stood among them and God's glory blazed around them. They were terrified.

(10) The Angel said: "Don't be afraid. I'm here to announce a great and joyful event that is meant for everybody, worldwide:

(11) A Savior has just been born in David's town, a Savior who is Messiah and Master.

(12) This is what you're to look for: a baby wrapped in a blanket and lying in a manger."

(13) At once the angel was joined by a huge angelic choir singing God's praises:

Looking at the parallel verses 8, 11, and 13, answer the following questions:
a. Where is the new and/or the focused information found?
b. Which (different) syntactic structures do the versions use to achieve their ordering?

In order to show you how to perform this analysis, I provide here an analysis of verses 7 and 9 in the Present-day English version above:

> 7: *Son/firstborn* and *no room in the hostel* are new/focused information. They are mentioned for the first time, as you will notice when you check the preceding context. *Son* is the object in an SVO clause and comes in final position, the normal position for new information. *No room* is complement in an existential *there*-clause, which is necessary here to put the entire new information in final position (compare: "the hostel had no room left," which puts part of the new information (hostel) in subject position).
>
> 9: Here, everything except for *them* (2x) and *they* is new information. The new information is put into subject position in the first sentence (*God's angel, God's glory*), which goes against information structure needs but is grammatically the best option, given SV order. *Suddenly* in initial position is focused information (compare: God's angel suddenly stood . . .).

3. Informational vs. interactive style

   Robert Hooke, an early empirical scientist, produced the text *An Attempt to Prove the Motion of the Earth from Observations* in 1674, from which the following passage is taken. Use the information in Table 8.2 and Table 8.3 above to place this text in the stylistic continuum. With regard to Table 8.2 you may want to concentrate on the following features:

   – the number of nouns in contrast to number of pronouns (Dimension A),
   – nominalizations (e.g., *appearance* from *appear*) (B),
   – prepositions (A),
   – *that*-deletion (A),
   – both types of passives (C),

- adverbial subordinators (e.g., *if*) (C),
- amplifiers (e.g., *very*) (A),
- hedges (e.g., *somewhat*) (A),
- contractions (A),
- final vs. pied-piped prepositions (e.g., *X on whom he depended* vs *X who he depended on*) (A, B).

I began therefore first to examine into the matter as it had already been performed by those who had asserted no sensible Parallax of the annual Orb of the Earth, and quickly found that (whatever they asserted) they could never determine whether there were any or no Parallax of this annual Orb; especially if it were less then a minute, which *Kepler* and *Riccioli* hypothetically affirm it to be: The former making it about twenty four Seconds, and the latter about ten. For though *Ticho*, a man of unquestionable truth in his assertions, affirms it possible to observe with large Instruments, conveniently mounted and furnished with sights contrived by himself (and now the common ones for Astronomical Instruments) to the accurateness of ten Seconds; and though *Riccioli* and his ingenious and accurate Companion *Grimaldi* affirm it possible to make observations by their way, with the naked eye to the accurateness of five Seconds; Yet *Kepler* did affirm, and that justly, that 'twas impossible to be sure to a less Angle then 12 Seconds: And I from my own experience do find it exceeding difficult by any of the common sights yet used to be sure to a minute. I quickly concluded therefore that all their endeavours must have hitherto been ineffectual to this purpose, and that they had not been less imposed on themselves, then they had deceived others by their mistaken observations. And this mistake I found proceeded from divers inconveniencies their wayes of observations were lyable to. As first from the shrinking and stretching of the materials wherewith their Instruments were made, I conceive a much greater angle then that of a minute may be mistaken in taking an altitude of fifty Degrees. For if the Instruments be made of Wood, 'tis manifest that moyst weather will make the frame stretch, and dry weather will make it shrink a much greater quantity then to vary a minute: and if it be Metal, unless it be provided for in the fabrick of the Instrument accordingly, the heat of Summer, when the Summer observations are to be made, will make the Quadrant swell, and the cold of Winter will make it shrink much more then to vary a minute: Both which inconveniencies ought to be removed. (LC, SciA1674)

4. Features of Jane Austen's letters

   Go to the website with a collection of Jane Austen's letters (http://etext.lib .virginia.edu/toc/modeng/public/AusLett.html).

In order to sample different types of letters I suggest you use the following: letter 67, letter 99 (to her sister Cassandra), letter 126 (to James Stanier Clarke, the Prince Regent's librarian), and letter 1817 (to her nephew Edward).

a. Apply Görlach's features (a) to (n) to letter examples as far as possible. Try to back up your conclusions with features of the text or with reasoned hypotheses about the situational/interpersonal context.

b. Which textual and linguistic letter conventions do you find realized in the letters? Are there any features that may point to some degree of orality/colloquialness?

Notes

I would like to thank Peter Grund for his helpful comments on an earlier version of this chapter.
1. For a full discussion of *thou* and *you* in English, see Chapter 9.
2. For a discussion of English corpora in general, see Chapter 5. Genre-specific corpora are treated in Chapter 10.
3. See Chapter 11 for general prescriptive tendencies.

9

Sociohistorical Approaches

PETER J. GRUND

Introduction

In a witness testimony from 1714, Ralph Coleman, a London butcher, relates the following dialogue that he overheard between the Reverend Robert Barry and Sarah Twycrosse (the here unnamed "Woman"), a hostel keeper.

> ... S˜ ['Sir'] I want
> to speake with you, to w^ch ['which'] the s^d ['said'] Robert Barry
> replyed, **Madam**, I have nothing to say to you
> wherto shee replyed, S^r I have something to say to
> you, & shall speake it in publick to wch the said
> Robert Barry replyed, Yes and Welcome & thereupon
> the said ∧{Woman} answeared him, Why then S^r I will. The
> Woman that I saw in bed with you is now with
> Child (ETED: London 1714–1715: F_4LD_London_003)[1]

We will leave aside whether Coleman accurately repeated what was originally said – we will have a closer look at the issue of textual reliability later. What is particularly interesting for us in this exchange is the way Twycrosse and Barry address each other. Twycrosse uses *sir* three times, and Barry responds once with *madam*. We can assume from modern conventions of address that this usage carried important social implications. After all, in modern contexts, the choice of address term (*sir, ma'am, professor, Mr., Ms., Mrs., Ralph, Sarah, idiot*, etc.) sends social signals about how we relate to (or perceive our relation to) the people we address: whether we see them as socially more or less powerful than ourselves, as socially close, etc. The selection may also reflect the particular situation we find ourselves in: whether formal or informal, or perhaps whether we feel happy or displeased with a person at a particular point. In the case of the early eighteenth-century exchange above, despite making quite a grave accusation against the clergyman, Twycrosse seems to politely acknowledge the social distance between them by using *sir*, a term normally used for a man of higher rank at the time. On the other hand, she may be emphasizing the distance between

218

them (considering the behavior she is accusing him of). The repeated, insistent use of *sir* may even carry a hint of irony: you may be a *sir*, but your behavior certainly does not reflect that status (intonation patterns, which we unfortunately do not have access to, would have been helpful here). Barry similarly uses the polite form *madam*, perhaps unaware of Twycrosse's social status or to (icily) distance himself. His use may also carry additional meanings, as *madam* could be used to signify a prostitute in the period (*OED*: s.v. *madam* n. 4b), which makes the politeness a bit more ambiguous or, indeed, no politeness at all.

Irrespective of the exact dynamics involved, what is important for us is the general picture that emerges: that interpersonal relationships and other aspects of individuals' situations are significant for language use, historically as well as present day. In other words, language is socially embedded, which means that various extralinguistic, social, and situational factors play a role in speakers' (conscious or subconscious) decisions about how to use language. It is this connection between society (broadly speaking) and language in past periods that sociohistorical approaches to the English language attempt to illustrate. This chapter describes some of the main ideas behind such approaches, the source material that researchers use, and the methodological challenges that they face (including disentangling the social implications of exchanges such as the one between Barry and Twycrosse above). The chapter ends with an in-depth look at two case studies. These studies highlight the powerful insights into the history of English that can come from approaching the language from a sociohistorical perspective. They also indicate the types of methodological decisions made by researchers in the field and the multidisciplinary nature of this kind of research.

Definitions and Concepts

Sociohistorical approaches to the English language are usually collected under the term "English historical sociolinguistics" (or less commonly "English socio-historical linguistics"). However, different scholars define and delimit this field in different ways, and there are several strands of research. Bergs (2005) and Nevalainen and Raumolin-Brunberg (2012) represent two partially overlapping, but also distinct ideas about the field. Both models stress its interdisciplinary nature. In Bergs's model, the field draws on, integrates, and elaborates on insights, theories, and methods primarily from history, the social sciences, and linguistics. Nevalainen and Raumolin-Brunberg's (2012) proposal is similar, but points to influences from a more fine-grained set of disciplines (including, among other areas, social history, corpus linguistics, and historical linguistics). One of the major differences between the models lies in how the authors view the relationship between modern sociolinguistics and historical sociolinguistics. Nevalainen and Raumolin-Brunberg see historical sociolinguistics as closely related to modern sociolinguistics, while Bergs (2005: 12, 21) suggests that historical sociolinguistics has and should have its own agenda, goals, and methods, which only partially overlap with modern sociolinguistics. The kind of data considered and the integration of insights from historical research are two aspects that set the disciplines apart.

Irrespective of how we understand the exact relationship between the two, historical sociolinguistics faces challenges that modern sociolinguistics does not. These challenges obviously arise out of the separation in time between us as researchers and the historical object of study. This is not only a question of finding relevant data sources, but also of understanding the conditions, structures, and values of past societies. On a very general level, English historical sociolinguistics relies on the "uniformitarian principle," as described here by Suzanne Romaine:

> ... we accept that the linguistic forces which operate today and are observable around us are not unlike those which have operated in the past. Sociolinguistically speaking, this means that there is no reason for claiming that language did not vary in the same patterned ways in the past as it has been observed to do today.   (1982: 122–123)

This principle provides a useful general grounding that sociohistorical approaches can build on: it suggests that we can look to results from modern sociolinguistic research for issues that may be of interest to explore historically. At the same time, we also know that there are significant differences between social structures and values in present-day and past societies. We can reasonably assume on the basis of the uniformitarian principle that, for example, social class/rank/status will play a role in linguistic choices and variation. But we cannot also simply assume that the social hierarchy will play exactly the same role in exactly the same way in modern and historical contexts. Instead, sociohistorical studies must carefully reconstruct the conditions of the particular historical context studied. To do so, we are very much dependent on input from historical research – economic, social, legal, political; historical sociolinguistics is by necessity a deeply interdisciplinary enterprise. This of course does not imply that the relationship between research in history and in historical sociolinguistics is a one-way street; rather, linguistic evidence can help point to aspects of past societies that are not revealed by other sources; moreover, some social categories are of course (co-)constructed through language, including class/rank/status and gender.

Most of the work in English historical sociolinguistics falls under what is usually described as "microsociolinguistics." This research strand focuses on charting the variation and change in language among and across communities and individual speakers, and takes into consideration the effect of a range of social factors (among others, gender, age, community and network ties, and class/rank/status). "Macrosociolinguistics" (or sometimes "sociology of language"), on the other hand, is concerned with larger societal patterns of language, including standardization processes and bilingualism or multilingualism (see Chapters 12 and 13). Such macrosociolinguistic perspectives are often part of descriptions of the history of English that trace the intersection between broader social patterns and linguistic usage (such as the status of French, Latin, and English during the Middle English period). Naturally, the two perspectives are often in close conversation and build upon each other.

Diachronic Approaches

Much of the work in English historical sociolinguistics is diachronic. It concentrates on the connection between various social factors and change over time; synchronic approaches, by contrast, focus on the social dynamics of language use at one point in time, as we will see later. In diachronic studies, scholars are often (implicitly or explicitly) guided by concepts from modern sociolinguistics. Explorations of social class/rank/status often appeal to the notions of "change from above" and "change from below." These notions can be understood in two different, yet overlapping senses: in terms of social hierarchy and in terms of awareness of the change. When a linguistic feature that is used or associated with the language of a higher class is adopted into the language of a lower class or becomes widespread in the language more generally, such a change would represent a change from above in the sense of the social hierarchy. The opposite would be a change from below. From the perspective of awareness, a change from below is subconscious (below the level of awareness), which means that language users are not overtly conscious of the change as it happens. When language users are instead aware of the change taking place, which is often connected with explicit commentary about the feature in the speech community, the change is said to be from above (the level of consciousness). Researchers have appealed to these two notions (in both senses) in explaining changes in English. Busse (2002: 284), for example, argues that Shakespeare very consciously transitioned from the use of *thou* forms to *you* forms in his comedies, a change from above (the level of awareness). Romaine (1982: 213), on the other hand, suggests that the introduction of the *wh*-words (*who, whom, whose*) as relative markers was accomplished in Middle English by a change from above (in the social hierarchy sense), influenced by French and Latin. Denison (2007) discusses a number of possible examples of changes from below (in both senses) in Late Modern English (e.g., the adoption of the passive form of the progressive, as in *The book **was being read***).

Most studies in English historical sociolinguistics interested in language development over time look at changes in "real time." This simply means that suitable and comparable texts from different periods are used to chart the development of a certain feature or the changing characteristics of two or more variants over time. However, "apparent-time" approaches can also be used: such approaches rely on collecting data from people of different ages at one point in time. The assumption here is that, for example, a 20-year-old, a 40-year-old, and a 60-year-old establish their linguistic repertoires at different points in time. A systematic difference between the three in the use of a given linguistic feature may point to a change that has taken place between the periods in which the three informants formed their linguistic habits. Although apparent-time approaches have been used in historical studies, they are not common outside studies of change in the late twentieth century and later. Until the LModE period, it is usually very difficult to identify appropriate material that allows us to study people of different ages where other parameters are equal (letters being a possible exception; see Nevalainen and Raumolin-Brunberg 2003). One might also raise objections about an underlying assumption made by apparent-time approaches, namely that people's linguistic behavior does not change significantly during their lifetime. This is where historical research can provide significant input to modern studies, as work on the history of English presents a great deal of counterevidence for this notion. Although a somewhat special case, Queen Elizabeth I changed a number of features of her language across her lifetime (Evans 2013). Elizabeth Montagu (1718–1800), author and leader of the Bluestocking literary circle, increased her use of contracted modals (such as *couldn't*) substantially in her letters over time (Sairio 2010).

Synchronic Approaches

While a great deal of sociohistorical work on the history of English is diachronic, there is starting to be a substantial body of research that is exclusively synchronic. Synchronic studies focus on the social embedding of language usage (especially linguistic variation) at a particular point in the history of English. Such research may be driven by questions of how very specific, situational concerns govern users' linguistic choices or how users deploy features very consciously to project certain social roles, signal authority, or indicate various attitudes. Such an approach is found in Grund's (2012) consideration of the employment of evidential markers (i.e., markers of source of information, such as *see, to my best understanding, believe*) during the witch trials in Salem, MA, in 1692–1693. The witnesses and recorders of their testimonies appear to use such markers, for example, to emphasize the witnesses' reliability and their central role during the proceedings. Sociohistorical work of this stripe has obvious overlaps with pragmatics (see Chapter 10), and it has even been suggested that cross-over approaches constitute their own distinct field: "historical sociopragmatics" (Culpeper 2011). A different strand of synchronic sociohistorical work is less concerned with the mechanisms of language and more interested in what insights linguistic usage can give into sociohistorical contexts and past communities (see the term "macrosociolinguistics" above). Townend (2000), for example, reviews a range of place-name evidence that points to the existence of "a bilingual society, and [to] the co-existence of speakers of Old English and Old Norse in the late Anglo-Saxon period" (2000: 99).

Source Material and "Bad Data"

One of the biggest challenges for sociohistorical approaches to the English language is accessing appropriate source material and finding sufficient contextual information to properly evaluate and interpret the data the sources yield – concerns that are shared especially by historical discourse analysis and historical pragmatics (see Chapters 8 and 10). Labov (1994:11) has famously referred to the data available as "bad data." He points to several problems with the textual evidence for language use in historical periods: the survival of texts is rather haphazard; we lack access to native speakers who can inform us about the social evaluation of linguistic forms at the time; and we have incomplete knowledge about the social structure of past communities. These problems cannot be denied: for a large part of the history of English, we lack access to materials produced by any language users other than a male, literate elite, and we often do not have a balanced body of texts that represents all relevant regions and social and situational contexts (see next section). However, researchers who approach language from a sociohistorical perspective have found ways of working around these problems or at least mitigating their impact.

Modern sociolinguistic research relies mostly on spoken rather than written data, drawn from interviews, questionnaires, corpora containing transcribed speech, and similar sources. For most of the history of the English language, such sources are obviously not available. Many researchers have therefore turned to informal, speech-based, or speech-related sources. The underlying assumption is that changes first occur in spoken language and only later take place in more formal, written contexts. Sources that have attracted special attention in this regard are (among others) letters, diaries, trial transcripts and witness testimonies, sermons, dialogues in fiction, and drama.[2] In addition to printed resources, a range of searchable linguistic databases and corpora is now available to access such materials, including (among others) those listed below.[3] These sources are carefully compiled to enable researchers to consider a broad range of sociolinguistic questions. CEECS and PCEEC, for example, contain a large number of letters by women from early periods of English.

- CED = *A Corpus of English Dialogues 1560–1760*
- CEECS and PCEEC = *Corpus of Early English Correspondence Sampler* (1418–1680); *Parsed Corpus of Early English Correspondence* (1410–1681)
- ETED = *An Electronic Text Edition of Depositions, 1560–1760*
- OBC = *The Old Bailey Corpus* (1720–1913) (see Exercise 3)

Each of the genres mentioned earlier comes with its own set of challenges, and those challenges must be carefully considered in light of the research questions that a study attempts to address. For example, using dialogues in fiction and drama for a study of women's and men's language will involve evaluating to what extent the author or dramatist has shaped the language in the texts for literary purposes. Along these lines, in their study of the functions of the verb *pray* in Early Modern English drama, Lutzky and Demmen (2013: 281) remind us that, when we view their gender-based results, "we cannot discount the possibility that this is a male-oriented, stereotypical perception or representation of the way people of both genders would have used *pray* forms." Research based on trial transcripts or witness testimonies, in contrast, has to consider the influence of the scribe who recorded the statements. Grund (2007), for instance, has shown that different versions of transcripts from the same pretrial hearings during the witch trials in Salem in 1692–1693 reflect the alleged spoken language differently (including variation in the recording of discourse markers such as *well*, *why*, and *oh*). Since the versions were written down by different recorders, the approaches of these recorders clearly impact the linguistic evidence we find in the transcripts.

Some researchers have questioned the emphasis on speech-related and speech-based texts. Bergs (2005: 14–20) proposes that historical sociolin-guists should not necessarily focus on recovering the "vernacular," that is, the most relaxed or unmonitored style of language. Bergs (2005: 18) instead argues that "there seems to be no objective reason why the study of the vernacular itself should be more rewarding than the study of any other defined or definable regular variety of language." In the case of some sociohistorical approaches, the alleged "spokenness" plays no role. Kopaczyk (2014), for example, draws on highly formal legal and administrative texts in Middle Scots (1380–1560) in order to chart linguistic conventions within a "community of practice" (see next section) consisting of clerks and notaries. She shows that the institutional context and audience expectations guided the scribes' careful linguistic crafting of documents.

We find a different kind of data source in the many comments and remarks on language presented in contemporaneous dictionaries, grammars, usage manuals, or other texts from a given period (see Chapter 11). Unfortunately, these comments do not become plentiful until after 1500, and it is far from always clear how to interpret the information that they provide. This can be illustrated by an observation made by the Fourth Earl of Chesterfield, Philip Dormer Stanhope, in an essay in the periodical *The World*, on December 5, 1754:

> Not contented with enriching our language by words absolutely new, my fair countrywomen have gone still farther, and improved it by the application and extension of old ones to various and very different significations. They take a word and change it, like a guinea into shillings for pocket money, to be employed in the several occasional purposes of the day. For instance, the adjective *vast* and its adverb *vastly* mean any thing, and are the fashionable words of the most fashionable people. A fine woman, under this head

> I comprehend all fine gentlemen too, not knowing in truth where else to place them properly, is *vastly* obliged, or *vastly* offended, *vastly* glad, or *vastly* sorry. Large objects are *vastly* great, small ones are *vastly* little; and I had lately the pleasure to hear a fine woman pronounce, by a happy metonymy, a very small gold snuff-box that was produced in company to be *vastly* pretty, because it was *vastly* little.   (Maty 1777: 171–172)

Chesterfield obviously sees certain innovations in language as connected to gender, attributing them to "my fair countrywomen" (although he also appears to ascribe the use of *vastly* to "fashionable people" in general). His larger point in the essay is to argue for the existence of a "genteel" language, "which owes both its rise and progress to my fair countrywomen, whose natural turn is more to the copiousness, than to the correctness of diction" (Maty 1777: 169). This comment illustrates the potentially very valuable sociolinguistic information we can obtain from this kind of source. The difficulty in interpreting Chesterfield's remarks lies in knowing whether his perception is indeed accurate, or whether he overgeneralizes from experience of the language of just one or a few women. Perhaps social or gender bias plays into his remarks? As modern sociolinguistics has shown, perception can sometimes differ significantly from actual usage (see, e.g., Coates 2004). Ideally, this kind of information should be put in a larger context and evaluated against the background of the time period and social and biographical details about the writer; data from primary and other secondary sources will also help establish (as far as possible) the reliability of statements such as Chesterfield's. A good illustration of such an approach is found in Tieken-Boon van Ostade (1994). She shows that Sir Horace Walpole's attribution of non-standard pronominal usage (such as *between you and I*) to women in particular in the eighteenth century appears to be incorrect. Her empirical study of letters by both men and women indicates that the usage is no more common in women's letters than in men's; in fact, it is rare in both.

Social Factors

Sociohistorical studies have shown that, not surprisingly, language was socially embedded historically; that is, a number of social factors play a significant role in linguistic usage at various points in the history of English. However, as we saw earlier, we are limited in our ability to investigate the possible impact of certain social factors: source materials that would enable their study are simply not accessible. In this respect, the different periods of English are not equals. In OE, the textual evidence is rather sparse, and the opportunities for sociohistorical approaches are therefore limited and complicated by the relatively narrow range of genres preserved. We do not have the sources to discover possible gender-based or class-based variation. At the same time, studies of regional variation and language contact phenomena have been crucial for our understanding of the connections between language and society in the period (see Chapters 12 and 13). The situation changes slowly during the ME period, where we see more textual evidence, more diversity of text categories, and more overt commentary on the social significance of (especially regional) variation (see Chapter 12). But we are still limited in other respects, such as access to data from certain social strata and from women, and in our ability to find evidence for the social significance of features across specific communities and the dissemination of a particular change. Once we enter the EModE period and certainly by the LModE period and later, we are better situated to carry out more systematic sociolinguistic work – diachronic as well as synchronic. We have access to a broad range of factors, and we are better able to reconstruct the social contexts of the texts, writers, and audiences. But even in these periods there is scarce access to systematic data from people on the very lowest steps of the social scale. These periods also see growing concerns about standardization, and we find frequent negative evaluation of (social) variation in a variety of sources (see Case Study: *h*-dropping). Indeed, understanding the development of the standard is key for our understanding of the dynamics of much social variation from the EModE period onwards (see Chapter 11).

It is important to remember in this context that the history of the English language becomes much more complex after the EModE period. Colonialization in the seventeenth, eighteenth, nineteenth, and early twentieth centuries has left a diverse linguistic landscape of Englishes. We are beginning to patch together an understanding of how social factors are connected with language usage in the history of English in the British Isles and Ireland, in North America, and in other geographical areas such as Australia and New Zealand, although much research remains to be done. However, for other varieties – Singaporean English, Hong Kong English, Philippine English (among others) – systematic research has just begun (see Noël et al. 2014). We will no doubt see great strides in linguistic research into these varieties over the coming years, not least from a sociohistorical perspective. As Schneider (2003) suggests in his outline of the "Dynamic Model" of the origins and development of World Englishes, social forces were crucial in the formation and establishment of new varieties of English (see Chapter 13).

The social factors that have been considered in historical work on the social embedding of language include those related to individual language users (e.g., gender, age, class/rank/status), those related to communities (e.g., social networks, discourse communities, communities of practice), and those that pertain to specific social contexts and situations; often several of these factors are combined. Not all factors can be reviewed in detail here, but we will have a closer look at a few. Among language user factors, "social class/rank/status" and gender have received the most attention. As the somewhat unwieldy label *class/rank/status* indicates, the categories and conceptualizations of general groupings in society have changed considerably over the course of the history of English. The modern notion of social class is not appropriate for most

Table 9.1 *Models of social stratification (adapted from Nevalainen and Raumolin-Brunberg 2003: 136)*

Models 1/2	Model 3	Model 4	
Royalty	Upper ranks	"Better sort"	higher
Nobility			
Gentry (upper and lower)			
Clergy (upper and lower)			
Social aspirers	Social aspirers		
Professional	Middle ranks	"Middling sort"	
Merchants			
Other non-gentry	Lower ranks	"Poorest sort"	lower

historical periods (and, indeed, the modern concept is not uncomplicated, as modern sociolinguists have shown, and not equally applicable to all English-speaking societies). Studying social class/rank/status therefore involves careful historical reconstruction based on historical research and contemporaneous description. The complexities involved in such reconstruction are illustrated by Nevalainen and Raumolin-Brunberg's (2003: 136) modeling of the social hierarchy reflected by their letter writers in a *Corpus of Early English Correspondence* (CEEC). Their reconstruction, based on work by social and economic historians as well as observations made in the EModE period, shows that multiple models can account for the same social reality (see Table 9.1). Each model has its strengths but also presents drawbacks. For example, a detailed hierarchy such as Model 1/2 may make it difficult to provide generalizations about the results since few data may be available for each category. A model that provides larger groupings (such as Models 3 and 4), on the other hand, may have the drawback of making more fine-grained patterns less clear.

Gender would seem to be a more straightforward category than class/rank/status, but it requires similar historical reconstruction. Like modern sociolinguists, sociohistorical researchers prefer to think of socially constructed gender rather than biological sex. Modern sociolinguistic research on gender has also emphasized the dynamic nature and performative aspects of gender. Gender is not something we have or are, but something that we "do" or perform in various contexts (see, e.g., Coates 2004: 138–139). In order to understand the linguistic significance of gender differences in a particular historical period, we therefore need to ask several questions: How were men and women viewed? What kinds of social expectations were put on men and women? What are men's and women's social standing in the period? Do particular historical contexts require a particular "performance" of gender? As is commonplace in modern sociolinguistics, most historical research is based on dividing informants into sex-based categories, at least as a starting point, but the results are understood in social terms; as Smitterberg (2005: 79) puts it, "'sex' [is] used as a classificatory and 'gender' as an interpretative variable."

Smitterberg (2005) shows that the use of the progressive form (e.g., *they are playing*) patterns differently for men and women in letters throughout the nineteenth century: women use more progressive forms than do men. The gender of the addressee of the letter also seems to play a role, especially for men, who use the progressive much less to other men than to women. Smitterberg argues that the progressive was mostly not a target of prescriptive comment and that its increased frequency was a change from below (the level of awareness). He therefore suggests that the more frequent use of the progressive by women may conform to Labov's (2001: 292, 293) principles that "in linguistic change from below, women use higher frequencies of innovative forms than men do" and that they "conform more closely than men to sociolinguistic norms that are overtly prescribed."

Different kinds of community construction have also been shown to be important in this context. Who you know and who you interact with was as important historically as it has been shown to be today. Modern "social network analysis" (L. Milroy 1987) has helped us recognize specific cases of how ties among individuals in historical periods allow a particular change to happen or how language usage is conserved. Social network analysis relies on the researcher being able to outline the relationships among language users in a network in some detail: whether the network is closed owing to strong (or multiplex) connections among the members, or whether the network is more open, allowing more influences from the outside. So, here again, careful socio-historical reconstruction is necessary. Letters have proved particularly useful for this approach, but it has also been applied to a variety of other types of sources (see Tieken-Boon van Ostade 2000b).

The reconstruction of a "community of practice" requires similar attention to details of social and interpersonal relationships, but also to the community members' actions and shared goals. A community of practice is characterized by the members' joint enterprise, mutual engagement, and a shared repertoire (of behaviors, actions, language, etc.); it may be a sports team, a company, or an academic department (Wenger 1998). The concept has been significant for modern sociolinguistic work over the past couple of decades (most notably in work by Penelope Eckert; see, e.g., Eckert 2000). Studies have suggested complex ways in which members use various linguistic resources (as well as other actions and behaviors) to signal their position and membership in the community. So far, few historical studies have explored this concept, again probably because of problems in reconstructing such communities and iden-tifying the linguistic resources that members employ to shape their commu-nity identities. But recent work has started to show various ways that the idea of the community of practice can be useful. It can help explain distinct linguistic patterns in texts produced in such different social contexts as ecclesiastical communities in Anglo-Saxon England or particular printing houses in the Early Modern English period (see Fitzmaurice 2010; Kopazcyk and Jucker 2014).

Language users also make linguistic choices depending on the type of social context they find themselves in, their communicative goals in that context, the persona they wish to project, audience expectations, and related factors. For example, the context of delivering a sermon may trigger usage that an everyday conversation would not, and vice versa (see Chapter 8). In historical periods, our access to such sociosituational (or sociopragmatic) usage is obviously limited to written texts produced in or reflective of such situations. Grund's (2012) study of evidentials in testimonies from the Salem witch trials, for example, reveals patterns of this kind. The linguistic choices made by the witnesses (or the recorders of their testimonies) reflect the particular trial setting that they found themselves in and the role the witnesses wished to play in the trial proceedings. From this perspective, at least some of the variation we find among genres in historical periods may, broadly speaking, be seen as reflecting language users' concern to respond to or align with expectations or norms in a particular socio-cultural setting. It is not always easy, of course, to reconstruct the nature of such norms, their origin, or their exact impact on the usage. The straightforward syntax of medieval (and later) recipes based on imperative verb forms and simple noun phrases (*take lard, boil for half an hour, mix with flour*) is presumably connected with the need for clear, sequential instruction as the food is being prepared. The use of a non-standard form in a private diary, on the other hand, may point to the writer's awareness that the diary is not written for an audience who might criticize the usage. Contemporaneous commentary and writing guides (such as letter manuals), as well as the genre patterns themselves, may help reveal the conventions and constraints.

Tieken-Boon van Ostade (2000c) discusses the problem of obtaining usage that reflects speakers' least monitored language in historical sociolinguistics. She suggests that many letters in the eighteenth century do not reflect "vernacular" language, in the sense of the speakers' least self-conscious usage. Letter writers were aware that a letter would often be read aloud to a broader audience than just the recipient. They would also be highly conscious of "a set of well-defined rules [for letter writing] to give [the language] a seemingly spontaneous, but at the same time polished form" (2000c: 455). Many writers of diaries or journals, on the other hand, were less self-conscious as they did not expect their work to be read by others. These diaries and journals are therefore often a better source for vernacular usage. In other words, writers' awareness of social conventions and audience expectations had a direct impact on language usage in the two genres.

Case Studies

Pronominal Usage: *Thou* and *You*

> Imedyately Rochester spake and sayde / god[es] ['God's']
> blud **you** vyle vylayne are **you** devowreng of a mayde
> in her mayster his gardeine and yf I wer by **the** ['thee'] I wolde
> thurste ['thrust'] my daggarde ['dagger'] in **the**.
>   (ETED: Norwich 1560–1566: F_1EC_NorwichA_023)

This extract from a witness testimony from Norwich, England, in 1563 reports on "Rochester's" discovery of two people having illicit sex and his indignant outburst. The extract illustrates perhaps one of the most intriguing and well-researched areas of the history of the English language: the alternation between the second-person pronouns *thou* and *you* (in bold in the extract). In our case, Rochester begins by addressing the "vyle vylayne" (here unnamed) with *you* but switches in the middle to *thou* (*thee*). Why would that be? We will return to that question below as we review three studies of this usage.

There are many interesting aspects of the story of *thou* and *you*:

- the complex interplay of social and situational factors that influenced the choice between the two pronouns;
- the drastic changes that the use of *thou* and *you* underwent from Old English to Early Modern English;
- the factors that ultimately led to the (virtual) disappearance of the pronoun *thou* (and its various inflected forms *thee*, *thy*, *thine*, and *thyself*) during the eighteenth century;
- and the current system where *you* serves both singular and plural uses but where other pronominal forms are competing with plural *you* in particular.

Work from a historical sociolinguistic angle has contributed significantly to our understanding of the complex development of *thou* and *you*, including (among others) studies by Wales (1983), Jucker (2006b), and Walker (2007). Looking at their approaches is instructive not only in terms of their findings, but also in terms of their methods, use of sources, and argumentation.

Wales (1983) responds to an earlier proposal by Brown and Gilman (1960) that the development of the use of *thou* and *you* (as well as equivalents in other European languages) can be seen as reflecting changes in a strict power and solidarity hierarchy. She notes that the development in English is distinct from that of other similar systems in Europe (e.g., German, French, and Russian), and the dynamic suggested by Brown and Gilman is unable to account for the variable uses found in English throughout the Middle Ages and early modern period. She suggests that in Middle English, the usage should be interpreted according to a number of sliding scales (Figure 9.1). These scales try to capture the tendencies but also the highly variable usage found in the period. For

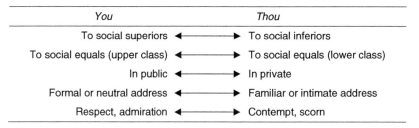

You	Thou
To social superiors ◄────►	To social inferiors
To social equals (upper class) ◄────►	To social equals (lower class)
In public ◄────►	In private
Formal or neutral address ◄────►	Familiar or intimate address
Respect, admiration ◄────►	Contempt, scorn

Figure 9.1 Thou *and* you *in Middle English (adapted from Wales 1983: 116)*

example, when addressing someone in private or in a familiar or intimate address, *thou* is more common, "but we have to recognize the possibility of variation from family to family; generation to generation; discourse to discourse, etc." In general, Wales (1983: 116) claims that "*you* can be associated with 'polite' usage, and *thou* with 'non-polite' (either 'familiar' or 'impolite'))."

Over time, of course, people increasingly preferred *you* where *thou* had previously been used. Wales relates this shift to a number of sociolinguistic processes. For example, she connects the increasing use of *you* with the emergence of a middle class, who would tend to use speech patterns perceived to be the most accepted and most polite language. In particular, she points to women as possible promoters of *you*. In doing so, she extrapolates from "present day evidence which suggests that middle class women favour 'standard' forms more than men" (Wales 1983: 119). *Thou*, on the other hand, would have been increasingly avoided when social distinctions became more unclear and there was a risk of insulting by potentially impolite usage. Wales's focus is on explaining the inadequacy of Brown and Gilman's strict model. She therefore paints the development mostly in broad strokes.

Jucker's (2006b) study demonstrates in detail the complex picture that Wales overviews. He stresses the flexible system of *thou* and *you* in a study of Chaucer's *Canterbury Tales*. He shows that the initial choice between the two pronouns is indeed guided by the well-known factors of familiarity, social status, and age, often in combination (as sketched in Figure 9.1). However, the use can change as power relations shift during the course of a conversation. Thus, a person who is initially addressed with *thou* as a social inferior by a social superior can gain the upper hand in a particular context and instead be addressed with *you* as an indication of that situational superiority. Jucker notes that this is in sharp contrast to the pronoun distinction found in some modern languages such as German and Polish (cf. Wales's point above): "[i]n these languages, choices of the appropriate pronouns remain relatively stable for any two people" (2006b: 61). Jucker demonstrates his point by looking closely at a number of Chaucer's Tales in which two people shift their pronominal usage during the tale. His discussion of the *Wife of Bath's Tale* will serve as an illustrative example. As a punishment for the crime of rape, a knight is charged to find out what women want most of all in the world, in order to preserve his life. In his quest, the knight encounters an old woman ("the loathly lady"), and they enter into conversation. Their first exchange is marked by deference. As shown in the extract below, they both use *you*-forms (in the original subject form *ye* and the possessive form *your*), "the lady because of the knight's higher social status, and the knight because of the lady's old age" (2006b: 63).

> Agayn the knyght this olde wyf gan ryse,
> And seyde, "Sire knyght, heer forth ne lith no wey.
> Tel me what that **ye** seken, by **youre** fey!
> Paraventure it may the bettre be;
> Thise olde folk kan muchel thyng," quod she.
> "My leeve mooder," quod this knyght, "certeyn
> I nam but deed but if that I kan seyn
> What thyng it is that wommen moost desire.
> Koude **ye** me wisse, I wolde wel quite **youre** hire."
>
> (as quoted in Jucker 2006b: 63–64; my emphasis)

> [This old woman got up at the knight's approach and said, 'Sir Knight, there's no road on from here. Tell me what it is you seek; that may be best, perhaps; we old folk know a great many things,' said she. 'Good mother,' the knight replied, 'the truth is I am as good as dead unless I can say what it is that women most desire. If you could tell me that, I'd reward you well.']
>
> (as quoted in Jucker 2006b: 64)

After this point the power relations shift, and so does the pronominal usage. "The loathly lady" has the upper hand in the interaction: she promises to help the knight if he in return promises to grant the wish she makes. In this interaction, she addresses him with *thou*, which reflects her newly gained situational status. She continues to address him with *thou* even at court when she (an old, lower-class woman) reminds him of his promise and requests to be his wife in front of the assembled nobles. The use shifts again as the two are married, but this time "the loathly lady" uses *you* as a sign of deference to her husband. He now responds with an insulting *thou* and accuses her of being ugly, old, and low-born: "**Thou** art so loothly, and so oold also | And therto comen of so lough a kynde" (as quoted in Jucker 2006b: 64; my emphasis). However, "the loathly lady" puts him in his place. She shows that she has power over him (this was the answer to the knight's initial question of what women most desire in the world: sovereignty over their husbands). The knight's polite response is suitably framed by a *you* address: "'My lady and my love, and wyf so deere, | I put me in **youre** wise governance" (as quoted in Jucker 2006b: 65; my emphasis).

What Jucker's study demonstrates, then, is that, yes, social factors are important for the choice of *thou* and *you* in Chaucer (especially in the initial address). However, as the power relationship develops during the course of a conversation, the usage can shift to reflect the situational status. Paying attention to the minute details and fluctuations in the sociopragmatic context is therefore crucial. It is of course difficult to determine with certainty if Chaucer's employment of *thou* and

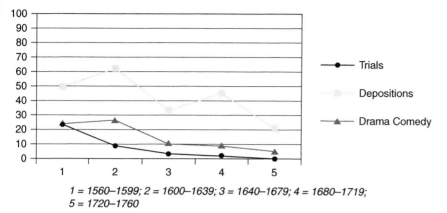

1 = 1560–1599; 2 = 1600–1639; 3 = 1640–1679; 4 = 1680–1719; 5 = 1720–1760

Figure 9.2 *Percentage of* thou *(in relation to* you*) in each genre in forty-year periods, 1560–1760 (from Terry Walker,* Thou *and* you *in Early Modern English dialogues. Amsterdam: John Benjamins, 2007, p. 288; reprinted with kind permission from John Benjamins Publishing Company)*

you is a reflection of broader usage: it could be a literary use of a system under development. However, we find in Walker's (2007) work similar, negotiable use in a range of genres and contexts in the early modern period. This makes it less likely that Chaucer's system was an idiosyncratic literary use, but he may of course have exaggerated it for literary purposes.

Walker's (2007) study is a corpus-based investigation of *thou* and *you* in the period 1560–1760. Her study demonstrates the importance of looking at different genres and of looking at how different social and situational factors interact in promoting *thou* or *you* in early modern England. Over the course of 200 years, *thou* declines substantially in the three genres Walker considers: Trials, Depositions (or witness testimonies), and Drama Comedy. However, as Figure 9.2 shows, *thou* is much more common in Depositions than in the other genres throughout the period. Even by the mid-eighteenth century, examples of *thou* amount to 21 percent of the address pronouns in Depositions. With the other genres, on the other hand, we see a much sharper decline, to a frequency in 1760 of 0 percent for Trials and 5 percent for Drama Comedy.

The purpose and nature of genres are clearly important for charting *thou* and *you* (see Chapter 8). In Trials, for example, the speakers (or the scribes who wrote down their statements) may have been guided by the formality of the situation. They therefore primarily selected the more formal and polite pronoun *you* (Walker 2007: 289). In Drama Comedy, the dramatist could clearly use the pronouns for literary effect, such as portraying a character as a particular type. The use of *thou*, for example, may mark a woman as a scold or a man as mad (Walker 2007: 232). For the depositions, the issue of region comes into play. Walker's depositions were collected from various geographical locations, including the north, the west, and the south-west, where *thou* survived in regular usage beyond the eighteenth century. The use of *thou* is indeed more robust throughout the 200-year period in depositions from these areas. The other genres do not contain this kind of regional material, and the difference in Figure 9.2 may therefore be at least partly a result of regional usage.

The use of depositions also raises a methodological question: whose usage is being represented? That of the person reporting a particular conversation? That of the person(s) whose usage is being reported? That of the scribe who wrote down the testimony? Or perhaps a combination? The following example shows how complicated it can be to interpret what motivates the pronominal switches in EModE depositions.

> ... she hard bullma*n* wyffe cauld
> styllinge nowghtie pak / who aunswerd what
> nowtynes know **y^u** by me / I am neythe*r*
> goossteler no*r* ~~stek~~ stege steiler I wold **yo^u**
> knew ytt / and y^n bullma*n* wyff said
> what noughty hoor caull **thou** me
> ~~nowghtie~~ goose steiler / nay mayry I know
> **the** fo*r* no such saith stillinge wyffe / but
> I thank **yo^u** fo*r* **your** good reporte whill*es* **y^u**
> & I talk further /
>
> (as quoted and highlighted in Walker 2007: 122)

> [She heard Bullman's wife call
> Styllinge "Naughty pack," who answered, "What
> naughtiness do you ['thou'] know about me?" "I am neither
> goose stealer nor gander stealer. I would like you ['you']
> to know it." And then Bullman's wife said:
> "What, naughty whore! Do you ['thou'] call me
> goose stealer?" "No, indeed, I don't know
> you ['thee'] for such," says Styllinge's wife, "but I
> thank you ['you'] for your ['your'] good report until you ['thou']
> and I talk further."]
>
> (my modern paraphrase)

Let's walk through the intricate details in this conversation between Margaret Bullman ("Bullman's wife") and Janet Styllinge ("Styllinge," "stillinge wyffe"). Styllinge has brought Bullman to trial for defamation (Bullman calling Styllinge whore) in the church court in Durham, England, sometime in the late 1560s, and a number of witnesses have been called to testify to what they heard. The witness who reported the above version is Agnes Wheitly, and she reports Bullman as using *thou* forms consistently, but she has Styllinge varying between *thou* and *you* forms. Interestingly, the exchange between the two women is reported very differently by two additional witnesses, including the use of the two pronouns. In both versions, the two female witnesses report Bullman and Styllinge as using almost exclusively *you* forms. Such variation reminds us that the linguistic evidence we find in depositions is often filtered. The witnesses may have portrayed the usage in a way that favored one side or another: we learn from the testimonies that Wheitly is Bullman's neighbor, and the other two witnesses are clearly pro-Styllinge. In addition to the influence of the witness, it is possible that the court scribe who recorded what the witness said modified the usage. In the case of Bullman's and Styllinge's conversation, that seems unlikely. After all, what they said to each other and how they said it was central to the case.

So, how exactly do we interpret the two women's use of *thou* and *you*? Walker (2007: 122–123) suggests that what needs explaining is not the use of *thou* forms, but Styllinge's use of *you* forms. *Thou* was probably the pronoun that the two women would normally have used, as they belong to the lower end of the social scale. The use of *you* would then have sent very clear signals of distancing or haughtiness. Basically, what Stillynge is implying by saying that she is not a goose or gander stealer is that Bullman is, and that is how Bullman perceives it. The "subtext" in Styllinge's phrasing and the use of *you* is, as Walker (2007: 123) puts it: "*you* are a thief and *I* don't want to be associated with you." Of course, Stillynge doesn't want to be sued for slander, even after Bullman calls her "whore" (the cause for the current law suit). So she lets it stand at "insinuation," switching back to the more familiar *thou*. But she again goes back to the distancing *you* when she thanks Bullman with an ironic tone for her "good report" (that is, calling her whore). "The point being made, Styllinge is reported as shifting back to [*thou*]" again, at the very end of the deposition (Walker 2007: 123). Dialogues are not always this complex, but this example clearly demonstrates how necessary it is to pay close attention to pronominal shifts on a very detailed level (as stressed by Jucker earlier).

A range of factors clearly had an impact on people's choices about pronouns, often in very complex and not wholly predictable ways. Gender, age, social rank, region, relationships, social context, and emotion all play a role in Walker's study (cf. Wales' model in Figure 9.1). Emotion, in particular, seems to have been able to trump any of the other factors. *Thou* may be motivated by anger, as is possibly the case in Rochester's switching between *you* and *thou* quoted at the beginning of this section. *You*, on the other hand, might signal haughtiness or distancing, as in the exchange between Bullman and Styllinge (see also Exercise 1). What we can see from Walker's study, then, is that sociohistorical approaches to *thou* and *you* require reconstruction on many levels:

- What is the larger sociocultural context of the evidence (i.e., what was the social hierarchy of the time, what specific sociosituational factors may have played into the usage, what is the purpose of the genre, etc.)?
- What are the situational relationships between the people who exchange *thou* and *you* (i.e., are there aspects of the conversation that may have shifted power relations or that indicate different kinds of emotional states)?
- What is the textual history of the evidence (i.e., has the language been filtered by scribes or other "reporters")?

Overall, the three sociohistorical approaches that we have reviewed reveal the complexities in the use of *thou* and *you*. The studies outline the dynamics of the use in various situations and show how we should understand the complexities in light of social and situational factors and in light of the context in which the texts were produced. Yet, this is hardly the final word in the story of *thou* and *you*. Many questions remain in the historical account. There are also many gaps in our understanding of what is happening now as forms such as *you guys, y'all*, and *you ones* compete with *you* (especially in the plural), and as even more complex forms with additional meanings emerge, such as *all y'all* in the southern United States.

H-dropping

> Habrams flattered himself that he knew a good deal about society, by darting into it from amongst his rhubarb bottles, about three times a-year, "on a haverage." "Not much in my way or Mrs. Habrams's," was his regular remark – but "hit's necessary to go hout – we mustn't be 'ermits – it inders the rust from haccumulating – keep on a par with the hothers – little social hintercourse – very pleasant, as I say to Mrs. Habrams."
>
> (*Country Crayons*. Sketch the Fifth "The country doctor." 1854, p. 287)

A mere glance at the short extract above makes it clear that something is up with the use of the letter *h*. It is left out where we would expect to find it (as in *'ermits*, *inders*), and it is inserted liberally where we would not expect it (as in *hout*, *hothers*, and *hintercourse*). The use is clearly intended to reflect the pronunciation of the speaker, a country doctor. This short story, *Country Crayons*, written by "the Druid" (aka Henry Hall Dixon), is exploiting a phenomenon known as "*h*-dropping" (which also includes insertion of *h*). But the question is why the doctor would be portrayed linguistically in this way. We will return to that question and the doctor's usage below.

The definition of *h*-dropping varies, but it is usually limited to cases where a word-initial phoneme /h/ appears before a vowel and is not pronounced, such as [ænd] instead of [hænd] for *hand*, or [ɪl] instead of [hɪl] for *hill*.[4] Nowadays, *h*-dropping is widespread in non-standard dialects in England and Wales, where it is often connected with working-class speech. But it is not found in other varieties, such as Irish English, Scottish English, and American English (at least not extensively). *h*-dropping is of considerable interest to historical linguists, and especially sociohistorical linguists, because its history is so complex and not yet fully understood and because over time it has become connected with various social characteristics. We will consider two very different approaches to the topic from two clearly separated periods in the history of English: Milroy's (1983; also 1992a) study of Middle English, and Mugglestone's (2003) discussion of eighteenth- and nineteenth-century usage. The two studies illustrate the type of evidence available and the challenges of interpreting it, and they highlight the social connections of *h*-dropping historically.

Milroy (1983) argues that *h*-dropping emerged much earlier in English than had been thought. While previous research had argued that there was little evidence of the phenomenon before the eighteenth century, he finds frequent spellings that lack an *h* in Middle English where we would expect one on historical grounds (as in "om" for *home* and "eld" for *held*). By contrast, there are also *h* spellings where we might not expect them (e.g., "hunkinde" for *unkind*). *h*-insertion in spelling may be seen as reflecting uncertainty on the part of users about where /h/ was pronounced. According to Milroy (1983: 42), this unhistorical usage of *h* (both dropping and insertion) is very frequent in texts from the south-east and the east Midlands in 1190–1320.

Milroy draws on both the historical context and insights from modern sociolinguistics in suggesting a number of sociolinguistic explanations for this usage. He sees *h*-dropping as a result of a language contact situation, in which speakers of English were influenced by French patterns. It is also likely that the usage carried some prestige, in Milroy's view, as it is mainly found in texts "from regions that were amongst the most important commercially and administratively," and mostly in texts "which are quite formal in style and learned in content" (1983: 47–48). The usage then diffused (as a change from above) from speakers of the higher social classes, who had contact with French speakers, to language users in the middle and lower part of the social scale.

Milroy's suggestions are thought-provoking, but some of his conclusions have been questioned. Studies have argued that there is evidence from other Germanic languages as well as other types of data in English that *h*-dropping began without influence from French (e.g., Minugh 1985; Häcker 2004). There is also the issue of how evidence from spelling should be interpreted. Before Milroy's study, the variable dropping and insertion of *h* in spelling had often been attributed to Anglo-Norman scribes' ignorance of how to use *h* correctly in English; or ME spelling was seen as an unreliable guide to pronunciation. Considering their frequency in a range of texts, however, Milroy sees the spellings as significant signs of the non-pronunciation of /h/. More recent research lends some support to this conclusion (see Crisma 2009; Schlüter 2009). We find the use of the article *an* instead of *a* with *h* words very frequently in early Middle English (as in "an handfulle" for *a handful*). This indicates that *h* was not pronounced, as an articulated /h/ would have triggered the article *a* (as it mostly does nowadays in standard varieties of English). There is also support from this type of evidence for Milroy's findings about regional patterns: *h*-dropping is frequent in the south and the Midlands, but it is hardly found at all in the north of England (Crisma 2009). It may have been associated with a certain amount of prestige in Early Middle English (judging by the texts in which it appears), and it was clearly connected with some regional dialects more than others (as is still the case in England and Wales).

If *h*-dropping was prestigious at one point, its fortunes had turned at least by the second half of the eighteenth century when it started attracting a great deal of social stigma. Mugglestone (2003) shows how this stigma develops during the eighteenth and nineteenth centuries in Britain. She considers recommendations and descriptions found in pronunciation guides, grammars, manuals of etiquette, and linguistic "self-help" books of the period (see Chapter 11). These types of sources do not show how people practiced or did not practice *h*-dropping. Instead, we get a picture of how certain writers saw the usage or attempted to dictate how it should be seen. At the same time, their commentary may of course hint at actual social or regional patterns, and they may give us a sense of how people reacted to perceived stigmas.

We find little social commentary before the second half of the eighteenth century, but after this period the non-pronunciation of /h/ is increasingly connected with uneducated, uncultured, low-status, "vulgar" usage (among other social connotations). The stigma of not pronouncing the /h/ is even extended to words borrowed from other languages (primarily French). In these words (in accordance with the original language), /h/ had usually not been pronounced in English even though an *h* appeared in the spelling (such as *hospital, hotel, humble*); nowadays, /h/ is usually pronounced in most of these words in standard varieties. By the 1850s and 1860s, the pronunciation or non-pronunciation of /h/ had become *the* sign of education and knowledge of the proper conventions of writing (or lack thereof). The strong feeling was that where *h* appeared in writing, it should also be pronounced (see Exercise 2).

Particularly interesting from a sociolinguistic perspective are certain stereotypes that appear in these descriptions, as they may point to people's heightened awareness of the social signals that the use of /h/ could send. Mugglestone (2003: 108–111) shows that the newly rich or the "self-made man" are often ridiculed for *h*-dropping, or perhaps even more commonly, the insertion of /h/ where it is not historically found. For example, the Honorable Henry H., the alleged author of *Poor Letter H: Its Use and Abuse*, a manual for the correct usage of /h/, discusses how he has

> heard a person, who was very well dressed, and looked like a lady, ask a gentleman who was sitting by her, if he knew whether Lord Murray had left any *H*eir behind him – the gentleman almost blushed, and I thought stopped a little, to see whether the lady meant a *Son* or a *Hare*.   (as quoted in Mugglestone 2003: 109)

The implication here is of course that the woman seems outwardly to be a lady, but she reveals her social origins to be more lowly by misapplying /h/. A similar example is found in the country doctor's speech that we saw at the beginning of this section. The doctor professes to know "a good deal about society." But the sprinkling of /h/ into his language (as indicated by the *h*-spellings) is clearly supposed to indicate that he does not, since he is not well versed in the most important linguistic convention of the time. Note that the *h*-spellings (or lack thereof) are the only features that would mark the country doctor as using nonstandard language.

Mugglestone (2003: 111) tentatively suggests that we can interpret /h/-insertion in sources of this kind by looking at results from modern socio-linguistic research. Such research has shown that people who are upwardly mobile or "insecure within the social hierarchy" are highly aware of prestigious forms, and may in fact overuse them, as a type of "hypercorrection." So there may have been some truth behind the "mispronouncing" lady in *Poor Letter H* and the country doctor. At least some newly rich or social aspirers in the nineteenth century may have been very sensitive to the use of /h/ because of the heavy emphasis on its proper usage in language manuals and guides. The overuse (or hypercorrect use) attempts to show mastery of the use of /h/ but mistakenly over-applies the "rule."

We get a good sense of the overwhelmingly negative associations of h--dropping found in the prescriptive literature of the time, and there is more evidence in literary works, such as *Country Crayons* and a host of novels cited by Mugglestone. The question is of course whether we actually find h-dropping used by certain groups in society as it is depicted in literary works or described in other sources. And did the prescriptions have any effect, and, if so, on whom? These are by and large questions that remain to be explored. But Schlüter's (2009) work on article usage with h-words (that is, whether h-words take *an* or *a*) does show us that there appears to be a steady decline of h-dropping during the eighteenth and nineteenth centuries. On the other hand, since this is a steady trend from the ME period onwards, it is unclear what role, if any, manuals and guides had in this development.

To sum up, we have seen two different sociohistorical approaches to h-dropping. They demonstrate the kinds of sources that are at our disposal when we want to investigate a phenomenon such as h-dropping: spelling, and social commentary in language manuals. Both types can clearly yield valuable evidence, but must also be treated with caution, as any one type of source is likely to yield only a partial picture of a complex phenomenon such as h-dropping. Drawing on findings from modern sociolinguistic research is useful, even if we cannot arrive at firm conclu-sions about the usage. As in the case of *thou* and *you*, there are many opportunities for new discoveries that will give us a better understanding of the development of h-dropping. Perhaps one of the most interesting questions is why we find a great deal of variation across different Englishes in terms of whether h-dropping occurs or not. This is especially interesting since h-dropping appears to have been present in English from at least the early ME period, that is, before the main era of English geographical expansion. If it was so common in the language, why doesn't it show up in all Englishes?

Concluding Remarks

The chapter has shown some of the major concerns and strands of sociohistorical approaches to the history of the English language. We have seen how taking the social context into consideration and using concepts and tools from modern sociolinguistics can help us shed light on the dynamics of linguistic usage and the mechanisms of language change in historical periods. The chapter has emphasized the need for careful selection of sources and detailed reconstruction of the sociocultural context of the language studied. We may lack access to materials that allow us to study certain features and social factors at particular points in time. Despite these gaps, the contributions of sociohistorical approaches to the description of the history of English are undeniable. They have illustrated again and again that society and language were intimately connected historically, just as they are now.

Suggestions for Further Study

Descriptions of (English) historical sociolinguistics are found in, e.g., Nevalainen and Raumolin-Brunberg (2003), Bergs (2005), Millar (2012), and Trousdale (2010: ch. 6). Early introductions are found in Romaine (1982), Milroy (1992a), and Machan and Scott (1992). Sociohistorical approaches for individual historical periods are found in Bergs (2012) for Middle English, Raumolin-Brunberg (2012) for Early Modern English, and Smitterberg (2012) for Late Modern English. For general principles in the field, see Labov (1994, 2001). Hernández-Campoy and Conde-Silvestre (2012) is a handbook of historical sociolinguistics, which covers a range of methodological approaches and topics. Although it does not focus on English, it covers many areas relevant for English. Research on English historical sociolinguistics is published in a range of journals, including *English Language and Linguistics*, *Journal of English Linguistics*, and *Journal of Historical Pragmatics*. A new journal, *Journal of Historical Sociolinguistics*, which covers all languages, has recently been launched (2015–).

Exercises

1. *Thou* and *you* in action
   a. Identify all second-person pronouns, singular and plural, used by First Murderer, Second Murderer, and George Plantagenet (Duke of Clarence) in the extract from William Shakespeare's *Richard III* (Act I, scene iv) below.
   b. In light of the discussion by Wales, Jucker, and Walker reviewed earlier, how would you explain the pronominal addresses? You may want to consider social rank/status in particular, and Jucker's suggestion of changing situational status.
   [The two murderers are going to kill George Plantagenet, Duke of Clarence, at the order of Richard III]

SECOND MURDERER.	Take the devil in thy mind, and relieve him not: he would insinuate with thee but to make thee sigh.
FIRST MURDERER.	Tut, I am strong-framed, he cannot prevail with me, I warrant thee.
SECOND MURDERER.	Spoke like a tail fellow that respects his reputation. Come, shall we to this gear?
FIRST MURDERER.	Take him over the costard with the hilts of thy sword, and then we will chop him in the malmsey-butt in the next room.
SECOND MURDERER.	O excellent devise! make a sop of him.
FIRST MURDERER.	Hark! he stirs: shall I strike?
SECOND MURDERER.	No, first let's reason with him.
GEORGE PLANTAGENET (DUKE OF CLARENCE).	Where art thou, keeper? Give me a cup of wine.
SECOND MURDERER.	You shall have wine enough, my lord, anon.
GEORGE PLANTAGENET (DUKE OF CLARENCE).	In God's name, what art thou?
SECOND MURDERER.	A man, as you are.
GEORGE PLANTAGENET (DUKE OF CLARENCE).	But not, as I am, royal.
SECOND MURDERER.	Nor you, as we are, loyal.
GEORGE PLANTAGENET (DUKE OF CLARENCE).	Thy voice is thunder, but thy looks are humble.
SECOND MURDERER.	My voice is now the king's, my looks mine own.
GEORGE PLANTAGENET (DUKE OF CLARENCE).	How darkly and how deadly dost thou speak! Your eyes do menace me: why look you pale? Who sent you hither? Wherefore do you come?
BOTH.	To, to, to—
GEORGE PLANTAGENET (DUKE OF CLARENCE).	To murder me?
BOTH.	Ay, ay.
GEORGE PLANTAGENET (DUKE OF CLARENCE).	You scarcely have the hearts to tell me so, And therefore cannot have the hearts to do it. Wherein, my friends, have I offended you?
FIRST MURDERER.	Offended us you have not, but the king.
GEORGE PLANTAGENET (DUKE OF CLARENCE).	I shall be reconciled to him again.
SECOND MURDERER.	Never, my lord; therefore prepare to die.
GEORGE PLANTAGENET (DUKE OF CLARENCE).	Are you call'd forth from out a world of men to slay the innocent? What is my offence? Where are the evidence that do accuse me? What lawful quest have given their verdict up unto the

	frowning judge? or who pronounced the bitter sentence of poor Clarence' death? Before I be convict by course of law, to threaten me with death is most unlawful. I charge you, as you hope to have redemption by Christ's dear blood shed for our grievous sins, that you depart and lay no hands on me the deed you undertake is damnable.
FIRST MURDERER.	What we will do, we do upon command.
SECOND MURDERER.	And he that hath commanded is the king.
GEORGE PLANTAGENET (DUKE OF CLARENCE).	Erroneous vassal! the great King of kings hath in the tables of his law commanded that thou shalt do no murder: and wilt thou, then, spurn at his edict and fulfil a man's? Take heed; for he holds vengeance in his hands, to hurl upon their heads that break his law.
SECOND MURDERER.	And that same vengeance doth he hurl on thee, for false forswearing and for murder too: Thou didst receive the holy sacrament, to fight in quarrel of the house of Lancaster.
FIRST MURDERER.	And, like a traitor to the name of God, didst break that vow; and with thy treacherous blade unrip'dst the bowels of thy sovereign's son.
SECOND MURDERER.	Whom thou wert sworn to cherish and defend.
FIRST MURDERER.	How canst thou urge God's dreadful law to us, when thou hast broke it in so dear degree?
	(Adapted from www.opensourceshakespeare .org/views/plays/play_view.php?WorkID=richa rd3&Act=1&Scene=4&Scope=scene)

2. *Hair* vs. *air*: Is there really that much of a difference?
The extract below is from Henry Alford's book *A Plea for the Queen's English: Stray Notes on Speaking and Spelling* from 1878 (pp. 40–41). In it, he comments on the pronunciation or non-pronunciation of /h/ ("the leaving out of the aspirate") in England.

> 51. I pass from spelling to pronunciation. And first and foremost, let me notice that worst of all faults, the leaving out of the aspirate where it ought to be, and putting it in where it ought not to be. This is a vulgarism not confined to this or that province of England, nor especially prevalent in one county or another, but common throughout England to persons of low breeding and inferior education, principally to those among the inhabitants of towns. Nothing so surely stamps a man as below the mark in intelligence, self-respect, and energy, as this unfortunate habit: in intelligence, because, if he were but moderately keen in perception, he would see how it marks him; in

self-respect and energy, because if he had these, he would long ago have set to work and cured it. Hundreds of stories are current about the absurd consequences of this vulgarism. We remember in *Punch* the barber who, while operating on a gentleman, expresses his opinion, that, after all, the cholera was in the *hair*. "Then," observes the customer, "you ought to be very careful what brushes you use." "Oh, sir," replies the barber, laughing, "I didn't mean the *air* of the *ed*, but the *hair* of the *hatmosphere*."

52. As I write these lines, which I do while waiting in a refreshment-room at Reading, between a Great-Western and a South-Eastern train, I hear one of two commercial gentlemen, from a neighbouring table, telling his friend that "his *ed* used to *hake* ready to burst."

(*Punch* ... A British satirical magazine published in the nineteenth and twentieth centuries)

a. What kind of sociolinguistic information about /h/ can we gain from this extract?
b. How would you evaluate the reliability of the information? How would you devise a study to check on the reliability?

3. *Can't* and *cannot*: A trial attempt
   You are interested in researching the variation between *can't* and *cannot* in the "spoken" language of the period 1770–1780. You decide to use the *Old Bailey Corpus* (OBC) for your study. Go to hdl: 11858/00-246C-0000-0023-8CFB-2, and run two searches (one for *can't* and one for *cannot*); make sure that you delimit the time period to 1770–1780 by clicking the box for "Year/period" and then specifying the date range. By way of a first survey of the data, look at the first 100 examples of each form.

   a. What social features recorded by OBC do you think will be useful to consider on the basis of your survey?
   b. What challenges do you see in considering those factors? (Here you might want to consider issues such as how gender and "social class" are constructed, the role of the speaker during the trial proceedings, the gaps in the OBC's record, the nature of the material, and similar issues.)

4. The field of historical sociolinguistics
   What are some of the advantages and challenges of seeing English historical sociolinguistics as a field (at least partially) distinct from modern sociolinguistics?

Notes

I am grateful to James W. Hartman, Amanda Sladek, Ingrid Tieken-Boon van Ostade, and Molly M. Zahn for comments on earlier drafts of this chapter. Naturally, any errors are entirely my own.

1. The text is given with the capitalization, punctuation, and spelling of the manuscript; bold face is added for emphasis. ETED refers to *An Electronic Text Edition of Depositions 1560–1760*.

2. For different ways of classifying these texts and for evaluating their "spokenness," see, e.g., Schneider (2013) and, as discussed in Chapter 5, Culpeper and Kytö (2010: chs. 1–2).
3. For more information on these corpora, see Chapter 10.
4. Most researchers only consider uses in stressed syllables (as in *hand* and *hill*), and therefore exclude the loss of /h/ in function words, such as [ɪm] for *him*, which is common in most varieties of spoken English.

10 Historical Pragmatic Approaches

LAUREL J. BRINTON

Introduction

The following passage from Geoffrey Chaucer's *Knight's Tale* (lines 2393–2401) in *The Canterbury Tales* might elicit a surprised reaction from twenty-first-century readers:

I am yong and unkonnynge, **as thow woost**	'I am young and ignorant, **as you know**
And, **as I trowe**, with love offended moost	And, **as I suppose**, most injured by love
That evere was any lyves creature,	That ever was any living creature,
For she that dooth me al this wo endure	For she that causes me to endure all this woe
Ne recceth nevere wher I synke or fleete.	Does not ever know whether I sink or swim.
And **wel I woot**, er she me mercy heete,	And **well I know**, before she may promise me mercy,
I moot with strengthe wynne hir in the place,	I must with strength win her in the lists
And **wel I woot,** withouten help or grace	And **well I know**, without help or grace
Of thee ne may my strengthe noght availle	Of you never may my strength ever avail'

(http://quod.lib.umich.edu/c/cme/CT/1:1.2.3?rgn=div3;view=fulltext)

Sprinkled in rapid succession among the lines of verse – in a part of the poem written in high, courtly style – are what we might consider colloquial elements (*as thow woost, as I trow, wel I woot*) similar to "filler" elements such as *y'know* and *I think* of Present-day English. However, as contemporary pragmatics has shown, these "comment clauses" are not mere fillers to be discounted, but are elements deserving serious study. They have been shown to serve important discourse-organizing and (inter)personal functions. Turning back to Chaucer, we can then ask: Do the Chaucerian forms serve functions similar to or different from those of Present-day English (or are they merely metrical expedients)? Or more generally, have language users always expressed such functions? If so, what forms have they used, and how has the inventory of such forms changed over time? How do such forms develop? Why are some forms lost and others preserved? Questions such as these are central to the approach called "historical pragmatics," the topic of this chapter.[1] After describing the field of historical pragmatics and its scope, its data, and its methodology, this chapter investigates two examples of historical pragmatic study: performative verbs/speech acts and comment clauses.

The Field of Historical Pragmatics

As the name suggests, historical pragmatics combines "pragmatics" – the study of language use in context – with "historical linguistics" – the study of language in historical periods and as it changes over time. As a distinct discipline, historical pragmatics is only about twenty years old, with its rise being attributed to a number of changes affecting both linguistics in general and pragmatics and historical linguistics specifically.[2]

According to Andreas Jucker (one of the pioneers in the field), historical pragmatics:

> studies historical language data by asking explicitly and systematically what the specific situation was in which the data was produced, who the writer was, and to what audience it was addressed. It studies the development of specific text types and specific forms of dialogue; it examines the development of specific linguistic elements which can only be described by reference to their pragmatic function in specific communicative situations; and it offers pragmatic explanations for language change.   (1998: 3)

The Scope of Historical Pragmatics

As the extended definition just given illustrates, the scope of historical pragmatics is quite wide-ranging, and a number of subfields can be identified. Like the field as a whole, these subfields have gone by different names (see Table 10.1). A brief discussion and illustration of the subfields is a good starting point for understanding the scope of historical pragmatic studies. In large part, the subfields depend upon whether the focus is on a particular point in time (synchronic) or on change over time (diachronic).

The first subfield ("pragmaphilology") is essentially synchronic, involving the pragmatic analysis of the conventions of language use at a particular point in time in the past. Hence it is historical, but not diachronic. The analyst seeks to understand the linguistic features or stylistic conventions of a historical text or texts by seeing them in their communicative and sociocultural context. For example, the use of *you* and *thou* address terms in Chaucer or in Shakespeare or of forms of insult in Old English might be so analyzed. On a larger scale, the genre conventions of medical writing in the ME period, of courtroom discourse of trials in the EModE period, or of newspaper reporting in the eighteenth century might be investigated. These studies typically depend upon a thorough

Table 10.1 *The subfields of historical pragmatics (adapted from Jucker 2008: 898)*

Subfield of historical pragmatics[a]	Characterization	Examples
1 historical discourse analysis proper OR pragmaphilology	study of the discourse-pragmatic features in one particular historical period	terms of address in Chaucer; politeness in Shakespeare; directives in OE
2 diachronic(ally oriented) discourse analysis OR diachronic pragmatics	study of the development of discourse-pragmatic features over time	history of speech acts; history of discourse markers
3 discourse-oriented diachronic linguistics OR pragma-historical linguistics	study of the discourse-pragmatic factors motivating language change	grammaticalization; word order change; topic/focus marking

[a] In each case, the first name is taken from Brinton (2015: 225) and the second from Jacobs and Jucker (1995).

knowledge of the (socio)historical contexts in which texts are produced, requiring research into social, legal, political, and/or scientific history.

A sample study of this kind is Moore's (2006) research into the language of depositions (testimony made under oath) in slander cases in Early Modern English. Moore shows that the Latin form *videlicet* 'namely, that is to say' is used in these texts – both those written entirely in English and those that mix Latin and English – as a "discourse marker." Discourse markers are typically short elements that are characteristic of oral speech, such as PDE *well, now, actually, in fact, after all, you know,* or *I mean.* They have little or no lexical content but rather function pragmatically to structure texts, denote speaker attitude, and signal interpersonal relations.[3] In EModE slander depositions, *videlicet* has a text-organizing function: it marks off the alleged speech of the defendant, occurring at the beginning of the representation of the slanderer's speech, either through direct quotation or indirect report, as in the following example from Moore (2006: 253):

(1)   thesaid william delve spake these following of thesaid Hugh mill with an intent to sla in a slanderous manner and verie disgracefullie **videlicet** Thou arte no Cuckold holding out two of his fingers to thesaid Mill in the manner of hornes (1615 Consistory Court of Exeter)

The fact that *videlicet* occurs in written texts and that its function is specific to the genre of slander depositions underlines the importance of textual considerations in all historical pragmatic studies.

The second subfield ("diachronic pragmatics") traces the development of pragmatic elements – pragmatic forms, functions, and genre conventions –

over time. Here, for example, an analyst might study the origin and development of a discourse marker or interjection, changes in the form of compliments or apologies, or differences in the stylistic convention of cooking recipes from Old English to the present.

A sample study of this kind is Jucker's (2011) study of the development of expressions of politeness in the history of English. He focuses on the concepts of "positive face" (the desire to be approved of) and "negative face" (the desire not to be imposed upon) that have been seen as central to politeness.[4] Contemporary society, he notes, is thought to emphasize "negative politeness"; we try to avoid imposing upon others by offering options and asking indirectly. In Anglo-Saxon England, since social relations were based on kin loyalty, the fixed position of interlocutors in the societal hierarchy, and mutual obligations, commands tended to be expressed directly, in (what looks to us) a face-threatening way (see below on directive speech acts). The importation of *curteisye* 'courtly conduct' in Middle English introduced "deference politeness." Here, the pronouns *you* and *thou* marked the relative status of the speaker and addressee and their relation to one another, but were not used to maintain face. In late Middle English, address terms become more varied and by Early Modern English, a system of face-based politeness seems to have become entrenched. But analyses of Shakespeare suggest that there was much more positive politeness (in-group identity markers, hedges to avoid disagreement, naming of admirable qualities) than negative politeness (indirect utterances and deferential expressions). Jucker attributes the subsequent change to a negative politeness culture to three causes:

(a) the replacement of *thou* by deferential *you*, which shows negative politeness (see Chapter 8);

(b) the replacement of *pray/prithee* by *please* (< *if you please*); *pray* expresses the speaker's wish for the hearer to do something and hence imposes on the addressee, whereas *please* is deferential and makes performing the action contingent on the addressee's will; and

(c) the replacement of *excuse me/pardon me/forgive me* by *sorry* in apologies; the older forms ask the hearer to forgive the speaker (again, an attack on negative face) while the new form is deferential.

Within both subfields, pragmaphilology and diachronic pragmatics, two approaches, or "mappings," are possible:

(a) from form to function, or

(b) from function to form.

In the first case, one begins with a linguistic form – e.g., a discourse marker, a speech act verb, or a set of address terms – analyzing its meaning at a point in time or tracing its changes in meaning over time. In the second case, one begins with a function – a speech act, (im)politeness rules, or genre expectations – analyzing its concrete manifestations at a point in time or changes in the realization of the function over time. Moore's study of *videlicet* proceeds from form to function, while Jucker's study of politeness proceeds from function to form.

The third subfield ("pragma-historical linguistics") is a study of the pragmatic causes of language change. Such studies have focused, for example, on the pragmatic motivations for word order change or on the inferential basis underlying semantic changes in grammaticalization (see Chapters 6 and 7). Much work on the English modal auxiliaries points to pragmatic motivations for the complex semantic changes they undergo. For example, Traugott and Dasher (2002: 120–137) argue that the original 'ability' meaning of the modal *must* changed to 'permission,' then to the two meanings still existent in PDE – 'obligation' (*You must leave now in order to arrive on time*) and 'epistemic possibility' (*This must be the right answer*) – via a set of invited inferences arising in the context of use.

Pragmatic Units

Another way to understand the scope of historical pragmatics is to consider the "pragmatic units" studied. There are three possible levels that can be investigated (see Jucker 2008: 898–902):

(1) expressions – e.g., discourse markers, interjections, address terms;
(2) utterances – e.g., speech acts;
(3) genres and domains of discourse – e.g., the genre conventions of personal letters, medical recipes, or prayers, or the language of medical or legal discourse.

Expressions. A prototypical pragmatic expression is a discourse marker, and the study of discourse markers has thus been central to the field of historical pragmatics. An important early study by Jucker (1997) looks at the origin and development of *well*, one of the most common and widely studied discourse markers in PDE. (Jucker's study of the development of *well* was discussed and exemplified in Chapter 7.) Like discourse markers, interjections have oral characteristics and marginal word-class status. In fact, there is considerable debate about what distinguishes interjections from discourse markers, with forms such as *oh* or OE *hwæt* 'lo, indeed, lit. what' being treated variously as belonging to both categories. One feature of interjections not shared by discourse markers, however, is their ability to constitute utterances in their own right, such as the complete utterances *Ouch!* or *Psst!*. The history of the interjection *gee!* (Gehweiler 2008) provides an interesting case study, as was also discussed in Chapter 7.

A wealth of scholarship relates to both nominal and pronominal address terms. As discussed in detail in Chapter 9, the second-person pronouns, *you/ye* and *thou*, assumed an honorific function in late Middle English and Early Modern English. The "rules" for the use of the pronouns were motivated by concerns of rank and gender as well as interpersonal relations. Traditionally, many studies of *you/ye* and *thou* examine literary usage, especially in Chaucer and Shakespeare (see, e.g., Busse 2002), where the use of – and switch between – the two pronouns can often indicate interpersonal relationships (intimacy, power relations, gender roles), (im)politeness, and emotional attitudes. Two quotations from Shakespeare's plays show this usage:

(2)   QUEEN: Hamlet, **thou** hast **thy** father much offended.
        HAMLET: Mother, **you** have my Father much offended.
        QUEEN: Come, come **you** answer with an idle tongue. (1600–1601
        Hamlet III.iv.12–14; www.folgerdigitaltexts.org)

(3)   HAMLET: ... I did love **you** once.
        OPHELIA: Indeed, my lord, **you** made me believe so.
        HAMLET: **You** should not have believed me, for virtue cannot so
        <inoculate> our old stock but we shall relish of it. I loved **you** not.
        OPHELIA: I was the more deceived.
        HAMLET: Get **thee** <to> a nunnery. Why wouldst **thou** be a breeder
        of sinners? ... Go **thy** ways to a nunnery. Where's **your** father?
        (1600–1601 *Hamlet* III.i.125–141; www.folgerdigitaltexts.org)

In the first quotation, Gertrude uses the intimate form *thou* with her son Hamlet. As is customary, Hamlet addresses his mother with the seemingly respectful *you*. But because he rebukes her for dishonoring his father's memory, she chides him in return by using *you*, which could be seen here as distancing. In the second quotation, Hamlet and Ophelia use *you* in addressing one another, following upper-class usage. But as Hamlet becomes suspicious of Ophelia's love, he switches to the informal – and here insulting – *thee* and *thy*, only to return to *you* in the end. An amusing use of *thou* is shown in the following excerpt from *Twelfth Night*. Here Sir Toby Belch advises the foppish and idiotic Sir Andrew Aguecheek on how to write a challenge to a rival suitor:

(4)   TOBY: If thou "thou"-est him some thrice, it shall not be amiss,
        (1600–1602 *Twelfth Night* III.ii.45; www.folgerdigitaltexts.org)

In addressing Sir Andrew using *thou* Sir Toby is expressing solidarity, while at the same time patronizing the gullible Sir Andrew. The recommendation that Sir Andrew use *thou* in his challenge ("thou-est") is intended to be a means of insulting his rival.

Utterances. Speech acts[5] have also been widely researched in the history of English. The speech act of "directives" is discussed in detail below, but here we look briefly at two other speech acts, promises and curses.

In a promise (what is called a "commissive" in speech act theory), speakers commit themselves to perform future actions, which they are both willing and able to carry out and which they believe the hearer wants. For the promise to be sincere, speakers must have the intention of carrying out the action (the so-called "sincerity condition"). The promise that the character Dorigan makes in

Chaucer's *Franklin's Tale* has been the subject of lively debate, among both students of historical pragmatics and literary critics. In order to get rid of an admirer, Dorigan promises to love him if he performs what she believes to be an impossible task (clearing the coastline of rocks). When he miraculously seems to have done this, she feels compelled to honor her promise. Using a speech act approach, Arnovick (2006) argues that Dorigan's statement does not in fact constitute a promise since it is uttered in the context of her assertion that she will always be true to her husband, and it is said "in pley" ('in jest') with the belief that what she asks "shal never bityde" ('shall never happen'). Dorigan – though she uses the conventional form of a promise – has no intention of fulfilling her promise and thus fails to fulfill the sincerity condition on promising. Rather, her utterance functions as a rejection of her erstwhile suitor: it is an "insincere promise embedded within a larger rejection" (Arnovick 2006: 170).[6]

Culpeper and Semino (2000) is a study of cursing, focusing on witchcraft narratives in Early Modern English. People accused as witches were typically poor and marginalized members of society, usually women. When these people reacted verbally to some wrong suffered at the hands of a more powerful neighbor, either by uttering a malevolent curse or simply expressing anger, they could be brought up on charges of witchcraft. In the excerpt given in (6), a witch is charged with "wishing her cousin harm," and this wish is seen as the cause of the cousin's lameness and death:

(5)   Further that **wished** her cosen Hobart **harme** and he fell lame and so continued till he died wch was wthin 3 days after she was questioned. (1645 *Suffolk Witches*, p. 293; Culpeper & Semino 2000: 103)

In Present-day English, these expressions would be a simple wish that something bad happen to the target with no causal connection (i.e., they would be "expressives" in a speech act framework, such as wishing a person 'good day'). But in the witchcraft context of the seventeenth century, these were interpreted as speech acts which would inevitably result in misfortune falling upon the target (i.e., they would be "declaratives").

Genres and domains. Studies of genres focus on the characteristic features of a genre at a particular historical period or trace the development of those features over time. They may also pay attention to the influence of genre on the selection and use of linguistic features.

In Chapter 8 we saw how studies have shown a "drift" from a more literate to a more oral style of writing up to the twentieth century, or the trend toward colloquialization in written forms in Present-day English.The genre of prayer, in contrast, has remained remarkably stable and conservative in the history of the language. Prayers in English became common in the EModE period, when they came to be collected in "primers." Primers were central in daily life and perhaps the most important product of print culture of the time. According to Kohnen (2012), prayers constitute an interactive and performative genre characterized by a high frequency of oral features: of first- and second-person pronouns, of explicit performatives – typically directives but also thanking, confessing, and praising – and of terms of address. Address terms are frequently followed by relative or appositional clauses, which explain the relevance of the point being made; a similar strategy is used in a conversational situation between two people who have known each other for a long time.

The use of "stance" markers (markers of personal attitude) has been shown to be affected by both genre and period. The range of stance markers includes:

- modals (e.g., *can, must*) and semi-modals (e.g., *have to, ought to*);
- stance adverbials (e.g., *certainly, evidently*); and
- *that-* or *to-*complement clauses (controlled by verbs [e.g., *predict, happen*], adjectives [e.g., *it is strange/likely*], or nouns [e.g., *hope, intention*]).

Biber (2004) looks at markers of stance from 1600–1990 in the genres of drama, personal letters, newspaper reportage, and medical prose. Overall, he finds that all markers of stance have increased over time, except for modals, which have witnessed a marked decline in all genres, especially in the last fifty years. The "popular" genres (personal letters and drama) have been in the vanguard in the increased use of stance marking; only medical prose has shown a decline. Biber concludes that the changes are not just a case of one grammatical system being replaced by another. Rather, he suggests that there is a change in cultural norms, with speakers being more willing to express stance, whether as a result of deliberate stylistic policies or popular attitudes.

On a higher level, entire domains of discourse – such as religious discourse, newspapers and pamphlets, scientific and medical discourse, literary discourse, and legal discourse – may be examined. In Chapter 8, the domain of letters was discussed in detail. Another important domain, news reporting, has undergone extensive change – even in respect to the physical format of newspapers – since its origins in the seventeenth century. Consider the two newspaper extracts given below, both describing a factory fire.[7] They show great differences in both style and content over the relatively short period of 150 years.

Destructive Fire! The Foundry in Ruins!

A heavy calamity has befallen our town. Another and most disastrous fire has visited us, laying in ruins one of the most extensive and prosperous manufacturing establishments in the Province. At about a quarter to three o'clock yesterday morning Mr. James Patterson, residing near the Foundry, being in attendance on a sick child, was alarmed by the reflection of a strong light thrown on a building immediately in front of his dwelling. In a moment he was in the street when he discovered fire issuing from the main building of J. Gartebore & Co's establishment. The alarm of fire quickly given, and as the residences of many of the workmen were in the vicinity, persons were quickly on the spot. The Town Engine and 5 or 6 of the portable ones were soon in full play, and every means which human ingenuity could devise was employed to arrest the progress of the devouring element . . .

For the information of persons at a distance, we will endeavor to describe the situation of the various buildings connected with the Foundry . . .

It is painful to contemplate the probably effects of this calamity . . .

Fortunately, no lives have been lost, though several of the men engaged in saving property were severely burned.

As to the origin of the fire nothing in known . . .

It will be in some measure a source of consolation to Messrs. Ewart and Gartebore in the season of heavy loss, to know that they command the deep sympathies of the entire population of the town . . .

(*The Globe*, October 6, 1846)

Police Clear Fire Area on Dundas

Police early today evacuated houses near Dundas Avenue West and Golden Avenue as a three-alarm factory fire shot flames high in the sky.

The blaze, which broke out shortly before 1:30 a.m., was in the rear of the factory. Within minutes after the arrival of firemen, the third alarm was sounded and extra equipment sent.

Police said flames and red ashes blew across the street. Police trucks towed cars away to give firemen more room.

Residents two miles away reported the sky so red they thought the fire only blocks away.

(*The Globe and Mail*, June 25, 1999)

Data and Methods in Historical Pragmatics

The "Bad Data" Problem

Contemporary pragmatics and discourse analysis have typically taken naturally occurring, spontaneous, face-to-face conversation and oral narratives as their source of data. Thus, the lack of audio recordings prior to the early twentieth century was initially felt to be a major impediment for historical pragmatics and excuses were often made for the lack of appropriate data (i.e., for "bad data"). However, it has come to be recognized that many forms of represented and recorded speech do indeed survive from the past, including witness depositions, court records, and parliamentary proceedings, dramatic dialogue, represented speech in narrative fiction and poetry, and didactic works in dialogic form. Moreover, more colloquial and dialogic forms of written language from the past, such as diaries, letters, sermons, pamphlets, and recipes, have also been preserved. Even within historical linguistics proper, such sources of data have proved increasingly important, as the emphasis has come to focus more on usage, variety, heterogeneity, on inferential processes of change, and on the importance of context (see Traugott 2008). While these "speech-based" sources must be approached with caution, as they may be heavily edited or redacted, we may glean from them at least some approximation of the everyday colloquial language of the past. It is also well-known that medieval texts had many "oral" features, such as discourse markers, historical presents, and formulae, and that historically we see a movement from more oral to more literate style, so the further we go back in time – for example to OE and ME texts – the closer we may come to uncovering colloquial forms of the language.

Ultimately, however, a more encompassing view of language has come to prevail, namely, that all forms of language, both written and spoken, are communicative acts, and thus even written language is a legitimate subject for pragmatic study. This view has come to be held even among pragmaticists, who originally considered written language artificial and hence unsuitable for study. The "communicative view," as Jucker and Taavitsainen term it,

> holds that both spoken and written language are forms of communication produced by speakers/writers for target audiences with communicative intentions, and language is always produced within situational constraints. Therefore, all forms of language that have survived and provide enough information to contextualize the use, are considered potential data for historical pragmatics.   (2013: 25)

In recent years, the compilation of genre-specific electronic corpora, including "speech-based," colloquial, and specialized written genres from earlier periods of English, has led to easier means of data retrieval and access to more relevant types of data. These have been mentioned in Chapter 9; Table 10.2 provides more complete details (but is itself not a complete listing).[8] The Chadwyck-Healey literary databases, designed in the first instance for literary use, provide invaluable tools in their TEI versions (which supply the texts in electronic form) for the collection of data. The Chadwyck-Healey *English Drama* database, containing 3,900 plays dating from the thirteenth to the early nineteenth century, may be pointed out as an especially valuable resource for historic pragmatic work, for as Culpeper and Kytö (2000) have shown, there is a "strong case" for seeing drama (compared to witness depositions, trial proceedings, and prose fiction) as closest to real speech. Although not available in electronic form, the *Records of the Salem Witch-hunts* (2013), provide an invaluable source of information about early, colloquial American English.

Historical Corpus Pragmatics

In its early stages, the methodology of historical pragmatics bore a resemblance to the traditional approach in philology (hence the early name "New Philology"

Table 10.2 *A partial listing of genre-specific corpora*

Corpus	Size	Contents
A Corpus of English Dialogues 1560–1760 (CED)	1.2 million words	"Authentic dialogue" (trial records and witness depositions) and "constructed dialogue" (comedy drama, didactic works, prose fiction)
Corpus of Early English Correspondence Sampler (1418–1680) (CEECS)	.45 million words	Personal letters sociolinguistically annotated with background information on the letter writers; additions to this corpus extend coverage to 1800
A Corpus of Late 18c Prose	300,000 words	The letters of Richard Orford dating from 1761 to 1790
The Old Bailey Corpus (OBC)	2.4 million words	A subset from *The Old Bailey Proceedings Online, 1674–1913*, a Part-of-Speech tagged corpus which provides sociolinguistic, pragmatic, and textual information
An Electronic Text Edition of Depositions 1560–1760 (ETED)	270,000 words	Witness depositions from all parts of England in original spelling
The Lampeter Corpus of Early Modern English Tracts (LC)	1.2 million words	Political, religious, economic, legal, and scientific tracts dated from 1640 to 1740
Early Modern English Medical Texts 1500–1700 (EMEMT)	2 million words	Texts ranging from more academic medical texts to popularized and utilitarian texts verging on household literature; there are also medieval and late modern corpora, bringing the effective range to 1375–1800

for historical pragmatics). That is, it was primarily qualitative, involving close readings of texts to extract data, focusing on the contexts of pragmatic forms to supply interpretations, and depending on a thorough knowledge of the social and cultural environment in which a text was produced. Such study remains an important part of historical pragmatics. But the methodology of historical pragmatics is also progressively moving toward corpus linguistics (see Chapter 5), creating a new discipline of "historical corpus pragmatics," or – if the orientation is more toward change over time – "diachronic corpus pragmatics." The use of corpora in historical pragmatics correlates with the rising use of corpora in both of the source disciplines, historical linguistics and pragmatics. Typically, the approach taken in historical pragmatics is corpus-based (or corpus-aided), in which the researcher begins with a predetermined linguistic feature or features about which he or she has formulated a hypothesis and then uses the corpora to extract data on that feature; the hypothesis is validated, refuted, or refined on the basis of the collected data.

The use of corpora, however, carries with it, as Jucker notes, "the risk of losing the philological sophistication of earlier research" (2008: 903), and hesitancy was initially expressed about the use of electronic corpora in historical pragmatics for a number of reasons. First, historical pragmatics studies were thought to be unsuitable for quantitative study in general. Second, it was felt that the easy extraction of data from large corpora would lead to "decontextualization," or the ignoring of context. Third, one of the advantages of a more objective and empirical methodology such as corpus linguistics – the replicability of one's results – could be problematic for historical pragmatics, as much of historical pragmatics involves interpretation of forms in context and is thus variable and subjective (to some degree). Fourth, the use of normalized spelling and edited texts in most corpora removed the researcher from access to original data important for pragmatic analysis.

Over the years, these reservations have been addressed in a number of different ways. The first historical corpus of English, *The Helsinki Corpus of English Texts* (see Chapter 5), was a multigenre, multipurpose corpus consisting of fairly short text extracts with little textual and contextual information and hence relatively unsuitable for historical pragmatic work. But as we saw above, this "first-generation" corpus has been followed by more recent corpora of single genre, speech-based texts, with fuller contextual information, much better suited for work in this field. As shown in Table 10.3, a search in *The Old Bailey Corpus* includes not only the search item and its immediate context, but also the sex, the social category, and the class of the speaker. A link takes one to the relevant section of *The Old Bailey Proceedings Online*, with the complete text (Figure 10.1a), information about the trial (this is the 1725 trial of Hester Gregory for fraud; verdict not guilty), and a link to an image of the original document (Figure 10.1b).

Jucker and Taavitsainen (2014: 12) see the pull between the two types of corpora, the large multigenre corpora and the specialized single genre corpora, as one of the "double binds" of historical corpus pragmatics: "On the one hand, scholars want to make use of ever larger corpora in order to achieve more sold and statistically valid generalizations, and on the other hand, they realize that they need rich contextualization in order to grasp the subtleties of language use in

Table 10.3 *Sample search result for* well *from* The Old Bailey Corpus

#	Left	Key	Right	Year	Sex	HISCLASS	HISCLAS (code)	HISCLASS (label)
19	rs, and so well acquainted with the Town too? 'Tis very strange!	Well	, says he, 'twas my own Fault, I was a rash Old Fool; I can blame	t17250827 -63	1725	f	3 – Medium-skilled workers	80320	Saddler and Harness Maker

See original

safely swear, that he had teiz'd my Mother 500 times to help him to a Wife: I myself have recommended him to at least 20 Women, all whom he left when he found their fortunes fell short of his Expectation. He was so continually importuning us to introduce him to Ladies, that at last we contrived to get rid of him, by dressing up my Maid in a young Lady's Apparel, and recommending her to him for a Barbadoes fortune, and the Plot succeeded beyond Expectation. I believe she's as modest a Woman as ever lived: Nor is she any thing below him, on account of her Father's being a Soldier, for his Father served in the same Quality under Oliver Cromwell . The Monday after his Wedding, he came to me, and told me he was Bit. Bit? says I, What a Man or your Years, and so well acquainted with the Town too? 'Tis very strange! Well, says he, 'twas my own Fault, I was a rash Old Fool; I can blame nobody but myself. But I should have bit her, if she had been so Rich as I expected; for I have made over all my Estate to my Brother's Son, except 130 l. a Year, a Third of which is all that she can come in for, I can't tell whether he did this before Marriage or since; but he desired both me and my Sister (the Defendant) to persuade his Wife to consent to a Divorce, upon Condition of his allowing her a handsome Reward. I told him I thought no Woman would be so much a Fool, as to swear herself to be a Whore, and so to lose her Husband for a little Money. Sh o, says he, there is no occasion for all that. I can manage it a much better way, if you can but get her to comply; I'll provide a Pre-Contracts betwixt me and another Lady, and get Witnesses to swear it.

Figure 10.1a *Text excerpt from* The Old Bailey Proceedings Online *(www .oldbaileyonline.org, version 7.0, March 24, 2012), August 1725, trial of Hester Gregory (t17250827-63). (Reprinted by permission)*

safely fwear, that he had teiz'd my Mother 500 times to help him to a Wife : I myfelf have recommended him to at leait 10 Women, all whom he left when he found their fortunes fell thort of his Expectation. He was fo continually importuning us to introduce him to Ladies, that at lalt we contrived to get rid of him, by dreffing up my Maid in a young Lady's Apparel, and recommending her to him for a *Barbadoes* rortune, and the Plot fucceeded beyond Expectation. I believe fhe's as modeft a Woman as ever lived : Nor is fhe any thing below him, on account of her Father's being a Soldier, for his Father ferved in the fame Quality under *Oliver Cromwell.* The *Monday* after his Wedding, he came to me, and told me he was Bit. Bit? fays I, What a Man of your Years, and fo well acquainted with the Town too? 'Tis very ftrange! *Well, fays he, 'twas my own Fault, I was a rafh Old Fool ; I can blame nobody but myfelf. But I fhould have bit her, if fhe had been fo Rich as I expected ; for I have made over all my eftate to my Brother's Son, except 130 l. a Year, a Third of which is all that fhe can come in for.* I can't tell whether he did this before Marriage or fince ; but he defired both me and my Sifter (the Defendant) to perfuade his Wife to confent to a Divorce, upon Coadition of his allowing her a handfome Reward. I told him I thought no Woman would be fo much a Fool, as to fwear herfelf to be a Whore, and fo to lofe her Hufband for a little Money. *Sh.o, fays he, there is no occafion for all that. I can manage it a much better way, if you can but get her to comply ; I'll provide a Pre-Contract betwixt me and another Lady, and get Witneffes to fwear it.*

Figure 10.1b *Page image from* The Old Bailey Proceedings Online *(Historical & Special Collections, Harvard Law School Library. Reprinted by permission)* all the extracts retrieved from the corpora." It is likely that both types of corpora will continue to have an important place in historical pragmatics studies in the future.

Along with refinements and advancements in the types of corpora available, various "work-arounds" have been developed in historical pragmatics for the use of corpora. In the form-to-function approach, searching an electronic corpus to determine the use or history of a specific pragmatic form, such as an interjection, a discourse marker, or a performative verb, can easily be carried out, as the search term or terms are readily available. It is here – especially in the study of discourse markers and processes accounting for their development – that corpora first came to the fore in historical pragmatics. In the function-to-form approach, however, for example in studying speech acts, implicit meanings, or the conventions of a genre, a suitable search term does not always exist. In the section below on speech acts, different ways in which this problem has been met will be discussed in detail.

To address the question of the distance corpora place between the researcher and the original text, scholars are turning to the use of texts in their original spelling. Some non-normalized spelling corpora have been produced, with aids for the researcher. ETED, for example, facilitates searching in the corpus by supplying a word list giving the variant spellings of all of the words. EMEMT provides a normalized spelling version that can be used for corpus searches as well as links to the original (non-normalized) texts in the *Early English Books Online* (EEBO) database. The use of such corpora requires more effort and time on the part of the researcher in retrieving desired elements. This reflects the pull between normalized (larger, more easily searchable) and non-normalized spelling (more faithful) corpora as the second "bind" of historical corpus pragmatics (Jucker and Taavitsainen 2014: 10). But the extra time spent with texts in their original spelling may reap rewards in and of itself in generating greater knowledge and understanding of the text and its context.

The remainder of the chapter discusses two case studies from historical pragmatics in greater detail, along with the problems and issues they raise: performative verbs and speech acts, and comment clauses.

Case Studies

Performative Verbs and Speech Acts

The study of verbs which are used to perform speech acts in the history of English can be carried out fairly straightforwardly, in form-to-function studies, whereas the historical study of speech acts has faced considerable challenges; it has even been suggested that it cannot be done, especially using a corpus pragmatic approach.

Performative verbs. Taavitsainen and Jucker (2007) provide an overview of the development of speech act verbs expressing insults, or verbal aggression. They recognize that speech act verbs can be used in two different ways, either performatively (in first-person present tense, as a means of carrying out the action denoted, as in *I challenge you to a duel*) or descriptively (as a means of labeling a speech act, as in *He challenged his rival to a duel*). The descriptive use, though indirect, is effective, they believe, in capturing the way in which the speaker conceptualizes the speech act. After locating all verbs containing 'insult' in their definition during the relevant periods using dictionaries, they then retrieved examples of these verbs from five corpora. They found no performative uses of the verbs in the OE and ME sections of the *Helsinki Corpus*, and only one in the EModE section:

(6)   ATTORNEY: All that he did was by thy Instigation, thou Viper; for **I thou** thee, thou Traitor. (Trial of Sir Walter Raleigh; Taavitsainen and Jucker 2007: 125)

Interestingly, the attorney here uses the second-person familiar pronoun *thou* as a verb of insult (see the Shakespearean example (4) above). Initially, speech act verbs of insult are localized in religious texts, often describing aspects of God's anger. In Early Modern English, they begin to be used in a broader range of contexts, importantly, between interlocutors when they are negotiating the communicative force or effect of the speech acts: *Do you mock me? Do not mock me!* The repertoire of topics constituting an insult by EModE times is consistent with what is found in contemporary insults: name-calling, impolite action; remarks on family relations; social standing, money; personal skills; breaking commitments; national insults.

    Focusing on the history of a single performative verb, *promise*. Traugott and Dasher (2002: 204–214; see also Traugott 1997) identify a number of pragmatic changes. First used as a speech act (non-performative) verb in the middle of the fifteenth century (as in *He promised to come again*), the performative use to make promises occurs by the end of the century (as in *I promise that I won't stop until the work is done*). This is a pragmatic change involving a shift from the domain of content semantics to the domain of pragmatic function. An epistemic parenthetical use, *I promise you*, develops at about the same time (as in *This will be a waste of time, I promise you*). This is a comment clause (see below) serving as a hedge or assurance, denoting the speaker's degree of certainty concerning the attached proposition. Traugott and Dasher argue that this use conventionalizes the commitment inherent in the speech act of promising but also signals that the hearer might have doubts about the speaker's message.[9]

    The form-to-function approach embodied by the study of performative verbs is, on the whole, not very fruitful. Performative verbs turn out to be quite rarely used in carrying out speech acts, they are often used non-perfomatively, and the same performative verb may carry out several different speech acts (e.g., *I promise* can be a true "commissive," as in *I promise to return this book tomorrow*, but also a very emphatic statement of belief, as in *I promise this is the funniest movie you'll see all year*). Only speech acts which tend to be performed in quite formulaic ways, such as thanks, greetings, or apologies, are amendable to the form-to-function approach.

Speech acts. The study of speech acts is the study of communicative functions (what are called "illocutionary forces"), and thus requires a function-to-form approach. But the use of a corpus calls for formal "search terms." Identifying all of the different realizations of a particular speech act can be difficult, if not impossible, since typically, a speech act may be carried out in a number of different ways, both directly and indirectly. When dealing with historical texts, the problems are obviously compounded as one does not have intuitive access to these different expression types. The problems here are twofold:

- the difficulty of compiling a complete inventory of forms which express a particular speech act, and
- the problem of what Kohnen (2007) calls "hidden manifestations."

Hidden manifestations refers to the fact that one might find, for example, a decrease of a particular way of expressing a speech act over time, but one cannot be certain whether this represents a change in the frequency of the speech act or whether other means used to express the speech act have come in to fill the void.

While it is obvious that the realizations of a speech act may change over time, a less obvious problem is that functions (i.e., illocutionary forces) are not necessarily stable and may change over time as well. For example, if we are studying compliments, we must recognize that what actually counts as a compliment may change as well.

Given these difficulties, the diachronic study of speech acts may seem to pose insurmountable obstacles. However, a number of expedients have been proposed. One may simply be the traditional philological method of reading the source texts and identifying all of the ways in which a speech act is expressed. This "bottom up" approach is very time-consuming and labor-intensive, though it usually ensures a high degree of accuracy. Kohnen (2004) suggests that our approach to speech acts is by necessity eclectic and incomplete. Either we can illustrate how a speech act is expressed during a particular period by selecting typical means of expressing that speech act, or we make a principled selection of forms used to express a speech act and study how they change over time.

More practical approaches have been proposed by Jucker (2013: 7–13):

(a)   The first involves focusing on "illocutionary-force-indicating" devices such as performative verbs but also words such as *sorry* for apologies or *please* for requests, or constructions such as subject–auxiliary inversions for questions. Such an approach will not retrieve all instances of the speech act, and it will retrieve some irrelevant examples, but if the search can be refined to include syntactic information, this approach can be quite effective. Example (7) shows *sorry* being used as an illocutionary-force-indicating device.

(b) The second approach is to select the patterns typical of a speech act. For example, compliments in Present-day English have been shown to frequently have the form *X is/looks (really) Y* (e.g., *This movie is really good*). But determining all of the relevant patterns, especially for older periods, and devising an appropriate search string can be challenging. In example (8) *sorry* is used in a typical pattern for apologies.

(c) The third approach is to focus on metacommunicative expressions, expressions used to talk about speech acts (*insult, greet*). *Sorry* is used in this way in example (9).

(7)   **Sorry,** but it's a fact. Give us our biscuits. (1882 COHA: NF)
(8)   But **I am sorry** I have put you to so much trouble. (1819 COHA: FIC)
(9)   **She was sorry**, and very penitent, before her death, for all that she had done to Juliet (1823 COHA: FIC)

Directives (orders, commands, requests) are perhaps the most prototypical type of speech act, the least susceptible to change over time, and the most independent of social and cultural variation. In a directive, a speaker wants a hearer to perform a future action and the utterance counts as such. The speaker must believe that the hearer is both willing and able to perform the action; for example, I cannot say to you *Grow taller!*. The issuing of a command may depend on a certain power relationship holding between the speaker and the hearer, or on the existence of an extralinguistic institution (e.g., military chain of command).

Directive speech acts may be realized in a large variety of ways:

- performatives (*I request/ask/command/order that you . . .*, *We ask that you . . .*) and hedged performatives (*I would like to ask you to . . .*)
- imperatives and periphrastic imperatives (*Be quiet for a minute!*, *Let's have pizza for dinner*)
- expressions of the hearer's obligation, modal (*You should . . .*) and otherwise (*You need to . . .*, *You'll have to . . .*)
- expressions of the speaker's wants (*I would like you to . . .*) or needs (*I need you to . . .*, *I must . . .*)
- questions of the hearer's abilities or willingness (*Can/could/would/will you . . . ?*)
- indirect idioms (*How about . . .*)
- hints (*The neighbors can hear you* = *Speak more quietly*)

These are roughly aligned from most direct to most indirect (from most face-threatening to least face-threatening), with at least the last three types being categorized as "indirect."

In a series of studies, Kohnen (2000a, b, 2004, 2007, 2008a, b) has examined the history of directives in English. An initial and quite dramatic finding was that performative verbs were seven times more frequent in Old English than in Present-day English, with Old English favoring what Kohnen calls "ask" and "order" verbs, where the addressor is subordinate or superordinate to the addressee, and Present-day English favoring less face-threatening "suggest" verbs, where the relative status of the interlocutors appears equivalent. This suggested to Kohnen that Old English has "a significantly larger proportion of (apparently) face-threatening acts" (2000a: 184), which he attributes to the strict hierarchy of Anglo-Saxon society and its oral culture. Later, more nuanced studies have complicated this picture. In these, Kohnen shows that overall Old English did not have as many strict directives as one might expect. Explicit performatives played quite a minor role, as did second-person imperatives and modals. First- and third-person modals, often expressing common ground or impersonality, were the most common form of directives. OE forms such as the *uton we* 'let's' + infinitive construction and the impersonal *(neod)thearf is* 'it is necessary' form appear to lessen the threat to face. However, Kohnen argues that because these are limited to religious contexts, they were not a strategy of politeness but a reflection of Christian ideals of *humilitas* and *oboedientia*. Kohnen concludes that "the choice of directive is – in many cases –not determined by face work" (2008a: 41).

Several important points arise out of Kohnen's studies of directives in the subsequent periods. In the fifteenth century there is an overall decrease in the number of directives, but at the same time a shift to the use of second-person modals, which signal the superior position of the addressor vis-à-vis the addressee. Thus, lower directive use is not associated with a less forceful and more polite style. In the EModE period, the increased use of indirect forms, both those focused on the addressor (*I would like* ...) and those focused on the addressee (*Can you* ...?), points to the rise of negative politeness (see Jucker's study summarized above). Present-day English continues this trend toward negative politeness with the rise of first-person modals, the *let's* construction, indirect forms, and performative verbs using "suggest/advise" verbs. Direct imperatives do not disappear, but tend to focus on mental rather than physical action and hence be less face-threatening.

Culpeper and Archer (2008) took a different approach to identifying speech acts, namely, by annotating a corpus (a subsection of the CED) for each instance of the speech act being studied. The annotation was done not on the basis of form, but on the basis of the effect of the speech act. That is, for the directives they studied, they looked to see whether it was either received by the recipient as a request or carried out. This technique, like traditional approaches, is quite time-consuming and labor-intensive. The results of their study of requests in drama and trials suggest that requests in the EModE period (1640–1760) are strikingly different from those in the PDE period. In the early period, requests belong to what they label the direct "impositive" category (imperatives, performatives, obligation and want statements) in 73 percent of the cases; indeed, nearly 76 percent of these are overt imperatives:

(10)   Lord President: If this be all that you will say, then, Gentlemen, you
          that brought the Prisoner hither, **take charge** of him back again (1650
          Trial of King Charles I; Culpeper and Archer 2008: 61)

In contrast, studies of requests in Present-day English have found that under
10 percent of requests are expressed by overt imperatives. Moreover, nearly one-
half of the directives in Early Modern English have no modification to soften the
blow. Vocatives and forms of *pray* (*prithee*) may occur, but "grounders" (which
give the reason for the request) – the most common present-day mitigator – are
not common. But Culpeper and Archer argue that one should not infer that Early
Modern English is "less polite." Rather, in the hierarchical society of the time one
could – depending on one's position in society – simply assume the right to make
a request, with no sense of infringing upon the rights of others. Indirect forms
also function differently in the two periods. In Present-day English, the use of
indirectness is ascribed to negative politeness, in which the least imposition
possible is placed upon the higher-ranked addressee; such indirect forms most
often question the addressee's ability (*Can/could you … ?*). In Early Modern
English, indirect forms are typically used by more powerful addressors and either
relate to the addressee's willingness to act or they grant the addressee permission
to act, thus being associated with positive politeness:

(11)   a. My Lord, Pray **let him know** what is done, to warn him, lest he fall
          into the same condemnation (1658 Trial of John Mordant; Culpeper
          and Archer 2008: 66)
       b. Then, Gentlemen, **will you sum up** (1696 Trial of Rockwood;
          Culpeper and Archer 2008: 66)

   In sum, these studies of directives in the history of English, while not entirely
comparable, have shown movement away from the direct directives to indirect
directives, and a concomitant shift from positive (or neutral) politeness to
negative politeness.

Comment Clauses

Comment clauses are parentheticals usually formed with first- or second-person
pronouns and simple present-tense verbs; like discourse markers, they may
express speaker (un)certainty, evoke speaker emotional attitude, or act as claims
on hearer attention, among a range of other pragmatic and politeness functions in
discourse. They are typical of spoken discourse, though not unknown in written
discourse. Below are some corpus examples from Present-day English:

(12)   a. It's definitely more, **you know, I guess**, spicy. (2012 COCA: SPOK)
       b. **I mean, I think, you know**, we keep rehashing sort of – all of the –
          the turn of events from the last few nights. (2012 COCA: FIC)
       c. He's mostly Irish wolfhound, **I think**. (2012 COCA: FIC)

As we saw in the introduction to this chapter, comment clauses occurred in earlier stages of English. Some can be dated to Old English (such as *that is (to say)*), while others arose in Middle English (such as *as it were, let me see, I (dare) say, I think/guess, I see, I find*). Studies of the history of comment clauses in English (e.g., Brinton 2008) have had two foci of attention:

    (a) the syntactic origin and development of comment clauses, and
    (b) the processes by which they develop.

An influential account of the syntactic development of comment clauses is that of Thompson and Mulac (1991), as was discussed in Chapter 7. Their proposal is a synchronic account of the origin of parenthetical *I think* and *I guess*, but it has been extended analogically to account for the diachronic origin of comment clauses. As shown in (13), Thompson and Mulac argue that the parenthetical comment clause begins as a main clause (*I think*); what will later emerge as the "host" for the comment clause is the complement *that*-clause (*that the weather is improving*) (13a). When the complementizer *that* is deleted, the syntactic status of *I think* becomes indeterminate, as either main clause or parenthetical (13b). Syntactic reanalysis of the main clause as a parenthetical allows for its movement to medial or final position (13c).

(13)   a. I think that the weather is improving.
         b. I think Ø the weather is improving.
         c. The weather is improving, I think./The weather is, I think, improving.

I think/I guess becomes a unitary, particle-like "epistemic parenthetical." For Thompson and Mulac, syntactic reanalysis depends on the frequency of indeterminate structures with zero complementizers (13b); there is a direct correlation between the frequency of first-person subjects/ *that*-less complements and the rise of *I think/I guess* as comment clauses. I have termed this the "matrix clause hypothesis" (Brinton 2008). Despite its intuitive appeal, there might be reason to question this hypothesis. Often, the diachronic record does not give evidence for a higher frequency of either the main clause forms or the *that*-less complements in earlier stages of the language.

    Let's examine the case of the comment clause *you see* in more detail.[10] In Present-day English, this has a number of forms (*you see, as you see, see*) and pragmatic uses: *(as) (you) see* ascertains the hearer's comprehension, continued interest, or agreement or expresses triumph, as in the following examples:

(14)   a. Kumari is the Hindu virgin goddess, **you see**, and Saraswati is the divine consort of Lord Brahma (2012 COCA: FIC)
         b. Astolfo was concluding: "So, **as you see**, the connections between possessor and possession are intimate and enduring." (2007 COCA: FIC)
         c. It's sick and ridiculous. Ridiculous. **See**, I have my own dictionary, (2006 COCA:MAG)

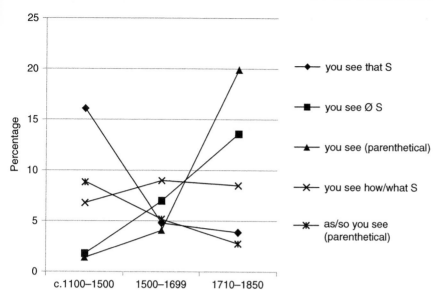

Figure 10.2 *Occurrences of* you see *constructions. Based on the* MED *quotation bank (for Middle English), the* OED *quotation bank (for Early Modern English, and CLMET[11] (for Late Modern English)*

Historically, Fitzmaurice (2004) has postulated the development of the comment clause from a main clause, namely,

you see that S > parenthetical *you see* (> *see*)

If we consider the frequency of the different forms (see Figure 10.2), we see that the changes generally follow the pattern expected by the matrix clause hypothesis. *You see that* S declines, *you see* without *that* increases, and *you see* parentheticals increase over time. However, none of the forms exceeds 20 percent; in fact, *you see* followed by an NP is the most common construction in all periods. At the point where parenthetical *you see* seems to take off in the Early Modern period, the most common form is *you see* followed by an indirect question (*how/what* S). More importantly, parenthetical *as you see* is much more common than *you see* in Middle English (examples from Brinton 2008: 144):

(15)   a. I am come here, in lyke wyse **as you see** (*c.* 1440 Generydes,
          A Romance 102; *OED*)
          'I am come here in like manner, as you see'
      b. God men, I am **als yee now her se**, An ald man (1400(a. 1325) *Cursor
          Mundi* (Vsp A.3) 5335; *MED*)
          'good men, I am as you now here see, an old man'

Thus, a postulated development from *as you see* to *you see* is more plausible and syntactically simpler than development from the matrix clause and complement *that* clause (whose frequency is under 5 percent), involving deletion of the complementizer (*as*) but no reversal of syntactic relationship.[12]

Conclusions from a range of diachronic studies suggest that there are several different syntactic sources for comment clauses (see Brinton 2006, 2008):

(a) matrix first-person clauses with a variety of clausal and non-clausal complements (*that* clauses, interrogatives, imperatives, noun phrases) (e.g., *I pray you/thee* > *(I) pray (you)/prithee, I'm afraid, I'm sorry, I promise you, (I) thank you, I say* > *say, I dare say, I/you admit*, and *I mean*)

(b) matrix imperative clauses (e.g. *(now) look (you) (here), mind you, see*)

(c) adverbial/relative clauses, involving either deletion of the complementizer (e.g., *if you please* > *please, as you say* > *you say, as I gather* > *I gather, as I find* > *I find*) or its retention (e.g., *if you will, as it were, so to speak*)

At least three different processes of change have been said to account for the development of comment clauses, and of discourse markers more generally: grammaticalization, lexicalization, and – a process unique to pragmatic forms – pragmaticalization. The following sections explore the question of which process most adequately accounts for the development of comment clauses and discourse markers.

> It would be helpful for you at this stage to review the discussion of grammaticalization and lexicalization in Chapter 6.

Many scholars have argued that comment clauses undergo the changes characteristic of grammaticalization. Like grammaticalizing items, comment clauses arise from verbs of general meaning (*say, see, look, mean, know, think*). Syntactically, they become fixed and (partially) fossilized, usually in the first- or second-person, simple present tense (*I mean, I think, you know*). Semantically, they are "bleached" of concrete meaning, while acquiring non-referential (pragmatic, politeness) meanings and undergoing (inter)subjectification. For example, the comment clause *you see* no longer denotes physical vision but claims mutual understanding and avoids a threat to negative face. These semantic changes often involve the conventionalization of invited inferences (see Chapter 7), as for example, the epistemic meaning of *look* resulting from the inference that 'what is seen must be believed.' The development of comment clauses can be seen as conforming to Hopper's (1991) principles of grammaticalization:

- decategorialization (loss of the behavioral characteristics of fully formed and complement-taking clause), e.g., *I think* or *I mean* exists as a syntactically frozen or defective clause, with a particle-like quality;

- persistence (the retention of some trace of the original meaning), e.g., *I find* retains some sense of 'discover by experience' even when functioning as a comment clause;
- divergence (the continued existence of the original functions in some contexts), e.g., *I think* continues to be a matrix clause governing a complement (variable in respect to subject/tense/aspect); and
- layering (the coexistence of older and newer forms), e.g., the newer appositional marker *I mean* coexists with the older forms *that is to say* or *to wit*.

But in some respects, the development of discourse markers and comment clauses diverges from what is thought to occur during grammaticalization. They do not seem to acquire the prototypical grammatical qualities that we expect in a fully grammaticalized inflection, that is:

(a) they rarely reduce phonetically and fuse with the preceding host form but remain independent items;
(b) they do not become entirely fixed either in form or position;
(c) they do not become an obligatory element in a grammatical paradigm; and
(d) they come to have increased scope over discourse rather than becoming more tightly bound to a host element.

Moreover, the resulting forms, discourse markers and comment clauses, while they resemble adverbials, belong to no identifiable grammatical class and occupy an extra-sentential position. Some scholars have gone as far as to say that their development scarcely resembles grammaticalization.

Ultimately, then, the question is whether items which are in some sense "agrammatical" can be seen as undergoing grammaticalization at all. This is a question to which we will return below.

Lexicalization may be seen as a process by which a free syntactic construction fossilizes, fuses, and coalesces, and thus comes to be treated as an unanalyzable lexical item. A complex unit becomes irregular, opaque, and often monomorphemic (see Chapter 6). This process might be seen as accounting for the development of comment clauses and phrasal discourse markers, which show some degree of coalescence and fusion (e.g., *is it not* > *innit*, *you know* > *y'know*, *me thinks* > *methinks*), ellipsis of phonological content (e.g., *look you* > *look*, *as you say* > *you say* > *say*), and semantic demotivation. That is, they come to be treated holistically as lexical items. For example, Fischer (2007a) argues that *I think* type comment clauses undergo bonding and come to form one lexical unit, while retaining much of their lexical meaning.

Since the processes pointed to as indicative of lexicalization – fossilization, univerbation, and coalescence – are common to both grammaticalization and lexicalization, some studies have argued that discourse markers and comment clauses result from a combination of grammaticalization and lexicalization.

The first to propose that discourse markers and comment clauses develop by a process distinct from grammaticalization and lexicalization were Erman and Kotsinas (1993) in a synchronic study of *you know* and Swedish *ba'*. They termed this distinct process "pragmaticalization." In pragmaticalization, a lexical element (with propositional meaning) develops directly into an element whose function is textual and interpersonal (with discourse-pragmatic meaning); there is no intermediate grammatical stage. Pragmaticalization has been distinguished from grammaticalization in a number of ways: by the non-truth-conditionality and optionality of pragmaticalized forms (see Aijmer 1997) or by the centrality of (inter)subjectivity and pragmatic strengthening to pragmaticalization (Claridge and Arnovick 2010). But in many respects there appears to be little to distinguish pragmaticalization from grammaticalization. Both involve the conventionalization of pragmatic meaning (invited inferences), the loss of phonetic content, increased frequency, optionality in the syntax of the sentence, subjectification, and scope expansion (over the whole proposition or utterance), as well as decategorialization, persistence, and divergence (in Hopper's sense, see above). Thus, the diachronic processes are "virtually indistinguishable" (Diewald 2011: 456).

The choice between the two processes seems to hinge on what is encompassed by "grammar." If grammar is viewed narrowly, as restricted to the morphosyntactic domain, and if grammatical items must have truth-conditional meaning, be obligatory, and fall strictly within the syntax of the sentence, then pragmatic elements are excluded. But it has been pointed out that many aspects of grammar – traditionally conceived – such as deixis, reference, tense, and modality have a discourse-pragmatic dimension, and many aspects of pragmatics, such as topic and focus, have a "grammatical" (syntactic) dimension. Moreover, some elements of grammar (such as sentence adverbials) are asyntactic (stand outside the clause) and carry scope over discourse. Thus, there seem to be good reasons for viewing grammar more broadly to encompass discourse functions. Diewald goes further to argue that pragmatic functions are "genuine grammatical functions which are indispensable for the organization and structuring" of discourse and "the fundamental features of grammar itself are rooted in pragmatics" (2006: 405; 2011: 451). Moreover, pragmatic elements could be seen as having "communicative obligatoriness" (Diewald 2010: 25) – i.e., not obligatory by language-internal criteria but by the "communicative intentions of the speaker."

Let's return, then, to the question of which process best accounts for the rise of comment clauses. *Contra* lexicalization, it can be pointed out that comment clauses do not behave like lexical items: they cannot be understood as belonging to any major lexical category, they do not express lexical (propositional, referential) meaning, but rather non-lexical (non-referential/ procedural) meaning, and, unlike lexical items, they are syntactically and prosodically constrained. Moreover, like grammaticalization, but unlike lexicalization, comment clauses typically increase in frequency and productivity, they involve decategorialization, they show semantic bleaching and (inter)subjectification, and they may show generality across languages.[13]

Contra pragmaticalization, we can argue that if pragmatic meaning is seen as foundational to grammar, then discourse markers and comment clauses "belong to grammar." Moreover, the similarities of the processes of change in pragmaticalization from grammaticalization entail that they are too close to be distinguished. Common to both are fusion and coalescence, idiomaticization (semantic demotivation), decategorialization, semantic/pragmatic expansion, inferencing or pragmatic strengthening, increased frequency, and gradualness. While there are differences from "classic" cases of grammaticalization – in respect to increased scope, syntactic fixedness, and lack of bondedness – it has been shown that no cases of grammaticalization exhibit all of the characteristic features. Pragmaticalization is thus a subtype of grammaticalization.[14]

In sum, we have argued that both the end result of change and the processes of change themselves point to grammaticalization as the appropriate way to account for the rise of discourse markers and comment clauses.

Concluding Remarks

This chapter has shown how the methods of pragmatic and historical linguistic study converged to produce the field of historical pragmatics. Though the major works in the field began to appear in the mid 1990s, historical pragmatics has deeper roots in traditional philological and literary study. In the twenty-five years since, the field has grown and diversified, overcoming some of the obstacles perceived to hold it back, such as the lack of appropriate data and methodological difficulties in the study of linguistic functions. As the two case studies discussed in detail in this chapter show, two major directions can be identified in historical pragmatics, one which is concerned more with sociocultural factors underlying pragmatic phenomena and moves more in the direction of historical sociolinguistics (see Chapter 9), and one which is concerned more with processes of lexical and grammatical change as they apply to development of pragmatic elements and often overlaps with grammaticalization studies (see Chapter 6). The future of historical pragmatics is to a large extent centered in corpus linguistics (see Chapter 5), though more traditionally oriented pragmaphilological studies continue to be important.

Suggestions for Further Study

The first major works in the field of historical pragmatics are Jucker (1995) and Brinton (1996). The field of historical pragmatics has been described in a number of articles, see Jacobs and Jucker (1995), Jucker (1998, 2006b, 2008), Traugott (2006), Taavitsainen and Fitzmaurice (2007), Culpeper (2010), Taavitsainen and

Jucker (2010, 2015), Taavitsainen (2012), and Brinton (2015). A comprehensive handbook of historical pragmatics containing state-of-the-art discussions is Jucker and Taavitsainen (2010); herein, see Archer (2010) on speech acts, Gehweiler (2010) on interjections, Brinton (2010) on discourse markers, Mazzon (2010) on address terms, and section VII on domains of discourse. A recent textbook in the field is Jucker and Taavitsainen (2013). The papers in Fitzmaurice and Taavitsainen (2007) focus on questions of methodology. Case studies on speech acts can be found in Jucker and Taavitsainen (2008) and on address terms in Taavitsainen and Jucker (2002). Taavitsainen, Jucker, and Tuominen (2014) contains articles focused on diachronic corpus pragmatics, and Brinton (2012) discusses some of the problems for such study. The *Journal of Historical Pragmatics* (2000–) publishes historical pragmatics studies from all languages and subfields, with occasional special issues devoted to specific topics, such as discourse markers, historical courtroom discourse, or letter writing.

Exercises

1. Directives in *Pride and Prejudice*

   In the following passage from Jane Austen's 1813 novel, *Pride and Prejudice* (ch. 20), Mrs. Bennet is upset that her daughter Elizabeth will not marry Mr. Collins and solicits her husband's help in convincing her daughter to accept the marriage proposal. The passage contains numerous directives.

   a. Identify the different forms used to utter these directives.

   b. Discuss whether all of these directives are successful speech acts. Remember that for a directive to "work" the action requested of the hearer must be future and voluntary. (Volition does not refer to one's liking to do what is commanded, but merely to its being humanly possible.) The speaker uttering a command must want or wish for the action to be carried out.

   c. The passage also contains a number of threats, which are a type of conditional "commissive" or promise, as the speaker expresses an intention to carry out an action under certain circumstances. Identify the threats in this passage and explain how they work.

   > "Oh! Mr. Bennet, you are wanted immediately; we are all in an uproar. You must come and make Lizzy marry Mr. Collins, for she vows she will not have him, and if you do not make haste he will change his mind and not have *her*."
   >
   > Mr. Bennet raised his eyes from his book as she entered, and fixed them on her face with a calm unconcern which was not in the least altered by her communication.
   >
   > "I have not the pleasure of understanding you," said he, when she had finished her speech. "Of what are you talking?"

"Of Mr. Collins and Lizzy. Lizzy declares she will not have Mr. Collins, and Mr. Collins begins to say that he will not have Lizzy."

"And what am I to do on the occasion? It seems an hopeless business."

"Speak to Lizzy about it yourself. Tell her that you insist upon her marrying him."

"Let her be called down. She shall hear my opinion."

Mrs. Bennet rang the bell, and Miss Elizabeth was summoned to the library.

"Come here, child," cried her father as she appeared. "I have sent for you on an affair of importance. I understand that Mr. Collins has made you an offer of marriage. Is it true?" Elizabeth replied that it was. "Very well—and this offer of marriage you have refused?"

"I have, sir."

"Very well. We now come to the point. Your mother insists upon your accepting it. Is it not so, Mrs. Bennet?"

"Yes, or I will never see her again."

"An unhappy alternative is before you, Elizabeth. From this day you must be a stranger to one of your parents. Your mother will never see you again if you do *not* marry Mr. Collins, and I will never see you again if you *do*."

Elizabeth could not but smile at such a conclusion of such a beginning, but Mrs. Bennet, who had persuaded herself that her husband regarded the affair as she wished, was excessively disappointed.

"What do you mean, Mr. Bennet, in talking this way? You promised me to *insist* upon her marrying him."   (www.gutenberg.org/files/1342/1342-h/ 1342-h.htm)

2. *See now* in *Gammer Gurton's Needle*

In the following passage from the 1575 edition of the comic drama *Gammer Gurton's Needle* (Act IV, scene iii), the playwright is playing on the form *see now*.

a. In some cases, the form can retain its literal meaning (as an order to the hearer to look at something), while in other cases it cannot. Try to distinguish the two. What contextual clues help to distinguish the literal from the non-literal uses?

b. As a comment clause in Present-day English, a number of different functions have been proposed for *see now*: as a means of ascertaining the hearer's comprehension, continued interest, or agreement, as an attention getter, and as an expression of triumph. Which, if any, of these functions can be identified in this text?

HODGE. By m'fay ['my faith'], sir, that ye shall,
          What matter soever there was done, ich can tell your maship [all]:
          My Gammer ['Grandma'] Gurton here, see now,
          Sat her down at this door, see now;
5   And, as she began to stir her, see now,

Her nee'le fell in the floor, see now;
And while her staff she took, see now,
At Gib her cat to fling, see now,
Her nee'le was lost in the floor, see now—
10   Is not this a wondrous thing, see now?
Then came the quean ['woman'] dame Chat, see now,
To ask for her black cup, see now:
And even here at this gate ['street'], see now,
She took that nee'le up, see now:
15   My gammer then she yede ['went'], see now,
Her nee'le again to bring, see now,
And was caught by the head, see now—
Is not this a wondrous thing, see now?
She tare ['tore'] my gammer's coat, see now,
20   And scratched her by the face, see now;
Chad ['If I had'] thought sh'ad ['she had'] stopp'd her throat, see now—
Is not this a wondrous case, see now?
When ich saw this, ich was wroth, see now,
And stert between them twain, see now;
25   Else ich durst ['dare'] take a book-oath, see now,
My gammer had been slain, see now.
(www.gutenberg.org/files/37503/37503-h/37503-h.htm)

3. The development of *after all*

After all is a discourse marker with the meaning 'in spite of any indications or expectations to the contrary; when all is said and done, nevertheless' (*OED*, s.v. *after*, adv., prep. and conj., def. 7c), as in the following example:

After all, what matters is what people do (2012 COCA: NEWS)

In the development of phrasal discourse markers such as *in fact*, *indeed*, and *besides*, Traugott (1995b) argues that there are four stages of development:

- a full lexical stage
- a predicate adverb stage – the adverb occurs within the predicate of the sentence with relatively concrete meaning and narrow scope
- a sentential adverb stage – the adverb is dislocated (usually to sentence-initial position) and assumes wider scope over the entire sentence
- a discourse marker stage – the adverb acquires new pragmatic functions which later become conventionalized, and the adverb may be further dislocated.

"Bridging" constructions, where the meaning is indeterminate between more or less literal meaning and the discourse-pragmatic meaning, will occur.

In the examples given below, see if you can trace the development of *after all* that Traugott postulates for other phrasal markers. What evidence can you use to classify examples? Is there further evidence of the grammaticalization of this discourse marker? Note here that the small context often makes interpretation difficult. You will also find that real historical data are often very "messy."

(i) He send his sond After alle þe wise men of his lond, And tolde hem alle his greuaunce. (*c.* 1330 *7 Sages(1)* (Auch) 290/1893; *MED*)
'he sent his son after all the wise men of his land and told them all his grievances'

(ii) Oure enditing ... assendiþ in þis book fro þe lowest þinges to þe hiȝest ... And after alle soche assencioun, it schal al be withouten voice, & al it schal be knittid to a þing þat is vnspekable. (a. 1425(? a1400) *Dionysius HDivinity (Hrl 674)* 8/21; *MED*)
'our writing ... leads in this book from the lowest things to the highest ... And after all such ascension, it shall all be without voice and al it shall be knitted to a thing that is unspeakable'

(iii) Intelligence ... iuggeth after all þat is in man, As he hath in þe exsaumple ydeall Conseyued þat non other may ne can. (*c.* 1450(1410) Walton, *Boeth.* (Lin-C 103) p. 309; *MED*)
'intelligence ... judges after all that is in man, as he has conceived in the ideal example that no other may not be able'

(iv) And he ful gentylly gate of ['got from'] hys fader the said book / and delyuerd it to me / by whiche I haue corrected my book / as here after alle alonge by thayde ['the aid'] of almyghty god shal folowe (1477–1684 Caxton, *Prologues and Epilogues*; HC)

(v) After all she was thrast unto the herte with a swerde. (1526 R. Whitford tr. *Martiloge* 138; *OED*)

(vi) and my lord bysshope Bonar of London did syng masse of requiem, and doctur Whyt bysshope of Lynkolne dyd pryche at the sam masse; and after all they whent to his plasse to dener. (1550–1563 Machyn, *The Diary of Henry Machyn*; HC)

(vii) there he made mee right welcome, both with varietie of fare, and after all, hee commanded three of his men to direct mee to see his most admirable Colemines; (1630 Taylor, *The Pennyles Pilgrimage*; HC)

(viii) If, after all ... he shall betake himself to the easiest and complyantest ways of accommodation. (1642 Ld. Digby in *Clarendon's Hist. Rebellion* (1702) I. iv. 338; *OED*)

(ix) After all, I will not be peremptory in the Negative. (1697 W. Dampier, *New Voy. around World* xvii. 485; *OED*)

(x) After all, these discoveries are not worth the candle. (*c.* 1700 *Gentleman Instructed* (1732) 556; *OED*)

(xi) What art thou asking of them, after all? Some mighty Boon ... ! (1712 J. Arbuthnot, *John Bull Still in Senses* x. 47; *OED*)

(xii) Men of a nice and foppish *Gusto*, whom, after all, it is almost impossible to please. (1727 Pope et al. *Peri Bathous* 11 in Swift et al. *Misc.: Last Vol.*; *OED*)

(xiii) Well, after all, Kitchen-Physic is the best Physic. (1738 Swift, *Compl. Coll. Genteel Conversat.* 154; *OED*)

(xiv) it was the wine of homecoming, and rejoicing, and gratitude. And afterall, he had been something of a prodigal, (1886 COHA: FIC)

4. The speech act of 'warning'

The speech act of 'warning' may be performed using the explicit performative verb *warn*, as in *I warn you that I am exhausting to live with*. If we look at the occurrence of this explicit performative in COHA, we find a frequency of 0.72/million words in 1820, rising to 2.99/million in 1900, but falling to 0.57/million in 2000. Can we conclude from this that people are uttering warnings less frequently now than in the past? Could this be a case of what Kohnen calls "hidden manifestations"? If so, how might one research this question in the COHA corpus?

Notes

For very helpful comments on an earlier draft of this chapter, I am grateful to Peter Grund and to graduate students in my historical pragmatics graduate class in 2014.

1. The approach has gone under a number of names, including "historical discourse analysis," "diachronic textlinguistics," "New Philology," and "historical dialogue analysis," but it is one of the earliest names, "historical pragmatics" (Stein 1985), which has gained the widest acceptance (for a discussion of the names, see Brinton 2015).

2. The changes affecting linguistics are set out by Traugott (2008), and Jucker and Taavitsainen (2013: ch. 1; Taavitsainen and Jucker 2015) discuss how these changes are responsible for shaping the field of historical pragmatics.

3. See Brinton (1996: 29–40; 2010: 285–287) for a fuller definition of discourse markers, or what may also be called "pragmatic markers."

4. On politeness, see Brown and Levinson (1987).

5. The classic discussion of speech acts is Searle (1969).

6. Pakkala-Weckström (2008) focuses on the essential condition of commissives, that is, the fact that the uttering of a promise places speakers under an obligation to do what is promised. She argues that in the highly honor-bound, chivalric society of Chaucer's *Franklin's Tale*, just the uttering of the words alone constituted a "binding promise" which honor dictated must be carried out, regardless of whether the speaker intended the utterance to place him or her under an obligation. Thus, the "essential condition" of the speech act worked differently than prototypical modern promises.

7. Texts reproduced from ProQuest Historical Newspapers: *The Globe and Mail*.

8. More information on these resources can be found in the "Corpora and Electronic Databases" section at the end of the text. See Kytö (2010) for a full description of all of these resources. A good summary of corpora may be found at www.helsinki.fi/varieng/Co RD/corpora/. For a discussion of multigenre, multipurpose corpora, which are also important for historical pragmatic work, see Chapter 5.

9. Another use of the verb *promise* arising in the late sixteenth century is a transitive construction in the sense of 'can be expected to provide, portend' (as in *The morning promised a fair day*), followed in the eighteenth century by a raising construction with nonfinite

complements meaning 'portend' (as in *He promises to be an extraordinary person*). These changes represent a separate path of development from the speech act verb (Traugott and Dasher 2002).

10. This study is based on Brinton (2008: ch. 6).

11. *The Corpus of Late Modern English Texts* (perswww.kuleuven.be/~u0044428/clmet.htm) has now been superseded by CLMET3.0.

12. As discussed in Brinton (2008: 148–154), the origin of *see* is more complex; it does not derive from *you see* by a process of shortening but from imperative *see*, with reinforcement from *did you see?*

13. For more on the differences and similarities between grammaticalization and lexicalization, see Brinton and Traugott (2005).

14. For a comparison of grammaticalization and pragmaticalization, see Degand and Evers-Vermeul (2015).

11

Perspectives on Standardization: From Codification to Prescriptivism

INGRID TIEKEN-BOON VAN OSTADE

Introduction

In 2014, a new edition came out of Sir Ernest Gowers' *Plain Words: A Guide to the Use of English*, originally published in 1948. Gowers (1880–1966) was a civil servant, and the new edition was produced by his great-granddaughter, the novelist Rebecca Gowers. *Plain Words* is a usage guide, a manual on how to use language correctly. Originally written for civil servants like Gowers himself, *Plain Words* became hugely popular. But the work is neither the first of its kind nor unique in history: English usage guides originated during the second half of the eighteenth century, and their popularity has increased enormously, particularly during the end of the twentieth century and the beginning the twenty-first, despite the fact that there are already very many of them. There is clearly a market for usage guides.

Such a market was already growing in England during the second half of the eighteenth century, though at first this new demand led to the publication of grammars, more than ever before. In some countries, grammars and usage guides, but also dictionaries, are published by an academy, an authoritative institution that is officially responsible for the regulation of the language. The best-known example is the Académie française, founded in 1635, but Spain has a language academy too, and so does the Netherlands, but it regulates Dutch spelling only. For English there has never been an academy, though at the beginning of the eighteenth century England came very close to having one. Instead of officially sanctioned publications, English grammars, dictionaries and usage guides came to be produced by individuals, writers from different backgrounds but all of them interested in language, often encouraged by publishers with an eye for the market.

Usage guides are neither grammars nor dictionaries because they deal with *all* aspects of language: pronunciation, spelling, vocabulary, grammar, and style. They originate from "normative grammars" like the one by the clergyman Robert Lowth (1710–1787), which presents a norm of correctness for those wishing to speak and write correctly. One of the reasons Lowth's *Short Introduction to English*

Grammar (1762) was so popular was that it had a chapter on syntax with numerous footnotes criticizing the grammatical mistakes of famous English writers. Because they were expected to provide a norm of correctness, normative grammars take both a *pre*scriptive approach (and so prescribe certain usages as correct) and a *pro*scriptive one (telling the reader what not to use). Modern grammars, by contrast, are primarily *de*scriptive, since they are expected to record and describe actual practice in language use instead of telling readers what is right and wrong. Lowth's approach to grammar is often called prescriptive, but analyzing his rules shows that he was just as often descriptive when discussing disputed features of language use. This is clear from the language he used: ending a sentence with a preposition, he wrote, is "an Idiom which our language is strongly inclined to; it prevails in common conversation, and suits very well with the familiar style in writing" (1762: 127–128). There is nothing prescriptive about these words. Lowth of course lacked the resources that allow modern linguists to do empirical research, like text corpora or databases (see Chapter 5), but he did have a collection of grammatical mistakes by famous English writers, and these formed the background of his discussions of linguistic correctness.

Lowth's grammar, and most of the other eighteenth-century works that will be discussed here, can be accessed through the database *Eighteenth Century Collections Online* (ECCO). An Advanced Search with his name under Author and with Title set to "short introduction to English grammar" produces many results, including different editions. Its influence on other grammars can be discovered through an Advanced Search in ECCO for "Lowth's grammar" (use quotation marks to mark the exact phrase), with "grammar" as part of the title and the dates set to 1762–1800. This produces a list of books that refer to Lowth as their source. Often, however, because of unacknowledged copying or plagiarism, Lowth's name is not mentioned. Searching instead for a phrase such as "noun of multitude," used by Lowth to denote collective nouns like *meeting* or *parliament* that can have either a singular or a plural verb form, and with the date set to 1762–1800, will show that his grammar had been plagiarized by Lindley Murray (1745–1826). Plagiarism was still fairly common among grammarians in those days, and Murray plagiarized several other grammars as well. His own grammar came out in 1795, and was frequently reprinted down to well into the nineteenth century. Because Lowth was Murray's main source, it is through the phenomenal popularity of Murray's grammar that Lowth's normative rules helped shape English grammar as it is today (see Exercise 1).

An older, less user-friendly but still valuable resource for accessing eighteenth-century grammars is R. C. Alston's series *English Linguistics 1500–1800* (Alston 1974).

Not long after Lowth's grammar, the first usage guide came out, called *Reflections on the English Language* (1770) by Robert Baker (flourished 1760–1779). Baker was a hack writer, who had lived in France as a young man. We know this from his other publications in ECCO, and from the preface of the *Reflections*, which includes quite a bit of personal information. While in France, Baker had learned French, so he was able to read a major publication by the French Academy, a usage guide published by Claude Favre de Vaugelas in 1647. A similar work for English might sell well, Baker believed. Though in the preface he claimed that he had never heard of Lowth's grammar, the two works contain many identical "usage problems" – items which show divided usage and about which readers needed to be advised, such as whether to write *different to* or *from* or why *the reason is because* is wrong and should be *the reason is that* instead. But Baker had not plagiarized Lowth. The only connection between them is the linguistic climate in which they lived: grammatical mistakes were frequently criticized in reviews of books that appeared in popular periodicals. This was discovered by Carol Percy, who set up a database with linguistic criticism found in the *Monthly Review* and the *Critical Review*, two influential eighteenth-century journals (Percy 2008, 2009). We know from references in their books that Lowth and Baker both read these journals, so that is where, each independently, they must have found the usage problems they discussed. The critical approach to language use taken by Lowth and Baker is typical of the second half of the eighteenth century, a period which was characterized by an increasingly pre-scriptive interest in language, not only in grammars or usage guides, but also in the popular press. Prescriptivism, in other words, became the spirit of the age, and it has remained so to this day.

Usage guides were eventually published in America as well, where people came to need advice on correct language use due to large-scale immigration from Europe around the middle of the nineteenth century. And in America, too, the new genre has boomed, with usage guides likewise being published in large numbers. An example is *Garner's Modern English Usage*, first pub-lished in 1998, and with a fourth edition already out in 2016. Bryan Garner is a lawyer, who also wrote books of language advice for lawyers. The title of his book reminds us of the well-known *Dictionary of Modern English Usage* by Henry Fowler (1858–1933), first published in 1926, and reissued as a second edition as *Fowler's Modern English Usage* by Sir Ernest Gowers (1965), with a more thoroughly updated third edition by Robert Burchfield (1996) and most recently a fourth edition by Jeremy Butterfield (2015). Fowler wasn't a linguist or lexicographer but a schoolmaster when he began to write usage guides. The first one was *The King's English* (1906), written together with his brother Frank. Henry Fowler not only left his usage guides to posterity, but also his name: *Fowler*, according to David Crystal in his preface to the facsimile reprint of the book's first edition (2010: vii), has "turned into a common noun," and there are various adjectives in the language that com-memorate the man and his work as well: *Fowlerian, Fowlerish*, and *Fowleresque*. However, it yet remains for these words to find their way into the *OED*!

This chapter focuses on the rise of prescriptivism, a subject which today is often regarded with considerable hostility. It will show when and why writers first became interested in linguistic correctness, and how, when the English academy project failed, grammars, dictionaries, and usage guides came to be written as part of separate attempts by individuals – entrepreneurs in the literal sense, like wealthy merchants and publishers – to produce works that would codify the language. As part of the English standardization process, this development led to a next step in the process, the birth of the English usage guide, in response to a real need among the people for linguistic guidance in an era characterized by social and geographical mobility. Drawing on original documents, and therefore giving a somewhat different account than what is usually found in English textbooks, this chapter also shows how research is done on the subject of grammars and usage guides, and it offers methods and even some data for more such research on prescription and prescriptivism.

Tracing the Roots of Prescriptivism

Usage guides originated from normative grammars, as is clear from Lowth's grammar, which was a kind of embryonic usage guide. This shows how one stage in the "standardization" of the English language can lead to another. English standardization as a historical process goes back to the fourteenth century (see Nevalainen and Tieken-Boon van Ostade 2006); the process mostly affected the written language, eventually resulting in a form of the language that showed relatively little variability and that was used largely by the more educated and well-to-do speakers in society (see also Chapter 8). Milroy and Milroy (2012: 22–23) divide the process into seven stages, the final two of which are called "codification" and "prescription." The codification of a language entails the laying down of its rules in grammars and dictionaries. According to Milroy and Milroy, the English standardization process is still unfinished today, since a language cannot be standardized in the strict sense of the word, like a system of weights and measures. Because of its function as an instrument in a society that is continually changing, it has to adapt to such changes, or it would become a dead language. Living languages therefore have to allow for variation in usage and for change, but it is precisely these two aspects of language use – variability and change – that are in conflict with the attempts to codify (or fix) its rules. This then accounts for the next stage in the standardization process, prescription, when language users have to remind themselves – or be reminded – about the existence of rules in the language.

The prescription stage saw the rise of the usage guide toward the end of the eighteenth century. Despite the new genre's continued popularity, it is also clear that imposing a norm of correctness on the language user, which was what the prescription stage was all about, has proved ineffective. Why that is so will be explained in this chapter, but first we will look at how and why prescription began, and why English never came to have an academy that might have played a role in this process. There were many people who pleaded for an English Academy around the beginning of the eighteenth century, and famous names in this respect were the writers Daniel Defoe (1660–1731), Joseph Addison (1672–1719), and Jonathan Swift (1667–1745). But the issue was first raised by the poet and playwright John Dryden (1631–1700), so it is to him that the first real interest in prescription can be traced. This interest arose from his revisions of Shakespeare's plays *The Tempest* and *Troilus and Cressida* during the 1660s and 1670s, well after Shakespeare's death. While revising these plays, Dryden made a number of grammatical changes as well, correcting:

- flat adverbs (adjectives without the adverbial marker *-ly*, as in *go slow*)
- double comparatives and double negation
- misuse of *that* for *who* or *which*, and of *whose* for *of which*
- mistakes in *who/whom, ye/you, you/thou*
- errors in the use of *be* as an indicative verb form and of *be, come*, and *have* in the subjunctive
- variation between *hath* and *has* and *doth* and *does*
- the use of periphrastic *do* in affirmative declarative sentences
- the incorrect use of verb tenses
- *like* used for *as*
- preposition stranding.

Double comparatives, to take one example, had been quite common in Shakespeare's time, and some examples are the following:

(1)   a **more larger** list of sceptres (1606–1607 *Anthony and Cleopatra*, III.vi.76)

(2)   to some **more fitter** place (1604 *Measure for Measure* II.ii.16)

That Dryden disapproved of the construction we know from his criticism of the poet and playwright Ben Jonson (1572–1637) in "Defense of the Epilogue" (1672). Whenever he found a double comparative in the plays by Shakespeare, he changed it: *more better* in *The Tempest* (I.ii.19) became simply *more*, and *more softer bowels* in *Troilus and Cressida* (II.ii.11) *more tender heart*.

In adapting Shakespeare's language Dryden was forced to acknowledge that English had changed: *thou* had given way to *you*, as is described in detail in Chapter 9; the pronoun *ye* was no longer very current in his time; and double negation had largely disappeared from the language of educated writers by the end of the seventeenth century. Other features in Shakespeare's language seemed grammatically incorrect, largely because Latin served as a model of correctness for Dryden, even for English. All educated writers, Dryden included, had been thoroughly schooled in Latin in their youth. This probably made Dryden correct Shakespeare's flat adverbs and what he perceived as errors in the use of the subjunctive, as well as instances of *who* and *whom* when they represented the wrong case: *who* should be used as the subject and *whom* as direct object. Yáñez-Bouza (2008: 265) quotes from Dryden's dedication to *Troilus and Cressida* to illustrate how Latin grammar served as an example for him:

> I am often put to stand in considering whether what I write be the Idiom of the tongue, or false *Grammar*, ... and have no other way to clear my doubts, but by translating my English into Latine, and thereby trying what sence the words will bear in a more stable language.

Translating his own English into Latin also drew his attention to the problem of preposition stranding: while in English preposition stranding, as in examples (3) and (4), has always been common, in Latin it wasn't, and Dryden corrected all cases of preposition stranding in Shakespeare. Having previously taken Jonson to task for stranding his prepositions, he was shocked to find that he did so himself, so he similarly corrected his own usage in a reissue of his *Essay of Dramatic Poesie* (1684), originally from 1668. Bately (1964) compared the two versions of the text, and identified changes like the following:

(3)   whom all the Story is built **upon** → **on** whom all the Story is built

(4)   this the Poet seems to allude **to** → **to** this the Poet seems to allude

Bately also studied Dryden's changes in the use of relative pronouns in this text: the changes show that he preferred *who* with personal antecedents and *which* with non-personal ones, though general usage was still variable at the time. The regulation of *who* and *which* along Dryden's preferences was later adopted by the eighteenth-century normative grammarians (Adamson 2007), and it is to them that we owe today's practice in this respect.

Dryden's work can be accessed through EEBO (*Early English Books Online*), another digital tool that is of great use for doing research on original documents. EEBO includes English books printed between 1473 and 1700, and searching for "Dryden" as the author and "Troilus and Cressida" as the title produces the revised play as the second hit. Unfortunately, EEBO (unlike ECCO) doesn't allow for full-text searches.

It is in the dedication to *Troilus and Cressida* that Dryden made his famous plea for an English academy. The dedication was addressed to a politician, Robert Spencer, to urge him to follow the example of Cardinal Richelieu, the initiator of the French Academy, in establishing an academy for English as well, to regulate the language. With the other calls for an academy, and the publication of Swift's well-known and influential "Proposal for correcting, improving, and ascertaining the English tongue" a little later in 1712, the project nearly succeeded: names of potential members were already circulating and the Queen had been secured as a patron. But it is largely due to the Queen's death in 1714 that the project failed, according to the historian John Oldmixon (1672/3–1742). The authoritative grammar and dictionary that the academy should have produced consequently never materialized. Instead, private individuals took the matter into their own hands, as they would do with another type of work that could have been produced by an English academy: the usage guide. Such a manual had already been published for French in 1647, as the Académie française's first official product. Strikingly, nearly all the grammatical features Dryden had stumbled upon when revising Shakespeare's plays and his own writings became part of the English usage guide tradition that started almost a century later.

Private Initiatives at Grammar Writing

The first grammar of English, William Bullokar's *Pamphlet for Grammar* (1585), dates from the late sixteenth century, but it is only in the second half of the eighteenth century that grammars were published in any numbers. Figure 11.1,

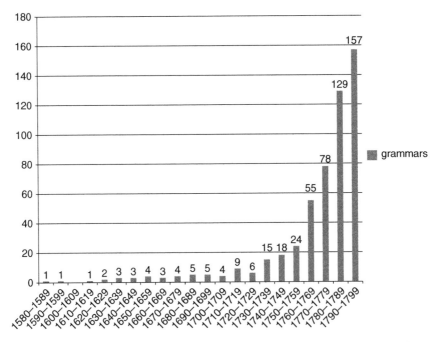

Figure 11.1 *Grammar production (new titles and reprints) from the earliest English grammar down to the end of the eighteenth century (adapted from Tieken-Boon van Ostade 2008a: 106 and 2008b: 2)*

covering new titles as well as reprints of older grammars, shows how, from the 1760s onwards, grammatical activity increased significantly.

> The data in Figure 11.1 are drawn from R. C. Alston's bibliography (1965) of grammars published since the introduction of printing, i.e., from the late fifteenth century down to 1800. Alston's important inventory contains full bibliographical details of these grammars (including all the other grammars discussed in this chapter), such as the authors' names, the dates of publication and the number of reprints that appeared. This allows us to assess their popularity, which helps us to determine how influential these early grammars were.

The grammars were not written by what we would nowadays call linguists: the authors came from every conceivable professional background. Lowth, already mentioned, was a clergyman, for instance. Biographical information on many other grammarians in Alston's bibliography is provided by the *Oxford Dictionary of National Biography* (*ODNB*), where you can learn, for example, that John Wesley (1703–1791), whose grammar came out in 1748, was the founder of Methodism, and that John Kirkby (*c.* 1705–1754), another clergyman, had published his *New English Grammar* two years earlier. Kirkby had served as a chaplain in the family of Edward Gibbon (later a well-known historian). Kirkby had also been the boy's tutor, teaching him arithmetic, English, and Latin. It is easy to see how in such a context an English grammar was written, but the work included a Latin grammar as well. Lowth's grammar had originally been written to prepare his son Thomas for the time when he would go to school and learn Latin, so this shows, too, that the teaching of *English* grammar was not at first a subject in its own right, but that it served to prepare boys for the learning of the grammar of Latin.

Some eighteenth-century grammarians were lawyers, like the American Noah Webster (1758–1843), though he never practiced law but became a lexicographer and grammarian instead. Lindley Murray, also born in America, emigrated to England in 1784, where he became a writer of extremely popular textbooks, including his famous *English Grammar* (1795). Some of the grammarians were scientists, such as the mathematician and inventor of microscopes Benjamin Martin (*c.* 1705–1782) and Joseph Priestley (1733–1804), best known for having isolated oxygen. Others were booksellers (or publishers, as we would call them today): Alston's bibliography includes at least one grammar by a bookseller (1788), John Binns, while the title page of another grammar (1797) simply reads "By a printer." Booksellers and printers were familiar with the booming trade in grammars, and they clearly tried to profit from it. There were also schoolmasters who wrote grammars, though we know very little about them (few of them have an entry in the *ODNB*): examples are Thomas Dyche (died *c.* 1733), John Collyer (flourished 1735), Daniel Fenning (1714/15–1767), and Peter Walkdenn Fogg

Figure 11.2 *A copy of an early London edition of Fenn's* Child's Grammar *(8x12 cms) (from the author's private collection of eighteenth-century English grammars)*

(flourished 1792–1796). What we do know about them often comes from information in their own books. We know more about eighteenth-century female grammarians (Cajka 2008). The most famous of them was Ann Fisher (1719–1778), who not only ran a girls' school but also, together with her husband who was a printer, "a shop, a printing press, and … the *Newcastle Chronicle*" (Rodríguez-Gil 2008: 151). Another important female grammarian was Lady Ellenor Fenn (1744–1813), who produced a spate of textbooks for children, including a tiny *Child's Grammar* (1799?) (Figure 11.2), but also a grammar for mothers wanting to teach English grammar to their children.

Competition among Grammarians

The graph in Figure 11.1 shows a little hump for the 1710s, preceding the peak of grammatical activity for the 1760s. This early period reflects a veritable "grammar war," as appears from the anonymous pamphlet *Bellum grammaticale* ('grammatical war'). Its year of publication, 1712, coincides with the loudest calls for an English Academy. The pamphlet deals with three recently published grammars: *A Grammar of the English Tongue* (1711), attributed to John Brightland (died 1717), James Greenwood's *Essay towards a Practical English Grammar* (1711), and *The English Grammar* by Michael Maittaire (1712). The pamphlet was published anonymously, but Buschmann-Göbels (2008) discovered that the author was Charles Gildon (*c.* 1665–1724), and that Gildon had also written the Brightland grammar. Gildon, she argues, wrote *Bellum grammaticale* to push his own grammar at the expense of the other two, particularly Greenwood's. Clues for all this are hidden in the grammar itself, in the form of the surname *Gildon* as an example of the pronunciation of /g/ in words in which it is followed by <i> (see Exercise 2). Parts of the grammar were included in a later work by Gildon, called *The Complete Art of Poetry* (1718), so his authorship of the "Brightland" grammar is beyond doubt.

Who was Gildon, and what was his relationship with John Brightland? What made him want to promote his own grammar to begin with? Gildon is described in the *ODNB* as a hack writer, and Brightland was the manager of a London insurance company, where Gildon worked for him "as company clerk and editor of the company's journal." Gildon left the company in 1712, the year the *Bellum grammaticale* came out. He had meanwhile got into an argument with Swift, accusing him of having stolen his own plan for an English academy. Gildon, then, was another advocate of an English academy, and one who felt slighted at not being credited with the idea (though he had not even been the first to raise it).

The title page of Gildon's grammar mentions that the work was "Printed for JOHN BRIGHTLAND," so Brightland had merely financed its publication. Publishing grammars anonymously was quite common at the time: even Lowth's grammar was published anonymously. If we hadn't known the author's name, we might have had to reconstruct the book's authorship, as in the Gildon case, by looking for clues in the work itself (Exercise 2). Lowth's name was so well known – many owners of the grammar scribbled it on the title page, as some of the copies in ECCO show – that it became a selling-point, as I will discuss in the next section. As for Brightland, we don't know much about him, but we can find some information about him in ECCO: his name comes up several times as a subscriber for particular books (a kind of crowd-sourcing avant-la-lettre), where he identified himself as a vintner from Southwark. Brightland was a merchant with money to spare, who could afford to subscribe to books and finance an English grammar. But the story continues, for, like Gildon, Oldmixon, already mentioned, had a bone to pick with Swift as well, concerning the "Proposal" for an academy of 1712. Oldmixon is often said to have opposed an English academy, though in fact he merely felt skeptical about whether Swift was the appropriate "person to suggest standards for the language" (Baugh and Cable 2013 [1951]: 262). What is of real interest is that Oldmixon wrote that "two *English* Grammars hav[e] been publish'd within this Twelvemonth [i.e. in 1711], and it remains ... to add a *Dictionary* worthy those Immortal Labours" (1712: 10): he was probably thinking here of Greenwood's grammar and the one by Gildon, which had been dedicated to Queen Anne, a strong supporter of an academy. As Oldmixon saw it, these two grammars merited the kind of recognition that would have been awarded to a grammar authorized by an academy; all that remained to be produced, he wrote, was a dictionary.

Publishers' Projects

That dictionary appeared in 1755, written by the well-known author Samuel Johnson (1709–1784) and published by Robert Dodsley (1703–1764) and several others. Johnson's dictionary was not the first English dictionary, but it became the most important one of the period, and remained so until well into the nineteenth century (see, e.g., Beal 2004: 35–65; Lynch 2009: 71–93). As in the case of the grammarians discussed in the previous section, Johnson was not a linguist or a lexicographer but a writer. His *Dictionary of the English Language* was a publishers' project (Reddick 1996), not because a group of publishers had financed it, but because Dodsley had taken the initiative for it. As the most important publisher of his time, Dodsley had a large network of writers whose work he published. He believed that his friend Johnson, who was in need of a new project, would be capable of compiling an English dictionary. Johnson's original response has been recorded by his biographer James Boswell: "I have been informed by Mr. James Dodsley," Boswell wrote,

> that . . ., when Johnson was one day sitting in his brother Robert's shop, he heard his brother suggest to him, that a Dictionary of the English Language would be a work that would be well received by the English publick; that Johnson seemed at first to catch at the proposition, but, after a pause, said, in his abrupt decisive manner, "I believe I shall not undertake it."   (Boswell 1791: 132)

Johnson did eventually write the dictionary, and Dodsley's initiative proved enormously successful.

Dodsley also published Lowth's grammar, together with his brother James and another publisher, Andrew Millar. This time the initiative came from Lowth, inspired by a request from one of his patrons, the politician Henry Bilson Legge, who wanted a copy of the grammar for his own son. The only way to make more copies of the manuscript would be by printing it, so Lowth approached Dodsley, who immediately spotted the grammar's potential. Johnson's dictionary contained an English grammar as well, though not a very good one, and Dodsley grasped the opportunity to publish what promised to be an authoritative grammar alongside the earlier dictionary.

Much of the account given here is based on an analysis of Lowth's private letters. I have collected these by searching libraries and archives, most of them in England, where Lowth lived. An important tool for locating letters like these is the website of the UK National Archives (www.nationalarchives.gov .uk). You can find an inventory of Lowth's letters as follows: click on "Discovery – our catalogue," then key in "Robert Lowth" (use quotation marks), and set the date to 1700–1799. You will receive 27 hits, including Lowth's correspondence with William Warburton, Bishop of Gloucester, and with the poet James Merrick, but also his will. Wills can be downloaded for a small fee, but for most other documents you need to visit the archives where they are held. Studying original documents is extremely important, and they formed the backbone of my book on Lowth, called *The Bishop's Grammar*

> (2011), in which I analyzed the publication history of the grammar and compared how his own language use corresponds to the rules of his grammar.

At the time, as an early effect of the Industrial Revolution, society was beginning to show considerable mobility (Fitzmaurice 1998): having more money, people could now attempt to climb the social ladder. Because they needed guidance if they wished to be accepted by the social classes above them, on matters of correct language use but also on skills like cooking, polite manners, and letter writing, cookery books, etiquette books, and letter-writing manuals began to flood the market. Lowth's grammar fit the need for linguistic guidance extremely well, largely because of the critical footnotes in his chapter on syntax; these offered advice on what was considered incorrect and therefore had to be avoided. But Lowth's was not the only grammar entering the scene at the time, and even Dodsley's own partner Andrew Millar published a grammar in the same year as the one by Lowth.

The Dodsleys promoted Lowth's grammar in amazingly modern ways. The *Short Introduction* was first published in only a small number of copies, and Dodsley brought out new editions (or reprints) in larger numbers every year, in various sizes and at different prices, usually advertised as "a new edition, corrected." All new editions were announced in the press because Dodsley knew that they would receive notice there. Though the grammar was published anonymously, Lowth's name always appeared in advertisements for the work, as in a *London Chronicle* advertisement for a sermon by Lowth published in 1764, which also read: "Of whom may be had, Two Editions of **Dr. Lowth's Introduction to English Grammar**; one printed on a fine Paper, Price 3 s. bound, and another on coarse [paper], Price 1 s. 6 d. in Sheep[skin]."

> Advertisements like these can be found in the database *British Newspapers 1600–1950* by searching for Lowth and his grammar. Today's equivalent of the price of books advertised can be calculated with the help of the Currency Converter developed by the National Archives (see Exercise 3).

Lowth's name became a selling point, as we can see from the title *The Easiest Introduction to Dr. Lowth's English Grammar, designed for the use of children under ten years of age* by John Ash (1766). Studying the publication history of Ash's grammar, Navest (2011) discovered that this edition, a reissue of an earlier grammar by Ash, had not been authorized by him. This, then, was another publisher's ploy to trade on Lowth's popularity and so gain a share in the growing market for English grammars. Searching ECCO for Lowth's grammar produces a second edition with his name – unusually – on the title page along with the words "To which are added, Observations on Style. By Joseph Priestley." This version of the grammar came out in Dublin as a so-called "pirated edition" – unauthorized by the author or the original publishers. Combining the names of two major grammarians was therefore another publisher's trick. Pirated editions of Lowth's grammar also appeared in America, from 1775 onwards. There, people were becoming interested in English grammar, too, and this interest becomes especially clear when the American Noah Webster published his *Grammatical Institute of the English Language* in 1784. By the time Murray's *English Grammar* (1795) reached America in 1800, true rivalry arose between these two writers, who both tried to dominate the market for English grammars there (Tieken-Boon van Ostade 1996).

From the Dodsley publishers' archives, reproduced in the edition of Robert Dodsley's letters (Tierney 1988), I have calculated that Lowth was paid £100 in copyright for his grammar by Robert Dodsley (see Exercise 3). This meant that Dodsley had the sole right to print the book – but only in England. Copyright did not extend outside the country. In fact, Alston's bibliography shows that Lowth's grammar was reprinted unofficially in Belfast and Cork in Ireland and in Basel in Switzerland, though also in Leeds and even London. The editions in the bibliography that do *not* have Lowth's name on the title page are authorized editions: all other editions which mention his name were published without his approval.

By the end of the century we see further activity of the publishers, when grammars that had been popular earlier on were all reissued. In all cases, the authors had died and copyright had expired, and a small group of publishers attempted to profit from this. Towards the end of his life, Lowth proudly recorded that his grammar had sold 34,000 copies, but Murray's grammar (1795) beat it all. As many as 1.5–2 million copies of Murray's grammar were printed down to 1850, in England and America but also elsewhere. Was his grammar a publishers' project as well? The print run sizes of Murray's grammar suggest that it might have been. Murray himself, however, never had any personal financial benefit from his publications, having sold the copyright to his publishers. He had been asked to write a grammar for a Quaker school for girls, Trinity Lane School, near York (Fens-de Zeeuw 2011), and the money he received for his work he donated to this school.

The Birth of the Usage Guide

Surprisingly, Robert Baker, the author of the first English usage guide, had never heard of Lowth's grammar. As he explained in the preface to his *Reflections on the English Language*, he hadn't known of Johnson's *Dictionary* either, until he stumbled upon its abridgement in a local library a few days before his own book would be printed:

> It will undoubtedly be thought strange, when I declare that I have never yet seen the folio Edition of Mr. *Johnson's* Dictionary: but, knowing Nobody that has it, I have never been able to borrow it, and I have myself no Books; at least, not many more than what a Church-going old Woman may be supposed to have of devotional Ones upon her Mantle-piece; for, having always had a narrow Income, it has not been in my Power to make a Collection, without straitening myself. Nor did I ever see even the Abridgement of this Dictionary till a few Days ago, when, observing it inserted in the Catalogue of a Circulating Library where I subscribe, I sent for it.   (Baker 1770: iv–v)

Baker found out about Lowth's grammar only when someone brought it to his attention, having noticed some overlap between the two works. This worried Baker, for in the first edition he had claimed that the book was "entirely [his] own" and that he "ha[d] consulted Nobody" (1770: iv). Baker repeated this claim in the second edition of his *Reflections* (1779):

> I here declare, as in the Preface to the first edition, that the performance is entirely my own. I have had no assistance from any friend; nor have I borrowed from any work. I even did not know, **till the late Dr. Salter shewed me** [Lowth's] **Introduction to the English Grammar**, that any thing of the kind had ever appeared among us.   (1779: xxiii)

Evidently, his friend, Rev. Samuel Salter, had discovered that "some (*not many*) of the observations [he] had made, had been already made by the author of that work." At the same time, Baker notes, there were similarities between his own *Reflections* and an edition of Lowth's grammar published *after* 1770, so borrowing might as well have gone the other way. Far from wishing to accuse Lowth of plagiarism, Baker did make an interesting point by noting that books like his own and Lowth's grammar before him contained many identical features. These eventually formed a collection of usage problems that has remained relatively stable over 250 years.

What makes Baker's *Reflections* a usage guide? How does it compare to today's best-known example of the genre, Fowler's *Dictionary of Modern English Usage*? Usage guides give advice on questions of divided usage or on usage which is considered incorrect, and they deal with all aspects of language: spelling, pronunciation, lexis, and grammar. In addition, they offer sociolinguistic comments, identifying linguistic phenomena with groups of speakers who are criticized because their language differs from standard English (Weiner 1988). A famous example of this is the split infinitive, as in the *Star Trek* trailer "To boldly go where no man has gone before." Here, the infinitive *to go* is "split" by the adverb *boldly*. Criticism of the construction goes back to 1834, with the *New-England Magazine* complaining about the language of "uneducated persons" (Bailey 1996: 248). As a usage problem it first occurs in the early American usage guide *Live and Learn: A Guide for All who Wish to Speak and Write Correctly* (Anon. 1856?), and a little later in Henry Alford's *Plea for the Queen's English* (1864) published in England. The split infinitive still occurs in usage guides published as late as 2010, Simon

Heffer's *Strictly English: The Correct Way to Write ... And Why It Matters* and Caroline Taggart's *Her Ladyship's Guide to the Queen's English*, though both mistakenly date the origin of the item to the eighteenth century.

So although recognition of the split infinitive as a usage problem post-dates Baker, he did provide usage advice on many other points. The first edition of his *Reflections* contains 127 items and the second 244, most of them lexical and syntactical usage problems, presented in no particular order (Vorlat 2001). An example is the use of *mutual*, which Baker says "is often improperly employed," adding that "[i]t ought to be used only when we would signify that there is an interchange," as in the case of "mutual love between [a man and a woman]" (1779: 26). A syntactical example is Baker's condemnation of *the reason is because*:

> This Expression ... is Nonsense; and it amazes me that our Writers don't perceive it. But, in short, they don't; and there are scarce any even of our greatest Authors that avoid this Way of speaking.   (1770: 80)

"Good Writers" are also criticized for using *different to*, which he claims "hardly makes Sense": "Is not the Word *From* here more natural than *To*?" (1770: 7). Baker explains his preference for *different from* by analogy with the verb *to differ*, which requires *from*, not *to*. The question of whether it should be *different to, from*, or even *than* has been a staple feature in English usage guides ever since, and different preferences are often assigned to different varieties of English, particularly American and British English (though, as we will see below, the reality is rather more complex).

Baker used quite strong language in criticizing usage: "improperly employed," "the Expression is Nonsense," "sounds contemptible." Such negative metalanguage is typical of the proscriptive approach taken by usage guide writers, as well as by the normative grammarians before them. Sundby et al. (1991), in *A Dictionary of English Normative Grammar 1700–1800*, made an inventory of the negative terminology found in eighteenth-century grammars. Proscriptive labels range from *absurd* to *vulgar*, which shows that normative grammarians did not mince their words. Though we no longer find such labels in today's grammars, they still occur in usage guides. Kingsley Amis (1922–1995), for instance, in his usage guide of 1997, used terms like *absurdly eccentric, improper, barbarism, offensive, unintelligible, not English*, and even *vulgar* when condemning particular usages. This kind of language is typical of usage criticism generally, not only in eighteenth-century normative grammars and usage guides, but also in linguistic complaints uttered by people today (Tieken-Boon van Ostade 2013).

Being a hack writer and not a linguist, Baker was no different from the grammarians of the period; nor does he differ in this respect from twentieth-century usage guides writers: Fowler was a schoolmaster, and Amis a novelist. And though Baker hadn't used Lowth as a source for his *Reflections on the English Language* – or indeed vice versa – the men did have a common source for the usage items they treated: the *Critical* and the *Monthly Reviews*. Usage criticism, calling attention to things like the confusion between *lie* and *lay*, first appeared in these periodicals in the 1750s, and many of the items discussed there became a fixed part of the usage guide tradition. The *lie/lay* problem was first discussed by Lowth and is still found in modern usage guides today. So it is in the popular journals of the period that the typical products of the final stages of the standardization process, grammars (codification) and usage guides (prescription), meet most directly.

Early Usage Guides in America

Live and Learn (Anon. 1856?) was the first American usage guide to list the split infinitive as a usage problem, but it was not the earliest usage guide to appear in America, nor was *Five Hundred Mistakes of Daily Occurrence* (Anon. 1856), from which the author of *Live and Learn* copied much of his material. The earliest one was Seth T. Hurd's *Grammatical Corrector; or Vocabulary of the Common Errors of Speech*, published in 1847 in Philadelphia (Figure 11.3).

Hurd describes himself in the preface as "a public lecturer upon the Grammar of the English Language … in [which] capacity, he visited successively almost every section of the United States" (1847: v); he had collected almost two thousand "common errors and peculiarities of speech." Nothing like his book, Hurd claimed, "has ever been published," a strong claim but one apparently based on thorough research, as his book includes a three-page list of English and American dictionaries, glossaries, and grammars. In contrast to Robert Baker before him, Hurd *had* studied Johnson's dictionary and Lowth's grammar, but neither Baker's *Reflections* nor the later *Vulgarities of Speech Corrected* (Anon. 1826) appear on the list. So although Hurd's *Grammatical Corrector* may be seen as a kind of bridge between the English and American traditions, the rise of the usage guide in America was an independent process.

Hurd dealt with all the features that are typically found in English usage guides except for spelling; in addition, he discussed many dialectal usages, criticizing them as linguistic mistakes. One example is the use of "LIKE, for *as, that, as though* … [which] is a very common error in the Middle and Southern States. It is frequently heard in New York – seldom, if ever, in New England" (1847: 47). On the use of *have went* Hurd commented:

> This is a gross and very common error in the southern part of Ohio, in Pennsylvania, and to some extent throughout the Middle and Southern States; not among the illiterate only, but among the educated, with whom it is an *unpardonable blunder*, as they must know it is a palpable violation of one of the plainest principles of the language.   (1847: 42)

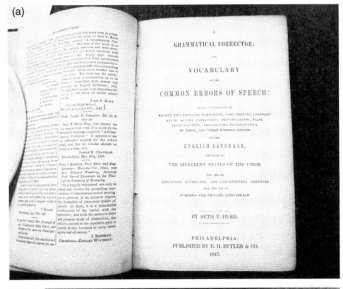

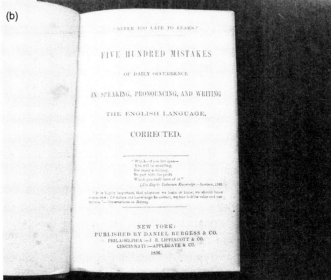

Figure 11.3 *Title pages of (a) Hurd (1847) and (b) the anonymous* Five Hundred Mistakes of Daily Occurrence *(1856) (from the author's private collection of English usage guides)*

The book includes a long list of variable pronunciations (1847: 77–90), such as *bile/boil, ketch/katch,* and *vollum/volyume,* with the first of each pair representing the incorrect pronunciation and the second the correct one. There is also a list of words with their accompanying prepositions (1847: 91–97), where we find, for instance, that *different* requires the preposition *from,* not *than.* Hurd's explicit focus on dialect gives a good insight into what was considered dialectal and what standard American English at the time, and this merits further analysis.

With the availability of electronic corpora for different periods of English (see Chapter 5), it becomes possible to check the statements of usage guides against actual usage. For example, a search of *different from* and *different than* in the 400-million-word *Corpus of Historical American English* (COHA), which ranges from 1810 to 2009, shows that Hurd was right: *different than* was indeed barely attested. The results also show a slow increase of *different than* since the 1920s, though this usage never became very frequent. Burchfield, in his edition of Fowler's *Modern English Usage* (1996: 212), claims that *different from* is the preferred British form during the twentieth century while *different than* was American. This is, however, not corroborated by the COHA evidence, which shows that *different from* has always been the preferred form in American English as well.

Another typical product of the prescription stage of the standardization process of American English is *Five Hundred Mistakes of Daily Occurrence* (Anon. 1856), which was much less systematically compiled than Hurd's *Grammatical Corrector*. The work is uneven – various items are dealt with more than once, while often the correct alternative is merely asserted without any explanation – but it is nevertheless important because it criticizes forms of usage typically found with Cockney immigrants. There is also a curious entry on the typical Irish pronunciation of the words *Irishman* and *Irish*:

> "The Duke of Wellington was an *Irishman*, but knew nothing of the *Irish* language:" beware of saying *Ierishman* for *Irishman*, or *Ierish* for *Irish*; a very common mistake, which the "Know-Nothings" are quick to detect.   (item 277)

This entry warns Irish immigrants against a powerful anti-immigrant political group called the "Know-Nothings," which had a large following between 1854 and 1856 (Mazo 2011: 242). The book therefore very likely originated in response to the many European immigrants at the time, from Europe but also, as references like these show, from England and Ireland. Usage guides like these continued to appear in America throughout the nineteenth and twentieth centuries.

Studying Usage Guides

To be able to study these and many other usage guides, we have compiled a database of usage guides and usage problems at the University of Leiden, called "Hyper Usage Guide of English" (HUGE). The database comprises selected usage guides and usage problems from 1770 down to 2010. HUGE includes thirty-seven American usage guides, published between 1847 and 2008, including well-known publications like Goold Brown's *Grammar of English Grammars* (1851), Alfred Ayres' *The Verbalist* (1911), William Strunk's *The Elements of Style* (1918), later reissued as Strunk and White (1959), Wilson

Follett's *Modern American Usage* (1966), and Bryan Garner's *Dictionary of Modern English Usage* (1998, 4th edn. 2016). The HUGE database offers information on the writers of these usage guides; Goold Brown, for instance, was a grammarian and Alfred Ayres a teacher. Information about these writers can also be found in the *American National Biography* Online (www.anb.org), where we read that William Strunk taught English composition at Cornell University and that Wilson Follett had "a versatile career as a man of letters." HUGE also includes usage guides by women, such as Josephine Turck Baker (1873–1942), who, according to Kostadinova (2014), made a career out of providing usage advice. She not only wrote many books on usage but also published a journal called *Correct English, How to Use It*. More recent American female writers of usage guides are Patricia O'Conner (1998) and Mignon Fogarty (2009); Fogarty is best known as "Grammar Girl," the persona behind a very popular website on usage advice. HUGE includes British usage guides as well, ranging from the first one ever published in England, Baker's *Reflections on the English Language* (1770), through Fowler's *Modern English Usage* (1926) to Simon Heffer's very critically received *Strictly English* (2010). These will be discussed in the next section.

Usage problems, like the split infinitive, double negation, the placement of *only* and all the others that have been discussed in this chapter, come and go, but throughout the years a stable body of items has developed. Their history across time can be studied in the freely available online HUGE database (http://huge .ullet.net/); such studies may answer questions like whether writers of usage guides have become more tolerant in the course of time. Apart from the 77 British and American usage guides, published between 1770 and 2010, the database includes an inventory of 123 usage problems, most of which deal with questions of grammatical correctness. Searching, for instance, for the usage problem *mutual* (for 'common'), discussed above, shows that this is a typical "old chestnut": it is treated in 43 of the 77 usage guides in the database, ranging from 1770, the very beginning, to 2010. (To search for this in HUGE, set the tab to Usage Guide, and the query to Problem Term, then fill in "mutual.") Further questions might be whether British and American prescriptions differ for this usage problem, and what kind of metalanguage is used, critical or otherwise, in proscribing this linguistic feature. For more information on HUGE, see at http:// bridgingtheunbridgeable.com/hugedb/, where a user manual may be found, as well as several sets of practice searches (see Exercise 4).

In an article about usage guides and usage problems, the linguist Pam Peters, who herself compiled two usage guides as well, on English generally (Peters 2004) and on Australian English (Peters 2007), refers to the publication of usage guides as an "industry" (Peters 2006). This is still so today, both in the US and in the UK, where one usage guide is published after another, most recently

Steven Pinker's *The Sense of Style* (2014) and Oliver Kamm's *Accidence Will Happen: The Non-Pedantic Guide to English Usage* (2015), respectively. Peters describes the development of the genre over the years, arguing that it has come a long way from just presenting the writers' private opinions on what was considered correct and what wasn't, to a reliance on data from text corpora. Usage guides, in other words, are believed to have become more descriptive over time. This is, however, not always the case. In a recent study, Matthijs Smits (2017) tested the claim made by Garner, the author of *Modern English Usage* (1998, 4th edn. 2016), that he is "a kind of descriptive prescriptivist" (3rd edn., 2009: xl). Smits did so by studying Garner's treatment of *different to/ from/than*, of *hopefully* as a sentence adverb (*hopefully it won't rain*), and of *snuck* for *sneaked* (*he snuck out of the room*). Comparing Garner's pronouncements concerning the acceptability of these selected items against data from COHA as well as from its present-day counterpart, the 520-million-word *Corpus of Contemporary American English* (COCA), Smits found that Garner's judgments did not always match actual usage. The data in HUGE, moreover, shows that the same usage problems occur again and again, and that views about their acceptability are slow to change. In his study of twentieth-century English Mair (2006: 18) notes that many usage problems have "gain [ed] a life of their own and [have] solidif[ied] into a body of folk-linguistic knowledge whose truth is taken for granted and no longer challenged even in scholarly publications." This is what makes usage guides so popular, since their function for those who consult them is to provide confirmation of what has always been considered to be correct.

The Fowler Brothers and Beyond

Kingsley Amis's posthumously published usage guide is called *The King's English* (1997). Why did Amis, a well-known English novelist, write a usage guide? And why did he give this title to a book published when the British monarch was a queen, not a king? His son Martin Amis, also a well-known novelist, claims that the title is a play on Kingsley's name, but the book contains so many references to Fowler that Amis's title should be interpreted as a tribute to the book's predecessor by H. W. and F. G. Fowler, which bears the same title (1906). Who then were these two men, and why did they write a usage guide? Their book was very popular, but how effective has their usage advice actually been?

Having tried their hand at different types of publications, the Fowler brothers drew up a plan for "a sort of English composition manual, from the negative point of view, for journalists and amateur writers" (McMorris 2001: 58). This became *The King's English* (1906). The book deals with vocabulary, syntax, punctuation, and miscellaneous other features, and it includes all the old chestnuts that have been discussed in this chapter: the split infinitive, *different to/from/than, that/ which/who, lie/lay, like* for *as, who/whom*, preposition stranding, and so on. The pronouncements are illustrated with examples from literature and newspapers, as in their discussion of *between you and I* which has quotations from Trollope and other writers, and *different to* which quotes from *The Times* and the *Daily Telegraph*. According to Jenny McMorris, Henry Fowler's biographer, the book had a mixed reception but nevertheless sold well (2001). One of the things the authors were accused of was not sticking to their own rules. Henry's next effort (alone this time, since his brother had died) became *A Dictionary of Modern English Usage* (1926), also an immediate success. As McMorris records, "more than 10,000 copies were sold in the first three months and 60,000 in the first year" (2001: 178). With three later editions (Gowers 1965; Burchfield 1996; Butterfield 2015) and the first edition reissued by Oxford University Press in 2009, Fowler's popularity over the years is evident, even in the United States. An echo of Fowler is found in the title of *Garner's Modern English Usage* (four editions between 1998 and 2016), but Follett (1966) already bore a similar title much earlier. Fowler had not wanted to write on American English, because he claimed he didn't know it well enough, so these publications filled a gap. Fowler's popularity can be assessed by performing a full-text search for his name in the HUGE database: this search produced more than 200 hits, and the usage guides which refer to Fowler include (in chronological order) Partridge, Gowers, Vallins, Follett, Wood, Bryson, Amis, Garner, Peters, Fogarty, Heffer, and others – British and American works alike.

How effective was Fowler's usage advice? In one instance at least his suggestion did not prove successful: Fowler proposed to assign clear roles to *which* and *that* in relative clauses – for British English, that is. He suggested that *that* might be confined to restrictive relative clauses (*Each made a list of books that had influenced him*) and *which* to non-restrictive ones (*I always buy his books, which have influenced me greatly*) (1926: 635). While his suggestion has been adopted in American English – see the advice of American Mignon Fogerty ("Grammar Girl") on her website QuickandDirtyTips.com – British usage continues to allow for both *which* and *that* in restrictive relative clauses (*Each made a list of books which/that had influenced him*), despite Fowler's proposal. Insistence on the "correct" use of *which* and *that* in American English has led to so-called "*which* hunts," and Deborah Cameron, in her book *Verbal Hygiene* (1995), discusses an absurd example of the rigorous requirements of American style guides in this matter. Conflict arose over the choice between *which* and *that* in a collection of academic papers by British and American authors. The collection was copy-edited for the American market following the *Chicago Manual of Style*, which prescribes *that* in restrictive and *which* in non-restrictive relative clauses. But the British authors revolted, and by way of a compromise all authors were allowed their national preferences (Cameron 1995: 50–51).

Two studies that have investigated the effect of usage advice by Fowler and others, like Gowers, Strunk and White, and Follett, on actual usage are Peters (2006) and Albakry (2007). These authors each discuss a number of case studies for which the prescriptive pronouncements were compared with data from existing or self-compiled text corpora. On the use of the subjunctive in English, which has been in decline for centuries, Peters found that despite Fowler's advice to avoid the mandative subjunctive altogether, there has been a sharp increase in British English usage (for the history of the subjunctive in English, see Chapter 5). She then looked at the use of the conjunction *like*, as in *It looked like* ["as if"] *it would rain*, which has been staunchly opposed. For example, Mittins et al. performed an acceptability survey in the late 1960s in British English and found a general acceptability of only 12 percent. There continues to be considerable opposition to *like* for *as if*; Taggart's *Her Ladyship's Guide to the Queen's English* reads: "[*like*] is one of the most overused and misused words in English – and was, even before the distressing colloquialism *And I'm, like, yeah, whatever* came into being" (2010: 76). (Note the negative metalanguage Taggart adopts when taking the opportunity to condemn the new and much criticized use of the discourse marker *like* in the same breath.) Peters, however, found that American writers consider usage of *like* for *as* or *as if* more acceptable than British ones. She also discovered different preferences in several varieties of English for the form of the pronoun occurring with the gerund, as in *they spoke of my/me being there*. Fowler recommended *my*, but British English today shows a preference for *me*, as does Australian and New Zealand English; in American English *my* prevails. Peters's fourth case study deals with *shall* and *will* as future auxiliaries, for which *shall* is recommended in the first person and *will* in the second and third (*I/we shall, you/he/she/it/they will*). Even when the rule was first drawn up in the 1650s – the first grammarian to formulate it was John Wallis (1653), and many later grammarians copied him uncritically – it did not reflect common usage, but in 1970 Mittins et al. identified a 56 percent general acceptability of *I will be twenty-one tomorrow*. Since then, usage of *shall* has decreased even further, and a survey I carried out within the "Bridging the Unbridgeable" project shows an acceptability of *I will* of over 90 percent.

In the late 1960s, Mittins et al. tested the acceptability of 55 grammatical usage problems, publishing the results in *Attitudes to English Usage* (1970). Informants were asked whether they considered sentences like *I will be twenty-one tomorrow*, *He refused to even think of it*, and *This process is very unique* acceptable in four different contexts: formal and informal speech and writing. To find out whether acceptability of these sentences had improved over the years, as might be expected given the growing informality of English (Mair 2006), the survey was repeated in different installments (11 usage polls dealing with 5 items each) published between 2011 and 2015 on the blog of the "Bridging the Unbridgeable" project (http://bridgingtheunbridgeable.com/usage-polls/). Two choices were added to the original format of the survey: whether usage was considered acceptable in so-called "netspeak" (communication on the internet or in social media) and whether it was believed to be "unacceptable under any circumstances." The results are freely accessible, and give an indication of trends of current acceptability of the items studied; such trends are worthwhile analyzing in greater sociolinguistic detail.

Albakry's five case studies are the following:

- starting a sentence with a coordinator (*and, but, or*)
- preposition stranding
- the split infinitive
- functional shift (e.g., nouns becoming verbs, as with *contact* and *host*)
- modifying absolute adjectives (*very unique*)

To check the effect of the proscriptive comments on these items against actual usage he compiled a corpus of texts from two important American newspapers, the *New York Times* and *USA Today*, published between 2001 and 2005. The first item proved quite common in both newspapers, while for preposition stranding and the split infinitive Albakry detected patterns of usage which possibly reflect different stylistic preferences characterizing the two newspapers. Searching for the last two items produced very few instances in his corpus, perhaps due to influence from usage guides or, indeed, the papers' style guides. For British English in the late 1960s Mittins et al. (1970) found that the sentence *This process is very unique* only reached a general acceptability of 11 percent, the lowest of all the features they examined. My own analysis carried out on the "Bridging the Unbridgeable" blog showed widespread general acceptability of *very unique* across different styles: 95 percent (fourth usage poll, 308 votes). General acceptability of the split infinitive similarly increased enormously: from 40 percent in the Mittins et al. survey to nearly 100 percent in my own (sixth usage poll, 221 votes). This indicates that users – those who contributed to the blog survey anyway – no longer seem to experience any problems with the split infinitive. Only one vote went to the category "unacceptable under any circumstances," which is much less than the figure for *very unique*: 4.6 percent (14 votes). The problem with anonymous online surveys like these, however, is that it is impossible to conduct a further, more sociolinguistically structured analysis of the data. It is, moreover, not unlikely that the responses of the informants taking the "Bridging the Unbridgeable" survey were influenced by the fact that the split infinitive is often used as an iconic example of what prescriptivism is all about: the first chapter of *The Language Wars* by Henry Hitchings (2011), for instance, is called "To boldly go." Still, these results give a good indication of increased acceptability of usage problems that have been around a long time; further analysis along actual sociolinguistic lines seems very promising indeed.

Concluding Remarks

Nearly 250 years of English usage advice has clearly proved ineffective: despite centuries of proscriptive comment, people continue to use singular *they* (*Will everyone pick up their coats please?*), to misplace *only* (*He only had one chapter to finish*) and to squabble over whether dangling participles as in *Summarizing, it may be said that* … should be considered acceptable or not (see Pinker 2014: 208–211). Even an Act of Parliament from 1850 prescribing the use of sex-indefinite *he* instead of singular *they* when the sex of the referent was undetermined (Bodine 1975) proved of no avail. The language has of course continued to change: not only are split infinitives, first-person *will*, and *who* as an object pronoun now widely accepted, different varieties of English have developed their own preferences for certain features of variable usage. Even different newspapers published within the same variety of English have their own preferences in this respect. There thus appears to be no single uniform norm of correctness for English, despite the fact that usage guide writers over the ages have assumed the contrary. But even among the eighteenth-century grammarians there was no agreement as to what was to be considered correct. Though they did attempt to impose order on the English grammatical system, largely drawing on Latin as their model (the three forms for the strong verb, as in *write – wrote – written*, or the assignment of *which* to inanimate and *who* to animate antecedents are good examples of this), preferences for many language features were divided. S. A. Leonard's *Doctrine of Correctness in English Usage, 1700–1800* (1929) includes a "Topical Glossary" with more than fifty pages of instances on which grammarians from the period disagreed. *It is I* had its advocates in the eighteenth century, but so did *it is me*, and the same applies to the pronoun in a phrase like *taller than I/me*. Arguments were presented to defend both choices: in the case of *taller than I*, the form *I* was to be preferred because of the underlying construction … *than I am* in which *than* was a conjunction, while for *taller than me* it was claimed that *me* was correct because *than* functioned as a preposition and therefore required an object pronoun. There is nothing against either argument, and they continue to be drawn upon whenever discussion arises today.

English never had an academy that might have pronounced on issues of divided usage like these. Despite continued attempts to compile usage guides, there has never been a single one that has managed to gain enough authority to assume such a role. Fowler may be an iconic usage guide, but much of its advice, as in the case of *which* and *that*, is idiosyncratic; rather than adopt *Fowler's Modern English Usage* as its official language advice manual, institutions like the BBC and the CIA and newspapers like the *Guardian* and the *New York Times* have compiled their own instead. The BBC, however, comes closest to having the role of an English academy in the UK. Because of its function as a national broadcaster financed with taxpayers' money, listeners expect it to uphold a standard of correctness, and they send in complaints whenever they detect allegedly failing standards of usage among newsreaders. In doing so they draw on a commonly identified body of features – the old chestnuts of the usage guides – that reflect an idealized notion of a norm of correctness that has become widely established over the centuries. According to Luscombe (2012), these listeners are predominantly southern, educated, and middle class as well as middle-aged. Because the BBC never initiates language advice but only responds to comments from listeners, its listeners constitute a social group of speakers that may be identified as the guardians of the language in the UK. Milroy and Milroy (2012) write that English has a well-established "complaint tradition" and that such a tradition is "typically found in communities that have highly developed standard languages" (2012: 39). The tradition finds expression not only in people criticizing alleged declining standards of correctness among BBC newsreaders but also in the phenomenon known as the letter to the editor (Lukač in progress). While the complaint tradition may not be as widespread internationally as Milroy and Milroy suggest – the Netherlands, for instance, does not have one: letters to the editor only rarely address issues of language – it may typically have arisen in England and other English-speaking nations because these countries never had an academy. Instead, as this chapter has shown, the codification of the language as well as the start of the subsequent prescription stage became the business of individuals with an interest in the language, strongly supported by the publishers who saw a market for grammars and, later, usage guides. And they still do so today. In contrast to countries that do have an Academy, whose business it is to impose from above a standard on speakers and writers of the language concerned, for the English language the latter end of the standardization process reflects a movement from below, in which self-appointed grammarians, lexicographers, schoolmasters, writers, journalists, and others with an interest in norms of correctness set themselves up as the guardians of the language, producing usage guides in ever increasing numbers. And though the genre of the usage guide may have originated for different reasons in England and America, this latter end of the standardization process is not really very different in both countries.

Suggestions for Further Study

This chapter has largely focused on grammar. This is because an interest in prescriptivism – going back to Dryden's revisions of Shakespeare – first expressed itself through changes in the grammar of that author. And many of the grammatical problems Dryden identified have remained as usage problems. In addition to grammar, usage problems have come to include a large body of other debated items, including lexical features (e.g., *teach* vs. *learn, infer* vs. *imply, loan* vs. *lend*) and perceived pronunciation problems (*REsearch, rePUtable, nucular*): see Burchfield's booklet *The Spoken Word* (1981), which he compiled for BBC announcers and newsreaders. Moreover, the codification and prescription of grammar represents only one part of the English standardization process; standardization also applies to pronunciation and the lexicon. A good study of the development of prestigious English accents may be found in Lynda Mugglestone's book *Talking Proper* (2007), and the prescriptivism of Johnson's *Dictionary of the English Language* is dealt with in papers in Lynch and McDermott (2005). Lynch (2009) provides a very readable account of aspects of prescriptivism that lexicographers were faced with as well.

As for further reading on the subject of this chapter, you could begin with Beal (2004) and Tieken-Boon van Ostade (2009), which are good introductions to the

LModE period during which codification and prescription occurred. A useful account of codification and prescription may also be found in Finegan (1999). Studies on various aspects of eighteenth-century grammars are included in Tieken-Boon van Ostade (2008c) while a detailed study of Lowth and his grammar in relation to the rise of prescriptivism is found in Tieken-Boon van Ostade (2011). The approach taken in this book might be equally profitable when applied to other grammarians of the period. On various aspects related to the ideology of standardization, read Bex and Watts (1999).

Exercises

1. Plagiarism as evidence for uncovering a network of borrowers
   ECCO (*Eighteenth Century Collections Online*) (see p. 277) is a useful source to find out who borrowed from whom within the eighteenth-century grammatical tradition. You only need a distinctive phrase that can be conclusively traced to an original source. Take the words "simply foretells" by way of an example. It comes from the translation of Wallis's famous rule for the use of *shall* and *will* to indicate future tense (1653): "In the first persons *shall* **simply foretells**; *will* promises or threatens. In the second and third persons *shall* promises or threatens; *will* **simply foretells**."
   Do an Advanced Search in ECCO for this phrase (with "grammar" in the box labeled Title and "simply foretells" in Entire Document).

   - How many results did you get?
   - Which of the grammarians discussed in this chapter drew upon Wallis?
   - Did Lowth plagiarize Greenwood, or Greenwood Brightland, or did Lowth make use of the Brightland grammar? (More creative detective work is needed to find out; see also Exercise 2.)

2. Doing detective work on eighteenth-century English grammars
   a. Finding Gildon in the "Brightland grammar"
      Go to ECCO, set the search options to Title, fill in "grammar of the English tongue," set the date to 1711, click on the result, and key in "gildon" into the space under "Search this Work." What do you find?
   b. Finding Thomas Henry in Lowth's *Short Introduction to English Grammar*
      In ECCO, set the search options to Title, fill in "short introduction to English grammar," set the date to 1762 (or later for later editions), and key in "thomas" in the box under "Search this Work." How would you know that Thomas was Lowth's son? You will find further clues by keying in "father" (though not in all cases).
   c. Finding evidence of Lowth's fame
      In ECCO, set the search options to Title, fill in "short introduction to English grammar," set the date range to 1762–1800, sort by "publication

date ascending," and look at all the title pages. Note that only the anonymous grammars are the authorized editions. Which ones have Lowth's
name added in handwriting and who would these writers be?

3. Converting eighteenth-century sums of money
   a. Did Dodsley pay Lowth a lot of money for the copyright of his *Short
      Introduction to English Grammar* (1762)?
      The National Archives has developed a Currency Converter so that we can
      calculate what older sums of money were worth by today's standards. Go
      to http://nationalarchive.gov.uk/currency/, click on Convert Old Money
      into New, key in "100" for pounds (£), "0" for shillings (s) and "0" for
      pence (d), and set the date to the nearest equivalent. How much did Lowth
      get in modern terms?
   b. Here is an advertisement in the *London Chronicle* in 1764: "Two Editions
      of Dr. Lowth's Introduction to English Grammar; one printed on a fine
      Paper, Price 3 s. bound, and another on coarse [paper], Price 1 s. 6 d. in
      Sheep[skin]."
      How much did the two editions of Lowth's grammar cost as advertised in
      the *London Chronicle* in 1764 by modern standards? How affordable
      would you say Lowth's grammar was in his day?

4. Learning to work with the HUGE database
   On the "Bridging the Unbridgeable" blog (http://bridgingtheunbridgeable
   .com/), click on HUGE db (under the banner), and apply for access. After
   registration, you will be given a username and a password. Then do the
   assignments under "HUGE for dummies"; after that, you may do any searches
   of your own, or proceed to the more advanced "Practice searches."

Note

This chapter was written in the context of the research project "Bridging the Unbridgeable:
Linguists, Prescriptivists and the General Public," financed by the Netherlands Organisation
for Scientific Research and directed by myself. It is based on much earlier work I did on the
subject, including Tieken-Boon van Ostade (1990, 1996, 2000a 2008a, 2008b, 2010, 2011,
2012a, 2012b and 2015) and Ayres-Bennett and Tieken-Boon van Ostade (2017).

12

Perspectives on Geographical Variation

MERJA STENROOS

Studying Variation

Variation in the Present and Past

Human language is, and always has been, variable. It is characterized, in the words of the linguist William Kretzschmar, by "extensive (really massive) variation in all features at all times" (2009: 3). This variability has functions that seem to be fundamental to human communication: the messages we convey depend not just on what we say, but how we say it. How we speak reflects who we are and where we belong, or would like to belong. It also reflects each situation, our purposes, roles, and attitudes.

The most obvious variation, that of which everyone is aware, has to do with geography. People speak differently in different places; and the differences generally grow with distance. Geographical variation – differences between "dialects" – was also the first kind of linguistic variation to be systematically studied, and dialectology remained for a long time the only discipline that studied linguistic variation. More recently, approaches such as sociolinguistics and pragmatics have come to focus on other kinds of variation. Sociolinguists study variation in relation to a wide range of variables, such as age, gender, social class, and ethnic and religious background; both sociolinguists and prag-maticists are concerned with different styles and domains, and pragmaticists are in particular interested in the different functions and uses of linguistic variants, such as politeness or insult (see Chapters 9 and 10).

Geographical and social variation were for a long time studied separately. Most early sociolinguistic studies focused on communities within large cities (as is reflected in the early term "urban dialectology") where geographical variation was not particularly relevant. Dialectology, on the other hand, tended to have an "antiquarian" interest: to record traditional dialectal forms before they died out, rather than to study the full scale of actual variation.

This division has now to a large extent disappeared. Sociolinguistic studies routinely take geography into account, and dialectology has become informed by insights both from sociolinguistics and from human geography. Dialectal variation is no longer seen only as a matter of physical distance: rather, it is a question of distance in terms of contact. People are not evenly dispersed over space, and they communicate much more in some directions than others: the linguistic forms used in a large city are much more likely to spread into other areas than are those used in a small isolated village.

This would have been the case also in the past. We can assume, of course, that physical geography mattered more in the days when communication could only move as fast as the traveller, and the fastest means of transport was on horseback. Even then, however, people would not travel evenly in all directions: a distance of 30 miles could be a comfortable day's journey along a good road, or an insurmountable obstacle in the form of a mountain or swamp; and people would gather in particular places for trade, worship, or education. Similarly, in all periods of history, people would have formed groups of various kinds, and communicated more with members of the same group than with other people; they would also have spoken, and written, differently in different situations.

This chapter is about the study of how English has varied during its history: what kinds of evidence we have, how we deal with it, and how this study differs from that of present-day linguistic variation.

A Thought Experiment

There are no recordings of speech from before the late nineteenth century. This means that we can have no direct evidence of the spoken language in earlier historical periods.[1] For these periods, we can only directly study written language, and everything we claim about speech is based on reconstruction – that is, informed guesswork on the basis of whatever evidence is available. If we go back far enough, not even written records survive, and we have to rely entirely on reconstruction.

Let us make a thought experiment in order to see what this means. We might imagine that all the recordings of spoken language produced in our time would disappear – as indeed they will in the process of time, unless continuously copied over into new formats. How might historical linguists in the future be able to reconstruct how we spoke, and how our speech varied?

Assuming that written materials were still available, the linguists might be able to reconstruct a great deal. For English today, there are vast amounts of written information about spoken variation, collected both by academic researchers and amateurs, and recorded both in print and on the internet. There are pronunciation dictionaries, phonetic alphabets, and transcriptions produced for linguistic research; and there are texts written "in dialect," usually for entertainment. Some novels also include dialogues in non-standard language, which may give a good idea about some aspects of spoken variation.

Such resources do not, however, cover more than a fraction of the actual spoken variation, and they do not exist for all languages. Assuming that this material would also be lost – perhaps in a period of global crisis when preserving the past would not be a priority – how would future linguists attempt to reconstruct how we spoke? The only direct evidence for language would, then, consist of whatever other written texts survived. The linguists would be working with scraps of randomly surviving text, perhaps having access to some genres in abundance while lacking others entirely, and not always quite understanding the function of a particular text.

Interpreting the material would be difficult. As everyone who has battled with English spelling knows, written language does not necessarily reflect speech sound for sound: future linguists might guess that *bough*, *tough*, *slough*, and *through* were rhyming words for us, and that *through*, *blue*, and *stew* were not – and they would be wrong. Also, most of the variation in spoken English is simply not recorded in writing: different pronunciations, many variant grammatical forms, and even a great deal of vocabulary never make it into standard writing. Written languages follow their own conventions; they often have a tendency to standardize; and they are in any case not meant to be accurate records of speech.

This also means that the kind of variation that does appear in writing has no necessary relationship to variation in speech. None of the differences between British and American spelling relate to different pronunciations: a British speaker does not have an extra vowel sound in *colour* or *mediaeval*, or pronounce the final consonant of *realise* differently from the American speaker who writes *color*, *medieval*, and *realize*.

There are, of course, other differences between written British and American English that do reflect spoken variation, such as items of vocabulary. Within the national standards, however, geographical variation is hardly shown in writing. Sometimes we can guess at a writer's gender or age from specific clues; however, most linguistic variation in written English reflects genre conventions more than anything else (see Chapter 8). Some genres are much closer to speech than others – compare the language of informal text messages to that of a book on linguistics. Future linguists may well work this out and try to get hold of as many informal notes as possible; however, books are surely much more likely to have survived.

With all their limitations when it comes to reconstructing speech, written texts are actual, real linguistic evidence. What if they had all perished? Historical linguistics, in fact, developed largely as a means of reconstructing a prehistoric language, Proto-Indo-European, through the comparison of living languages as well as well-recorded historical ones such as Latin, Ancient Greek, and Sanskrit. By comparing historically related words in different languages (for example, OE *fæder*, Latin *pater*, Greek *pater*, Old Irish *athir*, Sanskrit *pitár-* 'father') it was possible to work out regular correspondences and establish probable "proto-forms," in this case *$ph_2tḗr$ (the asterisk means that the form is a reconstruction). This method, known as the "comparative method" (see Chapter 2), may be used to reconstruct earlier stages of language on the basis of later developments, assuming that these are available.

However, the comparative method has some serious limitations. It can be used only to reconstruct forms on the basis of what has survived: there is no way of recovering those forms which have been lost without a trace. Also, the method assumes a homogeneous proto-language, with no variation. We now know that such homogeneous states of language do not exist: if there was a single language from which all "Indo-European" languages developed, it would have been variable just like present-day languages are. Variability means that languages can develop in complex and unpredictable ways: even if reconstructions may be interesting and instructive, they can only give vague hints about the reality that once was there.

The task of the hypothetical future historical linguists will, accordingly, depend greatly on what materials, if any, survive. This is precisely the kind of situation that we face when studying the language of historical periods. For some periods and communities we are lucky enough to have relatively plentiful materials, while others can provide us with only a few scraps. The questions that we can ask, and the features we choose to study, depend to a very large extent on what evidence is available.

The Evidence of Variation in Historical English

The Beginnings

The further back we go, the fewer written materials are likely to survive. This is both because a longer timespan means more chances of texts being lost, and because reading and writing, certainly in the case of English, were generally less common the further back we go.

The first writings in English that are more than occasional words date from the eighth century. The earliest texts are from northern England, where a Northumbrian culture flourished before the Viking raids: these texts consist mainly of short religious verse, cited in Latin texts or inscribed in runes on objects such as the large stone cross in Ruthwell, now in southern Scotland. The language of this early material is highly variable, reflecting the lack of a written tradition. This may be illustrated by two early Northumbrian versions, both from the early eighth century, of the same poem, *Cædmon's Hymn*, usually considered the first literary text in English:

> Nu scylun hergen hefaenricaes uard metudæs maecti end his modgidanc . . .
> He aerist scop aelda barnum heben til hrofe, haleg scepen
>
> Nu scilun herga hefenricæs uard metudæs mehti and his modgithanc . . .
> He ærist scop aeldu barnum hefen to hrofæ, halig sceppend
>
> 'Now we must praise the Heaven's Guardian, the Lord's power and his thought,
> He first created Heaven as a roof for the children of men, the holy Creator'

Even though the two versions are similar in language, they also show some striking differences. The form *aeldu* (in the second version) suggests an earlier genitive form in *-u*, that appears only occasionally in surviving OE texts, and *heben* (in the first version) suggests that the consonant usually spelt <f> in Old English – corresponding to PDE [v] – was pronounced as a bilabial sound, that is, produced with both lips, rather than involving the upper teeth. On the other hand, the form *herga* (in the second version) is an extremely early example of the loss of final *-n* in the infinitive form of verbs (cf. *hergen*). Other differences, such as the <d> and <th> in *modgidanc/modgithanc* 'thought' may simply reflect different choices in spelling: there was no dental fricative (the first consonant in *thought*) in Latin, the spelling system of which was the only available model.

Further south, texts in English do not appear until later. A number of ninth-century texts have been connected to Mercia, a large kingdom in the present Midlands, with power centers at Tamworth and Lichfield. From the tenth century onwards, the former kingdom of the West Saxons, Wessex, had become the main power center in England, with Winchester as the most important city. It is from this period that English texts start appearing in larger quantities, and include a range of genres, including official documents and law texts as well as chronicles, medical texts, religious prose, and verse, and (through a lucky escape from a library fire) the epic poem *Beowulf.*

It may be worth comparing a tenth-century translation of *Cædmon's Hymn* into West Saxon:

> Nu sculon herigean heofonrices þeard meotodes meahte ond his
>   modgeþanc . . .
> He ærest sceop eorðan bearnum heofon to hrofe, halig scyppend

Writings classified as West Saxon are characterized by a large number of vowel digraphs, in particular <ea>, <eo>, <ie>, as in *herigean, bearnum; heofonrices, meotodes*. These are in most cases held to represent diphthongs (both long and short) resulting from sound changes in this dialect.[2] However, there has been much debate about the extent to which the spellings actually reflect diphthongs (see Hogg 1992: 16–24 for an overview). As the "short diphthongs" seem to disappear without a trace by the Middle English period, some scholars have suggested that the spellings do not reflect diphthongs at all, but that the "extra" vowel symbols are either a purely orthographic convention or a diacritic indicating how the following consonant should be pronounced. This controversy is a good example of the challenges in reconstructing the sounds of the past: even though we can have a fair idea of the general picture, we can never be sure of how people actually spoke. Being aware of the variability of language does not make reconstruction easier, as the spellings could have "meant" different things for different people.

The use of Old English as a written language was remarkable for its time. During this period, Latin was completely dominant as a written language in Western Europe, and there are few examples of the use of mother tongue languages – or vernaculars – in writing. Latin was also used for the majority of texts in Anglo-Saxon England, but there is a considerable amount of surviving Old English writing. The corpus of surviving Old English texts, as published in the online *Dictionary of Old English Web Corpus* (DOEWC), which contains some but not all multiple copies of individual texts, runs to over 3 million words. From the point of view of the study of linguistic variation, the main problem with this material is its uneven spread in time and space (as was noted in Chapter 5): large parts of the geographical area are completely uncovered, and comparison is difficult as different areas have surviving texts from different periods (Northumbrian text production, for example, stops for a long while as the Viking raids begin).

The vast majority of surviving Old English texts have West Saxon characteristics, and show a relatively homogeneous usage that scholars traditionally refer to as "Late West Saxon." This usage is often known as the Old English "standard"; however, it should be remembered that it admitted a fair amount of variation (compared to present-day written standards), and there is no evidence for the kind of institutional control that is usually connected to standards.

The Middle English Period

After the Norman Conquest in 1066, the sociolinguistic situation of English changed dramatically. England became a highly multilingual society, with Latin, English, and French all being used by different users and for different purposes, a situation often referred to as *triglossia*. As positions of power were held by French speakers, who could not (to begin with) speak or read English, administrative texts were written in the usual written language of the time, Latin. Latin continued to be the universal language of learning and science and the medium of writing that was taught at schools (see Chapter 8). French also came to be used in administration, and in particular in the legal system, as well as for literary works.

English remained the spoken language of the vast majority of the population. The use of written English also continued locally, although its range was relatively limited, especially when it comes to original composition (see Treharne 2012 for a discussion). At Peterborough, the historical record known as the *Anglo-Saxon Chronicle* was continued until the mid-thirteenth century, and the chronicle entries, written down by consecutive scribes, provide a unique record of the changes that English underwent over time. In the southwest Midlands, especially Worcestershire and Herefordshire, there also seems to have been a continuous vernacular culture, as evidenced by a considerable body of early Middle English texts. In the North, however, virtually no writing in English survives from between the tenth and fifteenth centuries. This fact is important to keep in mind when we deal with the numerous examples of changes that are held to have started "in the North."

From the fourteenth century, English is used in an increasing variety of texts, and over the next centuries a "language shift" takes place in the written mode, with English taking over first from French and then from Latin. In the meantime, the lack of official functions (which could have encouraged the development of a standard variety) meant that written English had developed into an extremely variable medium. To take an example, a single line of the fourteenth-century poem *Prick of Conscience* in seven different manuscript versions, all dating from the late fourteenth or early fifteenth century, shows the following variation:[3]

   a.   That þei may haue no riȝt knowyng
   b.   That hy ne mowe haue no ryȝt knowyng
   c.   yat yei may haue non ryth knowyng
   d.   That þay may haue no ryght knowyng
   e.   þat þei may haue no right knowynge
   f.   that þey may haue noo ryht knowȳg
   g.   yat yai may haue no right knawyng
       'that they may have no accurate knowledge'

It may be noted that, with the exception of *haue* 'have,' not a single word is written alike in all the seven versions. Most of the differences have to do with spelling, but there are also grammatical differences: the (b) text shows an older negative construction with *ne ... haue* 'have not,' double negative *ne ... no*, and a plural form of the modal 'may,' *mowe*, found in none of the other versions.

Some scholars have treated written Middle English as though it was simply a transcription of speech. The nineteenth-century Austrian scholar Karl Luick famously stated that, in Middle English, "one wrote as one spoke," and Roger Lass (1997: 65) suggested that Middle English spellings could be treated like "a set of field-recordings of utterances." Other scholars assume that Middle English scribes, as any fluent writers, would have followed written conventions, even though these could vary. This implies that written variants do not necessarily reflect the speech of the scribe or author, but simply different conventions. Much of the written variation, in fact, is unlikely to relate to speech at all: for example, we assume that the variants *that*, *yat*, and *þat* relate to the same spoken form, simply using different spellings for the initial dental fricative.

As medieval English texts are always handwritten, there is a further consideration that complicates their use as evidence. When a text was produced in multiple copies, this was done by copying by hand. A popular work such as Chaucer's *Canterbury Tales* survives in 84 manuscript copies, and may have been produced in some hundreds or thousands. The copying did not take place at one specific center, or from a master copy, as with a printed book; rather, new copies were produced from existing ones, in different places, by different people and at different times, and any single surviving copy may be the result of a very large number of copyings.

For the most part, there was no expectation that the copies should follow the *exemplar* (text from which a scribe copies) letter for letter, or even word for word, and the texts could change considerably as they were translated from one dialect to another. This means that the language of a literary text is not necessarily the language of its original author, at least in detail. We also know that scribes did not necessarily translate texts uniformly into their "own" dialect, but could be greatly influenced by the forms in their exemplar. For example, scribes would, naturally enough, be likely to copy forms with which they were familiar but substitute less familiar ones with their own, a practice known as "constrained selection."

The indirect relationship between writing and speech, the practice of copying, and the fact that few manuscript books contain information about when and where they were produced, make this otherwise highly promising material rather "slippery" as evidence for linguistic variation. It may be problematic to recon-struct the speech behind the written form, and it is often difficult or impossible to pin down the time and place to which the linguistic variation could be related. This slipperiness of ME texts may be dealt with in different ways, which are discussed later in this chapter.

For the most part, ME texts stand alone as evidence of linguistic variation. There are extremely few contemporary comments, beyond the observation that northerners and southerners spoke very differently. Perhaps the best known of such comments is by the fourteenth-century scholar, John Trevisa, himself from the southwest:

> Al the longage of the North-humbres, and specialich at York, is so scharp, slytting, and frotyng and unschape that we Southeron men may that longage unnethe understand. Y trowe that that is bicause that a beth nigh to strange men and aliens, that speketh straungelich and also because that the kinges of Engelond woneth alwey fer from that contray.[4]

> 'All the language of the Northumbrians, and especially at York, is so sharp, tearing and grating and deformed that we Southern men are hardly able to understand that language. I think that it is because they live close to strange men and foreigners, who speak in a strange way, and also because the kings of England always live far from that country.'

Unfortunately, Trevisa gives no examples. However, his comment makes some important sociolinguistic points, not least the implied connection between "good" speech and the presence of the royal court. Northern speech is also famously imitated by Chaucer in the *Reeve's Tale* (see, e.g., Horobin 2001) and the first English printer, Caxton, recounts a story about confusing dialectal variation, citing *egges* and *eyren* for 'eggs' (see, e.g., Baugh and Cable 2013: 191). It is, however, not until the early modern period that an interest in "correctness" produces more substantial commentaries on contemporary speech.

The Modern Period

Earlier textbooks tended to date the "beginning of standardization" fairly pre-cisely, usually to the early or mid-fifteenth century. However, variation in writing continued throughout the Middle English period and far beyond, and it is not until the seventeenth and eighteenth centuries that we find the kind of codifica-tion in dictionaries and rule books that makes the term "standardization" appropriate (see Chapter 11). At the same time, geographical variation becomes less marked from the later fifteenth century onwards; this presumably reflects both the increased use of English for official, national purposes and the centralizing influence of printing.

Printed books are the characteristic medium of written text in the period between the Middle Ages and the breakthrough of digital communication. It should, however, be remembered that much writing was still produced by hand: personal writings and administrative documents are obvious cases, but also literary manuscripts were produced by hand and circulated by the authors. The language of handwritten texts, especially private ones, continued to be variable much longer than that of printed texts. With increased literacy, private writing became more common, and both early and late modern materials have recently been much studied by researchers concerned with pragmatics, and in particular with "ego-documents": texts with a personal voice, such as letters and diaries (see Chapter 8).

As writing becomes less variable, it no longer gives information about dialectal variation. From now on, the study of phonological variation must be based on spellings that are out of the ordinary: mistakes and "occasional spellings" that stand out from the norm. Letters and diaries by uneducated writers – or, basically, bad spellers – may provide information about spoken variation; such materials have been studied especially in early colonial sources, such as the writings of early settlers in the United States and South Africa.

During the early modern period, contemporary comments also become a major source of information on linguistic variation. An interest in correctness, and, as a result, an awareness of diversity, appears from the later sixteenth century onwards, with treatises on spelling and grammar, attempts at spelling reform, and, gradually, dictionaries. The problem with most of the early writers on grammar and spelling, known as *orthoepists*, is that their focus was prescriptive: they were intent on replacing bad language habits with good ones, and did not necessarily strive for accuracy in describing the bad ones.

A few early writers, such as Daniel Defoe, collected dialectal forms out of genuine interest. From the nineteenth century onwards, more or less systematic collections of dialect material begin to appear: early dialect surveys that are still of interest include those by Ellis (1889) and Wright (1898–1905, 1905); see also Ihalainen (1994). From the twentieth century, large and systematic dialect surveys, such as the *Survey of English Dialects* (SED) and the several surveys included in the *Linguistic Atlas Projects* of American English have produced vast collections of data, and there are now sound archives covering a vast range of varieties of English. At the same time, the digitization of printed texts makes it possible to compile vast text corpora for the study of written variation. For the last two centuries, the amount of available historical materials is extremely large, and the methods of dealing with them are approaching those of the study of contemporary variation, with two main differences: we cannot add to the data or revisit the informants, and we have to take into account the historical context.

Approaches to Variation in the History of English

Written or Spoken Language as the Object of Study

The approaches for studying historical variation have for the most part been developed by applying existing concepts and methodologies from contemporary study. Historical dialectologists therefore conduct dialect surveys and use "questionnaires" to collect written forms from their "informants" – in this case, the texts. Similarly, historical sociolinguists reconstruct social networks and define categories of social background in historical periods, and historical pragmaticists study speech acts and politeness in letters and drama texts, as discussed in Chapters 9 and 10.

At the same time, the approaches developed for present-day study are not always easy to transfer to the study of historical materials. A medieval text may not contain any clues as to the geographical or social background of its writer, let alone his/her social networks. Gender and religion are not necessarily very useful variables for the study of a community of writers, all of whom were male and Catholic. And, of course, we do not have direct evidence for the spoken language of historical speakers: what we are dealing with is written text. There have therefore been initiatives to develop concepts and methodologies specifically suited for the study of historical materials.

Perhaps the most controversial issue of all has been the lack of direct evidence for spoken language. There have been two possible solutions in dealing with this issue. The first – as was discussed in earlier chapters – is to try to reconstruct spoken variation while being aware of the limitations of the written evidence for this purpose. Scholars taking this approach tend to look for those written genres that may be assumed to be closest to spoken language: correspondence, diaries, drama text, court records such as witness statements (see, e.g., Culpeper and Kytö 2010). By comparing such genres it is then possible to try to reconstruct what the spoken language might have been like. As with any reconstructions, however, the problem is that we can only get glimpses of the actual variation that must have been there.

The other approach is to accept that our evidence for spoken variation is indirect and partial, and instead focus on that variation for which we have ample and direct evidence: the written variation itself. This approach takes as a starting point the notion that speech and writing are both valid forms of language and that written variation can form patterns that are just as interesting from the point of view of linguistic study as spoken ones, even when they do not actually relate to spoken forms.

This latter approach has met with some resistance. Within the structuralist tradition of linguistics, writing has generally been considered only a record of speech, used as a substitute when spoken communication is impossible. On the other hand, Angus McIntosh, who started the work on *A Linguistic Atlas of Late Mediaeval English* (LALME; 1986), suggested that written language could be studied as a completely independent system, as though its writers could not hear or speak (McIntosh 1961: 99). Few scholars would today take such a strict line. Even within the *Atlas* tradition, it has become accepted that the study of written variation has to take into account the fact that writers are also speakers, and that the two modes constantly interact. However, the overall principle that variation in writing should, first of all, be studied as writing, before making interpretations about the spoken mode, is very much a valid one, and is now taken for granted in many studies of historical variation.

Dialectology and the Concept of Dialects

The traditional approach to linguistic variation has been that of dialectology: the study of geographical variation, usually based on speakers with solid, native connections to an area. A considerable number of dialect surveys of English were carried out in the late nineteenth and twentieth centuries, and now provide plentiful data for the study of recent historical variation.

The choice of informants for the early surveys was based on different principles from those of the sampling methods used for linguistic studies today. For the most part, the purpose was to record traditional usage before it was lost, rather than to provide a representative picture of the overall linguistic variation at that point in time; this often meant that the speech of women and urban areas was underrepresented, a bias that must be borne in mind when generalizing from the data.

Most of the great dialect surveys of the late nineteenth and twentieth centuries were based on interviews with hand-picked informants, chosen to provide an "authentic" local dialect. Mainly in the 1950s, SED collected data from informants at 313 locations, mostly male and over the age of 65, as this group was felt to provide the most authentic and local dialect. Such informants have later been termed "Non-mobile Older Rural Males," or NORMs (Chambers and Trudgill 1998: 30). The collection was based on a questionnaire of more than 1,300 items, mostly of vocabulary but also items designed to collect information about pronunciation, morphology, and syntax.

To present and study geographical variation, the most obvious way is to display the data on maps, making major patterns easy to identify; much of the survey data collected has, consequently, been produced in the form of dialect atlases. The *English Dialect Dictionary* (EDD; 1898–1905) organized its findings in a dictionary format, while SED and the *Dictionary of American Regional English* (DARE; 1985–2012) have combined both formats. DARE is a unique resource for American English, combining a twentieth-century survey of live informants with a large amount of earlier historical data based on written materials, going back to the seventeenth century.

Dialect maps may be produced in different ways, depending on the type of data and the purpose of the map. The most straightforward representation is to mark the location from which a form is collected with a symbol, such as a dot, circle, or

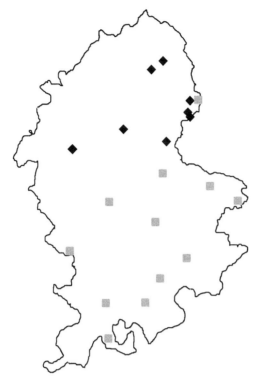

Figure 12.1 *Forms of "them" in Staffordshire, 1375–1450:* hom *(black diamonds) and* hem *(grey squares)*
Data from the Middle English Grammar Corpus *(MEG-C), version 2011.1, University of Stavanger*

diamond. The distribution of different variants may be shown by using different symbols for each variant (see Figure 12.1).[5]

To simplify complex maps, the areas within which particular forms are found are often separated by lines, known as "isoglosses" (Figure 12.2). Showing the distribution of different linguistic forms using isoglosses is very effective visually; however, the use of isoglosses can be misleading, as geographical variation is generally not as clear-cut as they suggest. Traditionally, dialectologists have used isoglosses to define "dialect areas," a concept that many scholars now find problematic.

The concept of dialect areas is closely related to the popular idea of dialects as clear-cut entities that may be used as labels for the ways in which people speak. The way different people define particular dialects may vary considerably, but they are generally thought to be real and precisely definable: non-linguists often have a very specific idea about what constitutes the dialect of their home town, and may argue at length about what is "authentic" and what is not.

In fact, as we have seen, no varieties of language are homogeneous, and neat boundaries are unusual in language. Unless there are major geographical

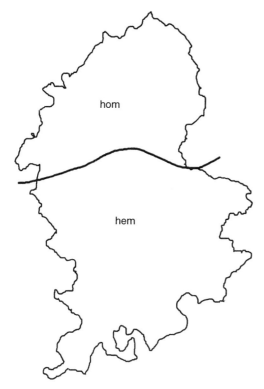

Figure 12.2 *Forms of "them" in Staffordshire, 1375–1450: a simplified version of Figure 12.1*

obstacles, such as high mountains or very broad rivers, dialects tend to form a "dialect continuum," in the sense that the geographical distributions of variants overlap. This means that, the more detailed a dialect survey is, the more difficult it is to draw sensible boundaries, within which a variety could be treated as discrete from surrounding varieties. Michael Benskin (1994: 169) illustrates this problem with the concept of "the Norfolk dialect":

> The boundary of "the Norfolk dialect" is the administrative county boundary of Norfolk, and that is that. Scholarly agonisings, of course, reflect the fact that dialectally Norfolk is not all of a piece: within the county there is marked dialectal variation. Similarly, features characteristic in Norfolk usage may be found across the county boundary . . .: "characteristically" does not entail "exclusively," though many have written as if it does.

Dialects, then, exist simply as helpful labels in our perception; they are not definable linguistic entities. Because of this, it generally makes sense to study and map the actual variation in a particular area (defined, like the county of Norfolk, on non-linguistic grounds), without trying to draw artificial dialect boundaries. For modern materials, where every informant can be placed at a precise position on the map (according to some consistent criterion, such as home address or place of upbringing), it is relatively easy to produce maps that reflect the full complexity of geographical variation, and study the changing patterns and frequencies of different forms. For earlier historical materials, however, mapping the variation is much more of a challenge.

Mapping Medieval Texts on Linguistic Grounds

To study geographical variation in Old English is highly problematic, even though spoken dialects must have varied greatly. There is simply not enough material from any single period that would allow for a geographical survey; in the late part of the period, from which materials are more plentiful, most writing adhered to the Late West Saxon model. Old English dialectology has therefore so far mainly been limited to discussions of particular features, as well as studies of individual texts and their comparison to the much more plentiful, and variable, Middle English materials (see Suggestions for Further Study).

For the ME period, dialect maps have been produced by numerous historical dialectologists, based on a range of approaches. These maps look superficially just like the maps produced on the basis of modern surveys: there may be dots representing informants, and the distribution of linguistic variants is marked either by individual symbols or by isoglosses. There are, however, fundamental differences between these maps and modern dialect maps, not only to do with the informants (written texts vs. speakers) but with the principles behind the localizations on the map.

Medieval materials are often impossible to connect to places, even though their language clearly reflects geographical variation. Most literary manuscripts give no clues about their geographical provenance. There have, basically, been two solutions to this problem. One is to turn the question around and localize texts on the basis of their language; the other is to focus on texts for which we do have evidence of provenance. The first approach has tended to dominate Middle English studies up to recent times.

Earlier dialectologists have usually taken the view that provenance in itself need not be relevant, as scribes could move from one part of the country to another: the dialect of a manuscript might therefore not reflect that of the locality where it was physically produced. This is essentially the same argument that lies behind the selection of NORMs for modern dialect study: if we wish to study the "authentic" dialect of a place, there is no point interviewing people who have newly moved in. Traditionally, Middle English texts have therefore been placed on the map wholly or partly on the basis of an assessment of the dialect they contain.

Two early dialect surveys, mainly based on literary texts, by Oakden (1930) and Moore, Meech, and Whitehall (1935) respectively, were based on grammatical and phonological data; that is, they were mapping sounds (as deduced from the spelling) rather than spellings. Both drew isoglosses on the basis of particular forms, in order to define dialect areas. These early surveys combined information about early manuscript associations with dialectal characteristics and resulted in fairly vague localizations. In contrast, the two major atlas projects of the later twentieth century, which were discussed in Chapter 5, *A Linguistic Atlas of Late Mediaeval English* (LALME) and *A Linguistic Atlas of Early Middle English* (LAEME), have produced very precise localizations for a large number of texts.

The methodology used in LALME and LAEME is basically a technique for localizing texts on the basis of their language: that is, working out by comparison with other texts where a particular text might belong in a reconstructed late Middle English dialect continuum. This method, known as the "fit-technique," was developed by Angus McIntosh in the 1950s, and has had an enormous impact on ME dialectology in the second half of the twentieth century.

To produce the atlases, texts with unknown origin were localized in relation to "anchor texts," that is, texts for which the geographical origin was known, usually local administrative or legal documents. Other texts were then placed in relation to what was already on the map, so that the more texts were added, the more precise the localizations would become. In LALME, approximately a thousand texts were placed on the map, and the digital version of LALME (eLALME) now includes a do-it-yourself localization tool replacing the traditional paper-and-pencil method described in Benskin (1991).

The LALME methodology is a very useful tool for comparing the dialectal characteristics of texts. At the same time, it is important to remember that the localizations do not reflect *actual* geographical locations: even if a text is placed at the position of a particular village on the real map, it does not necessarily have any historical connection with that village. The localizations simply tell us which texts are most similar in language, not where each text was produced or where its writer came from. The maps provide a reconstruction of an ideal dialect continuum: they are not intended to cover the whole range of variation in real, historical communities.

Adding Dimensions: The Expanding Concept of Variation

Ideas of linguistic variation have changed dramatically from the 1960s onwards. The concept of geography as a variable has itself been transformed: we now expect variation in language to reflect patterns of interaction rather than physical distance as such (see Britain 2002). Dialects demonstrably do not form a regular continuum where particular forms grow progressively more frequent and others become rarer, in a consistent fashion, as we travel in a particular direction. Rather, patterns of variation form clusters, and new innovations may turn up at several places, seemingly "missing" the areas between: this often happens in the case of towns, where people from different areas come into contact.

It has also become clear that geographical variation cannot be studied in isolation, as it forms only part of the whole complexity of linguistic variation. The scope of study has expanded to cover any variables that may be assumed to have significance for linguistic variation, as well as variation according to different styles, contexts, and uses. Sociolinguistic studies have come to include all kinds of speakers, as well as urban communities. This line of research has in general stressed the importance of quantification: the calculation of occurrences and the use of statistical methods of working out what variation is significant and what is coincidental. The findings of sociolinguistic studies are, accordingly, most often presented in diagrams or tables.

Because sociolinguistics arose partly as a reaction against traditional dialectology, it began with mainly urban areas, using quantitative methods. However, later sociolinguistic studies, and especially historical sociolinguistics, have come to include both rural areas and qualitative studies; in the latter, they often overlap with pragmatics, or the study of how language is used in interaction. Even though some scholars would still differentiate between sociolinguistic approaches to historical variation and "historical dialectology," all these directions have been informed by each others' insights to the point that drawing dividing lines is no longer necessarily useful.

At the same time, different approaches have generally shown themselves to be most appropriate for different periods, depending on the kinds of evidence available. Historical pragmaticists and sociolinguists have mostly (if not entirely) focused on the period from the seventeenth century onwards, as this provides plentiful materials for the study of speaker (or writer) interaction, including correspondence, court records and drama texts, as well as, generally, more information about the social backgrounds of individual speakers and writers (see the studies in Chapters 9 and 10).

Middle English materials, with their extremely variable writing systems, remain the focal area for the study of linguistic variation in relation to geography; here, however, insights from other fields have largely transformed the picture in recent years. The following three case studies deal with some of the fundamental issues within this field, all of which have implications for other periods as well: the localization of texts, the use of historical corpora, and the interpretation of written linguistic data.

Case Studies

Dealing with Data: *They* and *Hy* in Kent

Quantitative studies – whether in the general sense of studies involving figures, or in the sense of studies making use of statistical analysis – should be based on reasonably large amounts of comparable data: observations should preferably be counted in hundreds rather than tens, at least if studied in relation to several variables. For those periods from which surviving texts are plentiful, possibilities of study have expanded tremendously with the compilation of digital corpora and atlases (see also Chapter 5 in the present text). At the same time, such resources should be used with care, as they may give an impression of comparability, even though the underlying materials might be highly complex.

As an illustration, consider the following combination of texts, which makes up the material for the Kentish dialect of late Middle English in LALME (the Linguistic Profile codes used in LALME are given in brackets):[6]

- Small compilation of medical texts (5881) – fifteenth century
- Ordinances of St. Laurence's Hospital, Canterbury (9380) – late fourteenth century
- Administrative entries in a register of St. Lawrence's Hospital, Canterbury (5900) – first half of the fifteenth century.
- Sermons by Bishop John Sheppey (5940) – mid-fourteenth century
- Lyrics and a sermon (5950) – second quarter of the fourteenth century
- Religious poems by William of Shoreham (5960) – mid-fourteenth century
- Chaucer's *Canterbury Tales*, etc. (5970) – second quarter of the fifteenth century
- Chaucer's *Boece* (5990) – early fifteenth century
- Romance of *Merlin* (9470) – fifteenth century
- Religious treatises: Bonaventure and Rolle (5980) – fifteenth century

The datings given indicate that the corpus may stretch over a period of up to 175 years – a very considerable timespan. We might also note that most of the dates are very approximate, and that they are based on different kinds of information. When data from all these texts are shown on the same map, what look like geographical patterns may, in fact, represent changes over time or even genre differences.

To illustrate this, we can consider the distribution of forms of the third-person plural pronoun, "they," in the Kentish material. In the late fourteenth and fifteenth centuries, forms of the *thay, they* types (including spellings such as *thay, thai, they, thei, þay, þai, þey, þei*) appeared all over England and replaced the native pronoun (spelled *heo, hoe, he, ho, hi, hij, hy, hye*, etc.). It is usually assumed that the new forms were borrowed in the spoken mode from Scandinavian settlers well before the Norman Conquest, and became a feature of the northern dialects, from which they spread to the rest of the country in the late medieval period. The direction and detail of this spread are, however, difficult to verify, especially as there are few or no surviving earlier materials from the North, and from large parts of the North Midlands. In LALME, forms of the native pronoun remain in the south and in the eastern and western margins: forms such as *heo, hoe, ha, he* in the West Midlands, *he* in Norfolk and forms such as *hi, hij, hy* all over the South, including Kent.

Figure 12.3 shows the distribution of the forms of "they" in the Kentish material, using the LALME localizations. At first sight, it might suggest a pattern where the western part of Kent (which of course is the area closest to London) is more innovative (with a majority of *th-* forms), while only the native forms (spelt *hy*) appear in the eastern part.

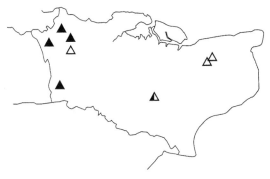

Figure 12.3 *Forms of the third-person plural pronoun in the LALME material for Kent: the* they *type (black triangles) and* hy *(unfilled triangles)*

However, if we look at the distribution of the forms in relation to the datings, we can also see a fairly clear chronological pattern:

hy	5,900 (early 15th century), 5,960 (mid 14th century), 9,380 (late 14th century)
they/thei/þei	5,970, 5,980, 5,990, 9,470 (all 15th century)
þey, hy	5,881 (15th century)

The data suggest quite a clear-cut change from the earlier *hy* forms to the *they* type (in various spellings), with all fourteenth-century texts showing *hy* only, and most fifteenth-century texts showing *they:* of the latter, one (dated to the first half of the century) shows *hy* only, and another shows *hy* as a variant form.

The pattern shown in Figure 12.3 cannot, therefore, be taken to reflect a synchronic pattern: as all the *they* type forms appear in fifteenth-century texts, there is no evidence for their use, or for any geographical patterning at all, in the fourteenth century. Instead, the pattern could be assumed to reflect a straightforward diachronic change, as in the rest of the southern materials in LALME, where the *hi, hy* type forms are mainly restricted to early materials.

In the fifteenth-century Kentish materials, on the other hand, *hy* forms are clearly confined to the east while *they* forms are concentrated in the west (Figure 12.4). However, the materials we are considering have now become so scanty as to make generalization impossible: two informants from the entire eastern part of Kent, both of whom show *hy*, are simply not sufficient evidence for a geographical distribution.

It should also be noted that all the texts which show only *they* type forms represent literary works that were not originally composed in Kent, while all the texts showing only *hy* originate in Kent (for the medical collection that shows both *they* and *hy*, 5881, we do not have any information about original composition). Bearing in mind what we know about scribal copying, this could mean that,

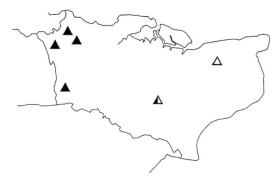

Figure 12.4 *Forms of the third-person plural pronoun in the fifteenth-century LALME material for Kent: the* they *type (black triangles) and* hy *(unfilled triangles)*

while Kentish scribes were familiar with *they*, and happy to copy it when they encountered it, the preferred form for writers in Kent was *hy*.

This means that the distributions in Figures 12.3 and 12.4 do not necessarily reflect geography at all, even though the patterns may look suggestive at first sight. Similarly, as all the texts with *hy*-forms originated in Kent, and all those with only *they* originated elsewhere, we cannot really use this material to make claims about chronological change either. Instead, all we can assume based on the material is the following:

- The form *hy* 'they' appears in texts composed and copied in Kent in the fourteenth and fifteenth centuries
- Forms of the *they* type appear in texts copied in Kent in the fifteenth century

In order to find out how and when the *they* type took over from *hy*, or to identify geographical patterns within Kent, we clearly need to have more material. This material should preferably be as homogeneous as possible, so that geographical patterns cannot be confused with variation related to other variables, such as the dialectal background of exemplars, or diachronic change.

What kind of variables, apart from date and textual background, could contribute to the patterns? Variables relevant for medieval written texts might include the genre or function of a text, its domain (religious, administrative, medical, etc.) and institutional connection. For example, many medical texts seem to contain certain combinations of dialectal forms that are usually connected to East Anglia or the central Midlands area (such as *silf(e)* 'self,' *ony* 'any,' *ȝouen* 'given'), irrespective of what dialectal features they contain otherwise; as medical texts form a very specialized group, they may well have developed their own written conventions, so that specific forms came to be considered appropriate in these texts by their users. Also, bearing in mind that writing is, to a much larger extent than speech, a learnt and conscious mode of communication, an institution (such as the Hospital of St Lawrence in

Canterbury) may well have had its own traditions with regard to written conventions; they may well, for example, have been particularly conservative with regard to forms such as *hy* 'they.'

To throw light on the development of "they" in Kent, we therefore need more texts, and more information about each one of the texts. Preferably, we would like to have large numbers of texts that are comparable – for example, all originating in Kent, and belonging to a single genre.

For the fourteenth century, it is unlikely that very much material can be added to what is already included in LALME. For the fifteenth and early sixteenth centuries, however, there are hundreds of administrative texts produced in Kent, most of which are precisely dated. Few such texts were included in LALME (in Kent only 5,900 and 9,380), as the compilers did not prioritize administrative texts from southern England. However, some 400 such texts have now been collected for an ongoing project, and are awaiting analysis. This material will eventually give us a much more detailed picture of what is going on in medieval Kent with regard to the third-person plural pronoun (and many other linguistic features), at least in administrative texts.

This example shows that the patterns we find on maps and in corpora could be misleading simply because they represent a very broad sample, consisting of few texts: in this case, ten texts with a date span of nearly two centuries and a mixture of genres and geographical origins of composition.[7] However, it also shows that, even for a "well-known" historical language such as Middle English, there are vast amounts of as yet unstudied materials and unanswered questions.

At the same time, the materials clearly cannot be augmented in all directions. We may not be able to say more about the fourteenth century, unless we find unexpected new information or materials (which, of course, may happen). Similarly, the administrative materials will not tell us what forms might have been used in other written genres in the fifteenth or sixteenth centuries, or indeed in speech. At the same time, they may give indications, especially in the case of quotations of direct speech, as in this witness statement from a 1514 Rochester adultery case:

> ye for god so I saide & And as **they** war to-gidder in the chamber as well whan hur husbound wass at home as whan he was owt by the space of an hoowre many tymes

> 'yes, by God, so I said, and that they were together in the room both when her husband was at home and when he was out for an hour, many times'

In this statement, which is written in a very oral style, *they* is used throughout – as one might, indeed, expect of an early sixteenth-century source.

For the moment, therefore, we need to leave the history of *they* and *hy* in Kent at an incomplete and general stage: all we know is that *hy* forms survived into the fifteenth century and were used at least at St. Lawrence's Hospital in Canterbury, perhaps at other places as well (for the medical manuscript, we have no information about provenance, as the LALME localization is based on language). To what extent they may have survived in other administrative materials, connected to other institutions, still remains to be seen.

Compared to present-day and recent historical materials, early historical sources limit considerably the research paths that we can take. At the same time, as the study of linguistic variation is no longer restricted to the study of patterns in space and time, we can focus on those research questions for which each kind of material is best suited. The materials that form the main focus of LALME – "literary" texts in a broad sense, including religious, historical, and even medical writings – provide splendid materials for the study of variation relating to variables such as genre and domain. However, if we wish to study in detail the geographical spread of innovative forms such as *they* in the late medieval and early modern periods, administrative texts are likely to provide a more promising starting point.

The Study of Local Documents

As LALME and LAEME placed texts according to their language, they produced (at least in principle) a neat picture where all the texts from a particular area show similar linguistic features. As with present-day variation, however, one may assume that the geographical variation in historical periods was complex, and reflected contact and communication rather than physical space alone. Recent studies of Middle and Early Modern English geographical variation tend to show more interest in the language actually produced in a given place than in reconstructing geographical dialect patterns. This kind of approach is generally informed by historical sociolinguistics, and tends to study the linguistic variation in texts for which we actually know, or can work out, the geographical origin.

For this purpose, most of the available material consists of what may be called "local documents": legal and administrative texts and letters, that is, texts that relate to actual people and places, and that often state directly when and where they were written. Even though many such texts are, in themselves, relatively short and may be formulaic, together they form a vast amount of material, including a wide range of genres: private and business letters, petitions, wills, court statements, rules and ordinances, and so on.

Local documents in English are generally only available from the early fifteenth century onwards: before that, administrative materials were written in Latin or French, and extremely few private writings survive. For the earlier period, onomastic materials – personal and place names – can provide some geographically located evidence. A survey by Kristensson (1969–2001) was based on English surnames collected from twelfth- and thirteenth-century documentary materials otherwise written in Latin. Such materials are, of course, limited in the evidence they can provide, and give, for example, little information about syntax: accordingly, Kristensson mainly mapped phonological variation, deduced from the spellings.

From the early fifteenth century onwards, however, local documents provide actual samples of written English that may be, to a large extent, connected directly to places on the map. Many documents provide clauses that state both the date and the place where the document was produced:

> Gifen at Cornay xxiij day of Janur in ye yhere of ye Reynge of kyenge henry ye sext next after ye conquest of yngland xvij

> 'Given at Cornay the 23 day of January in the seventeenth year of the reign of king Henry the sixth after the Conquest of England'

Other texts may be placed on the basis of places and people mentioned; for example, a receipt signed by the receiver of King's College, Cambridge, may quite confidently be placed in Cambridge.

We cannot always be certain that a given text was in fact produced where it claims to have been, and a text may have different kinds of connections to different places. However, we can fairly safely assume that the vast majority of texts that are associated with, for example, Cambridge were in fact produced there, and that most of the scribes were from that area. The main geographical patterns will therefore stand out if we carry out a study based on large numbers of documents.

Localizing texts strictly on the basis of this kind of non-linguistic evidence, irrespective of the kind of language they contain, makes it possible to study, not just the presumed "authentic" dialect of an area, but the actual development of written language in that area. This means that we can, for example, trace the gradual leveling of written variation – or "standardization" if we choose to use that term – in the fifteenth and sixteenth centuries.

The following example is based on a corpus of 238 local documents from the period 1400–1525, spread fairly evenly over the northern area, here defined as the historical (pre-1974) counties of Cumberland, Westmorland, Lancashire, Durham, Northumberland, and Yorkshire.[8] Figure 12.5 shows the gradual decline in frequency of four forms, typically identified as northern, over the fifteenth and early sixteenth centuries (sorted by royal dynasty):

- *sal(l)* spellings of "shall"
- *thay*-type spellings of "they" with <ay>
- *q*- spellings of "which" (e.g., *qwich, qwilk, quhilk*), and
- present participle forms ending in *-and* (e.g., *folowand*).

As the diagram shows, *sal(l), qwich*, and *-and* type forms have almost disappeared by the Tudor period, being gradually replaced by the "standard" variants *shal(l), which*, and *-ing*, while the *thay* type not only remains but actually grows slightly in frequency. It may be noted that *thay* forms spread further south as well during this period; this example goes to show that "standardization" in fifteenth- and sixteenth-century English was not a unidirectional process, nor did it imply the simultaneous displacement of all regional or local forms.

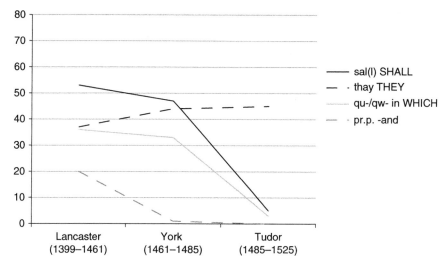

Figure 12.5 *The chronological development by royal dynasty of four northern features (as percentage of the total number of forms of each item). Data from the* Corpus of Middle English Local Documents *(MELD), version 2015.0, University of Stavanger*

Studying Sound and Spelling: *Wh-*

Standard English retains the spelling <wh> in words like *what, which, whale, whisky, whack*. This is one of several historical leftovers in English spelling: in earlier periods, *Wales* was pronounced differently from *whales*. Most English speakers today pronounce the initial consonant of both words as [w], though some accents still make a distinction: in most Scottish and some American accents, the *wh-* words are pronounced either with a voiceless *w*-sound, [ʍ], or with an aspiration – a clearly audible *h*-sound – before the *w*, [ʰw]. The loss of distinction between the pronunciation of words such as *Wales* and *whales* is the result of a sound change of a kind known as a merger: two phonemes, which we may represent as /hw/ and /w/, have merged into one. The merger of /hw/ and /w/ is part of a long trend of "*h*-dropping" in English, a development that may go back to the Old English period (Johannesson 2000; see also Milroy 1992b, Toon 1992).[9]

It is likely that [w] pronunciations of *what, which*, etc. started appearing quite early in some parts of the country. In Old English, the usual spelling was <hw>, but there are rare occurrences of <w>; in addition, in the northern Lindisfarne gospels, <chu> and <chw> appear as occasional variants: *chua* 'who,' *chwæm* 'whom,' *chuæt* 'what,' etc. In Middle English, we find three different main types of spellings of this initial consonant: <wh>, <w>, and a range of spellings beginning with *q*, including <qu>, <quh>, <qw> and <qwh>. The word "what" may, accordingly, appear as *what, wat, quat, quhat, qwat*, and so on.

If we examine the LALME maps for *wh-*, we find that the <wh> spellings appear everywhere, both in the north and the south, and that the <w> spellings are sprinkled fairly evenly across the south of England, with a few in the north as well. The *q*- spellings are, however, concentrated in the northern half of England, including the north-east Midlands and Norfolk. A similar distribution, with a southern limit that forms a diagonal line reaching down to East Anglia, appears for many of the "northern" dialectal forms mapped in LALME (see also the maps for *er* 'are,' *ilk* 'each,' and *sal*, *sulde* 'shall, should'). It is often connected to the historical Scandinavian settlement – several centuries before the late Middle English materials – in the Yorkshire and north-east Midland area, although it is by no means clear whether all the linguistic forms that show a concentration in this area have anything to do with Scandinavian contact.

What does this distribution suggest? First of all, with the benefit of hindsight, we might guess that the appearance of <w> spellings suggests that the merger of /hw/ and /w/ was already ongoing or had taken place, at least in some varieties. However, this does not necessarily follow from the <w> spellings alone: some writing systems could simply have merged the two spellings, using <w> to spell both /hw/ and /w/ (just as Present-day English uses <th> to relate to two different sounds, /θ/ and /ð/).

There is, however, other evidence to suggest that the two sounds had indeed merged, at least in some varieties. This is suggested by occasional inverse spellings in the material: that is, spellings such as *whas* 'was' and *whele* 'well.' Inverse spellings have been considered certain evidence for a merger, as they suggest that the writer is aware of the written distinction but makes mistakes since it is no longer supported by a distinction in speech (see Penzl 1969: 16, 18); that is, the writer is aware that the <wh> spelling often represents a /w/ sound and thus extends the spelling to words (also pronounced /w/) which never had that spelling. As we will see, however, once we are aware of linguistic variation, this is no longer an absolute rule.

The northern forms of the *qwat*, *quhat* types have also been held to reflect distinct pronunciations. Some scholars have suggested that northern speakers might have pronounced these words with a stronger fricative sound: [xw] rather than [hw] (see, e.g., Benskin 1989: 27; Bliss 1983: 12). In some varieties of northern English, the *wh* element might have come to be pronounced [kw] and merged with the initial consonant of words such as *queen* and *quick*. This is indicated, again, by back spellings such as *whick* 'quick.' We might, then, assume that there were three different systems (using the present-day "minimal pairs" for demonstration, even though whales and quails are fairly rare in medieval texts):

(1) /w/ in *Wales*, *whales*; /kw/ in *quails*
(2) /w/ in *Wales*; /hw/ or /xw/ in *whales*; /kw/ in *quails*
(3) /w/ in *Wales*; /kw/ in *whales*, *quails*

System (3) seems to have disappeared by the present date. However, both EDD and SED, recording late nineteenth- (and earlier) and mid-twentieth-century forms respectively; note occasional examples of [kw] pronunciations: in the Northumberland material in SED, these appear in the words *whey*, *whip*, and *white*.

We might note that earlier ideas of sound change did not admit that mergers could ever "unmerge" once they had taken place. However, once we are aware of linguistic variation, this is not a problem: in this particular case, we can simply assume that other pronunciations gradually became more frequent and that the [kw] pronunciations of *whales, whey*, etc. eventually disappeared.

So far so good; but in addition to the kinds of back spelling mentioned so far, we also get occasional spellings such as *wene* 'queen.' Might such spellings indicate that all the three consonants have merged in some varieties, ending up with *Wales, whales*, and *quails* all pronounced alike? The strict traditional view that back spellings always indicate mergers would suggest this. However, we are now aware that both spellings and pronunciations vary, often even in the repertoire of a single individual, and writers would in general choose conventional spellings rather than aiming at transcribing their own speech. There is good reason to assume that many individuals who wrote *what* actually pronounced the word with [w] – as most present-day speakers in England do.

How do we, then, explain a spelling such as *wene*? Margaret Laing and Roger Lass (Laing and Lass 2009; Laing 1999) have suggested that Middle English spelling tended to work with "substitution sets": that is, writers were aware that two or more spellings were equivalent in some contexts and might then treat them as interchangeable in other contexts as well. In this case, writers would have known that <w> and <wh> and <qu> were all valid spellings for the initial consonant of words such as *whey* or *whales*, and might, irrespective of their own pronunciations of the words, have extended this interchangeability to words of the *quail* type, to produce *wene* 'queen.'

This example shows, first of all, that some of the traditional rules about spelling as evidence for pronunciation, and of the regularity of sound change, do not necessarily hold when we take into account the variability of language – including, in historical periods, that of written language. The history of written <wh> is clearly different from that of the spoken element, even though there are important connections, and no single spelling can be treated as conclusive evidence of a particular pronunciation. This does not mean, however, that medieval spellings are useless as evidence. Confusing as they may occasionally appear, they are the most plentiful kind of direct data that we have for the study of linguistic variation. Taken on their own terms, they provide both indications about spoken variation – if in the form of puzzles rather than "field recordings of utterances"– and unique evidence about written variation, largely unavailable at the present day, except perhaps for some emergent usages in social media.

Concluding Remarks: Why Study Variation in the Past?

For a long time, it was natural for historical linguists to study past languages as though they were more or less homogeneous. Any variation was easily discarded as sloppiness, and "language" was conceived of as a regular system, just as it appears in the standardized and copy-edited text of a printed book. This expectation of regularity has meant that, even if the surviving written texts in a historical language do show variation, it has been common to focus on the most regular or most typical usage, often that of important literary works, and largely ignore the rest.

Given the limited evidence, is there any point in trying to reconstruct the linguistic variation of the distant past? Studying past stages of language as though they were homogeneous makes them, of course, easier to describe. And there is certainly no doubt that it makes them easier to learn: from the point of view of the beginning student, a homogeneous model variety (such as the "Late West Saxon" of Old English textbooks) is clearly an advantage, just as it is when we learn a modern foreign language.

At the same time, if variation is a central characteristic of human language, we cannot ignore it if we wish to understand what is going in the history of a language. Even when the actual variation cannot be recovered, acknowledging that it was there will allow us to look at the surviving evidence in a more informed way; this sometimes solves seemingly insoluble linguistic puzzles.

Several such puzzles have had to do with "reversed" sound change: Old or Middle English spellings that have suggested an unfinished or reversed change, something that could not be accommodated in earlier models of language. There is now no problem in explaining such spellings as the result of variation among speakers and writers. We no longer expect language to develop in an entirely linear way, with mathematical precision, because human communication simply does not work like that.

The study of linguistic variation has developed fast over the last decades, and many implications are still to be worked out when it comes to historical materials. The study of variation in the history of English has become a large field, including geographical, social, and pragmatic aspects, and with room for both quantitative, corpus-based studies and detailed, qualitative studies (see Nevalainen and Raumolin-Brunberg 2014: 26–28). It is not coincidental that such an integration has been more noticeable in the historical field than in contemporary linguistics. The nature of the historical materials means that we cannot pursue individual research questions in isolation to the extent that contemporary linguists can. Both because of the restricted amount of materials available and their "strangeness" from our point of view – belonging to a different historical context – we have to be careful about our generalizations. We can never reconstruct the entire range of variation, but with a broad range of viewpoints we can build up a vivid enough picture from those glimpses that we get.

Suggestions for Further Study

A classic and still useful introduction to dialectology is Chambers and Trudgill (1998). The concept of space in the study of linguistic variation is discussed by Britain (2013) and Meurman-Solin (2012); Williamson (2000, 2004) deals with space especially from the point of view of the "fit"-technique used in the LALME tradition. Kretzschmar (2009) deals with the study of geographical variation mainly in twentieth-century materials, but his theoretical and methodological discussion is highly useful for the study of all periods. Kretzschmar and Stenroos (2012) discuss the use of surveys and atlases in the history of English.

The specific challenges of OE dialectal variation have been discussed, at times intensively, in a succession of articles, including Crowley (1986), Hogg (1988), Toon (1992), Kitson (1993, 1995, 2004), Lowe (2001), and Trousdale (2005). The LALME methodology is described in Benskin (1991) and Benskin and Laing (1981); for more recent developments of this research tradition, see, e.g., Laing and Lass (2006), Williamson (2002). Relevant collections of papers include Laing and Williamson (1994) and Dossena and Lass (2004). LALME itself is now available as a digital version (eLALME), and sample transcriptions of approximately half the mapped texts are available in the *Middle English Grammar Corpus* (MEG-C).

Views on late medieval variation and "standardization" in English have changed greatly in recent years. Earlier studies that are still of interest include Samuels (1981) and Benskin (1992); for more recent views, see Machan (2016b), Nevalainen and Tieken-Boon van Ostade (2006), and Stenroos (2013). Especially on northern English, see Fernandez-Cuesta et al. (2008). Machan (2016a) contains several chapters on variation in medieval English. See also Chapters 5, 9, and 10 in the present volume for further reading on the study of variation in historical English.

Exercises

1. The problem of isoglosses

   Go back to Figures 12.1 and 12.2 and compare the two maps. Why can isoglosses be problematic? Can you see any problems with the isogloss in Figure 12.2, and might it have been possible to draw it differently?

2. Variant spellings of -ght

   Consider the spellings that are highlighted in bold in this thirteenth-century poem on the Virgin Mary. Then answer the following questions.

   > Heo is hele and lif ond **licte** / and helpit al moncunne;
   > 'She is health and life and light, and helps all mankind'
   > Ho us hauet ful vel **idiit** / Ho yaf us wele and wunne.
   > 'She has endowed ['dight'] us very well; She gave us wealth and happiness'
   > þu brutis us day and eue **nith** / heo brout wou, þu brout **rid**,
   > 'you brought us day and Eve [brought] night; she brought woe, you brought
   >   right'

þu almesse and heo sunne / þu do us merci, lauedi **brit**,
'you [brought] charity and she [brought] sin; be merciful to us, lady bright'
wene we sulin henne / ful wel þu **mit**
'when we shall [leave] hence; [as] very well you might'

a. How many different spellings can you find that correspond to the Present-day English cluster -*ght?* Do you think that any of them might relate to variant pronunciations?
b. Under what circumstances do you think that such an extremely variable spelling system could work? What might be the problems and/or benefits of introducing complete freedom into the spelling of English today, accepting all spellings? Would such a reform be imaginable?

3. Sound–spelling correspondences
   Consider the following three facts about Middle English spelling, and then use them to solve the puzzle below.
   a. In Middle English, there were two main spellings corresponding to the dental fricative (initial sound in *thousand* and *that*): <þ> ("thorn") and <th>.
   b. There were also two main spellings corresponding to the palatal approximant /j/ (initial sound in *York, you*): <y> and <ȝ> ("yogh")
   c. Especially in northern handwriting, the written forms of <þ> and <y> were very often identical, leading to forms such as *ye olde shoppe*, where the *ye* was always pronounced as "the."
   Now explain the form *saynt petir of thork*, produced by a Yorkshire scribe (MS Cambridge University Library Ee.iv.19, fol. 91 r, line 13, cited from Jensen 2012):

   for all brethir and sisters of our modir kyrke saynt petir of thork
   'for all brothers and sisters of our mother church, St. Peter of York'

   How do you explain the <th> in *thork?*

Notes

1. Recall the discussions of the "bad data" problem in Chapters 8, 9, and 10.
2. These changes include "breaking," "back mutation," and "palatal diphthongization" (see, e.g., Hogg 1992 or Lass 2006 for a discussion).
3. The *Prick of Conscience* survives in more than 120 manuscripts. The present excerpts are drawn from the following ones: (a) Oxford, Bodleian Library e Musaeo 76; (b) Oxford, Bodleian Laud Misc 486; (c) Oxford, Bodleian Rawlinson Poet. 138; (d) London, BL Lansdowne 348; (e) Oxford, Bodleian Ashmole 41 Part I; (f) London, BL Egerton 3245; (g) Oxford, Bodleian Bodley 99. In LALME, they were localized, respectively, in Essex, Gloucestershire, Norfolk, Staffordshire, Suffolk, and Yorkshire.
4. John Trevisa's translation of Higden's *Polychronicon*, 1385; cited from www.people.fas .harvard.edu/~chaucer/canttales/rvt/dialect2.html
5. Figures 12.1 and 12.2 have been adapted from Stenroos and Thengs (2012: figure 11).

6. LALME includes two more texts, for which no dating or content information is given.
7. It should be noted here that, for most counties, the LALME material is more plentiful and covers a narrower time span; however, the Kent material is not exceptional, and the same kind of problems appear in the study of most early historical materials.
8. *Middle English Local Documents Corpus* (MELD), working version 2015.0 (University of Stavanger).
9. See Chapter 9 for a full discussion of *h*-dropping.

13 Perspectives on Language Contact

EDGAR W. SCHNEIDER

Introduction: "Purity" versus Contact in the History of English

English is a Germanic language in origin: as is well known, it goes back to the settlement of the British Isles by continental Germanic tribes in 449. However, it has many properties which are quite untypical of this language family (Hawkins 2012: esp. 624–625). The examples under (1) illustrate some cases in point by juxtaposing some patterns of Modern English with their direct equivalents in Modern German, which has retained originally Germanic properties to a much stronger extent:

(1)   a. Der Hund beisst den Mann. = Den Mann beisst der Hund.
          The dog bites the man. ≠ The man bites the dog.
      b. Heute ist Maria nicht da.
         *Today is Mary not in.
         Mary is not in today.
      c. Ich las gestern Abend einen interessanten Artikel.
         *I read last night an interesting article.
         I read an interesting article last night.
      d. Ich kann Englisch.
         *I can English.
         I can speak English.
      e. Kommst du?
         *Come you?
         Do you come?
      f. Wenn man die Vorschläge des Augenarzts bedenkt, . . .
         Considering the oculist's proposals, . . .

In (1a), the inflectional endings of German (nominative *der* and accusative *den*) clearly identify syntactic functions and semantic roles, and the sequences of these constituents can thus be shuffled around rather liberally. English, in contrast, has lost the endings which it once had, and the identification of sentence functions is thus tied obligatorily to syntactic position within the firm SVO word order – so in the second example the fact that *man* precedes *bites* obligatorily implies the reading that the man performs the biting activity (however unlikely this may seem in reality). As (1b) shows, German is still a "verb-second" language, in which the constituent preceding the finite verb need not be the subject, unlike in English. Example (1c) illustrates another facet of the fixed word order of English: in German but not in English other constituents, such as a temporal adverbial, can be inserted between a verb and its direct object. In German, modal verbs still have full verb properties (of taking a direct object as in (1d), for instance); in English they have become auxiliaries which must be supplemented by a full verb. As shown in (1e), English requires an operator *do* in interrogatives (where full verbs cannot undergo inversion, unlike in German), and also in negatives. And (1f) illustrates the need to use Latin-derived words (*consider, oculist, proposal*) to render complex concepts which German can fully express using ancestral Germanic words (*be-denken, vorschlagen, Auge*). Quite a difference for two languages which once branched out from the very same roots! Why?

As it turns out, many if not all of these differences can be traced back to the fact that in the course of time the speakers of English have come to be in touch with speakers of other languages much more intensely than those of German. While the fact in itself is impossible to deny, its evaluation as well as the amount and importance of contact effects in English have been the subject of some controversy and debate, interestingly enough – for essentially sociopolitical, ideological reasons. Philology, the study (and interpretation) of language histories, is a child of the nineteenth century, a period marked by the establishment of nation states in Europe (and by Victorianism in England), so in line with the spirit of that age from its beginnings there has been a remarkable tendency in scholarship to emphasize the Germanic strength and "purity" of English. For example, in a once highly respected book Jespersen (1905: 2) attributed an "expressly *masculine*" character, with "very little childish or feminine about it," to the language. There has been a camouflaged tendency to regard contact effects as not really fundamental to the structural character of English (i.e., as constrained primarily to lexical borrowings) and as coming mostly from highly "respectable" donor sources (mostly Latin and French). In recent scholarship this rather narrow view has increasingly been challenged, however, with the argument that the role of contact in shaping modern English seems to have been more pervasive than was assumed before. This view was indirectly fueled by the growth of contact linguistics in general (see Hickey 2010b) and the recognition of important but not readily visible "substrate" effects in many other contact languages.

Modern Standard English is strongly a product of language contact (Schreier and Hundt 2013; cf. Pfenninger et al. 2014), more so than many other languages. This is not a thing of the past only, however, quite the contrary. Present-day English is characterized strongly by its role as the leading world language, and this expansion has even further strengthened the range of contacts between English and many other languages, and the effects of these processes. Today we are faced with many young or emergent varieties which have arisen in distinct contact ecologies in many countries around the globe, so that the notion of "Englishes," including "New Englishes" (Platt et al. 1984) or "Postcolonial Englishes" (Schneider 2007), has come to be widely accepted, and a new discipline of "World Englishes" has emerged (see Mesthrie and Bhatt 2008; Schneider 2011).

This chapter explores the impact of contact in the shaping of modern English throughout its history and in present-day varieties. The next section surveys some basic phases, processes, and categories which have played an important role in this context. Subsequently, I will discuss and characterize five case studies which illustrate important and typical contact scenarios, two from the history of British English and three more, with varying degrees of contact intensity, from globalization contexts.

Language Contact and English: a Survey

In the course of time speakers of English have come into contact with speakers of other languages quite frequently, and each of these encounters, permanent or not, left its linguistic traces. Textbooks of the history of English typically present a chronologically ordered line-up of contact situations, typically focusing on lexical influences because loanwords represent the most evident traces of these exchanges. This sequence of contact situations, some of which will be elaborated on later, includes the following:

- continental contacts with Latin, even before the settlement of the British Isles (i.e., roughly between the second and fourth centuries AD);
- contact with Celts who were the resident population when the Germanic tribes crossed the channel (in the fifth century and thereafter);
- the impact of Latin through Christianization (beginning in the late sixth and seventh centuries);
- contact with Scandinavian raiders and later settlers (between the seventh and tenth centuries);
- the strong exposure to French as the language of political power after 1066;
- the massive exposure to written Latin during the Renaissance;
- influences from other European languages beginning in the Early Modern English period; and
- the impact of colonial contacts and borrowings.

Until fairly recently the last of these categories has been dealt with as having contributed mainly some "exotic" vocabulary items to standard English – words such as *orangutan, maharajah, bungalow, chimpanzee, moccasins, taboo, boomerang*, and the like. But in fact it has been much more substantial, transforming English today in the contexts of colonization and globalization. Beginning with the foundation of the East India Company in 1600, English was transported as the colonizers' language to many foreign lands, mirroring and accompanying the global expansion of the British Empire. English became established as the language of administration, higher education, legislation, etc. in many colonies: in North America and the Caribbean in the seventeenth century, in South and South-East Asia in the seventeenth through nineteenth centuries, and then in Australia, New Zealand, Hong Kong, and the Philippines, many Pacific locations, and many parts of Africa. Indigenous languages were spoken in all of these places, of course, and so English coexisted with these for long periods of time, often through centuries – and of course mutual linguistic influences are inevitable in such contexts. Surprisingly, after the end of the colonial period around the mid-twentieth century, English was not removed from almost all of these regions but became even more strongly established – as a colonial leftover but more importantly a key to modernity and international structures and also, more often than not, an ethnically neutral code in multiethnic nations with many internal political and ethnolinguistic conflicts. All these contact scenarios yielded much more than a few loanwords; they produced the new local and regional varieties of English mentioned above. An appropriate current conceptualization of "English" as "a language" has thus to replace the idea of a single, largely coherent (standard) English by a range of "World Englishes," each with distinctive properties and usage conditions of their own.

The main determinant of these processes has clearly been extralinguistic history – after all, linguistic developments reflect social processes and the conditions of language usage very directly. This applies to all phases of the history of the language. In the early stages, it ranged from presumably rather light contact in trading exchanges between the continental Germanic tribes and the Roman military, via the indirect but potentially substantial impact of written Latin texts in Christianization and the Renaissance, and via conquest scenarios (experienced as the conquerors of the Celts but the ones conquered by the Anglo-Normans) to rather close coexistence in the later phase of Scandinavian settlement. In colonial expansion the intensity of linguistic exchanges depended strongly upon British motivations for moving abroad, which had an impact on the number of migrants involved, their duration of stay in the colonies, and ultimately on different colonization types. Trade colonization satisfied the desire of the homeland for exotic goods such as spices, and most likely resulted in limited exchanges between traders and natives, leading to lexical loans and sometimes pidginization. Exploitation colonies, such as India, were established permanently, and they produced long-lasting and often intense coexistence and communication needs, at least for some community members on both sides. The purpose of plantation colonies was large-scale agricultural production (of sugar, tobacco, rice, cotton, and the like), and mostly this colonization type involved huge and often cruel and relentless workforce relocation (of African slaves to the Caribbean or later of Indian laborers to many different countries, for instance; see Hundt and Sharma 2014); often these intense disruptions and new contacts produced creolization. And finally, English-speaking settlers from the British Isles transplanted the language to places such as North America, Australia, New Zealand, or South Africa, bringing it in contact with local vernaculars there.

Many of these contexts resulted in profound changes in the languages involved, with items and patterns from one language being taken over into another, and sometimes wholly new mixed codes emerging. Language contact theory attempts to explain both the social scenarios and their linguistic consequences (see Thomason 2001; Winford 2003; Matras 2009). The main prerequisite of one language strongly influencing another is bilingualism (or multilingualism): it is in the minds of bilingual speakers that forms and habits of a donor language cross over to and resurface in a recipient language (Matras 2009: 61–100; Hickey 2012a: 488–489). Since the work by Thomason and Kaufman (1988), two central points have been widely accepted. First, as stated above, "the history of a language is a function of the history of its speakers" (1988: 4), i.e., extralinguistic history predominates over internal processes of change. Second, there is a clear correlation between a cline of contact intensity on the one hand and an increasing range of contact effects on the other: social relations range from rather casual, occasional encounters via regular coexistence and exchange to full, often forced submersion and integration of one group into another; linguistic consequences range from light borrowing or regular lexical loans via some transfer and "replication" of morphosyntactic patterns to various kinds of full language mixture. Among the most extreme of these are pidgin and creole languages, which typically emerged in plantation contexts and slave societies, often with the vocabulary provided by the numerically smaller but socially dominant group (whose language thus is called the "lexifier") but with structural patterns and grammatical habits subconsciously transferred from an ancestral language or language type of the dominated groups. Caribbean English-based creoles have thus often been viewed as something like English-derived words combined by essentially African-derived grammatical structures (e.g., Alleyne 1980).[1] Thomason and Kaufman (1988: 49) proposed to regard creoles as completely unrelated to their lexifier languages, "new linguistic creations [without] any kind of transmission, broken or unbroken." Given obvious lexical continuities and far-reaching grammatical similarities also with English this is too extreme a claim; I believe (following Mufwene 2001 in that view) that it would be absolutely counterintuitive to deny the relatedness between both languages (similarly Winford 2012: 599). For example, see the transcript of a conversation in Jamaican Creole with a full account of the linguistic phenomena in it in Schneider (2011: 102–106); despite obvious differences, the similarities abound. But clearly the relationship is a complex and an interesting one, and English-based pidgins (such as the one discussed below) and creoles constitute noteworthy and important products of contact (see Holm 2000).

In fact, the growth of language contact theory in recent decades has also had direct ramifications for hypotheses on the nature of early stages of English itself. The recognition of substrate effects has inspired the "Celtic Hypothesis," to be discussed in the next section. Even more directly, in a few publications (Bailey and Maroldt 1977 on the role of French, Poussa 1982 on Norse) it was suggested that Middle English itself was basically a creole or a pidgin. Indeed, the amount of structural reorganization and simplification, most notably the far-reaching loss of inflectional endings, in Middle English as opposed to Old English is reminiscent of what has been found in modern pidgins as well (which are also typically structurally simplified and largely uninflected). But the thesis itself, certainly in its strong form, has been refuted convincingly (Thomason and Kaufman 1988: 306–315; Görlach 1990). It is quite clear that the conditions for full pidginization and creolization were not met at any time in the history of English, with the transmission of the language from one generation to another going on continuously without fundamental disruptions. Nevertheless, the idea pops up time and again, mostly in non-expert contexts. The reason for this is simply that some authors tend to use the terms "pidgin" or "creole" rather loosely and lightheartedly, for any processes involving simplification or contact, disregarding their precise definition (see also Fennell 2001: 125–131). Undisputedly, English is a language which has been strongly shaped and also transformed by contact processes, and in having become a largely analytic language it does indeed resemble some pidgins – but this is far from being the same as going back to a (former) pidgin itself.

So today's varieties of English can indeed be arranged along a continuum of varying degrees of contact influences and effects. Irrespective of one's views on whether or not creoles should be classified as separate languages, all linguists agree that their character, especially on the level of morphology and syntax, is strongly determined by their contact origins.

Not even creoles constitute a homogeneous class in respect to classification. Some "deep" creoles, like Suriname's Saramaccan, look radically different from English, and related words and phenomena need to be explained and cannot be directly recognized. But even disregarding such rather extreme cases, creoles, for instance those from the Caribbean, come in a range of degrees of "depth" and distance from English, somewhere between a few strong ones (like Jamaica's "Patwa") and rather "light" ones such as Bajan in Barbados, which are readily comprehensible to an English speaker (see Schneider 1990).

The "New Englishes" and "Postcolonial Englishes" fall in between, being clearly products of noticeable contact processes but also being clearly essentially dialects of English (see Schneider 2007). Settler varieties of English, like the New Zealand dialect, which will be discussed in detail below, have adopted more loanwords from local languages than "metropolitan" dialects in Britain or North

America. And of course, as has been emphasized repeatedly, even Standard English itself is a language whose properties can be accounted for as having emerged from contact processes to a considerable extent.

Case Studies

Early Vernacular Contact and Grammar

Within the first few centuries in England the British came into contact with two other large population groups, the Celts and the Scandinavians. In terms of social hierarchies they experienced this contact from two different ends: the Celts, originally resident in this area, were conquered by the incoming Germanic tribes, who thereby became British, while a few centuries later the then resident Anglo-Saxons were attacked and invaded by Scandinavian armies – who obtained residential rights later. This is a strange mixture of similarities – and this observation applies to a comparison of both processes in general, and also to the assessment of how strongly the Celts and Scandinavians, respectively, transformed English.

Conventional wisdom has claimed that the Celtic impact on emerging English in the years and centuries after 449 was "almost negligible" (Baugh and Cable 1951: 76 [2013: 72]). The idea is that the Celts were conquered fully and quickly; consequently, they were either killed or enslaved or driven off (to what later became the "Celtic fringe" in the northern and western regions of the British Isles), with limited opportunities for linguistic transfer, and as the subjugated people those who survived and stayed were forced to acquire the language of the invaders. The accepted assumption used to be that except for several place names and "fewer than a dozen words" (Townend 2012: 78–79) their Brittonic Celtic language left no traces in modern English. However, it has also been suggested that this conservative tradition, denying any serious Celtic impact, may also have been motivated in part by nineteenth-century nationalism, an implicit desire to construe English as an essentially Germanic language.

In contrast, recent research (e.g., Filppula et al. 2002, 2008; Fillpula and Klemola 2009), fueled by recognition of the substantial impact of substrate languages on the grammar of many contact languages, notably creoles, has suggested that Celtic did not vanish so invisibly, without leaving any traces. Sociohistorical and genetic DNA evidence support this (Miller 2012: 31–40), showing that many Celts continued to live side by side with the Germanic tribes, to some extent as servants and slaves, but also, and more importantly, as the concubines or wives of Germanic invaders (given that the composition of the conquering tribes was predominantly male, lacking women), who then gave birth to and raised the "Germanic" children. It seems not unlikely that Celtic women who were forced into a language shift passed on a form of Germanic dialects to their offspring which was strongly influenced by a structural substrate of their native tongue. Several distinctive structural properties of modern English have been suggested to have been shaped possibly by a camouflaged Celtic substrate, including the following (see Hickey 2012b):

- a double paradigm of the forms of the verb *be* (with verbs beginning in *b-*, like *be, been*, stemming from different roots than verbs beginning in a vowel or ending in *-s*, such as *am, is*);
- internal possessor constructions (personal pronouns for inalienable possession relations, as in *My head hurts*);
- the rise of the progressive construction;
- periphrastic *do* as an auxiliary in interrogatives, negation, etc. (presumably via south-western dialect, where this form was used long before its origin in standard English and where a Celtic language, Cornish, survived until the nineteenth century);
- patterns of verb inflection (notably, the "Northern Subject Rule" which states that an *-s* ending on verbs is favored unless it is immediately preceded by a personal pronoun, e.g. *children cries*; *they cry*; *they yell and cries*);
- answering decision questions by short sentences (e.g., *I will*) rather than *yes* or *no*.

This has remained a controversial issue to the present day, and given the temporal distance and the insurmountable methodological difficulty of the absence of very early vernacular records of the language it is unlikely to be fully resolved.

In the late eighth century Scandinavian sailors and later troops, mostly Norwegian Vikings and Danes as visualized in Figure 13.1, began to raid, attack, and invade the English coasts. After the Treaty of Wedmore of 878 they gained the right to settle down in large parts of the north and north-east of the country, the "Danelaw," so again we are faced with a situation of intense cohabitation between two peoples. This time, however, the original residents and also most likely the women in partnerships were the Anglo-Saxons, but again they were the socially superior group to which the others had to adjust to some extent, linguistically and culturally.

The substantial contribution of the Scandinavian contact language, Old Norse, to English is generally recognized, and explained by the strength of the interactions and interrelationships between the two peoples (which essentially merged in the long run). Linguistic traces are strong and impossible to ignore or deny. Of course words were borrowed from Scandinavian into Old English. Their number was large, and, more significantly, the borrowing process also affected core vocabulary – words for everyday notions and activities which normally tend to remain stable and unmodified by foreign contact. The most compelling example is perhaps the word *take*, which replaced Germanic *niman* (cf. German *nehmen*) – a highly frequently used concept and lexical item. Other cases in point include *bull, dirt, leg, want, flat, ill, call, die*, or, with respect to distinctive pronunciation features, *sky, get, give*, or *egg*. What is more, and has

Figure 13.1 *Viking raiders*
Source: *https://commons.wikimedia.org/wiki/File:Norsemen_Landing_in_Ice
land.jpg. Painting:* Norsemen Landing in Iceland *by Oscar Wergeland (1909).
Licensed under public domain via Wikimedia Commons*

been widely interpreted as a clear indicator of the intensity of the contact, is that
the Norse influences on English affected core components of the grammatical
system. A core grammatical element, a personal pronoun, was affected as well:
the third-person plural personal pronoun of Old English, *hie*, was replaced by
a Scandinavian form, *they* (with the onset consonant *th-* being a clear marker of
the Scandinavian roots of the form). The Old English paradigm in that subdomain
was relatively weak, since the male singular form *he* and the plural form *hie* were
phonetically similar, so that a danger of confusion existed and probably strengthened the need to mark the distinction clearly, but still, an exchange of pronoun
forms through contact is highly unusual and associated with intense contact
situations only. It is also interesting to see how the waves of this innovation
spread in England – the base form being followed by object and possessive
forms, and the Scandinavian innovation moving from the north to the south.

   Actually, the role of Scandinavian may have been even more substantial, with
an impact on the grammatical make-up of the language. There are a few syntactic
structures which may have resulted from or have been strengthened by
Scandinavian influence, including group genitives (*the king of France's men*),
complementizer *that* omission in object clauses, relativizer omission, or preposition stranding (Miller 2012: 134–147), but in most of these cases the evidence is
suggestive but not definitive. The strongest impact of Norse may have been an

indirect one, however. The articulatory weakness and reduction tendency of inflectional endings in English is a trend which has been shared by many Germanic languages and which was ultimately caused by the "Germanic Main Stress" rule, which fixed stress on the first syllable of words. But no other Germanic language has been transformed by this development as substantially as English, having lost almost all grammatical endings and having become largely an analytic language, a far cry from its erstwhile synthetic starting point. It has been hypothesized that this fundamental reorganization was not triggered but strongly reinforced by the contact conditions of the Scandinavian period. Both Old English and Old Norse were Germanic languages, which at that time had been drifting apart for just a few centuries. Most likely they were still mutually intelligible, with some difficulty – with similarities becoming more evident in lexical stems than in grammatical endings. That such a situation motivates speakers to drop suffixes seems plausible, and of course such behavior pushes the language gradually towards analyticity. (On the other hand, it is clear that such simplification trends and reductive developments were going on in early English outside the domain of Norse influence as well; for a cautious assessment, see Thomason and Kaufman 1988: 302–304.)

It is noteworthy that both the Celtic and the Scandinavian influence on Old English represent cases of what modern sociolinguistics would call contact-induced "change from below." Certainly these processes operated below the level of anybody's awareness (which is one perspective on this definition[2]), but clearly both processes also capture influences from "below" in the sense of 'socially inferior group/class': both the Celts and the Scandinavians had to shift linguistically to Old English; but they did so, similarly to many conquered groups in modernity, by bringing their original linguistic habits with themselves and transforming some of them into new habits of how to use English.[3]

Borrowing Ornate Vocabulary: French and Latin Loans

Unlike the vocabularies of all other Germanic languages, the word stock of modern English is strongly mixed in character. In fact, when it comes to lexical types, more than half of all the entries in dictionaries of English recognizably stem from Latin, often via French in between; for example, when I open my *Oxford Advanced Learner's Dictionary* at a random point, I get *provenance, proverb(ial), provide, province(ial/-ism), provision(al), provocateur*, ... – all Latin in origin. Many of these are little more than "dictionary words," however, used by journalists to vary their lexical expression or to show off but rarely used in real-life conversations. Conversely, when it comes to token frequencies (i.e., counting the same words repeatedly),[4] Germanic words predominate and constitute the backbone elements of texts, especially in oral and casual contexts or when it comes to denoting everyday activities, relations, objects, or qualities (such as *eat, drink, sleep, love; mother, son, sister; house, dog, finger; old, red*).

So in terms of both frequency relationships and sociostylistic function there is a strongly inverse relationship between the Germanic and Latinate vocabulary components: the former are smaller in number but they are used commonly and are indicative of informal or proximity contexts; in contrast, the latter are large in numbers of dictionary entries, but they are used relatively rarely, and they are indicative of more formal and distanced settings. And these latter properties derive from and continue the historical causes and conditions of their influx: French loans were borrowed during the Middle Ages as the "high" code in a diglossic setting, and Renaissance Latin borrowings were associated with learning and superior education. In other words, sociolinguistically speaking, both represent "change from above" (unlike the innovations discussed in the previous section), words more or less consciously taken over from higher classes and "respectable" settings.

As is well known, French was the dominant language in England after the Norman Conquest at the battle of Hastings of 1066, in which Harold, the last Anglo-Saxon king, was killed (see Figure 13.2 for the illustration of this scene in the famous "Bayeux Tapestry"). Subsequently, the leading roles of society, both nobility and clergy, were filled by Anglo-Normans, who spoke their northern variety of French (and often no English at all). This was a classic situation of diglossia, with French used in higher circles and for formal topics and contexts (Kibbee 1991), and English continuing in socially inferior contexts of farming and everyday life, but largely underneath the radar of written representation. As a result, we have deplorably few texts from English in a transition period between Old and Middle English, which would have been immensely interesting to observe in greater detail, because during that time major linguistic changes were rolling along (however, for a recent, alternative perspective on this, see Treharne 2012). Consequently, French words were used and became established in English predominantly for topics and domains of life where the ruling class was concerned or actively involved. Cases in point include the following (Baugh and Cable 1951: 167–174 [2013: 163–172]; Miller 2012: 164–167):

- aristocracy and government: *royal, reign, government, chancellor, minister, parliament, prince, peer, duke, baron,* . . .
- military matters: *war* (from an Anglo-Norman form of French *guerre*), *peace, battle, arms, siege, officer, lieutenant, sergeant, soldier, challenge, guard, enemy, danger, aid, prison, force, march,* . . .
- law and jurisdiction: *justice, judge, court, plaintiff, defendant, crime, summon, penalty, injury, felony,* . . .
- religious terms: *saint, savior, service, religion, trinity, preach, pray, miracle,* . . .
- social standing: *sir, madam; master, servant; command, obey; rich, poor; money, cash,* . . .
- pastimes and pleasures: *joy, pleasure, delight, ease, comfort; flowers, fruit,* . . .

Figure 13.2 *Harold's death at the battle of Hastings (as depicted in the Bayeux Tapestry)*
Source: *https://commons.wikimedia.org/wiki/File:Bayeux_Tapestry_scene57_ Harold_death.jpg#/media/File:Bayeux_Tapestry_scene57_Harold_death.jpg "Bayeux Tapestry scene 57Harold death" by Myrabella – Own work. Licensed under Public Domain via Wikimedia Commons*

- clothing and the arts: *dress, costume,* etc.; *beauty, colour, design, figure, ornament, paint; vault, pillar, aisle; palace, castle, manor, . . .*

There is a small set of loanwords which are commonly taken to reflect specific aspects of the social setting of the two languages in the Middle Ages. For example, there are many lexical pairs with words for animals being Germanic in origin but the words for their meat coming from French (e.g. *ox/cow – beef, calf – veal, sheep – mutton, swine – pork*) – implying that the English peasants had to raise the animals but the French nobility enjoyed the privilege of eating them. The fact that the conquerors of England were Anglo-Normans, i.e., speakers of a regional dialect of French and not of "respectable" Parisian French (with which relationships were established later), is illustrated by doublets such as *catch–chase, cattle–chattel,* or *warden–guardian,* with the first item showing northern French phonetic peculiarities retained in English and the latter displaying central French roots (earlier scholarship assumed a clear temporal sequence of these two stages, but this is no longer upheld; see Miller 2012: 152–160). Given that all these words are ultimately (vulgar) Latin in origin and (written) Latin itself also exerted its influence on English, it is no surprise that in some cases we actually have lexical triplets, with the same concepts being denoted by words of Germanic, French, and Latin roots (take *kingly*, *royal*, and *regal*, respectively), again typically associated with specific domains of life (so it is not a coincidence that we have a *royal* and not a *kingly* family, and that *regal* mainly co-occurs with abstract nouns such as *power*, *pomp*, or *influence*).

In fact, the amount of French influence on English has also been a contentious issue in recent scholarship, similar to that of Celtic influence, and interestingly enough the main thrust of the innovative arguments mirrors the opposite social roots of both donor languages: while for Celtic, a socially inferior substrate, a much stronger impact than assumed earlier was proposed, for French, the traditionally respected high-status donor, the novel idea is that its impact may actually have been not as far-reaching as originally assumed. Traditional scholarship regarded the French linguistic influence during the Middle Ages as all-pervasive, encompassing very many spheres of life and having been almost impossible to avoid (and thus having caused the strong lexical influence which modern English no doubt shows). Alternatively, it has been suggested that functional bilingualism, the prerequisite for strong linguistic contact, was restricted to some intermediate functionaries in society who had to deal with and mediate between both social and linguistic groups in England's society, with others – the high nobility including some kings who spoke no English at all and did not need to deal with the locals, and the lowly peasants who conducted their lives in regional Middle English only – not affected at all: "Outside of the highest level of the aristocracy and the monasteries French made few inroads into everyday life" (Kibbee 1991: 3). The strength of the linguistic traces of French seems to have been overrepresented unduly due to the fact that these bilingual agents were highly influential and active members of society, and they were the ones who produced the kinds of historical documents that have come down to us through centuries. Hence the relative strength of the French influence in formal and especially written styles became visible while its paucity in oral performance was widely disregarded.

It is not always clear whether words were borrowed into English from French or from Latin directly – forms of the same words in both languages were often very similar. Some French borrowings were actually re-Latinized at some stage, such as the word *aventure*, found in Middle English, which later received its full original Latin prefix *ad-* again and became modern *adventure*. Latin influence thus has many faces. As stated above, the earliest Latin loanwords go back to a time when English as such was not even in existence as yet: Germanic tribes, some of whom would later ferry across the channel to become the British, had contacts with Romans on the European continent, and took over words for concepts and things which they had not been familiar with and which reflected Roman superiority and cultural advancement, such as *street*, *mile*, *pound*, *mint*, or *wine* (all shared with modern German). (England was a Roman colony for a few centuries, of course, and it is a common misunderstanding that early Latin loans go back to that relationship, whereas in fact the Romans could not have met any "English" – in the modern sense – there because their ancestors came only later, almost half a century after the Romans left the island.) A few centuries later (after 597 and throughout the seventh century) the adoption of Christianity by the Anglo-Saxons brought a new wave of Latin words which were integrated into Old English, covering terms related to religion, obviously (e.g., *church, priest, rule, offer, candle*) and also education and other secular matters related mostly to learning and what in those days was modern culture (e.g., *master, verse, school, meter, circle*). These early Latin loans have been well integrated into English phonetically and semantically – their Latin origin is not really transparent and known to many speakers. Broadly, in sociostylistic terms they cover learned but still practically important concepts, and thus they fall between the even more mundane Germanic word stock and the more elevated post-medieval Latinisms.

The vast majority of Latin-derived words in modern English date back to the Renaissance period, however, the transition period between late Middle English and Early Modern English. Fundamental social changes like the end of the medieval feudal system and the rediscovery of human individuality, religious conflicts and the decreasing role of the church, an increasing emphasis on access to schooling, and so on triggered a reorientation toward antique thinking and antique texts – predominantly in Latin. So there was a huge demand for reading matter and translations of Latin texts into English; and for want of adequate English terms to denote sophisticated concepts in these texts very many Latin words (sometimes with quasi-paraphrases directly added, sometimes phonologically adjusted) were retained in English texts and thus gradually integrated into contemporary English. Many of them died out again, but many more have survived – some as regularly used words of modern English (e.g., *expect, consider, reflect, limit, usual*) but very many others as those rarely used dictionary items which motivate educated English persons to buy their *Concise Oxford Dictionary* (e.g., *coxcombical, excogitate, reverberate, resuscitate*). Not surprisingly, these strategies also introduced a sociolinguistic cleavage, of course, between those (usually clergy and higher social strata) who had enjoyed education in Latin and were thus capable of understanding such words and all the others for whom this was not the case (and to whom such words and texts thus remained largely opaque and inaccessible). Such Latinisms thus became known and classified as "hard words," and after the first tide of fashion, cherishing Latin borrowings, purist movements kept gaining ground, and the overuse of Latin words in English texts increasingly met with criticism. They became branded as "inkhorn words." Text 1, from that period, explicitly ridicules the widespread practice of overemploying Latinisms.

> **Text 1. Selection from "An ynkehorne letter," from T. Wilson's**
> ***The Art of Rhetorique* (1553) (reproduced from Görlach 1994:**
> **176)**
>
> Ponderyng, expendyng, and reuolutyng with my self your ingent affabilitee, and ingenious capacitee, for mundane affaires: I cannot but celebrate and extolle your magnificall dexteritee, aboue all other. For how could you haue adepted suche illustrate prerogatiue, and dominicall superioritee, if the fecunditee of your ingenie had not been so fertile, & wounderfull pregnaunt. Now therefore beeyng accersited, to suche splendent renoume, & dignitee splendidious: I doubt not but you will adiuuate suche poore adnichilate orphanes, as whilome ware condisciples with you, and of antique familiaritee in Lincolne shire. Emong whom I beeyng a Scholasticall panion, obtestate your sublimitee to extoll myne infirmitee. . . .

The contact of English with medieval and post-medieval French and Latin had its most obvious effects at the vocabulary level, but it did influence grammatical properties as well – although in these cases the influence is weaker, and sometimes difficult to really prove (see Miller 2012: 185–187). Phenomena of English which supposedly have been influenced (or increased numerically) by French and/or Latin models include:

- clause subordination, in particular the use of certain nonfinite constructions (e.g. infinitive object clauses such as *I want him to leave*, which resemble what in Latin grammar is called "accusativus cum infinitive," as opposed to Germanic finite object clauses);
- relative clauses, particularly those connected by *wh-* relative pronouns (which are supposed to derive from Latin *qui(s)* via French *que*);
- verbal nouns ending in *-ing*; and
- second-person plural pronouns used to address individuals politely, possibly after the model of French *vous*, and hence moving into the singular (so English *you* is originally actually a plural form which replaced the old singular *thou*).[5]

The Birth of a New Extraterritorial Variety – New Zealand English

As was stated initially, as a consequence of colonial expansion and globalization, the regularity and the geographical and typological range of contacts between English and other languages has increased dramatically, and these processes have repeatedly produced new contact varieties of English. Several types of settings of English in specific countries have been distinguished, including English as a Native Language (ENL, as in Australia or Canada), as a Second Language (ESL, e.g., India or Kenya), as a Foreign Language (EFL, e.g., Sweden or China), and intense contact situations which have produced pidgins and creoles (see Schneider 2011 for an overview).

"Extraterritorial" ENL nations are those to which English was transported by large groups of settlers from the British Isles who went there to stay for good and build a new life. Such "settler colonies" were established for a range of social reasons at home, in England, including a desire for religious freedom, over-population, overcrowding of prisons, strategic considerations, or simply a search for new economic opportunities. Typically, the settlers came to a territory where indigenous people were living, of course, so an important question is how these two groups interacted and got along with each other. In North America, Australia, and New Zealand (the topic of my case study in this section) the settlers came in large numbers, as invaders, and established themselves as the new majority of the population, often with disastrous effects on the original native population. In other places, such as South Africa in the early nineteenth and Kenya or (then) Rhodesia (today's Zimbabwe) in the early twentieth they remained cohesive and influential minorities. In the early phase of a young colony interethnic contacts tended to remain restricted to specific situations (such as trade or negotiations) and to some bilingual individuals (who for some reason were motivated to learn the other group's language – mostly these were indigenous people, who tended to be more interested in acquiring English than the other way around). With respect to contact processes, two phenomena are particularly characteristic of all early settlement communities. First, place names (and also names for local plants, animals, and cultural practices) are liberally adopted into local uses in English. Secondly, the fact that the settlers often come from widely different dialect regions leads to a process of mutual dialect accommodation known as koinéization, with extreme dialect forms, which are difficult to understand for speakers of other dialects, being communicatively unsuccessful and thus gradually dropped, and a moderate compromise dialect emerging in the course of time.

English came to New Zealand with Pacific sailors and whalers in the late eighteenth and some early settlers in the early nineteenth century. The real starting point for both the nation and its distinctive English variety is the Treaty of Waitangi of 1840, in which local Maori chiefs essentially ceded the islands to the British Crown (see a picture of the treaty in Figure 13.3). This opportunity initiated large-scale streams of organized settlement from the British Isles (including a linguistically and socially distinctive group of Scottish migrants who focused on the Otago region around the town of Dunedin – where to the present day the local dialect shows features of Scottish origin).

New Zealand English shows the characteristic features of early settlement communities, including heavy toponymic borrowing (very many place names originate in the Maori language) and massive koinéization, large-scale dialect contact effects (so that widespread southern British dialect input features have tended to survive

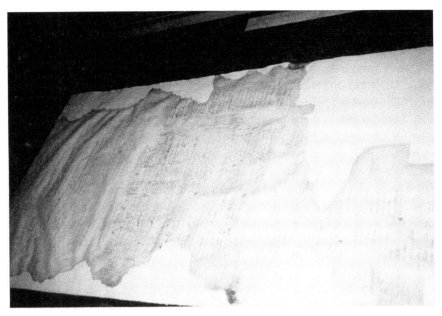

Figure 13.3 *The Treaty of Waitangi, on display in the National Archive in Wellington*
Source: *Photograph by author*

while rarely occurring ones from elsewhere have died out). Interestingly enough, these processes happen to have been unusually well documented through a voluminous archive of early sound recordings. In a research initiative known as ONZE (*Origins of New Zealand English Project*), the early stages of the emergence of distinctively New Zealand pronunciation features have been traced in some detail, and were dated to the late nineteenth century and associated with the first generations of locally born children (Gordon et al. 2004). These children selected and strengthened some of the varied input features brought over and offered by their parents' generation of original settlers, thus composing a new dialect. It has been shown that New Zealand English, like other so-called "southern hemisphere" varieties, continues developmental trajectories which apparently were built into and had just started to become effective in the southern English dialects which predominated numerically among the settler population. On the basis of such data Peter Trudgill (2004) developed his far-reaching claim that in contact between dialects, and in the birth of new colonial dialects in particular, the outcome is "inevitable," fully predictable on the basis of the numerical and linguistic composition of the contributors' groups and input variety components.

The original population of New Zealand, the Maoris, fared badly in all of this – even if perhaps not quite as badly as most Aboriginals in Australia and very many Native Americans in the USA. Attempts at resisting the massive influx of outsiders and the loss of their territories in the "Maori Wars" of the 1860s were unsuccessful, and to the present day some groups are struggling legally for land rights and compensation. Most of the Maoris underwent a language shift toward English (and in that process some pronunciation features may have been transferred: a dialect called "Maori English" has been postulated and described, though its traces are faint). Maori, their ancestral language, came close to extinction, with very small numbers of even the Maori population still speaking it and passing it on as a home language. Its fate has turned and improved after loosening ties with Great Britain, however, including some efforts at revitalization. The Maori language and culture have been recognized as important elements of New Zealand's heritage; the country is now officially bilingual, and all official documents and institutional names have to be bilingual (even if some of this clearly remains symbolic and of limited practical relevance). Contact effects on English are exclusively lexical, and they are strongly concentrated on the semantic domains to be expected: names of animals (*kiwi, tuatara*) and plants (*kauri*), and concepts and objects associated with Maori culture (*mana, hangi, whare, waka*, etc.). But there is some impact on New Zealand English in general as well. For example, the word *Pakeha* is generally used as the regular, unmarked term for white, European-ancestry New Zealanders.

There is another, fairly recent contact process and contact variety which has become increasingly visible and important in the country, namely so-called "Pasifika English." Over the last few decades many migrants from several Pacific islands have settled in New Zealand (now making up about 7 percent of the country's population) and constitute new cohesive social groups and speech communities, notably in Manukau in South Auckland. Many of these Polynesian people have been shifting to English, showing transfer features in their lexis, phonology, and (less so) grammar (e.g., omission of inflectional endings). Despite some remaining heterogeneity (and linguistic features restricted to, say, Samoans, Tongans, Niueans, or Cook Islanders only) a pan-ethnic variety encompassing speakers of many regional origins has emerged and been described (Starks et al. 2015). Shared features include words like *kai* 'food' or pronunciation traits such as unaspirated word-initial stops or devoiced word-final fricatives. Interestingly, some features are shared between Pasifika English and Maori English (which ultimately also has a Polynesian substrate), e.g., a realization of the short high front i-vowel in words such as *kit* or *tip* which is more fronted and higher than the centralized New Zealand English vowel in these words.

Singlish – The Birth of a New Vernacular

Singapore is a geographically small island state at the southern tip of the Malay peninsula; it is the most strongly anglicized ESL nation on the globe and a site of highly interesting and productive language contact. It would not

Figure 13.4 *Singapore's new Marina Bay area*
Source: *Photograph by author*

exist as such without British colonial interference: Sir Stamford Raffles
bought the island in 1819, recognizing its ideal strategic location, and founded
a colony there. It soon prospered indeed, becoming a primary center of naval
trade, and it grew rapidly, attracting people from afar. In addition to
a substantial number of British colonial representatives in various functions
and the native population of Malays, the vast majority of newcomers were
Chinese, and many Indians immigrated, too. Consequently, today's Singapore
is a highly multiethnic and multilingual state, with a strong Chinese-ancestry
population majority plus residents of other ethnicities as well, and with four
official languages recognized (Mandarin Chinese, Malay, Tamil, and
English). After independence in 1965 it prospered immensely and became
an extremely wealthy and strongly modernized "Tiger State," a world-class
urban metropolis – as shown, with its most recent and spectacular Marina Bay
development area, in Figure 13.4.

The government imposed a language policy which deliberately and obligatorily
invoked bilingualism for all children – teaching their Asian heritage languages to
strengthen cultural continuity and awareness and English as a pan-ethnic bond and
tool for modernization and international integration. In the long run, this approach
resulted in English becoming the country's most widely spoken language. All
public institutions and processes are fully anglicized, and the vast majority of the
population speak English, not only in international and interethnic settings but
increasingly also in intraethnic communication. In fact, Singapore seems to be
shifting gradually but persistently toward English. According to most recent
census data, between a third and a half of all children nowadays grow up with
English as their family language, and this percentage, just like related figures for
English literacy and usage especially among young speakers, has been increasing
dramatically. For many Singaporeans English is their first language now.

An interesting question, however, is: which English? Two major varieties are
conventionally distinguished, a standard one and a dialectal one. Singaporean
Standard English shows some distinctive pronunciation features but in general it
conforms to international or British linguistic norms. In contrast, Singapore
Colloquial English, popularly known as "Singlish," is strongly a product of
language contact, with transfer phenomena from some varieties of Chinese and

from the other local Asian languages occurring frequently and giving the language its distinctive flavor. A simple and common conversation could be *"Can or not?" "Can, lah!"* (meaning something like 'Are you able to do this or not?' 'Of course I am able ...'); and such utterances show the substrate impact of Chinese in a tendency to omit otherwise obligatory sentence constituents and complements, including the clause subject (see Bao 2015). Singlish is also notorious for its wide range of frequently used discourse particles borrowed from Chinese (of which *lah*, used for emphasis in this example, but also with other situation-dependent functions, is the best-known one).

Text 2 provides a short selection from a transcript of an informal conversation between young Singaporean males in Singlish. This short sample illustrates quite a number of contact-induced properties of the dialect:

- lexical interference from local Asian languages (here: *botak* 'bald,' from Malay);
- common use of local discourse markers (*lah, ah, lor*);
- reduplication for semantic intensification (*botak botak* 'very bald');
- zero copula (*He quite poor thing*);
- a distinctive relativization strategy using *one* to mark the end of a postmodifier (*The fella centre botak three side hair one* 'The man who is bald in the middle and has hair at three sides');
- lack of inflectional endings (no plural suffix in *three side*); and
- two instances of a peculiar syntactic loan construction, the so-called "*kena*-passive," which combines this Malay-derived function word with specific semantic constraints (the subject referent is affected by a negative incident).

It is noteworthy that despite the Malay loans in this text none of the three speakers is Malay himself.

Text 2. Transcript of a Conversation in Singlish

Source: Schneider (2011: 160–161); provided by Lisa Lim. Reproduced with permission.

C: The *botak botak* {fella
A: The fella centre *botak* three side hair {*one* ...
C: {Eh, that guy got problem *ah*, that fella ...
A: Lee was calling me his buddy yesterday.
B: He quite poor thing also *lor*, come to think of it.
C: Why?
B: At first, I dunno *lah*, I didn't really like him because he's just too ...
      his P.R. is quite bad *ah*.
C: Oh, P.R.

> B: That's why. That's the point *ah*. Come to think of it, okay *lah* ... he
>   also *kena* play out *lor.*
> C: By who?
> B: He *kena* sabotage *what*, the airport ... last minute, they send him to
>   Brunei, you know, instead of Taiwan.

For all we know, despite roots in long-standing contact, modern Singlish is largely a product of the post-independence era; most linguists date its gestation period to the 1970s and later, after independence and as a consequence of the implementation of the new bilingual language policy. For many Singaporeans it is a symbol of their multiethnic and multilingual background and surroundings. It is also the subject of an intense and at times fierce debate in the country, however. The Singaporean government (and with it some conservatives in society) strongly resent the use of Singlish, regarding it as an uneducated, bastardized and ultimately unacceptable variety which might endanger the international intelligibility and thus competitiveness of Singaporeans. For more than a decade the government has therefore run the "Speak Good English Movement" (SGEM), whose goal it is explicitly to eradicate Singlish. But, interestingly enough, while the government (from the same party since independence and backed by huge majorities in elections) usually steers the country with determination and success, in this case (the only one of its kind, as far as I know) it meets with persistent resistance: many Singaporeans cherish their dialect, continue to use it despite its official stigma, and defend it vigorously and with ingenuity. For many of its speakers Singlish is a language of the heart, a code of friendliness and proximity, and its mixed character is seen as a reflection of the ethnically mixed composition of the nation's population.

Actually, this is a nice illustration of the social embedding of contact effects and mixed varieties found in a similar fashion in many other locations as well. Innovative varieties in which English and indigenous languages are mixed liberally are found in surprisingly many countries – as "Hinglish" in India, "Taglish" in the Philippines, "Manglish" or "Rojak" in Malaysia, "Engsh" in Kenya, and so on. Typically, these varieties have been coined and are used by young and educated speakers, often in a playful mood; usually they are opposed and stigmatized officially by authorities but positively evaluated and upheld by their speakers as reflections of their multiethnic backgrounds.

Nigerian Pidgin English

So-called pidgin and creole languages are characterized by even stronger contact effects, so that in some cases the resulting speech forms are no longer mutually comprehensible with and recognizable as varieties of English (see above). Pidgins were conventionally defined as simplified (structurally and lexically reduced) speech forms for use in limited interethnic contact situations (such as trade), never spoken natively. Creoles, in contrast, were originally viewed as newly born and both structurally and functionally fully developed contact languages, native tongues which serve all social and linguistic needs of a speech community and show structural complexity. The traditional assumption was that creoles emerged when children in a pidgin-speaking community (e.g., on slave plantations) acquired a pidgin (i.e., structurally impoverished input) as their mother tongue and expanded it in this process. However, it has been found that this is too simple a view by far, given that contact influences are gradual phenomena which correlate strongly with certain types of social setup of mixed speech communities, with continuities or disruptions of speakers' and communities' fates, and with processes of linguistic restructuring performed to a considerable extent also by adults when the situation calls for extreme linguistic adjustments. Shared or similar structural properties and social settings of pidgins and creoles with various lexifier languages were observed for the first time in the 1960s, and since then these languages have been subjects of intense analysis and many discussions. In recent years many linguists have increasingly recognized the fuzziness of these categories, and it has been widely accepted that rather than producing clear-cut and distinct language types, contact effects come in varying degrees, as graded phenomena in direct correlation with degrees of social discontinuity. For instance, even if the idea has been proposed and is still defended by some, it has not been possible to define creoles on purely linguistic grounds: there is no single set of linguistic properties which only creoles but no other, non-creole languages share. There is a list of linguistic properties widely considered "typically creole" (such as preverbal markers to express time relations, lack of inflection, or zero copulas especially before adjectives), but practically all of these are fairly widespread in other languages as well, especially in analytic languages.

Nigerian Pidgin (NigP) is a nice illustration of this fuzziness. This begins with its label, which has been conventionally established but is in fact a misnomer. Structurally, NigP is a highly complex variety which shares many features with creole languages on both sides of the Atlantic, a far cry from the notion of a pidgin as characterized by short, simple patterns only. Functionally, it is used extremely widely in the country; reliable speaker numbers are impossible to obtain, but estimates go into many tens of millions. And socially it is acquired increasingly commonly as a mother tongue – often in families with parents of different ethnic backgrounds where the pidgin is then chosen as the home language; so technically speaking, NigP is actually often and in many respects "a creole." It is also not a homogeneous linguistic system but varies from simple, reduced versions to highly complex ones, by varying degrees of proximity to local forms of English, by speakers' backgrounds, and by contexts. Figure 13.5 illustrates a typical setting in which pidgin tends to be used, an urban market.

Figure 13.5 *A West African urban market*
Source: *Photograph by author*

Text 3 represents a developed, stable, and in some respects anglicized sub-variety, as used by some educated speakers.

Text 3. Extract from an interview with a female student from Lagos, on minimum wages for federal workers

Source: Deuber (2005): from sample V01-3 on CD. Reproduced with permission.

   I talk am say federal government put money// and di salary wey im carry go up/ e never start to dey reach people hand// even self na dis uh wetin dem dey call am? na only me sabi (na me sabi) na me know di problem of Nigeria/ na im dey cause all dis katakata wey we dey talk so// because federal government talk say/ okay o im go dey pay minimum wage of seven thousand five hundred// minimum wage na im be say/ di person wey dey bottom of government/ when e start for bottom/ e go dey earn wetin? seven thousand five hundred// but now e no hold meeting with di state government// so state government just wake up one day/ na im e say "wetin dey happen?" e say government don put money for deir salary// so state government say dem no be magician// how dem wan take pay di workers/ when money no dey inside deir pocket

Translation: 'I said that the federal government has increased salaries. But workers haven't even started to receive the increased salaries. It's this, what do they call it? Well, I know the problem of Nigeria, that's what causes all this chaos that we're talking about. Because the federal government announced a new minimum wage of seven thousand five hundred [naira]. Minimum wage means that the lowest government worker, when he/she starts at the bottom, he/she will earn what? Seven thousand five hundred. But it [the federal government] didn't consult with the state governments. So the state governments just woke up one day to find that the federal government had increased salaries. So the state governments said they weren't magicians: How could they pay the workers when they didn't have the money?'

Notice that while many words in this text can be identified as being English (especially those for formal, abstract concepts: *federal government, minimum wage, salary*), on the whole the text is in need of a translation and would be most difficult to grasp without one. Some words are distinctly local and need to be known: *na* is a pidgin copula or highlighter (here something like '(it) is'); *o* marks emphasis; and *katakata* suggests 'chaos' somewhat onomatopoetically. The word *sabi*, from Portuguese, is widespread in many pidgins and means 'know' or 'be able.' Some expressions can be recognized as being derived from English (*carry go up* 'raise,' *dey* from 'there,' *wetin* 'what,' lit. from *which thing*). And some forms and uses are fairly widespread in other pidgins and creoles but need to be known as such in order to be understood:

- *dey* is a copula ('is') or a marker of the progressive;
- *wey* is an invariant relativizer ('who, which');
- pronoun forms do not vary by subject / object function or gender (so *me, im/e, dem* are 'I, he/it, they');
- *go* is a preverbal marker of future time reference (so *im go dey pay* is 'it will be paying');
- *don* is a preverbal marker of perfective aspect (*don put* 'has put');
- *am* (from 'him/them') is a transitivity marker after verbs (so *talk am* is 'say [something]');
- *say* is a complementizer introducing an object clause (i.e. corresponding to 'that');
- forms are uninflected or invariant (*people hand* 'people's hands'; *be* 'is, are'); and
- preverbal *no* negates the following verb (*dem no be* 'they are not').

In practically all of these cases both roots in English and also significant distinctions and innovations, developments away from purely English speech habits, are evident – and this is a combination which appears typical of contact-induced varieties in general.

Historically speaking, it is not quite clear when Nigerian Pidgin originated (and the same applies to a range of similar pidgin Englishes spoken across West Africa). Trading contacts and coastal forts, also serving the notorious slave trade, go back to the seventeenth century, and must have led to contacts in simple pidgin. Some scholars claim, however, that the structural complexity of West African Pidgin Englishes and many of their properties in fact go back to the input of former slaves repatriated from North America and the Caribbean in the late eighteenth and early nineteenth centuries (originally to Sierra Leone and Liberia, respectively). In the mid-nineteenth century the empire's colonial activity and the hold of the British in Nigeria became stronger, and in the early twentieth century they also ventured further into the hinterland (Lagos became a British colony in 1861, and Nigeria itself in 1914). Clearly, NigP expanded and played a major role in these processes.

Today, Nigeria is an ESL country in which English predominates in formal national domains (like higher legislation, education, commerce, etc.), and it blends or competes with Pidgin in more informal contexts; in fact, many Pidgin speakers simply assume they speak English, and sometimes the boundary is difficult to draw. In a country torn by ethnic and religious conflicts and rivalries, this strong role of English (and, by implication, Pidgin as well) was originally promoted because of its ethnic neutrality – the fact that it is not any group's original language allows all ethnicities to adopt it and live with it (which would not be the case with any of Nigeria's strong African languages attempting to move into this role). Language ideologies and power discrepancies have a major impact on possible future developments, however. "Standard" English, with conservative and exonormative associations (i.e., continuing to accept British English as the external source of linguistic correctness), is officially called for (as the target of language education, for instance), but it has an air of being elitist and is accessible only to those in power. Pidgin, on the other hand, is stigmatized, and branded by gatekeepers and authorities (which indirectly clearly is also a step toward upholding power imbalances in the country). Nigerian Pidgin has occasionally been suggested as a candidate for the status as a new national language, because it is clearly African in origin, ethnically neutral, and without doubt the most widely spread and shared language of the country, but for the time being such a step appears to be inconceivable given the strong stigma which is officially associated with the language.

Such attitudes in broadly diglossic situations are in fact quite typical of many contact varieties and settings, including many other countries in which pidgins and creoles are spoken. English-based pidgins and creoles are found predominantly in parts and countries of the Caribbean and West Africa, and also in the south-west Pacific. Their social settings, a strange mixture of official stigma but covert prestige, are similar almost everywhere, and in structural terms especially the so-called "Atlantic" pidgins and creoles share a surprisingly large number of properties and even specific forms (for instance, *sabi* in Text 3). All of these languages and language varieties show strong and comparable contact effects, with words indirectly and often recognizably stemming mostly from English but grammatical patterns caused by transfer and restructuring processes and motivated by indigenous (and on both sides of the Atlantic this means mostly African) construction types.

Concluding Remarks: Contact Englishes in the Future

This chapter has shown that contact has played a major role in the evolution of English, both from the very beginnings of the language some 1,500 years ago and, perhaps increasingly so, to the present day. Recent research has tended to emphasize the increasing dynamics of the diffusion of English, in various forms and ways, to new contexts, as a consequence of its "transnational attraction" (Schneider 2014). English is expanding vigorously in countries where it is essentially a foreign language, so that nowadays the birth of varieties such as "Chinese English" is being projected (Xu 2010); and it simply constitutes a global resource which is being picked up, in bits and pieces and irrespective of norm concerns, by speakers in many different contexts and from all walks of life (Blommaert 2010; Meierkord 2012).

So – is English "fragmenting," ultimately bound to end up as a range of varying, mutually incomprehensible daughter languages? This is what happened to an earlier world language, Latin, roughly one and a half millennia ago, and interestingly enough it was "vulgar Latin," not the "classic" standard form, that became the base of all the modern Romance languages, just as today it is casual, informal varieties of English which show diversification. There are also countertendencies at the formal end: the conservative nature of writing conventions and the increase in international contact and exchange will secure a shared "common core" of some sort of a "standard English" with but limited variability. But on the ground, in grassroots contexts, English is being adjusted to new contexts and needs, being transformed further by all kinds of contact influences.

Suggestions for Further Study

A classic, non-technical and easily readable textbook on the history of English, with strong emphasis on extralinguistic history, is Baugh and Cable (1951 [2013]). Out of a very large number of books which survey the history of English and also highlight contact effects rather strongly, I recommend Fennell (2001), Hogg and Denison (2006), Mugglestone (2012), and Nevalainen and Traugott (2012), a monumental handbook inspired by recent research trends.

Specifically with respect to English viewed from a contact perspective, Miller (2012) looks into external influences up to the Renaissance period, and Schreier and Hundt (2013) address this phenomenon in a wider, more modern way, inspired by recent trends in linguistics. Introductions to language contact theory in general include Thomason (2001), Winford (2003), and Matras (2009).

A widely accepted theoretical framework which accounts for the growth of World Englishes is developed in Schneider (2007), a book which applies these ideas to many individual countries, including the ones discussed in this chapter. Schneider (2011) is an easily accessible textbook on this subject. New Zealand English is introduced to a wider audience in Gordon and Deverson (1998), and Gordon et al. (2004) document the emergence of the variety in a more technical and detailed perspective.

Several books on Singaporean English have been published in recent years, including Lim (2004), with a focus on structural properties, and Leimgruber (2013), who in addition to describing history and properties emphasizes the sociosymbolic "indexicality" of local varieties.

Holm (2000) explains the nature, spread, and properties of pidgin and creole languages. Deuber (2005) is an exciting source on Nigerian Pidgin, including many illustrative samples.

Exercises

1. Scandinavian pronouns in Middle English
   A line early in Chaucer's *Canterbury Tales* runs as follows: the pilgrims went to visit the tomb of the martyr . . .

   > . . . *that hem hath holpen when that they were seke.*
   > (literally, 'that them has helped when that they were sick')

   Given that Chaucer's language represents late fourteenth-century southern English, what do the pronoun forms in this line indicate concerning the diffusion of a Scandinavian innovation in time and space?

2. Latinisms in Early Modern English
   In Text 1, the "Ynkhorne letter," identify and mark the words of Latin origin. When in doubt, consult the *OED* or another dictionary which gives etymologies of words. How many and which of these words have survived into Present-day English? Compare the form of words which still exist in this Early Modern English (fake) letter to their modern forms and use this limited dataset to identify some strategies of anglicizing Latin-derived word forms.

3. The debate on Singlish
   Watch the YouTube clip "Speak Proper Singlish Campaign" www.youtube .com/watch?v=PbgsleSbUUg (Nov. 17, 2014). Collect and discuss the arguments brought forward in this clip in the light of the ongoing discussion on the acceptability of Singlish. Note also the title of the clip!

4. Understanding Nigerian Pidgin

   Using the brief grammatical explanations offered above, work toward a closer understanding of the precise composition of Text 3. I recommend a two-step strategy:

   a. produce a word-by-word rendition of the nearest English cognates or equivalents (e.g., at the end of the first line "the salary which him carry go up"), and

   b. then identify more complex meaning relationships.

5. English in international encounters: personal experiences

   Discuss your experiences with new, contact-derived forms of English in international travel (which, I assume, many of you will have had): In foreign countries, did you ever find somebody's English difficult to understand, or did you ever notice words, language forms, or expressions in such contexts which you recognized as derived from local languages?

Notes

I want to thank Lisa Lim and Dagmar Deuber for permission to use samples of Singlish and Nigerian Pidgin, respectively, from their work.

1. In a similar vein, for one of the most strongly contact-shaped "New Englishes," Bao (2015) shows how Vernacular Singaporean English has emerged via a filtered but systemic transfer of entire grammatical subsystems from its main substrate language, Chinese.

2. See Chapter 9 for a discussion of "change from below/above."

3. Compare, however, Lutz (2012: 509), who considers the impact of Old Norse on Old English as "superstratal" as well.

4. See Chapter 5 on the notion of "token."

5. See Chapter 9 for a discussion of *you/thou* in English.

References

Corpora and Electronic Databases

AE06 = *American English 2006.* (period 2003–2008) Compiled by Paul Baker (Lancaster University). www.helsinki.fi/varieng/CoRD/corpora/BE06/index.html

ANC = *American National Corpus* (second release). 2005. Compiled by Randi Reppen, Nancy Ide, and Keith Suderman. Philadelphia: Linguistic Data Consortium. www.anc.org

ARCHER = *A Representative Corpus of Historical English Registers 3.2.* 1990–1993/2002/ 2007/2010/2013. Originally compiled under the supervision of Douglas Biber (Northern Arizona University) and Edward Finegan (University of Southern California); currently managed by a consortium of participants at fourteen universities. www.alc.manchester.ac .uk/subjects/lel/research/projects/archer/

B-Brown = *The 1930s Brown Corpus.* 2004–2013. Compiled by Marianne Hundt (University of Zurich). www.es.uzh.ch/Subsites/Projects/BBROWN.html

BE06 = *British English 2006.* (period 2003–2008) Compiled by Paul Baker (Lancaster University). www.helsinki.fi/varieng/CoRD/corpora/BE06/index.html

B-LOB = *The B-LOB 1931 Corpus.* 2003–2006. Compiled by Geoffrey Leech and Paul Rayson (University of Lancaster). www.helsinki.fi/varieng/CoRD/corpora/BLOB-1931/ index.html

BNC = *British National Corpus*, version 3 (BNC XML edition). 2007. Distributed by Oxford University Computing Services on behalf of the BNC Consortium. www.natcorp.ox.ac.uk

British Newspapers 1600–1950. http://gdc.gale.com/products/19th-century-british-library-news papers-part-i-and part-ii/acquire/faqs/

Brown = *A Standard Corpus of Present-day Edited American English, for Use with Digital Computers.* 1964. Compiled by W. Nelson Francis and Henry Kučera (Brown University). www.helsinki.fi/varieng/CoRD/corpora/BROWN/

CED = *A Corpus of English Dialogues 1560–1760.* 2006. Compiled under the supervision of Merja Kytö (Uppsala University) and Jonathan Culpeper (Lancaster University). Available through the Oxford Text Archive. www.engelska.uu.se/forskning/engelska-spraket/elektro niska-resurser/a-corpus

CEEC = *Corpus of Early English Correspondence.* 1998. Compiled by Terttu Nevalainen, Helena Raumolin-Brunberg, Jukka Keränen, Minna Nevala, Arja Nurmi, and Minna Palander-Collin (University of Helsinki). www.helsinki.fi/varieng/CoRD/corpora/ CEEC/index.html

CEECS = *Corpus of Early English Correspondence Sampler (1418–1680).* 1998. Compiled by Jukka Keränen, Minna Nevala, Terttu Nevalainen, Arja Nurmi, Minna Palander-Collin, and Helena Raumolin-Brunberg (University of Helsinki). www.helsinki.fi/varieng/CoRD/cor pora/CEEC/ceecs.html

CEEM = *Corpus of Early English Medical Writing.* 2004. Project leaders Irma Taavitsainen and Päivi Pahta (University of Helsinki and Tampere). www.helsinki.fi/varieng/CoRD/corpora/CEEM/index.html

CLMET = *Corpus of Late Modern English Texts.* Compiled by Hendrik De Smet (University of Leuven). perswww.kuleuven.be/~u0044428/clmet.htm

CLMET3.0 = *Corpus of Late Modern English Texts* (version 3.0). Compiled by Hendrik De Smet (University of Leuven), Hans-Jürgen Diller (University of Bochum) and Jukka Tyrkkö (University of Tampere). perswww.kuleuven.be/~u0044428/clmet3_0.htm

COCA = *The Corpus of Contemporary American English: 520 Million Words, 1990–Present.* 2008–. Compiled by Mark Davies (Brigham Young University). http://corpus.byu.edu/coca/

COERP = *Corpus of English Religious Prose.* 2003–. Compiled by Thomas Kohnen et al. (University of Cologne). http://coerp.uni-koeln.de

COHA = *The Corpus of Historical American English: 400 Million Words, 1810–2009.* 2010–. Compiled by Mark Davies (Brigham Young University). http://corpus.byu.edu/coha/

COOEE = *Corpus of Oz Early English.* 2007. Compiled by Clemens Fritz. www.helsinki.fi/varieng/CoRD/corpora/COOEE/

CORIECOR = *Corpus of Irish English Correspondence.* Compiled by Kevin McCafferty (University of Bergen) and Carolina P. Amador-Moreno (University of Extremadura).

CoRD = *Corpus Resource Database.* www.helsinki.fi/varieng/CoRD/

Corpus of Scottish Correspondence. 2007. Compiled by Anneli Meurman-Solin. www.helsinki.fi/varieng/csc/

DCPSE = *Diachronic Corpus of Present-day Spoken English.* 2006. Compiled by Bas Aarts, Sean Wallis, et al. (University College London, Survey of English Usage). www.ucl.ac.uk/english-usage/projects/dcpse/index.htm

DOEWC = *Dictionary of Old English Web Corpus.* 2009. Ed. Antonette diPaolo Healey with John Price Wilkin and Xin Xiang. The University of Toronto, Dictionary of Old English. www.doe.utoronto.ca/pages/pub/web-corpus.html

EAF = *Early American Fiction Collection, 1789–1875.* 2000. Chadwyck-Healey (ProQuest Company). http://collections.chadwyck.com/marketing/products/about_ilc.jsp?collection=eaf2

ECCO = *Eighteenth Century Collections Online.* Thomson Gale. www.gale.com/EighteenthCentury/

ED = *English Drama.* 1996–2014. Ed. John Barnard et al. Chadwyck-Healey (ProQuest Company). www.proquest.com/en-US/catalogs/databases/detail/english_drama.shtml

EEBO = *Early English Books Online.* 2003–2015. Chadwyck-Healey (ProQuest Company). http://eebo.chadwyck.com/home

EMEMT = *Early Modern English Medical Texts.* Available on CD accompanying Irma Taavitsainen and Päivi Pahta (eds.). 2010. *Early Modern English Medical Texts: Corpus description and studies.* Amsterdam: John Benjamins. Also see www.helsinki.fi/varieng/CoRD/corpora/CEEM/EMEMTindex.html

ETED = *An Electronic Text Edition of Depositions 1560–1760.* Available on CD accompanying Merja Kytö, Peter J. Grund, and Terry Walker. 2011. *Testifying to language and life in Early Modern England.* Amsterdam: John Benjamins. Also see www.engelska.uu.se/research/english-language/electronic-resources/english-witness/

The English Language of the North-West in the Late Modern English Period: A Corpus of Late 18 c Prose. 2003–2010. Compiled by Linda van Bergen, David Denison, and

Joana Soliva (University of Manchester) http://personalpages.manchester.ac.uk/staff/david.denison/late18 c

FLOB = *Freiburg–LOB Corpus*. 1999. Compiled by Christian Mair (University of Freiburg). www.helsinki.fi/varieng/CoRD/corpora/FLOB/

Frown = *Freiburg–Brown Corpus*. 1999. Compiled by Christian Mair (University of Freiburg). www.helsinki.fi/varieng/CoRD/corpora/FROWN/

HC = *The Helsinki Corpus of English Texts: Diachronic and Dialectal*. 1991. Compiled by Matti Rissanen, Merja Kytö, Leena Kahlas-Tarkka, Matti Kilpiö, Saara Nevanlinna, Irma Taavitsainen, Terttu Nevalainen, and Helena Raumolin-Brunberg (University of Helsinki). www.helsinki.fi/varieng/CoRD/corpora/HelsinkiCorpus/

HUGE = *Hyper Usage Guide of English*, created by Robin Straaijer. www.huge.ullet.net

LAEME = *A Linguistic Atlas of Early Middle English, 1150–1325*. Version 3.2, 2013 [Version 2.1, 2008]. Compiled by Margaret Laing. Edinburgh: Version 3.2, 2013. © The University of Edinburgh. www.lel.ed.ac.uk/ihd/laeme2/laeme2.html

LALME = *A Linguistic Atlas of Late Mediaeval English*. 1986. Compiled by Angus McIntosh, Michael L. Samuels, and Michael Benskin. Aberdeen University Press.

LC = *The Lampeter Corpus of Early Modern English Tracts (1640–1740)*. 1997. Compiled by Josef Schmied, Claudia Claridge, and Rainer Siemund (University of Chemnitz). www.tu-chemnitz.de/phil/english/sections/linguist/real/independent/lampeter/lampr.htm; see also Siemund and Claridge (1997).

LOB = *Lancaster–Oslo–Bergen Corpus*. 1978. Compiled by Geoffrey Leech (Lancaster University), Stig Johansson (University of Oslo) (project leaders), and Knut Hofland (University of Bergen, head of computing). www.helsinki.fi/varieng/CoRD/corpora/LOB/index.html

MEG-C = *The Middle English Grammar Corpus*. 2011. Version 2011.1. Compiled by Merja Stenroos, Martti Mäkinen, Simon Horobin, and Jeremy Smith (University of Stavanger). www.uis.no/meg-c

MELD = *Middle English Local Documents Corpus*. Under construction by Merja Stenroos et al. (University of Stavanger).

NCF = *Nineteenth-century Fiction, 1782–1903*. 1999–2000. Chadwyck-Healey (ProQuest Company). http://collections.chadwyck.com/marketing/products/about_ilc.jsp?collection=ncf

The Newdigate Newsletters. Ed. Philip Hines, Jr. http://clu.uni.no/icame/newdigateeks.html

OBC = *The Old Bailey Corpus 2.0*. 2016. Compiled by Magnus Huber, Magnus Nissel, and Karin Puga. hdl: 11858/00-246C-0000-0023-8CFB-2; see also Huber (2007).

The Old Bailey Proceedings Online, 1674–1913. Ed. Tim Hitchcock, Robert Shoemaker, Clive Emsley, Sharon Howard, and Jamie McLauglin et al. (version 7.0, 24 March 2012) www.oldbaileyonline.org

ONZE = *Origins of New Zealand English Project*. www.nzilbb.canterbury.ac.nz/onze.shtml; see Gordon et al. (2007).

PCEEC = *Parsed Corpus of Early English Correspondence*, text version. 2006. Compiled by Terttu Nevalainen, Helena Raumolin-Brunberg, Jukka Keränen, Minna Nevala, Arja Nurmi, and Minna Palander-Collin, with additional annotation by Ann Taylor. Helsinki: University of Helsinki and York: University of York. Distributed through the Oxford Text Archive. www.helsinki.fi/varieng/CoRD/corpora/CEEC/pceec.html

PPCEME2 = *The Penn–Helsinki Parsed Corpus of Early Modern English*. 2004. Compiled by Anthony Kroch, Beatrice Santorini, and Ariel Diertani. www.ling.upenn.edu/hist-corpora /PPCEME-RELEASE-2/index.html

PPCME2 = *The Penn–Helsinki Parsed Corpus of Middle English*. 2000. 2nd edn. Compiled by Anthony Kroch and Ann Taylor (University of Pennsylvania). www.ling.upenn.edu/hist-corpora/PPCME2-RELEASE-3/index.html

Rostock Newspaper Corpus. 1996–2000. Ed. Friedrich Ungerer, Kristina Schneider, and Birte Bös. www.iaa.uni-rostock.de/lehrstuehle-abteilungen/sprachwissenschaft/rostock-newspaper-corpus/

YCOE = *The York–Toronto–Helsinki Parsed Corpus of Old English Prose*. 2003. Compiled by Ann Taylor, Anthony Warner, Susan Pintzuk, and Frank Beths (University of Pennsylvania). 1st edn. www-users.york.ac.uk/~lang22/YcoeHome1.htm

York Poetry corpus = *The York–Helsinki Parsed Corpus of Old English Poetry*. 2001. Compiled by Susan Pintzuk and Leendert Plug (University of York). 1st edn. www-users .york.ac.uk/~lang18/pcorpus.html

Grammars, Dictionaries, and Usage Guides

Alford, Henry. 1864. *A plea for the Queen's English*. London: Alexander Strahan.

Alston, R. C. (ed.). 1974. *English linguistics 1500–1800: A collection of facsimile reprints*. Menston: Scolar Press.

Amis, Kingsley. 1997. *The King's English: A guide to modern usage*. London: HarperCollins.

Anon. 1778. *The complete letter-writer; or, polite English secretary*. 16th edn. London: S. Crowder. ECCO: ESTC no. T162762

Anon. [1856]. *Live and learn: A guide for all, who wish to speak and write correctly*. New York: Dick & Fitzgerald.

Anon. 1856. *Five hundred mistakes of daily occurrence in speaking, pronouncing, and writing the English language, corrected*. New York: Daniel Burgess & Co.

Baker, Robert. 1770. *Reflections on the English language*. London: J. Bell. [2nd edn. 1779.]

[Brightland, John and Charles Gildon]. 1711. *A grammar of the English tongue*. London: John Brightland.

Bullokar, William. 1586 [1980]. *Pamphlet for grammar*. Ed. J. R. Turner. Leeds: University of Leeds, School of English.

Burchfield, R. W. 1981. *The spoken word: A BBC guide*. London: British Broadcasting Corporation.

Burchfield, R. W. 1996. *The new Fowler's modern English usage*. 3rd edn. Oxford: Oxford University Press.

Butterfield, Jeremy. 2015. *Fowler's dictionary of modern English usage*. 4th edn. Oxford: Oxford University Press.

Care, Henry. 1671. *The female secretary*. London: Henry Million. EEBO: Wing / C519

CIA style manual: *Style manual & writers guide for intelligence publications*. 2011. https:// fas.org/irp/cia/product/style.pdf

Day, Angel. 1586. *The English secretorie*. 2nd edn. London: Robert Walde-graue. EEBO: STC/6401.

Dryden, John. 1672 (1966). Defense of the Epilogue. In W. F. Bolton (ed.), *The English language*, 55–69. Cambridge: Cambridge University Press.

Dryden, John. 1684. *An essay of dramatic poesie*. London: Jos. Knight and Fr. Saunders.

Fenn, Ellenor. [1799]. *The child's grammar*. London: John Marshall.

Follett, Wilson. 1966. *Modern American usage*. New York: Hill & Wang.

Fowler, H. W. 1926. *A dictionary of modern English usage*. Oxford: Oxford University Press.

Fowler, H. W. and F. G. Fowler. 1906. *The King's English*. Oxford: Clarendon Press.

Garner, Bryan A. 2016. *Garner's modern English usage*. 4th edn. New York: Oxford University Press. [1st edn. 1998; 3rd edn. 2009, formerly entitled *Garner's modern American usage*]

[Gildon, Charles]. 1712. *Bellum grammaticale*. London: J. and M. Gerund.

Gowers, Rebecca. 2014. *Plain words: A guide to the use of English*. New edn. London: Penguin.

Gowers, Sir Ernest. 1965. *Fowler's Modern English usage*. 2nd edn. Oxford: Oxford University Press.

Grammar Girl: QuickandDirtyTips.com. www.quickanddirtytips.com/grammar-girl

Heffer, Simon. 2010. *Strictly English: The correct way to write … and why it matters*. New York: Random House.

Historical thesaurus of the Oxford English Dictionary, with additional material from A Thesaurus of Old English. 2009. Ed. Christian Kay, Jane Roberts, Michael Samuels, and Irené Witherspoon. Oxford: Oxford University Press.

Hurd, Seth T. 1847. *A grammatical corrector*. Philadelphia: E. H. Butler & Co.

Johnson, Samuel. 1755. *A dictionary of the English language*. 2 vols. London: J. and P. Knapton, T. and T. Longman, C. Hitch and L. Hawes, A. Millar, and R. and J. Dodsley.

Kamm, Oliver. 2015. *Accidence will happen: The non-pedantic guide to English usage*. London: Weidenfeld & Nicolson.

Kirkby, John. 1746. *A new English grammar*. London: R. Manby and H. S. Cox.

Lowth, Robert. 1762. *A short introduction to English grammar*. London: A. Millar, and R. & J. Dodsley.

Maty, M. (ed.). 1777. *Miscellaneous works of the late Philip Dormer Stanhope, Earl of Chesterfield*, vol. 2. Dublin.

MED = Middle English dictionary. 1952–2001. Ed. Hans Kurath and Sherman Kuhn. Ann Arbor: University of Michigan Press. Part of the *Middle English compendium*, Francis McSparran (chief ed.). http://quod.lib.umich.edu/m/mec/

Murray, Lindley. 1795. *English grammar*. York: Wilson, Spence and Mawman.

OED = Oxford English dictionary online. 2000–. 3rd edn. Oxford University Press. www.oed.com

[Oldmixon, John]. 1712. *Reflections on Dr. Swift's letter to the Earl of Oxford about the English tongue*. London: [sold by A. Baldwin].

Peters, Pam. 2004. *The Cambridge guide to English usage*. Cambridge: Cambridge University Press.

Peters, Pam. 2007. *The Cambridge guide to Australian English usage*. 2nd edn. Cambridge: Cambridge University Press.

Pinker, Steven. 2014. *The sense of style: The thinking person's guide to writing in the 21st century*. New York: Penguin.

Priestley, Joseph. 1761. *The rudiments of English grammar*. London: for R. Griffiths.

Strunk, William Jr. and E. B. White. 1959. *The elements of style*. New York: Macmillan.

Swift, Jonathan. 1712. *Proposal for correcting, improving, and ascertaining the English tongue.* London: Benj. Tooke. Available online: https://andromeda.rutgers.edu/~jlynch/Texts/proposal.html

Taggart, Caroline. 2010. *Her Ladyship's guide to the Queen's English.* London: National Trust.

Wallis, John. 1653. *Grammatica linguae anglicanae.* Oxford: Tho. Robinson.

Weiner, Edmund. 1983. *The Oxford guide to English usage.* Oxford: Clarendon Press.

Wright, Joseph. 1898–1905. *The English dialect dictionary.* 7 vols. London: Henry Frowde.

Wright, Joseph. 1905. *The English dialect grammar.* Oxford: Henry Frowde.

Primary Sources

Benson, Larry D. (ed.). 1987. *The Riverside Chaucer.* 3rd edn. Boston: Houghton Mifflin.

Boswell, James. 1791 [1970]. *Life of Johnson.* Ed. R. W. Chapman. Rev. edn. Oxford: Oxford University Press.

Burnley, David and Alison Wiggins (eds.). 2003. *The Auchinleck Manuscript.* Version 1.1. National Library of Scotland. http://auchinleck.nls.uk/

Dixon, Henry Hall (aka "the Druid"). 1854. Country crayons. Sketch the fifth: The country doctor. *The Sporting Review* (April), 286–293.

Fisher, John H., Malcolm Richardson, and June L. Fisher (eds.). 1984. *An anthology of Chancery English.* Knoxville: University of Tennessee Press. www.hti.umich.edu/c/cme

Honkapohja, Alpo (ed.). 2013. The Trinity Seven Planets. *Scholarly editing: The annual of the Association for Documentary Editing* 34. www.scholarlyediting.org/2013/editions/seven planets.html

Kiernan, Kevin (ed.). 2011. *Electronic Beowulf.* 3rd edn. London: British Library. Update for version 3.1. http://ebeowulf.uky.edu

Records of the Salem witch-hunts. 2013. Bernard Rosenthal (general ed.). Cambridge: Cambridge University Press.

Rosselli Del Turco, Roberto (ed.). 2013. *Digital Vercelli book (beta).* http://vbd.humnet.unipi.it/beta

Secondary Sources

Adamson, Sylvia. 2007. Prescribed reading: Pronouns and gender in the eighteenth century. *Historical Sociolinguistics and Sociohistorical Linguistics* 7. www.let.leidenuniv.nl/hsl_shl/index.html

Adger, David and Jennifer Smith. 2010. Variation in agreement: A lexical feature-based approach. *Lingua* 120, 1109–1134.

Aijmer, Karin. 1997. *I think*: An English modal particle. In Swan and Westvik (eds.), 1–47.

Aitchison, Jean. 2013. *Language change: Progress or decay?* 4th edn. Cambridge: Cambridge University Press.

Albakry, Mohammed. 2007. Usage prescription rules in newspaper language. *Southern Journal of Linguistics* 31(2), 28–56.

Alford, Henry. 1878. *A plea for the Queen's English: Stray notes on speaking and spelling.* New York: George Routledge.

Algeo, John. 2010. *The origins and development of the English language*. Based on the original work of Thomas Pyles. 6th edn. Boston: Wadsworth.

Allen, Cynthia L. 1995. *Case marking and reanalysis*. Oxford: Oxford University Press.

Allen, Cynthia L. 2007. Variation in the NP/DP in Old English: Determiner and possessive combinations. In Annie Zaenen, Jane Simpson, Tracy Holloway King, Jane Grimshaw, Joan Maling, and Chris Manning (eds.), *Architectures, rules, and preferences: Variations on themes by Joan W. Bresnan*, 3–20. Stanford, CA: CSLI Publications.

Allen, Cynthia L. 2016. Sifting through the evidence: Principles and pitfalls. In Machan (ed.), 166–187.

Alleyne, Mervyn C. 1980. *Comparative Afro-American: An historical-comparative study of English-based Afro-American dialects of the New World*. Ann Arbor: Karoma.

Alston, R. C. 1965. *A bibliography of the English language from the invention of printing to the year 1800*, vol. I. Leeds: Arnold and Son.

Ameka, Felix. 1992. Interjections: The universal yet neglected part of speech. *Journal of Pragmatics* 18(2–3), 101–118.

American national biography online. www.anb.org.

Andersen, Henning. 2006. Grammation, regrammation and degrammation: Tense loss in Russian. *Diachronica* 23(2), 231–258.

Anderson, Wendy and John Corbett. 2009. *Exploring English with online corpora*. Basingstoke: Palgrave Macmillan.

Anttila, Raimo. 1989. *Historical and comparative linguistics*. Amsterdam: John Benjamins.

Archer, Dawn. 2005. *Questions and answers in the English courtroom (1640–1760)*. Amsterdam: John Benjamins.

Archer, Dawn. 2010. Speech acts. In Jucker and Taavitsainen (eds.), 379–417.

Arnovick, Leslie K. 2006. *Written reliquaries: The resonance of orality in medieval English texts*. Amsterdam: John Benjamins.

Atkinson, Dwight. 1996. The Philosophical Transactions of the Royal Society of London, 1675–1975. *Language in Society* 25, 333–371.

Atkinson, Dwight. 1999. *Scientific discourse in sociohistorical context: The philosophical transactions of the Royal Society of London, 1675–1975*. Mahwah, NJ: Erlbaum.

Atwell, Eric. 2009. Development of tag sets for part-of-speech tagging. In Lüdeling and Kytö (eds.), vol. I, 501–527.

Auer, Anita. 2008. *Lest* the situation deteriorates: A study of *lest* as trigger of the inflectional subjunctive. In Miriam Locher and Jürg Strässler (eds.), *Standards and norms in the English language*, 149–173. Berlin: Mouton de Gruyter.

Auer, Anita. 2009. *The subjunctive in the age of prescriptivism: English and German developments during the eighteenth century*. Basingstoke: Palgrave Macmillan.

Ayres-Bennett, Wendy and Ingrid Tieken-Boon van Ostade. 2017. Prescriptivism in a comparative perspective: The case of France and England. In Tieken-Boon van Ostade and Percy (eds.), 105–120.

Bailey, Charles-James and Karl Maroldt. 1977. The French lineage of English. In Jürgen M. Meisel (ed.), *Langues en contact – pidgins – creoles – languages in contact*, 21–53. Tübingen: Narr.

Bailey, Richard W. 1991. *Images of English: A cultural history of the language*. Cambridge: Cambridge University Press.

Bailey, Richard W. 1996. *Nineteenth-century English*. Ann Arbor: University of Michigan Press.

Bao, Zhiming. 2015. *The making of Vernacular Singapore English: System, transfer and filter.* Cambridge: Cambridge University Press.

Barber, Charles, Joan C. Beal and Philip A. Shaw. 2009. *The English language: A historical introduction.* Cambridge: Cambridge University Press.

Bately, Janet M. 1964. Dryden's revisions in the Essay of dramatic poesy: The preposition at the end of the sentence and the expression of the relative. *Review of English Studies* 15(59), 268–282.

Baugh, Albert C. and Thomas Cable. 2013 [1951]. *A history of the English language.* 6th edn. Upper Saddle River, NJ: Prentice Hall.

Beal, Joan C. 2004. *English in modern times.* London: Arnold.

Beckner, Clay and Joan Bybee. 2009. A usage-based account of constituency and reanalysis. *Language Learning* 59, 29–48.

Benskin, Michael. 1989. Some aspects of Cumbrian English, mainly medieval. In Leiv Egil Breivik, Arnoldus Hille, and Stig Johansson (eds.), *Essays on English language in honour of Bertil Sundby,* 13–46. Oslo: Novus.

Benskin, Michael. 1991. The "Fit"-technique explained. In Felicity Riddy (ed.), *Regionalism in late medieval manuscripts and texts,* 9–26. Cambridge: D. S. Brewer.

Benskin, Michael. 1992. Some new perspectives on the origins of standard written English. In J. A. van Leuvensteijn and J. B. Berns (eds.), *Dialect and standard language in the English, Dutch, German and Norwegian language areas,* 71–105. Amsterdam: Koninklijke Nederlandse Akademie van Wetenschappen.

Benskin, Michael. 1994. Descriptions of dialect and areal distributions. In Laing and Williamson (eds.), 169–186.

Benskin, Michael and Margaret Laing. 1981. Translations and *Mischsprachen* in Middle English manuscripts. In Benskin and Samuels (eds.), 55–106.

Benskin, Michael and M. L. Samuels (eds.). 1981. *So meny people longages and longes: Philological essays in Scots and mediaeval English presented to Angus McIntosh.* Edinburgh: Middle English Dialect Project.

Benveniste, Émile. 1966. *Problèmes de linguistique générale.* Paris: Éditions Gallimard. [First published in *Journal de Psychologie*, July–Sept. 1958.]

Bergs, Alexander. 2005. *Social networks and historical sociolinguistics: Studies in morpho-syntactic variation in the Paston letters (1421–1503).* Berlin: Mouton de Gruyter.

Bergs, Alexander. 2012. Middle English: Sociolinguistics. In Bergs and Brinton (eds.), vol. I, 534–551.

Bergs, Alexander and Laurel J. Brinton (eds.). 2012a. *English historical linguistics: An international handbook* (Handbücher zur Sprachwissenschaft/Handbooks of linguistics and communication science/Manuels de linguistique et des sciences de communication 34.1–2). Berlin: De Gruyter Mouton.

Bergs, Alexander and Laurel J. Brinton. 2012b. Overview. In Bergs and Brinton (eds.), vol. II, 1289–1295.

Bermúdez-Otero, Ricardo. 2007. Diachronic phonology. In Paul de Lacy (ed.), *The Cambridge handbook of phonology,* 497–517. Cambridge: Cambridge University Press.

Berndt, Rolf. 1969. The linguistic situation in England from the Norman Conquest to the loss of Normandy (1066–1204). In Lass (ed.), 369–391.

Berndt, Rolf. 1976. French and English in thirteenth-century England: An investigation into the linguistic situation after the loss of the Duchy of Normandy and other continental dominions. Akademie der Wissenschaften der DDR (ed.), *Aspekte der anglistischen*

Forschungen in der DDR: Martin Lehnert zum 65. Geburtstag, 129–150. Berlin: Akademischer Verlag.

Bex, Tony and Richard J. Watts. 1999. *Standard English: The widening debate*. London and New York: Routledge.

Biber, Douglas. 1988. *Variation across speech and writing*. Cambridge: Cambridge University Press.

Biber, Douglas. 1993. Representativeness in corpus design. *Literary and Linguistic Computing* 8(4), 243–257.

Biber, Douglas. 1995. *Dimensions of register variation*. Cambridge: Cambridge University Press.

Biber, Douglas. 2001. Dimensions of variation among 18th-century registers. In Diller and Görlach (eds.), 89–109.

Biber, Douglas. 2004. Historical patterns for the grammatical marking of stance: A cross-register comparison. *Journal of Historical Pragmatics* 5, 107–135.

Biber, Douglas and Susan Conrad. 2009. *Register, genre, and style*. Cambridge: Cambridge University Press.

Biber, Douglas, Susan Conrad, and Randi Reppen. 1998. *Corpus linguistics: Investigating language structure and use*. Cambridge: Cambridge University Press.

Biber, Douglas and Edward Finegan. 1989. Drift and the evolution of English style: A history of three genres. *Language* 65, 487–517.

Biber, Douglas and Edward Finegan. 1992. The linguistic evolution of five written and speechbased English genres from the 17th to the 20th centuries. In Rissanen, Ihalainen, Nevalainen, and Taavitsainen (eds.), 688–704.

Biber, Douglas, Edward Finegan, and Dwight Atkinson. 1994. ARCHER and its challenges: Compiling and exploring a representative corpus of historical English registers. In Udo Fries, Gunnel Tottie, and Peter Schneider (eds.), *Creating and using English language corpora: Papers from the fourteenth international conference on English language research and computerized corpora, Zürich 1993*, 1–13. Amsterdam: Rodopi.

Biber, Douglas, Stig Johansson, Geoffrey Leech, Susan Conrad, and Edward Finegan. 1999. *Longman grammar of spoken and written English*. London: Longman.

Bliss, Alan. 1983. The history of English "wh." In E. G. Stanley and Douglas Gray (eds.), *Five hundred years of words and sounds: A Festschrift for Eric Dobson*, 11–20. Cambridge: D. S. Brewer.

Blommaert, Jan. 2010. *The sociolinguistics of globalization*. Cambridge: Cambridge University Press.

Bock, J. Kathryn. 1986. Syntactic persistence in language production. *Cognitive Psychology* 18, 355–387.

Bock, J. Kathryn and Zenzi M. Griffin. 2000. The persistence of structural priming: Transient activation or implicit learning? *Journal of Experimental Psychology: General* 129, 177–192.

Bodine, Ann. 1975. Androcentrism in prescriptive grammar: Singular "they," sex-indefinite "he," and "he or she." *Language in Society* 4, 129–146.

Boersma, Paul. 1997. How we learn variation, optionality, and probability. Paper presented at the Institute of Phonetic Sciences 21, Paris.

Bös, Birte. 2012. From 1760 to 1960: Diversification and popularization. In Facchinetti, Brownlees, Bös, and Fries (eds.), 91–143.

Bowerman, Melissa. 1988. The "no negative evidence" problem: How do children avoid constructing an overly general grammar? In John A. Hawkins (ed.), *Explaining language universals*, 73–101. Oxford: Blackwell.

Breivik, Leiv Egil. 1990. *Existential there: A synchronic and diachronic study*. Oslo: Novus Press.

Brems, Lieselotte. 2011. *Layering of size and type noun constructions in English*. Berlin: De Gruyter Mouton.

Bresnan, Joan, Ashwini Deo, and Devyani Sharma. 2007. Typology in variation: A probabilistic approach to *be* and *n't* in the *Survey of English Dialects*. *English Language and Linguistics* 11, 301–346.

Brinton, Laurel J. 1996. *Pragmatic markers in English: Grammaticalization and discourse functions*. Berlin: Mouton de Gruyter.

Brinton, Laurel J. 2006. Pathways in the development of pragmatic markers in English. In van Kemenade and Los (eds.), 307–334.

Brinton, Laurel J. 2008. *The comment clause in English: Syntactic origins and pragmatic development*. Cambridge: Cambridge University Press.

Brinton, Laurel J. 2010. Discourse markers. In Jucker and Taavitsainen (eds.), 285–314.

Brinton, Laurel J. 2012. Historical pragmatics and corpus linguistics: Problems and strategies. In Kytö (ed.), 101–131.

Brinton, Laurel J. 2015. Historical discourse analysis. In Deborah Tannen, Heidi E. Hamilton, and Deborah Schiffrin (eds.), *The handbook of discourse analysis*, 2nd edn., 222–243. Chichester: Wiley-Blackwell.

Brinton, Laurel J. and Leslie K. Arnovick. 2016. *The English language: A linguistic history*. 3rd edn. Toronto: Oxford University Press.

Brinton, Laurel J. and Elizabeth Closs Traugott. 2005. *Lexicalization and language change*. Cambridge: Cambridge University Press.

Britain, David. 2013. Space, diffusion and mobility. In Chambers and Schilling (eds.), 471–500.

Brown, Penelope and Stephen C. Levinson. 1987. *Politeness: Some universals in language use*. Cambridge: Cambridge University Press.

Brown, Robert and Albert Gilman. 1960. The pronouns of power and solidarity. In Thomas A. Sebeok (ed.), *Style in language*, 253–276. Cambridge, MA: MIT Press.

Brownlees, Nicholas (ed.). 2006. *News discourse in Early Modern Britain*. Bern: Lang.

Bühler, Karl. 1990. *Theory of language: The representational function of language*. Trans. Donald Fraser Goodwin 1990. Amsterdam: John Benjamins. [Translation of *Sprachtheorie*. Jena, 1934.]

Burchfield, Robert (ed.). 1994. *The Cambridge history of the English language*, vol. V: *English in Britain and overseas: Origins and development*. Cambridge: Cambridge University Press.

Buschmann-Göbels, Astrid. 2008. Bellum Grammaticale (1712): A battle of books and a battle for the market? In Tieken-Boon van Ostade (ed.), 81–100.

Busse, Ulrich. 2002. *Linguistic variation in the Shakespeare corpus: Morpho-syntactic variability of second person pronouns*. Amsterdam: John Benjamins.

Bybee, Joan. 1995. The semantic development of past tense modals in English. In Joan Bybee and Suzanne Fleischman (eds.), *Modality in grammar and discourse*, 503–517. Amsterdam: John Benjamins.

Bybee, Joan. 2010. *Language, usage and cognition*. Cambridge: Cambridge University Press.

Bybee, Joan and Paul Hopper (eds.). 2001. *Frequency and the emergence of linguistic structure*. Amsterdam: John Benjamins.

Bybee, Joan and Joanne Scheibman. 1999. The effect of usage on degrees of constituency: The reduction of *don't* in English. *Linguistics* 37(4), 575–596.

Bybee, Joan and Dan I. Slobin. 1982. Rules and schemas in the development and use of the English past tense. *Language* 58, 265–289.

Cajka, Karen. 2008. Eighteenth-century teacher-grammarians and the education of "proper" women. In Tieken-Boon van Ostade (ed.), 191–221.

Cameron, Deborah. 1995. *Verbal hygiene*. London: Routledge.

Campbell, Lyle (ed.). 2001a. *Grammaticalization: A critical assessment*. Special issue of *Language Sciences* 23.

Campbell, Lyle. 2001b. What is wrong with grammaticalization? *Language Sciences* 23, 113–161.

Campbell, Lyle. 2013. *Historical linguistics*. 3rd edn. Edinburgh: Edinburgh University Press.

Carpenter, Malinda, Nameera Akhtar, and Michael Tomasello. 1998. Fourteen- to 18-month-old infants differentially imitate intentional and accidental actions. *Infant Behavior and Development* 21, 315–330.

Chambers, J. K. and Peter Trudgill. 1998. *Dialectology*. 2nd edn. Cambridge: Cambridge University Press.

Chambers, J. K. and Nathalie Schilling (eds.). 2013. *Handbook of language variation and change*, 2nd edn. Oxford: Blackwell.

Chomsky, Noam. 1957. *Syntactic structures* (Janua linguarum 4). 's-Gravenhage: Mouton.

Chomsky, Noam. 1965. *Aspects of the theory of syntax*. Cambridge, MA: MIT Press.

Chomsky, Noam. 1993. A minimalist program for linguistic theory. In Kenneth L. Hale and Samuel Jay Keyser (eds.), *The view from building 20: Essays in linguistics in honor of Sylvain Bromberger* (Current Studies in Linguistics vol. 24), 1–37. Cambridge, MA: MIT Press.

Chomsky, Noam. 1995. *The minimalist program*. Cambridge, MA: MIT Press.

Chomsky, Noam and Morris Halle. 1968. *The sound pattern of English*. New York: Harper and Row.

Clackson, James. 2007. *Indo-European linguistics: An introduction*. Cambridge: Cambridge University Press.

Claridge, Claudia. 2009. Historical corpora. In Lüdeling and Kytö (eds.), vol. I, 242–259.

Claridge, Claudia and Leslie Arnovick. 2010. Pragmaticalisation and discoursisation. In Jucker and Taavitsainen (eds.), 165–192.

Claridge, Claudia and Andrew Wilson. 2002. Style evolution in the English sermon. In Fanego et al. (eds.), 25–44.

Clark, Brady. 2004. Early English clause structure change in a stochastic optimality setting. In Anne Curzan and Kimberly Emmons (eds.), *Studies in the history of the English language II: Unfolding conversations*, 343–369. Berlin: Mouton de Gruyter.

Clark, Brady. 2012. Subjects in early English: Syntactic change as gradual constraint reranking. In Jonas, Whitman, and Garrett (eds.), 256–274.

Clark, Herbert H. and Eve V. Clark. 1977. *Psychology and language: An introduction to psycholinguistics*. New York: Harcourt Brace Jovanovich.

Coates, Jennifer. 2004. *Women, men and language*. 3rd edn. Harlow: Longman.

Cole, Peter. 1975. The synchronic and diachronic status of conversational implicature. In Cole and Morgan (eds.), 257–288.

Company Company, Concepción. 2008. The directionality of grammaticalization in Spanish. *Journal of Historical Pragmatics* 9(2), 200–224.

Crawford, William. 2009. The mandative subjunctive. In Rohdenburg and Schlüter, (eds.), 257–276.

Crisma, Paola. 2009. Word-initial *h*- in Middle and Early Modern English. In Minkova (ed.), 130–167.

Crowley, Joseph P. 1986. The study of Old English dialects. *English Studies* 2, 97–112.

Crowley, Terry and Claire Bowern. 2010. *An introduction to historical linguistics.* 4th edn. Oxford: Oxford University Press.

Cruttenden, Alan. 2014. *Gimson's Pronunciation of English.* 8th edn. London: Arnold.

Crystal, David. 2003. *The Cambridge encyclopedia of the English language.* 2nd edn. Cambridge: Cambridge University Press.

Crystal, David. 2004. *The stories of English.* Harmondsworth: Penguin.

Crystal, David. 2010. Introduction to H. W. Fowler, *A dictionary of modern English usage,* vii–xxiv. Oxford: Oxford University Press.

Crystal, David and Ben Crystal. 2002. *Shakespeare's words: A glossary and language companion.* London: Penguin.

Culpeper, Jonathan. 2010. Historical pragmatics. In Louise Cummings (ed.), *The pragmatics encyclopedia,* 188–192. London and New York: Routledge.

Culpeper, Jonathan. 2011. Historical sociopragmatics: An introduction. In Jonathan Culpeper (ed.), *Historical sociopragmatics,* 1–8. Amsterdam: John Benjamins.

Culpeper, Jonathan and Dawn Archer. 2008. Requests and directives in Early Modern English trial proceedings and play texts 1640–1760. In Jucker and Taavitsainen (eds.), 45–84.

Culpeper, Jonathan and Merja Kytö. 2000. Data in historical pragmatics: Spoken interaction (re)cast as writing. *Journal of Historical Pragmatics* 1(2), 175–199.

Culpeper, Jonathan and Merja Kytö. 2010. *Early Modern English dialogues: Spoken interaction as writing.* Cambridge: Cambridge University Press.

Culpeper, Jonathan and Elena Semino. 2000. Constructing witches and spells: Speech acts and activity types in Early Modern England. *Journal of Historical Pragmatics* 1(1), 97–116.

Currency Converter. http://nationalarchives.gov.uk/currency/

Curzan, Anne. 2012. Periodization in the history of English. In Bergs and Brinton (eds.), vol. II, 1233–1256.

Dalton-Puffer, Christiane. 1996. *The French influence on Middle English morphology: A corpus-based study of derivation.* Berlin: Mouton de Gruyter.

Davidse, Kristin, Lieven Vandelanotte and Hubert Cuyckens (eds.). 2010. *Subjectification, intersubjectification and grammaticalization.* Berlin: De Gruyter Mouton.

Davis, Norman. 1965. The Litera Troili and English letters. *Review of English Studies,* new series 16, 233–244.

Defour, Tine. 2008. The speaker's voice: A diachronic study on the use of *well* and *now* as pragmatic markers. *English Text Construction* 1(1), 62–82.

Defour, Tine. 2010. The semantic-pragmatic development of *well* from the viewpoint of (inter) subjectification. In Davidse, Vandelanotte, and Cuyckens (eds.), 155–195.

Degand, Liesbeth and Jacqueline Evers-Vermeul. 2015. Grammaticalization or pragmaticalization of discourse markers? More than a terminological issue. *Journal of Historical Pragmatics* 16(1), 59–85.

Degand, Liesbeth and Anne-Marie Simon-Vandenbergen (eds.). 2011. *Grammaticalization, pragmaticalization and (inter)subjectification: Methodological issues in the study of discourse markers.* Special issue of *Linguistics* 49(2).

Dehé, Nicole and Yordanka Kavalova (eds.). 2007. *Parentheticals*. Amsterdam: John Benjamins.

Denison, David. 1993. *English historical syntax: Verbal constructions*. London: Longman.

Denison, David. 1998. Syntax. In Romaine (ed.), 92–329.

Denison, David. 2007. Syntactic surprises in some English letters: The underlying progress of the language. In Stephan Elspaß, Nils Langer, Joachim Scharloth, and Wim Vandenbussche (eds.), *Germanic language histories "from below" (1700–2000)*, 115–127. Berlin: Mouton de Gruyter.

Deuber, Dagmar. 2005. *Nigerian Pidgin in Lagos: Language contact, variation and change in an African urban setting*. London: Battlebridge.

Diessel, Holger. 2011. Review of Joan Bybee, *Language, usage and cognition* (Cambridge University Press 2010). *Language* 87(4), 830–844.

Diessel, Holger. 2015. Usage-based Construction Grammar. In Ewa Dabrowska and Dagmar Divjak (eds.), *Handbook of cognitive linguistics*, 296–321. Berlin: De Gruyter Mouton.

Diewald, Gabriele. 2006. Discourse particles and modal particles as grammatical elements. In Kerstin Fischer (ed.), *Approaches to discourse particles*, 403–425. Amsterdam: Elsevier.

Diewald, Gabriele. 2010. On some problem areas in grammaticalization studies. In Stathi, Gehweiler, and König (eds.), 17–50.

Diewald, Gabriele. 2011. Grammaticalization and pragmaticalization. In Heiko Narrog and Bernd Heine (eds.), *The Oxford handbook of grammaticalization*, 450–461. Oxford: Oxford University Press.

Diller, Hans-Jürgen and Manfred Görlach (eds.). 2001. *Towards a history of English as a history of genres*. Heidelberg: Winter.

Discenza, Nicole Guenther. 2002. The Old English Bede and the construction of Anglo-Saxon authority. *Anglo-Saxon England* 31, 69–80.

Dobson, E. J. 1968. *English pronunciation 1500–1700*, vol. I: *Survey of the sources*, vol. II: *Phonology*. 2nd edn. Oxford: Oxford University Press.

Dossena, Marina and Gabriella Del Lungo Camiciotti (eds.). 2012. *Letter writing in late modern Europe*. Amsterdam: John Benjamins.

Dossena, Marina and Roger Lass (eds.). 2004. *Methods and data in English historical dialectology*. Bern: Peter Lang.

Durkin, Philip. 2009. *The Oxford guide to etymology*. Oxford: Oxford University Press.

Durkin, Philip. 2014. *Borrowed words: A history of loanwords in English*. Oxford: Oxford University Press.

Eckardt, Regine. 2006. *Meaning change in grammaticalization: An enquiry into semantic reanalysis*. Oxford: Oxford University Press.

Eckert, Penelope. 2000. *Linguistic variation as social practice: The linguistic construction of identity in Belten High*. Oxford: Blackwell.

Ellegård, Alvar. 1953. *The auxiliary "do": The establishment and regulation of its growth in English*. Stockholm: Almqvist and Wiksell.

Ellis, Alexander J. 1889. *Early English pronunciation*. London: Trübner and Co.

Erman, Britt and Ulla-Britt Kotsinas. 1993. Pragmaticalization: The case of *ba'* and *you know*. *Studier i modern språkvetenskap*, 76–93. (Acta Universitatis Stockholmiensis, Stockholm Studies in Modern Philology, new series 10.) Stockholm: Almqvist and Wiksell.

Evans, Mel. 2013. *The language of Queen Elizabeth I: A sociolinguistic perspective on royal style and identity*. Oxford: Wiley Blackwell.

Evans, Nicholas D. and David Wilkins. 2000. In the mind's ear: The semantic extensions of perception. *Language* 76, 546–592.

Facchinetti, Roberta, Nicholas Brownlees, Birte Bös, and Udo Fries. 2012. *News as changing texts*. Cambridge: Cambridge Scholars.

Fanego, Teresa, Belén Méndez-Naya, and Elena Seoane (eds.). 2010. *Sounds, words, texts and change: Selected papers from 11 ICEHL, Santiago de Compostela, 7–11 September 2000*. Amsterdam: John Benjamins.

Fennell, Barbara A. 2001. *A history of English: A sociolinguistic approach*. Oxford: Blackwell.

Fens-de Zeeuw, Lyda. 2011. *Lindley Murray. 1745–1826: Quaker and grammarian*. Utrecht: LOT.

Fernández Cuesta, Julia, Mª Nieves Rodríguez Ledesma, and Inmaculada Senra Silva. 2008. Towards a history of Northern English: Early and late Northumbrian. *Studia Neophilologica* 80, 132–159.

Feynman, Richard. 1985. *Surely you're joking, Mr. Feynman! Adventures of a curious character*. New York: Norton.

Filppula, Markku and Juhani Klemola (eds.). 2009. *Re-evaluating the Celtic hypothesis*. Special issue of *English Language and Linguistics* 13(2).

Filppula, Markku, Juhani Klemola, and Heli Paulasto. 2008. *English and Celtic in contact*. London: Routledge.

Filppula, Markku, Juhani Klemola, and Heli Pitkänen. 2002. *The Celtic roots of English*. Joensuu: University of Joensuu, Faculty of Humanities.

Finegan, Edward. 1999. English grammar and usage. In Romaine (ed.), 536–588.

Finell, Anne. 1989. *Well* now and then. *Journal of Pragmatics* 13, 653–656.

Fischer, Olga. 2007a. The development of English parentheticals: A case of grammaticalization? In Ute Smit, Stefan Dollinger, Julia Hüttner, Gunther Kaltenböck, and Ursula Lutzky (eds.), *Tracing English through time: Explorations in language variation. A Festschrift for Herbert Schendl on the occasion of his 65th birthday*, 103–118. Vienna: Braumüller.

Fischer, Olga. 2007b. *Morphosyntactic change: Functional and formal perspectives*. Oxford: Oxford University Press.

Fischer, Olga. 2008. On analogy as the motivation for grammaticalization. *Studies in Language*, 32(2), 336–382.

Fischer, Olga, Anette Rosenbach, and Dieter Stein (eds.). 2000. *Pathways of change: Grammaticalization in English*. Amsterdam: John Benjamins.

Fischer, Olga, Ans van Kemenade, Willem Koopman, and Willem van der Wurff. 2000. *The syntax of early English*. Cambridge: Cambridge University Press.

Fitzmaurice, Susan M. 1998. The commerce of language in the pursuit of politeness in eighteenth-century England. *English Studies* 79(4), 309–328.

Fitzmaurice, Susan M. 2002. *The familiar letter in Early Modern English: A pragmatic approach*. Amsterdam: John Benjamins.

Fitzmaurice, Susan M. 2004. Subjectivity, intersubjectivity and the historical construction of interlocutor stance: From stance markers to discourse markers. *Discourse Studies* 6, 427–448.

Fitzmaurice, Susan M. 2010. Mr Spectator, identity and social roles in an early eighteenth-century community of practice and the periodical discourse community. In Pahta, Nevala, Nurmi, and Palander-Collin (eds.), 29–53.

Fitzmaurice, Susan M. and Irma Taavitsainen (eds.). 2007. *Methods in historical pragmatics*. Berlin: Mouton de Gruyter.

Gardner, Anne-Christine. 2014. *Derivation in Middle English. Regional and text type variation* (Mémoires de la Société Néophilologique de Helsinki XCII). Helsinki: Société Néophilologique.

Geeraerts, Dirk. 2010. *Theories of lexical semantics*. Oxford: Oxford University Press.

Gehweiler, Elke. 2008. From proper name to primary interjection: The case of *gee! Journal of Historical Pragmatics* 9(1), 71–93.

Gehweiler, Elke. 2010. Interjections and expletives. In Jucker and Taavitsainen (eds.), 315–349.

Geis, Michael L. and Arnold M. Zwicky. 1971. On invited inferences. *Linguistic Inquiry* 2, 561–566.

Gieszinger, Sabine. 2001. *The history of advertising language: The advertisements in "The Times" from 1788 to 1996*. Frankfurt am Main: Peter Lang.

Goldberg, Adele E. 1995. *Constructions: A Construction Grammar approach to argument structure*. Chicago: University of Chicago Press.

Goldberg, Adele E. 2006. *Constructions at work: The nature of generalization in language*. Oxford: Oxford University Press.

González-Alvarez, Dolores. 2003. "If he come" vs. "If he comes?", "If he shall come": Some remarks on the subjunctive in conditional protases in Early and Late Modern English. *Neuphilologische Mitteilungen* 104(3), 303–313.

Goossens, Louis. 2000. Patterns of meaning extension, "parallel chaining," subjectification, and model shifts. In Antonio Barcelona (ed.), *Metaphor and metonymy at a crossroads*, 149–169. Berlin: Mouton de Gruyter.

Gordon, Elizabeth and Tony Deverson. 1998. *New Zealand English and English in New Zealand*. Auckland: New House.

Gordon, Elizabeth, Lyle Campbell, Jennifer Hay, Margaret Maclagan, Andrea Sudbury, and Peter Trudgill. 2004. *New Zealand English: Its origins and evolution*. Cambridge: Cambridge University Press.

Gordon, Elizabeth, Margaret Maclagan, and Jennifer Hay. 2007. The ONZE Corpus. In Joan C. Beal, Karen P. Corrigan, and Herman L. Moisl (eds.), *Creating and digitizing language corpora*, vol. II: *Diachronic databases*, 82–104. Basingstoke: Palgrave Macmillan.

Gordon, Ian A. 1966. *The movement of English prose*. London: Longman.

Görlach, Manfred. 1990. Middle English – a creole? In Manfred Görlach, *Studies in the history of the English language*, 65–78. Heidelberg: Winter.

Görlach, Manfred. 1994. *Einführung ins Frühneuenglische*. Heidelberg: Winter.

Görlach, Manfred. 1999. Regional and social variation. In Lass (ed.), 459–538.

Görlach, Manfred. 2001. A history of text types: A componential analysis. In Diller and Görlach (eds.), 47–88.

Görlach, Manfred. 2004. *Text types and the history of English*. Berlin: de Gruyter.

Gray, Douglas. 2004. Chaucer, Geoffrey (*c.* 1340–1400). *Oxford dictionary of national biography*. Online edition, May 2012. Oxford: Oxford University Press. www.oxforddnb.com/view/article/5191

Grice, H. Paul. 1975. Logic and conversation. In Cole and Morgan (eds.), 41–58.

Grund, Peter. 2007. From tongue to text: The transmission of the Salem witchcraft examination records. *American Speech* 82(2), 119–150.

Grund, Peter. 2012. The nature of knowledge: Evidence and evidentiality in the witness depositions from the Salem witch trials. *American Speech* 87(1), 7–38.

Häcker, Martina. 2004. Intrusive [h] in present-day English accents and <h>-insertion in medieval manuscripts: Hypercorrection or functionally-motivated language use? In Christian Kay, Carole Hough, and Irené Wotherspoon (eds.), *New perspectives on English historical linguistics,* vol. II: *Lexis and transmission,* 109–123. Amsterdam: John Benjamins.

Halliday, M. A. K. and Ruqaia Hasan. 1976. *Cohesion in English.* London: Longman.

Hardie, Andrew. 2012. CQPweb: Combining power, flexibility and usability in a corpus analysis tool. *International Journal of Corpus Linguistics* 17(3), 380–409.

Harris, Alice and Lyle Campbell. 1995. *Historical syntax in cross-linguistic perspective.* Cambridge: Cambridge University Press.

Haugen, Einar. 1972. Dialect, language, nation. In J. B. Pride and Janet Holmes (eds.), *Sociolinguistics,* 97–111. Harmondsworth: Penguin.

Hauser, Marc D., Noam Chomsky, and W. Tecumseh Fitch. 2002. The faculty of language: What is it, who has it, and how did it evolve? *Science* 298, 1569–1579.

Hawkins, John. 2012. The drift of English toward invariable word order from a typological and Germanic perspective. In Nevalainen and Traugott (eds.), 622–632.

Heine, Bernd. 2002. On the role of context in grammaticalization. In Wischer and Diewald (eds.), 83–101.

Heine, Bernd. 2003a. On degrammaticalization. In Barry J. Blake and Kate Burridge (eds.), *Historical linguistics 2001. Selected papers from the 15th International Conference on Historical Linguistics, Melbourne, 13–17 August 2001,* 165–179. Amsterdam: John Benjamins.

Heine, Bernd. 2003b. Grammaticalization. In Joseph and Janda (eds.), 575–601.

Heine, Bernd, Ulrike Claudi, and Friederike Hünnemeyer. 1991. *Grammaticalization: A conceptual framework.* Chicago: University of Chicago Press.

Hernández-Campoy, Juan Manuel, and Juan Camilo Conde-Silvestre (eds.). 2012. *The handbook of historical sociolinguistics.* Chichester: Wiley-Blackwell.

Hickey, Raymond (ed.). 2004. *Legacies of colonial English: Studies in transported dialects.* Cambridge: Cambridge University Press.

Hickey, Raymond (ed.). 2010a. *Eighteenth-century English: Ideology and change.* Cambridge: Cambridge University Press.

Hickey, Raymond (ed.). 2010b. *Handbook of language contact.* Oxford: Wiley-Blackwell.

Hickey, Raymond. 2012a. Assessing the role of contact in the history of English. In Nevalainen and Traugott (eds.), 485–496.

Hickey, Raymond. 2012b. Early English and the Celtic hypothesis. In Nevalainen and Traugott (eds.), 497–507.

Hickey, Raymond. 2012c. Internally and externally motivated language change. In Hernández-Campoy and Conde-Silvestre (eds.), 401–421.

Hickey, Raymond (ed.). 2012d. *Standards of English: Codified varieties around the world.* Cambridge: Cambridge University Press.

Hilpert, Martin. 2013a. *Constructional change in English: Developments in morpho-phonology, word formation, and syntax.* Cambridge: Cambridge University Press.

Hilpert, Martin. 2013b. Corpus-based approaches to constructional change. In Thomas Hoffmann and Graeme Trousdale (eds.), *The Oxford handbook of Construction Grammar,* 458–475. Oxford: University Press.

Hilpert, Martin. 2014. *Construction Grammar and its application to English*. Edinburgh: Edinburgh University Press.

Hiltunen, Risto. 1990. *Chapters on legal English: Aspects past and present of the language of the law*. Helsinki: Suomalainen Tiedeakatemia.

Himmelmann, Nikolaus. 2004. Lexicalization and grammaticization: Opposite or orthogonal? In Walter Bisang, Nikolaus P. Himmelmann, and Björn Wiemer (eds.), *What makes grammaticalization: A look from its fringes and its components*, 21–42. Berlin: Mouton de Gruyter.

Hitchings, Henry. 2011. *The language wars: A history of proper English*. London: John Murray.

Hock, Hans Henrich and Brian D. Joseph. 2009. *Language history, language change, and language relationship: An introduction to historical and comparative linguistics*. 2nd revised edn. Berlin: Mouton de Gruyter.

Hoffmann, Sebastian. 2004. Using the OED quotations database as a corpus: A linguistic appraisal. *ICAME Journal* 28, 17–30.

Hoffmann, Sebastian. 2005. *Grammaticalization and English complex prepositions: A corpus-based study*. London: Routledge.

Hogg, Richard M. 1988. On the impossibility of Old English dialectology. In Dieter Kastovsky and Gero Bauer (eds.), *Luick revisited: Papers read at the Luick Symposium at Schloß Liechtenstein, 15–18.9.1985*, 183–203. Tübingen: Gunter Narr.

Hogg, Richard M. (general ed.). 1992–2001. *The Cambridge history of the English language*. 6 vols. Cambridge: Cambridge University Press.

Hogg, Richard M. and David Denison (eds.). 2006. *A history of the English language*. Cambridge: Cambridge University Press.

Holm, John. 2000. *An introduction to pidgins and creoles*. Cambridge: Cambridge University Press.

Holt, D. Eric (ed.). 2003. *Optimality theory and language change*. Dordrecht: Kluwer.

Hopper, Paul J. 1991. On some principles of grammaticization. In Traugott and Heine (eds.), vol. I, 17–35.

Hopper, Paul J. and Elizabeth Closs Traugott. 2003. *Grammaticalization*. 2nd edn. Cambridge: Cambridge University Press.

Horobin, Simon. 2001. J. R. R. Tolkien as a philologist: A reconsideration of the northernisms in Chaucer's *Reeve's tale*. *English Studies* 82, 97–105.

Huber, Magnus. 2007. The *Old Bailey Proceedings*, 1674–1834: Evaluating and annotating a corpus of 18th- and 19th-century spoken English. *Studies in Variation, Contacts and Change in English* 1. www.helsinki.fi/varieng/series/volumes/01/huber/

Huddleston, Rodney and Geoffrey Pullum. 2002. *The Cambridge grammar of the English language*. Cambridge: Cambridge University Press.

Hughes, Geoffrey. 2000. *A history of English words*. Oxford: Blackwell.

Hundt, Marianne. 1998. It is important that this study *(should) be* based on the analysis of parallel corpora: On the use of the mandative subjunctive in four varieties of English. In Hans Lindquist, Staffan Klintborg, Magnus Levin, and Maria Estling (eds.), *The major varieties of English*, 159–175. Växjö: Växjö University.

Hundt, Marianne. 2008. Text corpora. In Lüdeling and Kytö (eds.), vol. I, 168–187.

Hundt, Marianne. 2009. Colonial lag, colonial innovation, or simply language change? In Rohdenburg and Schlüter, (eds.), 13–37.

Hundt, Marianne (ed.). 2014. *Late Modern English syntax*. Cambridge: Cambridge University Press.

Hundt, Marianne and Geoffrey Leech. 2012. Small is beautiful: On the value of standard reference corpora for observing recent grammatical change. In Nevalainen and Traugott (eds.), 175–188.

Hundt, Marianne and Devyani Sharma (eds.). 2014. *English in the Indian diaspora*. Amsterdam: John Benjamins.

Ihalainen, Ossi. 1994. The dialects of England since 1776. In Burchfield (ed.), 197–274.

Israel, Michael. 1996. The *way* constructions grow. In Adele Goldberg (ed.), *Conceptual structure, discourse and langauge*, 217–230. Stanford, CA: CSLI Publications.

Jackendoff, Ray. 1977. *X-bar syntax: A study of phrase structure*. Cambridge, MA: MIT Press.

Jacobs, Andreas and Andreas H. Jucker. 1995. The historical perspective in pragmatics. In Jucker (ed.), 3–33.

Jäger, Gerhard and Anette Rosenbach. 2008. Priming and unidirectional language change. *Theoretical Linguistics* 34(2), 85–113.

Jensen, Vibeke. 2012. The consonantal element (th) in some Late Middle English Yorkshire texts. In Tyrkkö et al. (eds.). www.helsinki.fi/varieng/series/volumes/10/jensen

Jespersen, Otto. 1962 [1905]. *Growth and structure of the English language*. 9th edn. Oxford: Blackwell.

Jespersen, Otto. 1966 [1917]. *Negation in English and other languages*. 2nd edn. Copenhagen: Munksgaard.

Johannesson, Nils-Lennart. 2000. On the time-depth of variability: Orm and Farmon as h-droppers. In Magnus Ljung (ed.), *Language structure and variation*, 107–119. Stockholm: Almqvist & Wiksell.

Johansson, Stig and Else Helene Norheim. 1988. The subjunctive in British and American English. *ICAME Journal* 12, 27–36.

Jonas, Dianne, John Whitman, and Andrew Garrett (eds.). 2012. *Grammatical change: Origins, nature, outcomes*. Oxford: Oxford University Press.

Joseph, Brian D. and Richard D. Janda (eds.). 2003. *The handbook of historical linguistics*. Oxford: Blackwell.

Jucker, Andreas H. (ed.). 1995. *Historical pragmatics: Pragmatic developments in the history of English*. Amsterdam: John Benjamins.

Jucker, Andreas H. 1997. The discourse marker *well* in the history of English. *English Language and Linguistics* 1(1), 91–110.

Jucker, Andreas H. 1998. Historical pragmatics: An interdisciplinary approach. In Raimund Borgmeier, Herbert Grabes, and Andreas H. Jucker (eds.), *Anglistentag 1997 Giessen proceedings*, 3–7. Trier: Wissenschaftlicher Verlag Trier.

Jucker, Andreas H. 2000. *History of English and English historical linguistics*. Stuttgart: Ernst Klett.

Jucker, Andreas H. 2002. Discourse markers in Early Modern English. In Richard Watts and Peter Trudgill (eds.), *Alternative Histories of English*, 210–230. London: Routledge.

Jucker, Andreas H. 2006a. Historical pragmatics. In Keith Brown et al. (eds.), *Encyclopedia of language and linguistics*, vol. V, 329–331. Amsterdam: Elsevier.

Jucker, Andreas H. 2006b. "Thou art so loothly and so oold also": The use of *ye* and *thou* in Chaucer's *Canterbury Tales*. *Anglistik* 17(2), 57–72.

Jucker, Andreas H. 2008. Historical pragmatics. *Language and Linguistics Compass* 2(5), 894–906.

Jucker, Andreas H. (ed.). 2009. *Early Modern English news discourse: Newspapers, pamphlets and scientific news discourse*. Amsterdam: John Benjamins.

Jucker, Andreas H. 2011. Positive and negative face as descriptive categories in the history of English. *Journal of Historical Pragmatics* 12(1–2), 178–197.

Jucker, Andreas H. 2013. Corpus pragmatics. In Jan-Ola Östmann and Jef Verschueren (eds.), *Handbook of pragmatics (2013)*, 1–17. Amsterdam: John Benjamins.

Jucker, Andreas H. and Irma Taavitsainen (eds.). 2008. *Speech acts in the history of English*. Amsterdam: John Benjamins.

Jucker, Andreas H. and Irma Taavitsainen (eds.). 2010. *Historical pragmatics* (Handbooks of Pragmatics, vol. 8). Berlin: De Gruyter Mouton.

Jucker, Andreas H. and Irma Taavitsainen. 2013. *English historical pragmatics*. Edinburgh: Edinburgh University Press.

Jucker, Andreas H. and Irma Taavitsainen. 2014. Diachronic corpus pragmatics: Intersections and interactions. In Taavitsainen, Jucker, and Tuominen (eds.), 3–26.

Jurafsky, Daniel, Alan Bell, Michelle Gregory, and William D. Raymond. 2001. Probabilistic relations between words: Evidence from reduction in lexical production. In Joan L. Bybee and Paul J. Hopper (eds.), *Frequency and the emergence of linguistic structure*, 229–254. Amsterdam: John Benjamins.

Kaltenböck, Gunther, Bernd Heine, and Tania Kuteva. 2011. On Thetical Grammar. *Studies in Language* 35(4), 848–893.

Kemenade, Ans van. 1992. Structural factors in the history of English modals. In Rissanen, Ihalainen, Nevalainen, and Taavitsainen (eds.), 287–309.

Kemenade, Ans van and Bettelou Los (eds.). 2006. *The handbook of the history of English*. Oxford: Blackwell.

Kibbee, Douglas A. 1991. *For to speke Frenche trewely. The French language in England, 1000–1600: Its status, description and instruction*. Amsterdam: John Benjamins.

Kitson, Peter R. 1993. Geographical variation in Old English prepositions and the location of Ælfric's and other literary dialects. *English Studies* 74, 1–50.

Kitson, Peter R. 1995. The nature of Old English dialect distributions, mainly as exhibited in charter boundaries. In Jacek Fisiak (ed.), *Medieval dialectology*, 43–135. Berlin: Mouton de Gruyter.

Kitson, Peter R. 2004. On margins of error in Old English literary dialects. In Dossena and Lass (eds.), 219–239.

Kohnen, Thomas. 2000a. Corpora and speech acts: The study of performatives. In Christian Mair and Marianne Hundt (eds.), *Corpus linguistics and linguistic theory: Papers from the twentieth International Conference on English Language Research on Computerized Corpora (ICAME) Freiburg im Breisgau 1999*, 177–186. Amsterdam: Rodopi.

Kohnen, Thomas. 2000b. Explicit perfomatives in Old English: A corpus-based study of directives. *Journal of Historical Pragmatics* 1(2), 301–321.

Kohnen, Thomas. 2001. Text types as catalysts for language change: The example of the adverbial first participle construction. In Diller and Görlach (eds.), 111–124.

Kohnen, Thomas. 2004. Methodological problems in corpus-based historical pragmatics. The case of English directives. In Karin Aijmer and Bengt Altenberg (eds.), *Advances in corpus linguistics: Papers from the 23rd International Conference on English Language Research on Computerized Corpora (ICAME 23) Göteborg 22–26 May 2002*, 237–247. Amsterdam: Rodopi.

Kohnen, Thomas. 2007. Text types and the methodology of diachronic speech act analysis. In Fitzmaurice and Taavitsainen (eds.), 139–166.

Kohnen, Thomas. 2008a. Directives in Old English: Beyond politeness? In Jucker and Taavitsainen (eds.), 27–44.

Kohnen, Thomas. 2008b. Tracing directives through text and time: Towards a methodology of a corpus-based diachronic speech act analysis. In Jucker and Taavitsainen (eds.), 295–310.

Kohnen, Thomas. 2012. Prayers in the history of English: A corpus-based study. In Kytö (ed.), 165–180.

Kohnen, Thomas and Christian Mair. 2012. Technologies of communication. In Nevalainen and Traugott (eds.), 261–284.

König, Ekkehard and Johan van der Auwera. 1994. *The Germanic languages*. London: Routledge.

Kopaczyk, Joanna. 2014. How a community of practice creates a text community: Middle Scots legal and administrative discourse. In Joanna Kopaczyk and Andreas H. Jucker (eds.), *Communities of practice in the history of English*, 225–250. Amsterdam: John Benjamins.

Kortmann, Bernd. 1997. *Adverbial subordination: A typology and history of adverbial subordinators based on European languages*. Berlin: Mouton de Gruyter.

Kortmann, Bernd (general ed.). 2008. *Varieties of English*. 4 vols. Berlin: De Gruyter Mouton.

Kostadinova, Viktorija. 2014. Correcting English: Josephine Turck Baker and the American usage guides tradition. Paper presented at the conference "Margin(s) and Norm(s) in English Language(s)," University of Aix-Marseille, April 10–12, 2014.

Kretzschmar, William A., Jr. 2009. *The linguistics of speech*. Cambridge: Cambridge University Press.

Kretzschmar, William A., Jr., and Merja Stenroos. 2012. Evidence from surveys and atlases in the history of the English language. In Nevalainen and Traugott (eds.), 111–122.

Kristensson, Gillis. 1969–2001. *A survey of Middle English dialects 1290–1350*. Lund: Lund University Press.

Kroch, Anthony S. 1989. Reflexes of grammar in patterns of language change. *Language Variation and Change* 1, 199–244.

Krug, Manfred G. 2000. *Emerging English modals: A corpus-based study of grammaticalization*. Berlin: Mouton de Gruyter.

Krug, Manfred G. and Julia Schlüter (eds.). 2013. *Research methods in language variation and change*. Cambridge: Cambridge University Press.

Kytö, Merja. 2010. Data in historical pragmatics. In Jucker and Taavitsainen (eds.), 33–67.

Kytö, Merja. 2012a. Corpus linguistics. In Bergs and Brinton (eds.), vol. II, 1509–1531.

Kytö, Merja (ed.). 2012b. *English corpus linguistics: Crossing paths*. Amsterdam: Rodopi.

Kytö, Merja and Päivi Pahta (eds.). 2016. *The Cambridge handbook of English historical linguistics*. Cambridge: Cambridge University Press.

Labov, William. 1973. The boundaries of words and their meanings. In Charles-James N. Bailey and Roger W. Shuy (eds.), *New ways of analyzing variation in English*, 340–373. Washington, DC: Georgetown University Press.

Labov, William. 1994. *Principles of linguistic change, vol. I: Internal factors*. Oxford: Blackwell.

Labov, William. 2001. *Principles of linguistic change, vol. II: Social factors*. Oxford: Blackwell.

Laing, Margaret. 1999. Confusion *wrs* confounded: Litteral substitution sets in Early Middle English writing systems. *Neuphilologische Mitteilungen* 100, 251–270.

Laing, Margaret and Roger Lass. 2009. Shape-shifting, sound-change and the genesis of prodigal writing systems. *English Language and Linguistics* 13, 1–31.

Laing, Margaret and Keith Williamson (eds.). 1994. *Speaking in our tongues: Proceedings of a colloquium on medieval dialectology and related disciplines.* Cambridge: Boydell & Brewer.

Lakoff, George and Mark Johnson. 1980. *Metaphors we live by.* Chicago: University of Chicago Press.

Langacker, Ronald W. 1977. Syntactic reanalysis. In Charles N. Li (ed.), *Mechanisms of syntactic change,* 57–139. Austin: University of Texas Press.

Lass, Roger (ed.). 1969. *Approaches to English historical linguistics: An anthology.* New York: Holt, Rinehart, and Winston. [First published 1957.]

Lass, Roger. 1987. *The shape of English: Structure and history.* London: Dent.

Lass, Roger. 1997. *Historical linguistics and language change.* Cambridge: Cambridge University Press.

Lass, Roger (ed.). 1999. *The Cambridge history of the English language,* vol. III: *1476–1776.* Cambridge: Cambridge University Press.

Lass, Roger. 2006. Phonology and morphology. In Hogg and Denison (eds.), 43–108.

Leech, Geoffrey, Marianne Hundt, Christian Mair, and Nicholas Smith. 2009. *Change in contemporary English: A grammatical study.* Cambridge: Cambridge University Press.

Lefebvre, Claire, Bernard Comrie, and Henri Cohen (eds.). 2013. *New perspectives on the origins of language.* Amsterdam: John Benjamins.

Lehmann, Christian. 1985. Grammaticalization: Synchronic variation and diachronic change. *Lingua e Stile* 20, 303–318.

Lehmann, Christian. 1995. *Thoughts on grammaticalization.* Munich: LINCOM EUROPA. [2nd revised edn. of *Thoughts on grammaticalization: A programmatic sketch,* 1982.]

Lehmann, Christian. 2002. New reflections on grammaticalization and lexicalization. In Wischer and Diewald (eds.), 1–18.

Lehmberg, Tim and Kai Wörner. 2008. Annotation standards. In Lüdeling and Kytö (eds.), vol. I, 484–501.

Leimgruber, Jakob. 2013. *Singapore English: Structure, variation and usage.* Cambridge: Cambridge University Press.

Lenker, Ursula and Anneli Meurman-Solin (eds.). 2007. *Connectives in the history of English.* Amsterdam: John Benjamins.

Leonard, S. A. 1929. *The doctrine of correctness in English usage, 1700–1800.* Madison: University of Wisconsin Press.

Levinson, Stephen C. 1995. Three levels of meaning. In F. R. Palmer (ed.), *Grammar and meaning: Essays in honor of John Lyons,* 90–115. Cambridge: Cambridge University Press.

Levinson, Stephen C. 2000. *Presumptive meanings: The theory of generalized conversational implicature.* Cambridge, MA: MIT Press.

Lieberman, Erez, Jean-Baptiste Michel, Joe Jackson, Tina Tang, and Martin Nowak. 2007. Quantifying the evolutionary dynamics of language. *Nature* 449, 713–716.

Lightfoot, David. 1979. *Principles of diachronic syntax.* Cambridge: Cambridge University Press.

Lim, Lisa (ed.). 2004. *Singapore English: A grammatical description.* Amsterdam: John Benjamins.

Lindquist, Hans. 2009. *Corpus linguistics and the description of English.* Edinburgh: Edinburgh University Press.

López-Couso, María José. 2010. Subjectification and intersubjectification. In Jucker and Taavitsainen (eds.), 127–163.

López-Couso, María José and Belén Méndez-Naya. 2014. From clause to pragmatic marker: A study of the development of *like*-parentheticals in American English. *Journal of Historical Pragmatics* 15, 36–61.

Los, Bettelou and Erwin Komen. 2012. Clefts as resolution strategies after the loss of a multifunctional first position. In Nevalainen and Traugott (eds.), 884–898.

Lowe, Kathryn A. 2001. On the plausibility of Old English dialectology: The ninth century Kentish charter material. *Folia Linguistica Historica* 22, 67–102.

Lüdeling, Anke and Merja Kytö (eds.). 2008. *Corpus linguistics: An international handbook.* 2 vols. Berlin: Mouton de Gryuter.

Lukač, Morana (in progress). The public discourse of standard English usage. PhD dissertation, University of Leiden.

Luscombe, Anya. 2012. Sending the right message: Forty years of BBC radio news. PhD dissertation, University of Utrecht.

Lutz, Angelika. 2012. Language contact in the Scandinavian period. In Nevalainen and Traugott (eds.), 508–517.

Lutzky, Ursula and Jane Demmen. 2013. *Pray* in Early Modern English drama. *Journal of Historical Pragmatics* 14(2), 263–284.

Lynch, Jack. 2009. *The lexicographer's dilemma: The evolution of "proper" English, from Shakespeare to South Park*. New York: Walker & Company.

Lynch, Jack and Anne McDermott (eds.). 2005. *Anniversary essays on Johnson's dictionary*. Cambridge: Cambridge University Press.

Lyons, John. 1977. *Semantics*. 2 vols. Cambridge: Cambridge University Press.

Lyons, John. 1982. Deixis and subjectivity: *Loquor, ergo sum?* In Robert J. Jarvella and Wolfgang Klein (eds.), *Speech, place, and action: Studies in deixis and related topics*, 101–124. New York: Wiley.

Lyons, John. 1994. Subjecthood and subjectivity. In Marina Yaguello (ed.), *Subjecthood and subjectivity: The status of the subject in linguistic theory*, 9–17. Paris: Ophrys; London: Institut Français du Royaume-Uni.

Machan, Tim William (ed.). 2016a. *Imagining medieval English: Language structures and theories, 500–1500*. Cambridge: Cambridge University Press.

Machan, Tim William. 2016b. Snakes, ladders, and standard language. In Machan (ed.), 54–78.

Machan, Tim William and Charles T. Scott. 1992. *English in its social contexts: Essays in historical sociolinguistics*. Oxford: Oxford University Press.

Mair, Christian. 2006. *Twentieth-century English*. Cambridge: Cambridge University Press.

Markman, Arthur B. and Dedre Gentner. 1993. Structural alignment during similarity comparisons. *Cognitive Psychology* 25(4), 431–467.

Matras, Yaron. 2009. *Language contact*. Cambridge: Cambridge University Press.

Matthews, Robert J. 1979. Are the grammatical sentences of a language a recursive set? *Synthese* 40(2), 209–224.

Mazo, Jeffrey. 2011. The know-nothings. *Survival: Global Politics and Strategy* 53(6), 238–248.

Mazzon, Gabriella. 2010. Terms of address. In Jucker and Taavitsainen (eds.), 351–356.

McEnery, Tony and Andrew Hardie. 2012. *Corpus linguistics: Method, theory and practice*. Cambridge: Cambridge University Press.

McEnery, Tony and Andrew Wilson. 2001. *Corpus linguistics: An introduction*. 2nd edn. Edinburgh: Edinburgh University Press.

McEnery, Tony, Richard Xiao, and Yukio Tono. 2006. *Corpus-based language studies: An advanced resource book*. London and New York: Routledge.

McIntosh, Angus. 1956. The analysis of written Middle English. *Transactions of the Philological Society* 55(1), 26–55.

McIntosh, Angus. 1961. "Graphology" and meaning. *Archivum Linguisticum* 13, 107–120.

McIntosh, Carey. 1998. *The evolution of English, 1700–1800: Style, politeness, and print culture*. Cambridge: Cambridge University Press.

McMahon, April. 1994. *Understanding language change*. Cambridge: Cambridge University Press.

McMahon, April. 2006. Change for the better? Optimality Theory versus history. In van Kemenade and Los (eds.), 3–23.

McMorris, Jenny. 2001. *The warden of English: The life of H. W. Fowler*. Oxford: Oxford University Press.

McNamara, Timothy P. 2005. *Semantic priming: Perspectives from memory and word recognition*. New York: Psychology Press.

Meierkord, Christine. 2012. *Interactions across Englishes: Linguistic choices in local and international contact situations*. Cambridge: Cambridge University Press.

Meillet, Antoine. 1912. L'évolution des formes grammaticales. *Scientia* (Rivista di Scienza) 12(26), 6. [Reprinted in *Linguistique historique et linguistique générale*, 130–148. Paris: Champion, 1958.]

Meillet, Antoine. 1925. *La méthode comparative en linguistique historique*. Paris: Champion.

Mesthrie, Rajend and Rakesh Bhatt. 2008. *World Englishes*. Cambridge: Cambridge University Press.

Meurman-Solin, Anneli. 2012. Historical dialectology: Space as a variable in the reconstruction of regional dialects. In Hernández-Campoy and Conde-Silvestre (eds.), 465–479.

Meyer, Charles. 2008. Pre-electronic corpora. In Lüdeling and Kytö (eds.), vol. I, 1–14.

Meyer, David E. and Roger W. Schvaneveldt. 1971. Facilitation in recognizing pairs of words: Evidence of a dependence between retrieval operations. *Journal of Experimental Psychology* 90, 227–234.

Millar, Robert McColl. 2012. *English historical sociolinguistics*. Edinburgh: Edinburgh University Press.

Millar, Robert McColl (ed.). 2015. *Trask's Historical linguistics*. 3rd edn. London: Routledge.

Miller, D. Gary. 2012. *External influences on English: From its beginnings to the Renaissance*. Oxford: Oxford University Press.

Milroy, James. 1983. On the sociolinguistic history of /h/-dropping in English. In Michael Davenport, Erik Hansen and Hans Frede Nielsen (eds.), *Current topics in English historical linguistics*, 37–53. Odense: Odense University Press.

Milroy, James. 1992a. *Linguistic variation and change: On the historical sociolinguistics of English*. Oxford: Blackwell.

Milroy, James. 1992b. Middle English dialectology. In Norman Blake (ed.), *The Cambridge history of the English language*, vol. II: *1066–1476*, 156–206. Cambridge: Cambridge University Press.

Milroy, James and Lesley Milroy. 2012. *Authority in language: Investigating language prescription and standardization*. 4th edn. London: Routledge.

Milroy, Lesley. 1987. *Language and social networks*. 2nd edn. Oxford: Blackwell.

Minkova, Donka (ed.). 2009. *Phonological weakness in English: From Old to Present-Day English*. Basingstoke: Palgrave Macmillan.

Minkova, Donka. 2014. *A historical phonology of English*. Edinburgh: Edinburgh University Press.

Minugh, David. 1985. As old as the 'ills: Variable loss of *h* in Swedish dialects. *NOWELE* 6, 23–43.

Mitchell, Bruce. 1985. *Old English syntax*. 2 vols. Oxford: Clarendon.

Mittins, W. H., Mary Salu, Mary Edminson, and Sheila Coyne. 1970. *Attitudes to English usage*. London: Oxford University Press.

Moore, Colette. 2006. The use of *videlicet* in Early Modern slander depositions: A case of genre-specific grammaticalization. *Journal of Historical Pragmatics* 7(2), 245–263.

Moore, Samuel, Sanford B. Meech, and Harold Whitehall. 1935. *Middle English dialect characteristics and dialect boundaries: Essays and studies in English and comparative literature, 1–60*. Ann Arbor: University of Michigan Press.

Mufwene, Salikoko S. 2001. *The ecology of language evolution*. Cambridge: Cambridge University Press.

Mugglestone, Lynda. 2003. *Talking proper: The rise of accent as a social symbol*. Oxford: Oxford University Press.

Mugglestone, Lynda (ed.). 2012. *The Oxford history of English*. Updated edn. Oxford: Oxford University Press.

Mukherjee, Joybrato. 2009. *Anglistische Korpuslinguistik: Eine Einführung*. Berlin: Erich Schmidt.

Murray, James A. H. 1879. English language. *Encyclopedia Britannica*, vol. VIII. 9th edn. Edinburgh: Adam and Charles Black.

National Archives. www.nationalarchives.gov.uk

Navest, Karlijn. 2011. *John Ash and the rise of the children's grammar*. Utrecht: LOT.

Nerlich, Brigitte. 2010. Metaphor and metonymy. In Jucker and Taavitsainen (eds.), 193–215.

Nerlich, Brigitte and David Clarke. 2001. Serial metonymy: A study of reference-based polysemisation. *Journal of Historical Pragmatics* 2(2), 245–272.

Nevala, Minna. 2010. Politeness. In Jucker and Taavitsainen (eds.), 419–450.

Nevalainen, Terttu and Helena Raumolin-Brunberg. 2003. *Historical sociolinguistics: Language change in Tudor and Stuart England*. Harlow: Pearson.

Nevalainen, Terttu and Helena Raumolin-Brunberg. 2014. Historical sociolinguistics: Origins, motivations and paradigms. In Hernández-Campoy and Conde-Silvestre (eds.), 22–40.

Nevalainen, Terttu and Ingrid Tieken-Boon van Ostade. 2006. Standardisation. In Hogg and Denison (eds.), 271311.

Nevalainen, Terttu, and Elizabeth Closs Traugott (eds.). 2012. *The Oxford handbook of the history of English*. Oxford: Oxford University Press.

Noël, Dirk, Bertus van Rooy, and Johan van der Auwera. 2014. Diachronic approaches to modality in World Englishes: Introduction to the special issue. *Journal of English Linguistics* 42(1), 3–6.

Norde, Muriel. 2009. *Degrammaticalization*. Oxford: Oxford University Press.

Norde, Muriel. 2010. Degrammaticalization: Three common controversies. In Stathi, Gehweiler, and König (eds.), 123–150.

Nordlinger, Rachel and Elizabeth Closs Traugott. 1997. Scope and the development of epistemic modality: Evidence from *ought to*. *English Language and Linguistics* 1, 295–317.

Nurmi, Arja, Minna Nevala, and Minna Palander-Collin (eds.). 2009. *The language of daily life in England (1400–1800)*. Amsterdam: John Benjamins.

Oakden, James P. 1930. *Alliterative poetry in Middle English: The dialectal and metrical survey*. Manchester: Manchester University Press.

Oakes, Michael P. 1998. *Statistics for corpus linguistics*. Edinburgh: Edinburgh University Press.

ODNB: The Oxford dictionary of national biography. Online edition, www.oxforddnb.com

Orton, Harold et al. 1962–1971. *Survey of English Dialects* (SED). Introduction and 4 vols. in 3 parts. Leeds: Arnold.

Övergaard, Gerd. 1995. *The mandative subjunctive in American and British English in the 20th century*. Uppsala: Almquist and Wiksell.

Pahta, Päivi, Minna Nevala, Arja Nurmi, and Minna Palander-Collin (eds.). 2010. *Social roles and language practices in Late Modern English*. Amsterdam: John Benjamins.

Pakkala-Weckström, Mari. 2008. *No botmeles bihestes*: Various ways of making binding promises in Middle English. In Jucker and Taavitsainen (eds.), 133–162.

Palmer, Steven. 1975. The effects of contextual scenes on the identification of objects. *Memory and Cognition* 3, 519–526.

Patten, Amanda L. 2012. *The English it-cleft: A constructional account and a diachronic investigation*. Berlin: De Gruyter Mouton.

Paul, Hermann. 1891 [1880]. *Principles of the history of language*. Translated from the 2nd edn. of the original by H. A. Strong. London: Longmans Green.

Peikola, Matti, Janne Skaffari, and Sanna-Kaisa Tanskanen (eds.). 2009. *Instructional writing in English*. Amsterdam: John Benjamins.

Penzl, Herbert. 1969. The evidence for phonemic changes. In Lass (ed.), 10–24.

Percy, Carol. 2008. Mid-century grammars and their reception in the *Monthly Review* and the *Critical Review*. In Tieken-Boon van Ostade (ed.), 125–142.

Percy, Carol. 2009. Periodical reviews and the rise of prescriptivism: The *Monthly* (1749–1844) and *Critical Review* (1756–1817) in the eighteenth century. In Ingrid Tieken-Boon van Ostade and Wim van der Wurff (eds.), *Current issues in Late Modern English*, 117–150. Bern: Peter Lang.

Peters, Pam. 2006. English usage: Prescription and description. In Bas Aarts and April McMahon (eds.), *The handbook of English linguistics*, 759–780. Oxford: Blackwell.

Pfenninger, Simone E., Olga Timofeeva, Anne-Christine Gardner, Alpo Honkapohja, Marianne Hundt, and Daniel Schreier (eds.). 2014. *Contact, variation, and change in the history of English*. Amsterdam: John Benjamins.

Picallo, M. Carme (ed.). 2014. *Linguistic variation in the Minimalist framework*. Oxford: Oxford University Press.

Pintzuk, Susan. 1999. *Phrase structures in competition: Variation and change in Old English word order* (Outstanding Dissertations in Linguistics). New York: Garland. [Repr. Routledge 2014.]

Pintzuk, Susan, George Tsoulas, and Anthony Warner (eds). 2001. *Diachronic syntax. Models and mechanisms*. Oxford: Oxford University Press.

Plag, Ingo, Christiane Dalton-Puffer, and Harald Baayen. 1999. Morphological productivity across speech and writing. *English Language and Linguistics* 3(2), 209–228.

Plank, Frans. 1984. The modals story retold. *Studies in Language* 8, 305–364.

Platt, John, Heidi Weber, and Mian Lian Ho. 1984. *The New Englishes*. London: Routledge and Kegan Paul.

Pollock, Jean-Yves. 1989. Verb movement, universal grammar, and the structure of IP. *Linguistic Inquiry* 20, 265–424.

Poussa, Patricia. 1982. The evolution of early standard English: The creolization hypothesis. *Studia Anglica Posnaniensia* 14, 69–85.

Prentice, Sheryl and Andrew Hardie. 2009. Empowerment and disempowerment in the Glencairn Uprising: A corpus-based critical analysis of Early Modern English news discourse. *Journal of Historical Pragmatics* 10(1), 23–55.

Prince, Alan and Paul Smolensky. 1993. Optimality Theory: Constraint interaction in generative grammar. MS, Rutgers University Centre for Cognitive Science.

Quirk, Randolph, Sidney Greenbaum, Geoffrey Leech, and Jan Svartvik. 1985. *A comprehensive grammar of the English language.* London: Longman.

Ramat, Paolo. 1982. Ein Beispiel von "reanalysis," typologisch betrachtet. *Folia Linguistica* 16, 365–383.

Ramat, Paolo. 1992. Thoughts on degrammaticalization. *Linguistics* 30, 549–560.

Raumolin-Brunberg, Helena. 2009. Lifespan changes in the language of three early modern gentlemen. In Anja Nurmi, Minna Nevala and Minna Palander-Collin, (eds.), *The language of daily life in England (1400–1800),* 165–196. Amsterdam: John Benjamins.

Raumolin-Brunberg, Helena. 2012. Early Modern English: Sociolinguistics. In Bergs and Brinton (eds.), vol. I, 714–730.

Ray, John. 1674. *A collection of English words not generally used, with their significations and original.* Ed. Walter Skeat (English Dialect Society 6, series B). London: Trübner.

Reddick, Allen. 1996. *The making of Johnson's Dictionary 1746–1773.* Rev. edn. Cambridge: Cambridge University Press.

Richardson, Malcolm. 1984. The dictamen and its influence on fifteenth-century English prose. *Rhetorica* 2, 207–226.

Rissanen, Matti. 1999. Syntax. In Lass (ed.), 187–331.

Rissanen, Matti. 2009. Corpus linguistics and historical linguistics. In Lüdeling and Kytö (eds.), vol. I, 53–68.

Rissanen, Matti, Ossi Ihalainen, Terttu Nevalainen, and Irma Taavitsainen (eds.). 1992. *History of Englishes: New methods and interpretations in historical linguistics.* Berlin: Mouton de Gruyter.

Roberts, Ian G. 1985. Agreement parameters and the development of English modal auxiliaries. *Natural Language and Linguistic Theory* 3, 21–58.

Roberts, Ian G. 2007. *Diachronic syntax.* Oxford: Oxford University Press.

Roberts, Ian and Anna Roussou. 2003. *Syntactic change: A minimalist approach to grammaticalization.* Cambridge: Cambridge University Press.

Robinson, Orrin W. 1992. *Old English and its closest relatives: A survey of the earliest Germanic languages.* Stanford, CA: Stanford University Press.

Rodríguez-Gil, María. 2008. Ann Fisher's *A new grammar,* or was it Daniel Fisher's work? In Tieken-Boon van Ostade (ed.), 149–176.

Rohdenburg, Günter. 2013. Using the OED quotations database as a diachronic corpus. In Krug and Schlüter (eds.), 136–157.

Rohdenburg, Günter and Julia Schlüter, (eds.). 2009. *One language, two grammars? Differences between British and American English.* Cambridge: Cambridge University Press.

Romaine, Suzanne. 1982. *Socio-historical linguistics: Its status and methodology.* Cambridge: Cambridge University Press.

Romaine, Suzanne (ed.). 1999. *The Cambridge history of the English language,* vol. IV: *1776–1997.* Cambridge: Cambridge University Press.

Rosch, Eleanor. 1977. Human categorization. In Neil Warren (ed.), *Studies in cross-cultural psychology,* vol. I, 1–49. New York: Academic Press,.

Ross, John Robert. 1967. Constraints on variables in syntax. PhD dissertation, MIT.

Rudanko, Juhani. 2012. Exploring aspects of the Great Complement Shift with evidence from the TIME Corpus and COCA. In Nevalainen and Traugott (eds.), 222–232.

Säily, Tanja. 2014. *Sociolinguistic variation in English derivational productivity: Studies and methods in diachronic corpus linguistics* (Mémoires de la Société Néophilologique de Helsinki XCIV). Helsinki: Société Néophilologique.

Sairio, Anni. 2010. "If you think me obstinate I can't help it": Exploring the epistolary styles and social roles of Elizabeth Montagu and Sarah Scott. In Pahta, Nevala, Nurmi, and Palander-Collin (eds.), 87–109.

Samuels, Michael L. 1981. Spelling and dialect in the late and post-Middle English periods. In Benskin and Samuels (eds.), 43–54.

Sapir, Edward. 1921. *Language. An introduction to the study of speech.* New York: Harcourt, Brace, and Company.

Schendl, Herbert and Laura Wright (eds.). 2011. *Code-switching in early English.* Berlin: De Gruyter Mouton.

Schiffrin, Deborah. 1987. *Discourse markers.* Cambridge: Cambridge University Press.

Schlüter, Julia. 2009. The conditional subjunctive. In Rohdenburg and Schlüter (eds.), 277–305.

Schlüter, Julia. 2013. Using historical literature databases as corpora. In Krug and Schlüter (eds.), 119–135.

Schneider, Edgar W. 1990. The cline of creoleness in English-oriented creoles and semi-creoles of the Caribbean. *English World-Wide* 11, 79–113.

Schneider, Edgar W. 2003. The dynamics of New Englishes: From identity construction to dialect birth. *Language* 79(2), 233–281.

Schneider, Edgar W. 2007. *Postcolonial English: Varieties around the world.* Cambridge: Cambridge University Press.

Schneider, Edgar W. 2011. *English around the world: An introduction.* Cambridge: Cambridge University Press.

Schneider, Edgar W. 2013. Investigating variation and change in written documents: New prespectives. In Chambers and Schilling (eds.), 57–82.

Schneider, Edgar W. 2014. New reflections on the evolutionary dynamics of world Englishes. *World Englishes* 33, 9–32.

Schreier, Daniel and Marianne Hundt (eds.). 2013. *English as a contact language.* Cambridge: Cambridge University Press

Schreier, Daniel, Peter Trudgill, Edgar W. Schneider, and Jeffrey P. Williams (eds.). 2010. *The lesser-known varieties of English: An introduction.* Cambridge: Cambridge University Press.

Schwenter, Scott A. and Elizabeth Closs Traugott. 1995. The semantic and pragmatic development of substitutive complex prepositions in English. In Jucker (ed.), 243–273.

Searle, John. 1969. *Speech acts: An essay in the philosophy of language.* Cambridge: Cambridge University Press.

Seoane, Elena. 2006. Information structure and word order change: The passive as an information-rearranging strategy in the history of English. In van Kemenade and Los (eds.), 360–391.

Seppänen, Aimo, Rhonwen Bowen, and Joe Trotta. 1994. On the so-called complex prepositions. *Studia Anglica Posnaniensia* 29. 3–29.

Siemund, Rainer and Claudia Claridge. 1997. The Lampeter Corpus of Early Modern English Tracts. *ICAME Journal* 21, 61–70.

Sinclair, John McH. 1996. *EAGLES. Preliminary recommendations on corpus typology.* Available at www.ilc.cnr.it/EAGLES/corpustyp/corpustyp.html

Sloane, Thomas (ed.). 2001. *Encyclopedia of rhetoric.* Oxford: Oxford University Press.

Smith, Adam. 2013. Complex prepositions and variation within the PNP construction. In Hilde Hasselgård, Jarle Ebeling, and Signe Oksefjell Ebeling (eds.), *Corpus perspectives: On patterns of lexis,* 153–174. Amsterdam: John Benjamins.

Smith, Jeremy J. 1996. *Historical study of English: Function, form, and change.* London: Routledge.

Smith, Jeremy J. 2005. *Essentials of early English: An introduction to Old, Middle and Early Modern English.* 2nd edn. London: Routledge.

Smith, Jeremy J. 2007. *Sound change and the history of English.* Oxford: Oxford University Press.

Smits, Matthijs. 2017. "Garnering" respect? The emergence of authority in the American usage tradition. In Tieken-Boon van Ostade and Percy (eds.), 231–237.

Smitterberg, Erik. 2005. *The progressive in 19th-century English: A process of integration.* Amsterdam: Rodopi.

Smitterberg, Erik. 2009. Multal adverbs in nineteenth-century English. *Studia Neophilologica* 81(2), 121–144.

Smitterberg, Erik. 2012. Late Modern English: Sociolinguistics. In Bergs and Brinton (eds.), vol. I, 952–965.

Starks, Donna, Andy Gibson, and Allan Bell. 2015. Pasifika Englishes in New Zealand. In Williams et al. (eds.), 288–304.

Stathi, Katerina, Elke Gehweiler, and Ekkehard König (eds.). 2010. *Grammaticalization: Current views and issues.* Amsterdam: John Benjamins.

Stein, Dieter. 1985. Discourse markers in Early Modern English. In Roger Eaton, Olga Fischer, Willem Koopman, and Frederike van der Leek (eds.), *Papers from the 4th International Conference on English Historical Linguistics,* 283–302. Amsterdam: John Benjamins.

Stein, Dieter and Susan Wright (eds.). 1995. *Subjectivity and subjectivisation: Linguistic Perspectives.* Cambridge: Cambridge University Press.

Stenroos, Merja. 2013. Identity and intelligibility in Late Middle English scribal transmission: Local dialect as an active choice in fifteenth-century texts. In Esther-Miriam Wagner, Ben Outhwaite, and Bettina Beinhoff (eds.), *Scribes as agents of language change,* 159–182. Berlin: De Gruyter Mouton.

Stenroos, Merja and Kjetil V. Thengs. 2012. Two Staffordshires: Real and linguistic space in the study of late Middle English dialects. In Tyrkkö et al. (eds.). Helsinki: VARIENG. www .helsinki.fi/varieng/journal/volumes/10/stenroos_thengs/

Studer, Patrick. 2008. *Historical corpus stylistics: Media, technology and change.* London: Continuum.

Sundby, Bertil, Anne Kari Bjørge, and Kari E. Haugland. 1991. *A dictionary of English normative grammar 1700–1800.* Amsterdam: John Benjamins.

Suomela, Jukka. 2007. types1: Type and hapax accumulation curves. *Zenodo*. doi: 10.5281/zenodo.9860

Suomela, Jukka. 2014. types2: Type and hapax accumulation curves. *Zenodo*. doi: 10.5281/zenodo.9868

Swan, Toril and Olaf Jansen Westvik (eds.). 1997. *Modality in Germanic languages: Historical and comparative perspective*. Berlin: Mouton de Gruyter.

Sweet, Henry. 1874. *A history of English sounds from the earliest period*. Oxford: Oxford University Press.

Sweetser, Eve. 1990. *From etymology to pragmatics: Metaphorical and cultural aspects of semantic structure*. Cambridge: Cambridge University Press.

Taavitsainen, Irma. 2012. Historical pragmatics. In Bergs and Brinton (eds.), vol. II, 1457–1474.

Taavitsainen, Irma and Susan Fitzmaurice. 2007. Historical pragmatics: What it is and how to do it. In Fitzmaurice and Taavitsainen (eds.), 11–36.

Taavitsainen, Irma and Andreas H. Jucker (eds.). 2002. *Diachronic perspectives on address terms*. Amsterdam: John Benjamins.

Taavitsainen, Irma and Andreas H. Jucker. 2007. Speech act verbs and speech acts in the history of English. In Fitzmaurice and Taavitsainen (eds.), 107–138.

Taavitsainen, Irma and Andreas H. Jucker. 2010. Trends and developments in historical pragmatics. In Jucker and Taavitsainen (eds.), 3–30.

Taavitsainen, Irma and Andreas H. Jucker. 2015. Twenty years of historical pragmatics: Origins, developments and changing thought styles. *Journal of Historical Pragmatics* 16(1), 1–24.

Taavitsainen, Irma, Andreas H. Jucker, and Jukka Tuominen (eds.). 2014. *Diachronic corpus pragmatics*. Amsterdam: John Benjamins.

Taavitsainen, Irma and Päivi Pahta (eds.). 2010. *Early Modern English medical texts: Corpus description and studies*. Amsterdam: John Benjamins.

Taavitsainen, Irma, Päivi Pahta, and Martti Mäkinen (comps.). 2005. *Middle English medical texts*. Amsterdam: John Benjamins.

Taggart, Caroline. 2010. *Her ladyship's guide to the Queen's English*. London: National Trust.

Tagliamonte, Sali A. 2007. Quantitative analysis. In Robert Bayley and Ceil Lucas (eds.), *Sociolinguistic variation: Theories, methods and applications*, 190–214. Cambridge: Cambridge University Press.

Taylor, John R. 1989. *Linguistic categorization*. Oxford: Oxford University Press.

Thomason, Sarah G. 2001. *Language contact: An introduction*. Washington, DC: Georgetown University Press.

Thomason, Sarah Grey and Terrence Kaufman. 1988. *Language contact, creolization and genetic linguistics*. Berkeley: University of California Press.

Thompson, Sarah and Anthony Mulac. 1991. A quantitative perspective on the grammaticalization of epistemic parentheticals in English. In Traugott and Heine (eds.), vol. II, 313–329.

Tieken-Boon van Ostade, Ingrid. 1990. Drydens versies van *The Tempest* en Troilus and Cressida: De bewerker als purist. In *Traditie & Progressie. Handelingen van het 40ste Nederlands Filologencongres*, 161–169. 's Gravenhage: SDU Uitgeverij.

Tieken-Boon van Ostade, Ingrid. 1994. Standard and non-standard pronominal usage in English, with special reference to the eighteenth century. In Dieter Stein and Ingrid Tieken-Boon van Ostade (eds.), *Towards a standard English 1600–1800*, 217–242. Berlin: Mouton de Gruyter.

Tieken-Boon van Ostade, Ingrid. 1996. Two hundred years of Lindley Murray: An introduction. In Tieken-Boon van Ostade (ed.), *Two hundred years of Lindley Murray*, 9–25. Münster: Nodus Publikationen.

Tieken-Boon van Ostade, Ingrid. 2000a. Normative studies in England. In Sylvain Auroux, E. F. K. Koerner, Hans-Josef Niederehe, and Kees Versteegh (eds.), *History of the Language Sciences/Geschichte der Sprachwissenschaften/Histoire des Sciences du Langage*, vol. I, 876–887. Berlin: Walter de Gruyter.

Tieken-Boon van Ostade, Ingrid (ed.). 2000b. *Social network analysis and the history of English*. Special issue of *European Journal of English Studies* 4(3).

Tieken-Boon van Ostade, Ingrid. 2000c. Sociohistorical linguistics and the observer's paradox. In Dieter Kastovsky and Arthur Mettinger (eds.), *The history of English in a social context: A contribution to historical sociolinguistics*, 441–461. Berlin: Mouton de Gruyter.

Tieken-Boon van Ostade, Ingrid. 2008a. The 1760s: Grammars, grammarians and the booksellers. In Tieken-Boon van Ostade (ed.), 101–124.

Tieken-Boon van Ostade, Ingrid. 2008b. Grammars, grammarians and grammar writing: An introduction. In Tieken-Boon van Ostade (ed.), 1–14.

Tieken-Boon van Ostade, Ingrid (ed.). 2008c. *Grammars, grammarians and grammar-writing in 18th-century England*. Berlin: Mouton de Gruyter.

Tieken-Boon van Ostade, Ingrid. 2009. *An introduction to Late Modern English*. Edinburgh: Edinburgh University Press.

Tieken-Boon van Ostade, Ingrid. 2010. The usage guide: Its birth and popularity. *English Today* 26(2), 14–23, 44.

Tieken-Boon van Ostade, Ingrid. 2011. *The Bishop's grammar: Robert Lowth and the rise of prescriptivism*. Oxford: Oxford University Press.

Tieken-Boon van Ostade, Ingrid. 2012a. Codifying the English language. In Anne Schröder, Ulrich Busse, and Ralf Schneider (eds.), *Codification, canons, and curricula: Description and prescription in language and literature*, 61–77. Bielefeld: Aisthesis Verlag.

Tieken-Boon van Ostade, Ingrid. 2012b. The codification of English in England. In Hickey (ed.), 34–54.

Tieken-Boon van Ostade, Ingrid. 2013. Studying attitudes to English usage. *English Today* 29(4), 3–12.

Tieken-Boon van Ostade, Ingrid. 2015. *Five hundred mistakes corrected*: An early American English usage guide. In Marina Dossena (ed.), *Transatlantic perspectives on Late Modern English*, 55–71. Amsterdam: John Benjamins.

Tieken-Boon van Ostade, Ingrid and Carol Percy (eds.). 2017. *Prescription and tradition in language: Establishing standards across time and space*. Bristol: Multilingual Matters.

Tierney, James E. 1988. *The correspondence of Robert Dodsley 1733–1764*. Cambridge: Cambridge University Press.

Tomasello, Michael. 2003. *Constructing a language: A usage-based theory of language acquisition*. Cambridge: Harvard University Press.

Toon, Thomas E. 1992. Old English dialects. In Richard M. Hogg (ed.), *The Cambridge history of the English language,* vol. I: *The beginnings to 1066*, 409–451. Cambridge: Cambridge University Press.

Townend, Matthew. 2000. Viking age England as a bilingual society. In Dawn M. Hadley and Julian D. Richards (eds.), *Cultures in contact: Scandinavian settlement in England in the ninth and tenth centuries*, 89–105. Turnhout: Brepols.

Townend, Matthew. 2012. Contacts and conflicts: Latin, Norse, and French. In Mugglestone (ed.), 75–105.

Traugott, Elizabeth Closs. 1982. From propositional to textual and expressive meanings: Some semantic-pragmatic aspects of grammaticalization. In Winfred P. Lehmann and Yakov Malkiel (eds.), *Perspectives on historical linguistics*, 245–271. Amsterdam: John Benjamins.

Traugott, Elizabeth Closs. 1989. On the rise of epistemic meanings in English: An example of subjectification in semantic change. *Language* 57, 33–65.

Traugott, Elizabeth Closs. 1995a. The role of the development of discourse markers in a theory of grammaticalization. Paper presented at ICHL XII, Manchester 1995; Version of 11/97. www.stanford.edu/~traugott/papers/discourse.pdf

Traugott, Elizabeth Closs. 1995b. Subjectification in grammaticalisation. In Stein and Wright (eds.), 31–54.

Traugott, Elizabeth Closs. 1997. Subjectification and the development of epistemic meaning: The case of *promise* and *threaten*. In Swan and Westvik (eds.), 185–210.

Traugott, Elizabeth Closs. 1999a. The role of pragmatics in semantic change. In Jef Verscheuren (ed.), *Pragmatics in 1998: Selected papers from the 6th International Pragmatics Conference*, vol. II, 93–102. Antwerp: International Pragmatics Association.

Traugott, Elizabeth Closs. 1999b. The rhetoric of counter-expectation in semantic change: A study in subjectification. In Andreas Blank and Peter Koch (eds.), *Historical semantics and cognition*, 177–196. Berlin: Mouton de Gruyter.

Traugott, Elizabeth Closs. 2001. Legitimate counterexamples to unidirectionality. Paper presented at Freiburg University, October 17, 2001. www.stanford.edu/~traugott/ect-papers online.html

Traugott, Elizabeth Closs. 2003a. Constructions in grammaticalization. In Joseph and Janda (eds.), 624–647.

Traugott, Elizabeth Closs. 2003b. From subjectification to intersubjectification. In Raymond Hickey (ed.), *Motives for language change*, 124–139. Cambridge: Cambridge University Press.

Traugott, Elizabeth Closs. 2006. Historical pragmatics. In Laurence R. Horn and Gregory Ward (eds.), *The handbook of pragmatics*, 538–561. Oxford: Blackwell.

Traugott, Elizabeth Closs. 2007. (Inter)subjectification and unidirectionality. *Journal of Historical Pragmatics* 8(2), 295–309.

Traugott, Elizabeth Closs. 2008. The state of English language studies: A linguistics perspective. In Marianne Thormählen (ed.), *English now: Selected papers from the 20th IAUPE Conference in Lund 2007*, 199–225. Lund: Centre for Languages and Literature, Lund University.

Traugott, Elizabeth Closs. 2010a. (Inter)subjectivity and (inter)subjectification: A reassessment. In Davidse, Vandelanotte, and Cuyckens (eds.), 29–71.

Traugott, Elizabeth Closs. 2010b. Grammaticalization. In Jucker and Taavitsainen (eds.), 97–126.

Traugott, Elizabeth Closs and Richard B. Dasher. 2002. *Regularity in semantic change*. Cambridge: Cambridge University Press.

Traugott, Elizabeth Closs and Bernd Heine (eds.). 1991. *Approaches to Grammaticalization*. 2 vols. Amsterdam: John Benjamins.

Traugott, Elizabeth Closs and Ekkehard König. 1991. The semantics-pragmatics of grammaticalization revisited. In Traugott and Heine (eds.), vol. I, 189–218.

Traugott, Elizabeth Closs and Graeme Trousdale. 2013. *Constructionalization and constructional changes.* Oxford: Oxford University Press.

Treharne, Elaine. 2012. *Living through conquest: The politics of early English, 1020–1220.* Oxford: Oxford University Press.

Trotter, Derek (ed.). 2000. *Multilingualism in later medieval Britain.* Woodbridge: D. S. Brewer.

Trousdale, Graeme. 2005. The social context of Kentish Raising: Issues in Old English sociolinguistics. *International Journal of English Studies* 5, 59–76.

Trousdale, Graeme. 2010. *An introduction to English sociolinguistics.* Edinburgh: Edinburgh University Press.

Trudgill, Peter. 2004. *New-dialect formation: The inevitability of colonial Englishes.* Edinburgh: Edinburgh University Press.

Tyrkkö, Jukka, Matti Kilpiö Terttu Nevalainen, and Matti Rissanen (eds.). 2012 *Outposts of historical corpus linguistics: From the Helsinki Corpus to a proliferation of resources.* Hesinki: VARIENG. www.helsinki.fi/varieng/series/volumes/10

Ullmann, Stephen. 1957. *The principles of semantics.* 2nd edn. Oxford: Blackwell.

Ullmann, Stephen. 1962. *Semantics: An introduction to the science of meaning.* Oxford: Blackwell.

Ungerer, Friedrich. 2000. News stories and news events: A changing relationship. In Fredrich Ungerer (ed.), *English media texts*, 177–195. Amsterdam: John Benjamins.

Upton, Clive 2008. Received Pronunciation. In Kortmann (ed.), vol. I, 237–252.

van Gelderen, Elly. 1993. *The rise of functional categories.* Amsterdam: John Benjamins.

van Gelderen, Elly. 2004. *Grammaticalization as economy.* Amsterdam: John Benjamins.

van Gelderen, Elly. 2014. *A history of the English language.* Revised edn. Amsterdam: John Benjamins.

Vennemann, Theo. 1972. Rule inversion. *Lingua* 29, 209–242.

Visser, Fredericus Theodorus. 1984. *An historical syntax of the English language.* Part three, second half*: Syntactical units with two and with more verbs.* 2nd impression. Leiden: Brill.

Vorlat, Emma. 2001. Lexical rules in Robert Baker's "Reflections on the English Language." *Leuvense Bijdragen* 90(4), 391–401.

Wales, Kathleen M. 1983. *Thou* and *you* in Early Modern English: Brown and Gilman re-appraised. *Studia Linguistica* 37(2), 107–125.

Walker, Terry. 2007. *Thou and you in Early Modern English: dialogues.* Amsterdam: John Benjamins.

Waller, Tim. 2005. The subjunctive in Present-day British English: A survey, with particular reference to the mandative subjunctive. MA thesis, University College London.

Waller, Tim. 2016. The subjunctive in Present-day English: A study of recent syntactic change. PhD thesis, University College London.

Warner, Anthony. 1993. *English auxiliaries.* Cambridge: Cambridge University Press.

Weiner, Edmund. 1988. On editing a usage guide. In E. G. Stanley and T. F. Hoad (eds.), *Words: For Robert Burchfield's sixty-fifth birthday*, 171–183. Cambridge: D. S. Brewer.

Weinreich, Uriel, William Labov, and Marvin Herzog. 1968. Empirical foundations for a theory of language change. *Directions for historical linguistics: A symposium*, 95–188. Austin, TX: University of Texas Press.

Wells, John. 1982. *Accents of English.* 3 vols. Cambridge: Cambridge University Press.

Wenger, Etienne. 1998. *Communities of practice: Learning, meaning, and identity.* Cambridge: Cambridge University Press.

Williams, Graham. 2013. *Women's epistolary utterance: A study of the letters of Joan and Maria Thynne, 1575–1611*. Amsterdam: John Benjamins.

Williams, Jeffrey P., Edgar W. Schneider, Peter Trudgill, and Daniel Schreier (eds). 2015. *Further studies in the lesser-known varieties of English*. Cambridge: Cambridge University Press.

Williamson, Keith. 2000. Changing spaces: Linguistic relationships and the dialect continuum. In Irma Taavitsainen, Terttu Nevalainen, Päivi Pahta, and Matti Rissanen (eds.), *Placing Middle English in context*, 141–179. Berlin: Mouton de Gruyter.

Williamson, Keith. 2002. The dialectology of "English" north of the Humber, c. 1380–1500. In Fanego et al. (eds.), 253–287. Amsterdam: John Benjamins.

Williamson, Keith. 2004. On chronicity and space(s) in historical dialectology. In Dossena and Lass (eds.), 97–136.

Winford, Donald. 2003. *An introduction to contact linguistics*. Oxford: Blackwell.

Winford, Donald. 2012. Pidgins and creoles in the history of English. In Nevalainen and Traugott (eds.), 592–601.

Wischer, Ilse. 2000. Grammaticalization versus lexicalization: "Methinks" there is some confusion. In Fischer, Rosenbach, and Stein (eds.), 355–370.

Wischer, Ilse and Gabriele Diewald (eds.). 2002. *New reflections on grammaticalization*. Amsterdam: John Benjamins.

Woods, Anthony, Paul Fletcher, and Arthur Hughes. 1986. *Statistics in language studies*. Cambridge: Cambridge University Press.

Xu, Zhichang. 2010. *Chinese English: Features and implications*. Hong Kong: Open University of Hong Kong.

Yáñez-Bouza, Nuria. 2008. Preposition stranding in the eighteenth century: *Something to talk about*. In Tieken-Boon van Ostade (ed.), 251–277.

Glossary of Terms

"abduce" a grammar: in language acquisition, to form a hypothesis about the grammar producing the linguistic output that the child hears around him or her.

address term: a nominal or pronominal form (personal pronoun, title, endearment, etc.) by which one participant in a speech situation addresses another; the form chosen depends on the social relationship between the participants.

Affix Hopping (or affix lowering): a transformation that moves the tense affix from its "base-generated" position before the verb to its final position after the verb.

(a)melioration: a process of semantic change whereby a word or expression acquires a more favorable meaning, as in *knight*, which originally meant 'a boy employed as a servant.' *Compare* **pejoration**.

(American) structuralism: an approach to language which describes the structures of a language in terms of static patterns and does not seek to explain why one structure might be chosen by a speaker as more appropriate than an alternative structure.

analogical change: a process whereby an existing pattern triggers a change making some form conform to this pattern. This type of change includes proportional analogy, analogical remodeling, analogical maintenance, creation, and leveling.

analogy: the ability to perceive identities in relation, for instance the similarity between a shoplifter stealing a DVD from a shop and an internet user downloading a pirated movie from a website; in language, the ability to form, on the basis of the pattern *rake-raked*, the past tense of *bake* (*baked*).

analytic language: a language characterized by the use of function words and word order to express grammatical relations, and very few inflections, such as Present-day English or French.

anchor texts: in LALME, the texts for which the geographical provenance is known (typically administrative documents), and in relation to which other texts are localized on the basis of their linguistic forms.

annotation (and mark-up): an additional, separate layer of information in a corpus in the form of tags; some distinguish between mark-up (information on structural properties of the text such as "headline," "paragraph," etc.) and annotation (grammatical information such as **Part-of-Speech tags** (q.v.) and syntactic **parsing** (q.v.), as well as **lemmatization** (q.v) or **normalization**).

automatization: the change by which a sequence of deliberately executed actions, through extensive repetition, comes to be cognitively represented as a single action. Also known as "routinization," "entrenchment," and "chunking."

'bad data": for historical study, the haphazard survival of texts from earlier periods, the lack of access to native speakers and oral speech from the past, and our incomplete knowledge about the social structure of past communities.

bridging context: a specific context that invites an inference on the part of the reader/hearer but that is still compatible with the original meaning of the pattern/construction (and is thus cancelable). Bridging contexts may lead to new conventional grammatical meanings.

categorization: the ability to view things and ideas as belonging to a certain group, that is, as members of a category.

Celtic hypothesis: the hypothesis that the Celtic substrate in Britain supplied several structural properties to English.

change from above: (a) change in which a linguistic feature used or associated with the language of a higher class is adopted into the language of a lower class or language more generally, or (b) a change that is above the level of awareness.

change from below: (a) change in which a linguistic feature used or associated with the language of a lower class is adopted into the language of a higher class or language more generally, or (b) a change that is below the level of awareness.

change in apparent time: a change in language that is deduced from a systematic difference in a linguistic feature between speakers of different ages.

change in real time: a change in language that is determined by comparing texts from different periods.

code-switching: degrees of language mixing, ranging from clearly foreign words, phrases, or whole sentences being interspersed in an otherwise English text to the occurrence of non-, semi-, or even fully integrated borrowings

codification: the laying down of the rules of a language in grammars and dictionaries.

colloquialization: the trend toward a style which is more involved, more situated in context, and less abstract in style.

comment clause: a **parenthetical clause** (q.v.), typical of oral discourse, usually formed with a first- or second-person pronoun and a simple present-tense verb (e.g., *I think, you know, as you see*), serving a range of pragmatic and politeness functions in discourse.

community of practice: a group of language users characterized by their joint enterprise, mutual engagement, and shared repertoire (of behaviors, actions, language, etc.).

comparative method: the practice of comparing forms in two or more languages with a view to discovering regularities of correspondence or to justifying a postulated original form which is not attested.

competence: speakers' knowledge of the possible structures of their language.

complex preposition: sequences of two or three orthographic words (e.g., *contrary to, exclusive of, in terms of, by dint of*) that function in the same way as a simple preposition. Some linguists debate the existence of complex prepositions as a grammatical class.

concordance: all instances of the search word or structure in the context in which it occurs.

condensation: the shrinking of the scope of a grammaticalizing sign as it combines with structurally increasingly less complex constituents. One of the parameters of grammaticalization proposed by Lehmann (1985). Today, many scholars consider the development of forms that do not exhibit condensation (e.g., **discourse markers** [q.v.]) as examples of grammaticalization, too.

conditional subjunctive: the use of the subjunctive form in clauses following certain conjunctions such as *on condition that*.

constrained selection: a copying behaviour in which the copyist accepts those forms with which he/she is familiar, while translating less familiar ones to his own usage.

constraint: a general process which, on the basis of **Universal Grammar** (q.v.), limits or constrains the type of grammar a language learner can construct.

contact variety: a dialect which shows many features borrowed from different languages in contact.

"Cooperative Principle": the principle of conversational cooperation which interlocutors are expected to observe in order to achieve effective communication (see Grice 1975).

corpus: a principled collection of natural texts.

creole: a newly born and both structurally and functionally fully developed contact language, a native tongue which serves all social and linguistic needs of a speech community and shows structural complexity.

curial style: a style of (late) Middle English characterized by features which enhance precision and ceremoniousness, namely (i) nominal and verbal groups consisting of near-synonyms, (ii) extremely explicit cohesive devices, and (iii) Latinate (and often abstract) lexis.

database: a collection of texts or quotations, but one not designed to be used as a **corpus** (q. v.) (i.e., not aiming to be representative).

decategorialization: a process that results in the loss of (morphologically or functionally marked) features of a member of a grammatical category. For example, the nominal element in a **complex preposition** (q.v.) like *in line with* or *in view of* can no longer be pluralized or premodified by an adjective (**in straight line with*, *in views of).

degrammaticalization: the relatively infrequent process that turns items/patterns with a grammatical meaning into items/patterns with a lexical meaning.

deontic modality: the kind of modality which is concerned with the meanings of permission and obligation (e.g., *You must go home now*). Compare **epistemic modality.**

descriptive grammar: an approach to grammar which records and describes actual practice in language use instead of telling readers what is right and wrong.

diachronic pragmatics: study of the development of discourse-pragmatic features over time.

diachronic(ally oriented) discourse analysis: an approach which focuses on texts/genres/ registers as changing entities over time. *See also* **diachronic pragmatics.**

diacritic: a mark added to a letter to indicate a change in the corresponding sound value, e.g., the cedilla on the *c* in *façade* (indicating that the pronunciation is [s] rather than [k]).

dialect area: a geographical area considered to be distinct from adjoining areas in terms of dialectal usage, usually based on specific features and defined through the drawing of **isoglosses** (q.v.).

dialect continuum: the idea that language varies geographically in a gradual, non-discrete way.

dialectology: the study of geographical variation, usually based on speakers with solid, native connections to an area.

diglossia: the use of two languages within a single language community with socially unequal status (typically "high" and "low"). *See also* **triglossia.**

diphthong: a vowel sound characterized by a change (often referred to as a glide) in articulatory position, e.g., the [aʊ] in *how.*

directive: a speech act in which a speaker wants a hearer to perform an action (e.g., an order, command, request, question).

discourse marker (or pragmatic marker): a short element characteristic of oral discourse, such as *well, now, actually, in fact, after all, you know,* or *I mean,* having little or no lexical content but rather pragmatic meaning, functioning to structure texts, denote speaker attitude, and signal interpersonal relations.

discourse-oriented diachronic linguistics: an approach which examines what kind of role texts, genres, register play in the distribution of linguistic features, as well as in the origin and diffusion of changes. *See also* **pragma-historical linguistics.**

divergence: the continuing existence of the lexical origins of a form/pattern as it grammaticalizes; these lexical origins may undergo developments of their own. *See also* **layering**.

donor language: the source of loanwords in a language.

double comparative: the use of both the inflectional and periphrastic form of the comparative marker, as in *more larger*.

drift: in the history of languages, a gradual movement over time in a consistent direction, such as the movement in the history of English away from a synthetic language type, with many case endings and complex verb forms, to a more analytic type in which the morphology has been greatly simplified.

E-Language: the speaker's speech output.

ENL: English as a Native Language.

entrenchment: *see* **automatization.**

epistemic modality: the kind of modality which is concerned with the meanings of probability and possibility, qualifying degrees of speaker's commitment toward the truth of the proposition (e.g., *He must be home by now*). *Compare* **deontic modality**.

evidential marker: a marker of the source of information.

exemplar: the text from which a scribe copies.

exonormative: accepting another country's language behavior (an external one, often Britain) as one's own norm of correctness.

expletive: a taboo or euphemistic expression used as an **interjection** (q.v.) which conveys subjective meanings such as annoyance, surprise, or unexpectedness (e.g., *gee, gosh, my God*).

exploitation colonization: colonization for the main purpose of exploiting the natural resources and native population of the colonized land.

false positive: the result of a corpus search which incorrectly identifies the presence of a form.

fit-technique: a method of localizing texts on the basis of their linguistic features, based on the model of a completely regular **dialect continuum** (q.v.).

flat adverb: an adjective without the adverbial marker *-ly*, as in *go slow*.

focus: the element in a sentence which is most newsworthy, often contrastive and emphatic, as in *It was on Tuesday that she resigned*.

functional head: a phrasal head that carries grammatical rather than lexical information, such as tense.

functional load: the degree to which a distinction is utilized in a language; the smaller the load, the easier it is for elements involved in this distinction to be subject to merger or loss.

generative grammar: an approach which seeks to give a formal characterization of a native speaker's knowledge about what constitutes a grammatical sentence in his or her language.

genre: a collection of texts which share a specific communicative purpose and a conventional text structure. *Compare* **text type**.

gentrification: a related set of changes – including elaborated reference, informational and abstract style, and a preference for polysyllabic, abstract, learned vocabulary – driven by class-consciousness and a feeling of social propriety.

grammaticalization: the process that turns lexical items/patterns into grammatical ones (primary grammaticalization), or those that already have grammatical meaning into ones with more grammatical meaning (secondary grammaticalization).

Great Vowel Shift: a change in the values for long vowels, in which they were raised or diphthongized, beginning in the Middle English period and more or less completed after the age of Shakespeare.

Grimm's Law (Germanic Sound Shift) a sound change differentiating Germanic from the other Indo-European dialects, involving the shift of all voiceless stops to voiceless fricatives, voiced stops to voiceless stops, and voiced aspirated stops to voiced fricatives (and later to voiced stops).

***h*-dropping:** loss of a word-initial phoneme /h/ before a vowel; it may also involve the addition of /h/.

hapax legomenon: a word that is used only once in a corpus or for which there is only one attestation.

hiatus: the sequence of two vowels in adjacent syllables.

historical discourse analysis proper: an approach concerned with the linguistic/stylistic makeup of texts/genres, their communicative aims and their embedding in a sociocultural context at a certain point in time. *See also* **pragmaphilology**.

homonym: a word which is identical in sound (and spelling) to another word, but differs in meaning, such as *bear* 'an ursine animal' and *bear* 'to carry.'

hybrid formation: a form consisting of a foreign suffix attached to an English base, or an English suffix attached to a borrowed (e.g., French- or Norse-derived) base.

hypothetical subjunctive: the use of the subjunctive form in clauses following *(as) if, (as) though*, and *even if.*

I-Language: the speaker's internalized grammar.

illocutionary force: the way in which an utterance is to be taken, its communicative intent (e.g., as a promise, as a command, etc.)

impersonal verb: a verb that occurs only in the third person singular that has no specified agent. It may have a dummy subject (e.g., *it is raining*) or no subject at all.

implicature: a term used to refer to what speakers suggest to hearers beyond that which is explicitly uttered in a conversational exchange (see Grice 1975). Two types of implicatures can be distinguished: conversational implicatures, i.e., those which are not part of the conventional meaning of the utterance, and conventional implicatures, i.e., those which arise from the conventionalization of conversational implicatures and thus become part of the **polysemies** (q.v.) of a form. *See also* **invited inferencing**.

informant: a speaker or writer from whom linguistic data are collected in a dialect survey. In surveys of medieval materials, where many texts are anonymous and/or scribal copies, the texts themselves are usually considered the informants.

information packaging (= information structure): the way we order elements in a sentence so as to integrate it effectively into the surrounding text, following certain "rules," such as (i) given (old, known) information precedes new information in sentences and (ii) different clausal positions fulfill different functions in the so-called topic–comment structure. **Topics** (q.v.) are put in initial position.

inkhorn term: a Latin-derived word in English; the term ridicules the practice (in the sixteenth century) of overusing Latinisms.

interjection: a linguistic element (e.g., *oh, ouch, gee*) which is morphologically invariant and syntactically independent and typically constitutes an utterance in its own right; its function is expressive and emotional. *See also* **expletive**.

internal reconstruction: the use of evidence from within a single language to gain knowledge of an earlier stage, e.g., by examining the reflexes of older pronunciations. Such evidence is usually available in forms embodying unproductive processes which are themselves remnants of formerly active processes.

interpretable feature: a meaningful feature that the semantic component can interpret, such as number on nouns.

intersubjectification: "the development of meanings that encode speaker/writers' attention to the cognitive stances and social identities of addressees" (Traugott 2003b: 124).

invited inferencing: the process by which the meaning of utterances is enriched so that the overall interpretation is more than the compositional meaning of the words that are actually uttered. *See also* **implicature**.

"Invited Inferencing Theory of Semantic Change": a theory of semantic change developed by Traugott (1999a) and Traugott and Dasher (2002), which accounts for the conventionalization of pragmatic meanings as semantic meanings. According to this theory, semantic change follows certain predictable cross-linguistic regularities or trends.

isogloss: a line drawn on a dialect map, indicating the approximate distribution of a form, or the boundary between **dialect areas** (q.v.) defined on the basis of one or more features.

joint attention: the ability that children develop (at around 9–12 months of age) to engage in triadic joint attention, which allows them to focus on an object of interest together with a caretaker. This shared experience of an object facilitates word learning.

koinéization: the mixing of features of different dialects, leading to a new, compromised dialect.

language academy: an authoritative institution that is officially responsible for the regulation of the language.

language shift: the complete replacement of one language by another in a community.

layering: the existence of older and newer formal means of expressing a concept within one functional domain; e.g., in future time reference, the future auxiliary *will* for instance has been in the English grammar for longer than the BE *going to* construction (see Hopper 1991). In Hopper and Traugott (2003) layering refers to the coexistence of older and more recent forms of one and the same grammaticalizing form/pattern. For example, *be going to* can still be used to refer to a literal spatial movement even though the form has developed into a grammatical marker of futurity. Most authors follow this latter definition.

lemmatization: grouping all of the (inflected) forms of a word together under the head word in a dictionary entry ("lemma"); for instance, inflected words like *goes*, *going*, or *went* would be labeled with the lemma GO.

lexical semantic change: the processes by which lexical words and expressions change their meanings. Lexical semantic change draws on several pathways of change, notably metaphor and metonymy, broadening and narrowing, **amelioration** (q.v.), and **pejoration** (q.v.).

lexicalization: the process whereby new items are formed that are considered to be part of the lexical inventory of a language. For example, a free syntactic construction fossilizes, fuses, and coalesces, and thus comes to be treated as an unanalyzable lexical item; a complex unit becomes irregular, opaque, and often monomorphemic (e.g., *nostril, n'er do well, nuts and bolts*). The concept is highly theory-dependent and notoriously difficult to define. A major area of contention is its delimitation from the processes of **grammaticalization** (q.v.).

lexifier language: language of the socially dominant group which provides the vocabulary of a **pidgin** (q.v.).

linguistic variable: a form expressing the same – or nearly the same – (grammatical) meaning/function as another form, e.g., *-t* vs. *-ed* as past tense/participle endings in word pairs such as *burnt/burned, learnt/learned*, etc.

local document: a text that relates to actual people and places, and that often states directly when and where it was written, such as legal and administrative texts and letters.

mandative subjunctive: use of subjunctive verb forms in clauses following suasive verbs (*demand, suggest, require*), adjectives (*essential, important*), and nouns (*proposal, recommendation*).

"matrix clause hypothesis": hypothesis that **comment clauses** (q.v.) derive from full main clauses with deletion of complementizer *that* and syntactic reanalysis of the original main clause as parenthetical (i.e. *I think that we are right > I think we are right > We are right, I think*).

Merge: an operation that combines syntactic elements to build up a sentence step-by-step.

merger: a type of sound change, generally considered irreversible, where two sounds are reduced to one.

metaphor(ization): the process by which one semantic domain is understood in terms of another semantic domain. For instance, time is understood in spatial terms through the conceptual metaphor TIME IS SPACE (e.g., *a long time*).

metonymy (metonymization): the process by which a part of one semantic domain is understood in terms of another part of that semantic domain, or the entire semantic domain. For example, linguistic expressions such as *The violin has the flu today* show that the members of an orchestra can be metonymically referred to by the name of their respective instruments.

minimal pair: two words that are pronounced the same except for one segment (e.g., *cat–bat*), showing that the differing sounds are distinct phonemes.

Minimalism: the currently dominant program of generative linguistic inquiry, which seeks maximum economy in describing possible grammars of a human language, restricting to a minimum any necessary stipulations.

modal auxiliary: a verbal element such as *may* that shares a number of morphosyntactic characteristics with a core set (*could, can, should, shall, would, will, may, might,* and *must*) that set them apart from lexical verbs in English.

morphophonemic rule: a phonological rule that is restricted to a particular morpheme.

negative concord: a secondary negator accompanying the primary negator, as in French *ne ... pas*.

Neogrammarian hypothesis: the view that language change proceeds continuously for all elements which could in principle be affected by a change in progress. This view stresses the exceptionless character of sound change (German *Ausnahmslosigkeit*).

New Englishes: national varieties of English which newly originated in colonial and post-colonial contact situations, such as Indian English or Nigerian English.

NORM: acronym of "Non-mobile Older Rural Male," a term coined by Chambers and Trudgill (1998) for the typical **informant** (q.v.) of traditional dialect surveys.

normalization: (a) normalized frequency: determination of the number of attestations of a form in a given segment of text, often stated in terms of number of instances per 10,000 or 1,000,000 words; (b) level of annotation that abstracts away from the real variation in a text; e.g., giving standard spellings for historical variants.

Optimality Theory: the theory that speakers use language-specific rankings of universal constraints to produce the optimal or "least bad" output from a given input provided by their mental lexicon.

orthoepist: in the early modern period, a writer of dictionaries, grammars, spelling books or the like, who comments on contemporary usage from the point of view of **prescriptivism** (q.v.).

overgeneralization error: a child's application of a grammatical rule in a context where an adult speaker does not apply it, such as a child uttering *His doggie bited him* applying the past tense rule of *-ed.*

palatalization: a very common process in language change whereby the articulation of a sound is realized at the palate, the central, top part of the mouth. Often sounds which move to this region switch from a stop to an affricate or fricative articulation, e.g., Latin *quinque* 'five' with /k-/ and Italian *cinque* with /tš-/.

parallel derivative: formations with the same base but different suffixes that do not differ significantly in meaning, such as *idleness, idlehood,* and *idleship.*

parameters (principles) of grammaticalization: a set of changes or mechanisms that are intended to operationalize grammaticalization. Prominent examples are Lehmann's (1985) six parameters (including, for example, attrition and **condensation** [q.v.]), Hopper's (1991) five principles (including **layering** [q.v.] and **persistence** [q.v.]), and Himmelmann's (2004) three types of context expansion.

parameter setting: a choice the grammar of a specific language makes between two universally available grammatical settings, e.g., whether **Verb-Raising** (q.v.) is or is not possible in that language.

parenthetical clause: a clause which is appended to an anchor clause, is syntactically and prosodically independent from it, and serves different kinds of pragmatic functions, such as the expression of speaker viewpoint and the marking of speaker-hearer interaction. *See also* **comment clause**.

parsing: the analysis of a corpus with respect to phrase structure and syntactic functions.

Part-of-Speech (PoS) tagging: the (automatic) assignment of every token in the corpus to a word class and its labeling as such, e.g., 'NNS' (for plural noun).

pejoration: a process of semantic change whereby a word or expression acquires a less favorable meaning, as in *silly,* which originally meant 'blessed, innocent.' *Compare* **(a)melioration**.

performance: speakers' use of language, which might contain ungrammatical output or speech errors.

performative verb: a verb, typically in the first person, simple present tense, which explicitly signals a speech act, such as *I promise, I command, I challenge you.*

periodization: a (partially artificial and idealizing) process of defining historical or chronological units ("periods") of a language based on linguistic or historical criteria, or a combination of both.

persistence: the continuing presence of some traces of the original lexical meaning of a form/construction after it has grammaticalized, which may have a restricting effect on the grammatical distribution of the form (see Hopper 1991).

phonetic reduction: the loss of phonetic segments in frequently used linguistic forms, so that for example a string such as *I am going to* is pronounced as *I'm gonna.*

pidgin: a simplified (structurally and lexically reduced) speech form for use in limited interethnic contact situations (such as trade), never spoken natively.

pirated edition: the printing and distribution of a text which is unauthorized by the author or the original publisher.

polysemy: the existence of sets of conceptually related meanings which arise out of the process of **invited inference** (q.v.), as in the conjunction *since,* which has both a temporal and a causal meaning, the latter developing from the former.

population (in the statistical sense): the entirety of relevant data to be studied in empirical research; research typically defines a relevant target population – for historical corpora, this would be a (set of) text types or genres, for instance.

Postcolonial Englishes: forms of English which have arisen in former colonies.

pragma-historical linguistics: study of the discourse-pragmatic factors motivating language change.

pragmaphilology: study of the discourse-pragmatic features in one particular historical period.

pragmaticalization: a process by which a lexical element (with propositional meaning) develops directly into an element whose function is textual and interpersonal (with discourse-pragmatic meaning), with no intermediate grammatical stage. *Compare* **grammaticalization**.

precision: the number of relevant examples retrieved with a search (measured as a proportion against false positives).

preposition stranding: clauses with prepositions in final position which result from the fronting of the object of the proposition, as in *whom I spoke to, this I object to*.

prescriptive grammar: an approach to grammar which provides a norm of correctness, both prescribing and proscribing certain usages and codifying the rules of the language.

prescriptivism: the existence of rules in the language imposing a norm of correctness on the language user.

priming: the process by which the cognitive activation of one idea facilitates the subsequent processing of a similar idea, suggesting that human knowledge is organized in a network-like system.

productivity: the extent to which a word formation process is used to form new words.

prototype: the central member of a category that represents all features that characterize members of that category. More marginal members of the category share only some of those features.

psycholinguistics: the study of mental processes that underlie language processing, language production, and language acquisition.

questionnaire: the list of questions used in an interview to elicit data; also used of the set of items or features for which data are collected from a text or corpus.

reanalysis: a "change [by speakers] in the structure of an expression or class of expressions that does not involve any immediate or intrinsic modification of its surface manifestation" (Langacker 1977: 55); for example, when speakers change the analysis of a modal verb from an ordinary verb to an auxiliary verb in a special position.

recall: the success rate of retrieving relevant data (against instances that are missed).

register: language variety defined according to social use, a configuration of situational features, including subject matter, nature and roles of participants, etc.

representativeness (of a sample): the best approximation of a target population, with the aim of accurately reflecting the language (or period of language, genre of language, etc.) that it records.

rhotacism: a phonological change where /z/ (from an original /s/) changes to /r/, e.g., Old English *ceosan* 'choose,' past participle *gecoren* 'chosen' with an intervocalic /r/ from an earlier /z/.

rule inversion: in generative phonology, a historical change whereby a rule is replaced by its inverse, as in the reanalysis of the /n/ of *an* from being present in the underlying form and deleted by rule before a word beginning with a consonant to a sound that is not present in the underlying form, but inserted by rule before a vowel.

S-curve: the pattern describing a change which starts slowly, picks up speed, and proceeds rapidly but which stops – or at least slows down considerably – before it reaches completion, if indeed this final stage is actually reached.

sampling frame: determination of which text extracts from which (sub)period and which range of text types to include in the corpus (typically designed to achieve **representativeness** (q.v.) with respect to the target population).

search algorithm: a formula or search string used to extract relevant items of a (grammatical) structure from a corpus (typically making use of corpus software).

sincerity condition: the psychological state of the speaker which is necessary for the successful carrying out of a speech act.

size nouns: nominal expressions which in addition to their lexical meaning can synchronically designate (large or small) size, e.g., *bunch, heap(s), bit, scrap (of)*. This is hypothesized to be the result of grammaticalization (Brems 2011).

social class/rank/status: categories and conceptualizations of general groupings in society.

social embedding: the fact that language use is affected by a number of social factors.

social network analysis: analysis of language variation and change based on recognizing specific ties among individuals or the relationships among language users in a network.

sound law (from German *Lautgesetz*): a change or a series of related changes in the phonology of a language, such as Grimm's Law; a concept used by the Neogrammarians to stress the regularity of the change. *See also* **Neogrammarian hypothesis**.

source domain: in conceptual metaphor theory, the semantic domain that is used to make sense of and talk about a more abstract target domain. For example, an abstract target domain such as LOVE is understood in terms of a source domain that is more concrete, namely a JOURNEY.

speech act: an sentence which, by virtue of one's uttering it, constitutes an action, for example, commissives such as *I promise to pay you tomorrow* which perform a promise, or **directives** (q.v.) such as *I order you to open the window* which performs a command.

split infinitive: in infinitives, separation of *to* from the base form of the verb, usually by an adverb, as in *to quickly look*.

stance: the range of meanings associated with the speaker's personal feelings, attitudes, and judgments; stance is expressed by a wide variety of lexical and grammatical forms.

standard(ization): the development of a non-regionalized variety (typically a written variety) with little linguistic variability and maximal discourse functionality; the standard is used largely by the more educated and well-to-do speakers in society.

statistical significance: determination of whether results are likely to be due to chance or not.

structuralism: an approach to language and language change which focuses on the overall structure of language systems and the systemic effects of language change.

style: linguistic forms used not for functional but for aesthetic, idiosyncratic reasons – a conglomeration of textual features which are not inherently necessary for the register or genre but due to certain choices, for example aesthetic ones, by the language user.

subjectification: "the development of a grammatically identifiable expression of speaker belief or speaker attitude to what is said" (Traugott 1995b: 32) – which often accompanies grammaticalization but is not exclusive to it.

substratum: linguistic features of a contact variety which originate from the (often lost) ancestral languages of pidgin or creole language speakers; often camouflaged structural effects.

superstratum: linguistic features of a contact variety which originated from the socially superior (often lexifier) language.

suppletion: the appearance of a form from one paradigm in another paradigm in which it did not originally occur, e.g., *go* and *went* show parts from two original verbs, the second one is from *wendan*, an older word for 'go.'

syncretism: the conflation of inflections, as when *-um* and *-an* become *-en*.

synthetic language: a language characterized primarily by the use of inflections to express grammatical relations, such as Classical Latin or Modern German.

target domain: in conceptual metaphor theory, the semantic domain that speakers try to conceptualize using a more concrete source domain. For example, the highly abstract target domain TIME is understood in terms of the source domain SPACE.

text type: a collection of texts which share a cluster of linguistic features. *Compare* **genre**.

textual history: the history of successive copyings that lies behind a specific physical instance of a text.

***there*-sentence:** a sentence type used to provide information that is new to the reader (existential type: *there's no milk*) or new to the discourse (presentational type: *there remain two problems*).

token: the concrete occurrence of a linguistic form in a corpus. *Compare* **type**.

topic: what the clause is about; topics are typically given information and fill the initial position in a clause.

trade colonization: colonization which is primarily for the purposes of fulfilling the homeland's desire for exotic goods such as spices.

Transformational Grammar: the analysis of language as a dynamic system which involves more abstract underlying forms and processes which derive surface forms.

triglossia: the use of three languages with socially unequal status within a single language community. *See also* **diglossia**.

type: the number of different words or linguistic forms in a corpus; for instance, in *The students read the books*, there are four types (*the, students, read, books*) but five tokens (*the, students, read, the, books*) as the type *the* is attested by two tokens. *Compare* **token**.

umlaut: a process in which a high vowel or /j/ in a syllable (usually a grammatical ending) caused the vowel of the preceding syllable, if a back vowel, to be moved to a front position.

unidirectionality (hypothesis): the view that the processes of **grammaticalization** (q.v.) always proceed in the same direction, i.e., from less grammatical to more grammatical, from literal to abstract meaning, from independent to dependent lexeme, from free morpheme to affix, etc. A small number of counterexamples exist, which leads some scholars to question the general validity of the hypothesis.

uniformitarian principle: the belief that the linguistic forces which operate today are not unlike those that operated in the past.

uninterpretable feature: a purely grammatical feature that the semantic component cannot interpret; it must not be present at the end of the derivation of a sentence.

univerbation: the diachronic process of fusing a sequence of two or more orthographic words into a single new word.

Universal Grammar: the innate knowledge human beings are posited (especially by generative grammarians) to have about what constitutes a possible linguistic system.

usage guide: a manual giving advice on questions of divided usage or on usage which is considered incorrect and dealing with all aspects of language: spelling, pronunciation, lexis and grammar. It may also offer sociolinguistic comments, identifying linguistic phenomena with groups of speakers who are criticized because their language differs from standard English.

usage problem: a language phenomenon which shows divided usage (variant forms) and about which readers need to be advised, such as whether to say/write *different to* or *different from.*

usage-based linguistics: a family of linguistic theories sharing the idea that the forms of language and knowledge of language are shaped by language use, i.e., the experience of human beings communicating with language.

variable (non-linguistic): any parameter that shows variation in a population of speakers, writers or texts, that may be linguistically significant, such as geography, age, social class, or gender.

Verb-Raising: a process that raises a verb up to the position where verbal inflection resides.

verb-second (V2) word order: a word order pattern requiring the finite verb to appear in the second position; the first position is occupied by a single constituent which typically functions as the **topic** (q.v.).

vernacular: the most relaxed or unmonitored style of language. In medieval and early Modern Europe, the native language of a community, as opposed to a learned language such as Latin. The vernacular typically functioned as the "low" language of a **diglossic** (q.v.) situation.

vernacular(ization): in the context of Britain, the shifting from French and Latin to English.

X-bar theory: a theory which postulates that phrases of different types, e.g., NP and VP, conform to the same overall internal structure, usually assumed to be an optional specifier modifying a phrase containing the head and an optional complement.

Index